JOHN RAMSDEN is Professor of Modern History at Queen Mary in the University of London. He was in 1995–6 Visiting Professor of British History at Westminster College, Fulton, Missouri, in 2000 a Winston Churchill Fellow in New Zealand, and in 2001 a Distinguished Academic Visitor at La Trobe University, Melbourne. He is the author of three of the volumes in Longman's major specialised multi-volume History of the Conservative Party, and of many other books and articles on Conservative Party history. His much-acclaimed one-volume history, *An Appetite for Power*, was published in 1999. In 2002 he published *The Dam Busters* and (as general editor) *The Oxford Companion to Twentieth-Century British Politics*.

Also by John Ramsden

MAN OF
THE CENTURY

WINSTON CHURCHILL
AND HIS LEGEND SINCE 1945

JOHN RAMSDEN

HarperCollins*Publishers*

HarperCollins*Publishers*
77–85 Fulham Palace Road,
Hammersmith, London w6 8jb

www.harpercollins.co.uk

This paperback edition 2003
1 3 5 7 9 8 6 4 2

First published in Great Britain by
HarperCollins*Publishers* 2002

A catalogue record for this book
is available from the British Library

ISBN 0 00 653099 0

Set in PostScript Linotype Minion
with Castellar display by
Rowland Phototypesetting Ltd, Bury St Edmunds, Suffolk

Printed and bound in Great Britain by
Clays Ltd, St Ives plc

CONTENTS

LIST OF ILLUSTRATIONS

INTEGRATED

PLATE SECTION I

Churchill and Menzies

The mail of 'The Greatest Man Alive'. *Hulton Archive*

Churchill's funeral. *Hulton Archive*

Mary and Christopher Soames at the re-naming of the Avenue Churchill. *Associated Press*

Edward Heath at the unveiling of the House of Commons statue. *Hulton Archive*

PLATE SECTION II

Elizabeth II and President Chirac in homage before Churchill's statue. *Associated Press*

Churchill busts and statues

A double statue of Winston and Clementine Churchill

A double statue of Churchill and Franklin Roosevelt

Churchill with Australian soldiers. *Argus Newspaper Collection of Photographs, State Library of Victoria, Australia*

Churchill feeding his kangaroo. *Hulton Archive*

Churchill painting a landscape. *Hulton Archive*

The studio at Chartwell. *National Trust Photographic Library/Andreas von Einsiedel. Reproduced courtesy of Curtis Brown, London, on behalf of the Churchill Estate*

Commemorative Churchill street signs

Commemorative restaurant and bar signs

Churchill inscriptions

Churchill commemorated in shop, school, park and hospital signs

Disclaimer

While every effort has been made to trace the owners of copyright material reproduced herein, the publishers would like to apologise for any omissions and will be pleased to incorporate missing acknowledgements in any future editions.

ACKNOWLEDGEMENTS

I am most grateful to Queen Mary, University of London, for providing me with periods of leave during which this book could be worked on and completed, and to a number of colleagues there for advice on earlier drafts, notably to Peter Catterall, James Ellison and Peter Hennessy. I could not have done such extensive and geographically diverse research work at all without financial assistance with travel and accommodation provided by the Queen Mary History Department, and by the University of London, Westminster College, Fulton, Missouri, the UK Winston Churchill Memorial Trust, and La Trobe University, Melbourne. On each of these overseas research visits I was assisted by historians on the spot, and this is acknowledged in individual endnotes to the text. It has been a great pleasure to work on this book with Arabella Pike, Georgina Laycock and their colleagues at HarperCollins, with Peter James – surely the prince of copy-editors – and with my agent Giles Gordon.

For permission to see (and where relevant to quote from) unpublished papers, I wish to express my gratitude to the Master and Fellows of Churchill College, Cambridge (papers of Winston S. Churchill); the Harry S. Truman Presidential Library, Independence, Missouri (papers of Dean Acheson, Charles Ross and Harry S. Truman); the Dwight D. Eisenhower Presidential Library, Abilene, Kansas (papers of Dwight D. Eisenhower); the John F. Kennedy Presidential Library, Boston, Massachusetts (papers of Kay Halle and John F. Kennedy); the Lyndon B. Johnson Presidential Library (papers of Lyndon B. Johnson); the Minnesota Historical Society, St Paul, Minnesota (papers of Hubert Humphrey); the US National Archives, Washington DC (papers of the State Department); Westminster College, Fulton, Missouri (papers of the Winston Churchill Memorial); the English-Speaking Union, Washington DC Branch (papers of the E-SU branch, Churchill statue committee); the National Library of Australia, Canberra (papers of Richard Casey, Robert G. Menzies and the Returned Servicemen's League of Australia); the National Archives of Canada, Ottawa (papers of John

Diefenbaker, George Drew, Louis St Laurent and Lester B. Pearson); the Alexander Turnbull Library, Wellington, New Zealand (papers of Sidney Holland); New Zealand National Archives (papers of Peter Fraser).

PREFACE

The idea for this book emerged during the year in which I was Robertson Professor of British History at Westminster College, in Fulton, Missouri, an enlightened endowment which allows a different British historian each year both to experience the American academic environment in a small but distinguished College in the Mid-West and to travel widely in North America for academic purposes. The Winston Churchill Memorial and Library attached to Westminster College is one of the greatest shrines to the memory of Winston Churchill in the world. In this it is second only to Chartwell where he lived for forty years – though he spent less than one day of his ninety years in Fulton – and, possibly, to London's underground Cabinet War Rooms, a modern theme park dedicated to the memory of his 'finest hour'. The honouring of Britain as well as Churchill himself in the Fulton Memorial is slightly surreal for a visiting British historian, underlined as it is not only by a statue of Churchill in heroic mode on the College campus, but also by a Christopher Wren church, St Mary Aldermanbury, blitzed in London in 1941 and later beautifully re-erected (complete with Westminster chimes) in the state of Missouri. The Memorial's Museum and Library displays a large collection of Churchill memorabilia, hosts meetings and lectures on the theme of his life and example, and contains an enormous collection of books about him. It was these last that provided the germ of this book, for I was forcibly reminded by their physical presence on the shelves of the size of the post-war writing industry on Churchill themes, how far it was an international rather than a British or British Empire phenomenon, and (in some cases) how different the picture of Churchill given in such books was to the one with which historians of today have become familiar.

It was an especially fortunate coincidence that my year as the Robertson Professor happened to include March 1996, the fiftieth anniversary of Churchill's own visit to the College campus, the occasion both for an anniversary conference run in nearby Jefferson City by the

International Churchill Society (ICS), and many other commemorative events. The latter included not only a train ride and a motorcade, coast-to-coast coverage in the press and on television, and two banquets, but also a commemorative oration delivered by Margaret Thatcher. All of this drove home the extent to which so many Americans venerate the memory of Winston Churchill in the here and now, just as so many did when writing and buying books about him in the 1950s. The fact of his international appeal was more than made clear by my attending in that same academic year the ICS Conference, held in 1995 in Boston, where British, Canadian and American 'Churchillians' gathered to honour the sacred memory – but also to discuss it seriously and to listen to some fairly tough academic papers on the subject. All of this was 120 years after his birth and 30 years after his death. It was widely said when he died in 1965 that Churchill now 'belonged to History', but this was clearly no mere consigning of a popular and respected statesman to a dead and increasingly forgotten past. In America at least, the commemoration of Churchill continues today much as it did when he died, and criticism of anything he did is almost as difficult for a historian now as it was then – witness the outrage that greeted in some quarters critical books on him by Clive Ponting, John Charmley and (far more understandably) David Irving. Politicians around the world continue to invoke his memory, pray in aid his words of comfort or inspiration in difficult times, and treat him as a yardstick by which other men should be judged.

Clearly, this is a subject which needed to be properly investigated, and on a canvas wide enough to encompass so large and so widely dispersed a reputation. I was fortunately able to begin that process in North America during 1995–6, visiting numerous Presidential libraries and other archives over the course of the year, and revisiting many in the years since. The Robertson Chair awarded to me by Westminster College, under the auspices of the Fulbright Commission, was therefore the starting point of this quest, and I gratefully acknowledge its importance to everything that appears here. It was obvious enough, though, that Churchill had pitched his post-war appeal to 'the English-speaking peoples' as a whole, a favourite concept of his throughout a long career, and indeed one to which he remained faithful throughout a political life not otherwise notable for its apparent consistency. Was that appeal really as wide as it seemed, and how was it received in the further-flung reaches of the Commonwealth? It was essential then to investigate how Churchill was viewed beyond Britain and North America, and for this I needed to spend a good deal of time in the southern hemisphere. The award of a Fellowship by the (British) Winston Churchill Memorial Trust in 1999 allowed me to do the necessary research in New Zealand, and in 2001 I held a position as a Distinguished Academic Visitor in the Institute of Advanced Studies at La Trobe University in Melbourne, Australia. The former allowed me to research in New Zealand, while the latter not only facilitated the bigger task of investigating the diversity of Australian responses to Churchill, but also enabled me to review on a smaller scale the position of Churchill in respect of South-East Asia and the Southern Pacific, a whole range of places where English is still spoken, VCRs use VHS, and cars still drive on the left. To the WCMT and to La Trobe, I again acknowledge a considerable debt of gratitude.

Time and money did not allow for a similar extended foray into South Africa, one of the places where after all the Churchill legend was first born. Durban was the first English-speaking city to cheer him through its streets, in 1900 after he had escaped from captivity by the Boers, and Cape Town followed suit soon afterwards. But it was in the 1950s and 1960s that the true and lasting Churchill legend was established and fixed in the public mind, and during that period South Africa was passing gradually out of the British orbit. Churchill himself eventually stopped listing it among the most-favoured places in his speeches. Whereas in the 1930s he would have referred routinely to Canada, South Africa, Australia and New Zealand (often in that order), alongside Britain and the USA as 'the English-speaking peoples', by the 1950s the same list was often rendered as 'Canada, Australia, New Zealand and the others'. There have been museums and memorials to Churchill's memory in South Africa, for example at the Pretoria school-house in which he was once held prisoner and at the place in Durban where he spoke soon after his escape on the same adventure, while Estcourt in Natal made him a freeman of the town as late as 1964. But his association with the concept of Englishness put him somewhat out of fashion in (Afrikaans-speaking) government circles in South Africa well before the time of his death, and he has not been much commemorated there by such public acts as the erection of statues or the naming of streets. South Africa has had no branch of the International Churchill Society.

Churchill himself never ceased to praise his old friend Jan Smuts, and worked to ensure a proper memorial to Smuts in Britain, but once Smuts himself fell from power in South Africa in 1948, he did not concern himself overmuch with a country whose current politics he did not really like very much. He certainly regretted South Africa's ejection from the Commonwealth in 1961, much as he disliked Macmillan's 'winds of change' speech at Cape Town in 1960 (of which his doctor Lord Moran noted that 'he thinks Harold ought not to have gone to Africa, encouraging the black men'). But these were more the instinctively conservative reflections of a very old man than expressions of any real affection for the *Apartheid* regime and all that it represented. For better or worse, South Africa does not much figure here either.

Churchill's references to 'Canada . . . and the others' does, however, indicate some uncertainty about the exact nature of his concept of 'the English-speaking peoples' once the processes of British decolonisation had begun in 1947. Once India had become a republic, he assured New Zealanders that their country had become 'the brightest gem in the British crown', but, though New Zealanders themselves tended not to notice the fact, this was a highly conditional tribute, which clearly did not relate to *before* 1947, when India itself had been 'the jewel in the crown'. It has been represented to me that there may well be more English-speakers in India than in the whole of the rest of the world and that any analysis of Churchill and 'the English-speaking peoples' must include the sub-continent. It would be almost impossible to do this properly, however, for the range of diversity in Indian responses to the Churchill legend would be enormous, and it would make little sense anyway to research only those expressed in English. The most convincing reason for leaving out India, and indeed the whole non-white sector of the Commonwealth, is that this was clearly what Churchill himself did when he thought of the concept. Off the cuff and in private, he could be quite open about this, as in wartime Washington, when he remarked, 'Why be apologetic about Anglo-Saxon superiority? We are superior . . .' More often the matter was one of omission. In 1921, Neville Chamberlain had noted in a family letter a speech that Churchill made as Colonial Secretary during a conference of 'Dominion premiers and the Indian representatives'. Churchill 'showed his defects' when he:

clean forgot about India and talked about 'our race', 'English-Speaking Peoples' and 'the Four Great Dominions' so that I could not help asking myself What does Mr Sastri [an Indian delegate] think of all this. Towards the end of the speech someone handed up a card on which 'India' was written and Winston then produced an eloquent passage about the day when India would take her place on equal terms with the Dominions. But it was too late and when later on Sastri rose he delivered in perfect English and with perfect taste one of the most scathing rebukes I ever heard.[1]

Chamberlain concluded that 'W[inston] must have cussed a bit,' not least because the very fact that he was rebuked by an Indian in perfect English had exposed the deep fault-line in his argument. Even Churchill's self-correction here was pretty disingenuous, for he did not want to see India become a dominion anyway, and he almost wrecked his career in the 1930s by opposing with ferocity a Government of India Bill which half-heartedly offered to take India half of the way in that direction. Pandit Nehru, consulted some years before Churchill's death, had warmly agreed to attend his funeral, for his admiration entirely outweighed the fact that Churchill had always opposed Indian independence. In fact Nehru died first, but in Kenya Vice President Odinga Oginga, warily asked the same question by the British High Commissioner in 1965, replied simply, 'When Churchill was your Prime Minister, *I* was pro-British,' for his status as the 'saviour of humanity' was more important than his colonial views on Africa. An even less likely admirer of Churchill was Fidel Castro, who announced when visiting New York in 1964 that he was reading Churchill's war memoirs. Asked by a student how he could stomach such a great imperialist, Castro responded sharply that 'If Churchill hadn't done what he did to defeat the Nazis, you wouldn't be here, none of us would be here.' He then added, for the benefit of his American listeners, that 'We [Cubans] have to take a special interest in him because he too led a little island against a great enemy.' Each of these three men was an admirer of Churchill for his services to freedom in the world, but none of them saw him as a sympathiser with his own political cause or identity.[2]

I at least have not 'clean forgot' about India, but I am following Churchill's example in using what was in fact his practical definition of 'the English-speaking peoples', even if it was one that he would have been unlikely to acknowledge in public. That is to say that the English-speaking peoples were Britain, the 'white Commonwealth' and the United States, a racial concept that Churchill, Chamberlain and most Western contemporaries shared, as the above letter demonstrates. A quarter of a century later, in the curious little short-story-cum-political-testament that Churchill wrote in 1947 but never published, 'The Dream' of an imagined conversation with his father, he asserts that 'I have always worked for friendship with the United States, and indeed throughout the English-Speaking Peoples.' 'English-Speaking Peoples?' Lord Randolph repeats, 'weighing the phrase'. 'You mean with Canada, Australia, New Zealand, and all that?' 'Yes, all that.' 'Are they still loyal?' asks the father. 'They are our brothers,' Winston replies – but neither of them names South Africa and we are left to work out for ourselves if it is included in 'all that'. Winston would certainly not be including India among 'our brothers'.[3]

Those qualifications apart, this book therefore looks at the way in which Churchill projected himself across the world after 1945, how that self-projection was received, and how well it has stood the test of time. The first part looks at the extraordinary response to Churchill at the time of his 1965 funeral, delves back to the war years and before in order to see how that reputation evolved, and how after 1945 – partly through his own efforts – he came to be seen as 'the greatest living Englishman' and 'the man of the century'. The second part reviews the way in which this process was viewed from two very different nearby perspectives, in the Celtic parts of the British Isles and especially Ireland, and across Europe. The third part then considers in turn the way in which the different non-British parts of Churchill's English-speaking peoples received the message and made it their own. Finally, the last chapter looks at the way in which the Churchill legend has been fostered, used and on occasion abused, until the present day. Though *Life* did not make Churchill 'man of the century' as the twenty-first century began, many others did, and the terrorist attacks in New York in 2001 confirmed just how far his rhetoric, his image and his personality remained at the heart of Western ideas of leadership in international political affairs.

This book will perhaps seem more critical of Churchill than some of his greatest admirers will quite like, for, in charting the ways in which he acted as his own spin-doctor after 1945, and the manner in which his admirers managed to stifle legitimate criticism of the man and his record in his last years, it necessarily presents the figure of a man who was at times more petty, egocentric and selfish than almost any other British Prime Minister of modern times. But Churchill was a man who lived every part of his life on an epic scale, and his personal failings were therefore also large ones, as were his political failures, his misjudgements, and sometimes his wrong assessments of other people too. With the benefit of hindsight, none of this matters when compared to what he achieved in 1940–1, without which the world would still be a very different place. It is hard to express this appropriately in words other than his own, and nothing of Churchill's does it better than the assessment in his war memoirs of what had already been achieved by the end of 1940, just eight months after he took charge of the government and the British war effort.

> We were alive. We had beaten the German air force. There had been no invasion of the Island. The Army at home was now very powerful. London had stood triumphant throughout her ordeals . . . With a gasp of astonishment and relief the smaller neutrals and the subjugated states saw that stars still shone in the sky. Hope, and within it passion, burned anew in the hearts of hundreds of millions of men. The good cause would triumph, Right would not be trampled down. The flag of freedom, which in this fateful hour was the Union Jack, would still fly in all the winds that blew.[4]

It is difficult not to be carried way by such powerful words, especially for the British. But perhaps we should not try to resist, if we are fully to understand the impact that Churchill had on so many people, both at the time and since. The man, the message and the way in which he so effectively expressed it were and are indissolubly one.

Readers may reasonably ask where I myself stand. For my part, Churchill was a figure with whom I grew up. As a boy, I avidly read each week's instalment of the cartoon-strip serialisation of his life as 'The Happy Warrior' in the boy's magazine *Eagle*, and when the book version came out I re-read the story many times over. Shortly before leaving school, I watched Churchill's funeral on television and was intensely moved by the experience. As a young historian, I was occasionally able to meet and talk with those like A. L. Rowse and A. J. P. Taylor who had been among the first to celebrate his fame in historical terms, and to assert his uniquely historic position in modern British history, beyond that indeed to the history of the West. I now recognise that uncritical admiration is rarely a light that illuminates much truth; the Churchill legend which he and others so sedulously cultivated in the 1940s and 1950s – as this book shows – is only in part true, but the essence of what he did in the 1940s was of so great a historical significance that mistakes in other areas and at other times scarcely matter in the final measure of the man. When listeners to BBC Radio 4's *Today* programme were asked to nominate their British 'man of the millennium' as the twentieth century ended, they chose William Shakespeare for the title. As a lifelong believer in the power of the word – in English – Churchill might well not have dissented from that choice. But the only figure from the twentieth century and the only *politician* who came near to winning the poll was Churchill, just as he came near to winning – and certainly should have won – *Time* magazine's 'man of the century' title in 1999. Foibles and mistakes notwithstanding, Churchill *was* the towering personality of the century, and we are not yet done with him as the new century begins. Even four years before the bombing of the World Trade Center, Henry Kissinger was asserting that the memory of Churchill's life and the Anglo-American relationship for which he stood was as important to the post-Cold War era as it had been in the previous half-century – and would remain so after the millennium too. His Churchill Lecture, delivered appropriately enough at the English-Speaking Union in London in 1997, concluded like this:

> In a lecture dedicated to Winston Churchill, it is very important
> to remember that every great accomplishment was an idea before
> it became a reality, that cynics do not build cathedrals, and that
> the future really depends crucially on whether we can maintain
> the attitudes and the spirit that has brought us to this point.[5]

To be treated as a yardstick of international achievement in such a way, through the memory of his personality, his intellectual force and his sheer willpower, is the measure of what Churchill has become and remained since 1945. It seems, to say the least, worth trying to understand how that fame was created, perceived, marketed, spun and in some cases even fabricated. That is what this book sets out to do.

PART ONE

1

'The Greatest Dying Englishman': Churchill's Death and Funeral

WHEN INFORMED IN JANUARY 1965 that Winston Churchill had died, Charles de Gaulle is said to have murmured, without obvious regret, 'Now Britain is no longer a great power.' He was by no means alone at the time in viewing the second half of January 1965 as a natural punctuation point in British history, the end of an era. Nor were foreigners the only ones to see it that way. As Churchill's funeral train passed through Oxford, an All Souls' historian remarked dolefully, as 'the Western sky filled with the livid glow of winter sunset', that 'the Sun is going down on the British Empire'. In the *Illustrated London News*, Arthur Bryant announced that 'the age of giants has gone forever. For nobody now who can remember 1940 and the Second World War can expect to see in his lifetime anyone of the stature of this colossus of a man.'[1] Churchill's age – just over ninety when he died – his failing health and vitality over the last years and his increasing seclusion after about 1962 had all prompted expectations that he could not live much longer. Those planning memorials to the 'greatest living Englishman' had accelerated their efforts in the last months of his life. He was in those months, as *Private Eye* had put it with the characteristic lack of taste for which it was becoming famous even then, 'the greatest dying Englishman'. Then in January 1965 he suffered his final stroke and a week later died.

Given the debates of the time in British politics, it was perhaps inevitable that much of the immediate British commentary on Churchill's passing should have centred on his own 'finest hour' during the Second World War and be diagnosed as the end of that post-war epoch in which all had been overshadowed by 'Churchill's war'. As Churchill had aged towards his ninetieth birthday, however (for which he received 300,000 cards), he had become steadily more downbeat in his own assessments of what he had achieved in the war years. For the man who had proudly declared that he had not become the King's first minister in 1940 in order to preside over the liquidation of the British Empire had lived on to witness the devastating economic consequences of Britain's war effort of 1939–45, and at least the 'beginning of the end' of the Empire. He had also seen in 1962, and very probably deplored, Britain's first application to join 'Europe', a policy shift which involved a turning away from the British Dominions overseas, and to an extent away from the Special Relationship with the United States too. As he told his secretary, utterly refusing consolation, 'I have worked very hard all my life, and I have achieved a great deal, in the end to achieve NOTHING,' the last word falling from his lips 'with sombre emphasis'. The most he would concede when he was assured that he had been responsible for real and lasting achievements was just 'Perhaps.'[2]

January 1965 was thus to a large extent the end of the real 'post-war' period for Britain. With the passage of time, the phrase 'post-war' became more or less synonymous with 'since the war' and then just 'the second half of the twentieth century', whereas in the immediate aftermath of 1945 the phrase carried more specific, more useful and more comforting connotations. By the mid-1960s, the diplomatic and economic record of Britain since 1945 was no longer susceptible to the reassuring view that Britain had simply suffered a temporary setback after 1945, and would eventually reap 'the full fruits of victory'. In particular, the rehabilitation and economic success of the 'defeated' countries, Japan and Germany, had cast an inescapably gloomy shadow over the very idea of victory for Britain. This is a familiar argument, as is the view that in the early 1960s British policy-makers could still not bring themselves quite to draw the logical conclusions from it. The continuing life of Churchill, enjoying a steadily expanding place in the public's affection and esteem as he aged, was a barrier to any such fundamental reappraisal, as indicated by the panic within Harold Macmillan's Government when it seemed in 1962 that Churchill might come out publicly against British entry to the Common Market. It was absolutely commonplace for columnists – and even more so it may be suspected for pub conversationalists – to harp on the decline of British political leadership by contrasting Churchill with his successors. In 1965, the *New Statesman*'s cartoonist Trog drew Churchill as a Russian doll, from which a family of dolls – Eden, Macmillan, Home – emerged, each of a successively diminishing stature.[3] His son Randolph Churchill's blistering book on Eden, published in 1959, was based on the same premise, as were many of the dismissive remarks made about Sir Alec Douglas-Home's brief inglorious premiership. And critics were especially dismissive, though only after Churchill died, of Harold Wilson's assumption of Churchillian rhetoric during the difficult mid-1960s – an outstanding example, it was thought, of his tendency to be a 'Yorkshire Walter Mitty'. In such circumstances, it was particularly hard for political leaders to challenge those things that were inseparably mixed in the public mind with Churchill's own reputation. Churchill's death could thus have provided a real opening. The continuing assumption of the Churchillian mantle, by Wilson and in due course by Margaret Thatcher, could of course have the opposite effect.

About twenty years is the longest period that can usefully be described as 'post-[any]-war', and the critical reappraisal of Britain and its international position occasioned by the death and funeral of Winston Churchill in January 1965 makes a convenient milestone for this particular exercise in period demarcation. If we need antecedents, they can be found in the way in which both contemporaries and subsequent historians accepted that the deaths of Queen Elizabeth I and Queen Victoria had that significance. In each case this involved the disappearance of dominating national figures who had contentiously set the agenda of national life for a generation and then reached an unexpected apotheosis of popularity in old age, but whose departure both threatened and helped to unleash the deluge of radical change that their presences had held back. It is more than coincidental that Churchill rode to his funeral on the same gun carriage that had been used for Victoria herself in 1901, and that his state funeral had no precedent in living memory except those of the Windsor monarchs. There was no even more distant parallel other than the funerals of those eminent Victorians William Gladstone and the Duke of Wellington in the nineteenth century. The fact that Churchill had a state funeral at all was down to the Queen, for it was technically on her instruction, and only then with parliamentary acquiescence, that the decision was made. In contrast, in 1898 it was Parliament which had to beg a reluctant Queen Victoria to accord the same honour to Gladstone.[4]

But, if Victoria, Gladstone and Wellington were without doubt all titanic British figures, none had acquired the degree of international celebrity that Churchill's name evoked in 1965, and the celebration of their passing had no equivalent worldwide context. This is brought out clearly by an examination of the way in which the rest of the world, but especially the United States and the other English-speaking countries, was also swept up in memorialising Sir Winston, a process that was relatively late in beginning and only truly took off in the 1960s when he died. There were for example hardly any statues of Churchill anywhere in the world before 1960, but in the 1990s they were still being erected. The political consequences of President Johnson's inability to react appropriately to Churchill's death – despite his very best efforts to do so – will be presented here as evidence of that worldwide stage on which Churchill's obsequies were performed.

After he had broken his leg in 1962 (when he had been immediately flown home from Monte Carlo in an RAF Comet, to ensure that he would at least die in England), Churchill was not often seen in public, and even when granted the honorary citizenship of the United States in spring 1963 his only visible public reaction was to appear at the window of his home in Hyde Park Gate and wave to the London crowds, though press reports dwelt lovingly on the fact that he seemed in good spirits and had sported his familiar cigar. These photographs of Churchill were among the last to be taken, and were much used to illustrate newspaper editions carrying the news of his final illness and death, as were the few taken when he made without prior notice his final official visit to the House of Commons in summer 1964 – though his health did not allow him actually to be present when the Commons paid extraordinarily fulsome tributes to him as the Father of the House on his retirement in July. His ninetieth birthday in November was widely reported, the occasion of tributes, messages and presents from all round the world, but while such reports picked up on any sign of his continuing vitality (such as his recent ordering of a couple of new velvet zippered siren suits), the tone was more subdued than in past years, no doubt from the knowledge that the end could not now be long delayed. When it finally came, it was an unexpectedly long process, for Churchill like Charles II took an unconscionable time to die. His fight for life took a fortnight in fact, though only for the second week was it public knowledge. This was followed by a third week in which plans for his funeral were finalised and expectations built up for one of the great ceremonial pageants of British history.

That remarkable fortnight in London – described by at least one British newspaper at the time as likely to be the last time that the world would ever pay such attention to anything that happened in London – has remained etched in the memory of anyone old enough to remember it. The events were front-page news for two entire weeks, while the rest of public life came to an almost complete halt. They will be described here mainly from the pages of the *Guardian* (a paper that had not supported Churchill much once he left the Liberal Party proper to join Lloyd George in 1916, which had certainly resisted many of his later campaigns, and which was by 1965 a supporter of Britain's Labour Government) and from the *Daily Express* (a paper that was as Conservative, pro-Churchill and populist as the *Guardian* was radical, sceptical and dignified). As will be obvious, the more Conservative and more sensationalist papers gave the stories of Churchill's death and funeral even greater prominence and colour than *The Times* and the *Guardian*, but the relatively colourless *Guardian* may usefully be seen as the solid core of the British mood at the time. What was most striking in any case was how little difference there was in the views taken across the whole range of the national and regional press, all the way from the *Guardian* to the *Express*.

On Saturday 16 January 1965, the *Guardian*'s front page was headlined 'Sir Winston is seriously ill', the first story of his final stroke backed by a photograph taken during his final visit to the Commons in the previous summer. Prime Minister Wilson had visited him at Hyde Park Gate to pay his respects and had stayed for fifteen minutes, while other visitors had included his daughter Mary and her husband Christopher Soames, Randolph Churchill, and Churchill's doctor Lord Moran (who now achieved instant celebrity status as he read bulletins to the hundred photographers, pressmen and television technicians gathered outside). The London public had turned out too, as soon as the first news of Churchill's illness was broadcast on radio and television, and now formed a 'dense, murmuring crowd' in the street outside his house.

The crowd was an extraordinarily mixed one. There were sad looking Indians and emotional Americans. There were long-haired boys and short-haired girls to whom the name of

Churchill is only a legend. There was the respectably dressed middle-aged, standing quietly with an air of vigil, and the elderly ones extolling his praises and telling about his war years.

Worried by the numbers gathering and the danger that this might disturb the dying man inside, the police had in fact sealed off Hyde Park Gate (and fire engines and ambulances in that part of London had been ordered to switch off their sirens as they passed the end of the street for the same reason). But it was no use, for the public continued to stand four-deep at the entrance to the cul-de-sac, and 'were still determined to wait'.[5]

Neither the *Guardian* nor the crowd it was reporting would have foreseen that the vigil in Hyde Park Gate would last for a whole week, but once it was clear that this was indeed Churchill's final illness, crowds of about 250 people remained there despite cold weather and a good deal of rain, and the newspaper kept the story on its front page, often with photographs of the crowd itself to add variety to its coverage. On the following Monday, the headline was 'Sir Winston Losing Ground', and news of a 2 a.m. dash by Lord Moran to his patient's bedside hinted (wrongly) that the end was close. By then, there was international news to report too, with messages of condolence from the Pope, and related British stories such as special prayers for Churchill said at Westminster Abbey, in the Queen's presence at Sandringham, and even on BBC television before a Sunday-evening religious discussion programme. The breadth of world reaction was indicated in a warm tribute coming from the left-wing and anti-colonial President Nkrumah of Ghana, an improbable admirer of Churchill to say the least. But, as the Dean of Westminster had put it on the previous day, Churchill was 'a man whose rich and sure character has kindled the admiration of the whole world'.[6]

On Wednesday the *Guardian* headline was 'Sir Winston Sleeps through the Day', on Thursday, 'Condition of Sir Winston Worsens', a view based on Moran's twelfth bulletin on Churchill's illness with its reference to 'terminal decline'. Friday brought 'No Change to Sir Winston', and Saturday 'Sir Winston – Condition Worsens'. By the weekend, the story was still on page one, but had shrunk to about a third of a column, there being practically nothing by then left to say except how long it was all taking. This was though a story in itself, for other papers had already leaped into print with the opinion that 'the old warrior's

fight for life', even when comatose and doomed to failure, was a metaphor for his whole ninety years of gritty determination: the headline
'Fighting On' in the *Daily Express* on 19 January was fairly typical of
this. The *Guardian*, making the same point more prosaically, reported
a statement by the British Medical Association, to the effect that Churchill's 'answer to his illness is most remarkable, evidence of a terrific
tenacity and purpose in clinging to life'. In the meantime, the comings
and goings in Hyde Park Gate remained newsworthy. Almost all papers
printed photographs of Clementine Churchill in a headscarf looking
very strained. When the press shortly afterwards acted on Clementine's
request and moved their encampment, paraphernalia and television
lights out of Hyde Park Gate, where the effect on the neighbours had
become seriously troublesome on the fourth and fifth days of the vigil,
even such non-news photographs ceased to appear.

The Churchill story was as prominent as any other for almost the
whole week – being eclipsed only when on Friday it was necessary to
carry the news of the Foreign Secretary's defeat at a by-election in Leyton
and the appointment of a new Conservative Party Chairman, whereas
the rest of British political life had more or less stopped for the duration.
Wilson cancelled on Wednesday a visit to Bonn, 'in view of the nation's
concern about Sir Winston', and on the same day Iain Macleod postponed a television broadcast for the Conservatives. From within the
Treasury – and in the midst of an economic crisis – the economist Alec
Cairncross lamented in his diary, 'all kinds of government business
held up'. Editors were ingenious in finding angles which kept the story
interesting, sometimes with the arrivals of foreign visitors or returning
holidaymakers: Lord Avon (formerly Sir Anthony Eden) and Lady Avon
(herself Churchill's niece) had for example cut short a visit to the West
Indies to get back to London before Churchill died. Sometimes there
was a fortuitous angle that just wrote itself as a Churchill-related story,
as when on the day before he died Churchill unknowingly became a
great-grandfather.[7]

More often, the staple story was just of that crowd in Hyde Park
Gate, stealthily infiltrated by reporters even after the press was supposed
to have left the scene in the hope of a story that would illuminate the
enigmatic issue of Churchill's relationship with the British people. By
Tuesday the crowd numbered over seven hundred, 'the biggest yet', and
then, presumably fuelled by the press stories actually about the crowd

and the realisation that there would be time to get there and share in the 'vigil' before Churchill died, it continued to grow. Reporting on 'the long wait . . . drawn by heaven knows what mixture of motives' on 19 January, the *Guardian* noted that, 'in spite of the grumbles and the foot-stamping, the longing for a hot cup of coffee, the sheer depression of the occupation', the reporters, 'like the crowd, clearly feel an odd closeness to Sir Winston's struggle for life': 'The long-drawn out climax of his illness is so painfully in contrast with the decisiveness of his life, but it is also a final, pathetic manifestation of the astonishing Churchillian will.' The crowd waxed and waned as the day wore on, but reached its largest numbers in the evening as more people paused there for an hour or so on their way home from work, 'drawn, like moths, to the television arc lights' as the hour for the evening bulletin approached. Above all, the crowd was seen as a manifestation of popular memories of Churchill's part in the Second World War. Although the mood of the crowd was surprisingly upbeat, they remained hushed and:

> the grief of some could not be denied. One elderly couple almost tiptoed down Hyde Park Gate with a bunch of tulips and asked a policeman in a whisper if he could see they were taken to Sir Winston. There were words with an Inspector and the wife was invited to take them to the door herself. She had been in London all during the blitz, on war work. He had been at Dunkirk as well as in the First World War. Their faces looked stricken. 'We came because we felt that we had got to,' they said.[8]

On the following day, the *Daily Express* carried a long account by Rene MacColl 'from the house of destiny' where 'the Great Commoner, the mightiest man, surely, in all the wondrous history of England', lay dying. MacColl offered, unlike the unnamed *Guardian* reporter, a detailed and colourful physical description of the dramatic scene and its principal actors – the 'gaunt and stooped' Lord Moran, 'definitely of the old school. Not for him garrulousness about the patient', and Churchill's detective, 'as completely British as a pre-war five pound note . . . surely a brother under the skin of the great Lestrade'. Most of all he described the 'crowd of muted afternoon spectators – everyone instinctively speaks in low whispers'. There were 'the people in their parkas and suede jackets, with lambswool collar facings and old school ties, and the young girls in fancy stockings and the old ladies in severe hats, standing as though caught in a trance of unease and regret'. Across the street was the blue plaque recalling the residence of Sir Leslie Stephen, prompting MacColl to wonder how long it would be before the London County Council had one facing it to denote Churchill's time as a resident in Hyde Park Gate.[9] This captures the tone of the overwhelming mass of British reporting – unease as to a future without Churchill, fascination with the death of an immortal, and a determination to project the crowd of onlookers as both representative of the whole British people and conscious above all of the link of Churchill with the London of the Blitz when his words had so inspired these same people or their parents.

In view of the time and effort that the British dailies spent in keeping the Churchill story on their front pages for six successive editions when there was actually very little to report after the first day, they were extremely unlucky that when he died it came too late and over a week-end, so that the really important news of his death was broken by radio, television and (in parts of North America) the Sunday papers, before they had any chance to make any comment at all. Nevertheless, the fact that they had had a full week of advance notice of his death (and had anyway been preparing to announce it for years) meant that they were by no means caught unawares when it happened. On Monday 25 January the *Daily Express* front page carried only the words 'The Death of Churchill' and a full-page (wartime) photographic portrait of the great man in his most bulldog-like manner. Inside, the whole of the next four pages was devoted to announcing, analysing and commenting on his death, and to giving advance news of the funeral plans. For the *Guardian* too, most of that day's edition was given over to the Churchill story: the whole of the front page was the news itself, page four reprinted tributes already received from around the world, pages ten and eleven comprised a lengthy obituary, page fourteen was wholly given over to photographs of Churchill from his long career, and there was on page twelve a longish leader on Churchill's significance, taking an extremely positive, benevolent line. The delay over the weekend had at least ensured that the Monday papers could benefit from the first announcements of the funeral plans. The *Guardian*'s headline was in fact not the death of Churchill which its readers would have already known about, but 'State Funeral for Sir Winston', and the edition also gave details of the following Saturday's arrangements in detail, the route by road and river that the cortège would take, and plans for a lying-in-state in Westminster Hall.[10]

Having thus made the Churchill funeral as well as his death an item of front-page news, the British papers continued with it for the whole of the following week, when it was once again rarely off the front pages. There were more tributes to be printed from around the world, parliamentary tributes in Britain delivered on Monday the 25th and dominating newspaper accounts on the 26th (so allowing the *Guardian* a second editorial on Churchill as 'a good House of Commons man'), and reiterated assurances that the scale of the coming Saturday's obsequies would be large enough to befit the size of the man who was to be commemorated. So for example it was reported that BBC and ITV would pool their visual resources and commit no fewer than eighty-five television cameras to the coverage of the event, there would be a suitable number of troops and bands for the procession, the Queen would break with all precedent and come to the funeral of a commoner, and so too would at least four kings, three presidents, two vice presidents, six prime ministers, two chancellors and eleven foreign ministers (and these only from outside the Commonwealth, which would itself contribute to the glittering throng another vice president, five more prime ministers and five more foreign ministers). There was pride taken in advance for the meticulousness with which the Earl Marshal had planned the ceremonial, and preview pictures taken in the London streets as the funeral procession was rehearsed on successive mornings just after dawn to ensure that it would all go without a hitch.

Most of all, though, as the week bore on, the press and broadcasting coverage focussed on Churchill's lying-in-state in Westminster Hall, an event that practically nobody could remember ever happening to a commoner, and which because of the extreme antiquity of the building itself evoked regular assertions of Churchill's historic status. He was going, proclaimed the *Express*, 'into the Hall of Kings', a claim given added weight when the Queen herself came to pay him homage there, as did other visiting royalty and celebrity guests. Not to be left out, Harold Wilson, the other party leaders and the Speaker of the Commons came for a final act of homage on the last evening before the funeral, taking a turn in the places of the four soldiers who had been stationed around the catafalque. The *Guardian* reported that 'Crown and Commons pay last tribute', and the *Express* once again invoked the Churchillian language of wartime with 'Homage to a man owed so much by the Many'. The most reported and analysed part of the proceedings, however, was the interminable queue of ordinary people who waited patiently to view Churchill's coffin, its length and variety effectively captured by the *Express* as a running photograph across the top of four pages on 28 January.[11] On the Saturday itself, every paper carried again full details of the funeral arrangements, routes and broadcasting times, and several like the *Express* issued special Churchill funeral supplements. The fact that the main event was on a Saturday denied the dailies the chance to be the first to report it, but in this case the huge television audience for the live Saturday broadcasts had in effect scooped the entire press. All the same, every Sunday paper on the 31st and every daily on Monday 1 February devoted several pages to coverage of the funeral, dozens of photographs and yards of column inches, in some cases once again offering pull-out-and-keep supplements too. There was enormous national self-satisfaction in all this coverage, both from the brilliance and restraint with which the ceremonial had been staged, something that it was thought 'we British do so well', and from the reflected glory of the world's homage to Britain's greatest contemporary hero. The eloquence of the tributes paid on the air by America's Dwight Eisenhower and Australia's Robert Menzies was invariably cited in support of such a view, as was the sheer calibre of the world's representatives at the funeral.

In all that smugness, the British people and their opinion-formers would have been surprised but extremely gratified to know that the death and funeral of Winston Churchill attracted almost as much media attention across the rest of the English-speaking world as they did in London. All through from the first news of Churchill's stroke to the multitudes of photographs of his funeral (and television audiences too) the above account of the coverage in London's newspapers was broadly replicated not only in the *Scotsman* and the *Western Mail*, but also in the *Toronto Globe* and the *Vancouver Sun*, in both the *Sydney Morning Herald* and New Zealand's *The Dominion*. Indeed, though regional coverage varied much more in the United States, pretty much the same Churchill stories were covered in the same way on most days of that fortnight in late January 1965 in the *New York Times*, the *Boston Globe*, the *Los Angeles Times*, the *San Francisco Chronicle* and the *Philadelphia Inquirer*. The passing of Winston Churchill, though invariably reported as the end of a great Englishman, was also seen as an event of significance for the entire English-speaking world.

New Statesman, 5 February 1965

The death of Churchill then, whatever else it was, was certainly seen
at the time both as an event of historic importance in itself and as a
historic moment. The *Daily Express* editorialised that 'history was with
us while he lived', while the *Sunday Times* thought that the funeral had
been 'an act of history in itself'. Even Churchill's old adversary Charles
de Gaulle joined in the world's homage by attending the funeral, visiting
the lying-in-state and issuing a dignified statement asserting Churchill's
historic status. In the immediate aftermath of Churchill's death, the
United Nations, the Council of Europe, the US Congress, the NATO
Council and countless other international bodies all adjourned as a
sign of respect, and passed suitable motions of condolence. In Britain,
parliamentarians actually adjourned for almost a week between listening
to hours of tributes to Churchill and turning out in force for his funeral,
and in countless other ways, too, the fortnight between Churchill's illness
being announced on 15 January and his burial on the 30th was marked
by the suspension of normal events. The Prime Minister abandoned
trips abroad, and twice cancelled a party political broadcast, the Queen
changed her travel plans, football matches on the day of the funeral were
rescheduled and many shops closed for the day. Even the celebration of
the seven-hundredth anniversary of Parliament itself was postponed, as

a mark of respect for a lifelong parliamentarian. The National Association of Schoolmasters cancelled a strike because of the feeling that the time and mood were inappropriate for such things. *The Times*, famously, abandoned centuries of tradition by putting the news of Churchill's death on its front page; Big Ben did not chime all day on 30 January. London's Underground trains kept going through the night to cope with the crowds wishing to pay homage to the great man when lying in state and then for those gathering for the funeral. When the funeral train passed through the Home Counties on its way to Churchill's final interment in the village graveyard of Bladon in Oxfordshire, British Railways opened up twenty-one stations to allow in massive crowds to stand silently along the platforms as the coffin was carried past.[12]

The lying-in-state and the funeral were events of massive and long-planned pageantry on an unprecedented scale, beginning with Prime Minister Harold Wilson turning up in the Commons in a frock coat to deliver the Queen's message officially informing MPs of Churchill's death. Plans for the funeral had started in 1953 when Churchill had a stroke while still Prime Minister, and had been actively discussed with Churchill himself in the years since – needless to say receiving strong endorsement from a man who always liked a big emotional show. Following enquiries by the Earl Marshal, the Queen had suggested back in 1953 that Churchill should be given a send-off 'on a scale befitting his position in history', and the plans had been made and kept up to date ever since. Lord Mountbatten, who as First Sea Lord was involved in the funeral preparations, dined out for years on the story of how the funeral plans and lists of pall-bearers had constantly to be updated; as he told the story to Vice President Hubert Humphrey, 'the problem was that Churchill kept living and the pall-bearers kept dying'. On the main issue, though, Churchill got his way, and there was lots of good British military band music at his funeral. (He had once deeply upset Montgomery who had come to consult him on regimental amalgamations by taking no apparent interest in any part of the plans but the survival of their bands, explaining pathetically that he wanted to be sure that he would have a good funeral.) Hence, the detailed planning of procession, lying-in-state and funeral service had all been done years in advance. This was timed to the minute in some cases, mock-ups of such official documents as invitations had already been agreed with the College of Heralds, and a sort of 'war book' existed on a 'D-day plus x' basis for all the days between the death and the final ceremonials. It had long been seen that the funeral had to be on a Saturday, and Churchill's eventual death at a weekend duly allowed the plan to go smoothly and unhurriedly into action for the following week.[13]

The then considerable sum of £55,000 was spent on the ceremony, and even this figure would not have included any charge for the services of the police, armed forces, broadcasters and the Church of England. One hundred and twelve countries were represented at the funeral, mostly at a very high level. The Soviet Union among Britain's cold war adversaries sent a suitably eminent team of mourners led by the Foreign Minister. Only China refused to be represented at Churchill's funeral and in Europe only Ireland refused to broadcast the funeral live on television. British newspapers were highly critical of the United States when President Lyndon Johnson decided not to come in person, and their criticisms were reflected in the press as far away as Australia and New Zealand too, as well as in America itself. There was some compensation, however, in the fact that ex-President Eisenhower attended as a guest of the Churchill family, and from the touching tribute to his old friend that Ike broadcast on the BBC as Churchill's coffin was carried upriver from St Paul's Cathedral to Waterloo Station after the funeral service. It hit the appropriately emotional tone, on a day when many British people really let their feelings go – as they would not do again collectively until the Princess of Wales died more than thirty years later. American visitors were indeed both surprised and impressed by the extent to which British people standing in the London streets to watch the funeral procession gave way to floods of tears as it passed, but reassured themselves that this was only right and proper, for Churchill himself had been well known for his propensity to weep unashamedly in emotional circumstances. In this way too, then, Churchill's literal passing seemed only to emphasise the closeness of his historic link with the British people. As Laurie Lee put it, reporting the lying-in-state for the *Daily Telegraph*, 'the thousands still come, snow footed down the carpets of silence . . . not since the war has there been such shared emotion'.[14]

The expectation in Fleet Street – again reflected in the press in all the English-speaking countries – was that all the world would pay homage to Churchill, as indeed it mostly did. London has never again been the centre of the world's attention as it was in January 1965, and it seems unlikely indeed that the subsequent funeral of any long-retired British politician will ever generate such expectations. Nor is it probable that the broadcasting of such an event could attract a European television audience of 350 million people – a huge proportion of the total number of people with access to sets in 1965 – and a commensurately large one in the English-speaking world too. All of this may well be taken as a 'last rally', a point of finality along the lines of de Gaulle's comment about the end of British power. Churchill's personal detective disconsolately remarked that 'if the king is dead you can say, "Long Live the King". But now Sir Winston has gone, who is there? There's no one of his stature left.' In an important sense, then, although Churchill's state funeral was hailed around the world as demonstrating the British genius for public spectacle, it was not and could not be a celebration of continuity, as British royal pageantry has invariably been since that tradition was invented during the second half of the nineteenth century. Rather, it marked a point of finality, a view that was certainly reinforced by the funeral's public display of the ageing of many of Churchill's much younger political colleagues and rivals like Clement Attlee. As Alan Moorhead put it, 'one is touched suddenly to see how frail so many of these distinguished people are, how much they need their sticks . . . how they are determined to see the occasion through'.[15]

Within Britain, there is no doubting the degree of involvement in these funerary rites. While Churchill lay dying and crowds gathered in Hyde Park Gate, the Salvation Army distributed tea. This last point was frequently reported by British papers in the context of images of the Blitz of 1940–1, so closely were Churchill, the war, London and the British people enmeshed in the popular memory. There was a record British television audience of twenty-five million viewers for the funeral, but there were also vast crowds on the London streets, on a day so cold that there were even casualties among the police horses on duty. There was another huge queue in the churchyard at Bladon within a few hours of the private interment, and well over a hundred thousand people filed past Churchill's grave by the end of the day after his funeral.

Apart from the television audience, which at that size can have excluded few who were of an age to watch and were able to get to a set, it seems that the crowds on the streets were predominantly middle-aged and older people, many of whom told reporters that they were motivated directly by memories of 1940. As if consciously re-enacting the events of 1945, many in those crowds had brought with them children, determined that they should be able to say in later life that they had seen such a historic event. The most analysed part of the phenomenon was the mile-long queue that snaked around Westminster and over Lambeth Bridge as people waited their turn to troop past the coffin in Westminster Hall, memories of the Blitz once again kept alive by the uniformed Women's Voluntary Service who ministered to them with hot soup and sandwiches. Over three days and nights, nearly a third of a million people filed past Churchill's coffin, actually rather fewer than had been expected, though the bitter cold no doubt contributed to this. The total was about the same as visited the lying-in-state of George VI in February 1952, but less than half as many as turned out for the defiantly uncharismatic George V in the equally cold January of 1936. That lying-in-state occasioned some of Fleet Street's most purple prose, most notably from Vincent Mulchrone as the *Daily Mail*'s 'special cata-falque correspondent' – surely a unique by-line in the annals of British journalism. In the *Guardian*, John Grigg argued that it had been extremely difficult for thinking people to separate their 'exultation at the genuine grandeur' from the media's trivialising of 'phoney history, phoney religion and phoney emotion'. For such people, the dignified television coverage of the funeral of what Peter Black called 'the last of the great non-TV personalities' helped a great deal. Laurence Olivier's recruitment to the ITV commentary team may have put off some with his actorish histrionics, but Richard Dimbleby won as much praise for his role as the dignified anchorman of the BBC's programme as did the Duke of Norfolk for his stage-management of the pageantry itself.[16]

Some sympathy is perhaps due to the media anyway. It was after all a tough task for the editors to keep a story that just *had* to be front-page material going over a dozen consecutive daily issues. Almost everyone who could conceivably have a viewpoint was asked for an opinion on Churchill's significance, and some were asked more than once. Evelyn Waugh noted that the pathway to his house had been worn smooth by the shoes of telegraph boys delivering pleas that he should report the funeral for one paper or another. He attributed this to the fact that he had once written a novel about funerals, but it was more likely because he could combine a Churchillian way with words and a Falstaffian presence not unlike that of the focus of all the atten-tion.[17] But it is unlikely that Waugh's irreverence – not to mention his contempt for Churchill – would have been in step with the national mood in January 1965. Among the wits, Noël Coward was certainly nearer to that mood. In his *Cavalcade* manner, 'the Master' arranged for a party of friends to come round to his suite at the Savoy Hotel, and 'watched the funeral on television from 9.20 until 1.20 – in floods of proud tears most of the time. The arrival of the barge [en route for Waterloo Station] we could see from the window of my sitting-room, directly opposite us. A great and truly noble experience.' The 'elevated patriotism' that the *Sunday Times* detected in that week of solemn pageantry united Churchill's past with the country's present in a powerful brew of emotion; it was, the paper wrote, a mood 'without which Winston Churchill knew that the nation could not survive', but it was also an emotion that few others had ever been able to conjure up.[18]

Man is, as Dr Johnson once remarked, 'not on oath in lapidary inscriptions'. Overall, both the parliamentary and broadcast tributes which the press recorded, and the ones that they commissioned themselves, were written in a tone that confirmed all the inherited views about Churchill's role in 1940 and the impossibility of separating his 'finest hour' from that of the nation. Anthony Eden, for example, was generally congratulated for suggesting that the Government should institute a Churchill Day as a new bank holiday, timed to coincide with one of the great dates in the calendar of 1940, so that British history and Churchill's name would be imperishably combined. The *Observer* was almost unique in breaking ranks, arguing in an editorial that Churchill's finest hour had *not* been in 1940 at all, but the late 1930s when he had preached a message that almost everyone else had ignored. This view was certainly less self-congratulatory for the British people than the constant harping on 1940, but it was equally positive about Churchill (and could be said to have derived even more than memories of 1940 from Churchill's own cultivation of his personal history). It was also extremely rare, even on the left. When the playwright John Arden complained that even the *New Statesman* had departed from its usual standards by printing uncritical tributes to Churchill and glowing accounts of the funeral, he was attacked by several later correspondents who thought that the same editorial had been petty, carping and unimaginative. The flagship of the intellectual left rescued itself with a final, much praised article by V. S. Pritchett on the funeral itself. This combined an extremely upbeat account of the 'general emotion' rather than the 'private rhetoric' which had informed the day, and candidly admitted that Pritchett had himself been caught up in it all at the time. But it also offered a neat explanation: 'There was, I suspect,' he wrote, 'an undertone of self-pity. We were looking at the last flash of Victorian aplomb; we were looking at a past utterly irrecoverable. The whole machinery of life has altered faster in the space of two generations than ever before in human history.'[19] This was a characteristic view at the time. From within the then British Government, Richard Crossman thought the funeral 'a day of orgiastic self-condolence on the end of our imperial destiny – with Churchill as its symbol', while Anthony Wedgwood Benn (as he then was) believed it would prove to be 'the last great Victorian festival'.[20]

This last view – that, while the funeral reawakened all the emotional tugs of 1940, it did so for the last time – was not only to be found in writers and journals of the left. Harold Wilson told the Commons that 'we know, too, that with his death we are marking the end of an era'. Bernard Levin in the *Mail* was one of many who agreed that 'we shall not see his like again', in an article that stressed Churchill's link with Britain's greatness; without the man who could not be replaced, where would be the greatness? The *Daily Mail* editorial on the day of the funeral implicitly made the same point, emphasising at length how far Churchill's memory would always be linked with the war, but concluding with the words, 'and now it is over'.[21]

The weeklies were much more explicit about this theme, though sometimes just as ready to produce 'phoney history' in its support. *The Economist* thought that 1940 had shown that Churchill had been 'the best not the worst sort of Conservative' since he had always been ready to innovate and to welcome the future. He had – or so it was argued – shown great powers of decision and had been a great pro-European. This was all part of *The Economist's* campaign to replace Sir Alec Douglas-Home with the more pro-European Edward Heath as Tory leader, but the message was taken more widely too: 'the funeral is an end not a beginning. History has moved on. To so much of the world Churchill won immortality by fighting what appears not as the last great war, but as the last great European War.' The *Spectator* took exactly the same line, again recruiting the name of Churchill to the European cause that he had certainly never fully embraced: in the 1950s, after Churchill's retirement, Britain had failed to enter the EEC, but belatedly all sensible people had recognised that 'this was not Churchill's Britain, and we were not Churchills'. The *New Statesman*'s claim that Churchill had been 'able to prolong Britain's existence as a leading power by an entire generation – perhaps two', was a species of the same argument.[22]

But by far the most interesting analysis was John Grigg's weekly column in the *Guardian*. He began by suggesting that 'we have already learnt – indeed, we should have learnt – to live without Churchill', but went on in a vein that betrayed less confidence in that view. The funeral should be a national tonic, not a sedative, for Churchill had achieved 'a delusive victory for Britain' in 1945 as British power was actually shattered in the process. He added, in a tone that might well have been adopted by John Charmley in the 1990s, that Churchill 'successfully defied the power of our enemies, but he could not defy the power of our friends'. What then was the lesson? 'The death of Churchill robs us of an august and (in his old age) a well-loved presence, but it also relieves us of a psychological burden. England's great old men are, as it were, canonised, and for some years past Churchill's basic assumptions in foreign affairs have largely shared that immunity from criticism which Churchill himself enjoyed. Now we can take stock . . . face contemporary facts unblinkingly and shape our policies accordingly.' The withdrawal of British garrisons from East of Suez, planned shortly afterwards and accelerated into implementation as a result of a sterling crisis in 1967, was perhaps the first real sign that British Governments had by-passed the Churchillian roadblock to realistic planning. When intelligent contemporaries and recent historians reach such similar conclusions, we should take note.[23]

Back in 1965, *The Economist* concluded of Churchill's funeral that, 'with his end, an era, even the memory of an era, fades into the past. We participate today in a great recessional, and at a time to start afresh'. In taking that view, Alastair Burnett undoubtedly underestimated the staying power of mythology and tradition in British public and cultural life, but nevertheless, his point remained a good one. By about 1965, the 'post-war' era *was* over, but not the veneration of Winston Churchill, either at home or abroad.[24]

When reporting Churchill's funeral, *The Times* noted that 'the Anglo-American theme predominated' throughout that cold day in London; American as well as British flags flew together throughout the length of the procession, St Paul's Cathedral echoed to the singing of the 'Battle Hymn of the Republic' as well as to British anthems, and it was the American Eisenhower who delivered some of the most memorable words broadcast that day. Within the United States there was extensive media coverage, and the live broadcast of the funeral attracted the largest ever American television audience to date (higher than for John F. Kennedy's funeral only fifteen months earlier), and there was an equal concentration on the events in the other media too. But, for all this, the Churchill funeral accidentally caused an unfortunate hitch in Anglo-American relations – at least at the media level – and a nasty little political crisis for the Federal Government in Washington as a result. Nothing more clearly demonstrates the international aspect of Churchill's fame.[25]

The context for all of this was the extraordinary personal role that the post-war Churchill played as a mediator between Britain and the United States, at the level of popular as well as elite opinion, so that the celebration of his funeral was always likely to be difficult for the two Governments to get right. Churchill's dual parentage, his having an American mother and a British father, was important here, but so was his determination to use the fact to attract a personal audience in the United States, and thereby to give himself leverage in the harmonisation of Anglo-American relations. In this he was assisted by a number of Anglophile Americans, men like Bernard Baruch, Dean Acheson, Dwight Eisenhower and Henry Luce, who from their viewpoint saw the building up of the Churchill legend in the United States as a way of keeping America aware of post-war Europe and preventing it from descending back into its pre-war isolationism. In this process, the key moments were Churchill's own wartime radio appeals to America, from London and in speeches in Congress and at Harvard, his post-war triumphs in speeches at Fulton and at Boston, the tremendous impact of all his post-war visits, but especially that of 1946 when his wartime role was fresh in the American mind, and the 1959 visit to Washington and New York which was visibly the last appearance in his mother's homeland that the now declining Churchill would ever make. These events are described in Chapter Seven.

All of this climaxed in 1963 with the decision of Congress, after a spirited lobbying campaign by the American Churchillians, to make Churchill the first ever honorary citizen of the United States. Even this was an act of foreign policy as much as a purely ceremonial honour to a great old man in his final years, as the debates and lobbying showed,

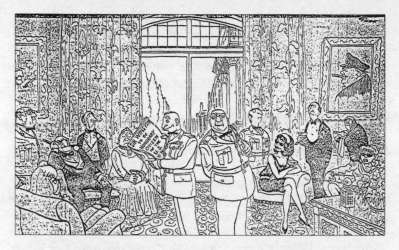

'Lay off referring to him as "That grand old American who won the war",
Lieutenant.' *Daily Express, c.* 10 April 1963

and there were even worries that America's wish to make Churchill a
favourite son would evoke jealousy in Britain. The popular British papers
welcomed the proposal anyway, but their cartoonists did hint at a little
submerged resentment. The *Daily Mail*'s Emmwood drew a vast American sergeant throttling a tiny Englishman in a pub with the words,
'Listen, Limey, smile when you mention the name of the greatest livin''
American,' while Giles in the *Daily Express* had a senior American officer
in an elite London club telling his aide to 'Lay off referring to him as
"That grand old American who won the war".' In both cases, at the
top and bottom of British society, the British pictured in the drawings
look less than enamoured with what the *New York Times* was calling
'the Americanization of Winston'. By 1965, Lyndon Johnson was indeed
referring to Churchill routinely and without qualification as 'the greatest
of all American citizens'.[26]

British sensibilities were meant to be smoothed over by an extended
piece contributed to the London *Daily Telegraph* by Arthur Schlesinger,
the historian and just then President Kennedy's counsel at the White
House. For Schlesinger, Churchill was truly a man with a foot in both
camps, educating the Americans mainly by his deeds in the war years,
the British mainly by his words.

He drove the dismal old stereotypes from respectable discourse and left them to the demagogues of the far Right and the far Left. As he made the Americans perceive the British as tough and virile, so he made the British perceive the Americans as adult and consequential ... The American people ... are celebrating in Churchill the man who by birth, by deed and by faith has made himself the first Atlantic citizen.

On this reading, Churchill the American remained no less Churchill the Briton than he had ever been. Churchill as a virility symbol for Britain was in itself a fairly common idea in the 1960s, though Freudians might have had even more of a field day with a man who was always anxious not to be seen in public with what would be seen as a 'comically short cigar'. Soon afterwards that idea was a central feature of Joe Orton's play *What the Butler Saw* (1969), though only after long battles with the censors. Sir Ralph Richardson, who had personally witnessed Kennedy making Churchill an honorary citizen in 1963 and was a fish out of water in that type of play, imposed his own censorship when he insisted on producing as a prop at the end of the play an enormous Churchillian cigar, instead of a piece of statue representing Sir Winston's private parts, as specified in Orton's text. To judge from the reactions of the West End public, neither version proved to be particularly popular, it being regarded as near-blasphemous to lampoon Churchill in that way, at a time when people were erecting statues of Churchill rather than blowing them up and making scurrilous fun of the 'parts'.[27]

Kennedy had for example agreed in 1963 to help sponsor the Washington statue of Churchill planned by the English-Speaking Union, specifically to repay the debt felt to be owed since the erection of Franklin Roosevelt's likeness in Grosvenor Square, London, for which the money had been raised by the Pilgrims Trust. Kennedy also agreed to become with Harry Truman honorary co-chairman of the Churchill Memorial planned for Fulton, where another Churchill statue would be placed.[28] The Fulton project and the Washington statue were to be the main focuses of America's physical commemoration of Churchill over the rest of the 1960s, but neither had been brought to fruition before the events surrounding Churchill's death and funeral had shed a remarkable light into the depths of what Americans felt about their new fellow citizen.

The length of time and the scale of the pageantry involved in Churchill's passing forced almost everyone in political life to take a public position on his role and importance. Both the press and broadcasting networks reported the progress of his illness and the preparations for his funeral daily for a full fortnight. Churchill and his funeral were also the subject of much discussion in the White House, of active diplomatic exchanges with American embassies and consulates around the world, and within the State Department, which set up a special Churchill Funeral Task Force to co-ordinate its activities.

In view of what followed, it is important to stress the fact that Johnson, Secretary of State Rusk and the Administration as a whole shared fully in the American elite's enthusiasm for Churchill. Rusk was personally involved in the plans to put up a Churchill statue in Washington (which he eventually unveiled), and his Department was quick off the mark in making plans. Already on 19 January, five days before Sir Winston died, all American diplomatic posts abroad were being asked to report to Washington on their host country's plans for marking his passing, and how they expected to be represented at his funeral. This urgency in itself occasioned some embarrassment, for example in Vientiane, where the Americans were told sternly that the Laotian Government were 'reluctant to consider funeral plans at this point, since they fear this would bring bad luck'; something similar happened in South Korea. From Poland, a different type of embarrassment was reported; the American envoy first consulted his British counterpart, who told him that he had no information on his Government's plans and was being 'snubbed' whenever he tried to get any, so he would be grateful if the Americans did not at this time raise the matter yet with the Poles. More often, though, foreign governments responded in a way that suggested that they well understood that this would be – even more than Kennedy's funeral in 1963 – a 'working funeral' at which all sorts of diplomatic business could be done by the official mourners as a by-product of the obsequies. It was reported for example that the King of Greece would be there and would like to meet LBJ or the Vice President to discuss issues of mutual interest. The Prime Minister of Jamaica planned to use the occasion 'to discuss bananas and citrus [fruit] with the British Government', while the Chileans hoped during their visit to London to discuss with various interested powers their boundary dispute with Argentina. Bangkok wanted talks 'at the highest level' about the future of the South East Asia Treaty Organization, and the American delegation at the UN reported that the Russians hoped that Mikoyan would be able to meet LBJ in London and so continue the thawing of the Cold War that had been discernible over the past year.[29]

Britain too was making a diplomatic virtue out of a funereal necessity, for early 1965 was also the moment when the Smith regime in Rhodesia was bracing itself for a unilateral and illegal declaration of independence (UDI). In Salisbury itself (now Harare, Zimbabwe), there was a 'magnificent service in the cathedral', attended by the Governor, cabinet ministers, judges, indeed the whole of the white social and political elite, an event seen by Alan Megahy as 'the last great "establishment" occasion in Rhodesia when the great and the good could feel part of the British tradition of which they had been so proud, and could recall again the dark days of 1939 and 1940 when the colony had played its part in the defence of the empire'. A few weeks later, the Governor initiated a Winston Churchill Thanksgiving and Memorial Fund for Rhodesia, following the example of Britain and the former Dominions, but the appeal was itself a casualty of the autumn UDI, when members of the planning committee refused to continue with its work in the absence of the Governor, who had by then been deposed by Ian Smith. Back in January, Harold Wilson had hoped to use Smith's presence in London for the Churchill funeral to hold talks about the colony's future and so prevent a UDI, but in this he was to be disappointed, and the recriminations about the cause of the failure of their talks indicated how desperate things had already become. Wilson planned to seize Smith at the Buckingham Palace reception for heads of government attending the funeral and whisk him off to Downing Street for talks with no pre-prepared agenda. But Smith did not turn up at the Palace, either because he was avoiding Wilson (Wilson's view) or because the invitation arrived too late, a deliberate slight to him (Smith's claim). When they finally began their talks later in the day, however, they managed to agree to a ministerial visit to Salisbury, the first of several doomed missions to head off UDI.[30]

Very few reports came in to Washington that suggested any lack of interest in the Churchill funeral, though the Irish Embassy reported that the Dublin Government's intention was to do only what was 'barely correct', since it had not forgotten Churchill's role in the Partition Treaty of 1921 or his 'vendetta' against De Valera over Irish neutrality in the war. The Irish, a Government source explained to the American

'... never was so much owed by so many...'
Daily Mail, 26 January 1965

Ambassador, would 'make no attempt to join the masses in paying tribute'. The Second World War was still a factor more generally too, for although most countries were limited to one official mourner at the funeral service, Britain's allies of 1939–45 each got two. This formula also allowed for two representatives to attend from South Africa, one of them Interior Minister de Klerk, without too much questioning of the country's current relationship with Britain since it had left the Commonwealth. Perhaps the saddest responses to the worldwide canvassing of diplomatic intentions came from the tiny and impoverished countries which were not equipped to join the rush to the airport that the concept of the working funeral involved. The Rwandan Government *might* be represented by its Ambassador to Belgium, who was also accredited to London, but he was too 'tied up' to go all the way from Brussels to London – though the American Ambassador suspected that this was a polite way of saying that the country could not afford his fare, and much the same turned out to be true of El Salvador. Whatever else might be said, the American diplomatic service was clearly trying hard to make the funeral as big an event as possible and to calibrate its own Government's reactions so as to offend absolutely nobody.[31]

From London, Ambassador David Bruce warned that it would be impolitic in the extreme if America were to jump the gun by announcing the name of its high-level official mourners before the British Government officially declared that there would *be* a state funeral, a warning that implied a poor estimation of Washington's diplomatic judgement. His fears would in any case prove to be well wide of the mark, for it was in the tardy and inadequate naming of the official mourners, rather than in moving too soon, that America's policy came unstuck, but there was no question of Johnson being a reluctant admirer of Churchill. As a Senator and as Vice President, he had assisted the congressional campaign for Churchill's honorary citizenship; he had taken up where Kennedy left off in the plans for a Fulton Memorial, so it was Johnson who formally launched the fundraising appeal; he was always quoting Churchill as a model for politicians to live by (or at least as a sort of virility test for their foreign and defence policies); and he was struggling in the very month of Churchill's death and burial to apply the lessons of Munich to South-East Asia. Johnson was indeed anxious to bring Australia and Britain with him into his increasing entanglement in Vietnam, and the celebration of all things Churchillian during January 1965 was at the least a convenient way of buttering up the British Commonwealth governments at that time, though Churchill himself had always resolutely refused to take the faintest interest in South-East Asia. In 1953 he announced to his doctor that he had 'lived for seventy-eight years without hearing of bloody places like Cambodia', and did not intend to start now.[32]

Johnson had picked up the inner essence of Churchill's message for post-war Americans, writing to him on his ninetieth birthday in 1964 that he had both demonstrated in his writings and proved in his life the moral that 'the price of greatness is responsibility'. He had happily signed the proclamation creating a Sir Winston Churchill Day to commemorate the honorary citizenship, and even made time in 1964 to sign a complete collection of Churchill speeches for a young British journalist Jeffrey Archer (on the assurance that they would be auctioned off in Britain for charity). During the week of Churchill's illness, Johnson personally oversaw the preparation of press releases and letters of condolence, in many cases redrafting them personally to add further superlatives to texts that were already fulsome – so that, for example, 'parliamentarian, faithful friend and honorary citizen' became 'superb parliamentarian, faithful friend and beloved honorary citizen'.[33] Even for so complex a character as LBJ, this accumulates to clear evidence of respect for Churchill, so the cause of his mishandling of the funeral arrangements has to be found in poor judgement during his own period of illness and stress in January 1965, rather than in a desire to insult Churchill's memory, or in a lack of concern for British feelings, as his critics alleged.

The real problem was that Johnson's illness – a bad cold acquired

when with Churchillian bravado he attended his Inauguration without
wearing a coat on a bitterly cold January day – was potentially more
serious than could be announced to the public, given his weak heart
(which was not a matter of public knowledge), and he was in hospital
for several days. As a result, the President delayed for too long the
decision on who should represent the United States at the Churchill
funeral, while he toyed with the idea of defying his doctors and making
a quick trip to London to lead the delegation himself. It would indeed
have been a quick trip if it had happened, for his security advisers were
positively neurotic about the dangers that he might be assassinated in
London. They would guarantee him security on his own plane, and if
a whole floor was booked for him in a major London hotel, but they
worried about his exposure out of doors for the funeral procession, and
seem not even to have been convinced that he would be safe at Buckingham Palace, should the Queen invite visiting heads of state to a buffet
lunch after the main event. By Wednesday 26 January, with half of the
week between Churchill's death and funeral gone, the USA was reported
to be the only country planning to attend which had still not named
its mourners, a source both of embarrassment and of increasingly urgent
telegrams from London. And the USA, like France and the USSR (and
no other country), was allowed three mourners at the funeral, which
made the balancing of the team a real challenge.[34]

Johnson only then bowed to the inevitable, took his doctors' advice,
and named as US delegates Secretary of State Dean Rusk, Chief Justice
Earl Warren, and London Ambassador David Bruce, though different
announcements contradicted each other as to whether Warren or Rusk
would be the chief mourner. The problem was then compounded by
Rusk catching influenza when he got to London, so that he too missed
the funeral (but, as British papers cuttingly pointed out, was thought
fit enough to fly home the same day). The USA was therefore represented only by Warren (who was a great Churchill admirer, but whom
few outside the USA had ever heard of) and Bruce (whom British
people regarded as virtually a London resident anyway). It was not a very
high-ranking team to put among the dozens of heads of state and reigning
monarchs that converged on London from everywhere else. And most
crucially, because the British order of precedence in which the mourners
processed and were seated in the Cathedral reflected the personal positions of the mourners rather than the international importance of their

countries, the official US mourners were well back in the line. The
United States deputation in fact processed between Finland and the
Ivory Coast, a fact noted with great pride in Helsinki, rather less so in
Washington. Since the television commentary tended as always to report
only the passing of the head of the procession and pictures showed only
the front rows in the Cathedral, many American television viewers were
unaware that their country was represented at all. They were outraged
and many of them wrote in to say so.

To say the least, this was a serious miscalculation – and a quite
unnecessary one, for there were plenty of people urging in advance of
the decision the importance of the issues involved. RCA's London director cabled Johnson on 15 January with the words, 'The President coming
to Churchill's funeral will be the greatest Anglo-American gesture of
century.' When it was clear that Johnson was not going, one irate New
York Democrat wired Harry Truman with the words, 'Get over to
England and give honour to that great warrior. This is an order.' But
Truman was also incapacitated by illness and had to refuse his personal
invitation to go like Eisenhower as a family friend. Likewise, the imaginative idea of sending the former war correspondent Ed Murrow to
London could not be pursued, though this was a gesture that would
have been warmly appreciated in Britain as another 'finest hour' link,
for Murrow was himself terminally ill by then. With the President ruled
out, it would have been easy enough to send Vice President Humphrey
in his place. Or, since Eisenhower was going anyway and had already
arranged to take a Presidential plane (on which the official mourners
now had to ask him for a lift), he could easily have been designated an
official American mourner too, much as ex-President Theodore Roosevelt
had represented America at the funeral of Edward VII in 1910. Eisenhower
would have started with the advantage of being widely known and
extremely popular in Britain, as his many post-war visits had shown, and
would also have seemed appropriate because of his wartime associations
with Churchill. White House staffers put this suggestion to Johnson with
the support of Ambassador Bruce, noting too that the appointment of a
Republican would be seen as a healing move after the recent, bruising
Presidential election. But Johnson was not a man to make such a magnanimous gesture, and never seems to have given the idea serious consideration, with the result that an American who attended the funeral in a
personal capacity completely upstaged the official mourners.

Eisenhower had been asked by the BBC to take part in the television coverage, and recorded a personal tribute to his old friend that was generally regarded as one of the best two tributes paid in the entire fortnight of eulogies. Ike had certainly felt Churchill's death deeply: his secretary noted that during the entire week of Churchill's last illness, 'DDE did not play golf,' for Ike the ultimate sign of respect. And the first draft of his funeral broadcast produced only a smudged copy from the secretary, who confessed that she had 'shed a tear or two while typing your tribute'. In drafting his broadcast, Ike had stated simply that he had 'no charter to speak for my countrymen', a harmless enough observation when written, before the US mourners had been chosen, but with a quite different resonance when broadcast on 30 January. At least sixty letters flowed in to his office, congratulating him on his words, but all contradicting that opening statement. A correspondent from Oregon wrote that 'LBJ had his representatives at the funeral of Winston Churchill. The American people had its representative also. For this we thank you.' And a writer from California told him that 'You said you did not have the charter to represent the American people at the services for Sir Winston. In our hearts you did have the charter, and may I thank you for representing us so beautifully.' Within a week of the funeral, Ike had been appointed by the English-Speaking Union to chair their fundraising for a long-term memorial to Churchill in the USA through scholarships, something that would keep him in the public mind, and linked with Churchill, for years to come. Any idea of healing breaches had gone sadly wrong.[35]

The fact that the President had missed the funeral because of 'a cold' now added to his troubles (not least when it was pointed out that the seventy-eight-year-old former British premier Attlee had managed to attend, though looking more dead than alive himself). Many of those who sent complaints to the White House doubted that Johnson had really been ill, and derided the President's later claim that he had been banned from going to London by his doctor, 'on the theory that I may be subject to reinfection'. For a President who saw Churchill as a virility symbol, the letter from Florida which argued that Sir Winston himself would not have let a bad cold get in the way of his duty must have been truly humiliating. Press stories that contrasted the sheer nobility of Churchill's funeral with Johnson's scheming pragmatism cannot have gone down any better, but the President's aides anyway revealed to journalists that as he had watched the ceremony on television he had become increasingly aware that he should have been there, whatever the risk. In a remarkable demonstration of the fact that the buck need not stop on the President's desk, Johnson actually had his doctor reply to complaining letters himself, thereby confirming that it really had been a medical decision. For those admirers of Churchill who knew well enough that he himself had rarely listened to doctors, this was presumably no more convincing. Finally, Johnson sent to Bethesda Naval Hospital for display there the first flag to be at half-staff when Churchill died – the one flown over the hospital itself while the President was in bed there, thereby setting up a permanent reminder that he *had* been ill when Churchill died. But trying to fight this storm of abuse was well-nigh impossible; as a State Department staffer noted on one extremely abusive letter, passed on to Rusk as an example of its own hate-mail, 'any answer we could give would be more likely to do harm than good'.[36]

In fact the flying of flags had been a good example of just what the critics deplored, an area where the Administration had started out with the best of intentions but finished up with a pragmatic compromise that satisfied nobody. Johnson was determined to do the right thing, and even while Churchill was dying a battle was fought out between the White House and the protocol section at State as to how long US flags should be at half-staff. Usual British practice was to lower flags on the day of a death and on the day of the funeral, but not on the days between. American practice on the other hand was for the half-staff flying to be from death to funeral, including all the days between, but State feared that this would be a dangerous precedent to adopt for a foreigner, even for someone who had been an honorary American citizen. State lost the argument for two reasons. It was discovered that the American practice had been followed when General Sir John Dill had died in America in 1944 (and half-American Churchill could hardly have less honour than wholly British Dill). And it was reported that in Canada the American practice would be followed, rather than the British practice as was usual, on the specific ground that Churchill was unique and so the occasion *should* therefore break precedent. Belatedly, the British Government then also adopted this practice. Johnson therefore issued an Executive Order on 24 January requiring American flags to be at half-staff until the funeral. This produced consternation among the military and American diplomats, who pointed out that this would mean that American flags would fly lower than those of Cuba and the USSR at such places as the United Nations in New York and at diplomatic posts overseas. After pressure from the Joint Chiefs of Staff, Johnson modified his order on the 25th so that the American flag would be lowered to half-staff only if this did not place it lower than flags flown by other countries at the same site. Churchill would thus be honoured as an American citizen, but only if there was no cost to the prestige of his adopted country by doing so, a striking contrast to the British readiness to place American and British flags at parity even in London that week.[37]

But if ordinary Americans who complained did so because they suspected the President's veracity, the media debate focussed on the more interesting political question of why the President had not sent Vice President Humphrey to London in his place. After all, Johnson, after not having a Vice President since he had moved up to the Presidency in 1963, had now just two weeks earlier acquired Humphrey in support. The veteran Churchill admirer and columnist Arthur Krock set the ball rolling with a story headlined 'New Game in Capital: Why Didn't Johnson Name Humphrey to Attend Churchill's Funeral?'[38] Attending funerals was after all typical of the trivial tasks which had been said over the years to be all that a Vice President was good for. Johnson's explanation to Humphrey himself was that, when he himself had been Vice President, Kennedy had given him nothing to do but such dogsbody tasks as funerals, and he was determined to save Humphrey from such a fate. Humphrey had resolved before taking up the Vice Presidency to allow no hint of a disagreement with the President to become public knowledge (as had been widely anticipated, given their very different backgrounds and political styles), a loyalty he practised until death. It is not therefore surprising that Humphrey never contradicted this explanation himself, though in later tape-recorded reminiscences – the parts that did not get into his autobiography – he returned over and again to the question of Johnson's real motive, which suggests that he at least did not believe the official story.

Critics in the press suspected a characteristically Johnsonian piece of intimidation, whereby the refusal to let Humphrey go to London alone, and perhaps meet the Russian leaders there, was calculated to show him at the very start of the Administration that LBJ was the boss.

This would certainly fit in with Humphrey's later memories of LBJ physically imposing himself, wrapping his long arms round Humphrey's shoulders, getting his face 'eyeglass close' and then bellowing in his ear. Some such deviousness in Johnson's decision was certainly suggested by the later conversation in which Muriel Humphrey, seeking to strike back when the President was needling her husband over dinner, asked him why he had not sent Hubert to London in 1965, a question that reduced Johnson to an unusually embarrassed silence.[39]

There was no doubt though that Johnson's absence and his failure to ensure a high-level team of mourners did cause some widespread concern in Britain as well as the United States, and US diplomatic posts were soon reporting that newspapers in other countries were also aware of British hurt feelings over Johnson's insensitivity. The consul in Vancouver was fairly typical in forwarding a newspaper story headed 'Britons claim Johnson snubbed Churchill rites', while the Helsinki Embassy's summary of the local press concluded that 'although admitted [that] President Johnson could not have foreseen Rusk's illness, some Englishmen find situation somewhat dismal, especially with Churchill's many American ties in mind'.[40] Faced with continuous American press probing in the week after the funeral, Johnson again called in the artillery. On 5 February, Senate Majority Leader Mansfield called for an end to the speculation, which he said was running down America's good name abroad, and things did then more or less die down.

Since 1965, even more fanciful suggestions have sometimes emerged, for example the answer given to enquirers by research staff at the Johnson Presidential Library in Austin, Texas, to the effect that Humphrey refused to attend Churchill's funeral because he had never forgiven Churchill for not coming to the funeral when Franklin Roosevelt died in 1945. Churchill had indeed intended to come to FDR's funeral, and the plane had been ready and waiting for him when he belatedly changed his mind, deciding that a funeral oration in Britain would actually be a better use of his time. It may indeed be the case that Churchill changed his mind and missed Roosevelt's funeral simply because he was reluctant to appear to upstage the new President at an American national occasion – that is anyway the explanation that Anthony Eden gave to James Forrestal in Washington a few days later. But there is not the faintest evidence that anyone, anywhere, bore a grudge about this. It was after all not that easy (or that safe) to cross the Atlantic at short notice in

1945, and Churchill still had a war to finish. Nor was Humphrey a man to nurse such a grudge for twenty years.[41]

The truth may well have been far more routine than all the excitement suggested. With the President ill, and a war going on in Vietnam, it would not have been wise to have the Vice President leave the country, a factor of which Johnson was particularly aware after his own experiences when Kennedy was shot in November 1963. But this was not an argument that he would have wished to refer to in public, not least because he would then have had to reveal the gravity of his heart condition. At a press conference on 4 February, Johnson acknowledged that 'I may have made a mistake,' but this meeting nevertheless showed the President at his sarcastic worst. The funeral story also produced a vintage piece of Johnsonian knockabout at Humphrey's expense. When he and Humphrey met with the National Council on Ageing in the same week, he promised them 'the very active understanding and co-operation of this virile, young Vice President', and, when Humphrey, beaming with pleasure, thanked the President for his words, Johnson added, 'if he is not out of the country attending some funeral'. He was as good as his word, for over the next four years, as Humphrey later recalled, 'there wasn't an important funeral that I didn't get to attend save one' (and to that one, for Prime Minister Holt of Australia, LBJ wanted to go himself as a personal friend of Holt's and as a thanks for Australia's Vietnam commitment). As Humphrey noted, the reverberations of this early run-in with the President went on throughout his Vice Presidency.[42]

The uproar over representation at the Churchill funeral indicated, then, the breadth of American admiration for Churchill and reinforced the determination of those Americans planning permanent memorials on US soil. It also guaranteed that the American Government would give favourable consideration to any scheme which came forward over the next few years to memorialise Sir Winston in the United States. There was therefore an active involvement of the US Government in fundraising for the Churchill statue in Washington and for the Fulton Memorial, and it seemed that anything Churchillian could attract their attention after the mess they had made of the funeral arrangements. President Johnson enthusiastically supported the plans to name the highest mountain in North America after Churchill, now the Churchill Peaks in Alaska. Johnson also wrote personally to Clementine Churchill on her birthday later in 1965, a copy of the BBC's film of the complete funeral broadcast was requested and placed in the Library of Congress, and American diplomats abroad were assiduous in attending the various memorial services that took place over the rest of the year, for example in Casablanca on 25 February.[43] What all of this demonstrates, of course, is just how far the image, language and reputation of Sir Winston Churchill had imposed themselves on the English-speaking politicians of his time. In order to explain this, we must go back to his, and the British people's, wartime 'finest hour', and then to the remarkable resurrection that he achieved after the British electorate buried him in 1945.

2

'Had This War Not Come, Who Would Speak of Winston Churchill?'

IN THE WEEK OF CHURCHILL'S FUNERAL, the same week in which his cabinet colleague R. A. Butler announced his own retirement from politics, the Treasury economist Alec Cairncross noted in his diary, 'Winston's funeral on Saturday. Had he retired like Rab at 62, he would have been thought an unsuccessful politician, rather unstable and reactionary.' Had Churchill indeed retired at sixty-two, after the Abdication Crisis in 1936 when his career was at one of its lowest ebbs, he would have had a career that would have almost exactly paralleled that of Sir Austen Chamberlain. Both Churchill and Chamberlain were the sons of famous political fathers – and both fathers had been famously maverick political figures too; both had an early start in politics because the family name ensured that talent would be noticed; both were in the Commons before the age of thirty and in the cabinet before they were forty; both suffered in the estimation of their party colleagues from their fatal fascination with Lloyd George and his centrist politics in 1916–22, but they returned together to the Conservative mainstream and under Baldwin held the two greatest offices of state below the premiership; both were excluded from the National Government when it settled into permanency in November 1931; both were highly critical of its defence policies by the mid-1930s, and both were persuaded by Baldwin to mute their criticisms when the possibility of cabinet office was dangled before their willing eyes. At this point their parallel careers diverged rather sharply, for Chamberlain died in 1937 at the age of sixty-four and is barely remembered by anyone except political historians, while Churchill became literally world-famous as a result of events that took place after he had passed the usual retirement age. Churchill notoriously remarked of Austen Chamberlain that he had always played the game and always lost, but if an epitaph on Churchill had been written in 1936, it would probably have been even more damning, for it must have been concluded that he had only rarely 'played the game' but had usually lost anyway. To write Churchill's life up to 1939, as Robert Rhodes James was to put it in 1970, was to describe *A Study in Failure*.[1] For his own part, Austen Chamberlain was fairly typical of the British political elite in the view of Churchill that he recorded in a family letter in May 1921.

> Winston has come back from Egypt as cross as a bear with a sore head & thinks that all the world is out of joint since he is not C[hancellor of the] E[xchequer] & the limelight is for the moment turned on to other players. He has so many good and even charming qualities & so much ability that it is tragic that he should not have a little more stability and judgement & a little less consciousness of self.

A month later, his half-brother Neville was writing about Churchill to the same sister, to the effect that 'I never quite know whether most to admire his great gifts or to be alarmed at his impulsiveness and hasty judgement.' Such views in the 1920s and 1930s could be multiplied a hundredfold from witnesses all over the political spectrum.[2]

It barely needs saying then that Churchill's reputation was transformed during the 1940s, not only during the Second World War but also in the remarkable come-back that he made from electoral defeat after 1945, through foreign policy speeches in the later 1940s and through the influence that his war memoirs had on perceptions of his own role as a war leader. It will be useful, though, to delve back briefly into the period before 1939, for the mature Churchill still carried a good deal of baggage from earlier in his career.

Churchill, in the first phase of his career in politics before the Great War, had an unusually sharp public image, but it was not a particularly positive one. He was widely viewed (as his father might well have put it) as a 'young man in a hurry', self-centred and over-excitable, possibly a medal-hunter in his army days and certainly a publicity-hunter in politics. There was for example his rush to the East End to take personal control of the Siege of Sidney Street when anarchists were cornered there by the police in 1911. However justified this might have been for a Home Secretary, it was widely *reported* as a determination to meddle, a sign of poor judgement and a desire to get into the papers on any pretext whatsoever. Churchill was thought to be a man always hugely enthusiastic for the project of the hour, but with ideas not obviously rooted in any firm political philosophy – hence his switch of parties in 1904 and the equally abrupt shift of the focus of his Liberal attentions from domestic social reform to imperial defence in 1911. He was certainly a mover and shaker in Asquith's 1908–15 Liberal Government, but he moved and shook its members rather more than most of them liked, and Edward VII soon decided that he was 'almost more of a cad in office than he was in opposition'.

The prevailing view of Churchill's hyperactivity was neatly summarised in a *Punch* cartoon of 1913, in which Churchill dozes in a deckchair on the Admiralty yacht *Enchantress*, while Asquith scans the newspapers: 'Any home news?' murmurs Churchill. 'How can there be, with you here?' responds the Prime Minister. Beside Churchill's deckchair are lying not only a cooling drink, but also a naval cap and telescope, and a cushion with a Union Jack for its cover. Lying on the flag, if we look closely, is the book he has been reading, *My African Journey*, the account of Churchill's own recent visit of 1908. Winston is thus reading his own autobiography. Indeed Churchill's whole persona at this point of his career seemed to illustrate Oscar Wilde's claim that absorption in one's own personality can be the beginning of a lifelong romance. About forty-five years later, Lord Beaverbrook's historical research assistant, when staying in the same villa as Churchill and 'the Beaver' in the South of France, happened on Churchill dozing with a book by the pool. When asked what he was reading, 'Sir Winston gave a guilty start. He was devouring a paperback edition, in comic strip form for American readers, of his [own] classic work *My Early Life*.' In the same period, his secretary Jock Colville asked Winston whether he had enjoyed reading his photographic biography edited by his son Randolph. 'It can't do any harm' was the initial response, but then the guards came down, and he conceded 'with a grim smile' that 'my vanity led me to spend two hours looking through it – I didn't go to bed until one forty-five. Perhaps, the public will not be as interested in it as I was.' His vanity had in fact correctly assured him that they would. Back in Edwardian times, the real Asquith was just as aware of Churchill's egocentricity as the *Punch* cartoonist. His daughter noted in 1914, for

UNDER HIS MASTER'S EYE.

SCENE—*Mediterranean, on board the Admiralty yacht "Enchantress."*

MR. WINSTON CHURCHILL. "ANY HOME NEWS?"
MR. ASQUITH. "HOW CAN THERE BE WITH YOU HERE?"

Punch, 21 May 1913

example, Asquith telling a story of Churchill seething with irritation during a Bonar Law speech, and saying that he 'wished he had the ability to answer him' (which Commons standing orders precluded). It was, Asquith added drily, 'the one modest remark he had ever heard Winston make'.[3]

Then there is the short story 'Ministers of Grace', first published by 'Saki' in 1911. In this charming political fantasy, divine intervention turns Britain's political leaders inside out, each taken over by a friendly Angel – Curzon becomes a cockney, Rosebery a man who categorically refuses to give opinions on any political subject at all, Lord Hugh Cecil calls for the disestablishment of the Church of England, and the quintessentially cool Balfour declares during a Commons speech, 'Gentlemen, I glory in the name of Apache!' The real Churchill, 'the well-known figure of a young Cabinet Minister, whose personality evoked a curious mixture of public interest and unpopularity', berates the narrator, in rolling, self-important paragraphs of empty prose. Then an angel called 'Quinston' takes his place, remarking modestly that *he* would much rather sit quietly and watch the ducks in the park than have to run about being politically active, 'like a spotted dog behind a carriage, getting all the dust and trying to look as if I was an important part of the machine. I must seem a perfect fool to you onlookers sometimes.'[4]

These are both cases of satire with sharp edges, but they also offer glimpses of an endearing personality who is liked rather more than he is admired – the very fact that even a Tory critic like Saki naturally called Churchill 'Winston' is fairly revealing, as is the fact that so early in his career he had that sharp profile. Asquith's daughter Violet, who became Churchill's lifelong friend, reviewing her father's cabinet when Churchill first joined it in 1908, deprecated all the 'rather commonplace people', and thought 'Winston the only in-the-least *unusual* one'. Not everyone shared the enthusiasm she had felt for Churchill even when first meeting him two years earlier. Returning home late, she 'burst' into her father's study and 'assured him that for the first time in my life I had met a genius'. Asquith calmly replied, 'Well, Winston would certainly agree with you there – but I'm not sure whether you will find many others of the same mind. Still, I know exactly what you mean. He is not only remarkable but unique.' Violet Asquith soon became aware of the overwhelming nature of Churchill's personality. She recorded in 1912 an occasion when, travelling through the Alps by train with the Churchills, Winston was describing at interminable length Napoleon's exact progress over the same route. Eventually, Clementine Churchill asked her 'rather weakly, "Violet, is Winston talking or reading aloud?" which is a very good demonstration of his conversational technique'. In 1911, Asquith was contrasting the effectiveness of Churchill on paper with the torrent of words that he used: 'I often wish he used the same economy in speech as in writing . . . I am not denigrating his conversational powers . . . but it's a question of time!'[5]

Even in that Edwardian period, however, Churchill's name became associated with two truly negative factors which had lasting consequences, in both cases most unfairly. First, as the son and self-confessed political heir of Lord Randolph, his advent into politics was greeted with considerable hostility in Ireland. This situation can only have been made worse by his barnstorming in 1900 as a hero of the Boer War – which many Irish nationalists opposed as an example of British colonialism, and some sufficiently so to go and fight for the Boers. His defeat in the parliamentary by-election in Manchester in 1908 was at least in part a consequence of the hostility of Irish voters, and this when he had barely uttered any public view on Irish matters. Thereafter, although Churchill was an enthusiastic supporter of Irish home rule and a key facilitator of the 1921 Treaty which gave most of Ireland its independence, he never established even the semblance of popularity with Irish opinion either at home or abroad. His greatest critics in Australia and in the United States, as well as in Ireland itself, all too often based their distrust on the assumption that Churchill was an enemy of Ireland, whence their ancestors had come. Churchill was himself a better hater than his admirers have generally conceded, and he reciprocated in later life at least some of Irishmen's negative opinions of him, delivering for example some choice remarks on Irish neutrality during the Second World War. But this was really a hostility with which he was born into politics, and from which could never escape.[6]

The second pre-1914 negative was the widespread impression that he was anti-working class, once again a grossly unfair label for one who had done so much to foster those social reforms of 1906–11, and who had defended them so robustly in trenchant speeches like those published in 1909 as *The People's Rights*. Here Churchill attacked such abuses as the unemployment which could be reduced by more government intervention in the labour market, casualisation of labour by unscrupulous employers, and the exploitation of under-age workers. He was also a staunch defender of his new system of labour exchanges, which would replace 'the present wasteful, heart-breaking aimless wanderings too and fro in search of work' with a system allowing the working man for the first time a 'free and fair market' for 'the only thing the great majority of people have to sell'. And he was equally vehement in defence of old age pensions and plans for health and unemployment insurance.[7]

The problem was that, despite the title of that book of speeches, he tended invariably to give the impression that social policies were being generously handed down by a benevolent government of the people's betters, rather than as a vindication of their 'rights', the combined product of his patrician background, of his uncompromising language when confronted with any strike action, and above all of the appalling misrepresentation of his actions as Home Secretary during the Welsh labour dispute at Tonypandy. This image too he found very hard to live down once acquired, and it was evidently still part of his problem with the British peacetime electorate when he was Tory leader in and after 1945. When New Zealanders took to commemorating Churchill in the 1950s and 1960s, they did not have much of an Irish community to obstruct the process, but there were some on the New Zealand left who had acquired a healthy distrust of Churchill as trades unionists in Britain before 1914. When tributes to Churchill from the New Zealand right became over-fulsome, Labour MPs like Walter Nash took to growling the word 'Tonypandy'.

The second phase of Churchill's career, between 1914 and 1939, darkened that overall image considerably, with his extrovert personality still to the fore but with considerably more emphasis on his lack of judgement as he acquired more ministerial authority and either took or shared in more difficult decisions. The catalogue of alleged Churchillian errors was a formidable one: Antwerp in 1914, Gallipoli in 1915–16, intervention in Russia against the Bolsheviks from 1919, opportunistic 're-ratting' (his own phrase) to rejoin the Tories in 1924, the return to the Gold Standard in 1925 with its consequences in overpriced exports and higher unemployment, the General Strike of 1926, opposing representative government in India in 1930–5, and taking the 'wrong' side in the Abdication Crisis of 1936.[8]

There was even some flirting with fascism. He was reported to be

Nazi Movement – Local Version
Daily Herald, 30 March 1933

'seeing a good deal' of Oswald Mosley in August 1931, by a diarist who
noted on the same day that Mosley 'is *very* interested in Hitlerism and
has made a close study of it'. Churchill did not hide in the later 1920s
his admiration for Mussolini as a 'Roman genius . . . the greatest lawgiver
among men', and refused to condemn Franco either during the Spanish
Civil War or even after 1945. In 1937, he was telling the House of
Commons that if forced to choose between Communism and the Nazis,
he would opt for the Nazis. A *Daily Herald* cartoonist could thus portray
him in 1933 making a fascist salute and carrying a paper labelled
'Thoughts on Gandhi by Adolf Churchill', the whole thing labelled 'Nazi
Movement – Local Version'.[9]

It matters not a jot that Churchill had a good case for the defence
on most if not all of these issues – as he sought tirelessly to prove
over Gallipoli, by appearing before the Dardanelles Commission and by
writing *The World Crisis* – for it was a reputation he could not lift from
his shoulders without an external agency such as a real Nazi movement,

German version, as was to be conveniently supplied in 1939. His relentless efforts to defend himself only seemed to provide more evidence of his egotistical special pleading, as when *The World Crisis* spoiled a good case by overstating his claims to be the political father of the tank. These and other errors were quickly pointed out in print, even before the end of the 1920s.[10] There were, however, whatever the rights and wrongs of each individual case, two salient continuities, the first and most obvious being that a politician who has to explain away alleged misjudgements quite so often during the course of a long career was not likely to go on being believed, even by his admirers, as the list got steadily longer. As his great friend F. E. Smith famously put it, 'Winston is often right, but when he is wrong, My God!' In the light of his opposition to appeasement in the 1930s after decades of 'failure', it might have been more appropriate to put it the other way round: 'Winston is often wrong, but when he is right . . .' For, as in the Tolstoyan fable of the fox and the hedgehog, Churchill was indeed thought to have been wrong on all too many things that later turned out to be 'little', but right on the 'one big thing'. As Adolf Hitler put it so graphically in a 1942 broadcast, 'Churchill, what has he achieved in all his lifetime? . . . had this war not come, who would speak of Winston Churchill?'[11]

The other great continuity is that Churchill never had the political gift either simply to wait on events or to agree to policies and then hide behind collective responsibility in case they went wrong. As Asquith's daughter and Churchill's lifelong friend Violet Bonham Carter put it, over the case of his impetuosity at Antwerp in 1914, 'he could not turn his back on action. Prudence . . . could never claim even a nodding acquaintance with Winston.' Stanley Baldwin once remarked that Churchill was quite easy to out-manoeuvre, since his inability to lie convincingly made him a bad conspirator. Over Gallipoli and over intervention in Russia, for example, he was only (as he and his biographers have been so keen to point out ever since) carrying out the Government's agreed policy as the responsible minister. But in each case he himself had originally harried the Government actually to take this action, when many others including the Prime Minister preferred to wait and see. Indeed Lloyd George thought that Churchill had completely lost his mental balance over Russia in 1919, so relentlessly did he set the pace on the issue. He thus became on both occasions the most visible advocate in public of dangerously contentious strategies, and he had therefore

Winston's Bag
Star, 21 January 1920

cast himself in advance in the role of scapegoat when things almost inevitably went wrong. He did not deserve the reputation he had over Russia, and he could not reasonably be held responsible for failures of army planning, logistics and training at Gallipoli, but this was far from obvious at the time, as the accumulation of past errors appeared to blot out his future hopes. When a British delegation consisting of George Bernard Shaw, Philip Kerr and the Astors visited Russia in 1931, Nancy Astor courageously berated Stalin to his face for keeping up such a large army. He replied charmingly, 'How do I know that Winston Churchill won't come back to power again?' Not a chance, they replied unanimously.[12]

Presented in its most critical form, Churchill's reputation by the inter-war years was very downbeat indeed. In 1919, for example, there appeared a fierce critique of Churchill by a former Liberal MP, with the title *The Political Gambler*. This made no attempt to deny Churchill's talents, describing his 'astounding versatility', oratorical powers, 'remarkable literary gift . . . many a true genuine impulse, and a fine show of humanity at times . . . Yes, Winston is really a man of genius. Had he more consistency and character, less ambition and egotism, what a really great leader he might be.' But this was the prelude to 'corruptio optima pessima', translated as 'the best man, when corrupted, becomes the most danger-ous'. The rest of the pamphlet retold Churchill's career in lurid terms, citing as examples of his gaffe-prone life Sidney Street, opposition to women's suffrage, Tonypandy, Antwerp ('a useless, ill-considered, ill-executed folly'), Gallipoli (of which he was 'the prime mover', causing 'thousands of lives lost, millions of treasure spent'), intervention in Russia ('he got up a scare' and 'schemed with Generals and Russian aristocrats'). In sum, he was 'a menace to the country and mankind . . . the essence of recklessness, militarism and reaction', while 'in disregard for veracity few can equal Churchill'.[13] Twelve years later a journalist and freelance writer published *The Tragedy of Winston Churchill*, which devoted three hundred pages to making very similar points about Churchill, and could now add the incidents of the 1920s like the General Strike to the catalogue of Winston's errors. It compared the expectations of Churchill in 1914, when he had seemed destined for a glorious political future, with the record since – hence the 'tragedy' of the title, a failure in middle life which had allowed obscure figures of 1914 like Stanley Baldwin to catch up and overtake him in the political race. 'What *has* been Mr Churchill's career in reality but the tragedy of a brilliant failure? . . . What is to be Winston Churchill's future? Will he reach his real goal, which is to be Prime Minister? One feels doubtful. What has he really got to offer *any* party?' The problem was that the public felt a 'latent distrust' for him, looking on him as 'brilliant, but rash, hot-headed, impulsive'.

> What sensible man is going to place confidence in Mr Churchill in any situation which needs cool-headedness, moderation or tact? The present writer, speaking to one of the Right Honour-able Gentleman's most enthusiastic admirers, posed the ques-tion point-blank: what would have happened in the last General Strike had Winston Churchill been a Conservative Prime Minis-ter? The answer came unhesitatingly: *The streets would have run with blood*.

In the press, Churchill often received a much better representation, not least because of his close relations with both journalists and press proprietors, and incidents within his career anyway lent themselves to a positive spin, but it would be hard to find any summation of his career as a whole from the inter-war years which was as positive as his critics were hostile.[14]

While having the undesirable reputation of a dangerous extremist, Churchill was all too often also suspected of being so self-centred that he would do anything to clamber into office. Lloyd George once exasperatedly remarked that Churchill would make a drum with the skin of his mother if he needed one to beat out his own praises. When Churchill thundered during the India debates, 'Fiat justitia, ruat coelum' ('Let justice be done, though the heavens fall'), his fellow Harrovian Leo Amery vastly amused the House by offering Churchill the alternative translation, 'If I can trip up Sam [Hoare], the government's bust.' His obvious ambition to get back into government was a handicap too when he was demanding faster rearmament in the mid-1930s, and his attempts to prevent Baldwin using this ambition to trip him up were not very effective. On one occasion, he actually went to Neville Chamberlain to ask if he was going to be offered a ministerial post, since if so he would pull his punches in a forthcoming speech, but if not he would really let himself go. We may now charitably concede that his desire to get back into the cabinet was motivated by the wish to change policy at least as much as by his desire for office itself, but that is certainly not how Chamberlain saw it at the time, deciding rather that Churchill's behaviour was 'an audacious piece of impertinence'. In the Abdication Crisis, many Tory backbenchers thought, however unfairly, that Churchill was on the side of the King simply because Baldwin was not, in the hope that the fall of the Government would propel him into office. When this alleged tactic failed, they labelled the crisis an example of his poor judgement as well. Robert Bruce Lockhart noted in December 1936 that 'ninety per cent of intelligent people regard the Beaverbrook–Rothermere campaign on [the] King's behalf as mischievous and irresponsible anti-Baldwinism. Winston is tarred with the same brush and has lost ground.' Interestingly, in view of Churchill's association by then with the idea of stronger defence policies, he added, 'de Margerie of the French embassy is worried by Winston's loss of ground'. The closeness of such views of his motivation to his own inner thoughts must have bothered even Churchill a little, for he had written to Clementine Churchill in 1929 that he was now in politics only for one thing, the premiership, and if that was not available then he might as well sell up, emigrate and earn his family some real money in Canada.[15]

In North America, Churchill had many friends in the American and Canadian political and business elites, built up over numerous visits since 1895. He was for example a close friend of Bernard Baruch, knew well Henry Luce of *Time* and Charles Sulzberger of the *New York Times*, and was an honoured guest of the media tycoon William Randolph Hearst at San Simeon. He also had a rather wider following even before 1940, as the large audiences for his extensive lecture tour in 1932 indicate (this being his last visit to the USA before Pearl Harbor). Even so, the theme of many of his addresses on that visit – the need for co-ordinated action by the English-speaking peoples to combat world depression – had great topicality, and this may have drawn in the crowds. If he actually had an 'image' in the United States in the 1930s it would have been as a very patrician Englishman – even the Anglophile *New York Times* was mistakenly calling him 'Sir Winston' in 1941, twelve years before he was actually knighted. Here was a great personality and a man with outspoken but increasingly unfashionable views on current events: he was for example pursued across America by Indian nationalists as well as by Irish ones during his 1932 tour and there were serious fears of an assassination attempt. Churchill did not then visit America again for nine years, and made no apparent effort to contact Franklin Roosevelt (whom he had actually met during the Great War, though Churchill had apparently forgotten the fact) in 1932 when he became President. It was thus Roosevelt rather than Churchill who initiated a correspondence between them when Churchill returned to office in 1939. Even though he was hard at work during the later 1930s on his *History of the English-Speaking Peoples*, a powerful historiographical appeal to the common inheritance, and though he was constantly calling on the British Government to involve the United States more in its foreign policy, his limited direct contact with Americans in America suggests that it was at that time a relatively low priority for him. After all, during the 1930s he had the time and needed the money, but he did not again try the American lecture circuit, whereas his appeal to Europeans was deliberately stepped up through syndication of his newspaper columns.[16] His visits to and involvement with Canada broadly matched those with the United States, and again he did not visit between 1932 and 1941.[17]

A revealing indication of Churchill's relatively limited impact on

North America before 1939, and the transformation of his standing soon afterwards, is the standard source *Bartlett's Familiar Quotations*. The final pre-war edition, published in New York in 1937, contained none of Churchill's words at all, though it did contain one remark by Hitler and six by Mussolini. Among British public figures, there were two each from Arthur Balfour and Lord Rosebery, three from Joseph Chamberlain, nine from Gladstone and no fewer than fifty-three from Disraeli (who had – though so did Churchill – the advantage of being a writer as well as a politician). The neglect of Churchill is even more remarkable when it is recalled that in his autobiography *My Early Life* (published in 1930 in the USA as *A Roving Commission* and a big seller there) he had offered the gratuitous tribute that 'it is a good thing for an educated man to read books of quotations. Bartlett's *Familiar Quotations* is an admirable work, and I studied it intently . . .' When a post-war edition of *Bartlett's* appeared in 1955, there were sixty-one quotations from Churchill, twelve of them from the pre-war period which had been ignored by the book at the time; by 1968, by which time Churchill had finally stopped talking, he was represented in *Bartlett's* by sixty-nine quotations, with three more added to the pre-war list. By then *Bartlett's* had also discovered what the young Churchill had thought of it and included that quotation as one of his edited highlights.[18]

Here the North American position closely matched that in Britain. There was no standard British work of reference of the same type until the 1940s – hence the young Churchill's recourse to *Bartlett's* – but when the first edition of the *Oxford Dictionary of Quotations* appeared early in 1941, having actually gone through the press during the Battle of Britain and the Blitz, Churchill received only a single entry. Again, many of his political contemporaries were represented by multiple entries – four for Balfour, two each for Bonar Law, Asquith and Lloyd George, for example. Even that single entry did not do much for Churchill's fame as an orator, for it was his use of the phrase 'terminological inexactitude' in 1906, as a way of calling another MP a liar without breaking the rules of the House of Commons. Post-war editions of the *ODQ*, like *Bartlett's*, sought to do the great man justice in retrospect: by 1953, it included twenty-six bits of Churchilliana, two of them from before 1939, and more recently the figure has gone up to nearly forty.[19] By 1954, when his recent words also occupied space in every public library and millions of home bookshelves, through his best-selling war memoirs, multiple volumes of collected speeches, gramophone records and such anthologies as *The Wit of Winston Churchill*, Churchill reminded MPs that 'you must remember that I have always earned my living by my pen and my tongue'. Even in his 'wilderness years' of the 1930s, Churchill remained a man whose way with words ensured an audience, those who could enjoy the performance even if rarely agreeing with the argument. At the close of one gloomy Commons philippic on rearmament, he sat down only to hear a Member mutter, 'Here endeth the book of Jeremiah,' and quickly responded with, 'Followed, I see, by Exodus,' for the Chamber was quickly emptying once he had finished speaking.[20]

All those partisan battles during the 1920s and 1930s tended to disguise the fact that there were some in the inter-war years who could see that Churchill in his fifties was potentially a different type of politician from the one they had so disliked in the past. He had been driven so much by relentless ambition for two main reasons. The first was the desire to appease the ghost of his hero-worshipped father, who had never thought he would amount to much. The second was his belief that men in his family did not live long and so needed to achieve things before they were forty. In 1924, though, in the month of his fiftieth birthday, he acquired the office that had been his father's highest political achievement, Chancellor of the Exchequer, and used indeed the same robes for formal occasions, robes which had 'slumbered in their tin box since January 1887'. Now even Churchill could begin to relax a bit and accept that he no longer had to prove himself on *every* day of the week. A perceptive biographer, calling himself 'Ephesian' (actually the journalist C. E. Bechofer Roberts), predicted in 1927 that 'age – if he ever grows old – which seems extremely doubtful – must mellow him, and, by rounding off the edges of his essentially dual personality, dovetail them into a more excellent unity. Puck will humanise Pitt; Pitt will moderate Puck.' The many people who after 1940 compared Churchill to the Elder Pitt as Britain's two greatest war leaders were picking up on this point, but the survival of Churchill's puckish elements even into his eighties, when in a sense he never did quite 'grow up', was an important part of his continuing appeal. Stanley Baldwin, a man of whom Churchill had so low an opinion that he said in 1947 that it would have been better had he never been born, did not reciprocate Churchill's antipathy, but had his reservations all the same. In 1936, he gave Tom Jones his considered view of Churchill. 'When Winston was born lots of fairies swooped down on his cradle with gifts – imagination, eloquence, industry, ability, and then came a fairy who said "no one person has a right to so many gifts", picked him up and gave him a shake and twist that denied him wisdom and judgement. And that is why we delight to listen to him in this House and do not take his advice.' Yet, after spending three hours with Churchill in 1943, Baldwin 'went out into Downing Street a happy man', full of 'pure patriotic joy that my country at such a time should have found such a leader. The furnace of the war has smelted all the base metals out of him.' In the late 1930s, though, when his call for speedier rearmament and a tougher response to Hitler dominated his political life, such a perception of the 'smelted down' unity of the Churchillian character was not achieved, his Pitt-like playing to the patriotic gallery fatally undermined by the general suspicion that he was all too often only trying to make puckish mischief.[21]

Nowhere was that more widely believed than on the British left, which explains in part the difficulty that he had in making allies within Labour's ranks for his anti-appeasement campaigns in the later 1930s. Even in the 1950s, Clement Attlee's private assessment of Churchill was 'half genius, half bloody fool', and when asked in December 1939 if Churchill should be recalled to office he had responded, 'Not Churchill. Sixty-five, old for a Churchill.' When opponents of the Government were trying to rally behind a single anti-appeasement candidate for the Oxford by-election, shortly after the Munich Crisis, one of their problems lay precisely in the fact that, as the future (and very moderate) Labour Foreign Secretary Patrick Gordon Walker put it, 'No one can argue that Churchill is safer than Chamberlain as a potential fascist.'[22] There was, then, some real irony in the circumstance that it was the refusal of Labour MPs to join a National Government under Neville Chamberlain in May 1940 that finally enabled Churchill to become Prime Minister. But that is to be explained not by Labour MPs' liking for Churchill so much as by their even greater distrust of Chamberlain, whom they thought ineffective as well as hateful – whereas Churchill's militancy was now an advantage since it could be turned on Germany rather than, say, the miners. As Paul Addison has put it, 'few now complained that he was a warmonger or a would-be Napoleon: the zeal with which he waged war was now a precious asset'. Even so, it seems clear enough that Labour would have served under Halifax rather than Churchill had that been the result of the King's soundings. At the Labour Party Conference, which happened to coincide with discussions of the change of government, voices were raised against co-operation with Churchill even in 1940. One Scottish delegate, for example, argued 'that [the] resolution asked for a vote of confidence in Winston Churchill and that was too much even in wartime [applause]. First he heard of him was in 1910 when he was doing down miners [applause].'[23] This deep distrust of Churchill on the left, as an anti-democratic class warrior with doubtful judgement, contrasts vividly with the public tribute paid to Churchill by the Labour leader Attlee in 1954, as 'the greatest citizen of the world in our time'. Or as one of Churchill's particular *bêtes noires* on the left, Emanuel Shinwell, described the change in 1964, 'there were times when it would have been regarded as heresy to praise Sir Winston', but 'aversions and dislikes had been replaced by admiration', and he too had become a reluctant admirer.

Opinion before 1939 was not much more favourable to Churchill in his own party, many of whose members could anyway not forgive his desertion to the Liberals back in 1904, and hardly any of whom regarded his behaviour after he rejoined the Conservatives in 1924 as demonstrating sufficient loyalty. He did not hold office between 1929 and 1939, even though the Conservatives dominated the Commons from 1931 onwards (when he was after all still only fifty-seven). He campaigned on India, the Abdication, rearmament and appeasement with little regard for the ruffling of party and ministerial feathers, and he wrote about politics in the press in ways that went well beyond the manner in which Conservatives were expected to behave in the public arena. There was for example his 1931 article on 'Personal Contacts', in which he regretted Lloyd George's exclusion from office by inferior (Conservative) Ministers.[24] His association with newspapermen, which went back to his earliest days as a war correspondent and had been assiduously cultivated when later he was both a Minister and a close friend of such press barons as Lord Beaverbrook, was in itself an object of further suspicion in a party which was in the 1930s often locked in combat with the press lords. When he spoke in the Commons in support of Anthony Eden after his resignation in 1938, a Tory backbencher wrote dismissively that this was merely 'another bid on his part to lead an Independent, perhaps Centre, party'. Loyalist Tories noted sourly even in 1939, when the press as a whole (including loyal Tory papers like the *Daily Telegraph*) was calling for Churchill's return to office as war approached, that he was in effect stirring up that campaign personally through his proprietor contacts. Lady Davidson MP wrote to the Prime Minister, on behalf of herself and her husband, a former Party Chairman:

> John and I . . . have been greatly worried in these last few days by the outrageous propaganda in practically all the newspapers on behalf of Mr Churchill. This kind of thing has happened before, frequently in fact, when Mr Churchill is wanting office . . . and I feel that I must write as a very ordinary backbencher to say how much I hope that you will *not* put him in the Cabinet.

It was such orthodox party insiders, and the official party whips, who initiated the moves in his Epping constituency which came close to deselecting Churchill altogether in 1938–9, and which while unsuccessful did nevertheless remove some of his freedom of action.[25] Even most Conservatives who agreed with his views on appeasement, such as Anthony Eden after he resigned in 1938, kept studiously away from Churchill and resisted any suggestions of joint action in the Commons or in the country, so as to avoid the appearance of disloyalty to their party by association with such a notorious outlaw. Once again, the contrast with the post-war years was stark, with Conservatives in the 1950s queuing up to praise their elder statesman as uniquely far sighted and gifted. Lord Hailsham, who had been first elected to Parliament as a Chamberlainite appeaser in 1938, with Churchill supporting his by-election opponent and telling the City of Oxford's electors not to send him to the Commons, hymned Churchill in 1961 as a 'political giant to whom my country and the world alike owe so much. Such men are not born more than once a century . . .'[26]

Churchill was, then, an improbable wartime national hero, a fact beautifully brought out in Graham Greene's 1943 novel *The Ministry of Fear*, for Greene's 'Arthur Rowe', after recovering from amnesia, is amazed to find who is now Prime Minister.

> He felt like Rip Van Winkle returning after a quarter of a century's sleep . . . Men of brilliant promise had lapsed into the Board of Trade, and of course in one great case a man who

had been considered too brilliant and too reckless ever to be trusted with major office was the leader of the country. One of [his] last memories was of hearing him hissed by ex-servicemen from the public gallery of a law court because he had told an unpalatable truth about an old campaign. Now he had taught the country to love his unpalatable truths.[27]

It is not hard to see, at a basic level, how such a change of perception took place, though it may not be so obvious that there was a change of the physical as well as of the personal identity in Churchill's public image. John Strachey thought in the later 1940s that Churchill 'looked like a Toby jug, a character out of Dickens', and since 1965 the toby jug has indeed been a favourite art form among the mass of commemorative Churchilliana. John Lukacs, on the other hand, was one of many for whom Churchill's round, hatted face evoked the image of the dome of St Paul's Cathedral, so far was Churchill linked in memory with the Blitz of 1940–1, a view that has also been cited by Peter Stansky. It was actually changes in Churchill's physiognomy during the war years that facilitated both of these comparisons. The American sculptor Bill McVey, who studied hundreds of Churchill photographs before starting work on the Washington statue of the great man, wrote that:

in about 1940 the mouth began to lengthen. The right corner gradually turned under and literally became mouth, while the left side dug deeper and warped and firmed against the cigar. As if to compensate for this, the tail of the left eyebrow tilted more pronouncedly, while both brows at the nose slipped below the eye-socket. The general head shape seemed to change from a long oval to something closer to a circle.

Lord Moran and others in his entourage simply noticed that during the early war years Churchill was – quite understandably – more short-tempered than before and scowled a great deal. Moran also thought that the scowl, 'not to be found on his face before', had been 'made to order', for (as he vainly told Graham Sutherland in 1965) it was import-ant never to 'forget that Winston is always acting'.[28]

Thus was formed under the actual strain of wartime leadership not only the toby-jug and dome-of-St-Paul's look, but also the bulldog look. The first cartoon representing Churchill as a bulldog came only in June

1940, from Strube in the *Daily Express*, while the first poster to make the association was issued in the USA later in the same year. There was also the 'angry lion' of Karsh of Ottawa's most famous Churchill photograph, taken during his visit to Canada in December 1941. Given by Churchill two minutes ('and I mean two minutes for one shot') in which to 'try to put on film a man who had already written or inspired a library of books, baffled all his biographers, filled the world with fame', Karsh was filled with dread, especially when Churchill 'marched in scowling'. By the simple device of depriving Churchill of his cigar, Karsh ensured that 'the scowl deepened, the head was thrust forward belligerently, and the hand [deprived of its usual prop] placed on the hip in an attitude of anger'. Karsh himself knew when looking back that 'it was the Churchill portrait of course that first won me international attention'. He felt that he had captured 'the image of England in those years, defiant and unconquerable', but it was an image of Churchill himself which simply could not have been caught on film two or three years earlier, because he had not actually looked like that. The photograph taken, Churchill conceded, 'Well, you can certainly make a roaring lion stand still to be photographed,' and allowed Karsh to take a second, smiling portrait. It was those Karsh photographs which became the most important visible representations of Churchill the war leader after he died in 1965, adorning millions of stamps and illustrating dozens of books. Something similar had occurred when the Society photographer Cecil Beaton took another famous wartime photograph of Churchill for the Ministry of Information. The Prime Minister was seated at the cabinet table and forced for a moment to give up his paperwork, 'glowering at the camera' and looking (as Beaton himself put it) 'like a bulldog guarding its kennel'. This then duly also appeared as the illustration on a commemorative Crown Ducal plate, with the inscription 'Britain's Fighting Premier'. When commissioning Bill McVey to sculpt Churchill for a Washington statue in 1963, the local English-Speaking Union knew that this was the image that they wanted too. Their chairman wrote:

> all of us have agreed that we would like a full-standing figure of Sir Winston with his famous hat, bow-tie and cane which were so characteristic and typical of him during the war years. Someone on the committee commented that the best period of his life would be World War Two or immediately after – the

early forties, and 'that he should have a dour look and be in an aggressive mood' . . . I am sure you are familiar with the picture of Sir Winston we have in mind.[29]

Indeed he was, and as a result he produced not only one of the best Churchill figures ever cast, but also one of the statues most evocative of the war years.

Churchill's star rose quickly even during the phoney war in 1939–40 when he was at the Admiralty. An army source in the survey organisation Mass-Observation reported in April 1940 that 'Churchill is far and away the most liked member of this government. Indeed his was the only talk I have heard a barrack room listen to on the wireless.' The organisation had noted even in the previous December that Churchill was often cheered by British cinema audiences when he appeared in newsreels.[30] Once installed as Prime Minister, he proved to be a formidable figure in the waging of war in both executive and inspirational terms. Drawing on his experience of the Great War, in which civilian control of the military had been a difficulty, he appointed himself Minister of Defence as well as premier, and so ensured that he could give instructions directly to the armed forces as well as lead the Government that managed them within the overall war effort. The knowledge that he was constantly prodding, exhorting, instructing, lecturing and when necessary sacking the leaders of the armed forces made this a very personal form of leadership, and in due course his war memoirs and books by close wartime associates ensured that people did indeed know this.[31] Admiral Sir William James MP in 1940 thought Churchill 'a gift from the Gods at this moment . . . Winston will of course be the Grand Panjandrum for all operations. He has a profound knowledge of war and one cannot imagine him "sitting back" when important decisions have to be made.' General Sir Ian Jacob later represented the change-over from Chamberlain's 'orderly fashion of working', as a result of which 'nothing was done', to Churchill's method, 'fertile with ideas . . . that personal touch which means so much', as the key moment, 'putting all Whitehall on its tiptoes and everything was done'. Patrick Cosgrave later heard from Jacob that he could date his belief in Britain's recovery from inertia to an actual moment on 13 May 1940, when 'I saw a Permanent Under Secretary in a corridor in Whitehall in his shirtsleeves, *running*. Then I knew that Churchill could shake up the machine.' Cosgrave also recounts the fact that the anecdote gave Margaret Thatcher 'enormous pleasure' when he told it to her himself.

Churchill was especially proud of the decision-making part of his war, and reacted sharply when others regarded his radio broadcasts as his biggest contribution. We should remember, though, that he was fortunate in the timing of his arrival in the premiership – though this was far from evident at first, given the immediacy of Dunkirk and the fall of France. Such crucial gearings-up as the tripling of fighter production in the first seven months of 1940, providing that bare margin of safety in the Battle of Britain, were just showing results in May; though he can share the credit as a member of Chamberlain's Government, he did not really deserve it all himself. Churchill generally argued after 1945 that he had not been the lion of 1940, only the man privileged to provide the roar, but very often added that he had also told it where to put its claws. And he 'complained' to Lord Moran even in 1945 that 'people say my speeches after Dunkirk were the main thing. That was only a part, not the chief part. They forget that I made all the main military decisions.'[32]

As a man who had been out of office for the pre-war decade, Churchill could not be held responsible either for the lack of armaments in 1940 or for the poor leadership of the armed forces where it occurred in 1940–1 – for example over the latter stages of the Battle for France or during early campaigns in the Western Desert. As the war progressed, however, there was more readiness to criticise his strategic judgement, though even then it was rare to do so openly. It is notable that the only occasion in the war years in which he came even remotely close to suffering a political fate like Chamberlain's in 1940 was in spring and summer 1942, when a string of unexpected defeats by the Japanese in the Far East and by Germany in North Africa and the North Atlantic (which by then could *not* easily be blamed on the pre-war Government) unleashed renewed fear of defeat and even of invasion. Churchill reacted to this political threat with characteristic boldness, buying time by dispatching his main political rival, Sir Stafford Cripps, to Moscow and then to India, where his reputation could only suffer since he had to deal there with intractable problems. Meanwhile Churchill gingered up the Middle Eastern armies with new munitions, new commanders and a personal visit to Egypt to cheer up the troops (faithfully captured on newsreel for the millions of soldiers and civilians who could not see it

By this time every man and woman in Britain was mobilized.
Daily Mail, 3 December 1941

in person, and then duly presented as a pivotal moment in the Oscar-winning documentary on the battle, *Desert Victory*, when it came out in 1943). Montgomery's victory at El Alamein in November 1942, and the subsequent rolling up of the German position in North Africa, was therefore widely seen as a consequence of Churchill's intervention, and since this 'end of the beginning' was followed by two years in which the Allies continued to advance towards victory, his personal reputation and political standing were never in any further danger while the war went on.[33]

Indeed Churchill made a positive virtue of his dependence on the House of Commons, taking care to report back regularly and in detail on the progress of the war, and ruthlessly demanding votes of confidence from its Members, though all that most of his critics wanted was the right to express genuinely constructive criticism of a war machine that was often far from perfect. Nevertheless, this visible dependence on the Commons ensured that the patrician Churchill was also visibly a leader of democratic forces in a five-year world struggle against totalitarianism. And that point was not lost either on his political contemporaries or on international observers. The war correspondent Ed Murrow reported to America in March 1941 that 'as long as Winston Churchill is Prime Minister the House of Commons will be given an opportunity to defend its traditions and to determine the character of the government that is to rule this country'. And when the war ended in 1945, there was deep emotion among MPs when Churchill told the Commons that 'the House had proved itself the strongest foundation for waging war that has ever been seen in the whole of our long history. He added whimsically that we had all of us made mistakes, but the strength of the parliamentary institution had been shown. At this there was a great outburst of cheering,' as a Labour MP noted in his diary.[34] For there was indeed no doubting Churchill's liking for firm government. Reviewing the final volume of *The History of the English-Speaking Peoples* in 1958, Michael Foot drew the inference that:

> Churchill dearly loves a great man. He sees most of them as a pale image of himself. Few can portray them with more enthusiasm. He has this quotation from Sir Robert Peel: 'The fact is people like a certain degree of obstinacy and presumption in a Minister. They abuse him for dictation and arrogance, but they like being governed.' How revealing that Churchill should have selected those words. Like the portrait painter, he can never exclude a hint of his own features.[35]

That Egyptian intervention in 1942 also revealed the other side of Churchill's personal contribution to the war effort, his ability to inspire the British people, both civilians and servicemen and women, with the need to fight, to make sacrifices and indeed to do everything that was necessary in order to win. In the first twentieth-century war, the Boer War of 1899–1902, Churchill had already seen that morale was a crucial factor in modern warfare, and that the media was itself now a weapon of war. As war correspondent of the *Morning Post* he had deliberately censored his own criticisms of the British generals, since to do otherwise would be to undermine the war effort in which he passionately believed, and he had – equally deliberately – managed to include cheerful and encouraging information even in dispatches that reported such dismal British defeats as the Battle of Spion Kop.[36] As a Minister during the Great War, Churchill knew a good deal about the extremely active, but largely covert, government propaganda campaign at home and abroad, and when his friend Beaverbrook became Minister of Information in 1918 he was directly involved in it.[37] Between the wars, Churchill had kept up this interest in the media and followed developments in the technology of film and radio – films being one of his favourite recreations. He therefore came to power in 1940 with a strong conviction that both at home and abroad the media – and his personal use of it – would be a weapon of the first order of importance. Even here, he put democratic values first, refusing for example to hold press conferences on the Roosevelt model, to the great irritation of international correspondents, so that MPs would hear Churchill's views in person in the Commons rather than reading them in the newspapers. His famous wartime speeches were written to be delivered in the Commons, then usually broadcast by the BBC later in the same evening, and often delivered a third time some hours later for live broadcasts to North America. 'Even the ace American reporter Quentin Reynolds only got to see him after a personal plea by Harry Hopkins. No Prime Minister of modern times had been so difficult for the Press to make contact with.'[38] There was no fear of the press in this distancing process, for, when in America on wartime visits to Roosevelt, Churchill easily adapted to the different conventions there. Arthur Krock of the *New York Times* felt that Churchill had in December 1941 turned in 'a bravura performance' with American journalists: 'the skill and success with which he met the questions of the American press, and his candour, alertness of intellect and concentration on the task in hand . . . matched the reputation Mr Churchill has acquired for all three'.[39]

Churchill planned indeed to use the media, but directly through his personal appearances and speeches rather than only through the distorting mirror of press coverage. On radio, then *the* medium for addressing the nation directly, Churchill established an immediate and unprecedented impact on the British population, and on other English-speaking audiences too. How fortunate Churchill was simply in the timing of his finest hour: a decade earlier, radio technology would not have allowed such penetration of the world's airwaves, and a generation later the key medium was television, which Churchill hated and at which he did not excel. But in 1940, it was (as Richard Dimbleby was to put it), 'as simple technically for him to address millions of people all over the world as it was to make a telephone call'. Sir Evelyn Wrench, abroad on government business for much of the war, later recalled witnessing the encouraging effect of hearing Churchill's radio voice in Canada, Australia, New Zealand, Singapore, and India. He was even told of the inspirational effect that it had had on the beleaguered British community in Kabul, when in 1940 Afghanistan was tempted to join the Axis powers at war. That same voice inspired Java in the Dutch East Indies to fight on when the Netherlands was occupied, the large hotels on the island placarded with photographic portraits of Churchill, alongside portraits of Queen Wilhemina and giant 'V for Victory' signs. It also won admiration among those who had no particular reason to like Churchill's imperial views or Britain: the young Nelson Mandela remembers that in 1940–1 he and his fellow students at a rural college in the Eastern Cape 'would huddle around an old radio and listen to Winston Churchill's stirring speeches'. Thousands of miles away to the east, a very different type of Methodist, Queen Salote of Tonga, listened to the same broadcasts, translated Churchill's words into Tongan and then rebroadcast them for her non-English-speaking subjects.[40]

Sometimes even the British had to draw inspiration from the radio voice when Churchill himself was far away. Cuthbert Headlam MP, no great Churchill admirer either before 1939 or after 1945, was nevertheless bowled over by hearing 'Winston's speech to the American Congress' in December 1941. 'It came over wonderfully well and certainly was one of his best efforts – "grim and gay" . . . He had a magnificent reception and was clearly enjoying himself.' For Richard Dimbleby, a wartime radio correspondent and no mean broadcaster himself, Churchill's magic was encapsulated by a story told to him by a German broadcasting official when the war ended. The official had once walked into the Hamburg radio studios late at night and discovered normal work at a standstill. 'Even William Joyce, then in the full foul flood of his radio oratory as "Haw Haw", was away from his desk. Asking what was up, the official was told to be quiet – "Churchill's broadcasting".'[41]

Despite his patrician background and relative lack of radio experience, Churchill had a voice and manner of address which showed the essential 'common touch, as his broadcast on the battle of the River Plate showed':

> Mr Churchill also revealed himself as the Government's Number One Broadcaster. Lacking the 'Oxford accent' he spoke as a Briton to Britons. 'Monty Viddio' was just what the man in the pub called that South American port. The Churchillian 'Narzi' sounded just as one imagined such an outsider should sound.

After hearing another Churchill broadcast a few weeks later, a Conservative MP wrote to thank him 'for filling our hearts with legitimate pride'. He added that although 'there might be difficulties, I wish you could talk to us every night!'[42] Another observer felt that the real effect of Churchill's first broadcast as Prime Minister was achieved by restraint, for 'people were more reassured by the half-dozen sentences that the Prime Minister barked into the microphone that Monday evening than they would have been by any lengthy, prepared oration.' This is certainly confirmed by the civilian diarist who noted a few days later that 'France's collapse was at first terrifying but we have grown used to the idea, particularly since Churchill's fighting speech on Monday night.' The Lord Mayor of Portsmouth recalled in 1950 that, after hearing Churchill promise to 'fight them on the beaches', the 'effect upon the people was almost instantaneous. I can well remember going round the City the following day, and noticing a marked difference on the faces of the people of Portsmouth.' But this was not because Churchill had encouraged the illusion that all was well; simply that he made people determined never to give in: 'You will remember that at this point we barricaded the Guildhall, gathered together a few rifles and hand-grenades, and, silly as it may sound now, were determined to defend that Guildhall against anything that came our way.' *Life* magazine's Walter Graebner thought that 'Churchill's great power and hold over the people rests as much on his romantic eloquence as on his solid wartime achievements. By words alone he can rally a worried, disgruntled nation or Parliament behind him. All Britishers now think Churchill is the symbol of their determination to beat Hitler, and to fight with their backs to the wall – to the death if necessary.'[43] In 1943, a very elderly correspondent assured readers of *The Times* that Churchill's oratory excelled in 'stout-hearted John Bullism' that of both

Palmerston and Disraeli (who had died in 1865 and 1881 respectively). The comparison was apt, for he had indeed deliberately mobilised British history to serve as part of the war effort, and rarely missed a chance to explain to the British people in 1940–1 how fortunate they were to be living at that historic hour. Visiting Harrow School for the annual Songs in December 1940, the midst of the Blitz, Churchill was greatly moved to find that new lines had been added to one of his old school's favourite songs, a verse celebrating his current achievements, but he nevertheless ventured to correct the way in which they had been described. As Arthur Bryant, another old Harrovian present on the occasion, recalled it, Churchill said that:

> there is one word in it I want to alter ... It is in the line 'Not the less we praise in darker days / The leader of our nation'. I have obtained the Headmaster's permission to alter *darker* to *sterner* ... These are not dark days: they are great days – the greatest days our country has ever lived ...

In the same year, he contributed a foreword to a reprint of William Pitt's war speeches of the 1790s, welcoming the timely reappearance of 'the historic speeches with which Pitt instructed and heartened the British people in their battle for freedom a century and a half ago'. It would be 'fortifying' for Britons to remember that they had already seen off Philip II, Louis XIV, Napoleon Bonaparte and Kaiser Wilhelm II in their quest for the domination of Europe, and they should now recall Pitt's voice, facing the very real threat of invasion with that 'just confidence which neither despises nor dreads the enemy', and bidding the Commons to remember that we were 'fighting for our very existence as a nation, for our very name as Englishmen, for everything dear and valuable to men this side of the grave'. The key word here was 'we', the continuous nation, called on once more to perform a historic task, but the conscious heir of those who had gone before and prospered.[44]

So likewise the 'finest hour' speech with its masterly evocation of the British past and the British future, delivered both to the Commons and later on the radio in June 1940, had in itself a galvanising effect on British morale, though those who experienced the speech twice thought that the radio audiences heard a much less effective rendition of the text than MPs had heard earlier in the day. The myth that Churchill was a natural and regular performer on the radio is deeply entrenched in the popular memory. In fact, he broadcast only rarely in the second half of the war, a mere five times in the whole of the three years 1942 to 1944; he had made as many broadcasts in less than six months when at the Admiralty in 1939–40. Those later efforts were also generally too long and less in tune with the public mood. He even missed out on some obvious opportunities to broadcast – nothing from Churchill was heard for example on D-Day (when the King, Eisenhower and President Roosevelt were all on the air) or on the death of Roosevelt himself in 1945. But there is nevertheless no doubting the impact that his voice and his words had on the British public in 1940–1.[45]

One woman listener was in September 1940 moved to compare the printed text of Churchill's warning of a possible invasion (from the next day's newspaper) with the radio address that she had heard. After analysing the methods by which the 'great orator' had achieved his results, she noted finally the extent to which the entire speech was founded on an assumption of trust between leader and followers, so that 'the monosyllable "I" occurs only four times in all the sixteen hundred words'. In much the same way, the theatre critic James Agate felt in 1943 that Churchill was 'the greatest orator this country has possessed in living memory', but that one of his greatest gifts was the ability to summon up at the critical moment not an original phrase of his own, but a quotation which the audience would remember, even if only dimly, and so give them a shared sense of possession in the speech – and therefore in its argument too. This was exactly the point that the editor of the *Oxford Dictionary of Quotations* had made in 1941, for though so few of Churchill's words got into the body of his text, his introduction was written entirely around the idea that such familiar quotations as those used by Churchill in his 1940 radio speeches were a subtle appeal to the common culture of speaker and audience, an effective if subliminal reinforcement of the idea that both were on the same side.[46] Nor is there the faintest doubt that in 1940–1 a Churchill radio address was a very important event indeed: the journalist Graham Cawthorne later recalled an occasion on which a local water board found that 'consumption of water stopped completely. Not a tap was turned on during the broadcast.' And on another occasion, the telephone exchange in Southampton did not deal with a single call for the fifteen minutes during which he spoke. This was the situation that provided the backdrop for one of the most widely circulated Churchill stories of the post-war period. In this implausible tale, Churchill is said to have needed to take a taxi to Broadcasting House to address the nation on the radio, but the driver says, 'Sorry, guv, can't take you there. I've got to get home quick to listen to the Prime Minister's speech on me radio.' Greatly pleased, Churchill offers a five-pound note, saying 'I'm in a hurry to get to that address,' and the cabbie responds, 'Get in, guv'nor. Frig the bloody Prime Minister – what's that address again?' This is without the faintest doubt spurious, but its inclusion in almost every anthology of popular Churchill stories from the 1940s onwards neverthe-less attests to the popular memory that in 1940–1 the entire nation was hanging on his broadcast words.[47]

The same rapport between leader and follower was aimed at – and to some extent achieved – by Churchill's visits to bombed areas on the day after a raid, 'encouraging, sympathising, and producing his silent V-sign gesture, chin thrust forth, clambering over rubble with the aid of a sturdy stick'. And he was very often accompanied by a newsreel camera, so that a wider public could once again feel a share in these events too. When he visited Plymouth, Mass-Observation found that 'for those who really got a see and sniff of him, the experience was profoundly moving', for he brought with him what one of the founders of the movement later called 'a breath of positivity, vitality and above all *concern*'. One M-O observer wrote in May 1941:

> It was impossible even for the most objective observer not to be deeply moved by the sight of this great man, fierce faced, firmly balanced on the back of the car, with great tears of angry sorrow in his eyes. He was so visibly moved by the suffering that he saw, yet so visibly determined to see that it spelt not defeat but victory. A man overflowing with human sympathy, an epic figure riding through this epic of destruction.

He was heard to keep saying 'God, bless you all!' and 'Well done, Plymouth,' invariably with tears in his eyes, while the crowds responded with 'Good old Winnie' and – most evocatively – 'He's like a *lighthouse*.' Paying a surprise visit to Manchester in April 1941, the scenes were much the same, and, though no official announcement of his arrival was made, news spread like wildfire, and he was soon being mobbed by crowds shouting 'Good old Winnie!' and being snapped by press photographers.[48] He was equally alert to the rather different photo-opportunities offered in Washington, for example demonstrating his famous zippered coverall suit to the photographers on the White House lawn – though ostensibly there only to feed the squirrels. In such cases, the V-sign, adopted by Churchill only in 1941, was invariably to the fore, and this too could be seen as a link with English history, for in its ruder, forward-facing version it dated back at least to the Battle of Agincourt, when the English bowmen had brandished their fingers to the French in defiance of a threat that all archers captured alive would have their first two fingers cut off to ensure that they could never draw a bowstring again.[49]

Such gifts – and indeed such arts of the master politician – contributed signally to the impact that Churchill had during the Battle of Britain in summer 1940 and the long-drawn-out endurance test of the Blitz over the following winter, but they also established for him the reputation of a man who was both a tough-minded leader and a warm human being. Sixty years later, Tony Benn and William Deedes from opposite sides of the political divide captured this dual quality remarkably well. Benn recalled 'his voice on the radio, his unmistakable figure, that wonderful billycock hat that he wore, the boiler suit, the personification of resistance – it was impossible to believe in defeat when he was there'. Deedes, more subtly, noted 'the amazing feature' of Churchill's 'mental robustness: the fact that it was a nature which had an altogether softer side, an altogether kindlier side'.[50]

Churchill therefore reached in his first year as Prime Minister a pinnacle of popularity – and indeed of actual *identity* between what he symbolised and what the nation most sought in a political leader – that was unprecedented in British politics and has not been matched since, not even in the high days of either Margaret Thatcher or Tony Blair. The writer Somerset Maugham, returning to Britain in June 1940 after a few weeks in France, found 'a very different England . . . [for] Winston Churchill had inspired the nation with his own stern and resolute fortitude. There was no more half-heartedness.' *Time* magazine made Churchill its 'man of the year' in March 1941, noting that 'he gave his countrymen exactly what he promised them: blood, toil, tears, sweat, and one thing more – untold courage. Those burning words summed up the nature of Britain's war, turned Britain's back on the weakness of the past, and set her face towards an unknown future.' Or in the more sober words of Britain's *Annual Register* for 1940, 'Under the inspiring leadership of Mr Churchill [Britain] finally cast off the slough which seemed to have settled on it at the time of Munich . . . Whatever might be in store for her in the coming year, there could be no question that a brilliant page of Britain's history had been written in the last seven months of 1940.'[51]

In many ways, Churchill seems to have retained elements of this almost superhuman image with some of the British public until the war's end. The *Spectator*, reviewing at the end of 1943 the fact that the premier's two attacks of pneumonia in the past year had caused 'universal alarm', felt all the same that 'we can no longer believe anything can happen to the Prime Minister . . . It is not simply that because the mind cannot conceive the scheme of things without Mr Churchill, the mind determines that the scheme of things will not be without Mr Churchill, but rather that we have acquired a deep conviction that there is something in the man himself that will keep him at his post, fit and active, till (in his own words) he has finished the job.' And even when the job, or at least the European part of it, was finished and a general election followed, many electors seem to have assumed that Churchill would somehow remain Prime Minister whichever party won the election. Even among the electors who voted against his party, some were devastated to find that its defeat meant that he would also have to resign; an Edinburgh elector was for example astonished to discover that Churchill could not now return to the Potsdam Conference, from which he had temporarily withdrawn in order to return home for the election results.[52]

Despite this, any movement from Churchill's pinnacle of popular support in the winter of 1940–1 could only be downwards, and there is in fact considerable evidence to suggest that this happened both quickly and substantially, once the threat both of invasion and of aerial destruction passed during the summer of 1941. The Nazi war machine then turned east and so, by invading the Soviet Union, ensured that Britain would no longer fight alone. Perhaps this in itself robbed Churchill's Britain of the collective siege mentality of self-conscious defiance that had fuelled the 'finest hour'. In any case, there grew during 1941, and especially from 1942 onwards, a tide of more radical popular opinion with which Churchill was seriously out of step. Whereas 77 per cent of the potential radio audience had heard his 1941 broadcasts, according to the BBC's own figures, the audience was down to 65.4 per cent in February 1942, and of these only 62 per cent approved of what he had said. This broadcast after the fall of Singapore produced overtly critical responses as well as admiration. A housewife in Bacup thought that 'what he said was good, but what he did not say more significant', while a Leeds social worker felt that this was his first broadcast 'that failed to convince and inspire'. Since Churchill spoke on the radio only four more times over the next thirty-six months, he can hardly have recovered this lost ground on his most favourable medium.[53]

At one level, support for Churchill seemed to be overwhelming, for opinion polls continued to record extraordinarily high approval ratings for the Prime Minister, sometimes approaching levels of 90 per cent of the surveyed population. But we need to be cautious in interpreting these as reliable indicators of public opinion: polling techniques were in their infancy and had never yet been tested in any British general election, while the mass movement away from home of large sections of the population made it almost impossible to compile proper samples for interview. Neville Chamberlain had also enjoyed his highest ever approval ratings in wartime, just before he lost power in a fall that was generally unlamented when it happened. It seems that questions about support for both incumbent premiers were seen as a test of patriotism rather than the chance to voice an opinion. In any case, even while Churchill's approval ratings remained staggeringly high by the standards of later years, the same interviewees also in every poll from 1943 onwards expressed an intention to return a Labour government (as indeed the electorate did in 1945 when it first had the chance), and parliamentary by-elections from 1942–3 demonstrated the same steady defection from Churchill's party by the voters.[54]

Mass-Observation, the self-consciously non-statistical research organisation which set out to record opinions qualitively, rather than merely count heads, found as early as the end of 1940 that a radical new spirit was abroad, that the very concept of a 'people's war' was leading to a questioning of the status quo and to demands for a whole series of social and economic changes in a planned post-war society. For their part, MPs were increasingly conscious during 1941–2 of the gap that was opening up between the public and their leaders on domestic policies. Meanwhile, surveys of opinion done for the Government itself, collected as Home Intelligence reports, demonstrated a steady increase of interest in such things as post-war employment policy, and an equivalent decline in interest in the war as such. Since Churchill had no time – in either sense of the phrase – for anything but the war, this necessarily reduced his impact on the public, especially when they looked towards a future in which there would be no war. Even as early as April 1941 when the immediate threat of invasion and the Blitz passed, Churchill's great friend and ministerial colleague Brendan Bracken remarked that for the Government 'the honeymoon is over. The grim realities of marriage must now be faced'. It is not clear, though, how far Churchill was ever aware of such changes of wartime opinion, for he certainly did not see them in their most formal presentations. When Lord Moran told him in early 1946 that the *News Chronicle* had been publishing for years before 1945 opinion polls predicting his defeat, this was clearly the first he had heard of it, but after expressing initial interest he lapsed back into his preferred view, that the electors had deserted him thoughtlessly and precipitately in 1945, after he had for five years enjoyed 'the trust and affection of the country'.[55]

As a result, there was an increasing distrust of Churchill's Government when the public reviewed the world after the war. Home Intelligence reports found in mid-1944 that 30 to 40 per cent of the home population was cynical about anything much being done about the popular Beveridge Report on social policy. One report recorded the widespread view that 'the Government is variously accused of slowness, vagueness, and making promises which are either beyond its intentions or its powers', while a Labour MP read to the Commons in 1942 a letter from a constituent which reflected that changing mood. The man had heard Churchill's last radio speech in the same pub in which he had heard the famous speeches of the earlier war years. 'Twelve months ago, you could have heard a pin dropping on the floor, everybody anxious to listen, but [this time] there was talk, laughter and jokes being expressed, and the proprietor had to turn off the wireless because nobody seemed interested in the speech.' He went on to report that 'all sorts of disrespectful remarks were being made about the Prime Minister', and that large numbers of people were now looking forward to the end of his Government. Increasingly in 1944–5, as the Labour Party managed to create a sense that it would back a more advanced social policy, and indeed a fully socialist policy, as Churchill and the Conservatives clearly would not, there was rising class antagonism, a mood that could only be harmful to the appeal of the unashamedly aristocratic Churchill, despite the common touch that he had so effectively shown in 1940–1.

This sense of an aristocratic leader of a party of privilege getting out of step with the democracy was picked up by American correspondents too, and reported in American newspapers, just as Churchill's speeches on the need to restore and rebuild the British Empire were also cited in America as evidence of his *passé* political mentality. When he sent Lord Louis Mountbatten to head the South-East Asia Command, the American joke was that SEAC stood for Churchill's efforts to 'Save England's Asian Colonies'.[56]

When Mass-Observation asked questions and reported conversations about Churchill himself, they picked up with remarkable regularity a fairly sophisticated duality of opinion within the British public. There was a significant group who remained strong supporters of Churchill as war leader but at the same time had not the slightest intention of voting for him as a leader once the national emergency was over. When he had been forced out of office in 1915, he had lamented that unemployment in wartime would be intolerable for him as he was 'a war person', while Baldwin had apparently reflected when not appointing Churchill to office in the mid-1930s that it might be as well to keep him in reserve – in case there was a war. It was now in the 1940s almost as though the public had formed a rational judgement on exactly that opinion of his worth. Much as they had transmuted pre-war (peacetime) suspicions into (wartime) enthusiasm in 1939–40, they were in 1943–5 again seeing the need for a peacemonger as leader. Already, at the end of 1942, a majority thought it would be better if Churchill stood down when the war ended, and by February 1944 this had risen to 62 per cent of the people surveyed. Reviewing all this evidence, Tom Harrisson wrote a 'Who'll Win?' article in 1944 which correctly predicted the result of the 1945 general election (when few others managed to read all the evidence correctly). The chief reason for this was that:

> supremely popular as [Churchill] is today, this is closely associated with the idea of Winston the war leader, Bulldog of battle etc. Ordinary people widely assume that after the war he'll rest on his magnificent laurels. If he doesn't, many say they will withdraw support, believing him no man of peace, of domestic policy, or of human detail. This comes up over and over again in diaries, letters, talk. It is harder for people to express such sentiments publicly about the chief loyalty figure and security

figure in wartime . . . but most people do not expect him to be the primary post-war leader.

From within the government, Cyril Radcliffe, the future law lord but then director-general at the Ministry of Information, and so on the receiving end of detailed reports on public opinion, had reached the same conclusion. Churchill would, he argued in October 1943, be 'an impossible post-war PM either as head of a coalition or of the Tory Party. His "invincible pugnacity" had been invaluable thro' the war but w[ou]ld not be helpful afterwards.'[57]

In this context, the result of the 1945 general election, when as Churchill ruefully put it the British people gave him the order of the boot rather than the order of the Garter, becomes easier to understand. Historians' debates about the significance of his ill-judged 'Gestapo' speech, or about the attractions of specific Labour pledges, fade into insignificance when it becomes clear that an irresistible tide had been building up for years, and that that tide included the rejection of Churchill the man as in some sense unsuitable for peacetime leadership, as well as the rejection of his party for its pre-war record. Ian Mikardo, standing for Labour in Reading, later pointed out however, just how counter-productive Churchill's broadcast was. Whenever the chairman of Mikardo's public meetings introduced him as 'Obergruppenfuehrer Ian Mikardo, prospective gauleiter of Berkshire, Buckinghamshire and Oxfordshire' there was a roar of approval, and when the Australian Russell Kerr, speaking for Mikardo, announced himself as 'a refugee from . . . Curtin's socialist gestapo in Australia', the audience 'erupted: I never heard such applause in my life'. It is hard not to see in such reactions to Churchill's broadcasts a rejection of the man as well as of his party. But during the actual campaign this was far from obvious, for Churchill paraded around the country in his motorcade and was generally received with huge outpourings of popular sentiment and gratitude. Yet none of this had anything much to do with voting intentions; as an East Ender told a bemused socialist canvasser who had seen the same crowd cheer Churchill *and* Labour's speakers, 'Just because we cheered the old bugger, it doesn't mean we're going to vote for him.' For many, that had been the intention all along, for what Stanley Baldwin called 'the greatest ever example of democratic ingratitude' had been callously premeditated by the voters over two or three years past.[58]

There remained though a second level at which the 1945 general election was misunderstood, and that was in the nearly universal assumption that it had terminated Churchill's career. It had not, for his rejection in 1945 proved rather to be the prelude to a remarkable fight-back which produced not only a second term as Prime Minister in 1951–5, but in the last twenty years of his life that quite astonishing apotheosis as an irresistibly lovable, renaissance man, indeed 'the man of the century'. How that happened is a quite different story, for much of Churchill's iconic status as the saviour of democracy was in fact rather carefully recrafted, on an international scale, for the post-war world, and with a good deal of input from the man himself. It might just be noted here that, when Eisenhower's aide Harry Butcher discussed with Churchill the idea of keeping a diary in wartime, the great man dismissed such ideas as only likely to make the diarist look foolish when subsequently published: 'for his part, the Prime Minister said, he would much prefer to wait until the war was over and then write impressions, so that, if necessary, he could correct or bury his mistakes'. Long before the war even ended, he was making plans to do just that.[59]

There is little doubting the public's sense of gratitude as the war ended, or of the close links that Churchill had established with British people of all types, evocatively captured by the *New Yorker* correspondent's account of VE Day.

> It was without doubt Churchill's day. Thousands of King George's subjects wedged themselves in front of the Palace throughout the day, ceaselessly chanting 'We want the King' and cheering themselves hoarse when he and the Queen and their daughters appeared, but when the crowd saw Churchill there was a deep, full-throated, almost reverential roar.

He had been seen first leading the procession of MPs to give thanks at St Margaret's Church, Westminster, when,

> instantly, he was surrounded by people – people running, standing on tiptoe, holding up babies so that they could be told later that they had seen him, and shouting affectionately the absurd little nurserymaid name 'Winnie, Winnie!' One or two happily sozzled, very old, and incredibly dirty cockneys who had been engaged in a slow, shuffling dance, like a couple of

Shakespearean clowns, bellowed. 'That's 'im, that's 'is little old lovely bald 'ead!'

There were cheers for Ernest Bevin, but Herbert Morrison was 'barely recognised', and nor were other cabinet Ministers, for 'the crowd had ears, eyes, and throats for no one but Churchill . . .'[60]

When he stood on that Whitehall balcony on VE Day, shortly before he conducted the cheering crowds in a riotous chorus of 'Land of Hope and Glory', Churchill shouted to the teeming throng, 'This is your victory!' 'No!' they shouted back (as they were perhaps meant to?). 'It's yours!' Thereafter there was a fairly careful Churchillian skate around this particular issue in his post-war writings, but he frequently settled for the concept put most definitively during his eightieth-birthday celebrations in Westminster Hall in 1954. Clement Attlee, when making the presentation, had referred to Churchill's efforts as a war leader, but Churchill himself rejected the claim that *he* had been the British lion of 1940, arguing rather that the British people all round the world had had the lions' hearts and that he had merely 'provided the roar'. Five years earlier, the idea that he had merely 'provided the roar' had already been neatly inverted in an influential review of volume two (the 1940 volume) of his own war memoirs. Rather, argued Isaiah Berlin, Churchill had 'the lion's share' in creating the remarkable mood of 1940, and not merely the right to voice it.[61] Confusion of this semantic type has remained in both popular consciousness and the literature ever since, and the lion invariably joined the bulldog in the Churchill iconography: when Churchill's pet lion cub, itself a gift from an admirer, died in London Zoo in 1956, the Lions' Club of Atlantic City, New Jersey, raised funds to send him a replacement. William Manchester's much later biography took the lion as the title-identity for Churchill's entire life.[62]

Where does a study of Churchill's wartime reputation come down within this conflict of animal imagery, between a war leader as merely instrumental and one that was both inspirational and strategically critical? Or is it a false dichotomy, since a leader without ready followers could have achieved little, and the British people leaderless in 1940 would surely have lost the war? Franklin Roosevelt got the balance of this argument pretty well when he noted in March 1941:

in this historic crisis Britain is blessed with a brilliant and a great leader in Winston Churchill. But no one knows better than Mr Churchill himself that it is not alone his stirring words and valiant deeds which give the British their superb morale. The essence of that morale is in the masses of plain people who are completely clear in their minds about the one essential fact – that they would rather die as free men than live as slaves.[63]

Maybe so, but that still begs the question of how – or by whose agency – they had got this so clear in their minds, as it certainly had not been clear in spring 1940. Others were less ambivalent, and so perhaps was FDR when he had got to know Churchill better. His special envoy Harry Hopkins was reporting back that 'Your "former naval person" [Churchill's wartime code name] is not only the Prime Minister, he is the directing force behind the strategy and the conduct of the war in all its essentials. He has an amazing hold on the British people of all classes and groups.' The *Sunday Times* thought a month later that 'Mr Churchill is not only Prime Minister, but the nation's leader. His position is unchallenged. The people trust him and look to him for guidance. Whatever he asks, they will do. No other British war statesman has ever had the nation so unitedly behind him.' Or as the cabinet Minister Leo Amery saw Churchill, in November 1941, 'He is the spirit of old England incarnate, with its unshakeable self-confidence, its grim gaiety, its unfailing sense of humour, its underlying moral earnestness, its unflinching tenacity.' This was of course the same 'old England' that the voters cold-bloodedly decided not to continue with in the post-war world, when they voted instead for Labour's 'New Jerusalem', and among other things threw Amery himself out of his parliamentary seat in Birmingham.[64]

During the depressing 1930s, Churchill had almost despaired of the possibility of strong leadership in the contemporary world, coming reluctantly to the conclusion that 'modern conditions do not lend themselves to the production of the heroic or super-dominant type'. But he could not resist contradicting himself when it came to the evaluation of the great men that he had known personally, and whom he wrote about in *Great Contemporaries* (1937). So for example his gripping account of the septuagenarian Georges Clemenceau in 1917: 'Clemenceau embodied and expressed France. As much as any single human being, miraculously magnified, can ever be a nation, he was France ... Happy the nation which when its fate quivers in the balance can find ... such a champion.'[65]

Such a champion was precisely what the almost equally aged Churchill became for Britain in 1940, and that conclusion is hardly undermined by the real evidence that his special status was inevitably temporary and largely conditioned by the transience of the war crisis itself. His great friend Jan Smuts, Prime Minister of South Africa, understood just this point when he asked himself in 1942 whether 'England would have stood without Churchill. Look what a fall France had – the greatest since Babylon – because they had a Pétain instead of a Clemenceau. The English are a better balanced people than the French, but they too needed a leader. And, thank God, they had one. Yes, the English and all of us may thank God there was a Churchill in England . . . [But] After the War?' That absolute centrality of Churchill was well enough understood in Nazi Germany too, as invasion plans indicated: a Chiefs of Staff paper of 1942 concluded that 'the elimination of Churchill must be an essential part of any attack on British morale. It would no doubt have an infuriating and therefore temporarily invigorating effect on the population, but that would wear off. And there is no other statesman who could possibly take his place as the focus and fountainhead of British morale.' This was the Tory MP Cuthbert Headlam's view too. Hearing that Churchill was after his American triumph of 1941 'quite rightly' going on to make a similar effort in Ottawa, Headlam noted that:

> the whole people not only here but throughout the Empire have decided that he is the organiser of victory. We are lucky to have such a man – for in war a 'leader' is absolutely essential – I suppose that L[loyd] G[eorge] fulfilled the same function of leadership in the last war, but nothing like to the same extent as Winston does in this war. In those days there were other men who might have stepped in to fill LG's place – today it is impossible to see anyone at all capable of replacing Winston.

How right they were, and no wonder that the achievement so completely transformed his standing in the world – even if the process had to be so carefully attended to and, in the best sense of the word, mythologised after 1945.[66]

For the process still remained to be done when Churchill fell from power in Britain as a result of the general election of 1945. The end of the European war was still too recent for any particular view of it to have become fixed in the public mind – hence the remarkable attention paid to Churchill's victory broadcast when for the first time the story of the war was set out in a single authoritative narrative. Little or no history of its strategy had yet been published, and the Japanese war was in any case still going on and was expected to last up to another couple of years. Even if press commentators generally agreed that Churchill's fame as a war leader was already imperishable, and had been in no way diminished by his election defeat, it had yet to be written up properly for posterity. So, if Churchill's war service was to be at the heart of any explanation of his extraordinary post-war fame, it was only in the post-war years that Churchill could permanently acquire the special status that such praise implied. The King's invitation to Churchill to share the balcony at Buckingham Palace with the royal family on VE Day and receive the cheers as the national leader gave official sanction to his unique status. Few recalled that Neville Chamberlain had been accorded the same honour by the same King, and with pretty much the same public reception, after the Munich Crisis. It could all have faded from the memory as easily as Chamberlain's triumph had done.

Sir Ernest Barker's biography, published in January 1945, concluded that there was indeed a danger of over-praising Churchill, for 'the genius of Britain is not the genius of the solitary great man'.[67] Along the same lines, the Ministry of Information published in 1942 an official account of wartime Britain by J. B. Priestley. This set Churchill in the egalitarian world of the 'people's war' and referred only to the leadership shown by 'Churchill, Cripps, Eden, Bevin and the rest' (there being no other reference to Churchill in the book's 118 pages). And when Priestley wrote of 1940 that 'the old lion roared', it was Britain rather than Churchill to which he was referring. Another British book of 1943 took the same line: there was a full-page portrait of Churchill opposite the title page, but there were then only two other references to him, while the text pays at least equal attention to Woolton, Bevin, A. V. Alexander, Attlee and Cripps. An extended newsreel film of the Victory Parade staged in London in the summer of 1946 had a similar feel to it: Churchill is credited as 'the architect of victory' in the opening sequence reminding viewers of VE Day a year earlier, but he is then mentioned only once more, as one of those gathered at the saluting stand, and the commentary then concentrates entirely on military leaders, servicemen and women, and ordinary civilians like the miners, bus drivers and land girls who are credited with seeing the country through its time of trial. The peroration is all about 'the little man of the free country' and *his* 'finest hour', and there is no further reference to leadership at all.[68] In many ways, then, the ideological atmosphere of the 'people's war' militated against the building up of a personal leadership mystique while it lasted, and the 1945 election demonstrated that many voters did not want Churchill as leader for the post-war world of welfare either. As an early post-war biographer put it, in 1945 'the British electorate concealed their enthusiasm for their hero'.[69]

Following that defeat, Churchill should, British, Australasian and American newspapers all agreed, rest on his laurels, accept a dukedom and take a long break from political life – and few expected that break to be anything but permanent. Nor was he as good a loser in 1945 as his admirers have sometimes suggested. He was immensely encouraged when Prime Minister Jan Smuts sent him from South Africa two 'heartfelt telegrams' on his defeat, but was then 'offended by the telegram he sent Attlee on his "brilliant" victory. Brilliant indeed. If he had just congratulated him on his victory it would have been different. Why brilliant? It wasn't brilliant at all.' Here Churchill was oblivious to the fact that Smuts had as South African premier to get on with Attlee, and indeed also to the fact that when in office he himself had behaved in exactly the same way, congratulating other countries' election-winners without a thought about how it might appear to the loser. Even his admirers were in 1945 gloomy about Churchill's prospects. Harold Nicolson recorded in his diaries in the first year after the war several accounts of younger backbenchers who thought Churchill 'too old' or simply 'too embarrassing' to lead their party. Having heard even Churchill's friend Jan Smuts voice similar opinions in May 1946, Nicolson concluded sadly that 'they all feel that Winston must go'. At the end of the year, Churchill's greatest admirer on the Labour benches, Hugh Dalton, noted in his diary:

> Winston is becoming rather a pathetic spectacle. The barber's shop downstairs at the House [of Commons] was all through the war decorated with pictures of Churchill in every possible pose. When the new Parliament assembled all this had been taken down . . . The barber . . . said to him, 'Sir, why don't you go right away? That would be much better than hanging about

this place like you're doing.' And in the country his stock has fallen right down . . .

Likewise, when Charles Andrews consulted sixty major political and military figures in the United States in 1946, only two of them thought that Churchill had any political future. And when Churchill dined with Henry Luce and the editorial staff of *Time* in New York on his way back from Fulton, an occasion on which he was on particularly good form after his recent triumph, one present nevertheless recorded that, while they all felt that they had entertained a great man, he was one whose future lay all in the past: 'the fire had unmistakably burned low'. Even in 1964, the film-maker Jack Le Vien was reluctant to end his *The Finest Hours* in 1945, as Churchill himself had suggested (on the perfectly reasonable ground that 'the real climax of his career was the winning of World War II'). But Le Vien could not bring himself to end the story with Churchill's loss of office, and went on into the post-war years, chronicling his return to office in 1951, his knighthood and his Nobel Prize. Post-war political recovery and honours were a crucial way to validate the wartime success, even for a fervent admirer like Le Vien.[70]

But if Churchill's fame still had to be consolidated in the post-war years and his post-war successes shed a new light on his wartime leadership, it remains to be seen how that process worked, and how far he contributed personally to the process.

3

'The Greatest Living Englishman'

WHEN HAROLD MACMILLAN, Britain's new Prime Minister, first met his Conservative supporters in January 1957, he told them – without apparent need of further explanation – that he had just come from having lunch with 'the greatest living Englishman', and proceeded to relay to them Churchill's advice. The phrase was neither original nor unusual, and on occasion in notes for speeches Macmillan and his contemporaries seem occasionally to have used 'GLE' much as Victorians talked and wrote of Gladstone as the 'G[rand] O[ld] M[an]'.[1] As Arthur Booth of the Press Association wrote after witnessing Churchill's reception all over Europe in the post-war period, 'Laurels were showered on him from all sides, irrespective of party, or of creed or of nationality. He was increasingly regarded as being not only the greatest living Englishman, but also the greatest man in the world.'[2] For the *New York Times* Churchill was to the world 'the statesman incarnate', and 'to the West a symbol of implacable resistance to tyranny'.[3] In the title of Neal Ferrier's biography published in 1955, Churchill was already *The Man of the Century*.[4] The last ten years of his life may have underscored the consensus, but it was substantially achieved by 1955. The historian A. M. Gollin wrote shortly afterwards that 'when he died, Churchill already belonged to history'.[5] Most obituarists took the same line in stressing Churchill's absolute singularity – no longer *one* of the great men of 1946, but by far and away *the* great man of the century; Alan Moorhead was being fairly cautious when in 1960 he wrote of Churchill as 'at least the greatest Briton since Wellington'.[6] (The fact that Wellington was born in Ireland and might better have been described as 'Anglo-Irish' seems to have escaped Moorhead, though to be fair it was also a description that did not appeal to the Duke himself, who once remarked that being born in a stable did not make a man a horse.) There was apparently no way of reviewing Churchill's career in 1965 without invoking the word 'great' or reference to his unique national and international status. The immense international response to his funeral was in itself a sign of this, but it was also the cue for his essential 'Englishness' to be widely celebrated, and for him to be compared – invariably to Churchill's advantage – to the great Englishmen of the past.

How then did Churchill become, in the catchphrases used both in 1955 when he retired and in 1965 when he died, 'the greatest living Englishman' and 'the man of the century'? An answer to this question depends on going back to the world before the serious Churchill books of today – the writings of Martin Gilbert, William Manchester, Norman Rose, Roy Jenkins and so on – to the multitudes of lesser writers who made the Churchill name in the 1950s and 1960s. Some of these were young scholars early in their careers, like Alfred Gollin and David Dilks, but mainly they were journalists and professional biographers. The Winston Churchill Memorial and Library at Fulton, Missouri, contains hundreds of such books, many of them collected and donated through 'Marshall Aid', the generosity of the book-collector John David Marshall. The point is not just the number of these sources, but the impact that even minor writers could have on the market. Robert Lewis Taylor, for example, had his Churchill book serialised in the *Saturday Evening Post*, selected for the Book of the Month Club, and translated into Swedish, Spanish, German, Hebrew and Norwegian, before acquiring a paperback imprint too.[7]

But, while Churchill's post-war careers as a politician and as an historian did undoubtedly contribute to this burgeoning fame, solidifying and giving permanence to 1945's perceptions of a great war leader (they will be considered in Chapter Four), the explanation of his unique status has to be found in other areas too. For the most part this will be considered in the British context, since the ways in which the process differed in other parts of the world are also dealt with in later chapters.

First, in establishing Churchill's singularity, there were the accidental – but quite exploitable – effects of time and political longevity. When Churchill became Prime Minister in 1940 he was only sixty-five, which was younger than either Chamberlain or Baldwin had recently been in the same post. But when he retired in 1955 he was over eighty and could be compared as Prime Minister only to Palmerston and Gladstone.

Comparability with Gladstone was the basis on which the British Government began in 1953 planning Churchill's state funeral and his lying-in-state at Westminster Hall, though as soon as planning began it was clear that it would dwarf the relatively restrained and civil – as opposed to military – festivities that had marked Gladstone's passing.[8]

The most recent state funeral with a strong military presence had in fact been that of the First World War general Earl Haig in 1928, for which Churchill had footed the bill as Chancellor of the Exchequer, but hardly anyone in 1965 seems to have remembered the fact. Haig was by then not a popular memory, and the news that there had been massive pageantry and great public involvement in his funeral would probably have amazed readers of British newspapers, but they were never in fact told about it. Haig was just not a man that the 1960s would compare to Churchill. Winston himself added another colourful and historical touch by requesting that for his funeral in St Paul's the massive candlesticks placed around the coffin should be those exhibited at the state funeral of the Duke of Wellington in 1852, which, amazingly, the Ministry of Public Building and Works was able to identify and produce when required in 1965. Wellington was a much more positive memory and comparator for a 'happy warrior' such as Churchill than was Haig.[9]

Nor did Churchill miss many opportunities to draw the appropriate moral from his ageing, which was what made such distant comparisons necessary. He pointed out in 1954 for example, in response to a tribute by Attlee, that the two of them were the only living premiers and ex-premiers, and that Churchill himself was now the only MP to have been elected in the reign of Queen Victoria. He was proud to become Father of the House of Commons in 1959, an honorary title previously enjoyed by both Campbell-Bannerman and Lloyd George, in whose governments he had served, but his service in the Commons for a total of sixty-two years was ten and thirteen years respectively more than the next longest-serving MPs of the entire century, Edward Heath and T. P. O'Connor. By 1963, Churchill could also claim to be the oldest ever ex-premier, since he was then older than Gladstone when he died in 1898, a fact deemed worthy of notice both at home and abroad.[10]

The fortuitous disappearance of all the other world leaders of the war years added to the impact of time: by 1947 Roosevelt, Hitler and Mussolini were all dead, de Gaulle in internal exile and Stalin had become *persona non grata* in the West. An enterprising Belgian publisher had produced in 1945 two sets of playing cards with the faces of Churchill, Stalin, Roosevelt and de Gaulle as the four Kings. Sadly, the suits allocated to the Kings in the two packs did not exhibit any consistent symbolism – Churchill represented Hearts in one pack but it was Stalin who was the King of Hearts in the other, when Clubs might have been more apposite. Such even-handedness would have been impossible even by 1947, and in all the later memorabilia Churchill almost invariably stands as a lone figure rather than as part of such a set.[11]

When Stalin died in 1953, with Churchill now back in office and de Gaulle still in the wilderness, the process was complete. The successors of the war leaders of 1942 were politicians of limited charismatic appeal, for Truman, Eisenhower, Attlee, Adenauer and de Gasperi each failed to make much personal impact outside his own country, and none of them could be called much of an orator. (Though they so often misquoted him, nobody ever insulted Churchill's prose as completely as did Oliver Jensen when he translated the Gettysburg address into 'Eisenhowese', beginning with 'I haven't checked these figures, but 87 years ago I think it was . . .') Churchill was left alone in the limelight, and the one man from the war generation who might have competed internationally was Eisenhower, but Ike devoted himself rather to building up the Churchill cult in the United States; there was scarcely an American book about Churchill to which he did not contribute a supportive foreword. The passage of time and the survival of Churchill came together, then, in the idea of Churchill as a singularly historic personage. As A. L. Rowse put it in 1953:

> In the end it is difficult not to exaggerate. For Winston Churchill sums up the whole first half of our century as no other statesman does . . . Now all the leading figures of the Second World War . . . are dead . . . Only Winston Churchill remains, incarnating how much of modern history in himself, a fabulous figure on the small stage of the modern world.[12]

The *New York Times* thought much the same, with a value judgement thrown in too, though one with which Rowse would have warmly concurred.

> He is the elder statesman of the free world, and a man who has won respect for more than the exercise of power. In his heyday

he had rivals in the greatness that comes with power, for Hitler and Stalin were, in their persons, men who could exercise more power than Winston Churchill, who was the leader of a democracy. Yet Sir Winston lived and fought for the noble things of life and this gives him a greatness the others could not touch.[13]

Increasingly a sense emerged that Churchill spanned the ages, as a man who had served every British monarch from Victoria to Elizabeth II, 'a Victorian who was ambushed at the Khyber Pass and lived beyond Hiroshima', and 'a complete anachronism – a royalist, an Imperialist, an Elizabethan thrust upon the stage of the twentieth century', as John Strachey put it. An American reporter, welcoming 'the Pickwickian figure' of Churchill on his first return to the United States as Prime Minister in 1952, pictured him as 'a Victorian gentleman at the door of a DC-6'.[14] This was in part the foundation of the veritable Churchill industry in publishing in the 1950s: Diana Coolidge wrote in 1960 that 'no man in his lifetime can have had more books written about him than Churchill', but this was quite explicable, for 'his life is the history of the first half of the twentieth century'.[15]

As time passed, Churchill was quite ready to add the mocking of his own antiquity to the act he put on for the world. When a Labour MP compared the lack of information on the contemporary Korean War to the scandal of the Crimea, Churchill replied to general hilarity that the 1850s 'were before even my time'. It was not quite so acceptable for others to make jokes about his age, though, even inadvertently. When Cecil B. De Mille visited him and assured him that the script for *The Ten Commandments* had been inspired by his essay on Moses, Churchill asked to be reminded in which of his books (of essays) this had appeared. Churchill's private secretary Anthony Montague Browne absent-mindedly suggested that it might have been in *Great Contemporaries*, and received a blast of disapproval which 'stunned' the guests: 'Damn your skin. That's not at all funny.'[16]

He was in fact ever acute to the advantage that could be wrung from the mellowing of opinion towards him as he aged. The Labour MP Woodrow Wyatt thought in 1958 that 'Churchill is the only man of our epoch to be declared a national monument in his own lifetime. All his parliamentary life he screwed the maximum advantage from every position. He was very sensible in his later years of the political advantage of the public's veneration while he enjoyed it.' Wyatt conceded that Churchill did not need such advantages in the Commons because he was well able to look after himself, and that in 'the great decade of his later maturity', 1945–55, he achieved an unprecedented domination over the Commons; his arrival prompted a sense of occasion and 'when he got up to go something of the vitality of the House went with him'. Churchill's performances in the Commons may also have gained something from their rarity in the 1950s, for in this last phase of his career he became a far less regular attender than he had previously been. James Humes points out that, after 1945, MPs laughed *with* Churchill rather than *at* him, because the Commons generally takes to an eccentric 'character' such as Churchill had now become. It was notable too that it was failure in the Commons in April 1954, suggesting that tolerance for his age was giving way to serious concern about his faculties, that really set alarm bells ringing among Churchill's colleagues as to the necessity for his retirement.[17] One British historian who visited the 1959 Parliament as an undergraduate later recalled the impression made on him by the respect for Churchill shown both by the House and by the public during his final years:

> How vividly I remember my only sighting of WSC . . . Edward Boyle was at the [dispatch] box for Question Time. Churchill was in his seat. Boyle was in mid-answer when Churchill got up and made his way slowly out of the House. Boyle stopped speaking, everyone in the Strangers' Gallery stood up, the clerks stopped writing. Churchill walked slowly but not over-slowly (as Macmillan used to do), clearly very old but still in control of his body. He left the Chamber. We sat down. Boyle resumed his answer, and the little vignette ended. It was a most moving incident, the more so because of the complete absence of comment – verbally or bodily – by the observers, except for their participation in it through their silence and their standing.[18]

Churchill's domination of the Commons was built on hard work and preparation for debates, but he was also allowed an unusual degree of latitude by the House because of what Wyatt called 'the huge volume of accumulated respect'.[19] This latter point was confirmed by Attlee, who pointed out in 1954 that despite Churchill being generally described in his own phrase as 'a child of the House of Commons', yet 'curiously enough he has never mastered the procedure of the House. He gives the impression that anyway the rules don't apply to him.' But because of the respect in which he was held he got away with it. In the same way, his apparently sudden conversion to the idea of East–West dialogue in 1953 changed the whole nature of the debate. Richard Crossman noted that this showed 'what an astonishing power Churchill still has ... The moment Churchill speaks, it becomes respectable,' whereas similar demands by the Labour left had been generally viewed as evidence of its weakness in the face of Communism. As Emanuel Shinwell put it in 1964, Churchill 'is no ordinary MP. He is one of our greatest institutions: the Throne, the Church, Parliament, the Press and Sir Winston Churchill.' John Strachey and Shinwell were old enemies who found that they could no longer hate the elderly Churchill. Strachey conceded in the late 1940s that '*everyone* calls him Winston. He's a national nuisance but one can't help being fond of him'. Even Nye Bevan was quoted as saying of Churchill that 'History itself seemed to come into the Chamber when he addressed us.' There have been others who have like Churchill survived long enough in active politics to live down their original image when they were demonised by the press as unstable and radical agitators. Manny Shinwell himself was a prime example of this process, while in 2001 Tony Benn was horrified to hear that he had been described by a British ambassador as 'a national treasure', indignantly denying that he was now a harmless old gentleman: 'I am old, I am a gentleman, but I hope I am not harmless.'[20]

Churchill's case, however, was an unique version of the common story, not least because his personal trajectory from radical Liberal to war hero and anti-Communist Conservative ensured that he was not just tolerated but actively celebrated by the media. Jealous though of this status as a veritable fifth estate of the realm, Churchill as Prime Minister in the 1950s took great care over his speeches and made sure to receive his share of the House's attention at Question Time. Junior Ministers programmed to answer questions before him gave only short replies, and when Hugh Gaitskell for the Opposition asked a Treasury spokesman a long supplementary question, Churchill, with his eyes on the clock, was heard to hiss, 'Don't answer him. Don't answer him.'[21]

The extent to which opinion mellowed as Churchill aged can be seen in the series of ceremonials that attended his last few years in office, a term that began in the acute political partisanship of the 1951 election, when one Labour slogan read, 'Vote for Churchill and reach for your rifle; Vote Labour and reach old age',[22] but ended with what was (as Roy Jenkins has put it) more like a pageant than a government.[23] The Labour left therefore got into quite a stew over how it should react to the national celebrations of Churchill's eightieth birthday, since it did not wish to give aid and comfort to a political foe, but neither did its members dare antagonise an increasingly pro-Churchill public mood. Crossman tried to organise a meeting of the Bevanite group of MPs to celebrate Churchill's birthday by absenting themselves from the occasion, only to find that Nye Bevan (due to dine with Churchill the following week) and Jennie Lee (part of the committee which had organised the parliamentary festivities and the person who had actually suggested Graham Sutherland as the man to paint Churchill's portrait) both refused to stay away. When Barbara Castle cancelled her subscription to the Churchill birthday fund in protest at his recent Cold War rhetoric, Bevan thought it an act of 'sheer demagogy', and exerted himself to ensure that almost all Labour MPs signed the parliamentary 'birthday book' for Churchill.[24]

In 1952, when the King died, sourness was still abroad; a Labour MP pointed out that Churchill's tribute to George VI harped on so much about 1940 that it was 'not only a fulsome tribute to the King; it was also an indirect eulogy of himself'.[25] But even that critic could not doubt the effectiveness of Churchill's parliamentary tribute to the new Queen: 'nobody in British public life today could compete with Winston Churchill in this form of eloquence. Connoisseurs of parliamentary oratory declared it worthy of the event, one which would go down into history as yet another masterpiece well worthy of inclusion in an anthology of Winston Churchill's immortal speeches.'[26] The Coronation of the following year was seen by some as 'Sir Winston's crowning glory as well as the Queen's', and there was much harmless fun poked at the old boy for his changing back and forth between the uniforms of the Garter and the Wardenship of the Cinque Ports as the day progressed.

There was, however, some uncertainty about why Churchill's coach had pulled out of the Coronation procession on the way back from the Abbey and taken a short cut back to Downing Street, distinctly upsetting the Crown Equerry who was in charge of that part of the proceedings. This extraordinary departure from protocol was variously attributed to the horses becoming over-excited or to Churchill himself being under the weather during a long and tiring day, but it is possible that there was another cause altogether. When collecting material for her book *Irrepressible Churchill*, Kay Halle interviewed Christopher Sykes, who knew the coachman who had actually driven Churchill in the Coronation procession, and noted down his account of the day. Initially, Churchill complained that the coach allotted to the Prime Minister had windows that were too small and that the public would not be able to see him, producing the reminder that this was supposed to be the Queen's day rather than his own, and so the royal family would get the best coaches. This point is confirmed by Lord Moran, who noted on 28 May 1953 that Churchill had been hoping to get the use of 'a big car with large windows' for the procession, rather than 'be hidden away in a box of a carriage', but it was difficult to envisage the 4th Hussars providing a mounted escort for a car. Consequently, he began the drive back from the Abbey in an uncertain temper and, after becoming increasingly jealous of the cheers for the Queen, he banged on the roof of the coach with his stick, near Admiralty Arch, and demanded to be taken home forthwith. The story then ends with the increasingly furious Churchill being unable to secure quick admittance to Downing Street from the rear because all the staff were out watching the event he had so summarily deserted. Halle did not print the story in her book, possibly because she had no confirmation of its accuracy from a more direct source, but more likely because it showed Churchill being *too* irrepressible to fit in with the heroic legend that had by then emerged.[27] Churchill's historic status was demonstrated on Coronation Day by his wearing the actual jewelled garter given by Queen Anne to his ancestor the first Duke of Marlborough and later worn by the first Duke of Wellington, but it also owed a good deal to what he actually did. Though Dick Crossman was unimpressed by the Coronation banquet in Westminster Hall ('rather fat New Zealand lamb and empire wines'), he conceded that 'I've never heard Churchill speak better. Despite the solemnity of the occasion, he made a light-hearted parliamentary oration . . .'[28]

The ceremony earlier in the year in which he had been installed as a Knight of the Garter – and, appropriately enough for 'the greatest living Englishman' this was on St George's Day – was a signal sign of royal approval and an addition to the growing impact of television in widening public awareness of such events. The Queen continued to demonstrate her view that Churchill was more than just her first Prime

Minister, coming to Downing Street to dine with the Churchills on the eve of his eventual retirement in 1955,[29] and then retiming the actual ceremony of resignation for a point earlier than planned on the following day so that her young children could be present to witness the historic moment. The dinner at Downing Street was widely reported to be breaking all precedents, the monarch for the first time dining formally with her premier at his residence rather than her own. In fact her father had done the same when Baldwin retired in 1937, and it was Churchill who wanted to follow the precedent with the first peacetime retirement since Baldwin. After the dinner, she wrote Churchill an eight-page letter of thanks in her own hand, which so moved Churchill that he spent a whole morning on his reply. The large crowds present in the streets on these occasions, and once again the television coverage, ensured that the Queen's personal favour would not go unnoticed, as did their presence being noted in all the contemporary biographies, one of which (by a Rumanian) proclaimed on the dust-jacket that 'le courage, dans tous les aspects a pris pour lui le visage, la forme et le nom de Sir Winston Churchill'.[30]

But the event of this period that most demonstrated the warmth of regard that Churchill had now achieved, both among the political elite and with the public, was his eightieth-birthday celebrations in November 1954. A Churchill birthday was always an event, and even his seventy-ninth in 1953 had produced more than two thousand cards,[31] but this was entirely dwarfed by the following year. The celebrations can only be compared to Victoria's Jubilees; there were presents from royalty, tributes from all parties, messages from countries all over the world, a special television programme in his honour from the BBC, and even a tribute from Eton to 'the greatest of all Harrovians'.[32] All in all there were thirty thousand birthday cards, and nine hundred actual presents – flowers, books, cigars and wine, and an illuminated address from the British Legion. Among the cards and letters were two which attracted additional publicity: one, from the Netherlands, bore only a photograph of Churchill pasted to the envelope, and the word 'England', while the other was a British card addressed to 'The Greatest Man Alive, London'. Both were delivered by the Kensington post office to Churchill on his birthday, and photographs of the covers appeared in the press.[33] A birthday collection eventually raised £259,000 from over 300,000 subscribers, which was placed in a Churchill Trust and used in part for the

Vintage Year
Daily Mail, 30 November 1957

foundation of Churchill College.[34] The three-foot-diameter birthday cake
weighed thirty-five pounds, and was decorated with copies in icing of
the covers of Churchill's major books, the insignia of the Garter and
the Cinque Ports, and such personal touches as a sculpture in icing of
his poodle Rufus.[35] The parliamentary aspect of the occasion, though,
did not lack seriousness, for two thousand of Britain's most prominent
citizens stood and cheered Churchill to the echo as he entered Westminster Hall to the strains of Elgar and as a drumbeat then pounded
out the 'V for Victory' morse message of 1940.[36] Attlee presented an
illuminated address from both Houses and the portrait by Graham
Sutherland that Lady Churchill later had burned because it so upset
Winston. Emrys Hughes sourly observed that Churchill did not like this
portrait because it showed the truth – 'it is the picture of a depressed-
looking old man thinking of the atom bomb'. This was perceptive, for
Churchill's private view, when having the picture painted, was that he
was 'more worried by the hydrogen bomb than by all the rest of my
troubles put together', but it was certainly not the image of himself that
he wished to project.[37]

'One man in his time plays many parts' – with congratulations to Sir Winston
Churchill, who tomorrow enters his 80th year
Sunday Times, 29 November 1953

Churchill in his own speech in Westminster Hall referred back to
1940 and his role in providing for Britain the lion's roar, but was also
careful to ensure that nobody missed the real point of the occasion.
'This is to me the most memorable public occasion of my life. No one
has ever received a similar mark of honour before. There has not been
anything like it in British history.'[38] More informally, at about this time,
he responded to a small boy who, when visiting Chartwell, somehow
managed to steal into the great man's room and pose the question, 'Are
you the greatest man in the world?', with the words, 'Yes, I am. Now
bugger off.'[39] So the unique status of Churchill was by the time of his
pending retirement well and truly established, and we even have his
own word for it. The *News Chronicle*'s cartoonist, Spencer, mischievously
parodying preparations for the birthday celebrations, drew two little
birds on a tree watching a bulldog (complete with Churchillian hat and
cigar). One of the birds is saying, 'Act like you can't make out who he's
supposed to be – it makes him furious.' The *Sunday Times*, more typically of the press, had its cartoonist draw the figure of History offering
the elderly Churchill a laurel wreath, while fourteen other Winston
Churchills – painter, soldier, historian and so on – look on in serried
ranks.[40]

Animal Crackers
'Act like you can't make out who he's supposed to be – it makes him furious.'
News Chronicle, 23 June 1954

The years 1953–4 were only the climax of a process. Churchill had indignantly refused in 1945 'to be exhibited as a prize bull whose chief attraction is its past prowess', as he put it,[41] and he also refused 'to retire in an aura of civic freedoms'. But that did not prevent him from accepting the freedoms, twenty-seven in all in the years 1946–51. He received a mass of prizes and awards all over Britain, Europe and the United States in the later 1940s, which both kept him permanently in the public eye and demonstrated the breadth and depth of admiration for his war work – no small advantage to a politician still seeking a return to office. When he later attended the Hague Congress as an ordinary Conservative Member, all the delegations from the European countries stood and cheered his entrance into the hall.[42] At Strasbourg, where he received the freedom of the city as well as making a major speech, it was clear that Churchill 'was the personality from Britain about whom the Continent knew most. He was the hero of the occasion.'[43] Some less tasteful proposals for honours had to be turned down, as was the idea of an English Mount Rushmore, with his face carved into the white cliffs of Dover, two hundred feet high, a huge red cigar permanently burning for the safety of shipping. But a carved wooden head of Churchill, large enough to merit an eight-foot-long bamboo cigar, did go ahead in the Australian outback and was said at one point to be the only significant landmark between Darwin and Alice Springs.[44]

The main focus of such honouring of Churchill was, however, in England itself, and the range and breadth of the honours awarded to him is a strong indication of the extent to which his fame and ordinary people's sense of their nation had become closely aligned. Some were most certainly awarded by those who wished to mark a specific association with the man, as was the freedom of the Borough of Wanstead and Woodford, which he had represented in the Commons since 1924, of Woodstock in Oxfordshire (where he had been born), of Harrow and of Brighton (where he had been at school), of Kensington (where his London house was situated), and of the City of Westminster (where Parliament itself, the site of so many of his triumphs and disasters, was located).[45] On the same principle, there was a cluster of honours associated with Kent, where he was both a weekend resident and Lord Warden of the Cinque Ports. Hence Churchill was made a freeman of (among other places) Beckenham, Margate, Rochester, Deal and Dover; he was also a deputy lieutenant for Kent, an honorary life member of the Association of Kentishmen and Men of Kent, president of the Deal, Walmer and Kingsdown Regatta Association, and a member of 'the Hastings fishermen's famous Winkle Club' (the last requiring Monty and Churchill to 'Winkle Up' when they visited the town together in 1955).[46] Beyond the areas of Britain where he had a local connection, there were certainly freedoms from places which would have been more than happy to celebrate a Tory leader like Churchill (Bath, Marlborough, Worcester, Eastbourne, Worthing, Colchester and Maldon, for example,[47] none of which had any real connection with his career), but he was also awarded freedoms in the Midlands and the industrial North, where Labour was at least as strong a presence as the Conservatives, for example in Birmingham, Darlington, Manchester, Leeds and Sheffield (the last of which had been under Labour control since 1933).[48]

The same breadth of response to Churchill is to be seen as we move from a geographical to a thematic analysis. Some honours related directly to his time as a soldier and to war leadership (vice presidency of the Royal Armoured Corps Club, Chesney Medal of the Royal United Services Institute, freedom of Aldershot and of Portsmouth),[49] some his claim to fame as a writer (life membership of the Athenaeum, fellowship of the Institute of Journalists, vice presidency of the London Library, Gold Medal of the Royal Institute of Arts, honorary fellowship of the British Academy). His post-war honorary degrees, from Oxford,

Cambridge and London among others, were all predicated partly on the same grounds.[50] Other honours reflected a leisure interest he had shown at some time in his life, such as the membership of the Shorthorn Society of Great Britain and Ireland and the honorary presidency of the Amateur Fencing Association.[51] But alongside all of these were ranged honours for which there was simply no particular Churchill connection at all. A small part of that list would include his fellowships of the Institute of Engineers and of the Royal Geographical Society, freedom of several London livery companies (including the Mercers, Shipwrights and Merchant Venturers), honorary membership of the Royal College of Physicians, the Institute of Municipal and County Engineers, the MCC, the Baltic Mercantile and Shipping Exchange, and the Glasgow Chamber of Commerce.[52] What all this cumulatively demonstrated of course is how far there was a desire by relatively low-level decision-makers all across England to own a piece of Mr Churchill and to claim him for themselves.

That point is borne out if we look in more detail at the way in which some of these honours were conferred and what was said by those making the decisions. Great significance was attached to such moments – nationally as well as locally: when Blackpool in October 1946 awarded the freedom of the borough to Churchill, a recording of the ceremony was broadcast on the Home Service of BBC radio. The timing was important here, for the decision was made when he was already known to be coming to Blackpool for the Conservative Party Conference – immediately after launching a ship in Liverpool – and this would provide an opportunity to make the presentation. As we shall see, getting Churchill actually to come and collect honours was far more difficult than persuading councillors to vote for them. It was a great festivity for western Lancashire, and there was a heavy local demand for tickets, both for the ceremony itself and for the party rally which he would address at the end of the party conference. Tickets for the ceremony were said to be changing hands for five guineas each on the local black market, but since he drove in state for eight miles along the famous promenade in an open-topped car there were plenty of chances for the locals to see him – and to witness the cigars, the V-signs and the rest of the personality on show. When he entered the town hall, loudspeakers were broadcasting recorded extracts from the council debate in which the freedom resolution was passed, and then extracts from Churchill's own broadcasts in 1940. He certainly lived up to the expectations, speaking of his earliest political activities as a candidate 'in this famous Palatinate', and he told the 'privileged thousands' in the ceremony that 'no cheers fall so sweetly on my ears as British cheers'. Finally, seizing the freeman's scroll from its casket, he flourished it to the audience with the words, 'This shall hang on my walls that my descendants may know that there was a time when I was well spoken of in Blackpool!' Blackpool women (noted 'Phyllis' in her column in Blackpool's *Gazette and Herald*) had also risen to the occasion with a fine repast, even in that year of austerity. The menu included a 'Churchill Pudding', a dish hopefully closer to cabinet pudding than to Woolton pie. The cheering was deafening, the choruses of 'For He's a Jolly Good Fellow' were prolonged, and Lancastrians bid farewell with cries of 'Cheerio, Winnie.'[53]

Brighton awarded its Churchill honour in exactly the same way, in October 1947, when the Conservatives moved from the west to the south coast for their conference, though the council had actually voted it through in wartime. This official Churchill visit had the combined purpose of receiving the freedom of the borough and opening Churchill House, an ex-servicemen's social and welfare centre which had been set up as a sort of war memorial, after collection of funds by the Brighton and Hove Thank-you Committee. The appeal for funds asserted that 'it seems right and proper that the man who led the nation to victory should be permanently associated with the building which is being bought to commemorate for all time the achievement of the men and women who made that victory possible'. The naming for and by Churchill would thus link his leadership with the war of the common people. Unfortunately, though, while the appeal did well enough to raise £15,000 to buy and equip Churchill House, it did not manage also to endow it. With many of the twelve ex-service bodies which initially used it withering away, and with inadequate funds for its ordinary activity, Churchill House, rather than existing 'for all time', closed down in 1949, and a similar fate soon overtook the social club for the officers and men of the Royal Sussex Regiment which Churchill had formally presented to the regiment on the same visit. The visit itself was viewed as part of a series of links which through collective memory and their regular revisiting in the local press did indeed give the impression of a connection for all time. During the 1946 visit, Churchill spoke fondly of his early school days in Hove, and he recalled too the visit that he had made in 1940, when with General Montgomery he had toured possible invasion areas and watched the Grenadier Guards sandbagging the kiosks along the Brighton seafront. Typically, as he rose to speak at a civic lunch in the Dome, he spotted 'a comrade of the Boer War . . . with four or five clasps on his medals', the sight of whom aroused memories of days 'when we used to sing "Soldiers of the Queen" and did our best to secure a free and broad future for South Africa'. The oldest member of Brighton Council, offering a tribute to Churchill, even recalled attending a dinner held in Liverpool in 1900 to celebrate Churchill's escape from Boer captivity. And so it went on, replete with nostalgia for the three major wars in which Britain had been involved since 1900, in all of which Brighton could claim a link with the great man. Naturally, not a note of criticism was to be heard, and Churchill himself remarked that 'you have said a great deal about me which it is not good for a man to hear until he is dead'.[54]

Thereafter, the 1946 visit itself became the focus of nostalgia, with several columns recounting the story in the town and county papers. When Churchill died, there was a full tribute by David Marlowe, Hove's Conservative MP since 1941, which retold Churchill's heroic story and its Brighton context for a new and younger audience. Churchill had been 'cold-shouldered' by the establishment in the 1930s, but he had come through in 1940.

> At that time he was, as it were, fighting the war almost single-handed. We had no allies. France was defeated. America had not yet come in, and we were woefully deficient in weapons. But, thank God for it, we had one matchless weapon – the faith and courage of this man who hurled defiance at the enemy with words and deeds which inspired us all to make the supreme effort. Let none of us ever forget that we owe our survival to him.

Marlowe was not blind to Churchill's deficiencies, even in wartime, but he knew too that he had witnessed the best moments of 'the greatest man in British history. Stormy, tempestuous, competitive and obstinate, perhaps the most remarkable aspect of his character was that he always evoked affection, even from those who disagreed with him.' The last point was often associated by later writers with the crowds and cheers in Brighton in 1946, when his car could barely get through the streets to reach the various places of ceremonial, because of that spontaneous affection. But the message had subtly changed since 1947, for when the freedom of Brighton was actually conferred the emphasis was on the link between the ordinary people's war record and Churchill's lead. By 1964–5, it had become a much less complicated matter of the homage paid to a great man by his admirers.[55]

Portsmouth proved a rather different story, largely because Churchill had visited far more regularly, often in the course of his connections with the Royal Navy, but he had first been there in 1898 to deliver one his very earliest political speeches, just after returning from the Sudan, and even then nostalgic references were made to the speech Lord Randolph Churchill had delivered in the same hall in 1880. He had returned in 1901 to lecture on his escape from the Boers, had visited 'almost every weekend' when as First Lord of the Admiralty in 1911–15 he had personal use of the Admiralty Yacht *Enchantress*, had gone there in 1934 to speak in support of Admiral Sir Roger Keyes at a by-election, and most memorably had visited in 1941 when Portsmouth was blitzed. It was even suggested that the 'loud cheers' which ensued when he sat down after speaking in 1898 caused many locals to hope that he would become Portsmouth's MP, but Oldham got him first. All of this was included in a tribute to Churchill on his birthday in 1948.[56]

Portsmouth had in fact decided to make Churchill a freeman soon after he visited with Harry Hopkins in 1941, but had to wait until 1950 for a visit at which the honour could be conferred. The city had ensured that the Lord Mayor who now conferred the honour should be the same one who had welcomed Churchill back in 1941, and Alderman Sir Denis Daley duly obliged with a stirring tribute to Churchill's record as the nation's war leader, but with its focus carefully adjusted to ensure that every possible local and naval link was stressed. Churchill had been 'the Captain of the ship' of Britain's war effort, who 'was continuously on the bridge', and whose 'own picked men' worked 'as men had never worked before, to ensure that the Ship of State might be brought into calmer waters'. Churchill, whose naval connection had already been emphasised by a visit the same day to the Portsmouth dockyard and the battleship HMS *Vanguard*, picked the same themes in his response. He cited his friendships with naval heroes like Fisher, Power, James and Vian (and Power's name would hardly have been recognised in any other town), he remembered playfully how much fun it had been to be First Lord (compared to the Home Office, 'a dreadful office', and the Exchequer, 'another dreadful office'), and spoke emotionally of the losses suffered in Portsmouth town and dockyard in 1941. The emphasis, once again, was on leadership rather than a 'people's war', and on the shared experience of 1941 and – because of the naval tradition which they shared – over the whole of Churchill's career. It is tempting to wonder how much all this hero-worship of the still politically active Churchill affected the results in the parliamentary elections of 1950 and 1951, when the Conservatives held all three Portsmouth seats, including one that had been lost in 1945. It can certainly have done their chances no harm.[57]

Once again, later news items about Churchill were able to refer back to the 1950 ceremonials, and especially to Churchill's own avowal that the freedom of Portsmouth was 'an event outstanding in my life'. He visited the city for the Coronation naval review in 1953, and again to welcome *Britannia* back from the Queen's world tour in 1954. When he retired in 1955 and when he died in 1965, the local press recycled the story of 1950 as well as 1941 to indicate that the city had a special link with 'the greatest of all Englishmen'. Since he was a freeman, the Lord Mayor in 1965 sent a special condolence to Churchill's widow, and was able to attend the funeral at St Paul's in person – but on behalf of all the citizens of Portsmouth.[58]

Bristol too could claim both a real link with Churchill, for he had been Chancellor of the University since 1929 in succession to his old cabinet colleague Haldane, and a chance to see him in person when he came to University degree ceremonies. The *Western Daily Press* in April 1945 saw this as a sign of the city fathers' perception, for 'they could have had no idea of the celebrity he was destined to achieve', so limited were expectations of Churchill's future in 1929. It also took a retrospective swipe at those who had opposed his appointment as Chancellor on the ground that he was 'primarily a politician', for his national status now proved his supporters in 1929 to have been 'men of shrewder judgement than many might have imagined' at the time. The freedom ceremony was seen as the city's dress-rehearsal for VE Day, and Churchill drove through Bristol in an open-topped carriage. The involvement in the ceremony of the Royal Navy's HMS *Bristol* highlighted both Churchill's naval connections and the city's own part in the war, but this was anyway emphasised in all the speeches, including Churchill's own, and by the presence of Churchill's daughter in uniform.[59]

Manchester could also claim kinship, for he had represented the city in Parliament for two tempestuous years, and, though his constituents had rudely ejected him at a by-election in 1908, this had not much disrupted his ministerial career. He seems as a result not to have developed the dislike for Manchester that he had for Dundee, when losing his seat there in 1922 began his lowest period of electoral fortune. He had never set foot in Dundee again and allegedly ensured that the blinds were down in his compartment when he had to pass through the city by train, but he had happily revisited Manchester on a number of occasions. He had first been there officially in 1904, to address the inaugural meeting of the Free Trade League, and, apart from his duties as a Manchester MP, had visited again in 1907 for a banquet of the British Cotton Association, and in 1909 for a 'great political meeting' on the Lloyd George budget in the Free Trade Hall. He did not visit again until he came in January 1940 to review 'the first five months of the war to a crowded audience' in the same hall, but was back in 1941 to inspect sites of bomb damage. In June 1945, during his election tour, Manchester 'gave a tumultuous reception to the great war leader. One of the greatest crowds ever assembled in Manchester greeted Mr Churchill in Piccadilly.' All these quoted words, and the review of his six official visits to the city, are taken from the brief provided for the Lord Mayor in advance of the 1947 freedom ceremony, a brief which did not mention the fact that two weeks after his 1945 visit Manchester elected nine Labour MPs and only one Tory, so that many of those Mancunians who cheered him plainly did not vote for him to remain in office. By then, however, he was already on the way to becoming a Manchester freeman, for the City Council had passed the resolution in July 1943, with only one dissentient, an independent councillor.[60]

At the 1947 ceremony, the triangular relationship of Churchill, Manchester and the recent war was on full display. The casket containing the freedom scroll was made in mahogany and metal salvaged from the ruins of the old Free Trade Hall, blitzed in December 1940, decorated with the city's coat of arms and a suitable inscription, but also with 'numerous panels indicative of the city's war effort . . . exemplified by water colour drawings of HMS *Manchester*, a "Churchill tank", and a "Lancaster" bomber.' There were further panels representing worldwide trade, the cotton industry, commerce and engineering. And since Mancunians were not noted in the 1940s either for frivolity or for waste, provision had been made for the removal of the scroll and the mounting on which it was placed in the casket, so that it could be used as a cigar box.[61]

When the freedom resolution was passed in 1943, it was observed by the *Manchester Evening News* that 'the ceremony . . . was robbed of much of the spectacular significance which would have crowned it by the unavoidable absence of the premier', and it was hoped to confer it on him in person later in the year. In the event it took four years to organise the ceremony, and Churchill then gave Manchester only three weeks' notice of the day he would come (combining it with a speaking engagement at a Conservative rally at Belle Vue). But Manchester then made a great deal of the occasion. The *Manchester Guardian*, remarking that 'the weather did not help' (but reflecting that this at least made it a true Manchester event of the sort he would remember from before 1914), nevertheless reported a massive crowd whose welcome was 'spontaneous and affectionate', and which prompted Churchill to an 'admirable and felicitous speech'. Noting the goodwill indicated by a council with a substantial Labour majority carrying out this particular ceremony, Churchill was on his best, above-party behaviour, invoking 'the most precious things in our national heritage, especially the continuance in our political life of personal good feeling and relations – all part of "the tolerance and freedom which have been our glory and our happiness and an important element in our success"'. Though his train had arrived early, the denseness of the crowds meant he was already twenty minutes late by the time he arrived at the Town Hall. The people there assembled, seeing 'his left hand raised in the familiar salute' and the doffing of his hat, gave him 'the loudest cheer Manchester has heard for many a day'. After the ceremony in the council chamber, Churchill returned to where the crowd was patiently waiting, and delivered an impromptu address, 'smiling broadly enough to take in every one of the "Men and Women of Lancashire" – the warmer style of address with which he supplemented the formal "Ladies and gentlemen"'. That impromptu address, though only five minutes long, included a tribute to Manchester in the war, an optimistic prediction for the future of the textile industry, and the obligatory reference to Britain's victory over 'Narsi tyranny'.[62]

At the Belle Vue rally of fourteen thousand local Tories on the following day, Churchill was hailed by the Conservative Party Chairman Lord Woolton as 'a Manchester man', but Woolton then added that he saw it as a disgrace that the North-West should have so few Conservative MPs. Both Woolton and Churchill himself made tub-thumping party speeches, and banners proclaimed the Conservatives' determination to 'set the people free', not from 'Narsi tyranny' but from the tyranny of Clement Attlee's Labour Government. 'Mr Churchill said he wished to set forth some broad, plain truths, irrespective of whether they were immediately popular or not,' and proceeded to lambast the 'morbid fallacy of socialism'. Despite this rapid descent from good feeling to political abuse, Churchill's official visit to Manchester remained one which the city referred back to often and affectionately, notably when his eightieth birthday came in 1954, his retirement from the premiership in 1955 and his ninetieth birthday in 1964. Manchester had made good its claim to a Churchill connection and would not let go. At the end of the century, though Winston's Restaurant in the Portland Hotel had been renamed after a popular television chef, the city centre still had its Churchill pub, with a bulldog on its sign and a chip shop next door advertised as 'the chippie next to Churchill's'; nearby Bolton had another.[63]

Sheffield could make no such claims about the city's closeness to Churchill, though over his long career he had in fact made seven official visits, the first in 1903 for a Conservative Party Conference, the most recent to inspect war damage in 1941. It was at least able to ensure that the new freeman came to collect his honour in person, probably by timing the 1951 ceremony to coincide with the annual Cutlers' Feast, a banquet then frequently addressed by national leaders, given the importance of Sheffield-made cutlery to the export trade. Nor had Sheffield suffered especially badly during the war, though it had had one particularly bad night of bombing which was given a good deal of attention during Churchill's visit. On the day of the ceremony, 16 April 1951, the *Sheffield Telegraph* editorialised 'with proud memories' on Churchill, the war, and the Sheffield Blitz of 1941, noting that Ernest Bevin's recent death had reminded everyone of the all-party support that Churchill had received in the war. The following day it devoted three of its six pages to reporting the visit, the ceremony, the speeches and the cheering crowds, with lots of pictures of happy smiling faces, and on the 18th there were three more pages, this time reporting the Cutlers' Feast, now with the city's business elite pictured in evening dress, but substantially going down the same memory lane to 1941. Pointing out that the city had already honoured in this way Lloyd George, Ramsay MacDonald, Smuts, Australia's Robert Menzies and New Zealand's Peter Fraser, as well as A. V. Alexander, a former railwayman who had risen to Lord Mayor and then become Churchill's wartime colleague, the paper smugly remarked, 'so does Sheffield delight to honour men – and women – for their distinguished service to the State regardless of their political allegiance'. The city practised just this approach, putting on a big show for the man that the local Labour leadership would otherwise have been attacking with no holds barred. There was a parade of Sheffield's war disabled, and a school choir of four hundred singing Parry's setting of 'This Royal Throne of Kings'. Representatives of the city's youth movements and grammar schools (of which Labour was then extremely proud) were included in the main audience of three thousand Sheffielders in the City Hall, two thousand more hearing the ceremony by direct relay in overflow meetings. Buses were diverted and tram routes suspended to allow large crowds to gather in the streets, and several hundred were still waiting for a glimpse when at almost midnight he emerged from a car bringing him from the civic banquet back to his hotel, their persistence rewarded by the familiar 'V-sign for Sheffield', 'God bless you all,' and (to an eleven-year-old) 'It's time you were in bed.' Since all the speeches concentrated on the war, things remained good-humoured, the mood caught by Churchill's reference to the Churchill tanks made in Sheffield, which had been named after him 'only after a very serious defect had occurred, and he hastened to add that the defect was of design and not handiwork'. For his part, the Lord Mayor drew laughter, applause and a Churchillian beam of approval when he spoke of the Nazi threat, and then, turning to his guest, corrected himself by saying 'Narsi'. Offered the canteen of cutlery to which Sheffield's freemen were traditionally entitled and asked for the traditional halfpenny in return, Churchill triumphantly drew from his pocket one that he had as Prime Minister had specially minted for the occasion and handed over as if it were still hot – a souvenir that soon found its way into the city museum.[64]

Neither Birmingham nor Leeds was so fortunate, for in neither case did Churchill visit the city to be honoured. Birmingham's freedom was conferred at Churchill's London home in 1946, but the *Birmingham Post* covered the story fully and over several days, as had happened in Sheffield. The freeman's scroll was once again placed in a casket designed with several symbolic points in mind. Made in silver and ivory, it had four supporting figures at the corners, representing courage, faith, wisdom and steadfastness, embossed figures on the top representing 'the four Dominions', and a carved ivory figure of St George and the Dragon (so collectively celebrating the English-speaking world and Churchill's Englishness at the same time). The casket also bore three inscriptions, one from Wordsworth's 'The Happy Warrior', and two translated from the Latin, 'Always shall thy name and thy honour abide', and, most significantly, 'One man by his drive saved the State for us'. There is, however, some restraint in the tone of the Birmingham press reports, compared to the euphoria of Manchester or Sheffield. After all, it was not demanding much to expect an opposition politician actually to go a mere hundred miles to receive the highest honour the second largest English city could confer. Hardly anybody said so, but Birmingham was clearly disappointed, and one senior figure, Labour's Alderman Lewis, actually refused to join the civic deputation to make the presentation. Though asserting that 'the City was well represented without me', the fact that he had been chairman of the council committee which initiated the freedom for Churchill suggested vexation.

> I am speaking for the majority of our citizens when I say they did expect Mr Churchill would at least be able to spare a few hours necessary to receive the freedom [here]. Birmingham is the hub of the area which produced one-third of the war material, and this would have been his opportunity to say 'thank-you.'

Churchill telling a few local leaders how much he valued his relations with a city which had frequently been the site of his and his fathers' political exploits, celebrating his work alongside the Chamberlains (whom few in Birmingham in the 1940s wanted to be reminded of), and having his speech recorded so that it could be played later in Birmingham, was simply no substitute for going there and being the focus of attention.[65]

Reluctance to believe that Churchill did not actually rate Leeds' affairs very highly in his own order of priorities was no doubt the reason that the *Yorkshire Post* headlined its 1953 report 'Premier hopes to come

North when time permits'. His conversation with his doctor on the morning of the Leeds ceremony suggests that this was a pretty empty hope, for he was not even looking forward to meeting the people of Leeds in London. Moran found Churchill 'reading a book. He put it down reluctantly.' He would have to prepare for cabinet, chair it, take parliamentary questions, have an audience with the Queen (all of these actually being things that he loved doing). After all that, 'a deputation had come from Leeds to give him the Freedom of their City. It was going to be a long day. He gave a great yawn' – and returned to the more interesting business of discussing with Moran Sir Walter Scott's *Quentin Durward*.[66]

Unsurprisingly, Churchill did not manage to visit either Darlington or Stafford either, and the reasonable explanation given to Leeds, that he was recovering from 'a slight indisposition' (actually a stroke, but this was not publicised), did not apply in these other cases. Stafford had decided to honour Churchill with the freedom of 'this ancient borough' in the euphoria that followed VJ Day in 1945, prompted by the presentation of his bust to the town by a local sculptor. It was hoped that he would come and unveil the bust and also receive the freedom. This proved unexpectedly controversial. Labour's Alderman Owen, though stating that he had 'no objection' to the resolution, nevertheless suggested that it be postponed until after the coming borough elections, in case there was 'a change in the political position of the council'. Labour had taken the Stafford parliamentary seat a few weeks earlier, Stephen Swingler ousting Peter Thorneycroft, and would indeed take control of the borough a few weeks later. It is not clear whether Owen was suggesting that a Labour majority would not honour Churchill or whether he just wanted Labour to have the honour of doing so, but another Labour alderman suggested that there were at least reservations on their side of the chamber. Though Churchill was 'the greatest war leader the country had ever possessed', he had also 'developed into the greatest mudslinger the Tory party had ever put forward', an obvious reference to his Gestapo speech about twelve weeks earlier. Embarrassed by the revelation that Churchill had already been approached before the Stafford council had voted on the matter, the Tory majority nevertheless fought back effectively. Alderman Adamson deprecated the introduction of party politics into such a delicate matter.

He thought they all agreed – the whole world agreed – that Mr
Winston Churchill had very admirable qualities as a war leader.
The distinction they proposed to confer upon him was in recognition of his war services, and had nothing to do with his being a
member of any political party. 'I don't think anyone will quarrel
with me when I say that Winston Churchill in his own way has
been one of the greatest men that Great Britain ever produced.'

The Mayor added the procedurally helpful advice that Churchill
had only been consulted as to whether he would accept the honour if
offered, and had not yet actually been offered it. Though Labour continued to grumble that Churchill had been consulted more than had
Stafford's own minority party, the party eventually caved in, allowing
the resolution to pass unanimously on the understanding that it was
only about the war. Even then, there were a few parting shots. Councillor
Reynolds 'paid an eloquent tribute to the way in which Mr Churchill
had rallied the nation in its darkest days, and to the way that he had
fought Fascism and helped to bring about the triumph of democracy',
but added that there was still, 'at the back of his mind, a broadcast Mr
Churchill made to the electorate on the eve of the last election. He
regretted that on that occasion, even in the opinion of some of his
followers, he fell from the very altitude of achievement to the level of
a political deceptionist.' It is not likely that Churchill would ever have
gone to so small a place as Stafford, where he had neither personal
connection nor political business, but if he was ever advised of the tone
of the debate that surrounded the award of his freedom there that would
certainly have persuaded him to stay away.[67]

Darlington managed things rather better. The town proceeded to
make Churchill a freeman in 1947, shortly after Montgomery had visited
to unveil Churchill's portrait, the central element of a 'victory panel'
installed in the public library. A delegation of fifty local worthies, 'representing the civic, professional and industrial life of the city', travelled
up to London and installed their new freeman in Apothecaries' Hall,
during a ceremony from which politics was conspicuously absent. Churchill spoke of the event as one that proved 'the national unity which
transcends party divisions', while the Labour Mayor said that 'Mr Churchill's courage, leadership and comradeship would never be forgotten
... No other man could have given to the British people the same will

and determination.' Everyone queued up to get his autograph on the commemorative programme ('as if we were schoolboys and he were Don Bradman') and a good, morale-boosting time was had by all. Nevertheless, there was submerged resentment that he had not made the trip to Darlington, indicated in the *Northern Echo*'s headline, 'Mr Churchill may yet visit Darlington', a view which attributed far more weight than it deserved to Churchill's usual promise to visit if and when time allowed (he was after all saying exactly the same thing to New Zealand). More positive was the usual link made between the town's own war effort and Churchill's freedom of the borough. He spoke gratefully but unspecifically of the North's role during the war, and this prompted the local paper to editorialise on 'the great part played by the workshops of the North in forging the weapons with which the war was won'. His reference to Darlington as a railway town 'proved' that he was aware of 'the share taken by transport in achieving victory'. Since it had plenty of readers on the farms and in the shipyards too, the *Echo* added its own tribute to 'the North's broad fields' providing the nation with airfields, and to the local rivers which had 'launched the ships and carried the supplies that were vital factors in the conflict', though Churchill had himself made no such allusion. Everyone had to have their share in the man, his war and his honouring.[68]

The sticky political debate at Stafford in 1945 indicates, however, that there remained, not far from the surface, reservations about Churchill on the left which could erupt into outrage if things were not well managed. Even during the war, the debate on Churchill's freedom of Dundee had shown this clearly enough. The city's Conservative leaders made the cardinal errors of not consulting Labour before proposing the freedom of the burgh for Churchill, and then not holding back when a meeting of the Lord Provost's committee showed that there was dissent within the council on a matter which needed to be unanimous or not touched on at all. But since they had already – as later at Stafford – consulted Churchill as to whether he would accept the honour (perhaps suspecting his low opinion of the city since 1922) they would have found it hard to retreat without awkwardness anyway. The full council meeting was therefore a source of deep embarrassment to the city and its leaders in time of war. Labour councillors attacked Churchill's management of the Norwegian campaign in 1940 as showing his fallibility as a warrior, suggested that the Conservatives were only proposing the honour now (a most inappropriate moment for such ceremony when all were being urged to tighten their belts) because they knew they would lose control once the war ended and elections were resumed (as indeed they did), and reminded the Lord Provost to his face that he had said in 1922 that Dundee's decision to throw Churchill out of Parliament was the greatest day in its political history. The Lord Provost, having earlier conceded that even Churchill had made mistakes ('why rake up a man's past against him?'), now added unhappily that he too had made mistakes, his worst being in 1922. Interestingly, the strongest objection from the left came in terms of 'people's war' rhetoric, exactly the factor that was limiting the Churchill appeal while the conflict lasted. Councillor Hirst bluntly asserted that 'to make the claim that Mr Churchill as an individual had saved Britain and the British Empire was to castigate the generals and soldiers who had done the fighting, and the workers who had made the munitions'.

With the council polarised on party lines, the majority party's motion inevitably passed, but only by sixteen votes to fifteen. The Lord Provost ruled out of order a Labour request that the voting figures should be insultingly included in the letter to Churchill offering the freedom of Dundee, but he could not prevent Labour from refusing to serve on the committee appointed to make the arrangements for the ceremony. There was, however, no such ceremony, for the local furore was reported in the national press, and Churchill would therefore have known about the contested vote even before receiving the Lord Provost's letter. Ten days later a special meeting of the council heard the Lord Provost read an extremely curt note from Churchill's secretary, declining the honour without any explanation. The local paper offered no editorial comment, and printed in the following days no letters from Dundonians on the matter, though it is inconceivable that it received none. It was all too embarrassing, and silence was the only possible course of action.[69]

Rather more improbably, since there was neither previous closeness nor earlier hostility, the same embarrassing scenario was re-enacted in Luton in 1948. Though once again the root cause seems to have been poor local political management, the violence of passions unleashed is real testament to continued hostility to Churchill on the left. The *Luton News* headed its first account of the story with a three-decker headline: 'Storm Over Luton Offer to Churchill / Blatant Wangle Says Labour / "Menace to the Well-Being of the Country"'. The problem stemmed from the fact that Churchill was due to address a mass Conservative rally at Luton Hoo in June 1948, so the town's Conservative leaders decided to confer on him the freedom of the borough, on the occasion of the visit. But they failed to take the precaution of first squaring the local Labour leaders, who felt deeply insulted by being ignored and suspected that it was simply a stunt to improve the Conservative vote in a marginal constituency. They therefore proposed the reference back of the committee report proposing the freedom, and were outvoted by nineteen votes to twelve, just as in Dundee on a straight party vote. Their chief argument was that the honour should be given only on a non-political visit, not as an adjunct to a party rally, and they were unimpressed when the Mayor pointed out that it was 'only a convenience' to do it on the same day. It was more likely Luton's only chance to get Churchill to accept the freedom in person, but he could hardly say this. As the debate proceeded, however, Labour's anger increased, with one alderman denouncing Churchill as 'the most vicious anti-working class Conservative leader who has ever disgraced the House of Commons'. Another alderman claimed that 'trade unionists in Luton regarded Mr Churchill as one of their greatest enemies', while a councillor added that 'ever since the war Mr Churchill has been making wicked, lying, irresponsible statements about the Labour Party. Since losing the elections he has been acting like a big baby.' Another pointed out that if it had really been about just the war then it was strangely belated, and that Churchill had anyway done nothing much for Luton. 'I say this man is a menace to the well-being of the country. We are agreed on his war leadership, but what he did before and what he has done since far outweigh any good he did then.' Few would have gone so far, but it is important to remember that Churchill's *post*-war partisanship was just as unpopular on the left as his behaviour before 1939 had been. Most admirers of Churchill on the left would therefore have practised a sort of 'Don't mention anything *but* the war' policy in such debates.

The resolution having passed, there followed a great volume of letters to the editor, at first all supporting the majority view and claiming that ordinary people in Luton wanted to honour Churchill, and that Labour councillors had proved that they were 'not fit for public office', but with Labour stepping up its counter-attack as the weeks passed. By 20 May 1948, three weeks after its initial report, the *Luton News* was wearily headlining its correspondence column 'Still debating Mr Churchill' and deploring the tone of many of the letters that it received. The following week, though, it reported that Churchill had declined the offer of Luton's freedom, another story which he could easily have read about in the national press. The paper conceded that he had been left with no real choice in the matter, but the terms in which he had actually refused the offer of the freedom rather suggested that Labour had a point in attacking him for his partisanship. Luton's offer was turned down because of 'so much Socialist bitterness', and because 'I should not like to distress them' by accepting it. But he did accept the Mayor's invitation to drive through the town in an open-topped car and be received at a civic lunch, so that he could 'salute' the ordinary people of the town for 'the good work they did in the war'. A month later, Churchill did just that, and the ordinary people of Luton flocked out on to the streets to cheer him. Since the attendance at the Conservative fête was a massive 100,000 people, and must have included many thousands of Lutonians, it seems likely that on this occasion at least the local Conservatives had their fingers more on the pulse of the town than Labour. As he listened to the crowds singing 'For He's a Jolly Good Fellow', Churchill said happily that he 'felt it most exhilarating to be up-borne by the goodwill, friendship and support of his fellow countrymen', a palpable hit at Labour for being both divisive and lacking in goodwill. None of this can have done any harm to the Conservative position in the town, and in 1950 the wartime 'radio doctor' Charles Hill (a neat selection to stress the Churchill link) duly recaptured the parliamentary seat from Labour.[70]

Dundee and Luton were probably unique, but they show how Churchill's party status could still be an obstacle to his honouring as a national hero. Freedoms were of course only one of many ways of honouring Churchill, though to seek to list the others would be lengthy and tedious. Jacob Epstein was already at work on a Churchill bust by early 1946, and another was unveiled later the same year at the offices of the Wembley Conservatives. A new waxwork of Churchill was commissioned for Madame Tussaud's, for which Churchill himself provided the clothes, and even its damaging by a vandal in 1954 was thought a news item worthy of report (readers were assured that the damaged 1951 head had been quickly replaced by the 1943 head, kept in store in case of emergencies and not simply melted down like most redundant waxworks, so Churchill remained defiantly on display). In addition to the Frank Salisbury portrait commissioned by Darlington, one by Oswald Birley was hung in the House of Commons, and another was bought by the parliamentary press gallery and unveiled by Churchill himself in 1952, to be hung alongside the commemorative panel already installed.[71]

All this activity tended to tail off when he became Prime Minister again in 1951, but when he was out of office again in the later 1950s the pace picked up quite a bit. A Churchill bust in London's Guildhall had been proposed in 1953, but the City decided to go further and commission Oscar Nemon to do a full statue, duly unveiled in 1955. Portraits were acquired by, among others, the City of London, the Institute of Directors (with the white cliffs of Dover placed behind the central figure to evoke wartime memories), Harrow Council and the Ministry of Works, busts by the British Embassy in Paris, Buckingham Palace (Oscar Nemon being personally chosen by the Queen for the task), Conservative Central Office and the National Trust. Memorial plaques appeared in Hove, at Harrow School (as well as memorial scholarships), at Bristol University and at Wookey Hole. Dudley produced in 1968 a large Churchill Memorial Screen in a shopping centre. Copies of the limited edition of Epstein's bust occasionally changed hands, Lord Bath acquiring one at auction in 1963, but he had to pay 2,600 guineas, the highest price that had then been paid for any Epstein bronze. Though it was among the sculptor's finest works, combining a physical likeness with a texturing that implied the granite-like qualities of the man, it seems likely that the status of Churchill as well as the status of Epstein had combined to push up the price.[72]

These were only uncontroversial if they offered a physical representation of Churchill which was at the same time benign, heroic and human, a range of objectives not easy to combine in one work of art at the best of times, but especially difficult when those who had raised the money and the public who had subscribed to the funds were generally looking for a fairly conservative artwork, while many of the best practitioners in the 1950s and 1960s were modernists. It is this tension that explains the furore over Graham Sutherland's portrait of Churchill presented in 1954, and never seen in public again. The City of London had some difficulty with its statue for the Guildhall, a massive and unconventionally sitting figure, though it was officially explained that it was the sculptor himself who had had second thoughts, and at the unveiling Churchill said that 'it seems such a very good likeness'. The 1969 statue on Westerham village green, another seated statue with some modernist tendencies, did not satisfy everyone's taste either. These disputes remained within reasonable bounds, but the proposal to erect a statue on Woodford Green in Churchill's constituency became a long-running and nationally reported dispute. Opposition by local councillors to the design submitted by the sculptor David McFall, allied to persistent rumours that the Churchill family did not like it either, led on to redesigns and to the unveiling being twice postponed. The initial design was unacceptable 'because it depicted an old man' – Churchill then being well over eighty, but it was his 'finest hour' that had to be commemorated. The less than flattering view of an American newspaper was that 'this piece of work looks like a moronic – indeed an apelike – lug dug out of a Limehouse flophouse and dressed up by some prankster in an old suit of clothes a couple of sizes too big for him'. When redesigned, completed and unveiled two days after Churchill's eighty-fifth birthday it was generally praised, but the road to this conclusion had been a rocky one.[73] The committee of MPs chosen to supervise the Churchill statue in the Palace of Westminster had a somewhat easier task, and Oscar Nemon produced a design for a widely accepted bronze figure. But when it came to the Parliament Square statue, there was once again a long-running dispute about its size, design, placement, and even the direction in which it should face. When unveiled, its brooding, massive, overcoated presence was not much liked. Ironically, those who did not have to carry the responsibility were sometimes more impressed than those who did. The sculptor's model of the Wanstead and Wood-ford statue was bought by Glasgow City Corporation as its own Churchill Memorial, while by the end of the century the capitals of the Czech Republic and of Australia, Prague and Canberra, had both erected copies of the statue standing in Westminster's Parliament Square – in each case reduced to life-size and placed on a lower plinth, and therefore looking more appropriate than the original.[74]

Namings were another widespread form of commemoration, and not only of streets. Charing Cross Hospital had a Churchill Ward, and the Church Army an old people's housing scheme, both in 1945. Over the next few years, Churchill was commemorated by name with a British Railways locomotive, a college and a forest in Israel, a scholarship at Sedbergh School, a housing scheme in Pimlico, an RAF convalescent home, a bell at St Andrew's parish church, Chinnor, a nuclear sub-marine, a chair at Cambridge University, a scout patrol, a gliding award, a prestigious London hotel, a school for the deaf in Woodford, a series of memorial concerts, an extension to the Royal Military College, an Oxford hospital, and an insurance company (actually a subsidiary of a Swiss company, the name 'Churchill' chosen to denote trustworthiness for British clients) – to name but a few.[75]

After 1955 Churchill also resumed his triumphal progress, with the last few British freedoms, and with visits to Geneva, Aachen (where he received the Charlemagne Prize), Paris (where he belatedly got the Croix de la Libération from a bemused de Gaulle) and Washington for a dinner at the White House, as well as receiving his freedoms at Rochester, Harrow and Maldon.[76] In Washington, President Eisenhower's secretary took copious notes on all the events of the week of Churchill's 1959 visit, because it was to her:

> the most historic and memorable event of all the years at the White House, simply because to me Churchill symbolizes Anglo-American unity, and statesmanship in every sense of the word, and gallantry and courage. And I can never forget his voice as I used to listen to it at 4:00 AM coming from belea-guered Britain in the early days of the war. That grand, that wonderful voice, and that eloquence.[77]

In case such fervour ebbed, the regular revisiting of 1940–5 in anniversaries and memoirs ensured that neither 'that wonderful voice' nor its owner's identification with Britain's 'finest hour' faded from the memory. To take just a couple of examples from many, in 1949 and again in 1950, Churchill was guest of honour at the annual Alamein reunion in London, where some ten thousand Eighth Army veterans gathered to celebrate past triumphs, and from which the speeches of Montgomery and Churchill were broadcast live all over the world; Montgomery was only slightly exaggerating when claiming in 1951 that this had already become 'one of the great events of the year'.[78] Twelve years later, on the thirtieth anniversary of the Atlantic Charter, President Kennedy issued a press release praising Churchill's foresight and wisdom, and in a covering letter told Churchill himself that 'your own name will endure as long as free men survive to recall'. The war remained central to the Churchill story in other ways too. Ben Tucker's *Winston*

Churchill: His Life in Pictures first appeared in 1945, and devoted two-thirds of its length to the six years since 1940. The 1950 reprint added nothing at all since 1945, and when Churchill retired in 1955 a mere sixteen pages were added to record his post-war career of ten years, compared to more than two hundred on the six war years.[79]

As we have seen, Churchill was always scrupulously careful to assert that he had only been instrumental in mobilising the British national effort in 1940, a view that was often repeated and reached its definitive statement in the 1954 birthday celebrations. 'I was very glad that Mr Attlee described my speeches in the war as expressing the will not only of Parliament but of the whole nation. Their will was resolute and remorseless and, as it proved, unconquerable. It fell to me to express it, and if I found the right words you must remember that I have always earned my living by my pen and my tongue. It was a nation and race dwelling all round the globe that had the lion's heart. I had the luck to be called upon to give the roar.'[80] But this and other disclaimers like it were a typical piece of understatement, the self-pride that projects itself as modesty, as were his refusals of the offer of a dukedom. It is after all even better to be generally known as one who can refuse such honours than to accept them – and that contrast remained right through to his burial in a simple parish cemetery after the biggest state funeral in history. Churchill's intended title had he taken a peerage, 'Duke of London', indicates no great self-abnegation, for no previous peer had been called after the capital city, as does his initial response, 'Can't you guess?', when Anthony Montague Browne asked him the question. There was, though, a certain appropriateness to the choice, as Churchill himself well knew. Over the course of his political career he had represented constituencies in three different counties, been born in a fourth, and lived at Chartwell in a fifth, while actually spending more time in London as a national politician than anywhere else. For fifty years, Churchill's constituency was in fact the whole country, and his taking its capital for his title would have been perfectly natural to him – and in the 1950s to many other people too.[81]

The plain name and dates on his gravestone and the Westminster Abbey plaque with only the words 'Remember Winston Churchill'[82] are each testament to the assumption that his deeds were already too well known to need description. Mollie Keller thought the latter an 'odd' inscription, because it was obvious to her that nobody would ever forget

Tory Dream
News Chronicle, 30 May 1945

him anyway. He would no doubt be delighted that an American book of 1971 could conclude that 'today . . . to many, Blenheim is better known as Churchill's birthplace'. This is demonstrated by the fact that Blenheim Palace was in the 1980s attracting only about twice as many tourists as visited Chartwell, despite the fact that as a house Chartwell has virtually nothing special about it, except the fact that Winston Churchill lived there, while Blenheim was one of the nation's greatest architectural treasures – and also has associations with another of Britain's greatest men of the past, Churchill's ancestral first Duke of Marlborough. At the end of the century, Chartwell was continuing to attract about 160,000 visitors a year, tenth out of all properties administered by the National Trust and more than double the figures for such gems of Britain's architectural heritage as Knole, Petworth and Charlcote – and this despite the connections of the last of these to William Shakespeare.[83]

By the time Churchill disclaimed in 1954 any but an instrumental relationship with Britain's finest hour, his assertion had been generally dismissed anyway, mainly through the reception of his own war memoirs. The key review was that of volume two, *Their Finest Hour*, by Isaiah Berlin, which had the rare privilege of republication as *Mr Churchill in 1940* and achieved a substantial circulation in its own right.[84] For Berlin, without discounting the resolution under fire of the mass of ordinary people, Churchill's role was more than instrumental, for 'he had the lion's share' in creating Britain's mood in 1940 and that was what had given him the right to voice it. Sir Isaiah clearly did not bear a grudge for the occasion late in the war when Churchill had mistaken the songwriter Irving Berlin for his academic namesake and been told (by the man he thought to be an eminent philosopher and historian) that he felt his best work to be 'Alexander's Ragtime Band'. 'After he had spoken', wrote Berlin,

> as no one else has ever before or since, [the British people] conceived a new idea of themselves which their own prowess and the admiration of the world has since established as a heroic image in the history of mankind, like Thermopylae or the defeat of the Spanish Armada. They went forward into battle transformed by his words. The spirit which they found within them he created within himself from his inner resources, and poured it into his nation, and took their vivid reaction for an original impulse on their part, which he merely had the honour to clothe in suitable words. He created the mood and turned the fortunes of the Battle of Britain not by catching the mood of his surroundings (which was not indeed at any time one of craven panic or bewilderment or apathy, but somewhat confused: stouthearted but unorganised) but by being stubbornly impervious to it, as he had been to so many of the passing shades and tones of which the life around him has been composed.[85]

These words, written in 1948, surely convey the gist of what historians have been trying to say – and indeed have said – about Churchill in 1940 ever since. The impact of such an elevated view of Churchill in his own finest hour has done much to colour all accounts of Churchill's war record and of his pre-war views on defence, not least because of the formidable intellectual standing that Sir Isaiah himself acquired. When Arnold Toynbee and George Steiner were asked to write on Churchill near the end of his life, each of them explicitly endorsed Berlin's judgement on Churchill's wartime role.[86]

The weight that Churchill himself gave to Isaiah Berlin's views was indicated clearly enough by the fact that he was one of only a small group who were asked to comment at an early stage on the whole of the first volume of the memoirs, *The Gathering Storm*; that Churchill responded positively to Berlin's fairly trenchant views and that he sent him a cheque for two hundred guineas for services rendered. Some might feel that after this Berlin should not have been reviewing the book at all, since he was in a sense complicit in its writing. At the time, when this insider dealing with Churchill was not known, he was criticised rather more as an ideological traitor from the left. The Churchill-hater Harold Laski, for example, complained that Berlin had written a hagiography of Churchill, in an essay which ignored his 'lack of magnanimity, his power to be meanly aggressive, his long-term capacity for revenge' and his 'coarse and often malignant brutality'. A Russian émigré friend who did not dissent from Berlin's judgement on Churchill nevertheless argued that 'it is not the business of a member of the Labour party [which Berlin was] to write an "objective" account about the role of Churchill, it is after all not an obituary, it is a heroisation of the still alive and acting Churchill, appearing 2 months before an election'. Berlin, an uncomfortable Labour Party member anyway, was not convinced by this line, but he had anyway already published his key work on the subject and could hardly now recant – it was a 'panegyric' which became, as Michael Ignatieff has put it, 'one of the essays that created the Churchillian myth'.[87]

The ungrudging, entirely unforced endorsement of Churchill by intellectuals who considered themselves to be independent-minded men of the left may indeed be seen as a peculiarly British version of the age-old story of the *trahison des clercs*, the fascination of men of the pen for one who could himself wield both a pen and a sword. Or as Andrew Roberts has put it, referring to the admiration of Churchill by the very different Arthur Bryant and E. H. Carr, they belonged to 'that species of historian so fascinated by power that he fails to discriminate objectively between those wielding it'. But such admiration for Churchill also clearly owed a great deal to such men's intellectual honesty and to awareness of the fact that the British left and British intellectuals had been just as wrong as the right in their reluctance during the 1930s to face up to the need for armed resistance to fascism. This was a fact of which a good party man like Laski would have been equally aware but could hardly admit. Such support did, however, sometimes require mental gymnastics. When Arnold Toynbee, already mentioned as having accepted Isaiah Berlin's view of Churchill, was made an honorary member of the French Academy in succession to Churchill himself, both the Academy's president and Toynbee devoted their speeches to the significance of Winston Churchill in fighting for the liberties of the world in 1940 and proclaiming a 'European' future after 1945. 'The Europe of tomorrow, as Winston Churchill used to say, is as unthinkable without Britain as without France,' remarked the Frenchman. Toynbee, rather more tactlessly, argued that Britain's scepticism about Europe was all the fault of Joan of Arc, who had 'taught us to turn our backs on Europe' by inflicting heavy defeats on the invading English in the fifteenth century. But they could effortlessly agree about 1940, for, as Toynbee put it,

> the fact that Britain finally emerged on the side of the victor
> after the Second World War was due to the association of the
> British people and Churchill at the critical moment. Churchill
> won the confidence of the British people because he had confi-
> dence in himself.[88]

A. L. Rowse, though proud to call himself 'a lifelong socialist', and a Labour parliamentary candidate in his native Cornwall during the 1930s, had a slightly different impact from Berlin's, more negative and far more polemical. He had published in 1940 one of the most vicious of all the retrospective attacks on the appeasers, 'Reflections on Lord Baldwin', and in due course included it in his book of essays called *The End of an Epoch*. He would later add his *All Souls and Appeasement*, and numerous other reflections on 1930s diplomacy in various other autobiographical works. In that first essay he had proudly referred to 'Mr Churchill and I' having warned the country against appeasement, exactly as if they alone had been a 'happy few' who had together won their scars while the rest of the country had been merely 'gentlemen of England now abed'. Alas, this unqualified admiration for Churchill had not always been so evident at the time. Rowse's *Politics and the Younger Generation* (1931) made several unflattering references to the great man. He had been in his prime before 1914 (and by implication past it by the 1920s, when the Government in which he had been Chancellor of the Exchequer was described by Rowse as completely lacking in ideas); he was a selfish defender of the interests of property, because he was from the propertied class; and, most cuttingly, he embodied the 'connection of militant nationalism with capitalism' and this made him far too fond of armaments. 'It is always the Winston Churchills and the George Lloyds who are so shrill for a strong hand in Egypt or India, or shriek that we are letting down the navy when there is any question of disarmament.' But these reservations were all pre-Hitler, and it is only fair to add that Rowse's convergence with Churchill (as for so many others in the 1930s) legitimately changed his mind, and such hostile views were no longer put forward. By 1940, even when he was writing on Baldwin, Churchill was for Rowse the hero of the story and the claimed personal link one that Rowse was intensely proud of, quoting indeed far more of Churchill's words than those of Baldwin himself. His *The Spirit of English History* (1943) was dedicated to 'the Right Honourable Winston S. Churchill, historian, statesman, saviour of his country', and in it he was proud to claim a kinship with Churchill as a fellow historian and as the embodiment of what Rowse felt was English history's spirit. Churchill and Lloyd George in 1916–18 were 'men in the tradition of Marlborough, the Pitts, Canning ... The historian cannot but feel a deep satisfaction that at such a fateful moment as the present the nation has found a leader of uttermost courage, whose vision is rooted in the historic sense of our past.' This was because he was descended on one side from 'the great Marlborough' and on the other from the puritan stock of early modern England, which had gone out and founded a sister English-speaking nation in America.[89]

In the post-war period, Rowse too took Churchill's shilling, as an adviser on the *History of the English-Speaking Peoples*, and then commended in reviews the books that he had helped to write, but Rowse had at least demonstrated his support for Churchill as a national saviour as early as 1940, and never then budged from his opinion. When writing his book on the Churchill family, he decided (as he rather vainly put it later) 'to make Winston's acquaintance', mainly so that he could get access to the family archives at Blenheim. But it was not until he was invited in 1955 to offer his opinion on the second volume of the *History of the English-Speaking Peoples*, reading draft chapters during the course of a day at Chartwell, that they met again, and even from Rowse's own account it is clear that he was easily impressed, for he had already been venerating Churchill for over fifteen years. Churchill sent a car to collect him, 'a very grand affair' flying the flag of the Lord Warden of the Cinque Ports, and then shortly before lunch 'the figure all the world knew entered: striped blue zip suit, blue velvet slippers, with WSC worked in gold braid, [facing] outwards, in case anybody didn't know who was approaching'. Over lunch, he heard Churchill discourse on Hitler, the war, his memories of Stalin and so on, and was so overwhelmed by the experience that, though generally a teetotaller, he did not resist offers of sherry, hock and cointreau, after which 'he toddled out with his stick; I toddled out wondering if I was not a little sozzled'. Over the afternoon, he had tours of the house, garden and grounds (including, he noted delightedly, the wall dating from the 'wilderness years'), was shown memorabilia and paintings, and heard Churchill himself declaim passages from his *Marlborough*, 'read with approbation and tears of appreciation as he turned the pages'. As he left this glimpse of a great man and a lifestyle that was light years from his own, Rowse noted the Churchill flag flying over Chartwell, as if he were a medieval magnate secure in his castle. If Rowse had not already been entirely Churchill's man, that day at Chartwell would surely have completed the process. When Churchill in 1958 sent him a signed copy of the final volume of the *History of the English-Speaking Peoples*, Rowse replied with a fawning, grovelling letter of sheer adulation. Now that the set was complete, he wrote, it made up 'a splendid fabric – comparable to Blenheim itself, with its wings and porticoes and courts, and the resplendent view all round'. He had learned things he did not know from all the volumes, but he was now mainly writing to draw Churchill's attention back to his own book on the family, and to express the hope that Churchill would write some more autobiography, since he had found the gaps such as the 1920s difficult to fill in when covering them in *The Later Churchills* – a comment very revealing on Rowse's method of wherever possible recycling Churchill's own view of his life. Rowse concluded, 'When I came to tackle your own career at the end of the story, I could not hope to do it justice, but I hope that something of the admiration and gratitude for all you have done and been came through.' Indeed it did, but should a historian ever be writing in such tones to his subject?[90]

Among other established figures of the historical profession, we may usefully review Sir Lewis Namier and George Macaulay Trevelyan. G. M. Trevelyan, from the same patrician world as Churchill himself, a near contemporary at Harrow, and a leading figure in the Liberal establishment of which Churchill had formed a part in 1914, managed largely to resist the Churchill legend. Churchill had as Prime Minister made Trevelyan Master of Trinity College, Cambridge, in 1940, but could not persuade him to remain in consideration for the governor-generalship of Canada in 1945. Though he was not particularly favourable to Labour, Trevelyan voted for the party in 1945 because Churchill's election broadcasts persuaded him that it was 'the lesser of two evils'. He certainly admired Churchill as a historian, and they had indeed much in common as writers, each seeing history as a literary form aimed at the mass reading public, and in the 1930s at least each working on the same period, the 1710s. But Trevelyan was a keen appeaser in the 1930s, and too honest a man to claim otherwise when events proved him to have been wrong. As he put it in a letter to his daughter, 'Baldwin and Chamberlain and the "appeasers", including to a considerable extent *ourselves*', had been shown to be in error, while 'dire events' have 'proved . . . Winston right'. He came indeed to admire Churchill rather more during wartime, writing to him in 1940 to say that at Harrow he had admired 'the driving force of your great character, which is now our nation's great support'. Nevertheless, Trevelyan never wholly surrendered, fastidiously noting that while Churchill was 'a great parliamentarian' his 'lapses in taste are an essential part of Churchill, the price we pay for him'. In the post-war years, then, though there was a respectful correspondence between them and a regular exchange of books whenever either published a new one, there were no ringing reviews by Trevelyan of Churchill's war memoirs to lend his own reputation to the establishment of Churchill's burgeoning fame, and this was no doubt some part of the reason for Rowse's reservations about a man he regarded as the head of his profession, reservations which sometimes had remarkable consequences. Writing on Trevelyan much later, Rowse regretted that, even when Trevelyan had belatedly seen the error of his ways over foreign policy, he had continued to regard Baldwin as superior to Churchill on the domestic scene. Not so, thundered Rowse, for

Baldwin had made any number of errors with the economy, one of them the return to the Gold Standard in 1925 – and he seemed not even to recall that Churchill had actually been Chancellor of the Exchequer at the time.[91]

With Sir Lewis Namier, though, more a man of the right than the left anyway, without the patrician disdain for Churchill's lapses of taste felt by Trevelyan, and with the refugee's love for all things British which Churchill seemed to incarnate, admiration was more or less unbounded. Though predominantly a historian of the eighteenth century, Namier wrote three books on the Nazi period, the most important of which was *Diplomatic Prelude* (1948), which came out alongside Churchill's own *The Gathering Storm* and carried a very similar message. Inspired in part by his 'hatred of Germany, which was connected with both his Jewishness and his Polish origins', he mounted a polemical attack on the appeasing governments of the 1930s, but his 'historical judgement' was 'coloured by his warm admiration for Chamberlain's great critic, Winston Churchill'. Deeply enamoured of the British aristocratic world in earlier centuries, which he mainly studied, he displayed a 'passionate bias' as an apologist for such elite groups in his own century, 'elite groups from which he was himself excluded'. Hence the upper-class Churchill, Eden and Cranborne were natural patriots while the provincial business class typified by Chamberlain were not, a view that made sense only if equally aristocratic appeasers like Halifax were simply ignored. Such social and economic determinism, allied to a belief in aristocracy, was presumably what A. J. P. Taylor had in mind when he called Namier a 'Tory marxist', but exactly the same view was often expressed by A. L. Rowse, who was neither a Tory nor a marxist, even as late as 1961. Appeasing Ministers, according to Rowse,

> did not have the hereditary sense of the security of the state, unlike Churchill, Eden, [or] the Cecils. Nor did they have the toughness of the 18th century aristocracy. They came at the end of the ascendancy of the Victorian middle class, deeply affected as that was by high-mindedness and humbug. They all talked, in one form or another, the language of disingenuousness or cant, it was second nature to them – so different from Churchill.

Such a view owed more to snobbishness than to evidence, but, though its superficiality becomes obvious once pointed out, it was virtually never challenged by reviewers at the time. The idea was in fact fairly consistent with Churchill's own table-talk, for in Beaverbrook's absence – he would never have dared in his presence – he used the supposed failings of Bonar Law to build an entire social theory of political leadership, as Lord Moran noted in December 1947.

> He spoke scornfully of Bonar Law as a narrow, doctrinaire Glasgow profiteer, and of Baldwin in terms so inaccurate that even [Lord] Camrose demurred. On this slender basis of their supposed incompetence, Winston . . . impulsively built a theory that politics was a whole-time job to which men should devote their lives. It was priesthood, a profession. He, Winston, felt vaguely that there should be some test which members of the House of Commons must pass before taking their seat.

As indeed there had been under Namier's admired, eighteenth-century aristocracy. The acceptance of such crude ideas coloured attitudes at the top of British Conservative politics for a generation. Churchill's three successors as Tory leader were all from the aristocratic mould, Eden from the County Durham squirearchy, Macmillan the son-in-law of a duke, and the fourteenth Earl of Home. The first two of these could properly claim to have been war heroes in 1914–18 and to have opposed appeasement in the 1930s. (If Eden's claim to be an anti-appeaser was pretty tenuous, it was at least given the official endorsement of Churchill's war memoirs.) Home was more of a problem, having been Neville Chamberlain's bag-carrying parliamentary private secretary at the time of Munich, but Macmillan reassured himself when fixing the succession for him in 1963 that he had had little to do with policy in the late 1930s, and would if the right age indeed have been one of the heroes of the trenches in 1914. Fascinatingly, the chief casualty of the Conservatives submitting to this generation of the *noblesse d'épée*, a step backwards from the industrial capitalist world of Bonar Law, Baldwin and the Chamberlains, was R. A. Butler, passed over for the leadership in both 1957 and 1963. And Butler was a scion of both industrial capitalism and Cambridge rather than the old aristocracy, and had been Halifax's appeasing Under Secretary in 1938. An alternative view of the sociological significance of Churchill was offered by Nikita Khrushchev, when he asserted in 1959 that Churchill had been for Stalin 'a worthy opponent, a clever and refined politician', but that he was now an old man, 'old and shaky like the social order of his party'. After losing office in 1964, the Conservatives tended to accept Khrushchev's version rather than Rowse's, since they leapfrogged both a generation and several social classes to elect Ted Heath as Home's successor.[92]

Rowse rarely let go of these arguments over the rest of a long reviewing life, praising books that confirmed his views and writing very critically indeed about those that did not. He was for example happy to point out that 'Namier's *Diplomatic Prelude, 1938–9* greatly impressed me', while he denounced Robert Rhodes James for daring to speak favourably of Baldwin in his *The British Revolution*, and Maurice Cowling for suggesting that Churchill was actually seeking to get back into office in the 1930s. At times, he came close to contending that Churchill was infallible. Since Churchill had said that Baldwin was wrong about Germany, then Baldwin *must* have been wrong, while the fact that E. M. Forster hated Churchill only went to show how poor was Forster's judgement.[93]

Among contemporary historians, the only writer who came near to matching either Churchill's prolixity or his readership was a fellow non-professional, Arthur Bryant, knighted on Churchill's own recommendation in 1954. He had like Trevelyan been a supporter of appeasement, though a staunch party Tory rather than a Whig, and had propagandised tirelessly in the 1930s on behalf of Baldwin and Neville Chamberlain, notably through a biography of the first and an edition of the speeches of the second. He was, to the disgust of his great friend Rowse, slow to abandon his faith in the appeasers, and had the temerity even to publish a spirited defence of appeasement as the war began in 1939. Thereafter, however, a natural patriot like Bryant could not but rally to Churchill and the way in which he personified the British war efforts – or, as Rowse cattily put it, describing the career of his friend once he had died, 'after 1939 he rehabilitated himself (he was very good at climbing on bandwagons)'. Bryant wrote, spoke and corresponded unrelentingly for wartime causes, and through his trilogy on the Napoleonic Wars did much to reinforce Churchill's reiterated claim that Britain had stood alone often enough before and come through safely. In *The Years of Victory*, Bryant was even more explicit, for, after recounting the story of Nelson at Trafalgar, he asserted that 'to the end of time Churchill's signal will fly with Nelson's'. This could hardly fail to appeal to a Prime Minister who both kept a bust of Nelson in his

Chartwell study and called the Downing Street cat 'Nelson' too – and who then indignantly remonstrated with the poor thing for showing signs of fear during the Blitz: 'Come out, Nelson! Shame on you, bearing such a name as yours, to skulk there while the enemy is overhead!' In 1945, Churchill announced that Bryant was his 'favourite living historian', as indeed he was also Clement Attlee's.[94]

Nor would Churchill have demurred from Bryant's description of D-Day, delivered incidentally during a lecture to the Churchill Club in Westminster, a social facility for British, American and Commonwealth officers: 'The whole English-speaking world was one brotherhood that day.' Thereafter, Bryant was fairly conventionally pro-Churchill and, since he wrote so much ('an inveterate scribbler', thought Rowse, whose own hundred or so books did not exactly suggest another Flaubert), he added at regular intervals to the Churchill legend. He was the only writer other than Churchill himself to receive the Chesney Medal for a war book in the decade after 1945, and eventually achieved a sort of status in the literary world not too dissimilar to Churchill's in the political, his partisan past forgotten in an autumnal glow. They first met after Churchill's defeat in 1945, when, as Rowse later put it, Bryant 'fell completely for his magic'. Though their relationship must have been distanced somewhat by Bryant editing for publication in the 1950s the Alanbrooke diaries (which will be dealt with in Chapter Four), Churchill can only have approved of a man for whom, above and beyond even the titanic figures of the British past, the greatest hero was the English people. Bryant's 'love of England', as an American reviewer noted, was 'positively Churchillian and it gleams through his writing with a Churchillian radiance'. Nowhere was this truer than in his final book, *Spirit of England* (1982), which said of George VI that 'like his Minister, Winston Churchill, he embodied and stood for all the ancient, enduring virtues of his country'. More expansively, in another part of the book, he wrote:

> Shakespeare and Milton, Elizabeth I and Cromwell, Chatham and Churchill, Drake, Nelson and Wellington, Wren, Purcell, Dr Johnson, Newton and Darwin ... have been a remarkable harvest for one small island ... And Washington, Jefferson, Lee and Lincoln were of the same argumentative, versatile stock.

Apart from Bryant, Churchill was the only post-war British historian who could have written such lines.

Arthur Bryant was, however, no mere patriot-worshipper of his newly discovered hero, and though his uncompleted history of the English people was often compared by reviewers to Churchill's *History of the English-Speaking Peoples*, such reviewers were also wont to point out that, while Churchill's history was the sort of thing he had learned at Harrow in the 1880s, Bryant's was surprisingly up to date – in every way that is except its tone and focus. He retained the same scholarly awareness of the evidence in relation to Churchill himself, infuriating his friend Rowse more than once by insisting on what would soon become a historians' commonplace, that Churchill's actual successes before 1939 had been nothing much to write home about. They almost had a mortal breach – not difficult with Rowse – when Bryant insisted that Churchill had to share part of the blame for Britain's weak armaments when Hitler came to power, since he had been at the Treasury when the 'ten-year rule' had been imposed to limit defence spending. Bereft of any real argument against this modest reservation as to Churchill's infallibility, Rowse fell back on bluster: all the appeasers naturally protested too much, but 'Fancy blaming Churchill . . .'[95]

Nevertheless, the most influential single historian in propagating Churchill's view of the world and his own importance in it was a younger man with left-wing views which Churchill himself came nowhere near to sharing, Namier's Manchester protégé A. J. P. Taylor. A near Communist in the 1930s rather than a Labour moderate like Leslie Rowse, Taylor too had been a strong anti-appeaser at the time, and an early convert to Churchill as the man for the job of war leader. Thereafter Churchill was simply 'one of his heroes'.[96] Since Taylor was so widely read over the period after the mid-1950s when Churchill's fame might well have waned, this was of considerable importance and has remained so. When Chris Wrigley asked a group of sixty-two history undergraduates in 1977 to list the names of historians they knew, living or dead, thirty-nine mentioned Taylor, while Churchill himself came second with twenty-nine mentions, each of them well ahead of the likes of Hill, Elton, Trevelyan and Trevor-Roper. Surprisingly, Taylor, who reviewed very widely indeed in the British press in the 1940s and 1950s, hardly ever seems to have reviewed a Churchill book, and there were therefore no highly quotable Taylorian aphorisms endorsing *The Gathering Storm*.

Given the fact that Taylor's early writings frequently praised Churchill most for his espousal of a Russian alliance in 1941, when he was by the time Taylor wrote reviews rather seen as a prophet of the Cold War, it may well be that Taylor avoided reviewing Churchill's books simply so that he need not criticise the hero. This is certainly suggested by the fact that his autobiography makes only scant references to Churchill in the war, almost all related to the Russian alliance.

Taylor did, though, suggest in asides in other reviews that he thought very highly of the war memoirs, noting for example in 1954, when reviewing General Spears' *Assignment to Catastrophe*, that 'Churchill and Sir Edward Spears are the only two writers who have written books of superlative excellence about both wars.' As a CND man and unilateral disarmer in the 1950s, Taylor allowed himself some criticisms of Churchill's support for deterrence, while Churchill would not have been impressed by Taylor's advocacy of unilateralism on the ground that 'perhaps we shall shame the rulers of Russia into following our example' – nor would Taylor have been impressed if the same argument had been applied to Hitler. As Churchill's life drew to a close, Taylor urged his *Sunday Express* readers to 'Let Winston Stay!' as a Member of the House of Commons rather than retire in 1964, without either the need to be elected or to have a constituency. 'In 1940 we stood alone. Sir Winston Churchill raised us up . . . He saved us all. He embodied the British people. They loved him in 1940. They love him now.' Shortly afterwards he was telling the same readers that 'We bless his name on his 90th birthday and on every day when we draw breath as free men.' Later the same year, he wrote of 'the man who gave us our finest hour' and concluded that he was 'the saviour of his country and the saviour of freedom throughout the world'.

In 1965, Taylor transferred this viewpoint from a Sunday newspaper to an authoritative textbook. He included early in his 1914–45 volume of the *Oxford History of England* a short biographical footnote on Churchill which tersely concluded with the words 'the saviour of his country', and more generally he gave a positive view of Churchill's life and career, differing from him only when their respective writings diverged on the course of 1930s diplomacy. He wrote an intensely personal and emotional account of 1940, presenting Churchill again from a perspective on the left, a people's leader who had called in the people against the discredited men at the top. Reviewing Lord Moran's published diaries in 1966, he returned to the fray and reached the same conclusion. 'Anyone can run up an account of Churchill and find plenty of faults. They weigh not a feather in the balance. There has never been anyone like him, and that is all there is to it. He was the saviour of his country at the most critical moment in its history . . .' In Taylor's own academic writings, Churchill came pretty well out of *The Origins of the Second World War*, even though Taylor distanced himself from Churchill's own account of the same processes, and Churchill's 1930s critics anyway received a severe mauling in the book, so that he again seemed far-sighted by comparison. He was hardly undermined by Taylor's essay in *Churchill: Four Faces and the Man* (unconvincingly and inappropriately marketed in America as a shocking and revisionist account), and then even emerged as a posthumous co-author, when Taylor edited in 1969–71 a deferential part-work based on and named after *The History of the English-Speaking Peoples*.

It was sometimes remarked at the time that Taylor's endorsement of Churchill came oddly from a man on the radical left, noted as an iconoclast and with little time for aristocratic leadership. But this was to miss the real point, for they also had much in common – not least a populism shared with their mutual friend Beaverbrook, a deep distrust of Germany, and a robust pro-British patriotism. It may even have been an expression of Taylor's tendency to do the unexpected, rather than its denial, that led him into this self-appointed task of telling a large readership over three decades about Churchill's greatness. But Taylor was too much of an individualist to fit into the Churchill team of historical admirers, and many of those like Rowse who saw the 1930s as a simple moral fable in which Churchill had been uniquely right were affronted by *The Origins of the Second World War* because it took a more sceptical line. Isaiah Berlin believed that through the book Taylor was 'spitting on Namier's grave', while the 'affronted' Rowse thought he was wrong to have diverged from the Churchill line on Munich. More generally, the book was 'utterly irresponsible' in denying Hitler's culpability, and anyway departed from all standards of fairness by exonerating Taylor's friend, the arch-appeaser Beaverbrook, from any share of the blame, a good and fair point. Rowse cannot have been much impressed by Taylor's demonstration that Churchill's early warnings about German armaments were based on exaggerated figures of German strength – 'Churchill, Winston, British Statesman: wrong on

German rearmament . . .' is indeed the first line of an index reference worthy of Churchill himself. He will not have liked Taylor reminding readers how much Churchill had admired Mussolini, or his description of *The Gathering Storm* as 'the record of a critic, with occasional bits of solid information'. Taylor's verdict was that Churchill's work after 1940 outweighed all his earlier mistakes, but that those mistakes were nevertheless part of the historical record, while Rowse could not bring himself to accept that Churchill had ever been wrong. It is not hard to see who emerges from the exchange as the better historian.[97]

As we shall see in the next chapter, it was hard to get an audience for anything critical of Churchill but many never faced this problem because they did not want to criticise anyway. Sir Arthur MacNalty suspected that 'the carping critic' of his book would find that it 'seems to err "on this side of idolatry"' but asked, 'in what other vein can a citizen of this country write when he chronicles the deeds of this great Englishman?'[98] Interviewed by Alistair Cooke in 1970 for the BBC, President Eisenhower made a similar adjustment to his memory, recalling that American officers in wartime Britain always spoke of Churchill with 'respect, admiration and affection. Although they loved to chuckle at his foibles, they knew he was a staunch friend.'[99] Some indication of the turning tide of opinion can be given in the successive editions of the biography of Churchill by the Labour MP Emrys Hughes. In 1950, under the title *Winston Churchill in War and Peace*, he still allowed himself quite a lot of criticism from the perspective of the left (including a chapter on 1941–5 called 'Appeasing Stalin'), but by the time of the 1955 edition, now entitled *Winston Churchill, British Bulldog*, the earlier chapters are unchanged, but the period from 1940 onwards has been bathed in a mellow glow of admiration.[100] An American writer thought in 1952 that 'by now Churchill has developed an immunity to censure'.[101]

This development owed something to the breadth and depth of the Churchill character placed before the public in the post-war years. The 1940s emphasised his qualities as an orator, statesman and military man for all to see, and his writing of contemporary history linked these together. As Isaiah Berlin put it, reviewing Churchill's written words as though they were a part of the oratory, 'like a great actor – perhaps the last of his kind – upon the stage of history [Churchill] speaks his memorable lines with a large, unhurried and stately utterance in a blaze of light . . . His narrative is a great public performance and has the attributes of formal magnificence.'[102] His books would, thought Berlin, 'like all he has said and done, reinforce the famous public image, which is no longer distinguishable from the inner essence and the true nature of the author'. On the other hand, the reception of his war memoirs, and subsequently of his *History of the English-Speaking Peoples*, presented Churchill as a writer of real quality, where he would have appeared before 1939 more as a jobbing writer, though one who could rise to greater heights in such matters of familial piety as his *Marlborough*. In the 1950s it was not unusual to find a chapter on Churchill in anthologies of the great historians, alongside Macaulay, Carlyle, Froude, Gardiner, Trevelyan and Tawney,[103] a judgement much reinforced by his Nobel Prize for Literature in 1953. His secretary noticed that he was 'frightfully excited' when told that he had won a Nobel Prize, but that his face fell when he discovered that it was for Literature, whereas the Peace Prize that year went to General Marshall.[104] There was a good deal of consolation to be found in beating off the claims of Ernest Hemingway, who was also nominated for the Literature Prize in 1953. Hemingway, being as bad a loser as Churchill himself could sometimes be, commented on the 1953 award that Churchill was 'the greatest master of the *spoken* word', which was not what the Nobel Prize for Literature was supposed to be for, though Churchill's war speeches were indeed included in the citation praising his literary efforts. This was of course to miss the point, for since he read his speeches and dictated his books, the two were essentially the same thing. By getting the Literature Prize, however, Churchill achieved something that only Rudyard Kipling, John Galsworthy and George Bernard Shaw among Britons had previously achieved (as Churchill himself pointed out in his acceptance speech).[105] Such a deliberate, reiterated association of Churchill's name with the most eminent comparators from the British past over a wide range of fields was in effect what then established cumulatively his claim to a historic uniqueness.[106] Dwight Eisenhower had given exactly this issue much thought. He assured a correspondent in 1954 that Churchill had 'come nearer to fulfilling the requirements of greatness in any individual than I have met in my lifetime'. The essential point was that Churchill's greatness was multi-faceted, and that he was therefore, like Martin Luther, 'a great man', while Eisenhower thought Napoleon the specialist to have been merely 'a great general'. Given the range of talents Churchill was thought to have, this distinction mattered. Ike concluded that 'I have known finer and greater characters, wiser philosophers, more understanding personalities, but no greater man.'[107]

Alongside literature there was painting, a hobby that Churchill had first taken up in the trenches in 1915 but which he practised far more seriously with time on his hands after 1945. After advice from the top people's aesthetic impresario of the age, Eddie Marsh, his own former private secretary, Churchill in 1947 submitted two paintings anonymously to the Royal Academy, and when they were accepted he allowed his name to be known and then submitted paintings in most subsequent years. Herbert Stewart thought that Churchill's interest in painting was a natural consequence of the vivid word-painting in his prose, a view reflected by *The Times*'s comment on the Fulton speech: 'the phrase "iron curtain" only summarised a cogent argument, but it vividly painted the background against which all thinking about foreign policy had to be done'.[108] Painting then became another well-known side of Churchill's life, and the subject of another of his books, *Painting as a Pastime*, while in these post-war years painting provided a further link with Eisenhower, who was also a keen amateur painter.[109] Showing off his canvases became a favourite way of entertaining visitors that he wanted to impress – as when he first met Walter Graebner of *Life* magazine, though he also read to him extracts from the secret documents he was then working on for his memoirs.[110]

Eventually, after being shown first in the United States, Canada (even in such provincial centres as Fredericton, New Brunswick), Australia and New Zealand, a Churchill painting exhibition was put on public display in London in March 1959. This exhibition by what *The Times* called 'the most distinguished amateur painter in the world' would be mounted because 'his talent is not, in all essentials' amateur. After a week, the exhibition had to be temporarily closed so that the sixty-two paintings could be rehung, allowing the larger-than-expected crowds actually to see them properly. Forty-eight thousand people had seen the paintings during the first three weeks, a figure that compared to 39,000 who had visited the British Academy's Leonardo da Vinci show in 1952. A month later, by which time the total was up to 91,000, Churchill was toasted at the Academy's annual dinner – as well he might be, given the number of paying customers he was bringing in. It proved necessary to extend the exhibition for several weeks after its intended closing date, and by the time it ended in early August there had been 141,000 visitors, half as many again as had attended the FA Cup final. By the last weeks, foreign visitors made up a large proportion of the visitors (as they would no doubt also have done for Leonardo), many of them Americans. *Bottlescape* appeared to be one of the visitors' favourites, partly no doubt because it is indeed one of Churchill's most assured paintings, but in all probability also because the subject seemed appropriately his, and the invented title characteristic of his highly personal approach to life and the use of words. As in other countries where Churchill art had been on show, viewers were determined to find a link with the man through the pictures.[111]

In addition to painting and writing there was press coverage of Churchill's outdoor careers as landowner, farmer, racehorse owner and bricklayer (notably his lengthy battle to acquire membership of the building labourers' trade union). A Winston Churchill Stakes was run each year at Hurst Park from 1946 (with extracts from his war speeches reprinted in the race programme);[112] wins by his horses were loudly cheered by racegoers rather like victories by the royal horses, and his visits to the courses were equally popular.[113] The word 'Winston's here' is said to have buzzed around Kempton Park when he came to see his horses run, and when he accompanied a winner into the paddock it was noticed that spectators removed their hats – a mark of respect normally paid by the racing fraternity only to visiting royalty.[114] Churchill was received with much the same respect in other social circumstances too. In August 1952, Jock Colville noted that 'he got a great welcome' when going to see a play in the West End ('but embarrassed us by being unable to hear and asking questions in a loud voice'), and when he went a few weeks later to see *The Yeoman of the Guard* in Streatham, 'the PM was received with immense acclamation by the audience'.[115]

Even above and beyond these accumulating fields of glory, Churchill acquired a great reputation as a wit and a wordspinner, and books of 'The Wit and Wisdom of Sir Winston' began to appear.[116] A. P. Herbert, who was no mean judge of such things, thought Churchill to be 'the greatest British humorist of his day', outclassing Belloc, Coward and Wodehouse, but he also noted that the written word did not do him full justice. The real impact would be missed, 'without some knowledge of the scene, the circumstances, the unique and vibrant voice, the pause, the chuckle, the mischievous and boyish twinkle on the face, and all the tiny signs that something grander than wit is on parade'. It was all, as Frank Carson would later put it, in 'the way you tell 'em', and James Humes thought that Churchill could set up a punch-line with all the timing of Jack Benny or Groucho Marx. Anthony Montague Browne recorded one cross-talk act well worthy of such a comic, when a German visitor to Chartwell arrived in the company of two Mormons. When offered a drink, one defiantly replied, 'May I have water, Sir Winston? Lions drink it,' to which Churchill responded *sotto voce*, 'Asses drink it too.' The second offered the severe opinion that 'Strong drink rageth and stingeth like a serpent,' only to be topped by Churchill's muttered riposte that 'I have long been looking for a drink like that.' Congratulated on his wit after their departure, Churchill self-deprecatingly conceded that 'None of it was original. They just fed me a music-hall chance.' This further evidence of a quite outstanding memory on display, and of course the confidence to use it, goes far to explain why Churchill has been so often credited with jokes that were actually much older than his own first use of them, such as the nineteenth-century crack that wherever the Virgin Islands might be, they were certainly nowhere near the Isle of Man. Churchill had referred to himself as 'the star turn' when in his autobiography he described his appearances in Oldham in 1900, and an enterprising potter had produced a figure of him with this on the plinth when he returned to the Admiralty in 1939. He certainly would have topped the bill against almost any competition in the 1950s. In view of Churchill's well-merited reputation as a comedian, there is some irony in the fact that when an American proposal to name a nuclear submarine after him fell through, the name chosen instead was USS *Will Rogers*. When the British public voted at about the same time for a new Cunard liner to be named after Churchill, he was again passed over, this time in favour of Queen Elizabeth II, a falling-off that deprived the British press of some wonderful opportunities for nostalgia when the *QE2* went to war in the Falklands conflict of 1982.[117] The *Queen Mary*, now moored permanently as a floating hotel at Long Beach, California, does however have a cabin and a restaurant still named in his memory.

The quality of wit had always been at Churchill's command, but the relaxed confidence that he allowed himself, after his great wartime triumph, removed the antagonism that sarcasm and conversational bullying had often generated in the past. He never did grow old (in the sense of growing up), but the mellowing process that took place made him by the 1950s an impossible man to hate, and an easy man to love. The *Manchester Guardian*'s political correspondent, for example, noted in February 1954 that 'the Prime Minister has grown in the affection of the whole House in the most striking way in these recent months.' In June 1955, it was reporting his reappearance in the Commons after retirement as Prime Minister in a similar way, his first return to the back benches since 1939. When he first appeared a Labour MP was speaking, but involuntarily interrupted himself with the exclamation 'Churchill!' In a moment, everyone was standing, cheering, clapping and waving order papers, and noticing with tears in the eyes that Churchill had automatically resumed his seat below the gangway from which he had delivered in the 1930s his warnings about Hitler. Bob Menzies, who had had a stormy relationship with him in 1940–1, found that by 1948 Churchill had 'mellowed marvellously', so that he could now take part in a real dialogue rather than simply be required to listen to a monologue: 'Conversation is now a two-way affair.' That change was an important constituent of Churchill's post-war persona, though more noticed by people like Menzies who did not see him very often and then generally only on social occasions, than by his British colleagues. Another Australian, Richard Casey, made exactly the same point when he lunched with Churchill in 1952: instead of comparing Churchill to Henry VIII as he had done in his diary in the past, he observed in a tone of surprise that he had 'talked freely and, what is more, listened well . . . Winston is notably quieter and less belligerent – more inclined to listen and discuss and less liable to lay down the law – more calm and cautious than six years ago.' Lord Moran, who had seen him more often at close quarters than either of the Australians, nevertheless detected in 1945 much the same thing: 'Winston has been purged of the frailties which have prevented so many of his immediate colleagues from fully accepting his greatness – and when you get beneath the self-indulgence which he has allowed himself throughout his life, there is a fine character, staunch and truthful, loyal and affectionate.' In 1953, he recorded Lord Woolton marvelling that 'Winston is positively good-tempered these days' and a Labour MP asking, 'What have you done to Winston? There is something almost serene about him.' One of Churchill's friends answered that 'of course he has mellowed', but Moran's own view was that 'Winston has got on top of his pugnacity.'[118]

The new warmth that such perceptions fostered undoubtedly contributed to his command of the Commons. How else could MPs react to a man who responded to Nye Bevan's calling all Tories 'lower than vermin' by declaring that the Minister of Health had become the Minister of Disease? Churchill also suggested that Bevan register himself as the first patient in his new National Health Service, 'since he so obviously needs psychiatrical attention'.[119] Or what reaction but laughter could there be to one who mused in Rabelaisian mood on the implications of his colleagues' names, so that Clive Bossom MP became to Winston 'neither one thing nor the other'? Or to one who, when he made one of his least favourite politicians, Harry Crookshank, Lord Privy Seal and then heard that Crookshank himself had remarked that he was 'neither a Lord, nor a Privy, nor a Seal', himself murmured, 'He's wrong about one of those.'[120]

Both the wit and the wisdom were deeply politically incorrect even in the 1940s, but so too was the material of most contemporary stand-up comics. When asked how he kept fit as he aged, Churchill responded that he now mainly took his exercise as pall-bearer to younger friends who had lived healthier lifestyles. A variant on this was to say that he took his exercise by feeding his Chartwell goldfish, while in 1957 he told a Japanese diplomat that he attributed his long life and good health to 'a lot of drinking, a lot of eating and eight or nine hours' sleep, most of it in the daytime'. Sir Stafford Cripps, declared Churchill (when not descending to the irresistible spoonerism of *that* name), 'has all the virtues I dislike and none of the vices I admire'.[121] Asked by King George VI on a cold morning at the airport whether he would take something to warm him, Churchill replied gravely that 'when I was younger I made it a rule never to take strong drink before lunch. It is now my rule never to do so before breakfast.'[122] The *Manchester Guardian*'s Malcolm Muggeridge had suggested – even twenty years earlier – that 'to succeed pre-eminently in British public life, it is necessary to conform either to the public image of a bookie or of a clergyman; Churchill being a perfect example of the first'.[123] Nevertheless, like all attempts to fit Churchill into any general scheme of things, this does not capture the whole man. Perhaps George Lichtheim came closest of all, describing Churchill's public career as 'something midway between Homeric epic and Rabelaisian fantasy', larger than life in both of these directions. When Sir John Rothenstein told Churchill that his only virtue was that he was a non-smoker, he replied sternly that 'there is no such thing as a negative virtue. If I have been of any service to my fellow men, it has never been by self-repression, but always by self-expression.' This was entirely consistent with what Churchill had told his mother as early as 1898: 'I should never care to bolster up a sham reputation by disguising my personality. Of course – as you have known for some time – I believe in myself. If I did not, I might perhaps take other views.'[124]

There were even political points to be made out of self-indulgence. Lord Moran once told the *Daily Express* that 'Stalin thinks the Prime Minister is a broth of a boy. Stalin does not like a man who lives on nuts and soda water' – another palpable hit at Cripps.[125] And in 1951 Harold Macmillan recorded:

> conscious that many people feel that he is too old to form a Government . . . he has used these days to give a demonstration of energy and vitality. He has voted in every division; made a series of brilliant little speeches; shown all his qualities of humour and sarcasm; and crowned it all by a remarkable break-fast (at 7.30 a.m.) of eggs, bacon, sausages and coffee, followed by a large whisky and soda and a huge cigar. This latter feat commanded general admiration.

In the same year, Robert Bruce Lockhart reflected on the fact that the British public thought Churchill 'a wonderful old boy' when they read that he had spent three days in Denmark, flown back one morning to see his racehorse run for the sixth time in succession, and then flown straight on to Blackpool in the afternoon for the party conference, all this at the age of seventy-six. The moral he drew from all this was that 'the English always preferred physical prowess to intellectual ability' (Bruce Lockhart himself being a 'Scot of the Scots'). 'Ah,' replied Anthony Eden, when offered this view, 'Winston's always been a wonderful showman.'[126] When, rather later, Churchill entered the Smoking Room in the House of Commons and was offered a cup of tea by a nervous young Conservative MP, he snapped back, 'No. Don't be a bloody fool. I want a *large* glass of whisky!' Self-indulgence and defiance of the ageing process contributed irresistibly to his burgeoning popularity, for, as *The Times* wrote when the actor Robert Morley died, 'few qualities are more likeable than the ability to give the impression that one is enjoying oneself hugely'.[127]

Add wit and wisdom to the other ingredients – politician, soldier, writer, orator, gourmet, farmer, painter and historian – and the picture of Churchill that was being offered to the public by 1950 was of a veritable renaissance man whose energies never flagged even in his eighties, and who failed at nothing he attempted.[128] Even in his hobbies he was measured by the highest standards; in a volume of essays issued for his eightieth birthday, his paintings were evaluated by the director of the Tate Gallery, his racehorses by the Aga Khan, his histories by Sir Charles Webster, and his wit by A. P. Herbert.[129] Although he was not especially interested in gardening, he was nevertheless adopted as an icon by the horticultural fraternity, and by 1955 the name 'Churchill' had been added to varieties of chrysanthemum, Michaelmas daisy, fuchsia, gladiolus, hyacinth, sweet pea and rose.[130] More significantly, these various interests and associations provided never-ending opportunities for photo-calls, magazine articles and public appearances. As Pauline Bloncourt wrote, 'in the 1950s, his broad presence touched every facet of English life'.[131]

Alongside that range of Churchilliana can be placed the size of the personality now on permanent and relaxed display. In her wartime social survey work on Anglo-American relations, the anthropologist Margaret Mead had pointed out that Americans in particular often confused 'bigness' with 'greatness'[132] (so that many GIs wondered how Britain could be 'Great' when you could travel its entire length in a few hours). John Rothenstein noticed that in *Painting as a Pastime* Churchill himself applied the same principle, by using 'great' as an adjective to describe his larger canvases, and, when shown Oscar Nemon's 'larger than lifesize' bronze statue of himself, by announcing that 'it seems to be such a very good likeness'.[133] Churchill's larger-than-lifesize personality therefore contributed to the idea of his 'greatness' as a man, and thus also as a leader. Dean Acheson was clearly using that analogy when, in introducing Churchill as a speaker at a dinner, he referred to him as a great man who greatly lived and who when he erred also erred greatly, and Churchill himself enthusiastically accepted the tribute.[134] Virginia Cowles believed that Churchill was 'a titan amongst his fellow men' because both his mistakes and his triumphs were all on the same epic scale.[135] Isaiah Berlin applied a similar approach, when he wrote of 1940 that Churchill was 'able to impose his imagination and his will upon his countrymen precisely because he appeared to them larger and nobler

'Why don't you make way for someone who can make a bigger impression on the
political scene?'
Daily Express, 29 January 1954

than life and lifted them to abnormal heights in a moment of crisis'.
And in 1949 Berlin thought that Churchill was still 'a man larger than
life, composed of bigger and simpler elements than ordinary men, a
gigantic historical figure during his own lifetime, superhumanly bold,
strong and imaginative, one of the two greatest men of action his nation

has produced ... the largest human being of our times'. It is not clear who Churchill was being compared to here but it seems likely that Berlin was thinking of Oliver Cromwell, another parliamentary personality who was also a man of action, though Churchill's reception of Graham Sutherland's portrait in 1954 made a marked contrast to Cromwell's insistence that he be painted 'warts and all'. Berlin's phrase about 'the largest human being' was extensively quoted, often unconsciously, so far did it enter into the general vocabulary of Anglo-American Churchilliana. In 1963 a Virginian journalist was surely thinking of it when applying to Churchill Walt Whitman's self-description, 'I am large. I contain multitudes.'[136]

From here it was a short step to the application of the word 'great' and many who used it after personal encounters were clearly overwhelmed by the Churchillian personality, and with the impact of meeting face to face a legend in his own lifetime. An American visitor to Downing Street spoke of 'shaking hands with history' and a Norwegian said that he had spoken to 'the man who wrote history, lived history and made history'.[137] Virginia Cowles decided in 1953 that only Leonardo da Vinci could be compared with Churchill's range of talents, but that the Churchillian presence also imposed a 'feeling of awe' on anyone who met him or heard him speak. Arnold Toynbee argued along the same lines in 1964, that one of the things that made Churchill so historic a person was his defiantly 'unmodern' *range* of interests.[138] The *Christian Science Monitor*, reporting an honour given to Churchill by Colonial Williamsburg in 1955, wrote that 'it simply does not matter where you hear Churchill – or what he says. The aura of greatness encircles the man. You may not understand why, but you cannot escape it when you get within range.'[139] This aura rubbed off on to his properties too; enormous crowds visited Chartwell on the single day on which it was opened to the public when first made over to the National Trust, but even on ordinary days it was not unusual to have respectful groups gathering at the gates in the hope of getting a look inside.[140] If Churchill himself could be glimpsed then something memorable would be anticipated for, as Walter Graebner put it,

> even in moments of greatest ease and leisure, even in his most desultory table conversation, I, like all who approached him, was always aware of his inherent greatness. Everything about

him was on a larger and grander scale than is customary in ordinary mortals. There was a certain *éclat* even in his pottering around the fishpond or passing the port to a guest at dinner, for whatever he turned his attention to became, for the moment, lifted out of the commonplace.[141]

Dean Acheson thought that 'a bathrobe could no more disguise his eminence than a toga could Caesar's' – a strange comparison to choose when it is borne in mind that eminent Romans treated the toga as a *mark* of eminence – but he added that 'even in pajamas, an aura of command hung about the man'.[142]

Isaiah Berlin's conclusion, 'the largest human being of our times', could be endlessly reiterated in appreciations of Churchill, and prevented the image taking flight into absolute unreality; Churchill was perceived as a man on a great scale but possessed of ordinary human foibles – of actual humanity – on an almost unimaginable scale too. The *Reader's Digest* concluded epigrammatically in 1965 that 'his life seemed super-human, yet there has never been a more human figure'.[143] Mollie Keller thought that it was deliberate, that in the post-war years 'Winston turned himself into a "character", a larger than life figure, a legend everyone could share', as a conscious act, and that his cigars, hats, uniforms and romper suits, his pets, practical jokes, birthday parties and weeping in public, were all part of a deliberate love affair with the British public in which nothing was to be held back.[144] Churchill had recounted in a 1930s essay on 'Cartoons and Cartoonists', later anthologised in *Thoughts and Adventures*, that 'one of the most necessary features of a public man's equipment is some distinctive mark which everyone learns to look for and recognise', such 'props' as Chamberlain's monocle, Disraeli's curl or Baldwin's pipe. Since, he argued, he did not have such a piece of equipment, cartoonists had simply invented one, after he was spotted during an election campaign in Southport in 1910 wearing an odd-looking hat, actually a borrowed one that did not fit properly.

Ever since, the cartoonists and paragraphists have dwelt on my hats; how many they are; how strange and queer; and how I am always changing them; and what importance I attach to them, and so on. It is all rubbish, and it all founded on a single photograph. Well, if it is a help to these worthy gentlemen in their hard work, why should I complain? Indeed, I think I will convert the legend into a reality by buying myself a new hat on purpose!

This was more than a little disingenuous: if it was not a 'prop' of that sort, what then was the Churchill cigar, already very much his own by the 1930s and so much his symbol by 1945 that many presents from people whom he had never met came to him in that form? But Churchill's cigar smoking (and just as often his unlit-cigar-chewing), his distinctive style in straight-sided billy-cock hats for ordinary occasions and his eccentric choices for special ones, like his known preference for the comfort and convenience of velvet siren suits, were all adjuncts to the art of self-projection, all seized on by cartoonists and 'paragraphists', and an invaluable aid in making him, his photographs and his cartoons instantly recognisable.[145]

To an extent, then, this was a series of rehearsed and repeated acts; it was notable, for example, that Churchill refused to begin his 1946 motorcade through Fulton until he had found a match to light his cigar, on the ground that that was what his public would expect, and that on other occasions he would 'time' his cigars so that he was not photographed with a cigar that looked 'comically short'. In the same way, he perhaps delayed arrival at public events to make himself late, so that he could 'make an entrance'; his late arrival at Westminster Abbey for Princess Elizabeth's wedding in 1947 allowed the assembled company to give him a standing ovation. As the producer of his complete wartime speeches put it when they were reissued on long-playing records, 'Sir Winston has always had a streak of the ham, you know.' There is of course nothing unusual in a public figure tending his own image in this way, but there is considerable irony in the fact that a worshipper of Churchill like A. L. Rowse could find Baldwin's comparable posing with his pipe to be clear evidence of the man's absolute insincerity, and of his 'pandering to the gallery'.[146] But the one thing that differentiated Churchill from other publicity-hungry politicians was the undisguised openness of his craving for the limelight: when in Washington in 1952 President Truman and he were autographing for each other photographs taken at Potsdam in 1945, Churchill complained that even the best picture showed only the back of his head, and Truman had to promise to find and send him a better one. Seven years later, Ann Whitman, in Eisenhower's White House, could see through the Churchill perform-

HATS THAT HAVE HELPED ME.

Mr. Winston Churchill (*trying on Colonial headgear*). "VERY BECOMING—BUT ON THE SMALL SIDE, AS USUAL."

Punch, 26 January 1921

ance all right, but nonetheless fell for it. 'People here say that he is merely the master of showmanship. Master of showmanship or not – and I grant that he is (witness the ten gallon hat, the bow ties of this visit) – he has taken me in completely and totally.'[147]

The visible signs all seemed to show that excess of fallible humanity which it was impossible not to love in a man who had in the war years shown clearly enough that he was an achiever and not just a show-off. There was for example the irresistible boyishness of an eighty-year-old who insisted on flying the flag of the Cinque Ports at Chartwell whenever he, the Lord Warden, was in residence, and even flew it over airliners when he was aboard.[148] Walter Graebner most remembered in 1965,

> his vivid and extraordinary personality – his exuberant spirits, his fearlessness, his deep emotional capacity, his robust enjoyment of life and his stubborn refusal to compromise with the second rate. He was English to the core, with an old-fashioned swashbuckling Elizabethan Englishness that expressed itself grandly and without petty restraint. Therein, I think, lay the secret of his greatness, and of the power he had to capture the admiration and affection of the whole world. He was the epitome of all that was best in the English character . . . He was John Bull himself, the true English bulldog.[149]

In the same year, another American journalist, in London during the funeral, wrote that 'the English are supposed to be a restrained lot, but during this last week of January 1965 they let go wholly and without embarrassment. Many recalled Churchill himself in tears, of pride, of humility; the stories and photos of Churchill weeping were relished.'[150]

But it was not only Americans who thought that Churchill summed up something archetypally English. The identification of Churchill with quintessential Englishness had originated in the war years, deriving as much as anything from his own appeal to English history in his speeches of 1940, so that some American biographers of 1941 titled their book *Mr England*, and another American thought him even then to be 'something between a bulldog and Mr Pickwick, very much a British Everyman'.[151]

As in many areas, images and concepts hurriedly conscripted into the war effort in the early 1940s were given permanent shape only when the fighting ended. Here the high priest of the cult was undoubtedly A. L. Rowse, but not only for his writings on contemporary affairs. At the end of the war Rowse published *The English Spirit*, in which he proudly claimed the Churchills as a West Country family and presented Winston as the inheritor of a peculiar genius of English history from the heroic Tudors and Stuarts. This theme was fully worked through in

his two-volume family history *The Churchills* published in the later
1950s, by which time Rowse was well known and widely read as an
historian of the early modern period through his seminal *The England
of Elizabeth*. No fewer than five chapters of his second volume on the
Churchill family, 136 pages, are devoted to an uncritical account of the
life of Winston Churchill. Just as Churchill had written that he felt in
1940 that his whole life had been a preparation for office in wartime,
Rowse suggested that the history of the family – even English history
itself – could be viewed in the same perspective.[152] To Rowse, Churchill
was 'among the greatest Englishmen known to history', and he could
suggest only Cromwell, Chatham and King Edward I as possible rivals
for the title, comparators that once again only did honour to Churchill
by association.[153] Rowse was supported by multitudes of lesser writers
playing the same tune, notably Sir Arthur MacNalty in *The Three Great
Churchills*, but the theme was not necessarily limited to the family.
Stephen Graubard wrote a triangular biography of Burke, Disraeli and
Churchill, presenting them as three English conservative writers who
had epitomised 'the politics of perseverance',[154] while the poet of English
cricket, Aubrey de Selincourt, wrote the lives of *Six Great Englishmen*,
in which Churchill was put alongside Drake, Nelson, Keats, Dr Johnson
and Marlborough. For both Marlborough and Churchill, de Selincourt
relied entirely on Churchill's own books, so much was he taken at his
own estimation.[155]

Perhaps the oddest company in which Churchill ever found himself
in such anthologies of greatness was in Donald McFarlan's *Four Great
Leaders*, where he shared the laurels with Franklin Roosevelt (no problem
there), Gandhi and 'Aggrey of Africa', each one representing a different
continent. This was in effect a lesson in civics for young English-speaking
Africans in the Gold Coast colony (shortly to become independent as
Ghana). Thus McFarlan's account of Gandhi was highly flattering to
British rule in India, while the life story of 'Aggrey of Africa' (not exactly
a household name outside the Gold Coast itself) was recounted as an
example of another man under colonial rule who had renounced violence and devoted himself instead to bettering educational provision for
his people.[156]

The assumptions of Churchill's inherent Englishness could even be
applied as a test to others: Rowse thought Ernest Bevin to be Labour's
'most Churchillian figure', after Churchill 'the most John Bullish of

Englishmen'. Emrys Hughes noted that in the Commons Churchill never attacked Bevin, whom he thought of as 'a sort of Labour "John Bull"', while Bevin returned the compliment: when the Soviet Minister Vishinsky said after Fulton that Churchill was 'as bad as Hitler', he had the Foreign Office send a 'stinging retort' that cited at length Churchill's anti-fascist credentials. They were not alone in making that identification, for Bevin's own Transport and General Workers' Union gave, in memory of Bevin rather than Churchill, a large sum to the Churchill birthday appeal in 1954.[157] Rowse was also keen to protect his anti-appeasement All Souls friends from the general condemnation of their College and the policy. This was often done by somehow tying them into Churchill's circle: Leo Amery had fought side by side with Churchill 'but in vain', Isaiah Berlin had opposed appeasement as well as admiring Churchill, while Quintin Hogg had been 'not really a Chamberlainite; he was naturally a Churchillian'. The latter claim sits uncomfortably alongside the fact that Hogg had first got into Parliament at a 1938 by-election in which he had staunchly supported Chamberlain, while the united anti-appeasers, discreetly supported by Churchill, had proclaimed that 'a vote for Hogg is a vote for Hitler' (a slogan coined by the Oxford philosopher J. L. Austin, and dubbed by A. J. P. Taylor 'the only proposition of Austin's I ever managed to understand').[158]

Among major post-war British politicians, only the fifth Marquess of Salisbury like Churchill could trace his ancestry back to those who had taken a leading role in national life centuries earlier, and it is not difficult to see how, had the political wheel turned differently in 1940 and 'Bobbety' Salisbury become the wartime hero, the likes of A. L. Rowse would have been writing eloquently of ancestors who had defied the Spanish Armada and the Gunpowder Plot, and how Hatfield rather than Chartwell and Blenheim would have become the popular place of pilgrimage. And interestingly Rowse considered writing just such a book, at the suggestion of 'Dicky Cecil', before deciding to do the Churchills instead.[159] But, for Churchill, that distant ancestry was part of the real story of his life, kept constantly before the public by his own biographies of both his father and his greatest ancestor, and through regular references back to them in his speeches. Churchill would not have been at all amused by the back-handed tribute offered by the writer who argued that English people 'might have thought that the guilt of the ancestor, who betrayed two sovereigns and served his own ends with consummate zeal [Marlborough], was extinguished – expiated – by the fealty of the descendant, who has served six sovereigns with his sword, his genius, his will, and his heart'.[160] In order to reinforce a conservative political message, it could even be hinted that 'breeding' as such was an essential part of Churchill's story. The 'lifelong socialist' Rowse came dangerously close to this, and an American reviewer certainly thought that he had proved that 'to understand Churchill it is essential to view him with three centuries of national and family history as background. This is precisely what Mr Rowse has provided . . . an eloquent and patriotic achievement.'[161]

An unlikely aspect of Churchill's Englishness to attract attention was his idiosyncratic religious opinions: Archbishop Fisher thought that Churchill 'had a very real religion, but it was a religion of the Englishman. He had a real belief in Providence, but it was God as the God with a special care for the values of the British people.' He recalled that for Churchill (who was not, thought Fisher, a Christian believer in any meaningful sense) the dome of St Paul's surrounded by the fires of 1941 nevertheless had an acute appeal that was both emotional and national. He had been brought up firmly within the Anglican tradition, and in his post-1945 short story, 'The Dream', when he seems to meet the ghost of his father while dozing over a painting of him, he instantly responds to Lord Randolph's question about his religion with the word 'Episcopalian'. (He also once joked that there could never be an American pope, since no infallible leader could be allowed to say 'I guess . . .') As Prime Minister Churchill did not devote much attention to the ecclesiastical patronage that came with the job, though he hotly resented it if anyone pointed out the fact. But that prodigious memory included for easy quotation not only all the verses of dozens of Anglican hymns, but also long stretches of the King James Bible and the (unrevised) Prayer Book. His verdict on the decolonisation of Africa and Asia was for example drawn from Isaiah ('Thou hast multiplied the nations and not increased the joy'), his condemnation of the Munich settlement from Daniel ('Thou art weighed in the balance and found wanting'), and his support for harsh punishments for offences committed against children from St Matthew ('Whosoever shall offend against one of these little ones . . .').

Often such quotations were mere acts of conversational bravado, just like his fondness for quoting at length songs by Gilbert and Sullivan, or English and American poetry, but on occasion they could have deeper significance. Many noticed, for example, the emotional pull exerted by the paragraph of a wartime radio broadcast beginning with a reference to the imminence of Trinity Sunday, with its evocation of the shared British Anglican inheritance. Margaret Mein has indeed taken this argument further, tracing the way in which Churchill having been brought up in 'the world of Christian faith and culture' influenced his language at key moments. His 'finest hour' speech was thus a subtle appeal to fellowship by use of the Anglican liturgy for the first Sunday after Trinity. However, while his regular references to common citizenship, as at Harvard in 1943 or Zurich in 1946, had a similar background in the ethics of Western Christendom and can indeed be paralleled by de Gaulle's 'Appel aux Français' broadcast from London in 1940, in Churchill's case such appeals when in Britain had a specific link to a British – Anglican – linguistic inheritance too. When he referred to the American Secretary of State, John Foster Dulles, looking and acting like a Methodist, it was clearly not intended as a compliment, though his habit also of quoting Bunyan in his speeches gave them a more ecumenical appeal, albeit once again only within the English-speaking world.

Churchill was surely not a Christian believer, as the choice of the words 'Operation Hope Not' as the planning title for his funeral arrangements made extremely clear, but he had a latitudinarian Anglican's respect for the tradition itself. In the Prayer Book debate in the Commons in January 1928 he therefore appealed for the Church to be given more time to reach a consensus, for 'I do not wish to see the mitred front of the one great remaining Protestant Church in Europe irretrievably broken into discordant factions.' However, when he argued that more effort should be made to preserve 'those English institutions which have largely formed the nation, and which are ancient because they are flexible', it is not clear whether he was referring to the Church, the Book of Common Prayer or both. The importance to him of Anglican liturgical language is, however, beyond dispute. The volume of the *History of the English-Speaking Peoples* covering the reigns of the Tudor and Stuart monarchs does not even mention Shakespeare and the great flowering of English literary culture at the end of Elizabeth's reign, but it refers to Cranmer's Prayer Book as being written in 'shining historical prose', to which the 1662 Act of Uniformity provided 'valuable additions'. It also devotes an entire page to the translation and publication of the Authorised Version of the Bible in 1611, which, thought Churchill, 'may be deemed [King] James's greatest achievement', printed by the 1950s in at least ninety million copies. The important thing, though, was that this English translation, as well as being loved, honoured and learned by the English themselves, had been taken in their luggage by transatlantic migrants along with Shakespeare (and, later, also *The Pilgrim's Progress*, another Churchill prose favourite), and so forged 'an enduring link, literary and religious, between the English-speaking peoples of the world'.[162]

From here it was a short step to such automatic associations as that given by Eisenhower in a book preface, that 'Winston was the authentic Englishman.' C. E. M. Joad had long ago said the same thing in a subtler way, arguing that the wartime Churchill was 'the average Englishman, but the average Englishman raised to the *n*th degree', a concept that neatly combined representativeness with exceptionality.[163] A sign of how far the press at least accepted this idea of Churchill's identity with the British people came in their annual pilgrimages to the East End of London for suitable quotations to mark each Churchill birthday and anniversary, such as 'Cor, 80! 'E's 'ad a run for it,' or the lorry driver quoted as saying, 'Look at the old ****. Got to 'and it to 'im, mate. Wish we 'ad more like 'im. Real Englishman, 'e is.'[164] Arthur Booth wrote in 1958 that, when Churchill was the first post-war premier to speak at the rebuilt Guildhall in the City of London, he was 'watched by the battered [note the unstated but unmissable reference to the Blitz here] statues of Nelson, Pitt and Wellington, among the ... famous heroes of the illustrious past, to which his own statue was added in his lifetime, an unparalleled distinction'. Churchill was extremely aware of the point being made here, telling his doctor that he liked the grand and imposing Guildhall statue 'as much as he had disliked Graham Sutherland's portrait', but adding 'how agreeable' it was to be commemorated along with Gog and Magog, 'between Nelson and Wellington, with Pitt and Chatham'. Not a hint of modesty, whether false or otherwise, there.[165]

When the public's voracious appetite for Churchilliana tempted his staff into print, and 'insider' memoirs appeared, written by his detective, his typist and his valet, they only confirmed this patriotic picture; his valet, for example, told the world that Winston liked above all else, 'good red beef, which was no doubt a symbol to him of the England he loved so much'.[166] It seems hardly to have occurred to Norman McGowan that Churchill might simply have liked the taste of beef. Nonetheless, asked which tree he would choose to plant at Chequers to commemorate Churchill's premiership, his secretary suggested an oak, but Churchill immediately corrected him with, 'An *English* oak.' (Neville Chamberlain's choice of a yew tree, with its redolence of the English churchyard, seems somehow just as appropriate in its way. Clem Attlee, who actually lived in Woodford, rather than representing it in Parliament as Churchill did, imaginatively chose the hornbeam, common locally in Epping Forest.) The constant use of such emblems as John Bull, the British bulldog, the roast beef of old England, Mr Pickwick, Dr Johnson, Wellington and Falstaff – Walter Elliott indeed thought in 1955 that Churchill was Falstaff and Prince Hal rolled into one[167] – greatly underlined his association with the colourful pageant of Britain's past, though it could hardly have been further from the reality of post-war Britain, with its ration books, its grimy working-class slums and its petty squabbles about the cost of the welfare state. Here perhaps is the key to the paradox. Was it not especially comforting for the British people to have such a visible symbol of continuity back to the heroic ages of ruffs and knee breeches, buccaneers and musketry, in the very period in which the atom bomb and decolonisation were challenging their sense of identity and of Britain's place in the world?

Dean Acheson had a similarly encouraging perspective in mind when explaining Churchill's international appeal: 'at a time when man has seemed to be dwarfed by his own creations, you have shown us anew', he wrote when Churchill retired, 'the grandeur and greatness which the human spirit can achieve.' Churchill had in effect applied for just this reputation by speaking on the subject fairly frequently, for example in his Nobel Prize acceptance speech, in which he asserted that 'the power of man has grown in every field except over himself. Never in the field of action have events seemed so harshly to dwarf personalities.' Half a century later, this seems a very strange way to describe a generation dominated by Hitler, Stalin, Roosevelt and Churchill himself, and it was perhaps never intended even that the audience of 1954 should agree with Churchill on this point.[168] Dwight Eisenhower, in a statement to be read at a Churchill exhibition in New York in 1965, wrote that Churchill memorabilia would 'remind us how much one individual can accomplish in one lifetime, in the cause of peace with freedom'. And

David Dilks, in the same year, reviewing the scientific developments and the conflict between worldwide political creeds that had shaped most of recent history, remarked that Churchill 'never believed that events should be left to drift and take their course. Great men and great efforts may alter history, and there will be few who will now deny that Churchill was the saviour of Britain at a time when she was fighting for her life.'[169] Churchill's public image thus reinforced the optimistic view that man is able to master the vast impersonal forces that seemed to submerge the contemporary world. The biographer of Thomas Jefferson, rejecting the argument that it was illogical for anti-colonial America to honour the imperialist Churchill, argued that Churchill was 'a continual reminder that there are today, as there were yesterday, vigorous, cour-ageous and eloquent leaders'. Only a few weeks earlier, reviewing Chur-chill's own *History of the English-Speaking Peoples*, Harold Nicolson claimed that both the book and its author 'proved' that great men could alter the course of history.[170] Unsurprisingly, Margaret Thatcher also took this view. On the fiftieth anniversary of Churchill first becoming Prime Minister in 1940, Mrs Thatcher made a speech which reviewed various theories of history, and concluded:

> Winston Churchill illustrates dramatically that whatever theory one espouses, a place has to be found for personality, for leader-ship, for individual drive and determination, for history has shown many times that the fortunes of nations can be trans-formed, for good or ill, by the character and deeds of individuals.

The 'iron lady' at least shared with 'the great Winston', with whom she often invited self-comparison, his tendency to mix history and auto-biography.[171]

The popular association of Churchill's 'Englishness' with that distant period of English history in which the first prominent Churchills had flourished enabled Anglophile Americans to claim this as their own heritage, and his more uncritical association with 'olde Englande' may anyway have fitted transatlantic perceptions better than those in Britain itself, where the reality was more obviously at hand. This is underlined by the various guidebooks to 'Churchill's England' issued from the mid-1950s, with an obvious eye to transatlantic visitors; one such includ-ing Blenheim and Bladon, Harrow, Chartwell, Westerham, Walmer Castle (residence of the Lord Warden of the Cinque Ports), the House of Commons and the War Rooms of 1940, all described in purplish prose as representing historic England. The same is true of lavishly illustrated coffee-table books such as *Heritage of Britain*, Walmer Castle, Blenheim and Chartwell again figuring prominently, and with Churchill's connection pointed out.[172] Churchill's proclamation of a 'new Elizabethan Age' when Queen Elizabeth came to the throne in 1952 fitted in with this splendidly, for, as Lord and Lady Longford pointed out, while Churchill had a great gift for getting inside and evoking the real past, it was nevertheless a romantic vision of the past that he used for mainly political purposes in the present.[173]

After his death, Americans took at least as prominent a role as Britons in ensuring that Churchill's career and the messages to be drawn from it should never be forgotten, but they were also convinced that Churchill was quintessentially English. Among the many tributes paid to Churchill in the US Congress when he died – no fewer than forty in the House of Representatives (including a very perceptive one by Gerald Ford) and eighteen in the Senate, plus many more who read into the record editorials from newspapers in their home states, there were many who spoke of Churchill's Englishness. Senator Bartlett of Arkansas, after reading to his colleagues both Henry V's Agincourt oration *and* Elizabeth I's Tilbury speech against the Armada, concluded that 'Churchill in 1940 made freedom invincible.' Senator John Tower of Texas, in the same session, compared Churchill to Richard I, Edward III, Elizabeth I, Wellington, Nelson and Disraeli, but concluded that Winston had been 'the greatest Englishman of them all'. Those were indeed the days, when Texans knew that much British history.[174]

In these multiple ways, then, Churchill came to be seen as quite unique; in 1954 the philosopher Gilbert Murray applied to him Cicero's verdict on Julius Caesar, that all other statesmen were at root just ordinary men, 'but this portent, this prodigy?'[175] Churchill was viewed as the reincarnation of Julius Caesar, Cromwell, Palmerston, Gladstone, Edward I, Kipling, Shaw, Galsworthy, Dr Johnson, Burke, Disraeli, Drake, Nelson, Marlborough, Wellington, Leonardo da Vinci – and this is to limit the list to only some of the actual historical characters and to leave out all of the fictional ones. One biographer even argued that Churchill's comparison with fictional heroes added to their standing, rather than the other way around: 'He was the only living character remotely comparable with characters in books by Dumas and Baroness

Orczy. He made their heroes credible.'[176] This was an impressive catalogue of peers to be placed alongside the living Churchill, and accumulating to an absolutely unique status. The comparison of Churchill with
Julius Caesar was no doubt particularly apt, for he too had written the
history of his own wars and so set the agenda for historians' versions
of his life for years to come. As Shakespeare has a fifteenth-century
English prince say,

> That Julius Caesar was a famous man:
> With what his valour did enrich his wit,
> His wit set down to make his valour live.
> Death made no conquest of this conqueror,
> For yet he lives in fame though not in life.

So it was to be with Churchill. A *Punch* cartoon in the 1920s had
already made exactly this point, depicting Churchill saluting Caesar's
bust, and saying, 'We have both made history and we have written it.
Let us exchange headgear.' Churchill's hat being offered in exchange
for Caesar's laurel wreath was clearly not seen *then* as a fair exchange,
but it would have been after 1945.[177]

A variation on the same theme was the book *Heroes of History*,
published in 1968. Here Churchill's own 'favourite historical characters'
were given short biographies in extracts from his *History of the English-
Speaking Peoples*; there are chapters on King Alfred, Harold and William
the Conqueror, Henry II and Beckett, Richard I, Henry V, Joan of
Arc, Henry VIII, Elizabeth I, George Washington, Nelson, Wellington,
Lincoln and Lee, and Queen Victoria. With presumably unconscious
irony, the editor contributes a fourteenth chapter to the roll call of
Winston's heroes, devoted to Winston himself (but the story again told
in his own words).[178]

It is surprising that even American writers seem not to have noticed
the closest actual comparator to Churchill, Theodore Roosevelt. Both
were born to the purple but always short of money; both practised a
populist political style which led to collisions with their own parties;
both were writers with a principal interest in history as literature; both
enjoyed lifelong love affairs with their own personalities; and both lived
their lives at a rate which would have killed lesser men. Although Churchill and Roosevelt expressed a wary admiration for each other from
afar, they did not get on at all well when they actually met, presumably

MR. CHURCHILL AND FRIEND

WINSTON : " *We have both made history and we have both written it.*
Let us exchange headgear."

Punch, 14 February 1923

because each had finally encountered a rival for the dominating position
in conversation – it is unlikely that any third person present would have
had much chance of getting a word in. It is also possible that Roosevelt
never quite forgave Churchill for bagging a white rhino on his 1908

Kenyan trip, which the great hunter never managed on his own African safari. Roosevelt in his lifetime was compared, among others, to Julius Caesar, Andrew Jackson, Napoleon and Kaiser Wilhelm II, and, when he received an honorary degree from Oxford in 1910, the Chancellor, Lord Curzon, described him as 'peer of the most august kings ... yet the most human of mankind', a verdict strikingly like the one generally applied to Churchill in the 1950s.[179] Roosevelt, however, met only the brash young man that Churchill was in the Edwardian period, exploding to Violet Asquith (in a tone that suggested that he really did recognise the similarities of their dispositions, though he would never have admitted the fact), 'I hate it when a man obliges *me* to act like a swine – to prevent *him* from behaving like one. I had to *ask* him to go and say goodbye to his hostess – and to take his cigar out of his mouth when he did so.' Perhaps it was just such traits that led an American newspaper, seeking to Americanise Winston for the American market in 1940, to dub him 'the Rough Rider of Downing Street'.[180]

Faced with a similarly negative reaction to Churchill from Charles Masterman, one of his cabinet colleagues, Violet Asquith sympathised but counselled perseverance. 'Winston is disconcerting because he is so self-absorbed – and has very little loose, roving attention – but if you once manage to seize and rivet it you will find him amazingly appreciative.'[181] The mature Churchill was much better behaved than this, but something of the problem nevertheless remained, until the changes wrought on him by the Second World War, and the post-war status that he achieved through his own continuing efforts turned a love–hate affair with the British (and to an extent the American) people into a love feast. They had finally riveted their attention on Churchill's good qualities and become 'amazingly appreciative'. Lord and Lady Longford thought in 1973 that the war years had been the catalyst, but that the real change came later: 'the English people, having once given him their trust, loved him increasingly. It was hardly credible that it should have taken him so many years to win their hearts.'[182]

4

'I Must Justify Myself
before History': Fulton and
the War Memoirs

HOW WRONG THE HISTORIAN ARTHUR BRYANT WAS, even in his highly sympathetic expectation of Churchill's future after election defeat, in a letter of August 1945.

> Yes, it's sad about Winston – it seems ungrateful and un-gracious. Yet from his own point of view, how that defeat secures his place in history! It is as though he'd been assassinated like Lincoln in the hour of victory: 'Now he belongs to the ages'. Yet he still remains above the earth he loves so well to enjoy good brandy, good company ... and a few years of his own immortality.[1]

These and many similar judgements were wrong, because all such assessments grievously mistook their man in assigning to him so passive a future. Churchill was not ready to retire in a blaze of honours, not indeed ready to retire at all, for as he later remarked, 'I always believed in staying in the pub until closing time.' Moreover, while he remained active, he was also a man whose actions would continue to shape the public's perceptions of himself, his personality – and his past. The previous chapter described the relatively passive part of Churchill's rise to a unique status, while this one looks at the other side of the coin, the way in which his post-war role as an international statesman and writer shaped these same processes.[2]

Churchill's journey to the campus of a small college in a remote town in the heart of the United States, Westminster College in Fulton, Missouri, in March 1946, to deliver what has been variously known as the 'iron curtain' speech[3], or the 'sinews of peace' speech, or just the 'Fulton speech', has acquired a mythic significance both in evaluations of the great man's post-war career and in investigations of the point at which the Cold War went into superfreeze. For Churchill, the speech at Fulton was the first of a series of major orations, almost all on foreign affairs, which kept his name and his reputation alive internationally during his six years out of office after his election defeat in 1945. It would be followed by similar international triumphs at Zurich, Strasbourg, MIT (Boston) and The Hague, so that journalists who followed him on the international circuit found that he remained better known across Europe and in the United States than were either the British Prime Minister or the Foreign Secretary.[4] These successes, beginning with the extraordinary attention paid by the international community to the purely personal opinions he expressed at Fulton, helped both to persuade Churchill against retirement and to provide the platform on which his comeback could be staged.[5]

The speech has a quite different significance in the historiography of international relations, where it tends to be interpreted as a milestone along the way to growing antagonism between the Soviet Union and the West. Whereas it was once typically argued that Churchill alone saw the need for a strong Western response to Russian expansionism, and that his courageous call for such measures at Fulton had itself awakened the sleeping giant of American arms in defence of freedom, more recent historians have rightly pointed to the extent to which American elite opinion was already tending in that direction before Churchill went to Fulton.[6] In support of this view they cite the gradual shift in the views of President Harry S. Truman towards a tougher response to Stalin over the winter of 1945–6, the insistent reports of Averell Harriman from Europe which argued that action would be all that Stalin would understand, and especially the 'long telegram' that George Kennan was encouraged to send in from Moscow, which set out the case for a strong response to Stalin at its most cogent and in the words of a man recognised as one of the State Department's most informed minds where Soviet affairs were concerned. Secretary of State Byrnes was still more reluctant over the impending tilt of policy and Truman seemed unwilling to overrule him, but the assumption remains that with or without

New Statesman, 4 December 1954

Churchill the United States would have shifted its international policy in a tougher direction, and sooner rather than later.

These two viewpoints do not coincide, though even without knowledge of the detail it is not hard to surmise that Churchill's personal views and those of Washington's experts on Soviet affairs may simply have converged, reaching similar conclusions from much the same experience of Russian policy. Most analyses have, however, suffered from the same problems. First, Churchill's visit to Fulton was claimed to be (and was reported as) a purely personal one, and his speech was prefaced with a clear statement that he did not speak on behalf of anyone but himself. When the speech produced a hail of criticism both in Britain and in the United States, the British and American Governments each reiterated that view and officially detached themselves from everything that Churchill had said. As a result of these insistent denials, neither Truman in America nor Attlee and Bevin in London could plausibly claim a share of the credit when after an interval – largely as a result of Russian reactions to the speech, or at least of Russian actions

'Beware the bogy man ...'
Daily Mail, 13 March 1946

soon after Fulton – Churchill's speech came to be seen as uniquely prophetic. (By comparison with the instantaneous debate on Churchill's speech, Harriman's opinions on Russia, Kennan's telegrams and the other policy influences in the same direction as the Fulton speech did not become generally known until memoirs and historians added them to the debate several decades after the event.) Churchill's solo warning about the threat to freedom posed by Stalin fitted neatly with the reputation that he already had of being uniquely right about Hitler before 1939. And so it passed into the mythology, he himself doing some at least of the mythologising.

But was it true that the Churchill speech was a solo effort, or was it carefully contrived by – or at least with – the British and/or the American Governments to achieve a pre-calculated effect?[7] Was it in other words simply convenient for Attlee and Truman to have Churchill go out on a limb at Fulton, given that their complicity could easily be denied if the need arose (as indeed it did)? And how far was Churchill himself aware of his own convenience to others in this process? Only with the opening of the Churchill papers can we now answer that central question.[8]

Second, reactions to the speech itself have often tended to miss the extent to which his later speech in New York, just ten days after he had spoken at Fulton, readjusted the balance of the policy recommended, corrected misunderstandings and allayed fears. But even in the short period between those two speeches, between 5 and 15 March 1946, Stalin's violent speech in reaction to what Churchill had originally said and the actuality of Russian policy in Iran had changed the balance of the argument anyway. We need not only to establish just what Churchill meant to say, but also how he adjusted it very quickly in response to a rapidly changing international crisis. We need to begin then by looking at what the two speeches actually said, and by seeking to establish from where in Churchill's thinking and previous experience the key concepts came. Only then can we discuss how far the British and American Governments were involved in the speech and may be presumed to have shown either foreknowledge or *post facto* approval of Churchill's views. Finally, we can consider the impact on the United States that Churchill's speeches actually had.

It is quite clear that Churchill saw from the start that the invitation to go to Fulton had given him a wonderful opportunity to bring off something big. He told Truman in January 1946, 'I have a message to deliver to your country and the world,' and Truman's reply picked up and repeated the phrase: 'I know you have a real message to deliver at Fulton.' The speech eventually given was longer than any that Churchill produced during the two years after the war, except only for the party conference oration which in October 1946 was needed to re-establish his party leadership, and the preparations for Fulton were on a suitably elaborate scale. He had decided that the original invitation to give a series of four lectures was too much for him in his exhausted post-war condition, but he well understood that Truman's endorsement of the Westminster College invitation produced an opportunity for a major media event. In advance of the speech, Churchill told the President of Westminster College that 'in the circumstances, it will be a political pronouncement of considerable importance', and, as they left the College gymnasium in which the speech was delivered, he told President McCluer that he hoped he had 'started some thinking that will make history'.[9] On the train back to Washington, Churchill proclaimed that it had been 'the most important speech of my career'.[10]

What were the special circumstances which enabled history to be made? In accepting Truman's fairly casual invitation, he committed the

President to rather more than had probably been intended: 'if you . . . would like me to visit you in your home State and would introduce me, I should feel it my duty – and it would also be a great pleasure – to deliver an address . . . on the world situation under your aegis'. When beginning the speech at Fulton, Churchill then drew attention not only to the fact that the President had invited him personally, but pointed out that Truman too had travelled over a thousand miles 'to dignify and magnify our meeting'. Elaborate plans had been made for press coverage, the speech was put out almost in full by all three of the major press services in the United States, newsreels filmed the speech, and the entire speech was broadcast live, coast to coast (and in Canada) on CBS radio. Because of the importance of the event, Churchill did, however, veto television coverage, since he 'deprecate[d] complicating the occasion with technical experiments'.[11]

In preparation for the big event, he took his personal secretary with him to America, at considerable additional expense both to himself and to his American host Colonel Frank Clarke, for she alone would be able to give him the experienced support of someone who knew his working habits. This proved to be important when as usual the final version of the speech was produced only at the last moment, for (as she explained) 'on such occasions Mr Churchill makes alterations and additions on the spur of the moment'. Nothing was done to damp down rising interest in the coming speech as an event, but equally Churchill refused all prior interviews so as not to give away in advance what he intended to say in Fulton. When asked by reporters in Miami on 12 February whether he had discussed relations with Russia during his recent visit to Truman, Churchill replied, 'No comment,' and then added with a grin, 'I think "No comment" is a splendid expression. I am using it again and again.' Meanwhile Truman somewhat disingenuously reassured the more pro-Russian members of the Administration like Henry Wallace by telling them that Churchill's speech would just be 'the usual "hands across the sea" stuff' like his 1943 speech at Harvard. No other Churchill speeches of importance were arranged for the period between his arrival in America and the Fulton meeting, though he did agree to several engagements over the fortnight following, and in particular to speak in Richmond, Virginia and in New York, so that his favours would be spread equally across the South, the Mid-West and the North-East, only the Far West being entirely deprived of his attention. When Westminster

College announced early in January that only ticket-holders would be allowed to attend, it received within a fortnight fifteen thousand requests for the three thousand or so available places, and demand continued to rise over the next six weeks until the event itself.[12]

Expectations were therefore high when Churchill, following a triumphant motorcade through the city, rose to speak at Fulton on 5 March 1946, and he did not disappoint. In brief, the speech outlined the threat that Communism posed to the free world, with pointed descriptions of 'police government' under a 'privileged party', and he juxtaposed this with the common law background that had made Magna Carta, the Bill of Rights and the US Declaration of Independence the joint inheritance of the British Commonwealth and the United States. He then explained that 'the crux of what I have travelled here to say' was that the prevention of another war at an early date depended entirely on 'the fraternal association of the English-speaking peoples. This means a special relationship between the British Commonwealth and Empire and the United States.' The United Nations might develop into a peacemaking court of world opinion, but peacemaking required sheriffs as well as judges, with the English-speaking peoples cast in the role of the law-enforcers of the world. This implied – but he did not quite dare to call for – a military alliance between Britain and the United States. A first step toward this, the joint American–Canadian defence agreement, could be extended to the rest of the Commonwealth, but he did not rule out future co-operation reaching even to common citizenship.

Ten days later in New York, by which time he had come in for some heavy attacks both from Stalin and from the British and American left, Churchill proclaimed that 'when I spoke at Fulton . . . I felt it was necessary for someone in an unofficial position to speak in arresting terms about the present plight of the world'. Here came a long pause to increase audience tension as to what he was going to say next, and then, speaking slowly and with great force, he added, 'I do not wish to withdraw or modify a single word.' 'The only question', he insisted, was whether the United Kingdom and the United States united to *prevent* a world war, 'or in the course of that struggle' as in 1941. Nevertheless, at New York Churchill did tone down some parts of his message and amplify others; he was careful to accept that Russia did not want war, at least 'at the present time', and to pay a warm tribute to all that Russians had done in the war against the Nazis, pointing out that if the

Russian Government managed to forfeit the world's admiration for the Russian people then the fault would be entirely its own. He was even more careful than at Fulton to emphasise that he wanted a friendship with the United States that extended to practical co-operation, and *not* a military alliance. But America's great economic and military power, he insisted, imposed duties and responsibilities that must not be shirked.[13]

Where then had these thoughts come from? On the extent of the threat to peace, Churchill's views had certainly shifted during the winter of 1945–6. In a Commons debate on demobilisation in October 1945, he had accepted the Government's plans to run down the armed forces on the basis that 'it is common ground that this possibility of a major war may rightly be excluded, at any rate that we have an interlude of peace'. Three weeks later he deleted, presumably as too scare-mongering, a paragraph from his Commons speech on foreign policy which would have described the horrors of the recent war and forecast 'a period of still more hideous conflict ... One cannot but feel a sense of danger, the menace of vast, descending tribulations.' By the time he spoke at Fulton, the equivalent passages remained in the speech, and he took a much darker view of the potential risk of war than he had done in public before. In much the same way, his view of Soviet Russia – or at least what he said about it – darkened over the same period. He had also deleted from his 7 November Commons speech a claim that Truman 'would not tolerate wrongly-headed, unfair, tyrannical governments', while adding at the last stage of drafting a reassuring sentence arguing that closer Anglo-American relations did not exclude Russia from friendship with both those countries, though in private conversation with Canada's Mackenzie King he took a much harder line. Although he again upped the rhetorical level of his anti-Communism at Fulton in his references to the 'iron curtain' and to 'barbarism', he was also ready to retreat somewhat when he spoke again in New York.[14]

On one theme, though, Churchill's argument never wavered, and that was on the necessity for closer working relations between Britain and America, which he invariably saw as both natural and beneficial to world peace – it was perhaps more than coincidental that it was while sailing to America that Churchill resumed work on his *History of the English-Speaking Peoples*, abandoned in 1939. In the Commons on 7 November, he argued that Britain and America 'come together naturally' as a result of their linguistic, legal and literary background, and that on all important issues 'the English-speaking peoples of the world are in general agreement'. His peroration argued that 'We should fortify in every way our special and friendly connections with the United States, aiming always at a fraternal association for the purposes of common protection and world peace.' The Fulton speech did not materially advance that argument, and although it contained the first formal usage of the phrase 'special relationship', back in November 1945 Churchill had already been talking of 'special and friendly connections', and he even used the phrase 'special relationship' in that speech, but in the narrower context of Anglo-American–Canadian nuclear co-operation. When at Fulton he applied it to Anglo-American relations in general, the phrase added a subtle appeal to a common kinship to the usual claim of joint self-interest.[15]

And so the theme went on through the winter. Even when addressing the Belgian Senate and Chamber in Brussels on 16 November, Churchill had to explain that 'it is evident of course that the affairs of Great Britain and the British Commonwealth and Empire are becoming ever more closely interwoven with those of the United States, and that an underlying unity of thought and conviction increasingly pervades the English-speaking world'. Quite what moral the Belgians were supposed to draw from this was not clear, but some Europeans certainly thought it an alarming sign of Britain turning away from Europe.[16]

In the Commons in December, Churchill was on an even stickier wicket, for the bulk of his own party thought that the Americans had extracted unduly vindictive terms from Britain in negotiations for a post-war loan, and it was the most that he could do to prevent Conservatives as a whole from voting against the proposal. Even under these trying circumstances, he made a plea for closer relations, for 'united, these two countries can, without the slightest injury to other nations or to themselves, almost double each other's prosperity, and united they can surely double each other's power and safety'. Once in America in January 1946, inhibitions disappeared and Churchill's language became more eloquent. In an impromptu address at the University of Miami, he quoted Bismarck saying that 'the most important fact in the world was that the British and American people spoke the same language', and rhapsodised over the 'noble inheritance of literature' which 'unites us as no such great communities have ever been united before'. He was therefore well prepared for the appeal that he made at Fulton, and on this issue there was no modification over the following weeks. At Richmond, he said:

> In these last years of my life there is a message of which I conceive myself to be a bearer. It is a very simple message which can be well understood by the people of both countries. It is that we should stand together ... among the English-speaking peoples of the world there must be the union of hearts based upon conviction and common ideals.[17]

And remarkably, for such a quintessential Englishman as Churchill was so often seen by Americans, he made an admission during the train journey to Missouri which would not have gone down at all well if quoted in London; he suddenly said to his fellow poker-players of the Presidential party that there was only one country in which he would now wish to be born into, one country which had an unbounded future. When asked to say which country that was, he exclaimed, 'The United States of America.'[18] There was, however, a price for this celebration of everything American, for Churchill called at Fulton and again in New York for America to take up the main burden in the new relationship, a point that he had also made quite explicitly to Truman in the previous November. 'The United States', he wrote, 'has reached a pinnacle of glory and power not exceeded by any nation in the history of the world, and with that come not only opportunities literally for saving misguided humanity but also terrible responsibilities if those opportunities cannot be seized'.[19]

With the question posed in these epic terms, and with a speech at Fulton that had been set up in a way that guaranteed the attention of the world's press, it is not surprising that reactions were strong. The myth that almost everyone in the United States was hostile to the Fulton speech and only saw the light later was long ago demolished by Fraser Harbutt. Taken as a whole, opinion was fairly evenly divided, but with regional concentrations of support for Churchill in the press on the East and West Coasts and with the main area of hostility in the traditionally isolationist Mid-West. Even to that pattern there were significant exceptions, for William Allen White, editor of the influential *Emporia Gazette* in Kansas, was one of the first to rally to Churchill, telling him that if his speech 'fail[ed] to pull the democratic world together to meet the crisis, I don't think that anything else can succeed'.[20]

What cannot be denied, though, is the violence of feeling on both sides in the few days after the speech was delivered. As he prepared for his speech in New York on 15 March, Churchill was deluged with telegrams which variously urged him to go home, to stop talking about freedom and democracy – at least until Britain got out of Ireland – or conversely to stick in there and keep pitching. A Baptist clergyman cabled the message, 'Ignore the boos. They're all dirty rats. Pull no punches'; a golf-club president from Brooklyn chimed in with 'Attaboy Winnie, give Uncle Joe the needle. 100 million behind you'; while 'a disabled veteran' asked, 'Don't you believe you have caused enough trouble? It's time you went back to your island.' The British Consul-General in New York had the thousand or so letters and telegrams sent to Churchill analysed and found that only about 18 per cent were actually hostile, and that these tended to show 'a marked similarity of wording [which] made the sudden spate of abuse seem anything but spontaneous'. It was very noticeable, however, that hardly any of the thousand letters were in any way neutral or borderline – all came down for or against. And since some of those that were against came down very hard indeed, it is unsurprising that the Truman Administration took the opportunity to deny its involvement, stand back and await the firming up of opinion. For example, the National Maritime Union, exactly the type of blue-collar group on which Truman's Democrats relied for support, expressed very trenchant views indeed:

> The Tory wail of Winston Churchill to the American youth of Westminster College in your native state is repugnant and insulting ... Loyal Americans [are] aghast at the crass impudence and lack of respect evidenced by a subject of another nation over-enjoying our hospitality ... We cannot believe that you willingly or knowingly lent aid and comfort or accepted his proposal to save the crumbling Empire at the cost of one American boy's life.

In the US Senate, Claude Pepper of Florida, later a great admirer of Churchill, argued even that Churchill had now thrown in his lot with the old Chamberlainite Tories, 'who strengthened the Nazis as part of their anti-Soviet crusade'. The most imaginative response in a critical tone came from the American Communists, who declared that 'the Sun never set on the British Empire because God did not trust Winston

Churchill in the dark', a joke that so amused Churchill himself that he insisted on hearing it again.[21] When he heard of the attacks on him in *Pravda*, he thought it 'an orchestra of abuse and vilification', but, being Churchill, was happy to be the centre of attention even in such unpromising circumstances. 'This in itself is flattering ... If *I* had been turned loose on Winston Churchill I would have done a much better job of denunciation.'[22] Whatever else he had done, Churchill had certainly got his proposals into the debate.

None of this could have happened without at least the acquiescence of the British Government, but in some areas it was more a case of active support than acquiescence. British diplomats in the United States treated Churchill more like a visiting premier than a private citizen, and thus undoubtedly contributed to the impression that many Americans seem to have had that his was, despite all the disclaimers, an official visit on behalf of Britain. Churchill was in any case fond of emphasising the continuity of British policy since Eden had been replaced at the Foreign Office, something that neatly obscured the gap between Government and Opposition. The British Information Service in New York sent down to Churchill in Miami copies of all the BBC's news bulletins, and regular digests of the London press; the British Consul-General in New York looked after 'the details of Mr Churchill's schedule there and [was] responsible for providing transportation etc.'; British consuls in Miami and New York dealt with all the casual letters written to Churchill by ordinary Americans, almost two thousand letters in Florida alone (three hundred of which included such gifts as cigars, brandy and sides of ham), sorted them, analysed them and presumably answered them too; the Foreign Office bag was made available for Churchill's correspondence with his party colleagues in London, and when a cable went astray it was the British Ambassador who received the complaint rather than the cable company.[23] Churchill seems indeed to have taken such back-up as his right in 1946; he wrote to the Ambassador, Lord Halifax, that he would expect him to 'shelter' him while he was in Washington. Although the Foreign Office bag was supposed to be only for 'important communications', he used it among others things to send his French watch back to Paris for repair. And he seems to have felt no great obligation to be helpful in return; when the Washington Embassy asked Churchill to give some time to a visit from a Congressman who had been 'of great help to the British authorities in connection with the British economic

situation after the War and with the loan', the telegram was unceremoniously marked 'No', by Churchill himself, and no interview was granted.[24]

But British Government help went further than administrative and
logistic support, for without the Government's approval of the trip
Churchill could never have got across the Atlantic in the first place.
Shipping and air transport were still rigorously controlled in the winter
of 1945–6, and Churchill had to assure the Minister of War Transport
that his visit had been cleared with the Prime Minister and Foreign
Secretary before he was able to secure berths for his large party. In case
this seems no more than a technical matter, the application to Churchill
of general regulations that were not meant to apply to persons such as
himself, another piece of transatlantic business needs to be considered.
As a consequence of his American trip, Churchill was asked to send a
contribution to a fund to restore the Jerome family church of his ancestors, but his request to the Cabinet Office to allow him to dispatch the
scarcely extravagant sum of £25 to this good cause was sternly turned
down, by a civil servant in the first instance and by Hugh Dalton when
Churchill appealed to the Chancellor himself, even though Churchill
reminded them that his 'family association with the United States ha[d]
been of public advantage during the War and might still be of public
advantage'. No exceptions could be made to the policy of exchange
control, even for Churchill. In response he thundered that he did not
consider 'this particular exercise of arbitrary power is an instance of
wise or sensible judgement'. But when he decided instead to send the
Jeromes a dozen signed photographs which could be raffled in New
York (and which presumably raised far more than £25), he found that
he had to apply for a special export licence before he could do even
that. Earlier in the year, he had asked the Government for the use of
an aeroplane to take him to Metz so that he could receive its freedom
and make a major speech, only to be told that the use of a Government
plane would cost him two hundred pounds. It is quite clear then that
British Ministers could very easily have obstructed his American visit
in 1946 had they wished to.[25]

It was of course highly unlikely that they would do so, for in many
and various ways a Churchill visit would be helpful to Britain's interests
in North America, whatever he actually said in the big speech. Sarah
Churchill told her father when the trip was over that he had 'contributed
much to the world cause, quite apart from what you did for poor old

England', and the diplomats seem to have agreed. The British Consul in Baltimore reported that Churchill's visit to Virginia had done 'more in twenty-four hours to help us than we could have accomplished in months'.[26] In part this was a matter of putting him on display so that he could meet prominent Americans, and of the private meetings with the more famous that the Embassy was able to schedule, for example with New York's Governor Dewey. In part it was simply that, for Americans who were pro-British, Churchill in their midst was a reminder of all that he had symbolised since 1940; one Miami pressman, who heard only an impromptu Churchill address from the balcony of the Yacht Club, nevertheless found that Churchill's voice revived his admiration for 'Old England, which has always held aloft the banner of freedom ... It re-lit memories of those dark days when, huddled with others about a radio in a small United States village, I heard, "We shall fight them on the beaches ...".' Churchill understood very well the impact that his reputation could now have on American opinion: as he told Attlee a few weeks later, when seeking permission to use cabinet documents in his forthcoming war memoirs:

> I think [the memoirs] could win sympathy for our country, particularly in the United States, and make them understand the awful character of the trials through which we passed, especially when we were fighting alone, and the moral debt owed to us by other countries.[27]

American critics of Churchill's speech at Fulton were also aware of this, for many of them complained precisely about Churchill using his hold over American opinion to influence future policy. One telegram argued to Truman that 'British expectations as exposed by Churchill for eternal lend–lease is only typical,' and another urged Churchill to 'go home and quit begging for more dollars'. The sort of reaction to Churchill that such people feared was typified by the Southerner who wired, 'Just heard your speech. You talk like a Texan, you act like a Texan, and God bless you. And we are with you for all the English-speaking peoples.'[28] At a time during which the Foreign Secretary was desperate to keep American troops in Europe, such sentiments could only be helpful to Britain's case.

Beyond this general advantage to Britain from Churchill's visit, Attlee's Ministers had nothing much to lose from encouraging it to take place. Responsibility for a Conservative politician's speech was much more deniable for a Labour Prime Minister thousands of miles away than for the American President who had arranged it and witnessed it in person, and while the American press scarcely treated Truman's denial of foreknowledge as remotely credible, the British press showed no equivalent scepticism about Attlee and Bevin. The Labour Government could therefore benefit from the military and diplomatic consequences of what Churchill had said while continuing to proclaim the unlimited goodwill towards Stalin that the Labour Party wanted to hear. Almost a year after the Fulton speech, 'Cassandra' was still telling his *Sunday Pictorial* readers that Ernest Bevin's main foreign policy aim was to improve relations with Russia, and denouncing Randolph Churchill's recent 'incendiary' lectures in the United States as even more irresponsible than his father had been. Randolph Churchill was, said 'Cassandra', 'explaining to the American people the details which his father carefully omitted to supply when he made the Fulton speech. What Winston Churchill considered to be too inflammable to explain at length, his incendiary son ignites with . . . reckless gusto.' This was unfair, for Randolph was for once trying to remain entirely within his father's careful bounds. He reminded American listeners to his *Europe Today* broadcast on CBS that Churchill had not called for a military alliance at Fulton, but for a fraternal understanding such as the USA already had with Canada, and that Churchill's 'so-called "denunciation" of Russia' at Fulton had been 'mild and restrained' when compared with what had been heard since from 'responsible government spokesmen, like Mr Byrnes, Mr Bevin and Mr Attlee'. The problem with the Fulton speech, thought Randolph, lay not in its content, but in the 're-write men and headline writers' who had inaccurately summarised it and sensationalised its message.[29]

But, whatever 'Mr Bevin and Mr Attlee' said over the next year, did the British Government have foreknowledge of what Churchill was to say at Fulton, and was their denial of responsibility therefore disingenuous? Churchill told Lord Halifax that he had accepted the invitation to Fulton to talk about 'foreign affairs' only after the Foreign Office had indicated that it would be 'agreeable to them', and he told the Labour Minister Alfred Barnes that he had 'made the Foreign Secretary and the Prime Minister acquainted with this project of mine some time ago, and have been informed by them that, as far as they are concerned in the matter, they view my movements with approval'.[30] Although Churchill reported the same conversations to Truman rather more positively – saying that Attlee viewed his visit 'with favour' – the wording of his letter to Barnes (who could check with Attlee, and would therefore be told the truth) suggests something less than close involvement. There is no evidence of much further contact on the subject between Churchill and the British Government until the actual speech, and the report that Churchill sent Attlee on 21 February was positively misleading, indicating only that he was likely to speak along the lines of his Harvard speech of 1943, which had been for closer Anglo-American relations without being against Russia. This perhaps shows among other things that Churchill and Truman had also agreed in advance on the smokescreen that they would use to deflect interference. Churchill eventually sent to Attlee and Bevin a full account of what he had said, why he had said it, and how in his opinion all of this fitted into developing American Administration attitudes to Russia, but not until 7 March. This six-hundred-word cable (which will be discussed below) produced after a week's delay a characteristically laconic response from Attlee, expressing thanks for Churchill's 'long and interesting telegram' but making no comment whatsoever on anything that Churchill had said either at Fulton or in his telegram. He could hardly have communicated less if he had simply cabled 'Glad you are having a good time'. There is however a suggestion in the diary of the Chancellor of the Exchequer, Hugh Dalton, that he at least was in some way complicit in advance of the Fulton speech. Dalton had been an ally of Churchill in his battles against appeasement in the 1930s, and a close wartime ministerial colleague. He had hoped to use Churchill's American visit to build up support for the American loan to Britain, but he also agreed on 25 February 'to send Churchill some material for his forthcoming speech at Fulton . . .'. It is hard to see from the speech what this economic material might have been used for, if indeed it was used at all, but it is typical of Churchill's semi-detached position at the time that he would use yet another informal and personal link for the gathering of information, rather than simply going through official channels.[31]

The British Embassy in Washington could not take so distanced a view, and the fact that it was headed until May 1946 by Churchill's appointee and former Tory colleague Lord Halifax made detachment from Churchill's project even more unlikely. Halifax wrote to welcome

Churchill's American visit with the partisan reminder that 'your American friends . . . are still frankly puzzled at what seemed to them the great ingratitude of the British people'. To those who recall Halifax only as Churchill's opponent over foreign policy in the 1930s (and Churchill's desire to get him out of office in 1940), this may seem surprising, but despite earlier conflicts and Halifax's recent irritation with Churchill's refusal to vote in the Commons in support of the American loan on which he had expended such effort, Halifax and Churchill remained on good personal terms. Churchill wanted Halifax back in his shadow cabinet as soon as he returned from Washington, and Halifax resisted this only on the ground that he could not take a partisan line so soon after being Labour's Ambassador.[32]

Once Churchill was in America, Halifax not only helped make the arrangements, but also told him what he should say in his speeches. Before Fulton, he suggested ways in which the coming speech could be made amenable to American opinion, and endured Churchill trying a good deal of it out on him as an audience, 'with tears almost rolling down his cheeks as he thought of the great strategical concept of the future'. After Fulton, when Churchill was preparing his New York speech, Halifax sent a far more detailed set of recommendations. First, he deprecated 'U[ncle] J[oe Stalin]'s speech' as 'pretty insolent, but I suppose he would say that you began it. Any public argument between you will get the world nowhere except into a worse temper.' He therefore suggested that Churchill explain that Stalin had misunderstood what he had said at Fulton, but that the Soviet leader also 'does not appear to appreciate any of the causes that are responsible for the present anxiety about Russian policy'. Churchill should go on to pay a warm tribute to Russian sacrifices during the war and positively refuse to allow Anglo-Russian friendship 'to be frosted over'. And he should therefore offer to go on from America to Moscow for 'a full and frank discussion' of world affairs with Stalin. Halifax believed 'that something of this kind would have a profound effect both in the US and at home, and that it might do something that neither Attlee nor Truman could do'. If Churchill were to take up the idea of personal diplomacy in Moscow, Halifax volunteered to recommend the idea to the British Government on his own behalf.[33]

Churchill's New York speech followed these prescriptions fairly closely. Surprisingly – in view of his faith in personal diplomacy, his conviction that he alone among Western statesmen could handle Stalin, and his later adoption of just such a summit-meeting strategy for winding down the Cold War from 1950 onwards – he did not suggest a trip to Moscow, but all of Halifax's other suggestions found their way into the New York speech, and the Ambassador was accordingly very enthusiastic about what Churchill said to the New Yorkers. He cabled his 'warmest congratulations on your last night's speech ... Dorothy and I listened in and I felt much better for it.'[34] Halifax was pursuing a very personal line here, having failed in a devious attempt to get his Foreign Secretary to come into line with the new anti-Soviet policy in advance, and apparently without briefing him on Churchill's intentions. But, though coming adrift from his own Government, Halifax kept in step with the American Administration. That need to consult may explain why it took nine of the ten days that passed between Churchill's Fulton and New York speeches before Halifax made his proposals by urgent telegram, and why the idea of a trip to Moscow had a curious similarity to Truman's own reaction to Stalin's denunciation of Churchill, which was to invite the Russian leader to come to America and make a speech of his own at the University of Missouri in Columbia (though Truman's offer to transport Stalin to the United States on the USS *Missouri* hardly made the paranoid Russian leader's acceptance likely).[35]

In public, in any case, Attlee and Bevin kept their distance, and it was reported all across the world that 'official sources' in London had denied that Churchill 'had the approval of the British Government'. That view was maintained even when Churchill himself sought advice; when he received the congratulations of the Brazilian Christian Democrats on his American speeches, the Foreign Office suggested that 'in view of the somewhat controversial nature of the message, we feel that it would be wiser to send no acknowledgement'. Nevertheless, despite the need of the Labour Government to keep its own left-wingers happy, in the Cabinet as well as in the Commons, it was by then receiving hawkish advice from Britain's Ambassador in Moscow, Frank Roberts, in a tone remarkably similar to what George Kennan was sending back to Washington, and Foreign Office analyses of the Russian press indicated a breakdown of Russo-American relations on both sides. These were developments that Bevin could hardly ignore, and if he was not going to be trapped into giving public support for Churchill, neither was he going to be cornered into repudiating him. Attlee later claimed not to have known in advance of Churchill's intentions, and to have been worried that the Fulton speech would actually be counter-productive by antagonising Americans, until Churchill's own assurance that he had Truman's backing reassured him.[36]

A second and definite channel of communication relates to Canada, for Prime Minister Mackenzie King (at that stage moving rapidly into an anti-Communist mood as the Ottawa trial of Russian spies threatened his Government) was also involved actively in forwarding Churchill's 'project', having already agreed when they met in London in the previous November with Churchill's objective of bringing the United States and the British Commonwealth closer together. In advance of Churchill's speech at Fulton, he sent him a copy of the Ogdensburg Agreement of August 1940, by which Canada and the USA set up a joint board of defence, 'which may be of some use in connection with your forth-coming address'. This suggests at the least some detailed foreknowledge of what Churchill was going to say, possibly from Churchill's discussions with the Canadian Ambassador during his trip to Washington. As is demonstrated in Chapter Eight, King refused to come to Washington to be consulted just before the speech was delivered, since this would have removed any line of retreat if the response to Churchill's speech proved to be hostile, but he did have the Canadian Ambassador in Washington, the future Prime Minister Lester Pearson, go over the speech with Churchill and make helpful suggestions. On the day after Fulton, King not only sent Churchill 'heartiest congratulations on what I believe is already generally regarded as the greatest and most significant of your many epoch-making public addresses', but he also cabled Attlee with the advice that the Fulton speech was 'the most courageous utter-ance that I have ever heard from a public man', helpfully sending a copy of this cable to Churchill himself. When Churchill was criticised after Fulton, King wrote again, urging like Halifax that when he spoke in New York he should stress the idea of practical co-operation rather than a binding Anglo-American alliance, for 'I can see no justification whatever for an attack being made on the extension of what is already in existence and warmly approved by the US.' When Churchill in New York followed his advice – or at least spoke along the same lines – King was even more jubilant: 'What you said', he cabled Churchill, 'seemed to me, in the light of the discussion which has taken place since your address at Fulton, to be just what was needed in the way of supplement.'[37]

Watching over the Mother of Parliaments: Churchill's brooding presence
in Parliament Square, 1973.

ABOVE Churchill with the Empire's political leaders, 1944 (left to right): Mackenzie King of Canada, Jan Christiaan Smuts of South Africa, John Curtin of Australia and Peter Fraser of New Zealand.

BELOW Churchill addressing a typically enormous crowd while campaigning in 1945.

ABOVE Churchill, with Harry Truman, acknowledging cheers from the train on the way to Fulton, Missouri, 1946.

RIGHT Churchill dwarfed by 'the long fellow', Eamon de Valera, Downing Street, 1953.

ABOVE European leaders applaud a tearful Churchill, after he calls for a United Europe at The Hague Congress, 1949.

BELOW The Churchills have the Windsors round for dinner, on the eve of his retirement, 1955.

ABOVE Robert Menzies, with Earl Alexander of Tunis and Keith Holyoake to his left, launches the Winston Churchill Memorial Appeal, 1965.

BELOW Churchill listens to Menzies, in the garden of Number Ten, 1953.

ABOVE The Kensington post office exhibits the mail of 'The Greatest Man Alive', 1954.

BELOW Churchill's funeral, St. Paul's Cathedral, 1965.

Mary and Christopher Soames at the re-naming ceremony of the Avenue Churchill in Paris, 1966.

OVERLEAF Edward Heath dwarfed by the legacy of Churchill, at the unveiling of the House of Commons statue, 1969.

It seems unlikely that the Foreign Office were unaware of these attempts at least to get Churchill to modify what he had said at Fulton, even if they had no foreknowledge of the original speech, and there remains at least the suspicion that the British Government felt that it had got too close for comfort to Churchill during his American trip. Although Churchill and Bevin remained on friendly terms after his return to London, and agreed without difficulty not only on the timing of foreign policy debates but also on which issues should and which should not be raised, the Government nevertheless resisted Churchill's demands that he continue to be briefed at a high level on international developments and nuclear policy. Churchill became increasingly irritated by this and eventually complained to Attlee, reminding him that he had generously taken Attlee even to Potsdam with him in 1945. Attlee's reply was a classic 'Clem' put-down which among other things reminded Churchill that Britain had been in the midst of a general election in June 1945, an election which Churchill had called against Labour advice. He pointed out that as Labour's leader from 1935 onwards he knew all the precedents, so that he could tell Churchill just how little his Tory predecessors had involved the Opposition in the making of policy. But Attlee's letter also included a paragraph that unmistakably referred back to Fulton:

> You are, I am sure, aware of the tendency of certain Foreign
> Powers to believe that speeches by eminent persons like yourself,
> must have been concerted with the Government. This has been
> an embarrassment to us, and doubtless to you.

And if Churchill did indeed remain briefed much like a Minister, Attlee felt, then it would impose restraints on him of the type that an Opposition ought not to have to face. That last point was prophetic, for when in 1949 Attlee again briefed Churchill and other senior Conservatives, on Privy Council terms, on details of defence policy, it was eventually Churchill himself who broke off the talks because inside knowledge to which he could not refer in public did indeed inhibit his position as Opposition leader. Attlee's claim that Stalin saw Churchill as still a representative of the British Government was borne out by a conversation that the British Ambassador had with Stalin in May: he reported that 'When I insisted that Mr Churchill had spoken as a private individual', Stalin replied chillingly that 'There are no such private individuals in this country.'[38]

Curiously enough, the people who remained most in the dark about Churchill's activities in America were not the Labour Government but the Conservative Opposition. Anthony Eden certainly did not know in advance what Churchill was going to say, and had difficulty fielding journalists' questions about the speech, both before it was delivered and afterwards. Paradoxically, it was Attlee rather than Churchill who provided Eden with a copy of Churchill's telegram explaining what he was up to. Privately, Eden deplored Churchill's increasingly anti-Russian rhetoric, and told a friend that he sometimes suspected Churchill of trying to start another war simply to get himself back into office. But in this suspicious response Eden was out of line in a party which had never much liked the Russian alliance and which was now most unlikely to condemn its leader for being too anti-Communist. Duff Cooper reassured Churchill that his speech had been 'well-received in Conservative circles' and the shadow cabinet had the Conservative Chief Whip cable their leader with 'sincere congratulations on a magnificent speech'. This was the telegram that went astray, and Churchill's reaction when it eventually came to light indicates his uncertainty as to how even his supporters would react to Fulton: 'I should have been much comforted to have had it at the time.'[39]

When we move to the question of the American Administration's involvement, the issues become clearer. Most obviously, Truman pulled out all the stops to ensure that Churchill had an enjoyable trip. His personal pilot carried messages for Churchill, he sent his own aircraft to ferry Churchill to Cuba and back, and later to Washington, and would have provided a USAAF plane for prospective visits to Trinidad and Brazil had Churchill's health not prevented these additional forays. He seems to have assisted with the provision of a brand-new Cadillac and chauffeur, put at Churchill's disposal for his two months in the United States, he was ready to entertain the whole Churchill party on his Presidential yacht off the Florida coast as well as at the White House, and he intervened personally to ensure that the authorities in New York left the exhausted Churchill alone when he first arrived. His staff made the arrangements for the visit to Missouri, and Clementine Churchill stayed with Bess Truman at the White House while her husband and the President were in the Mid-West, so saving her the fatigue of the journey. When Churchill at the last moment changed his mind and asked if he and Truman could travel to Missouri by train rather than by air, the President rearranged his schedule at a fortnight's notice and committed two additional days to getting to Missouri and back. This last point suggests that Presidential support went well beyond the good manners expected even of a host with a distinguished guest.[40]

The change from aeroplane to a convivial all-male party that would spend three days together on a long-distance train journey made a social difference of the first order. Several of the participants had vivid recollections of Churchill's 'zippered black-out suit', his high spirits (particularly after the speech had been delivered), his inability to grasp the rules of poker, and how far 'he and the President got on famously', as press secretary Charles Ross put it. Over several games of late-night poker – during which the President first told his card-playing staffers that they must not be seen to allow Churchill to win, but later reversed the advice when Churchill's losses mounted alarmingly – Churchill and Truman became good friends rather than just political allies. 'If I am going to play poker with you, Mr President,' declared Churchill, 'I am going to call you Harry,' to which Truman replied, 'All right, Winston.' This became a permanent rather than a temporary change of protocol; Churchill's letter to Truman after Fulton began with the words, 'My dear Harry (you see I am obeying your commands)', and was accompanied by signed sets of Churchill's war speeches and of his *Marlborough* biography as a further sign of personal goodwill. An indication of how close the relationship became is to be found in badinage recorded during that famous train ride. On one occasion Churchill explained that he had only one complaint to make about Americans, which was that they stopped drinking during mealtimes, and when Truman rejoined that the custom was just dandy since it allowed Americans to save enough money on wines and spirits to bail out Great Britain with post-war loans, Churchill countered that 'the great American pastime these days seems to be twisting the loan's tail'.[41]

Thereafter, Truman was on the list of those who routinely received birthday and Christmas messages and complimentary, signed copies of each Churchill book, and throughout their later correspondence and meetings there were almost obligatory references back to the trip to Missouri in March 1946. They discovered that they had things in common over and above politics, for example in each having daughters in the arts of whom they were inordinately proud. When Truman discovered that Sarah Oliver (née Churchill) was appearing in a play in

Maryland in 1949, he took a full Presidential party down from Washington to see her in action, and had himself photographed with the cast. Winston duly received prints and Truman later also sent photographs showing their two daughters together when they met in Atlanta, gestures that were warmly appreciated by the always family-conscious Churchill. When Churchill met Truman in Washington in 1952, personal relations were cordial enough to allow Truman to take a seat at the piano (he was a fine pianist) and accompany Churchill's rendition of a number of old songs.[42] Churchill's precarious health and the danger that bad weather conditions could prevent them from getting to Missouri at all if they relied on air transport, the reasons given by Churchill for preferring a train ride, were plausible enough, but in view of Churchill's known preference for personal diplomacy it seems likely enough that he was also motivated by the desire to get Truman to himself for a few days, aiming at exactly the result that he got. The unbuttoned atmosphere of the train journey encouraged the Americans to tell Churchill things about their developing policy that he had not discovered in earlier, more formal meetings, and so to judge more precisely the impact that his speech would make. And it was still not too late, for final adjustments to the text were made during the train journey. The most famous paragraph in the speech, referring to the 'iron curtain', seems only to have appeared at that late stage, within a few hours of the speech's delivery.[43]

Perhaps the best way to analyse the evidence is as a convergence of views between Churchill and Truman that began as early as the autumn of 1945, when the Missouri visit was being set up. The story began with Truman's Navy Day speech, delivered on 27 October 1945, generally regarded as his first shot across Stalin's bows, the first hint of a tougher American policy to come. Churchill received a copy of Truman's speech when he was preparing his own first speech on foreign policy since he had ceased to be Prime Minister, for the Commons debate on 7 November. In that speech he described what Truman had said as 'momentous' and urged the Commons to concentrate on Anglo-American relations as 'the supreme matter'. He returned to Truman's speech later in his own remarks, summarised what Truman had said as committing the United States to defend democracy even at the risk of war (which was rather further than Truman had gone) and warmly endorsed Truman's approach. On the very next day, Churchill wrote to Truman to accept his invitation to go to Fulton, an invitation sent to him a couple of weeks earlier (in other words, while Truman had been preparing *his* speech). 'I dare say you will have seen from the speech I made yesterday', wrote Churchill, 'how very much I admire your recent declarations and my great desire to carry forward the policy which you announced by every means in the power of the Conservative Party.' Interestingly too, in the context of possible British foreknowledge of Churchill's Fulton speech, that letter from Churchill to Truman was hand-delivered by Attlee's secretary Leslie Rowan, accompanying his master to meet Truman in Canada. It seems inconceivable that Attlee would not already have grasped the turn of events by November 1945, five months before Fulton. When they met at the White House in February, the diary of Truman's Chief of Staff demonstrates just how close their views had become in private, and Fraser Harbutt has indeed argued that it was during the couple of days during which Churchill was with Truman in mid-February that American policy towards Russia actually changed. By early March, convergence had become public, and, reflecting on his Fulton speech in his telegram to Attlee, Churchill concluded:

> Having spent nearly three days in most intimate, friendly contact with the President and his immediate circle, and also having had a long talk with Mr Byrnes, I have no doubt that the Executive forces here are deeply distressed at the way they are being treated by Russia, and that they do not intend to put up with treaty breaches in Persia or encroachments in Manchuria and Korea, or pressure from the Russian expansion at the expense of Turkey in the Mediterranean. I am convinced that some show of strength and resisting power is necessary to a good settlement with Russia. I predict that this will be the prevailing opinion in the United States in the near future.[44]

Churchill's own views, his assessment of US Government opinion and his prediction of future events after Fulton were by then all in step.

How much, though, was this merely implicit convergence, and how far was the speech actually the result of collusion with American officials? Despite repeated denials, which, as a New York paper remarked, had convinced nobody, it is clear that the Truman Administration knew in advance exactly what Churchill meant to say at Fulton, and thoroughly approved of it in private, even while denying its complicity in public.

As far back as November 1945, Churchill had assured Truman, 'Naturally I would let you know beforehand the line which I propose to take ... so that nothing should be said by me on this occasion which would cause you embarrassment. I do not however think this likely to happen, as we are so much agreed in our general outlook.' On 29 January, soon after arriving in America, Churchill reminded Truman that 'I need a talk with you about our Fulton date. I have a message ... and I think it very likely that we shall be in full agreement about it.' During February, Churchill flew to Washington to meet Truman and other members of the Administration, and Secretary Byrnes flew to Miami for further discussions with Churchill. Truman also received from the American Ambassador in Cuba the most detailed account of a dinner conversation with Churchill in which he had outlined his views in full, and which would have told Truman almost everything that would be said at Fulton even if he had had no other source. In respect of the speech text itself, Churchill reported to Attlee that he had first showed it to Admiral Leahy, Truman's Chief of Staff, who 'was enthusiastic'. On the evening before boarding the train, he showed the latest draft to Byrnes, who 'was excited about it and did not suggest any alterations'. Finally, during the train journey, Churchill showed the text to Truman himself, who 'told me he thought it was admirable and would do nothing but good, though it would make a stir. He seemed equally pleased during and after' the speech's delivery. It was only because Truman had been careful to read 'a mimeographed reproduction', rather than 'the exact text' from which Churchill read, that he could claim that he had not seen 'the speech' before it was delivered. But this was a transparent evasion to those who were in the know, and the Presidential press secretary was not at all happy about the regular denials that he was instructed to issue. Even so, some Democrat newspapers at least went along with the fiction that they were being fed from the White House, and explained (as an editorial put it in 'the old reliable' *News and Observer* of Raleigh, North Carolina) that 'Truman Didn't Know'. To his mother, Truman wrote less misleadingly: 'I think [the speech] did some good but I am not ready to endorse it yet.'[45]

Churchill's declaration to Attlee that 'I take complete and sole responsibility for what I said, for I altered nothing as the result of my contacts with those high American authorities' was almost equally disingenuous. There was no need to change the speech when these 'high ...

Authorities' agreed with it anyway, but the extent to which he had consulted them in advance surely showed that he would have been prepared to make modifications had they asked him to, which is anyway what he had said privately to Truman from the start. It did not at all suit Churchill's 'project' in America to get out of step with what US officials *really* thought, though he recognised clearly enough that he might need to get out of step with what they could yet say in public. As he joked when speaking in Virginia three days after Fulton, he would not touch on foreign policy, for 'I might easily, for instance, blurt out a lot of things which people know in their hearts are true but are a bit shy of saying in public [laughter]. And this might cause a regular commotion and get you all into trouble.' This curious status as the only preacher of a truth that others recognised but dared not own merely increased Churchill's standing among his American admirers, and for some it seemed even to prove the truth of his Fulton message. A businessman from New York cabled on 15 March to express his support for 'someone who has the guts to speak so honestly . . . while our State Department seems to be following the pattern of Neville Chamberlain. If Joe Stalin can scare members of our State Department away from your [New York] dinner tonight, it shows the extreme need for more blunt speeches.'[46] This last jibe was a reference to Under Secretary of State Dean Acheson's hasty cancellation of his attendance at Churchill's New York meeting, for in view of the row going on since Fulton the State Department did not want to be seen to be lending open support to Churchill, a reversal of course of which the Anglophile Churchill-admirer Acheson was thoroughly ashamed. He went instead to a private Embassy lunch to meet Churchill and there assured him of his support.[47]

Finally, from this viewpoint, what did members of the Administration say privately about the speech while they were all busily denying foreknowledge and responsibility in public? In almost every case, they were expressing unqualified approval, much as Acheson was doing, and the liberal Henry Wallace's confident assertion that 'Churchill undoubtedly is not speaking either for the American people or their government' showed only how successful Truman's smokescreen had been – and how soon Wallace himself would be forced out of the Government. Navy Secretary Forrestal told Churchill on 8 March that 'Averell [Harriman] is back and in good form. I do not think you would find him in any profound disagreement with your observations of last Thursday,' which from its tone does not suggest much disagreement by Forrestal either, a view that is certainly not challenged by his published diary. When Harriman himself wrote on 19 March, he was unequivocal in his support for the speeches that Churchill had been making in America. Truman was more cautious than the most hawkish members of his Administration, but close reading of his personal letter thanking Churchill for going to Fulton finds an endorsement all the same. He did not directly refer to the content of the Fulton speech, but the letter concluded that 'the people of Missouri were highly pleased with your visit and enjoyed what you had to say'. When it is remembered that Truman was hugely proud of his home state and had at one time a notice placed on the Presidential desk bearing the words, 'I'm from Missouri,' the coded message becomes clear: the President was one of those 'people of Missouri'. It was in any event much nearer the truth than the words he used in actually introducing Churchill to speak at Fulton, when he had declared that 'I do not know what Mr Churchill is going to say.'[48]

The Administration's public reticence owed much to the violence of the criticism which the Fulton speech initially provoked, but by the time that Churchill sailed for home on 20 March the tide had already turned decisively in favour of what he had been saying. The mass of New Yorkers who heard Churchill speak on 15 March thoroughly approved of his message, as he was assured by various observers who went to the event as much to read the reaction as to hear him speak. The Consul-General's analysis of Churchill's mail also found that the pattern had changed within the fortnight after Fulton: at first almost all were favourable, then there was a surge of (probably organised) hostility, but after the New York speech almost every letter was favourable. This rather confirms the importance of the modifications that Churchill had added for New York, changes that both reduced the negative reaction and accentuated the positive. Events were of course as important as what Churchill said after 5 March, but the change of opinions was certainly dramatic: an opinion poll just after Fulton had found only 18 per cent favouring an Anglo-American alliance, while a month later the figure was 85 per cent. In a message to him from J. D. Rockefeller on 19 March, Churchill could feel that his core message had really got through in influential quarters: 'Your various utterances,' wrote Rockefeller, 'so gracious and kindly and yet always so sincere and challenging, have directed again the attention of America to the great opportunity and the equally great responsibility that rests upon it.'[49]

In the middle of April, a month after Churchill returned to London, Halifax wrote:

> I am quite sure that there has been a steady movement of understanding what your Fulton speech was about and appreciating it. Many people of a kind I should hardly have expected to take that line have said to me what an immense service you rendered by stating the stark realities, and what an effect that had had upon the thinking and the policy of the Administration. I have very little doubt that it is true.

By the following October, Truman could assure Churchill that 'your Fulton . . . speech becomes more nearly a prophecy every day'. By then the myth of Churchill's solo effort was so well established that the British Ambassador and the American President had both come to believe it, though at the time they had known better.[50]

How then was it possible for the speech to have such a considerable impact? Probably for two main reasons – who Churchill actually was in relation to American opinion, and the extremely fortuitous timing of the speech. Frank Clarke thought that it was 'almost incredible that the timing could have been so perfect', for Churchill's speeches (which he believed would have been influential even a year before the event) had in fact 'directed the intense spotlight on the dangerous international situation within less than a month of the crisis'. This is persuasive, for early March 1946 was indeed the eye of the storm in the development of the Cold War. On 28 February, Secretary Byrnes warned the Russians not to push America too far, but on 1 March the Russians announced that they would halt their withdrawal from Iran, a pull-back that a treaty of 1942 required. On the very day of Churchill's Fulton speech the United States delivered two stiff notes of protest about Russian policy, in Iran and in Manchuria. The *New York Times* pointed out that 'One would have to go far . . . to find two United States protest notes to one power on two different issues on the same day.' Even as Churchill journeyed to Fulton, he was told confidentially that the US Administration had decided to send home the body of the recently deceased Turkish Ambassador, but with a full naval escort including a battleship, two aircraft carriers and many other warships, the nucleus of what was to be the permanent American military presence in the Eastern Mediterranean. This was a pivotal moment in the US deployment to confront Russian expansion, and, although the decision was not announced until 6 March, Churchill immediately grasped its strategic significance, telling Attlee that it was 'a very important act of state and one calculated to make Russia understand that she must come to reasonable terms of discussion with the Western democracies'. Nor did timeliness end with the speech at Fulton, for on the eve of his New York address the US press was reporting that Russian tanks had been sighted within twenty miles of Tehran, and even more virulent Russian denunciations of Churchill added again to the impact of Russian policy. After Fulton, Stalin was in a double-bind over the growing crisis in Iran, for if he pulled back then Churchill's argument that Communists respected only a show of force would be vindicated, whereas if he went forward he would prove Churchill's claim of a growing Russian threat and encourage world opinion to unite against him at the United Nations, as happened at the end of March. His decision first to go ahead and then to climb down was perhaps the ideal one – from Churchill's perspective. As a correspondent told Churchill, 'the reaction of the Russians to your Fulton address has done more to make America understand' than anything else. So 'ripeness was all' in relation to the speech; had it come before the Iran crisis, it is likely that Churchill's message would have been generally disregarded, while, as Churchill himself said only seven months later, 'if I were to make that speech at the present time and in the same place, it would attract no particular attention'.[51]

Finally, where did Churchill's own status with Americans fit in, allowing him to make the most of the opportunity that timing gave him? Before departure, he had told his doctor that 'I think I can be of some use over there; they will take things from me.' When he had completed the mission, Frank Clarke summarised his success in the same terms. The typical American, he wrote, had previously 'eliminated from his mind the possibility of further war', but,

> since you sailed it is becoming more and more evident that your warnings have caused a realization in this country that a strong and definite foreign policy is the only 'overall strategic concept' – to use our own words – which will offset the same drifting, compromising attitude of laissez faire which led up to

Munich and the war with Hitler ... Certainly plain talk was needed. Actually you were the only one to whom this country, and for that matter the democratic peoples of the world, would listen ... You have impressed all freedom-loving people with your honesty of purpose and your knowledge and experience of world affairs, and when you speak and send a warning, they are all forced to look the situation squarely in the face.

Churchill's unique status, deriving from his record in the 1930s and the war years, was thus the catalyst in persuading Americans to engage with the emerging international situation, and although it clearly emerges from the archival evidence that the British and American Governments were in different degrees each complicit in his Fulton 'project', it remains clear that the change in informed opinion across the democratic West, which those Governments sought but dared not yet openly demand, owed a great deal to Churchill's personal efforts in March 1946. As Pierson Dixon of the British Foreign Office put it in his diary on 6 March: 'I must say Winston's speech echoes the sentiments of all. None but he could have said it.'[32]

The fact that he did say it, and could then be given the credit both for prophetic powers and for courage, was of crucial significance for the maintenance of Churchill's worldwide reputation. After Fulton, Churchill was quick to point to the speed with which other people had caught up with the views that he had expressed. He was already saying so by summer 1946, and this soon merited a section in every Churchill speech on foreign affairs. At the Massachusetts Institute of Technology in March 1949, he argued definitively that:

three years ago, I made a speech at Fulton ... Many people here and in my own country were startled and even shocked by what I said. But events have vindicated in much detail the warnings which I deemed it my duty to give at that time. Today there is a very different climate of opinion.

Sometimes indeed he made the claim to foresight even more cheekily. In an article published both in America in *Life* and in Britain in the *Daily Telegraph* in April 1947, he referred back to the 'commotion' that had followed his Fulton speech. 'Statements of this character', he added modestly, 'are not challenged in any part of the world today,' except behind the iron curtain. He also pointed out that the West had at last belatedly woken up to the strategic importance of Greece and Turkey, whereas he himself had on his own authority already rescued Greece for the free world by sending British troops to Athens in 1944–5.[53]

Where Churchill led, his admirers were quick to follow, but this time the key interpreter was not Isaiah Berlin or A. L. Rowse, but the Dutch writer J. H. Huizinga, son of the famous medieval historian, whose 1948 article on the Fulton speech was quoted by Randolph Churchill when editing his father's speeches and then regularly anthologised by others. For Huizinga 'the prize for moral leadership should surely go to Mr Churchill'.

> Who dared to call a spade a spade and a Russian an enemy of democracy? ... Who turned the 'cards on the table' face upwards and showed the public what sort of cards they were more than a year before this salutary revelation received its official blessing? In other words, who led and who followed?

This of course ignored the fact that it was Harry Truman who actually arranged that Churchill go to Fulton, knowing well what he would say when he got there. It was Truman's own trip to Missouri that ensured that the world press reported the Churchill speech, and it was the British Foreign Office which helped to make the logistical arrangements. But all of these people denied their complicity when the speech produced its storm of 'warmonger' outrage, and this had left Churchill and his admirers free to claim all the credit for him when the tide of opinion turned.

Summarising much recent writing, Rowse mused in 1954 that 'we wonder now what all the fuss was about, for Churchill was only, as so often before, pointing out what was in front of people's noses. To do that in politics is the prerogative of genius ... At Fulton he merely pointed out the obvious.'[54] From there it passed into the orthodoxy of history. As the journalist and former wartime American broadcaster from the London Blitz, Quentin Reynolds, summarised the popular view, 'Many people criticised Churchill for being so harsh with Russia in that Westminster [College] speech, but time proved him to be right.'[55] In 1966, Martin Gilbert wrote of Fulton that 'even in his old age, Churchill's wisdom was considered mere irresponsible prattle. Yet within a

year' he was vindicated by events, and Gilbert reached the same conclusion in the official biography in 1988.[56] In other words, he was still
ignoring the alternative historiographical school which has argued for
years that the 'iron curtain' speech, by alarming Stalin, actually helped
to provoke the Cold War rather than merely announcing its arrival,
that Churchill's warning was in effect self-fulfilling. At least at a personal
level, Churchill seems to have been aware of this. When eating *Time*'s
caviar in New York, a couple of days after warning about Russian
expansionism, he remarked that 'Uncle Joe [Stalin] used to send me a
lot of this, but I don't suppose I'll be getting any more.'[57] This is not
to argue that those revisionist writers who have argued that it was the
West that started the Cold War have won the historians' argument,
for they certainly have not done so. They have, however, contributed
significantly to the more balanced overall view that now predominates.
Only writers on Churchill seem to ignore the fact.

The Fulton speech had in any case a secondary impact on Churchill's
reputation, because of the way in which he had put his own judgement
on the line in asserting the need for strong measures. At Fulton, Churchill made direct comparisons between the Nazi threat in the 1930s and
the Communist threat in the 1940s, in what David Cannadine has called
his apocalyptic tone: 'Last time I saw it all coming and cried aloud to
my own fellow-countrymen and to the world, but no one paid any
attention.' He argued that an unnecessary world war had been the
consequence of ignoring his warnings, exactly the historiographical
orthodoxy that he was even then establishing through his war memoirs.
Given that Churchill's reputation for good judgement over his long
career was – to say the least – mixed, and that his warnings about the
Nazis in the 1930s were then seen as his clearest success, it was indeed
a courageous act to risk all that with a second try in 1946. When it came
off, though, it provided a perfect way for his admirers to link pre-war
and post-war crusades in foreign affairs, each of them lone battles against
the prevailing opinion in which Churchill had been vindicated by events.
Fulton thus set Churchill apart from his international rivals for the
supreme position, and demonstrated the historic nature of his qualities.
The *Daily Telegraph* thought in 1950 that 'even when he has been in
opposition, the inherent force of his themes has made history'.[58]

The popular memory of the 1930s, substantially shaped by Churchill's own speeches and writings, was a powerful tool with which he

could now shape perceptions of the post-war world. In 1951, his biographer J. G. Lockhart wrote of Fulton:

> as had happened so often before, his warnings were decried by many, and he himself was denounced as a mischievous, even a warmongering man. And as had happened so often before, events were soon to show who was right ... His opponents might sometimes deprecate his counsel, but could not ignore it, for graven in the memories of all were the thirties, the years the locust had eaten, when a prophet, without honour in his own land, had told the truth and been rejected.[59]

If these thoughts were indeed graven in the popular memory, then Churchill had himself done much of the chiselling. It is notable for example that Lockhart himself had misquoted a biblical phrase ('the years that the locust hath eaten', Joel ii: 25), which had first been applied only to the *early* 1930s by Sir Thomas Inskip, but to which Churchill had given more general currency in *The Gathering Storm*. A few years later, *The Locust Years* could be routinely chosen as the title of an American study of Britain in the entire inter-war period, so pervasive was the influence of both Churchill's vocabulary and his viewpoint. There is much then to be said for Diana Coolidge's view that the post-Fulton 'outcry' against 'that old Russian-hater, that warmonger Churchill', merely preceded a time in which 'it was seen that Churchill's position in his country and the world was subtly altered. Instead of becoming the obstinate old man who would not retire he had come forward once again as a leader and a statesman.' All other positive developments in Churchill's post-war reputation would be contingent on this 'subtle transformation' in the aftermath of Fulton and of his war memoirs.[60]

The *New York Times* had already reached this conclusion by 1953, publishing a political obituary under the mistaken impression that Churchill's third stroke would compel his retirement. But, for the *New York Times*, Churchill had already in 1953 become 'a part of world history for half a century. His great decisions – to fight on in 1940, to oppose Stalinism in 1946, altered its course . . .' – note the parity given to these two achievements in the summary of Churchill's contribution to world history. So 'the first rough draft of history', as the quality press's political coverage has been dubbed, was setting the tone for all that would follow,

and the many uncritical biographies of Churchill in the 1950s and 1960s
duly did follow, quoting such pressmen's verdicts on Fulton as independent confirmation of their authors' own views.[61]

The press was not of course left to its own devices, for Churchill
never gave up his lifelong habit of cultivating newspaper proprietors,
such men as Lords Beaverbrook and Camrose in Britain, or Henry Luce
and Charles Sulzberger in the USA – hence the dinner with Luce and
his senior managers on *Life* shortly after Fulton. And he never visited
Washington after 1941 without visiting the National Press Club, for
discussions which (he assured the British Ambassador) were scrupulously confidential. Reporting to the White House, the Ambassador
assumed that this must be one of Winston's little jokes, since anything
that he said there was always quoted in full in the next day's papers.
Much of the first draft of history was therefore more or less in Churchill's
handwriting. As Churchill himself told the National Press Club in
Washington in 1954, referring back to Fulton, 'I got into trouble being
in front of the weather that time. But it's all come out since – I won't
say all right, but it's all come out.' This was almost exactly the phrase
that Churchill had long ago applied to Joseph Chamberlain in *Great
Contemporaries*. 'Joe', he had written, was the man who 'made the
weather', and shaped the political agenda with which others then had
to deal. As Roland Quinault has shown, Joe Chamberlain was also a
man who succeeded brilliantly in getting himself measured against his
own estimation of his worth, a spell that he has cast over biographers
and historians as much as over his contemporaries. So it is no wonder
that Winston so admired Joe. For the 'iron curtain' speech at Fulton
and the writing and reception of his Second World War memoirs demonstrated that – on a global scale – Winston Churchill could not only
'make the weather' but to a large extent write the weather reports too.[62]

Having established at Fulton the reputation of an international
statesman whose career was certainly *not* over, as had been generally
assumed only a few weeks earlier, and having had a considerable boost
to his own morale and confidence from the whole American visit of
1946, Churchill never looked back. March 1946 in effect purged for him
the shame of election defeat in July 1945, and he returned to Britain
raring to go, determined to become Prime Minister again. He told his
doctor in August 1946 that 'a short time ago I was ready to retire and
die gracefully. Now I am going stay and have them out . . . I'll tear their

bleeding entrails out of them.' At about the same time, one Churchill crony, Brendan Bracken, was happily assuring another, Lord Beaverbrook, that 'Winston is determined to lead the Tory Party until he becomes Prime Minister on earth or Minister of Defence in Heaven.' Though these views were expressed in terms of domestic politics, since only there could he win the electoral battle to take him back into Downing Street, it was surely the acclaim that greeted him abroad that produced the turnaround in his own view of the future, for his actual involvement in domestic politics in that first year after the war was extremely tenuous.[63]

After the summer of 1946, that international standing was reinforced by regular triumphs of a similar type, beginning with his speech on European unity at Zurich in September. The very fact of his Fulton success ensured that whenever he was billed to speak internationally afterwards expectations were pitched at the highest level. This sometimes put him under considerable personal pressure, for he had reached a level of fame from which he could only move downwards, and hence when he was not intending his remarks to be taken as a great pronouncement, as at Metz in July 1946, he made sure that this was known in advance and then kept to a fairly light, bantering, anecdotal tone in the speech itself. Such low-key speeches had their value too, in putting his more avuncular side on display, but it was important that his audience should have the right expectations.

Elevated expectations also ensured, however, that the world's press would be on hand to hear and report his words, that radio and newsreels would record them for a wider audience and for posterity, and that they would in due course appear and be read in successive volumes of his speeches too. These collected editions continued to have a wide circulation, ten thousand hardback copies being produced of *The Sinews of Peace* (speeches of 1945–6), and slightly more for *Europe Unite* (1947–8). Each was also separately published in the United States, and welcomed by reviewers there. Churchill took considerable trouble over these orations, but he also ensured that they would conform to one of his most fundamental beliefs about what made a 'great speech', that it should contain only a single theme. He also took great care – again as at Fulton – to ensure that the theme matched with the location in which it would be delivered. Hence, the Zurich speech dealt only with the issue of European unity, and especially with the need for closer understanding between France and Germany, an idea that had an especially strong appeal to the Swiss, divided as they were between the two linguistic communities. Later speeches at Brussels (1949) and at Strasbourg (1949 and 1950), each city already becoming pivots of the European entity, were devoted to the same theme, as was his big speech at The Hague in 1948, but, with the development of the European idea over those years and his own close association with it, he was able to keep the message fresh (if not always unambiguous). For his speech at the Massachusetts Institute of Technology, Boston, in 1949, he again took up the issue of East–West relations for an American audience, extremely topical in the month in which the NATO treaty was finalised. Cumulatively, then, these international triumphs kept his name on the front pages of the world's press, and no doubt gave him an enormous boost in his quest to impress the British electorate with the constructive side of his statesmanship.[64]

Nonetheless, over these years Churchill took little active part in the conduct of the Conservative opposition at Westminster. Though he was again taking considerable trouble over a few speeches annually to large Conservative rallies – more of course in election years like 1950 – he devoted the bulk of his time in the Opposition years 1945–51 to writing six volumes of war memoirs, published pretty well annually between 1948 and 1954.

It was generally recognised that Churchill's Second World War writings, like his other publications, were to an extent autobiographical. As his wartime ministerial colleague Malcolm MacDonald put it, Churchill 'acted as his own Boswell to his own Dr Johnson – and no more zealous Boswell ever scribbled about a grander Johnson', while Herbert Stewart compared Churchill's writings to Julius Caesar's campaign memoirs, written for the same self-glorifying political purpose.[65] But these memoirs could not be discounted as mere egotism, as many had considered Churchill's The World Crisis to be. As Stephen Graubard pointed out, quoting the popular 1920s joke that Churchill had written his autobiography and called it the world crisis, 'in 1948 such witticism would have been meaningless and impossible. Churchill's position in the Second World War made his personal history and that of the nation indivisible; the presentation of one was the representation of the other.' Or as the citation read when Churchill was given the first ever freedom award by Colonial Williamsburg, 'The history of these battles which he

wrote could be in large measure autobiographical.'[66] Writing of the
similar case of Abraham Lincoln's part in the American Civil War,
Emerson had claimed that 'there is properly no history, only biography',
for Lincoln 'is the true history of the American people in his time'. But
even Lincoln did not survive to write the standard six-volume history
of his own presidency.[67]

Beyond this, as his historian–collaborators Bill Deakin and Maurice
Ashley have pointed out, in Churchill's war memoirs the autobiographical aspect was artificially and deliberately reinforced, for example by
printing far more of Churchill's own dispatches, letters and Cabinet
papers than the replies that they elicited. The impression that Churchill's
leadership was always a matter of 'action this day' owes much to that
basic literary stratagem. As John Connell pointed out,

> there was no indication [in the memoirs] of the way in which . . .
> subordinates reacted to the endless series of questions, vigorous
> prods and stern summonses to 'action this day'. Their explan-
> ations, their protests, their occasional outraged and absolute
> negatives were not given. The memoirs, therefore, give a one-
> sided picture of the war's conduct and administration, but as
> [Churchill] himself would have said, *some side*.

This was sometimes noted and resented when the books came out.
The wartime Minister of Information John Reith, for example, told Lord
Moran that 'I intensely dislike your man,' and when asked if he found
Churchill 'wanting in consideration', replied:

> No. You cannot expect consideration from a Prime Minister in
> war. But Winston prints in his war book innumerable directives
> and never once lets us see a single answer. Why, he vituperated
> me for not doing something, though I had been trying to get
> the Government to do the very thing for months. And even
> when I wrote to him and explained this, the same directive
> appeared unaltered in the next edition.

Field Marshal Earl Wavell took exactly the same view: the war
memoirs included 'all his own minutes, orders and actions, and not a
word of anyone's reactions to them'. Wavell, like Alanbrooke, was
equally irritated by Churchill's claim to personal credit for strategic
decisions which others remembered as collective: 'not a word, too, of

giving credit to [General] Dill' for sending the Armoured Division to the Middle East in 1940. 'This – boldest decision of war – he just described as "I took the grave decision" etc.' In December 1950, Robert Bruce Lockhart summarised in his diary many recent conversations on the Churchill war memoirs, including talks with Churchill admirers like Ismay and Hollis. 'What Anthony Eden and everyone else in the know says' was that 'as history his memoirs are grossly unfair, that only the successes are recorded whereas numerous failures and turned-down suggestions are omitted, and that future historians will get a very wrong view from the book.' Bruce Lockhart not only recorded this emerging (but very private) consensus from those 'in the know', but endorsed it too, with the authority of a sharp observer of the contemporary scene and an author of considerable repute in his own right – and a man indeed who was certainly not hostile to Churchill.

> I agree. Indeed, I go further. I say that if these errors of a very great man are not contradicted now, historians of the future may take them as true. Some people believe that in time truth will out. I am far from sure. I think that unless someone contemporaneous can get a sight of it, there is very poor chance of it emerging unemasculated later.

Other Churchill admirers, it must be said, took a far less critical view even in private. Hugh Dalton, for example, noted in August 1948 that 'I have read Winston's *Gathering Storm* – I spent three solid days on it. It is a magnificent achievement. Nowhere can you say that he is wrong...'[68]

Lord Boyd-Carpenter in 1988 suggested that no other politician has ever 'liberated so much material from the Public Record Office so quickly' as Churchill did, though he might well have added, 'but published it so selectively'.[69] Churchill alone among historians of the time was given access to the public records, before there was any programme at all for their general release to scholars; indeed he used some papers in the 1940s which still seem not to have been released for anyone else to consult half a century later. Churchill's attitude to the actual publication of recent documents in this last phase of his career was highly opportunistic. Early in the process of his memoirs, he appealed to Harry Truman when the State Department had refused his request to publish his wartime correspondence with Franklin Roosevelt. Churchill stressed

that this eight-year-old material was all 'past history', but rather contradicted this view that it was uncontroversial by offering to keep the
documents out of public view until after the forthcoming US Presidential elections. He also applied leverage by reminding Truman that earlier
American accounts like that of Eisenhower's naval aide Harry Butcher
had been 'none too favourable to me', so making the writing of his
memoirs seem like a necessary defensive act. Truman concluded that
he could hardly prevent Churchill from quoting his own cables, but
insisted that he only paraphrase Roosevelt's replies.[70] Churchill and
Truman then played the same game in 1953, when Churchill reached
the point in his memoirs in which Truman began to figure as President
in 1945; he was again able to publish his own cables but not to quote
Truman's, since Truman was by then also at work on memoirs and
wanted to reserve his words for his own book.[71]

Churchill adopted a similarly 'open government' tone when asking
in 1951 for permission to publish the 1943 Quebec Agreement on nuclear
policy, a request motivated by his recent discovery that Britain's rights
under the treaty had been surrendered by the Attlee Government and
by his wish to attack the Labour Party with the information. This
eight-year-old story, he argued, 'belongs to the past and to history'.[72]
Though he failed on that occasion to convince the American Government, he blurted the secret out anyway in a Commons debate in 1954.
In 1952, as Prime Minister, he was all prepared to publish secret information on Korea only two years old, for the same purpose of embarrassing Labour, until headed off by the Americans, this time successfully.
In this last case, the information was so secret that even the State
Department in Washington was not thought secure enough to contain
a copy of the document that Churchill proposed to read to the Commons. He made his point, however, by reading to the Commons in 1952
details of another understanding that the previous Labour Government
had reached with the Americans but never told its own supporters, and
so achieved the aim of sowing dissension in Labour's ranks. This was,
noted the scarcely left-wing Hugh Gaitskell in his diary, 'an interesting
example of his complete unscrupulousness'. No wonder that Gaitskell
found this difficult to reconcile with Churchill's generosity to a man he
had always disliked, Stafford Cripps, to whom in 1952 he sent flowers,
books and several letters when he was hospitalised.[73]

Conversely, Churchill consistently opposed publication in America of documents from his wartime premiership that could not be accessed in Britain, where the privacy rules were tighter. In 1948 he was 'very angry' (as Beaverbrook told Robert Bruce Lockhart) about Robert Sherwood's edition of *The White House Papers of Harry Hopkins*, 'resents certain revelations and thinks that Sherwood should have consulted him personally much more than he did'. In 1955, he strongly opposed American publication of papers relating to the Yalta Conference of 1945, and when the general principle of non-publication had been lost he sought to reserve from view interpreters' records of his private meetings with Stalin.[74] In 1962, he was still refusing to allow Eisenhower to reprint in his Presidential memoirs a letter that Churchill had written in 1954 in support of American policy in Indo-China; the reason given, that the letter dealt with issues 'of quite recent date and still alive', would have outlawed most of Churchill's six volumes of memoirs had it been systematically applied.[75]

Churchill managed to secure access to masses of documentary material, and not only from his own archives and from the public records (to which as a former Minister he had access). Just as after 1918 he had used all his political connections and friendships to secure access to other sources and records too, for *The World Crisis*, so after 1945 he exploited his political and military friendships both at home and abroad for the same purpose.[76] This meant that the marshalling of so much material was in itself a fearsome task, and it is an enormous tribute to both the research staff and to Churchill himself that the processes by which the books were written produced such coherent and dramatic narratives. So much could easily have been submerged among the multiplicity of files of paperwork, or sections could have been simply delegated to other writers and the shape of the overall product lost in the process (as happened to an extent with the *History of the English-Speaking Peoples*, when after 1955 Churchill's intellectual powers had waned). At times, though, the selection of which documents to include and which to leave out of the war memoirs went so far as subtly to amend the judgements that the documents were supposed to underpin. *US News and World Report* picked up in 1952 the rumour that Churchill would shortly publish his account of the last year of the war, and was 'critical of General Dwight Eisenhower for not wanting to take Berlin, instead of leaving it to the Russians, when the chance was open in 1945. The wartime British Prime Minister does not want these criticisms to get deeply entangled in US politics.' When Eisenhower became President in 1953, and Churchill looked forward to the renewal of their harmonious wartime partnership, he was uncomfortably aware that the imminent publication of *Triumph and Tragedy*, his final volume of war memoirs, would have to describe those Anglo-American disagreements in 1945 during which the two men had been on opposite sides. Churchill not only went over the book again to take out any reference 'which might imply that there was in those days any controversy or lack of confidence between us', but then also invited Ike to read the manuscript and make further revisions if he wished. With Jock Colville, Churchill:

> lamented that, owing to Eisenhower winning the presidency he must cut much out of his War History and could not tell the story of how the United States gave away, to please Russia, vast tracts of Europe they had occupied and how suspicious they were of his pleas for caution.

This conversation invites several comments. First, in private, Churchill was not bothering to pretend that this was anything other than a history of the war. Second, he was – both before and after he 'revised' the final volume in 1953 – projecting an account of 1945 in which someone other than himself was to blame for the failures. Finally, though he did not include in the book any very overt criticisms of either Roosevelt or Eisenhower, by entitling it *Triumph and Tragedy* he was offering up those criticisms to discerning American readers anyway. Churchill himself was cast as the architect of the triumph, with others left to take the blame for the tragedy, but with nothing (at least on the surface) to threaten Anglo-American harmony. Robert Eden is surely right to suggest that the aim of cementing the Anglo-American alliance was one of Churchill's chief rhetorical projects in the whole of his war memoirs, and not just in the detailed senses described here.[77] This pragmatic approach consorted badly with Churchill's statement that 'I prefer to be judged by what I wrote at the time, rather than rely on present narrative and argument which is liable to be influenced by after-events.'[78] Truman's literary adviser, after checking the texts attached to the Churchill letter which contained these impeccable sentiments, noted detailed ways in which on past form Churchill was likely to distort the record in using Truman's words, and concluded sadly that 'Mr Churchill is an honorable man – but a British statesman with typical British retrospective flexibility, no matter what he says in his letter to the contrary.'[79]

The 1930s were as subject as were the war years to Churchill's 'retrospective flexibility', as an examination of *The Gathering Storm* will shortly indicate. Donald Cameron Watt has shown how far Churchill was misleading in portraying Neville Chamberlain as motivated by his anti-American instincts and Eden as pro-American in the political crisis that led to Eden's 1938 resignation, a key moment in the political descent to war, on Churchill's view of the process. But in 1948, it made good sense for Churchill to align his deputy and likely successor behind his own insistently pro-American views as they had emerged by that time (though, ironically, Eden did not share such views either in 1938 or in 1948), and if *The Gathering Storm* could contribute to that process, so much the better. In the case of Eden's 1938 resignation, Churchill may however have been as much the victim as the orchestrator of the documentary manipulation, for Eden's own stage-door army of friends and admirers had provided Churchill's researchers with a carefully filleted collection of 1938 documents which would present their hero in as flattering a light as possible.[80]

Nevertheless, the publication of so many documents in Churchill's war memoirs gave them a distinctive aura of authenticity and sometimes impressed even the best informed, hence Churchill's insistence that they remain in the text, even though receiving from his literary agent Emery Reves a battery of letters arguing that they should be pruned or relegated to appendices, so as not to slow down the dramatic thrust of the story. Dwight Eisenhower told Churchill in 1949 that his reading of 'the historic memorandum you wrote to General Ismay on the 4th of June 1940' had deeply impressed him when published in the second volume, *Their Finest Hour*:

> I never before saw it in verbatim form, although I knew of its existence from the very day that I first met the British planners in January 1942. To see it in print brings home to me again, and with emphasis, the virtue and farsightedness of your leadership in those dark days. The aggressive and completely practical concept of applicable strategy expressed in that memorandum is worthy of any so-called 'captain of history'.[81]

Ordinary reviewers invariably referred to the authenticity of Churchill's documentary account, for example when Hanson Baldwin, headlining his review of *Triumph and Tragedy* 'Churchill was right', explicitly rejected earlier American accounts which had tried to vindicate US policy in 1944–5 and credited Churchill with a unique farsightedness – credit that depended almost entirely on the selection of 1944–5 documents that Churchill had printed.[82] In all this self-quotation, Churchill had the quite inestimable advantage that the documents of his official life, unlike almost anyone else's, were such a good read: his texts could be larded with quotations from his telegrams, cabinet papers and military instructions without any danger of boring the reader. As John Kenneth Galbraith perceptively argued, when reviewing in 1978 documentary volumes of the official Churchill biography, 'it is hard to think of any misfortune for any politician [considered for the Nobel Prize] that would be as devastating as the release of his official prose. Churchill survives.'[83] When Eden followed Churchill's example and filled his own memoirs with documentary 'proof' of their authenticity, the result was to render them well nigh unreadable.

Churchill knew well that, by writing about world-shattering events in the portentous tone of voice that he anyway preferred to use even in routine writing, he was elevating the stature of the major participants in the war. As he told Eisenhower when Ike's former naval aide Harry Butcher published his diaries in 1946, thus becoming one of the few to beat Churchill himself to the draw:

> The articles are, in my opinion, altogether below the level upon which such matters should be treated. Great events and personalities are all made small when passed through the medium of this small mind. Few people have played around with so much dynamite and made so little of it.

As David Reynolds has suggested, this sort of thing was characteristic of Churchill's entire great-man view of history, one that 'naturally privileges the significance of the individual and the uniqueness of events'. Many of those who were critical of his *History of the English-Speaking Peoples* in the 1950s took exactly the same view when he applied that philosophy not just to his own life and his own family but to the entire history of the race.[84]

Eisenhower, who correctly divined that Churchill placed him among the great minds in this summary division of mankind, took much the same view. When Montgomery cheekily wrote to him to ask for a copy

of Kay Summersby's book which described her alleged wartime romance
with Ike and for Ike's guidance on how he should reply to questions
about it, he replied that he had not read the book, and would not know
how to find a copy, dismissing as pointless all 'inquiries arising from
inconsequential, personal accounts of anything that was as big as the war
was'.[85] Nobody would ever accuse Churchill of penning 'inconsequential
accounts' of the war. Indeed reviewers of his war memoirs wrote again
and again about the perfect match between the topic and the prose,
each on a suitably epic scale: 'When before,' asked the *Spectator*, 'through
all the centuries of this island's history, has such a theme matched such
a pen?' 'What a theme for the painter in words . . . the master-work of a
mastermind,' enthused the *Yorkshire Post*. Such judgements contributed
significantly to the perception of Churchill himself as both uniquely
historic and historically unique.[86] It was this idea that ensured that
wherever Churchill went in his last fifteen years – for example in New
York in 1959 – people flooded out on to the streets in their thousands,
so that they would be able to claim later in their lives that they had
actually *seen* Winston Churchill.[87]

The official answer to any critics who felt that Churchill's war
memoirs magnified his own role and opinions was that he was offering
only 'a contribution to history', and that it would be for others to decide
how much his autobiography contributed. The same view was taken
privately by friends who did not utter a word of criticism. General Sir
Hastings ('Pug') Ismay, head of Churchill's Defence Office, while agreeing with Ike that Churchill both in the war and in his memoirs had
placed 'a wholly disproportionate emphasis . . . on the importance of
the islands in the Eastern Mediterranean', reported that earlier drafts
had been so obsessed by the Mediterranean as to be 'downright boring',
and that though 'we got him to cut a good deal of it . . . on the main
issue he was, and still is, as obstinate as a mule'. But while confiding
that he also agreed with Ike's view that Churchill's talents lay in grand
strategy rather than in the logistics and mechanics of modern warfare,
on which 'he was, and still is, completely ignorant', he felt that none
of this really mattered. 'The great thing to remember is that his book
does not profess to be history; it is merely the story of the Second World
War as it struck him personally. And I have no doubt that when the
full history comes to be written, many of his contentions will not hold
water.'[88]

However, as the Churchill bibliographer Frederick Woods conceded, the very fact that Churchill was writing about a time when he himself was war leader 'gave the work an authority and a weightiness that tended to obscure the fact that it *still* presented only one man's view' – and, we might add, *some man!*[89] When he was Prime Minister after 1951, Churchill sent unofficial personal messages to world leaders, a tactic that enabled him to bypass the need for cabinet and Foreign Office 'censorship' (his word), and conveniently ignored the fact that his words were treated as coming from his Government. So in his war memoirs he time and again had it both ways, writing what was billed as only a 'personal' account, but with the extra authority of a man who had made the history before writing it. Confusion on the point was added to by the publishers and book clubs who, when marketing the actual volumes, used only the series title *The Second World War*, which certainly sounded more like a history than a personal memoir. This was all that appeared on the spine and title pages of the books, apart from the volume number and Churchill's name.

Churchill was of course well aware of what he was doing. The Conservative Research Department director, visiting Chartwell on party business, found himself on one occasion waiting for a considerable time while Churchill laboured with his research staff on his memoirs. Eventually the great man returned to the present, apologised with his usual charm for the delay, and explained the vital importance of what he was doing with the words, 'I must justify myself before history.' Justification perhaps came before history in both senses of the phrase. As Lord Moran reflected in 1953, 'for five years he has tried to justify to posterity in the six volumes of his book all that he did in the war'. A year later, he quoted Churchill at length (perhaps too great a length indeed to be trustworthy as direct reportage, but reliably representing the gist of what he had said). Discussing the onset of the Cold War in 1945, Churchill had insisted that:

only one thing mattered now – it was often in his mind – when his record came before posterity they must be fair to him. All this talk about the war having been fought in vain made him angry. At any rate he was not to blame. To get that quite clear he had added a sixth volume to his book and called it *Triumph and Tragedy*. He would remember then how Camrose and his publishers tried to persuade him that it was a mistake to bring out another volume. But he would not listen to them. For he was resolved to make known that he wanted to take precautions against some rather ugly possibilities in the spring of 1945, at a time when the Americans were still making friends with Stalin and had not woken up to the danger of Communism.

This was, however, the same volume from which he then took *out* so much when Eisenhower became President, his desire to justify his past in his war memoirs clashing with his desire to make more history in the future. One or two reviewers (but very few and all from the left) pointed out these weakness in the war memoirs at the time, even with *The Gathering Storm*. Emanuel Shinwell acidly observed that Churchill had written a novel with himself as the chief character. Michael Foot, though as critical as Churchill of the appeasers, wrote of his 'clothing his personal vindication in the garb of history . . . In 500 pages Churchill hardly allows himself one admission of weakness or false judgement on his own part.' Then Foot added, most provocatively, that although the book was 'vastly more enjoyable and instructive than Hitler's *Mein Kampf*', yet 'in personal conceit and arrogance there is some likeness between the two'. Such voices were not much heard, though, in the hubbub of adulatory reviews, and the fact that they came only from those who had been lifelong critics of Churchill anyway ensured that they made virtually no impact outside their own circles.[90]

In any case, the problem with the argument that this was merely a personal account that others could correct if they wished – apart, that is, from the fact that other historians could not see the documents and decide for themselves whether Churchill had selected from them fairly – was that such people as Ismay and Eisenhower, who could well have placed in print as their own 'contributions to history' alternatives to the Churchillian authorised version, resolutely refused to do so. Ike certainly permitted himself, when writing his own account, some criticisms of his British military subordinates that ruffled their feathers, but not a syllable of doubt about the military wisdom of Churchill. When Alanbrooke had the temerity to publish his wartime diaries, documents that had as fair a claim on the attention of the reading public as Churchill's reprints of cabinet papers, Ike was incensed, writing that 'I could not imagine myself as being guilty of writing anything, ten years after

the war was over, that could be construed as disparaging the accomplishments of the wartime Prime Minister.' Ismay took the same view, only
more so: he was gratified to find that his own exceptionally discreet
memoirs were well received when published in 1960, for 'my purposes
in writing the book were to show, first, that so far as the UK was
concerned, Winston Churchill was head and shoulders above anybody
else. Secondly, that his relations with his military advisers were, on the
whole, very friendly . . .' Ismay, as Jock Colville put it, 'loved and vener-
ated Churchill', and had been an admirer even before 1940 (a key test
for Churchillians, though one that Colville himself would not have
passed). He knew 'by heart whole passages of *The World Crisis*', but
would say privately that Churchill 'can be relied on to make a century
in a test match, but he is no good at all in village cricket'. Both in
wartime as his military secretary and in the post-war world of the
memoirists, Ismay appointed himself as the man who would do for
Churchill the 'village cricket' part of the job. Unsurprisingly, when
Ismay's draft memoirs were sent to Churchill in manuscript in 1958, he
was 'fascinated. He could not put them down.'[91]

If such key witnesses recognised that Churchill had written autobiography rather than history but then wrote in support of his version
rather than offer correctives to it, it is difficult to see how other historians
were supposed to reach a more balanced verdict. At times Churchill's
friends did not even pretend that they should, Ismay privately writing
of his own book that 'if I could have found any more superlatives to
apply to Winston I would gladly have used them. And I hope that when
his full-scale biography comes to be written some fifty years hence, the
pen picture that I have drawn of him will be taken as accurate.'[92] And
Ike, having collaborated in the doctoring of *Triumph and Tragedy* so
that it would say nothing to embarrass Anglo-American relations ten
years after the event, then congratulated Churchill on 'this final volume
of your masterful *history* of World War II'.[93]

This point is made the more telling when it is borne in mind that
Ismay and Eisenhower, and all of the inner group of Churchill admirers
like them, knew from personal experience exactly how cavalier Churchill
could be with documents. When asked to comment on specific questions
about the military direction of the war, Ismay reminded Ike that 'I was
not present at many of the talks that you had with Winston, and he
was often rather naughty about not telling me what had transpired. Nor

did he invariably show me your written communications, unless they were in exact accord with his own arguments.'[94] If Churchill's instruction to Maurice Ashley when he came to work on the *History of the English-Speaking Peoples* – 'Give me the facts, Ashley, and I will twist them the way I want to suit my argument' – was clearly a joke, it was, like many good jokes, one that diverted attention away from the truth, in this case from Churchill's pragmatic view of the craft of the historian. For, as Martin Gilbert has put it, 'Churchill had no illusions about the role of history and historians (himself included).' Asked by Jock Colville if Beaverbrook's *Politicians and the War* and *Men and Power* books on the politics of 1914–18 were 'true', he responded that they were 'Max's interpretation of the truth'.[95]

As significant as the Churchill-centred content was the impact that the war memoirs made on the worldwide market. The US serial rights alone brought in a million dollars from *Life* magazine and prompted Churchill to jest that 'I'm not writing a book. I'm developing a property.'[96] Churchill's claim to Moran that he was outselling every previous book but the Bible was plausible enough, for the six volumes of the British edition alone printed about a quarter of a million hardback copies each, the first two volumes at least selling out within hours. An American edition, which actually began to appear four months before the British version (so important was the American audience for Churchill's message), was printed in editions of about sixty thousand copies per volume. There were also concurrent Canadian, Australian, Taiwanese and Book Club editions of all six volumes, with translations appearing at the time of original publication in Danish, Dutch, French (three different versions for Belgium, France and Switzerland respectively), German (two versions again, one for the Swiss), Greek, Italian, Norwegian, Portuguese, Russian, Spanish, Swedish and Turkish. By the time of his death, these had been added to by editions in Arabic, Hebrew, Japanese, Korean, Polish and Serbo-Croat. Churchill generously acknowledged the critical importance in all this of Emery Reves, who had 'buzzed around the world for a year making contacts'. During Churchill's lifetime, the original editions were joined in the English-speaking market by an abridged edition, a pocket-sized reprint edition, school editions, an illustrated 'Chartwell edition' with deluxe bindings, and both British and American paperback editions. Thereafter many other editions of the volumes appeared in hard and paper covers, including a complete slip-cased set from Penguin. The original books were dispatched as soon as published in special leather-bound presentation copies to politicians, military men and other leaders of opinion in Britain, America and the Commonwealth, and apparently read avidly as they arrived.[97]

A comparison with Churchill's First World War memoirs is instructive here. The initial British edition alone of *The Second World War* sold about twenty-five times as many copies (and much more quickly) as *The World Crisis*, and then went on reprinting and selling for much longer. They remain in print half a century after the event, and still command a pretty good second-hand price, a remarkable feat for books that so swamped the market when first produced. Between 1948 and 1954, then, the six volumes of war memoirs were serialised in eighty magazines and newspapers worldwide, and then appeared in hardback in fifty countries in all the appropriate languages. Moreover, the sheer extent of the extracts that were serialised is staggering to a generation which sees four or five extracts from a new book in a newspaper as successful exposure. Extracts from *The Gathering Storm* appeared in no fewer than forty-two daily editions of the *Daily Telegraph*,[98] and in commensurate quantities of exposure in the *New York Times* and the *Sydney Morning Herald*, and even in such outposts of the English-speaking world as Singapore's *Straits Times*.

The shape and structure of the books were also of considerable significance, and in this Churchill had – and occasionally even took – expert advice. The first volume was originally to be called 'The Downward Path', and was at one stage to be called 'Towards Catastrophe'. Publishers, especially those in the United States, did not like this apparently downbeat start to a series for which they were paying so much (and had therefore to generate enormous sales merely in order to get their money back). Emery Reeves eventually came up with 'The Gathering Storm', which sounded suitably apocalyptic but had the right 'crescendo' feel for the first part of a series. The effect of the title and of a structure which concluded the first book with Churchill becoming Prime Minister was to highlight from the start his own personal trajectory from 'wilderness' to Downing Street at least as much as the world's path to war.[99]

Churchill was thus able to produce at considerable length and for a colossal audience of international readers a coherent narrative of the

1930s and the war years that would have a long head start over any competitor – quite apart from the stamp of authenticity given by his name and his inimitable prose style, and by all those cited documents. As Robert Blake pointed out as recently as 1990, while Churchill's *The World Crisis*, published in 1923–4, was already being debunked by such military historians as Charles Oman in 1927, 'no one has tried to do a similar *critique* of the six volumes on the Second World War'.[100] The Book of the Month Club all too plausibly claimed in 1955, 'He retires, but never from history!'

Beyond the books themselves came dramatisations and films, generally more adulatory than the books had been. When ABC set out to serialise the war memoirs as *The Valiant Years* in 1960, the writers were instructed that 'we must make it a cardinal principle of this series that Winston Churchill is our leading man, and every creative and dramatic device must be used to bring him to life'. The producer's concept of the Second World War was that it had been a duel between Hitler and Churchill: 'it will be like a Western; Winston Churchill hiding behind rocks as a sharpshooter or leading the charge down the valley. We have a good leading man and a good heavy.' The flavour of the programmes when completed is conveyed by the press advertisements: 'dominating the scene, investing the vast scope with immediacy and theatric splendour are the deeds, the words, the voice, the very presence of that man called by many the greatest of the century – the Right Honourable Sir Winston Spencer Churchill, KG, OM'; three-quarters of each full-page advertisement was taken up with Churchill's portrait. The added comment, however 'pridefully' it was made, that the series 'takes its place in the roster of adult, informed programs' was unduly optimistic.[101] When Jack Le Vien then condensed the million-and-a-quarter-words of war memoirs into a single feature film, *The Finest Hours*, the even greater compression led to a still less balanced account. *The Times* was moved to point out that even Churchill had admitted to making *some* mistakes during the war (which the film did not), though it was left to the *Daily Worker* to remind moviegoers that the Red Army had actually taken part in the Second World War too. But such was the adulation of Churchill in his ninetieth year that this uncritical stuff was hailed by most British reviewers as 'a simple yet thrilling eulogy', and then later by Bosley Crowther in the United States as 'a grand hymn in Sir Winston's praise'. In Washington, the *Evening Star* thought it 'a factual film that flows like fiction' but also noticed a subtlety in the title. 'In *Their Finest Hour* [the title of volume two of the war memoirs] Churchill was saluting the British for the way they faced World War II; *The Finest Hours* salutes Churchill for the way he led the British and the rest through that conflict.'[102]

The tone of Le Vien's television and cinematic representations of Churchill may be fairly easily be demonstrated from the book of the television series, *The Valiant Years*, itself a big-selling publication in Britain and in the United States. The acknowledgements page begins, 'Our deepest appreciation is expressed to Winston S. Churchill, who inspired this history of the Second World War. Without his leadership at a time of great crisis for mankind it would have been impossible to publish this book or any other expression of free opinion.' Almost three hundred pages later, the book ends with Churchill accepting his 1945 election defeat philosophically and without bitterness, whereas it is quite clear from contemporary sources that the defeat actually plunged him into a self-pitying slough of despond which took most of a year to surmount – entirely understandably. In Le Vien's version, though, he drinks a glass of champagne as he prepares for a well-earned rest, urges his family and friends to 'Never, *never* indulge in self-pity,' and raises his glass, 'the bubbles dancing golden and joyful in it, and offers a toast, "To the *future*"'. If the scene was not actually imaginary, it was certainly so unrepresentative as to be quite misleading.[103]

In due course, *Young Winston* and on television *Winston Churchill: The Wilderness Years* followed on in the same vein. *Young Winston* was the pet project of the American writer and producer Carl Foreman, so committed to the project that he took a good deal of persuading not to play Lord Randolph Churchill himself. His script, thought the director, Richard Attenborough, was a deliberate act of homage, 'based on a profound knowledge of the subject matter and born of a deeply felt admiration for Winston Churchill, increased perhaps by virtue of his welcome in his now adopted country [Britain] following his self-determined exile from the United States', during the McCarthy period. The film, for which for Churchill had already signed away his rights in 1941, produced nevertheless an income of £100,000 and 6 per cent of the gross takings for him when eventually made twenty years later. It hardly needs pointing out then that in turning Churchill's *My Early Life* into the film *Young Winston*, neither the scriptwriters nor the film-makers paid any attention to the errors of fact in the book that contemporary eye-witnesses like General Sir Hubert Gough had pointed out from personal knowledge. Gough had come to have great veneration for Churchill during the Second World War, and did not put his reservations on the record when he published his own memoirs. Shortly after *Young Winston* was announced, though, his thoughts on the subject were made clear enough in pencilled annotations discovered on a (borrowed) copy of *My Early Life*, annotations that were confirmed as his by a handwriting expert for *The Times*. In these asides he dismissed parts of Churchill's accounts of both Indian and South African campaigns in such terms as 'disregard of strict truth', 'pure fabrication', 'Bunk. Pure fabrication. I was there with the transport animals . . .' The few who read about this discovery in the quality press in 1971 would have been dwarfed by the millions who saw then and later the film's uncomplicatedly heroic account. And though these critical revelations came too late to affect the account of Churchill's campaigning in 1897–1900 given in Randolph Churchill's second volume of the official biography, neither were they mentioned when Martin Gilbert reached in 1976 the volume of the official biography covering the period in which Churchill had written *My Early Life*. *Young Winston*, coming out a year after these revelations, also took no account of them, and even *The Times*, which had itself broken the story about Gough's revelations, saw no need to refer to them when reviewing the film. In much the same way, Churchill's romanticised account of himself as a failure at school and therefore owing everything of his later success to himself and little to others, easily disproved from the Harrow records, was once again restated by the film, in this case in contradiction of the official biography too. In such summary forms, then, through the entertainment media as well as the book market, the various books of Churchill's memoirs were thus passed on from his own partisan viewpoint to further generations.[104]

Because of the advantages that surrounded its initial publication, Churchill's general view of the war and its origins was not seriously contested for twenty years, and it became almost impossible during his retirement to criticise him in print at all. An example that makes this point squarely is the extent to which Churchill's account of his campaigning against appeasement in the 1930s remained the received truth for so long, though it told the story in a highly partisan manner. There

was little in *The Gathering Storm*, for example, to explain the economic
and imperial problems within which Baldwin and Chamberlain had
to make foreign policy; little acknowledgement that the ruination of
Churchill's reputation over India and the Abdication (and by his ceaseless pursuit of office from the appeasing premiers he later affected to
despise) made sensible people reluctant to listen to him. He shyly admitted that he had in fact been campaigning for rearmament with what
turned out to be exaggerated figures of German strength, but seemed
not to be aware that this tendency to exaggerate ('In these endeavours
no doubt I painted the picture even darker than it was') made it less
likely that he would be believed by Ministers with access to at least
equally reliable figures of their own. No reference at all is made to the
fact that Churchill had been utterly and consistently wrong about Japan.
In an article in 1938, he had confidently asserted that the Japanese would
never dare to risk war ('it would be madness') with the English-speaking
nations, for they could wage war 'at a level at which it would be quite
impossible for Japan to compete'. Nor did such confidence wane even
as war actually approached in 1941. Indeed, anyone who still thinks of
Churchill as infallibly prophetic on military matters at that time should
ponder on his observation, just a week before Pearl Harbor was bombed,
that in the event of war the Japanese would 'fold up like the Italians'.
'The Japs', said Winston, were 'the wops of the Far East'. Even as a
whistling-in-the-dark-to-keep-cheerful remark, this was extraordinarily
unperceptive.[105] If such a phrase had ever been uttered by Neville Chamberlain, it would have been hanging round his neck as an historical
albatross ever since, much like 'Hitler has missed the bus.'

Nor did Churchill ever substantiate his core argument that Hitler
could have been painlessly stopped by early action by the democracies,
because there was no way to evaluate reliably his belief that internal
German resistance would have overthrown Hitler if the democracies
had opposed his aggressive plans. Writing in *The Gathering Storm* of
the Rhineland Crisis of 1936, he thundered that if the French had mobilised, 'there is no doubt that Hitler would have been compelled by his
own General Staff to withdraw; and a check would have been given to
his pretensions which might well have been fatal to his rule'. Note the
way in which that sentence slides imperceptibly from a confident 'there
is no doubt', via two hopeful 'would have been[s]' to a suggestive 'might
well have been'. It was on such a frail thread of syntax that hung

Churchill's oft repeated claim that (as he put it at Fulton), 'there never was a war in all history easier to prevent'. But there was as a matter of fact considerable doubt about the premise on which his logic rested, and while we might now agree that war could well have been prevented from breaking out in 1939, that would only be because it would already have started in 1936 or 1938. A war started over the Rhineland or Czechoslovakia would perhaps have been a lesser and shorter war which killed far fewer people – no inconsiderable matter, even if it was not what Churchill himself ever claimed – but it would have been war nevertheless, with all the costs, risks and uncertainties that any war brings in its train. Nor does it need hindsight to reach the view that Hitler would not have accepted a permanent setback achieved simply by bluffing him: he did in fact decide that he had been bluffed in 1938 at Munich, and it was partly because of this that he could not be deterred in 1939. Even at the time, Chamberlain put it rather well when he argued that the expectation of Hitler accepting humiliation without a fight was 'not a reliable estimate of a mad dictator's reactions'. In any case, Churchill was not, as the memoirs would have us believe, 'a lone voice calling for rearmament in the 1930s, but one of a number of actors – in office, officialdom, the military and parliament – engaged in a complex bureaucratic battle to shift the government from its early ignorance and complacency', as David Reynolds has put it (a point echoed at the same 2001 conference by Stuart Ball). Within that campaign, his priorities were only proved to be correct because his judgement was not, in that his call for priority for the air force was vindicated by the RAF's victory in September 1940, but the Battle of Britain was only necessary anyway because of the failure of the French army in May and June, a subject on which he had shown no better foresight than anyone else. It is at least arguable that, had the British Government followed Churchill's advice before 1939, it would have been scarcely better prepared than it actually was to avoid the terrible circumstance of fighting on alone in 1940.[106]

The intuitive 'counter-factuals' – and the literary devices with which they were persuasively put forward – that Churchill used to draw such sweeping conclusions from the Rhineland Crisis of 1936, or from Eden's resignation in 1938, or from the chances of an effective alliance with Russia to deter Hitler, were an old trick. Robin Prior has shown just how extensively Churchill had used the same devices when writing *The*

World Crisis. He had for example spun such a complex series of 'if onlys' around the Dardanelles episode, and over the development of the tank, that the reader finds it extremely difficult to disentangle serious possibilities from sheer fantasy. And in almost every case the issue was what great things might have been achieved 'if only' Churchill's advice had been followed more closely, with little rigour applied to the analysis of what chances there had ever actually been for such an outcome. As in revisiting the Great War in the 1920s, so Churchill worked in revisiting the Second World War after 1945, except of course that this time he had a far better record to defend. But it would be over-critical to assume that Churchill used these devices simply in self-defence. His private secretary, Anthony Montague Browne, noted rather that they were simply part of his conversation, the way he naturally viewed historical narratives. He had long ago published a fascinating essay on 'If Lee had not won the Battle of Gettysburg' (so achieving a double-bluff effect), and 'rather liked building an ephemeral but fascinating narrative on the radical consequences of a different single political or military decision'.[107]

Equally, though, it is difficult to match *The Gathering Storm*'s account of a six-year lone crusade with the fact that Churchill did not cast a single vote against the Government on foreign or defence policy before the Munich Crisis, while he did cast adverse votes over India. He denounced Gandhi in even stronger language than he applied to Hitler, while refusing to attack Franco at all. The Spanish Civil War, for most contemporaries the acid test of anti-fascist credentials, is notable mainly by its absence from *The Gathering Storm*, for Churchill's record on Spain was no better than Baldwin's or Chamberlain's. More broadly, as Richard Powers long ago showed from an analysis of his Commons speeches, Churchill did not quickly denounce the Naval Treaty made with Hitler in 1935, he hoped for a deal with Mussolini to split the fascist dictators, he did not at first support effective action against Mussolini over Abyssinia, he was apparently relieved when Britain and France did *not* act quickly to kick Hitler out of the Rhineland, and he only began even to abstain in foreign policy divisions in May 1938. Late in 1937, Churchill was still advocating the return to Germany of colonies confiscated in 1919, as part of a general settlement of European grievances, a policy that has been more generally associated with Chamberlain than with Churchill. It would be hard to grasp from *The Gathering Storm* the optimism that Churchill felt when Neville Chamberlain became Prime Minister in 1937, but that is certainly what he told readers of his column in *Collier's* at the time, rejecting any idea that Chamberlain was cold and unfeeling, and asserting rather that he had a passionate belief and a good record as an advocate of rearmament. And when Eden resigned the Foreign Office in February 1938, Churchill was fourth quickest of four hundred Tory MPs to sign a round robin that expressed undiminished confidence in Neville Chamberlain.[108] In this last case at least, *The Gathering Storm* works hard to give exactly the opposite impression.

But throughout the 1950s such things were just not said, and not until the mid-1960s did any official papers appear that would provide evidential support for revisionist accounts of the war years either. When well-argued new views did appear, for example in A. J. P. Taylor's *The Origins of the Second World War* in 1961 and Martin Gilbert and Richard Gott's *The Appeasers* in 1963, they tended to find new ways to denounce the makers of British policy in the 1930s rather than re-evaluate the role of Churchill in his wilderness years. Taylor, by arguing persuasively that the Second World War had been virtually caused by the appeasers, reinforced what Churchill had always claimed – if on different grounds. Apart from Powers' little-known and now well-forgotten article, only Donald Cameron Watt subjected Churchill's own 1930s views on defence to serious scrutiny before the official papers and the arrival of committed defenders of Baldwin and Chamberlain transformed the debate anyway in the 1970s, and far too few of the writers of secondary literature took any account of their findings anyway. As Professor Jack Plumb put it in 1969, other historians of the war had mainly moved down 'the broad avenues which he [Churchill] drove through the war's confusion and complexity . . . Churchill the historian lies at the very heart of all historiography of the Second World War, and will always remain there.'[109] The relatively uncritical collaboration of the major figures of the British historical profession in this process, discussed in the previous chapter, goes a long way to explain its durability.

In innumerable ways, then, the exaggerated myth of Churchill as a lone figure, single-mindedly and unrelentingly warning the world of an avoidable war and the need for strong defence measures entered the vocabulary of politics throughout the English-speaking world and was recounted endlessly, both in celebration of Churchill himself and in support of whatever strong-arm policy the speaker wished to justify. In

1954, President Eisenhower, applying the lessons of Munich to Indo-China, argued to Churchill himself that 'we failed to halt Hirohito, Mussolini and Hitler by not acting in unity and in time ... May it not be that our nations have learned something from the lesson?' Even though Britain and France were then celebrating the fiftieth anniversaries of 1904's Entente Cordiale, Churchill remained unmoved by such appeals and would not commit British troops to back the French in their faraway colony of which he knew little and cared even less.[110] He had after all, only a few months earlier, announced that he had reached his seventy-eighth year without ever hearing the word 'Cambodia' and did not intend to start now – though this was just as likely to be the effect of the elderly premier switching off his hearing aid or just 'switching off' mentally whenever topics of conversation bored him.

When Lyndon Johnson struggled ten years later over the key decision to commit American ground troops to Indo-China, he was heard frequently intoning the message of Munich as Churchill had told the story – and it cannot have helped that these crucial Washington debates actually occurred in the period of Churchill's final illness, death and funeral, weeks in which the entire world went mad over all things Churchillian. With the decision made, Johnson was defending it later in 1965 on familiar terms: 'from Munich until today, we have learned that to yield to aggression brings only greater threats and brings even more destructive wars'.[111] In the same year, Harry Truman, equally keen to discover Munich in Vietnam, reiterated the story of Churchill preaching in the 1930s against an avoidable war, 'but although his solitary voice calling for action in the thirties to prevent the last War was wasted, the world seems to have learned its lesson'.[112] The next Democratic President felt much the same; it was reported in 1980 that Jimmy Carter was 're-reading Winston Churchill's history [sic] of World War II, studying in particular that part where Hitler moves unchallenged into the Rhineland in 1936. "Nobody sent a clear signal to Hitler," says the President, "War became inevitable. We are not going to let that happen."'[113]

Even with the cold warrior Ronald Reagan in office in 1983, the *Washington Post* turned a review of the BBC's *Winston Churchill: The Wilderness Years* into an appeal to 'struthious politicians' (those who like ostriches buried their heads in the sands) to recognise the re-emergence of a Russian threat under Andropov. 'So far have we drifted from the lessons of World War II, that it is now chic in some academic circles to disparage Churchill as a warmonger.' Later in the same year, Senator John Tower was asking despairingly, citing Churchill in the 1930s, 'have we learned nothing from history?' It was clear too that the *New York Times*, when reviewing Martin Gilbert's *Finest Hour* volume of the official biography on Churchill in 1940–1, detected contemporary parallels in offering the Churchillian theme for the volume as 'How the British people held the fort ALONE till those who hitherto had been half blind were half ready'. Unlike Randolph Churchill for volumes one and two, Gilbert eschewed the adoption of great over-arching themes for the later volumes of the official biography. So the *New York Times* picked its own by quoting one from the war memoirs, and thus (characteristically) allowed Churchill in effect to review posthumously a biography of himself.[114] It was clearly Margaret Thatcher's 'iron lady' stance that was in mind here, and the same Churchillian parallel was emphasised in the following year when her Government's decision to open Churchill's wartime Whitehall bunker to visitors came to fruition. Her speech on that occasion had, said *The Times*, 'more than a hint of patriotic nostalgia'. When the Foreign Secretary Geoffrey Howe ventured a mild note of dissent from her support of America's invasion of Grenada, the Prime Minister lectured her colleagues for quite some time on the need to stand up to aggressors, ending with an appeal to them not to become a cabinet of appeasers. As one of them privately told John Cole of the BBC, the rest 'kept [their] heads below the parapet, hoping we could soon get on to discussing milk quotas'. Arguably, then, they were indeed a cabinet of appeasers, though not quite in the sense that she had in mind.[115]

The simplistic idea of appeasement that derived from an over-eager acceptance of a concept that Churchill's memoirs had anyway simplified in the first place proved to be a trap for most of his successors. In 1956, the Labour leader Gaitskell identified Nasser as a new Hitler, and Prime Minister Eden diagnosed the nationalisation of the Suez Canal Company as 'the Rhineland phase' of the new dictator's expansionist plans. Dean Rusk, while acknowledging that the fact that Hitler was an Austrian and Mao Tse-tung Chinese did make a difference, nevertheless insisted on the Munich analogy for his Far Eastern policy in the 1960s. This was rarely helpful, for the Churchillian legend of 'Munich' could all too easily become a virility test which engendered a wholesale loss of perspective, as

Churchill himself privately noted of Eden over Suez. Indeed Arthur Schlesinger, suggesting in 1967 that the use of 'Munich' as a political icon in the post-war world would make a splendid topic for a PhD thesis, wondered whether the student might not find that 'the multitude of errors committed in the name of "Munich" may exceed the original error of 1938'.[116]

Even Churchill the politician had to struggle to escape from the restraints imposed by the rhetorical success of Churchill the historian. He was already explaining to the House of Commons by 1950 that 'No appeasement':

> is a good slogan for the country . . . However . . . it requires to be more precisely defined. What we really mean, I think, is no appeasement through weakness or fear. Appeasement in itself may be good or bad according to circumstances. Appeasement from weakness and fear is alike futile and fatal. Appeasement from strength is magnanimous and noble and might be the surest and perhaps the only path to world peace.

This amounted to a near-restatement of what British policy had been in the 1920s when Churchill had been a Minister and the country had *dis*armed, and it came perilously close to saying that there actually were no generally applicable lessons from the 1930s, since it would all be 'according to circumstances'. But he might have saved his breath, for the word 'appeasement' steadily declined into an over-used term of abuse, and even Churchill himself had to change his language and talk of 'easement' when seeking – unsuccessfully – to get support for winding down the Cold War in and after 1952. He was unsuccessful partly because his American allies had all read *The Gathering Storm* and therefore knew that you must never show weakness when dealing with a dictator.

By the time of his death, and as a result of his post-war speeches and writings as much as of his actual war record, Churchill was seen (as Malcolm MacDonald observed) as 'a paragon of all the virtues in both peace and war'. When Viscount Alanbrooke and General Sir John Ferguson each published books in which their real admiration of Churchill was tempered by criticism of his judgement and temperament, they came under heavy fire. The *Daily Telegraph* urged such 'authors of vinegary memoirs' to abstain from publication, and invited them to remember that they, 'however eminent, are certainly lesser; however

Daily Mail, 2 November 1959

honest, are no more humble; however qualified, are not so qualified' as Churchill, either to lead or to write about leadership.

Churchill and Alanbrooke had formed a crucial but always stormy relationship at the heart of Britain's war machine, but they had never felt much personal sympathy for each other. Churchill was often incandescent with rage at Alanbrooke's stubborn refusal to waste time on evaluating his wilder strategic ideas, and by his frequent direct negatives which he regarded almost as insubordination, while the organised and tidy-minded Alanbrooke regarded Churchill's methods of working ('the reverse of orderly', as even Jock Colville put it) as a terrible waste of his and other people's time when there was no time to spare. After the war, they rarely met, but Alanbrooke invited Arthur Bryant to publish his diaries in 1954 as a response to the way in which Churchill had portrayed him in his war memoirs. He had carefully read and critically annotated the books as they came out, and found some of Churchill's dismissive accounts of his wartime role extremely wounding, some of Churchill's claims to credit for military successes unhistorical and unjustified. Bryant initially responded (writing actually on Churchill's eightieth birthday) that 'because of their complete truth and frankness ... the diary and notes cannot be published in full for many years'. When the first volume, *The Turn of the Tide*, was published in 1957, Alanbrooke contributed a nervous foreword that explained that any criticisms and carping about Churchill that now appeared should be seen in the context of a broad admiration for his inspiring leadership. 'Such scattered expressions of irritation or impatience at the defects that arose out of his very greatness are insignificant when set against the magnitude of his achievement.' Churchill, he wrote, was 'the most wonderful man I have ever met; it is a source of never-ending interest studying him and getting to realise that occasionally such human beings make their appearance on this earth – human beings who stand out head and shoulders above all others'. Just how much critical material was left out altogether in the attempt to appease devotees of Winston Churchill was only clear when a full edition of the diaries came out more than forty years later.

Nevertheless, the diaries' publication became a great publishing *cause célèbre*, for William Collins had made a big thing out of their appearance (presumably hoping to reap similar benefits from those that had attended Churchill's memoirs), invited twelve hundred people to a launch party at the Dorchester, and secured extensive serialisation in the *Sunday Times*. First Bryant, who was after all by then a great admirer of Churchill, began to get cold feet and sought unavailingly to withdraw the most anti-Churchill extracts from the press, and then almost all those lined up to speak at the launch party became equally jittery, including Alanbrooke himself, so the whole affair turned into an extended act of apology rather than the celebration of an important book. Despite even this much contrition, the press was especially hostile, most of all that part of it owned by Lord Beaverbrook, though hostility extended to such impeccable reviewers as the *Times Literary Supplement*. Bryant and Alanbrooke had the feel of men who had done something that deserved to be celebrated in a Bateman cartoon rather than something that contributed to the historical record, though the general view was that this was Bryant's fault rather than Alanbrooke's, Churchill and his circle as ever underestimating Alanbrooke. Churchill himself had never been personally close to Alanbrooke, who lacked all those extrovert qualities of personality that made for a congenial conversationalist.

When he first saw an advance copy of the published diaries, he seemed not to mind too much (and had not perhaps read them with great attention), but as his friends and family became ever more indignant, he took the same line and was said to be deeply upset. This breach then upset Alanbrooke more than Churchill and his friends, so impregnable was the Churchillians' armour of self-assurance about the war. Martin Gilbert quotes in the official biography the letter that Churchill sent to Alanbrooke, thanking him for the *inscription* in the book, but, since this was also a pointed way of not thanking him for the book itself, it may not be quite right to describe the action as 'generous as ever'. Indeed, according to Jock Colville, Churchill soon afterwards 'deliberately and ostentatiously' turned his back on Alanbrooke rather than talk to him, the only person he ever saw Churchill treat that way. This was a response then that was less than generous, but it probably never even occurred to either Churchill or his admirers how much he had upset proud men like Alanbrooke among his wartime entourage by claiming all the credit for 'my strategy' in the war memoirs.[117]

Interestingly, it was the appearance of Alanbrooke's critical diaries that finally convinced G. M. Trevelyan of Churchill's greatness, because they offered documentary proof from a critic that Churchill had been an outstanding war leader.

So far from lowering my estimate of Winston, this book, to me, has raised it. He was not very considerate of his advisers in the matter of taking counsel at two o'clock in the morning etc., but the great impression left on me by the facts of the book is this: he asked for advice and very often took it, sometimes contrary to what he had first thought himself. This habit of taking counsel, combined with his own personal qualities, is what won the war. Napoleon fell because he could never take counsel. His Marshals were only his servants, whereas Winston treated his generals as his advisers.

A. J. P. Taylor took much the same view, reviewing Bryant's second volume of the Alanbrooke diaries, *Triumph in the West*, as demonstrating that Churchill 'emerges from the record greater than ever – impossibly difficult to deal with in private, but always rising to the challenge of events when it came to the point'. As Bryant himself reassured Alan-brooke in 1957, Churchill emerged from the published diaries as 'more human', and thus more believable, than 'the rather boring and infallible image which a stupid propaganda is creating'. Those who had retained their critical faculties could see this and recognise Churchill's greatness all the more clearly when stripped of its excesses of unnecessary adulation, but there have in truth been few chances to do so of the type offered by Bryant and Alanbrooke in 1957.[118]

Alanbrooke's colleague General Sir John Kennedy used the same tactic as Alanbrooke had attempted, admitting in the foreword to his book that 'we sometimes longed for a leader with more balance and less brilliance', but following this remark with a diary extract that concedes that 'despite [Churchill's] strategical vagaries, he is a great leader'.[119] The same literary tactic adopted by Alanbrooke and Kennedy was used even as recently as 1993, by the naval historian Richard Ollard. He prefaced an essay on 'Churchill and the Navy' – a devastating catalogue of the great man's lack of strategic insight, absence of feel for the real naval perspective, and faulty judgement – with the remark that, for those old enough to remember the war, 'no criticism of Churchill can be more than a scholiast's note on the imperishable achievement of his having saved the country and, arguably, civilisation itself in 1940'.[120] Nevertheless, even with these types of disclaimers, such books invariably created an outcry, though Kennedy's probably did not do as much as Alanbrooke's to dent Churchill's self-assurance. After reading that Kennedy had written disparagingly of Churchill's war leadership in *The Business of War*, and had cited Menzies himself as one of Churchill's wartime critics, Robert Menzies sent to Churchill a statement which he had had placed in the Australian press, taking Churchill's side of the argument. He also sent a letter expressing his regret that a great man's retirement should be disturbed by such petty squabbles. Churchill's reply was warm but disingenuous. He thanked Menzies for 'your very kind remarks' but claimed that 'I myself cannot recollect Kennedy either, though I no doubt met him.' Since Kennedy had held a senior post at the War Office for most of the war, while Churchill was Minister of Defence, and they had met often and explosively, this part of Churchill's own history had clearly been erased from the mental record.[121] It may indeed be the fact that Alanbrooke was too well known to be so easily ignored that ignited such a controversy over his diary.

One of the more temperate responses to these early independent assessments of Churchill was Lord Ismay, who advised Americans to remember that 'the British people the world over should thank God that in the hour of their trial their principal servant was the greatest Englishman of his time, perhaps of all time', a view with which the likes of Alanbrooke would easily have agreed, but which did not deal with his evidence of how difficult Churchill was to deal with. However, as Lord Moran wrote a few years later, nervously thinking no doubt about the effect of publishing his own diaries,

> there was a feeling of dismay when [Alanbrooke's] *Diaries* were published that the legend had been scratched. Nobody, it appeared, wanted to argue about Winston's skill or lack of skill in planning the strategy of the war, though that is the crucial issue raised by the *Diaries*. Nobody was prepared to see him treated dispassionately as an historical figure. People disliked the *Diaries* because they loved Winston.

The inviolability of Churchill's good name was even more apparent in the last years before his death. When the just-founded *Private Eye* directed its attention to him in 1963, he became the first man successfully to sue it for libel. One of the *Eye*'s writers commented apprehensively after the action that 'the whole establishment is hanging over our heads like a damned sword of Damocles'. In February 1964, Richard Crossman unwisely suggested in a newspaper article that Churchill arranged for the unnecessary bombing of Milan in 1943, as a 'savage reaction' to a propaganda coup brought off by the Political Warfare Executive (in which Crossman himself was involved), a raid that took place in bad weather and therefore caused unnecessary RAF casualties. Under a hail of criticism and the threat of a libel action, Crossman rapidly withdrew the claim, offering Churchill the most abject of apologies. He accepted that his article had been 'false, defamatory and reckless' – an extremely damaging admission from someone who hoped shortly to be a cabinet Minister, and made a 'substantial' donation to the RAF Benevolent Fund.[122]

Occasionally, in their enthusiasm, Churchill's defenders scored own goals, as when Monty lectured his fellow military autobiographers in 1957; he told an ITV interviewer, adopting the same method of auto-biography in the mirror that Churchill himself favoured:

> I think [that Churchill] was a tremendous national leader and I think that he played a part in winning the war greater than

any other single person. I am very grieved at the sniping at home which goes on in these books, saying what a difficult man he was to get along with. All great men are difficult.[123]

Now, who else *could* he have had in mind?

Churchill's apparent immunity from criticism in the 1950s was even extended backwards from 1939 to his early life, which had been open season for criticism in the past. When Trumbull Higgins wrote critically on Churchill and the Dardanelles, the *New York Times* complained that he had merely found little faults of detail and ignored the big plus of Churchill's service to humanity in two world wars.[124] Tom Harrisson thought that the wartime Churchill had already become a sort of 'emotional deep shelter' for the British people, which is largely how he remained, and hence an attack on Churchill was resented as a threat to the source of needed reassurance; Peter Clarke more recently argued a similar viewpoint, that Britons in the 1950s ignored the realities of the post-war situation which were blindingly obvious to foreigners, simply by 'closing one's eyes and thinking of Winston Churchill'.[125]

In this context it is important to remind ourselves that his reputation did not *have* to soar in this way in the post-war period. After all, Montgomery, whose popularity as a war hero with the British people stood second only to Churchill's own in 1945, then went steadily downhill, so that he ended his life generally regarded as foolish, egotistical and eccentric – a decline caused to a large extent by memoirs that backfired badly and a post-retirement career that was *seen to be* a desperate, demeaning search for publicity, Churchill managed both manoeuvres far more skilfully. Montgomery's most recent biographer argued that Monty's fall from grace was due to inherent character defects, in that he lacked subtlety, grace, flexibility of mind, cunning, charm and the ability to see and exploit other people's weak points. Anthony Eden was only one of the many who became after 1945 exasperated by Monty's too obvious search for fame, and the accumulating evidence that he had been carefully working on this as early as 1942, a reflection occasioned by his receipt in 1946 of Montgomery's *Ten Chapters*, effectively an album of tributes to himself collected and given to those who might do him good in future. Montgomery's overbearing manner was in any case more reminiscent of Churchill during the war than of the mellowed figure of later years. Lord Moran for example recorded a tale of Montgomery instructing Vi Attlee on the croquet lawn at Chequers, though she was by far the better player (and a formidable character in her own right). Eventually she laid down her mallet with the words, 'I know a great deal about croquet. Please don't order me about. It is quite intolerable.' Montgomery was for a time abashed by this unexpected sign of resistance, 'but after a little he again began directing the game. He cannot help it.'[126]

But Winston Churchill had each of the necessary weapons in his personal armoury and used them all to great effect. He derived considerable pleasure from the fact that Britain's main battle tank of the later war years had been named after him, but it was often a self-mocking pleasure that noted that 'Churchills' had been prone to mechanical breakdown. He would certainly never have made any remark equivalent to Montgomery's to Jock Colville in 1947, that he thought that British soldiers would like to be known as 'Monties' rather than 'Tommies'. General Sir Leslie Hollis recounted to Robert Bruce Lockhart in 1948 the story of how the 1943 victory parade in Tripoli had been filmed, for the documentary *Tunisian Victory*.

> Monty put on a tremendous show on the square for Winston, but really of course for himself. When Winston arrived, the bands played and Monty strode forward to greet him with the most fulsome flattery, such as 'You are the greatest Prime Minister that Britain has ever possessed, and I am happy to have the honour of greeting you here on this wonderful occasion.' [Churchill], a little abashed, felt he had better reply in the same manner and started off with, 'You are the greatest general . . .'

When Churchill saw the film, however, he insisted that this material be not used in the documentary, since 'it makes me almost as big a cad as Monty'. It is, alas, hard to believe that Montgomery himself would ever have applied the same self-denying ordinance.[127]

Victor Feske has shown how Churchill as a 'public historian' came at the end of a tradition that went back to Lord Macaulay and had in the twentieth century included Belloc, the Hammonds, the Webbs and Trevelyan. The 'public historian', on this reading, not only aimed to appeal directly to the public through a mass readership, but also sought to inculcate an optimistic, liberal-valued view of the country's present and future through the reinterpretation of its past. This essentially

nineteenth-century view of the role of history, as something more than
an academic discipline, became increasingly disconnected from the realities of 'the terrible twentieth century', as Churchill himself frequently
described it, since it was becoming so hard to remain cheerful about a
liberal future. G. M. Trevelyan's 'retreat' to the narrowness of academic
Cambridge and to centuries other than his own as subjects for his
research and writing seems to Feske to embody the problem. After 1945,
there was in fact a more general European retreat from contemporary
history. This shift of emphasis in several countries recently occupied by
the Nazis produced wonderful insights into other cultures and earlier
periods, for example through the *Annales* school of social history in
France, with its concentration on the early modern period, but little
writing on the times in which its practitioners lived. In the 1920s, the
Liberal journalist Peter Wright had applied exactly the same analysis to
Churchill himself. The volumes of Churchill's *World Crisis* recorded for
Wright:

> a life's disappointment. For Mr Churchill does not want to be
> merely a man of words and a rhetorician, but a man of acts
> and a ruler ... But he must console himself, and reflect that
> hardly anyone has ever done great things and written fine books.
> In life a choice must be made. If he did not vindicate the
> superiority of English fleets to the rest of the world, he has
> asserted the superiority of English letters, and that may give
> him a higher and more enduring fame.

After 1945, however, Churchill could fit the bill on both counts. He
related to and used academic historians but remained their master in
the books he wrote, and he both practised and preached history to the
mass market. Because he had an unusually Tory slant to his respect for
liberal democratic values, he could incorporate a respect for power
politics and an understanding of national defence into the story. On
this reading, the liberal values in Churchill's histories became vastly
stronger, since they had acquired the means to defend themselves from
the most terrible forms of contemporary attack, militaristic and totalitarian aggression. In Churchill, therefore, liberal optimism seemed also
to be realism. He noted for example, in an article in 1935, that the
possibility of another war was being described by many writers as like

the inevitable onrush of a Niagara Falls, with the 'helplessness of man' swirling 'amid the current of destiny'.

> Nevertheless, I shall continue to proclaim that it is still in our power to ward off war, to curb barbarism, to preserve liberty, and to avert our doom. For what else indeed is free choice given to Man, and wherefore was this unique biped endowed with his glorious comprehension and mystic powers?

It was exactly this message that could inspire during the 1930s – on the opposite American coasts – the young John Kennedy and the young Caspar Weinberger, each of them deriving inspiration from *The World Crisis* before Churchill's rehabilitation even began in 1939, and each true to the faith even in the sceptical environment of an isolationist Harvard. As we have seen, many contemporaries compared Churchill to Julius Caesar, in that each refused to choose between a life of action and being a man of letters. Feske's analysis concludes in 1939, since that is where the focus of his book ends, incorporating the *History of the English-Speaking Peoples* into his argument since it was substantially written by 1939, but barely touching on the war memoirs. Those six volumes of war memoirs were, however, the crowning glory of Churchill's work as a liberal, 'public historian', for they chart the way in which democracy's weaknesses could be overcome even in a battle with its greatest foes, how a leader committed to democratic values could inspire his people and their allies, and how optimistic a future this holds out before us if it is properly understood. Being even more of a Tory and far less of a liberal than Churchill, Arthur Bryant tried valiantly to become his successor in this field of public history, but, since his ideal world was always in the past rather than the future, he could only partially succeed and gradually came to be seen more as an outdated survival rather than as a Churchillian beacon of hope.[128]

The story does not end quite here, for Churchill's writing of history and his career in making it had always been indissolubly linked. His Fulton speech, explicitly drawing on memories of the 1930s and re-cycling them to illuminate the post-war world, and the rallying of the Western democracies to resist Communist totalitarianism which this facilitated, was therefore the activist half of the story. However, during exactly the same years Churchill was using his war memoirs to achieve the same purposes more reflectively. If, as Sir Walter Scott once wrote, all historians secretly despise themselves for not being able to take part personally in the great events about which they write, then no wonder that the British historical fraternity was so in awe of Churchill, the man who 'lived history', 'made history' and 'wrote history' – if not always necessarily in quite that order.[129]

PART TWO

5

'The Maker of Modern Ireland'?
Churchill and the Celts

IT MIGHT BE EXPECTED that the reputation of 'the greatest living Englishman' would have been viewed very differently in 'the rottenest parts of these islands of ours' which 'we've left in the hands of three unfriendly powers' (as Flanders and Swann were unflatteringly putting it at about the time of Churchill's funeral). This is not the less interesting when it is remembered that Irishmen had fought for and won a qualified independence during Churchill's actual political career, processes in which he had been closely involved, while Scotland and Wales were just beginning to take their quests for separate national identities into party politics during his last years. The non-English parts of the British Isles provide, however, not a single model of differentiation from the English, but a fascinating pattern of variation. Cornwall and Wales received the Churchill legend rather less positively than England. Often called near the end of his life 'the greatest living Cornishman', A. L. Rowse was proud both of that sub-Churchillian title and of his own work in propagating Churchill's fame and legend. His county of Cornwall was another matter, and, when dragging up every possible example of the contribution of Cornwall and Cornishmen to British history in order to impress an audience of Devonians, he was not able to produce a single Churchill contact apart from his own, which was 'brief but not without significance'. There are no memorials to Churchill in Cornwall, he received no freedoms there, and there seems to have been only one thoroughfare named in his honour, and that one is in Saltash, almost within sight of the Devon border. By way of contrast, the other five South-Western counties of England have thirty-seven Churchill streets between them, and none has fewer than five. Scotland, on the other hand, was extremely supportive, though in a way quite distinct from England, and Churchill was always willing to parade his personal links with Scotland, even if never quite forgiving Dundee for throwing him out as its MP in 1922.

Ireland, entirely predictably, offered two opposed responses to the Churchill myth. In the Irish Republic, responses were heavily conditioned by Churchill's lifetime duel with Eamon de Valera and by the issue of Irish neutrality in the Second World War, so that almost alone in Europe the Irish made very little of Churchill's death and funeral in 1965. North of the border, Ulster paraded its fealty to Churchill as a core value within post-war Loyalism, and Belfast probably celebrated Churchill's eightieth birthday and his death and funeral more elaborately than any English city. Unionist politicians and newspapers reassured themselves in the post-war period that Churchill had 'become' a staunch supporter of Ulster – a word which hinted at earlier anxieties but which was well justified by his warm tributes to the wartime role of Northern Ireland and his reiterated assurances after 1922 that Ulster would never be coerced into an Irish union. This was, however, a majority response, and Catholic, Nationalist opinion in Ulster largely opted out of such Unionist demonstrations of loyalty to Churchill's embodiment of the United Kingdom. Nothing brought out that divide more starkly than the fact that Belfast's 'united' church service to memorialise Churchill in January 1965 was actually a union only of Protestant groups but was attended by most of the Northern Ireland Government, while no Catholic memorial service seems ever to have been held.[1]

The Welsh case is perhaps dealt with most easily, for Churchill rarely went to the country and almost certainly did not think of it as being any more materially different from England than was, say, Yorkshire. He had after all grown up in a generation which took such things for granted, and did not even consider Monmouthshire to be part of Wales anyway.[2] It is notable for example that when he came to describe in his *History of the English-Speaking Peoples* the conquest of Wales by Edward I and the incorporation of Wales into the English Parliament by Henry VIII, he did so in terms which suggested that these events had been unequivocally a good thing for all concerned. Nowhere indeed was Churchill more a Whiggish historian than when writing about the development of the United Kingdom, but even there he was more sensitive to the national separateness of Scotland and Ireland than he ever appears to have been about Wales. When during his second premiership he was asked questions about Welsh devolution, he offered uncompromisingly bleak responses, considerably more insensitive than replies to equivalent questions about Scotland, and on one occasion even replied to a Parliamentary Question on the subject in Welsh, the two words that he had specially learned for the occasion then being translated (by Churchill himself) as 'Nothing doing'.[3]

Churchill seems rarely to have gone to Wales, there being for example no equivalent of the annual conference of Scottish Unionists which required his regular attendance in the decade after 1945. And though he did speak as party leader at the main party conference in 1948, when it was held in Llandudno, in those days the leader did not attend the conference as such and merely descended at the end of the week to address a mass rally, a visit that required him to spend only a few hours in the Principality. Similarly, he visited Cardiff in February 1950 to address an election rally in the city's Ninian Park football stadium, and, though he made graceful remarks about the country and its history, he also spoke defensively and at length about Tonypandy and rejected outright the case for a Welsh parliament: 'it would not be good for you and it would not be good for us'. The truth was that the Conservatives had only four Welsh MPs after the 1945 election, and only six when Churchill became Prime Minister for the last time in 1951, so Wales was never going to attract much of his attention. That election speech contained warm references to Lloyd George (which can hardly have been what Welsh Tories wanted to hear) but none of the usual tributes to local valour in the world wars with which he laced every address in Scotland and in Ulster.[4]

Churchill had begun the Ninian Park address by remarking that 'it gave me great pleasure to drive along the splendid road you have named after me', Churchill Way in the centre of Cardiff, so named in 1949 (though against vocal opposition from Labour councillors, who even then brought up memories of Tonypandy). He had also agreed to accept the freedom of the city of Cardiff in 1945 (though the city could not attract enough of his attention actually to confer it until 1948), and was also by that time a freeman of Pembroke. What is striking here is that Cardiff and Pembroke are rightly considered to be the most 'English' of the South Walian towns, that there was no move to erect a statue or any equivalent memorial to Churchill in the Welsh capital, and that very few Welsh municipalities followed the example of Cardiff by naming streets after him either. Apart from the freedom of Aberystwyth, conferred in 1951, in the Welsh-speaking areas of West and North Wales, and in the coalfields of the South, there would be no freedom or similar honour offered and apparently no Churchill thoroughfares either.[5]

Churchill's post-war discourse with Wales largely centred on two issues, the memory of Lloyd George and the myth of Tonypandy. Lloyd George was celebrated after his death by Churchill partly through genuine respect for an early political sparring partner and a man he had thought of so highly that he had even offered him ministerial office in 1940. He paid an emotional parliamentary tribute and was strongly supportive of the schemes to erect a statue of LG in the House of Commons (though he refused to support a backbencher's motion that the conventional ten-year interval after a death before a statue could be proposed should be reduced to two in the case of LG. In Churchill's own case, of course, he was willing to be commemorated even in his own lifetime.)[6] His pleasure at being able to appoint Lloyd George's son Gwilym to ministerial office in 1951 had, however, little to do with his Welsh blood, rather more to do with his desire to unite his Liberal past with his Tory present, so that he was disappointed not to be able to pull off the double by including Cyril Asquith too. More often, Churchill's praise of David Lloyd George was merely the prelude to an attack on his *bête noire* Aneurin Bevan and a repudiation of the idea that Bevan had now become a 'second Lloyd George', embodying the left-inclined Welsh national will as the first had done.

Tonypandy was, however, a real issue because the Labour Party insisted that it be so in Wales at any election when Churchill led the Conservatives. Churchill recognised the threat and sought to head it off, with speeches and even with threats of legal action. At Ninian Park, before he had said anything at all about Conservative policy or his party's criticisms of the Labour Government, he asked his listeners to:

> allow [him] to tell you about an incident which, though it happened a long time ago, was a cause of controversy . . . I am told that the Socialists and Communists continually spread the story that I used the troops to shoot down the Welsh miners and that the story of Tonypandy will never be forgotten.

He was quite content that it be remembered, 'provided that the truth is told', and he then explained at length what that truth was – from his own perspective of course. That delving into an incident forty years old took up more than a tenth of his speech in Cardiff, and showed just how seriously he treated Labour's charges.[7] Labour clearly felt itself to be on a winner when shouting about Tonypandy in Wales, and resurrected the charge at each general election. In 1945 it hardly mattered, given all the other factors working against the Conservatives, and in any case Churchill's personal popularity as war leader may have made opponents wary of mounting personal attacks, but in 1950 the charge was very firmly made. Ness Edwards, Labour MP and former miner, returned to the attack after Churchill's own speech in Cardiff, and subjected his account of the events of 1910 to close scrutiny. Offering documentary evidence from the contemporary *Western Mail* and from Sir Neville Macready's autobiography (Macready commanded the actual troops in 1910) he concluded that the true version was what Labour had always said, and that it had been recorded 'not by a romantic Tory politician but by the Tory newspaper at the time, and by the commanding officer of the forces employed. Mr Churchill did use the military against the miners at Tonypandy and the miners will never forget it.' Over the next few days, Churchill's measured reply to Edwards, stressing constitutional issues (the Home Secretary did not have any power to do what Edwards said Churchill had done), was met with further vituperation from Edwards about Churchill's 'masquerade of the truth'. Others now joined in, almost entirely to Churchill's disadvantage: the Mineworkers' President Sir William Lawther, for example, argued that:

It has taken Mr Churchill 40 years to give an explanation of the Tonypandy episode in 1910 . . . and his explanation of 1910 is as far wrong as his explanation of the facts of 1950. But it does show that his friends of 1910, like his friends of 1950, had no objection to using oppressive and repressive measures against the workers. It was his treatment of the miners of that period that has helped the miners to understand that neither in 1910 nor in 1950 are either he or his associates the friends of the miners or anyone else outside the charmed circle in which he moves, lives and has his being.[8]

Lawther was from Northumberland rather than Wales, and was speaking to the Leicestershire miners when he made those claims. In other words, Tonypandy was a convenient stick with which to beat Churchill anywhere in the heavy industrial areas. In this sense, the use of Tonypandy by Labour hardly differed from the use of Churchill's record in the General Strike or the more generalised Labour claim that his past record showed that he was 'anti-working class'. The mining areas of the North-East and of Yorkshire were no more likely than South Wales to forget such things, and there would be no more Churchill streets in such areas than in Wales.[9] Churchill's past kept coming up to haunt the Conservatives in the early post-war general elections, exploited by Labour for all it was worth in order to consolidate the additional working-class vote that had come its way in 1945, and what was happening in Wales was merely a more specific local example of that process.[10]

Churchill himself took it a good deal more personally, resenting the continual reiteration of what he saw as a wicked lie (as for the most part it was)[11] about an event in which he had actually behaved with uncharacteristic caution and discretion. Whether it was wise to keep on about it on the political platform is another matter altogether, and it is noticeable that few other Conservatives rallied to their leader's defence, preferring rather to concentrate on other issues on which they might expect to score more runs. One final point might be made. Nursing the grievance that his past was being horribly misrepresented, as he did, Churchill was apparently enthralled when Josephine Tey's historical detective story *The Daughter of Time* came out in 1952, demonstrating that most of what was popularly believed about Tonypandy was completely false, as a prelude to the book's main focus on the 1480s. Unfortunately, he seems to have concluded that if the author could be so right about his own past, then she was to be trusted on other historical matters too. This caused considerable difficulty for the team working on the *History of the English-Speaking Peoples*, since he now urged them, with encouragement from both Jock Colville and the Lord Chancellor, to consider the possibility that Richard III was innocent of the deaths of the Princes in the Tower. The professional historians gradually wore him down, difficult though it was to persuade him to abandon the romantic defence of a historical underdog. He was then at least spared from further irritating the Welsh by questioning the veracity of the

'Look you! Our man? Indeed to goodness!'
News Chronicle, 30 October 1951

Welsh Tudors' own account of the death of the Princes – and indeed
the entire Tudor claim to the throne for that matter.[12]

A fascinating footnote to Churchill's relationship with Wales came
in his centenary year of 1974, indicating the uneasy relationship of the
greatest by-then-dead Englishman with one of Wales's own major icons
of the period, Richard Burton. When Churchill had still been Prime
Minister in 1953, he visited the Old Vic Theatre to see Burton play
Hamlet, complimenting him on the virility of his characterisation. During the interval he visited Burton in his dressing room (asking 'My Lord
Hamlet' if he might make use of his lavatory) and then met the cast
and shook hands with them on stage after the performance. Burton later
recalled the extreme difficulty of performing in front of 'this religion, this
flag, this *insignia*', especially since the great man was sitting near the
front of the stalls and muttering 'To be or not to be?' and much of the
rest of the play along with the eponymous hero. A few years later,
Burton earned $100,000 for recording Churchill's own words for the

soundtrack of the television series *The Valiant Years*, based on Churchill's war memoirs, and was apparently chosen for the part by Churchill himself ('Get that boy from the Old Vic . . .'), arguably one of the best things he ever did. He managed to convey the inner feel of that gravelly Churchillian voice without actually mimicking it, and he was thereafter much in demand for soundtracks requiring Churchill's words, for example in Jack Le Vien's *The Finest Hours*, much as Robert Hardy would be in the next generation. Even then, Burton was fairly defensive about just what he was doing, claiming that he had based his Churchill voice 'slightly on a Peter Sellers imitation I once heard of an upper class Englishman, dropping aitches and changing Rs into Ws'. By making such claims, as he did from time to time on television chat shows (usually reminding audiences that this was a long way from the real Burton, for 'I'm the son of a Welsh miner'), he was implicitly undermining the idea of Churchill as an epic figure, though that was certainly what his Churchill voice actually sounded like. And anyway the famous Sellers impersonation that he was surely referring to, 'Party Political Broadcast', was based on Anthony Eden and did not sound remotely like either Churchill himself or Burton's version of him.

The problem was, as Burton told Kenneth Tynan in 1967, 'I am the son of a Welsh miner and one would expect me to be at my happiest playing peasants, people of the earth. But in actual fact I am happier playing princes and kings . . .' He was in fact unhappy being Churchill partly because he had found in himself a tyrannical, domineering person – quite right for the part but hard to live with and not the way he liked to think of himself. This inner dichotomy came suddenly and damagingly to the surface when in 1974 he was cast *as* Churchill in a centenary television play about his opposition to appeasement in the 1930s, a joint BBC–NBC production sponsored by Hallmark Cards. Actually appearing as Churchill rather than merely providing a voice for his words clearly upset Burton greatly, though by this stage of his life his drinking problem was beginning to overwhelm him anyway and his processes of thought were at times affected by it. Just a few days before the programme was to be shown on both British and American television, interviews with Burton appeared in the American press in which he confessed that 'to play Churchill is to hate him' and asked himself what the son of a Welsh miner was doing in a celebration of a man who was the enemy of his class and his nation, a 'toy soldier child' who had never grown up and (thought Burton the actor) was himself always playing a role. He now recalled that meeting Churchill had been like 'a blow under the heart', so overwhelming was his presence. 'I cannot pretend otherwise, though my class and his hate each other to seething point.' A few days later, by which stage he was under severe attack in both countries, receiving shoals of (unanswered) letters of complaint from friends like Robert Hardy, and had been banned from BBC Drama for life, he went even further: 'Churchill has fascinated me since childhood – a bogeyman who hated us, the mining class, motivelessly. He ordered a few of us to be shot, you know, and the orders were carried out.'

So even in the week of his centenary, the myth of Tonypandy was still around to haunt Churchill's memory. Burton too was of course playing a part here too, for his lifestyle was now way beyond the comprehension of Welsh miners. Jack Le Vien was quick to point out that Burton's new views had nothing in common with the admiration for Churchill that he had expressed in all their previous conversations, the most recent only a month earlier, that he had a Churchill bust which was one of his 'most treasured possessions', and that he had recently met both Clementine Churchill and Churchill's grandson and told both of them how much he admired 'the old man'. In the Commons Conservative MPs were outraged. Norman Tebbit, just then gearing up for his life's work as the polecat of parliamentary and tabloid invective, observed that this was 'merely an actor past his peak indulging in a fit of pique, jealousy and ignorant comment'. Neville Trotter spoke for rather more of the silent majority with the measured avowal that 'if there were more Churchills and fewer Burtons we would be in a very much better country'. As his career and life deteriorated around him and the fog of alcohol descended, Burton was trying desperately to play the man he had been long ago, and he at least knew what young Welshmen had been expected to believe about Winston Churchill. He was not asked to play either part again.[13]

In the case of Scotland, Churchill may well have had to overcome some personal aversion in order to establish – or at least claim – a real rapport. He was not much more regular a visitor to Scotland than to Wales, and in this case sheer distance from the golden triangle of Chartwell, Chequers and Woodford, all close to London and within which his career mainly operated from the 1920s onwards, would have been reinforced by the Seasonal Affective Disorder from which he probably suffered and which dictated holidays in warmer climates and with long hours of sunshine whenever he had the choice. Writing from Stack Lodge, Lairg, where he had been enticed for the fishing in 1927, he began a letter to Clementine with the words, 'Here I am at the North Pole!'[14] Yet Churchill could and did claim positive connections with Scotland (as he could not with Wales), usually in the post-war years in much the same form of words that he used when receiving the freedom of Aberdeen in 1946. First, he congratulated the Aberdonians on their connection with 'your own' 51st Highland Division, and spent half his entire speech celebrating its wartime achievements. He also listed his several links with the country: he could claim no Scottish blood, but he had at least been born on St Andrew's Day, he had found a wife in Scotland, he had commanded a Scottish regiment on the Western Front in 1915, and he had represented a Scottish constituency in the Commons for nearly fifteen years. On such a celebratory occasion it no doubt passed without comment that none of these claimed connections with Scotland was less than twenty years old, the characteristic of the day being more the presentation of flowers, cigars and chocolate than rigorous textual analysis. When a year later he became a freeman of Ayr, he delivered almost the same speech, except that he could now dwell more on his own connections with the Royal Scots Fusiliers than on generalised praise of Highlanders' prowess. Ayr was not only a recruiting area for the RSF, but the regiment's base there was now in the Churchill Barracks. Ten thousand people heard him speak in Ayr that day, and four thousand more crowded an overflow meeting. When he visited Perth for a party meeting in 1948 there were similar scenes, with spontaneous singing of 'Land of Hope and Glory' as a part of the 'real Highland welcome' he was given. The eight Labour councillors apparently felt rather foolish over their decision to boycott the ceremony when it was so obviously popular in the town.[15]

Churchill certainly did receive honours aplenty in post-war Scotland, just as he had been more warmly received in Glasgow and Edinburgh than anywhere else in his election tour of 1945: the Conservative press happily recorded then that his progress between the two cities had been 'forty-five miles of cheers . . . At almost every place through which he passed the Premier's car was brought to a complete standstill by the crowds which surged from the pavements, broke police cordons and thronged round.' Falkirk had produced a crowd of five thousand, Princes Street Gardens in Edinburgh produced fifteen thousand, he was presented with cigars in Linlithgow, and in Glasgow was received as 'a conquering hero'.[16] He was over the last ten years of his active career awarded the freedoms of Aberdeen, Ayr, Perth, Stirling and Inverness, that of Aberdeen coming along with an honorary doctorate of laws from the University. When he visited the city to receive these honours in 1946, big crowds again turned out to greet and cheer him, and it was necessary to arrange an overflow meeting.[17] Dundee too had offered the freedom of the burgh during the war, but since it was carried on a narrow party vote, the Unionist supporters of the motion only just outvoting Labour opponents, he bluntly refused to accept it. As we have seen, though he regularly travelled through the city on the way to Balmoral, Churchill had indeed never set foot in Dundee since the day on which he had lost his parliamentary seat there in 1922, a defeat that ushered in the darkest period of his career with three election defeats in less than eighteen months. He of all people can in any case hardly have seen the funny side of being defeated by a worthy but obscure local man with no pretensions to national office and whose policy preferences included prohibitionism. He had probably not dissented much from T. E. Lawrence's succinct response to Churchill's defeat in 1922 ('What bloody shits these Dundeeans must be!') and there may therefore have been some of the sweetness of revenge in his later refusal of Dundee's highly conditional offer of its freedom.[18]

However, whereas the Conservatives under Churchill had little to gain from wooing the Welsh, they had much at stake in Scotland, and this no doubt contributed to Churchill's greater efforts there. The rousing reception that he received in 1945 was followed by an election result in which Scotland swung to the left less than almost every other region (though this also reflected in part at least Labour's better-than-average performance in some Scottish regions in 1935, when the seats had last been contested). What cannot be doubted is that the Conservatives recovered from the 1945 defeat in Scotland as in England, that they did even better in 1951, and reached in 1955 – at the point of Churchill's retirement – the zenith of their post-war performance there, winning more than half the Scottish vote and capturing thirty-six of the seventy-one Scottish seats. This clearly owed at least something to Churchill's determined wooing of the Scots, partly through the assiduous promotion of his own political image there no doubt, but partly too through a dangerous tactic of encouraging separatist feelings so as to attach them to his own party. He no doubt saw no such danger, arguing often that the old antagonisms of English and Scots had now happily died away, and that each was a loyal member of a united English-speaking world. Putting the same point more ironically in 1950, he described a character-istically fervent welcome in Edinburgh, in which the crowd sang 'For He's a Jolly Good Fellow', as an 'admirable demonstration of the Scottish hatred for the English'.[19]

Just before the 1945 general election, Churchill summarily dismissed calls for a referendum on Scottish independence, but he did so in terms that both characterised the stance he would adopt for the next ten years and showed how far his attitude to Scotland was coloured by the Irish experience. Scotland's future, he argued, was inherently tied up with that of England, but the actual government of Scotland ought to be put more into Scottish hands, especially so because Labour's 'centralising' tendencies would be inherently hostile to Scottish aspirations.[20] At Perth in 1948, he set this out at its starkest, a fairly crude populist appeal to Scottish national opinion:

> But over-centralisation in Whitehall or other English head-quarters [laughter] affects Scotland in a serious manner, and alters the conditions that have prevailed since the happy union of the two countries. Scottish enterprise and contrivance, and her thrifty management, will be increasingly baffled by the intrusion of the English parliamentary majority into whole fields of Scottish national life until now left entirely free.

To give this broad argument some focus, he then claimed that the nationalisation of steel by Labour would be the 'crucial test'.[21] This was neat, but it also reflected a genuine determination to make changes as well as a desire to win votes. Once the Conservatives' post-war policy review was well under way, he was able to announce that a Churchill government would devolve a great deal of the administration of Scottish policy to Edinburgh, and from 1948 onwards every speech on Scottish affairs contained such a pledge, summarised approvingly in a *Scotsman* headline as 'Scottish control of Scottish affairs'. Every speech also con-tained a claim that this devolutionist Conservatism was starkly opposed to Labour's determination to erode Scotland's separate identity and the influence of Scotsmen over their own affairs.[22] During the 1950 election this position was reiterated in a speech in Edinburgh's Usher Hall, when 'speaking of the Nationalist movement in Scotland, he said that he would never adopt the view that Scotland should be forced into the serfdom of socialism as a result of a vote in the House of Commons', urging that a vote for the Scottish National Party would simply be a vote denied to the Conservatives' crusade to protect Scotland's independence.[23] When in due course the 1951 election returned Churchill to office with a small majority, the *Scotsman* at least believed that the Conservatives' three gains in Scotland, crucial to his chances of governing for a full Parliament, could be attributed at least in part to former SNP voters deciding to give the Tories a chance to show what they could do to allow Scotland 'to have more control of its own affairs'.[24]

Back in office from 1951, he did indeed introduce a substantial programme of administrative devolution from the Scottish Office in London to St Andrew's House in Edinburgh, including the appointment of a Minister of State normally resident in Edinburgh, and he rarely thereafter missed a chance to demand Scottish gratitude for what he had done.[25] The problem was that this would work well as a strategy only so long as it was contrasted with Labour's offer of even less to Scotland – in effect it would work until it was actually carried out. But it would be not *administrative* devolution but *legislative* devolution that would be at the heart of Scottish national aspirations in the decades to come, and it is probably no accident that in 1959, when his administrative devolution had had a few years to show how little it could offer, the Conservatives lost votes and seats in Scotland even though they gained them everywhere else. Three years later, the Scottish National Party were seriously on the march again at a by-election in West Lothian, proclaiming that administrative devolution was all smoke and mirrors, since real power remained with the Government in London. This view had been given some weight ten years earlier when Churchill was still Prime Minister, over the symbolic issue of the Stone of Scone, stolen from Westminster Abbey (where it had lain under the Coronation Throne ever since it had been stolen from Scotland in the first place in medieval times). When the police recovered the Stone (or at least one very like it), and once the Queen was safely crowned above it, the Churchill Government had to face the tricky question of where it should be placed in the future. The Prime Minister took his time over this

'And you'd better review the relation of the British government to Britain – and
with reference to self-government!'
Daily Worker, 28 July 1952

question but eventually announced that it would remain in Westminster
Abbey, claiming that this was also the overwhelming view of Scottish
opinion that the Government had consulted, but declining to list any
of the Scots who had offered such advice. Nothing was more symbolic
of Scottish aspirations to nationhood, nothing more indicative of Churchill's (or at least his Government's) limitations when it came to
satisfying those aspirations which he had himself helped to reawaken.
It may not be entirely fanciful to liken his policy to – in his own words
on another occasion – 'feeding a tiger with buns'.[26]

For Churchill's personal fame in Scotland, none of this mattered
much, and any effect on his party was anyway delayed long past his
retirement. Scottish newspapers and television marked the later rituals
of Churchill's life – his eightieth birthday, retirement, golden wedding,
death and funeral – with as much pomp and circumstance as occurred
anywhere in the Commonwealth, and on each of these occasions were
at pains to find photographs and quotations which would link Churchill
directly to Scotland itself, for example by recalling his long friendship
with General Sir Ian Hamilton. Obituaries tended not only to give
laudatory accounts of Churchill's life in general, but also to stress exactly
those links with Scotland that he himself had spent so many words in

establishing – his wife's Scottish ancestry, his war service with a Scottish regiment, his parliamentary constituency at Dundee, and his tributes to Scottish martial valour. Scotsmen and women, like so many others around the world, wanted to *own* a share of Winston Churchill at the end of his life.

He was commemorated by the end of the century in the names of a couple of dozen Scottish streets, including one in Dundee. Some like Churchill Street in Rosyth and Churchill Square in Helensburgh clearly commemorate him among naval heroes, others place him alongside other war heroes (such as Roosevelt in Kirknewton) or British Prime Ministers (as in Johnstone). More often, the proximity of a Chartwell Road (as in Bishopton) or a Winston Way indicates a specific commemoration of Churchill as the national leader. And although there are few streets named after him in the Edinburgh area (Churchill Street in Morningside being a corruption of Church Hill) and no Churchill statue even in a capital city awash with them, Edinburgh does boast a Winston's Bar in Corstorphine, where the bar itself is surmounted by a huge ceramic bulldog, bearing round its neck on a chain the label 'Winston'. The symbolism of the 'finest hour' still apparently has its appeal in Scotland.

Churchill visited Ireland only extremely rarely over his long life, but his earliest political memory was of seeing a statue unveiled there by his ducal grandfather, and of the fear of Fenians in the 1870s in Dublin, to which Lord Randolph Churchill had prudently withdrawn himself and his family after deeply offending the Prince of Wales. He was not yet twelve when Lord Randolph came out against home rule for Ireland, declaring ringingly that 'Ulster will fight, and Ulster will be right,' and from the start of his own parliamentary career in 1900 Ireland provided a continuous counterpoint – sometimes indeed the chief melody – of his many political ups and downs.[27] There was, though, as the *Belfast Telegraph* grudgingly accepted when he died, 'an underlying consistency in his views' on Ireland, often obscured by the vehemence with which he took up short-term positions on the subject. He had declared 'my own personal view' in *The World Crisis* in 1923, stating baldly that 'I would never coerce Ulster to make her come under a Dublin Parliament, but I would do all that was necessary to prevent her stopping the rest of Ireland having the Parliament they desired. I believe this was sound and right.' If this implicit endorsement of the actual

partition of Ireland in 1920–1 owed a little to hindsight, it was nevertheless consistent with both his earlier opinions and his ministerial actions.
It was certainly consistent with his views and actions after 1923.[28]

Churchill had been a strong Empire man since the Boer War, when
he was with soldiers from the Dublin Fusiliers on an armoured train
when captured by the Boers, while the Boers themselves were aided by
an Irish Brigade which included Arthur Griffith in the ranks – but he
had never taken a purely imperial view of Ireland. Though an avowed
apologist for Lord Randolph, who had scarcely done any wrong in
his son–biographer's eyes, he was nevertheless already by 1903 overtly
anti-colonial in his views on both South Africa and Ireland (possibly
indeed influenced in this by the views of such Irish friends as the
American Bourke Cockran), and he was happy to be reassured by Wilfrid
Blunt after he had read Winston's *Lord Randolph Churchill* that Lord
Randolph had not in fact been a deep opponent of home rule, except
as it affected the tactics of electoral politics in 1885–6. As a result of
this, his cross-over from the Unionists to the Liberals was a less difficult
one than might have been expected for the son of the man who had
played 'the orange card' in 1886. But that was hardly the way in which
Unionists saw it, as witnessed by the violent reception that he had when
he addressed an open-air home-rule rally in Belfast in 1912. His public
belligerence in defending the policy of the Liberal Government before
1914, even to the extent of ordering battleships to Lamlash to overawe
Unionist Belfast, masked his continuous attempts within the cabinet to
secure a form of federal 'home rule all round', or at least the exclusion
of Protestant Ulster from the proposed Dublin Parliament. Fascinatingly,
though, when contributing a supportive foreword to a Liberal speakers'
handbook on the case for home rule in 1912, Churchill stressed not the
national rights of the Irish, but the benefits to the British Empire of
moving towards federation under the Crown, and the advantage to the
'English-speaking races' as a whole of removing an obstacle to closer
relations between Britain and the United States. Since even Irish Nationalist MPs were hardly aware of the conditionality of his support for
their cause until rather late in the day, Irish opinion was outraged when
he then emerged after the First World War as the Minister responsible
for the Black and Tans, as a man prepared to threaten even worse rough
measures to combat IRA activities, and as a key architect of the Treaty
of 1921 which partitioned the country.[29]

Turning the tables
Daily Express, 11 April 1914

Unlike most of the other British participants, Churchill embarked on those Anglo-Irish talks in 1921 knowing exactly what outcome he wanted to achieve: Ireland should be offered full dominion status within the Empire, just like the Canada which he had by then come to love and admire as a separate but loyal settlement of the overseas British. He was therefore as unflinching as any negotiator in defence of such sticking points as the oath of loyalty to the King and continuing access to Irish ports for the Royal Navy, and was quite prepared to make further war on the Irish in defence of such principles. In his fascination with the mercurial Michael Collins whom he was ultimately able to persuade, Churchill seems never to have grasped that it was exactly such principles, denying as they did the core idea of Irish nationality, that would ensure that other Irishmen would never accept the deal or regard it as in any way final. In the event, and after the misunderstanding, cajolery, sharp practice and verbal coercion on which historians can still not reach consensus, the Irish delegates agreed to sign the proposed Treaty with all these principles still in it. Thereafter, Churchill professed for the rest of his political life to be defending a constitutional arrangement which had the special status of a treaty freely entered into by two nations, and would never accept even the legality – much less the desirability – of any changes to it. As Colonial Secretary he played over the next year a key role in implementing the treaty through detailed plans which brought the Free State into being, and it was in this sense at least that he can be claimed as a 'founder of modern Ireland'. Collins' final message, shortly before he was ambushed and shot by opponents of the Treaty, was, 'Tell Winston that we could not have done it without him.' Yet even in that year, with the more pliable Collins at the helm, Churchill had been inflexible on the terms of the Treaty, intervening for example to prevent Collins bringing into his Government Treaty opponents as a means of avoiding civil war, and both urging and facilitating Collins' subsequent military action against his opponents in Dublin, action that began the Irish civil war. If Churchill was indeed the 'founder of Ireland', as William Manchester has argued, then it was of a state divided not only within the island but as a free state wracked by deep internal divisions over the nature of its very existence and character. Even if, as Churchill clearly expected and frequently stated, he expected partition to be short-lived and Ulster soon to be peacefully integrated into an Ireland within the Empire, in the South itself it would have taken decades to heal the scar tissue of 1921–3.[30]

From Churchill's viewpoint, then, the Irish constitutional issue had reached finality in the 1921 Treaty, awaiting only the reincorporation of Ulster, but there were two deep flaws in this view of the situation. First, the pledges that had been given to Ulster in 1920 and reiterated to secure Unionist acceptance of the Treaty of 1921, that Ulster should never be coerced, though consistent with his own long-term opinions and often repeated thereafter, removed any likelihood that the built-in Protestant majority in the North would ever vote to join 'Ireland'. This in itself would poison Anglo-Irish arrangements for the rest of the century, with one side taking its stand on the autochthonous nature of Ireland as a nation, and the other asserting the rights of a democratic Ulster to decide on its own future. Each was a respectable argument, but since they begin from quite different premises there was no ground for pragmatic compromise. Second, though the anti-Treaty forces led by Eamon de Valera were defeated in the Irish civil war, and then frustrated and marginalised during Fianna Fáil's boycott of the Dáil, they were able to regroup in the 1930s and win power in Dublin. Once he was Ireland's democratically elected Taoiseach, de Valera devoted himself to undoing in stages all the hated parts of the 1921 Treaty, and set about creating not a dominion like Canada but a theocratic, Catholic republic – a process which only reinforced (if that were possible) the Northern Protestants' determination not to come in. Over the course of the 1930s and 1940s, Ireland repudiated the Treaty itself as a founding constitutional document, the right of the Westminster Parliament to issue such a document, the right of the Royal Navy to use Irish ports, and in due course the British monarchy itself (whereas Churchill had in 1921 insisted on the oath to the King partly as a means of keeping Republicans like de Valera out of power in Dublin). In the war years after 1939, de Valera pursued with courage and single-mindedness a policy of neutrality, lest the internal discord that had so recently brought civil war should erupt again.

Just as he had failed to grasp that many Irishmen would not accept the 1921 Treaty precisely because they thought of Ireland as a nation that need not and should not be bound by such imposed compromises, Churchill watched all this with great concern, seeking to exclude Ireland from the liberalising provisions of the 1931 Statute of Westminster, arguing in 1932 that de Valera only represented 'Irish hatred of England', and vowing that he would support Ulster 'as if it were Kent or Lancashire. We could no more allow hostile hands to be laid on the liberties of the Protestant north than we could allow the Isle of Wight or the castles of Edinburgh or Carnarvon to fall into the hands of the Germans or the French.' Privately he could be even more bellicose: when the Australian Prime Minister Robert Menzies tried to mediate between Churchill and de Valera in 1941, Churchill told him bluntly that nothing good could come from negotiating with 'that murderer and perjurer'. He never seems to have understood that de Valera's policies were deeply popular in the twenty-six counties of the South, and, as a result of this gap in comprehension, simply could not restrain himself from acting – and in particular from speaking – in ways that inflamed the situation. Whatever the respect for him as a British war leader, he was never popular in the later part of his career with majority opinion in Ireland, or minority opinion in Ulster. This indeed goes far to explain why it was Irishmen abroad who took such a leading role in opposing the burgeoning Churchill legend in their own countries, as they did for example in Australia.[31]

Such delvings into the more distant past are absolutely necessary if we are to understand what followed from the 1940s, as is so often the case in Irish history: Flanders and Swann after all also reminded their listeners in the 1960s that the Irish 'blow up policemen, or so I have heard, and blame it on Cromwell and William the Third'. Churchill was well aware himself of the centrality of history to these processes, brutally dismissing Irish neutrality in 1941 as the product of '700 years of hatred and six months of pure funk'. Though he had produced parliamentary rumblings against any Irish Government policy that threatened 'his' Treaty, it was Neville Chamberlain's Anglo-Irish Agreement of 1938, relinquishing all British claims to naval use of the Treaty Ports on the south-western Irish coast that first unleashed Churchill's vituperation against de Valera. This was in essence all part of his oratorical campaign in favour of British defence preparations for a war against Germany. It seemed to him wilfully short-sighted of Chamberlain to give up such important bases, which had proved vital in 1917–18 in combating the threat of German submarines, and he did not mince his words; Ireland must know that Britain had to have these ports again if the country's survival were at stake, but if Ireland chose to remain neutral in an Anglo-German war (or, worse, if Ireland sought to trade belligerence for Ulster), then Britain would have to invade Ireland to retake the ports or suffer the loss of masses of merchant shipping to German torpedoes. The fact that de Valera was himself a noted appeaser, and that he and Chamberlain regularly paid warm tributes to each other's good sense, would have done little to reassure him. It is only fair to add, though, that Churchill was to an extent right in his warnings and almost the only politician in Britain who foresaw the probability of Irish neutrality in a German war. In his war memoirs, he duly revisited this issue, arguing that Chamberlain's surrender of the Treaty Ports in 1938 had been a cardinal act in the folly of appeasement: 'a more feckless act can hardly be imagined, and at such a time. Many a ship and many a life was soon to be lost as a result of this improvident example of appeasement.' Note that in this sense appeasing de Valera was placed squarely alongside appeasing Hitler in Churchill's use of such apocalyptic language.[32]

When war actually began in 1939 and Ireland did indeed remain neutral, Churchill went to the Admiralty and hence had ministerial responsibility for dealing with the ports issue. He kept up over the winter of 1939–40 a ceaseless flow of demands that the Irish ports be regained for the navy by any means available, diplomatic if possible and military if not, pointed out the losses in ships and merchant seaman that followed from the navy's inability to base convoy escorts there, and effectively argued that British sailors were dying to get seaborne goods through to Ireland as well as to England. The ports issue then rumbled on throughout the war, though the fall of France in 1940 made them strategically less important than they had been either in 1917–18 or in 1939–40. Thereafter, most convoys had anyway to take the northern route around Ireland towards Glasgow or Liverpool, so as to avoid German ships and aeroplanes based in western France, and bases in Northern Ireland became more important than those in the south-west. Nevertheless, Churchill kept up his complaints, and it was the ports issue that provided the sharpest focus for the ill-considered attack on Irish policy in his 1945 victory broadcast, of which more later.[33]

The Treaty Ports were but one of a series of matters that divided Churchill from de Valera's Irish Government in the years when they were both Prime Minister, 1940 to 1945. Irish neutrality itself was the real point at issue, and here the dispute was mainly symbolic, for in most practical matters, at least once Britain had avoided early defeat in 1940–1, Irish policy was heavily supportive of the Allies. The British Colonial Office Minister Malcolm MacDonald wrote later that de Valera 'could scarcely have promised more benevolent cooperation short of declaring war against the enemy', and even at the time the Foreign Secretary Anthony Eden was telling his secretary that 'de Valera is doing all he can for us.' For example, whereas the Irish Government's draconian censorship policies banned even the printing and broadcasting of weather forecasts, lest they should inadvertently be seen to help one of the belligerents in Irish waters, Irish meteorologists were actually sending their readings straight to London to assist the Royal Navy and the RAF. When Belfast was blitzed, much of the Dublin fire brigade went north to help put out the fires, and then when the worst was over was hastily recalled lest this should look like an act of war. The Irish security services were also working hand in glove with the British (and from 1941 American) intelligence services to ensure that German spies were unable to function effectively in Ireland, though they were also asserting their independence at the same time, and refusing to be pushed around by MI5 or the American OSS. The point is that none of this was generally known at the time, since both de Valera and Churchill had their own reasons for keeping it secret. There were also masses of Irish volunteers in the British forces, never counted accurately and completely unreported in Ireland itself under the censorship, but certainly exceeding a hundred thousand people. These volunteer servicemen and women won 780 British military decorations for their war services (eight of them Victoria Crosses), twice as many as were awarded to citizens of Northern Ireland and almost as many awarded to its armed forces by Canada. In addition to this, there were thousands more who migrated to Britain and played a crucial part in the war economy, perhaps as much as 15 per cent of eligible Irish workers – even if they did so in part because of the lack of jobs in a moribund domestic economy. From Churchill's viewpoint, all of this was fine so far as it went, but it did not deliver either strategic reassurance or the endorsement in principle of the rightness of the Allied cause that he craved.[34]

In 1940–1, the reassurance that Churchill wanted related to Ireland's ability to defend itself if Germany invaded – a historian like Churchill could hardly fail to remember 1798 and 1916, when Britain's enemies in earlier life-and-death struggles had sought to invade Ireland or to supply Britain's Irish enemies. He certainly would not have been reassured by such intelligence reports as the one from Ireland which stated in 1940 that 'the German Gauleiters of Eire are already here ... Up to 2000 leaders have been landed in Eire from German U-Boats and by other methods since the outbreak of war.' The IRA's shadowy links with Germany would have provided further justification for such fears had de Valera not summarily locked up most of its members for the duration of 'the Emergency', though the British could not of course be so sure of this. The most that de Valera could be coaxed into saying was that he would accept British military aid if Germany invaded, whereas Churchill wanted to send British aid to deter German invasion, and this was anyway balanced by de Valera effectively saying that he would also ask for German help if Britain invaded Ireland. (An Irish joke of the time was 'Ireland is neutral, but who are we neutral against?') Churchill fumed, insisted on plans being made (by General Montgomery) to rush troops to Ireland in the event either of German landings or of the absolute need to seize the ports, but in the end did nothing, and since Germany did not invade Ireland either (in part to give Britain no excuse for doing so, so expertly had de Valera played off both sides against the middle) these plans were never activated.[35]

Later in the war, the British need for reassurance related more to espionage than to more overtly military matters, there being some suspicion that German advance knowledge of the disastrous Dieppe raid had been forwarded through Dublin. With the re-invasion of France pending in 1944, Britain and America stepped up the pressure to close down the German Legation in Dublin, and took the unusual step of making these demands public, so as to brand de Valera for posterity as a man who had refused to help in the liberation of Europe and the destruction of Nazism.[36] They got absolutely nowhere with him on this or any other occasion, though these diplomatic exchanges did have the effect of isolating Ireland for a decade once the war was over. Ireland itself refused to join NATO because of partition, but it was the Soviet Union that blocked Irish participation in the United Nations, on the ground that (as Andrei Gromyko put it in 1947) 'we all know Ireland was on very good terms with the Axis powers and gave no assistance whatsoever to the Allied Nations in their struggle against Fascist States'. In the short term, Churchill intensified the economic pressure on Ireland and made it more difficult to travel between the two countries or from Ireland to other neutral states, so as to restrict the flow of information from which the Germans might learn in advance about D-Day.[37] The final dispute of this type came when in 1945, with the war over and Germany surrendering, the Allies demanded of de Valera possession of the German Legation in Dublin and all its papers and contents, so that they would be able to tell at least retrospectively if their fears had been justified, and if any of their own nationals had been acting traitorously. Since the Allies were now in control of Germany itself and the German Government no longer existed, this was a more difficult demand to rebut, but de Valera managed to play for time by consulting his legal advisers, and when the Legation was eventually handed over, there was nothing left inside worth reading.[38]

All these running battles could have been resolved to Churchill's satisfaction only by Ireland abandoning its neutrality and joining the Allied side in the war, something to which he devoted considerable if intermittent attention, but with negligible and even counter-productive results.

Shortly after he became Prime Minister in 1940, with Ireland's neutrality policy already a year old but with the crisis of the war in the west fast approaching, Churchill sanctioned an extraordinary approach to de Valera in which Ireland was promised a defence council for the whole island and the best offices of the British Government to achieve Irish unity after the war, in return for Ireland coming into the war on the Allied side. To ensure that this offer was at least seriously considered in Dublin, the approach was made through Neville Chamberlain, whom de Valera still greatly respected and whose removal from the British premiership he had lamented.[39] But this should probably be seen alongside the offer of perpetual union with France made by Churchill at about the same time – a grand gesture at a desperate time, rather than a considered proposal for constitutional change. When Churchill was asked in the Commons in 1944 whether future Irish unity could be discussed as part of the peacemaking, he replied with a curt negative. De Valera immediately perceived in 1940 that Ireland would have to join the war now, that a defence council would mainly benefit Britain's war effort rather than Ireland itself, and that Irish unity would merely be talked about later. He would not have been reassured to know that the Northern Ireland Prime Minister, rushing to London when he heard of these proposals, went back to Belfast content with Churchill's traditional reassurance that Ulster would never be coerced.[40]

Nevertheless, this was the last time that cross-border institutions were offered by the British Government until the 1970s, and a positive Irish response could at least have begun a dialogue, from the logic of which Britain would have found it hard to escape, just as Irish participation in the war would have narrowed the gulf between Dublin and Belfast, whereas neutrality on one side and belligerence on the other certainly widened it. De Valera effectively prevented any progress towards a deal in 1940 though, by putting forward a counter-suggestion that Ireland be immediately united and declared neutral in the war. This would have been a huge strategic setback for Britain in its hour of peril, for which it would have gained nothing in return, and so the offer was tantamount to a breaking off of negotiations. Churchill later returned to the attack, sometimes indirectly as with suggestions that American troops or ships be invited to Ireland to guarantee Irish integrity, if British forces were unacceptable, but this was rejected as equally impossible for a sovereign state. (Indeed, when American forces arrived in Ulster in 1942, de Valera protested formally to the American Government, since the Irish Government did not recognise either the regime in the North or Britain's right to invite its allies to go there, protests that were not at all welcome in Washington.) The Japanese attack on Pearl Harbor provoked Churchill's final attempt to wear down de Valera, an approach apparently stemming from the delusion that even if Irishmen hated Britain then they at least loved the United States and so might now join the Allies. Even this odd logic ignored the fact that a conservative, Catholic country like Ireland would also have had to join in alliance with the Communist Soviet Union, an issue on which de Valera was a good deal less pragmatic than Churchill. Roused from his sleep by the British Embassy, given the news of the Japanese attack and of the imminent arrival of a Churchill message in the middle of the night, de Valera was bemused to receive not a studied diplomatic communication but a terse and emotional appeal that Ireland should seize its chance to become 'a nation once again' – a Nationalist slogan from Churchill's home-rule past. Attributing the message more to Churchill's excitement and to his fondness for brandy than to any serious purpose, the Taoiseach went back to bed, and when a reply was eventually sent it was as uncompromising as ever.[41] Joseph Lee's comment on the crisis provoked by the half-hearted proposal to introduce conscription into Northern Ireland may be applied here, and indeed to much of the Anglo-Irish wartime relationship: 'the British approach was vague, chimerical, histrionic, very Irish! The Irish response was cold, clinical, calculating, very English!'[42]

Churchill frequently asserted in his wartime table-talk that Irish neutrality was of dubious legality, since Ireland had rejected the dominion status he felt that he had achieved for it in 1921 but had not (yet) rejected the King who had declared war on Germany in 1939. Such logic-chopping entirely missed the point, in refusing to see that the Irish majority accepted de Valera's claim of Ireland's sovereign rights, and that almost the entire Dáil and the vast majority of opinion in the country backed neutrality as the best policy for Ireland. Those few voices that had once been raised in dissent, like the *Irish Times* and the Fine Gael leader James Dillon, candidly accepted by 1941 that they constituted a small minority of opinion and must accept the majority view. That view could be shared even by strong supporters of Britain's war: the self-proclaimed 'West British' journalist Brian Inglis had volunteered for the RAF, but when he heard that Churchill might send troops to take the former Treaty Ports against the will of the Irish Government, he vowed to resign if such a thing ever happened, even if it meant being court-martialled. For a lifelong democrat, Churchill was astonishingly deaf to the voice of Irish democracy in 1940–5, somehow convincing himself that Ulster loyalists and the Southern men who volunteered for service with Britain were the true voice of Ireland, which had been stifled by the devious machinations of de Valera, using his censorship to mask the evil truth about the Nazis. Effective that censorship certainly was, at least for Irishmen who had for generations been brought up to doubt the truth of England's word anyway: when Hitler's death camps were liberated in 1945 and the fact of the Holocaust was for the rest of the world inescapable, Irish censorship at first refused to allow the stories to be printed at all. When the war ended and the truth became printable even in Dublin, it was all too often attributed to British propaganda: it was apparently believed in Kilkenny that the British newsreels had shown an invented Belsen, using 'starving Indians' as faked evidence. More generally, this was why much of Irish opinion refused outright to be conscripted for an alliance to fight for freedom, Britain itself simply not appearing as a credible ally in such a crusade. Nicholas Furlong recalled being at school in Wexford during the war, when 'taunts of . . . German atrocities . . . were met with a query about Amritsar, a million murdered Zulus, Bloody Sunday, Macroom, India, Kevin Barry, the Six Counties . . . and "What about the Black and Tans?"' For Hugh Leonard's father, who was 'anti-English and pro-nobody, but he could never grasp the distinction', Adolf Hitler seemed 'the greatest man barring de Valera that ever trod shoe leather'. Pro-German feeling did exist in its own right in wartime Ireland, but a great deal of Irishmen's pro-German sympathies was at root just anti-Englishness. This de Valera understood well, and played on for all he was worth: the American Ambassador reported in 1940 that 'the politician in Ireland who has custody of the Lion's tail is the one who retains power. If Mr De V. let this object out of his hands he would be lost.'[43]

After 1941, it was mainly the American Government which kept up the wartime pressure on de Valera, partly because David Gray, the American Ambassador in Dublin, was less diplomatic than Sir John Maffey who represented Britain, partly no doubt because Roosevelt knew that de Valera was doing all that he could through his influence with Irish Americans to undermine his presidency at home. Churchill was, though, always a willing accomplice in the Allied pressure on Dublin, and more than once went a step further in his public statements than was entirely wise. After one such intervention, Maffey despairingly asked himself how political bulls could be persuaded to stay out of his diplomatic china shop. With victory in May 1945, however, Churchill really let himself go, with terribly self-defeating effect. He was undoubtedly incandescent with rage when he heard that de Valera had responded to the news of Hitler's suicide by visiting the German Legation in Dublin in person, so as to offer his condolences. This was clearly a terrible blunder on the Taoiseach's part, and the Allied leaders had merely to keep quiet or express sorrow rather than anger to reap the benefit in Irish embarrassment. Nor was even supportive Irish opinion much impressed by de Valera's argument that he had acted exactly as he had done when Franklin Roosevelt died a month earlier, so reiterating the even-handedness of Irish neutrality, and that he did not wish to insult the German Minister, who had always treated him kindly (unlike the British and the Americans). The extent of the potential divisions in Ireland is indicated clearly enough by the deep regret voiced by the *Irish Times*, and the fact that newspapers that supported the Government did not even report de Valera's visit to the German Legation, or at least did not report it until it was the subject of angry attacks in the British House of Commons. The hostile British press did not point out that other neutrals such as Portugal had behaved exactly as Ireland had done – but then the British press had never accepted that Irish neutrality was equally valid.[44]

On VE Day, while Belfast was the scene of bonfires and wild celebrations comparable to what has happening in London, Dublin ordered no official celebration at all. Irritated by this, the (mainly Protestant) students of Trinity College hoisted the flags of the Allied nations above the College walls. Things then got seriously out of control, when an angry, anti-British crowd gathered outside on College Green, prompting some of the wilder spirits within to burn the Irish flag in full sight of the growing crowd. In retaliation, a Union Jack was then burned by (Catholic) students from University College, one of them the future Taoiseach Charles Haughey. As the evening wore on the threat of a major riot loomed, the British and American Embassies were stoned, as were such other haunts of the 'West British' ascendancy as the Wicklow Hotel and Jammet's restaurant. The police eventually had to make several baton charges in order to clear the streets and restore order. There was everything to be gained by Churchill in letting this pot simmer, as the end of Irish censorship gradually allowed more people to learn the truth about the war and the Nazis. Even after Churchill had missed his chance, memories of de Valera's actions in 1945 could still irritate some Irishmen: when his Fianna Fáil Government was struggling to fight off a non-confidence motion in the Dáil in 1953, his supporters argued that 'Dev' had saved Ireland by keeping it neutral, provoking a hostile Independent TD to shout back, 'It was Churchill that saved Ireland'.[45]

Churchill, however, leaped into the fray regardless in his BBC victory broadcast of 13 May and scored a spectacular own-goal in the process. In a wide-ranging review of the entire war, he spent several minutes celebrating the loyalty and patriotism of Ulster, and the thousands of Irish volunteers in the British forces, noting how many had been decorated for their bravery, and naming one by one the Irish winners of the Victoria Cross. This positive face of Ireland was then contrasted with the shameful spinelessness of the Irish Government, whose refusal to rally to the forces of good against the forces of evil in 1940–1 had almost brought Europe to disaster, and had anyway cost the lives of countless British sailors. Worse even than that brutal claim, Churchill argued that Britain could easily have been compelled to invade Ireland in 1940 to secure the navy's use of the Treaty Ports, and so begin a new chapter in bloodshed and hatred between Britain and Ireland. If this had happened, and he clearly took the view that Britain would have been within its rights had it done it, then the fault would have been de Valera's alone. This was harsh, unforgiving stuff, and it was celebrated in the British press with all the mood of spectators at the end of a fox hunt, de Valera apparently about to be torn apart by the Churchill pack of hounds.

The reaction in Ireland was, however, what mattered now, and the varying ways in which Irish newspapers responded tells an evocative tale. The *Irish Times*, though critical of both Irish neutrality and de Valera's Government, administered a dignified rebuke which demonstrated just how far Churchill was thought to have insulted the whole of Ireland, and not just the Government. An editorial pointed out ironically that 'we have an uneasy feeling that possibly he went just a little too far', picking out for example Churchill's remark that de Valera had been left to 'frolic with the Germans and the Japanese' as 'to say the least of it, a slight overstatement'. For Irish neutrality had in practice been 'almost wholly benevolent' to Britain. Equally interesting was the fact that most other Irish newspapers printed news stories about Churchill's verbal attack on Ireland but offered no comment whatsoever. The *Belfast Telegraph* indeed noted gleefully that their having advance copies of Churchill's speech did not seem to have helped them to generate any editorial thoughts at all. It also reported that 'when the premier began his address there were few sets in Eire that were not tuned to the BBC and remained on BBC stations for the entire 35 minutes Mr Churchill spoke'. The *Telegraph*'s own view was succinctly summed up in an editorial headed 'How the North Saved Eire', and in reporting the Presbyterian preacher in Londonderry who had spoken of de Valera's 'shame', now exposed by Churchill to the whole world. Nor was it only Conservatives and Unionists who took such a hostile view. Labour's Hugh Dalton began a speech to supporters on 2 May with the words, 'If I were Mr de Valera – thank God I am not – I would open my remarks by condoling with you on the death of a painter . . .'[46]

Since so many ordinary Irishmen in the South heard Churchill's speech for themselves, and almost all would have read about it in the newspapers but seen no comment or official reaction, there was a widespread sense of national anticipation when de Valera was billed to deliver his own radio address a few days later. This was a masterly performance, controlled and sensible where Churchill's had been reckless and self-indulgent, and it had a lasting impact on Churchill's status in Ireland. More in sorrow than in anger, de Valera congratulated Churchill for *not* invading Ireland in 1940–1, but robustly maintained that such an act would have been one of unprovoked aggression against a sovereign state, without a shred of legality. He did not hide behind any claim that Ireland had actually been pro-British, but instead met head-on Churchill's claim that Ireland had been standing aside in a battle between good and evil, arguing that neutrality had a higher moral value than belligerence and that Ireland's fight for the rights of small nations against aggression had gone on for hundreds of years, not just since 1939. He concluded in statesmanlike vein with the hope that past divisions could now be put behind both countries in the expectation of better understanding for the future.

The impact of the speech was immediate and profound. The relatively pro-British *Irish Times* thought the speech to have been 'as temperate as it was dignified', and an editorial gave it a full-hearted endorsement. The press mouthpiece of Fianna Fáil, the *Irish Press*, reported the story under the headline 'United Nation Acclaims Taoiseach's Broadcast', and this seems to be borne out by the avalanche of congratulations that flowed in to de Valera in letters, telegrams and telephone calls. When he entered the Dáil on the next day, only five Fine Gael members failed to join in a standing ovation. Newspapers in Dublin sold out within hours of appearing on the streets, since 'they all wanted the speech'. The *Irish Independent* concluded that de Valera had spoken 'with dignity and reason' for the overwhelming majority of Irish people who had always favoured neutrality and the defence of Ireland's rights, and it was surely right in its judgement. Joseph Lee, noting that de Valera's broadcast had evoked a 'rapturous response', has also pointed out that it continued the fine balance that the Taoiseach had maintained throughout the war, pragmatism towards the Allies sufficient to deter them from intervening, and rhetoric that 'satisfied national psychic needs'. Churchill's own reaction was striking, as Randolph Churchill later recalled. After hearing de Valera's broadcast, he was uncharacteristically quiet for a considerable time, clearly recognising that his Irish opponent had won this particular joust and that he himself had created the opportunity for him to do so. He later told Randolph that it was a speech that 'perhaps I should not have made in the heat of the moment. We had just come through the War and I had been looking around at our victories. The idea of Eire sitting at our feet without giving us a hand annoyed me.' Significantly, the Churchill speech was toned down (in fact it must have been deliberately misquoted) when later cited in his war memoirs. Churchill's official biographer quotes this inaccurate version of the speech and makes no mention at all either of de Valera's reply or of any effect that their exchanges had on Anglo-Irish relations. It has plainly become an incident that Churchill and his apologists wish had never taken place at all.[47]

Only in the six counties of the North was de Valera's speech of 17 May 1945 received with hostility, a further indication of how far their respective neutrality and belligerence had widened the gap. Ulster had had its own victory broadcasts (with recorded contributions from Churchill and Montgomery) and several victory services, as well as celebrating the important contributions to the British war effort of such Ulstermen as Field Marshal Alexander and General Templar. The Unionist press happily printed letters from Irish soldiers who were appalled by de

Valera's offering condolences at the German Legation, and editorialised loyally on the 'Golden Circle of the Crown', the fine job done by George VI in uniting the wartime nation. As Ulster prepared for its own post-war general election, the Unionists welcomed letters of support from Churchill (in which he wrote that they had 'my best wishes and the gratitude of the British race in every quarter of the globe'), and the *Belfast Telegraph* returned the compliment with an article endorsing Churchill's own campaign for re-election ('Winston Churchill – He'll Win the Peace'). The newspaper also subjected de Valera's broadcast to critical scrutiny, and lamented 'Mr De Valera's short memory': his wartime neutrality was sardonically contrasted with his eloquence as chairman of League of Nations gatherings in the 1930s, in which he had urged the need 'to hold aggressors in check'. His arguments would only be acceptable to:

> people who had extremely short memories and who have been living under a censorship which has blacked out the moral issues of the war . . . Never was there a war in which spiritual issues were so supremely at stake, and yet Eire has stood aside. Nothing Mr De Valera said on Wednesday night is likely to alter history's verdict on that decision.

After ramming home the point that Irish neutrality had depended entirely on British naval protection, for which the country had refused to pay its dues, and lamenting the censorship which had allowed de Valera to claim that 'Eire saved herself alone', but only 'at the cost of truth', it concluded prophetically and unforgivingly:

> On Wednesday night his understanding of opinion outside Eire was plainly as limited as ever when he talked of the experience of the war years as affording a fresh beginning towards mutual comprehension. That is most unlikely. That visit to the German Minister to condole with him on the death of Hitler will not be forgotten easily either here or in Britain.

If Churchill's final duel with de Valera in May 1945 was then won by de Valera, because he understood opinion in Eire while Churchill did not, then it was equally true that de Valera's ignorance of – or indifference to – opinion everywhere else had done the cause of Irish unity further and lasting harm.[48]

Thereafter, while Churchill's last two decades were followed with

Listen and learn
Dublin Opinion, June 1945

interest and enthusiasm in Ulster, in the rest of the English-speaking
world and to a great extent in the rest of Europe too, they were either
ignored in Ireland or treated as having no relevance to the bulk of the
Irish people. His great foreign policy speeches of the later 1940s, for
example, were reported simply as foreign news in the Irish press, not
as involving Ireland itself. If Irish Ministers were asked for comments
on them, they did not volunteer any in the way that was common in
the rest of the Western world, nor did Irish newspapers (except the
more internationalist *Irish Times*) ever editorialise on them.[49] The fact
that Ireland had been excluded from the United Nations and excluded
itself from NATO undoubtedly reinforced this inward-looking tendency, but Ireland did participate in the movement towards European

co-operation, and in 1949 Churchill almost met de Valera for the first time in Strasbourg. They had not met during the 1921 Treaty negotiations because de Valera had craftily sent others to London for this task, so freeing himself in advance to repudiate any deal that they made, and he was out of office when Churchill as Chancellor of the Exchequer had to deal with the Irish Government over outstanding debts in 1925. In the 1930s, when de Valera was Taoiseach and so meeting British Ministers at Commonwealth conferences and in direct economic negotiations, it was Churchill who was out of office. Finally, during the war years, Churchill's various offers to meet de Valera to discuss closer co-operation were always courteously rebuffed. (Though Churchill couched these offers in terms that suggested meeting 'at any time', it was clear that he expected de Valera to come to London for the purpose, rather than he himself going to Dublin, and since this would appear like the mountain going to Mahomet, it was highly unlikely that de Valera would ever accept such an invitation. In Churchill's war memoirs this was obscured by the substitution of the words 'I am ready to meet you wherever you wish' for what he had actually said to de Valera in 1941: 'Am very ready to meet you at any time.')

Now at last they almost met on neutral territory, but could not quite bring themselves to do so. That non-meeting in 1949 did not receive comment in the press at the time, and has been the subject of different interpretations by historians since. De Valera's official biographers quote him as saying that 'at Strasbourg, Churchill was treated as a hero and honoured accordingly. When I approached the foot of the steps leading to the entrance to the hall, I noticed Churchill at the top of the steps and surrounded by photographers and newspaper reporters. Some of the photographers looked over at me and wanted me to go up and be photographed with Churchill. This I refused as I did not want to be snubbed publicly by Churchill.' Tim Pat Coogan even more negatively argues that de Valera 'refused either to be photographed or to fraternise with him'. Other accounts, though, have Churchill smiling encouragingly in de Valera's direction (whether de Valera's already very poor eyesight would have picked up such facial expressions at a distance is far from clear) but making no attempt to move towards him. Pride dictated that neither would take the first step, and it is hard to avoid the conclusion from de Valera's own words that jealousy was present too, Churchill now being the centre of attention in international

gatherings as he himself had often been in the 1930s. The actual occasion
was not propitious anyway, for the Irish delegation was trying to raise
the issue of partition, finding it ruled out of order, making attacks on
Britain anyway within speeches on other subjects and being roundly
attacked for their pains in the British press.[50]

As in the thawing of his initially frosty relations with Bob Menzies,
Churchill's return to office in 1951 seems to have had its effect. He sent
de Valera a warm message on his seventieth birthday in 1952, and in
the same year, when de Valera sent condolences on the death of George
VI, Churchill replied that it had been 'a most kind message of sympathy',
adding that 'it gives me much pleasure to receive this telegram from
you. You know, I am sure, that I bear sincere goodwill to your country
and admire the faith and culture of the community you have built
amidst so many difficulties.' In the following year, Churchill had de
Valera's congratulations on the award of the Garter, and in 1954 a
message on his own eightieth birthday. By then, the two old adversaries
had also finally met for their one and only conversation, when de Valera
visited Churchill in Downing Street as part of an international tour in
September 1953. Not all Churchill's staff were as magnanimous. After
contemplating making a citizen's arrest of the Taoiseach on a charge of
murder at the actual door of Number Ten, Anthony Montague Browne
decided instead to content himself with a refusal to be present on the
day of reconciliation. Churchill accepted this with equanimity, telling
him, 'I will do violence to no man's conscience,' but the incident is
nevertheless a useful reminder that, as in the case of the post-war reconciliation with Germany, Churchill's refusal to bear old grudges produced criticism as well as praise, even among his closest admirers.

This time, though, Churchill and de Valera did indeed pose for a
photograph, on the steps of Number Ten, de Valera having to stoop
noticeably even to reach Churchill's hand, so much taller was the 'long
fellow'. The *Irish Press* reported that amid the many shouts of 'Churchill,
Churchill', there had been a few London cheers for de Valera too, and
one ominous voice that had been heard to declare, 'Partition is dead,
and I will kill it.' Churchill told his doctor that he had liked de Valera
now that they had finally met, and it was reported that they had mainly
talked about 'the higher mathematics', this being de Valera's subject as
a teacher (though how Churchill kept up his end on this particular
subject is something of a mystery). Churchill did not tell Lord Moran

that they had also discussed Ireland and found virtually no common ground, though de Valera recorded that Churchill 'went out of his way to be courteous'. When de Valera spoke of unification, Churchill responded uncompromisingly that 'they could never put out of the United Kingdom the people of the Six Counties so long as the majority wished to remain with them. There were also political factors which no Conservative would ignore.' This last point presumably referred to the fact the Ulster Unionists currently constituted almost the whole of Churchill's parliamentary majority, which at least suggests that their discussion was frank and to the point.

When de Valera asked about the return of the body of Sir Roger Casement, dishonourably buried in an English jail since his execution in 1916 but regarded by Ireland as a martyr, Churchill was a little more hopeful, but said that he must consult legal opinion and referred again to the problem of opinion in Ulster. In due course he wrote to tell de Valera that his Government would not sanction the return of Casement's bones, and when de Valera wrote to protest further he did not reply. Not until Harold Wilson was Prime Minister and in the year of Churchill's own death were Casement's remains reinterred in Ireland. De Valera astounded his host, however, by explaining that if he had remained Prime Minister through the later 1940s he would not have taken Ireland out of the Commonwealth as the Costello Government had done, a matter on which Churchill had been sharply critical at the time. As de Valera left, Churchill apparently 'waved a cheerful au revoir as the car moved off'; while one Irish paper offered as 'the opinion in informed circles' the view that 'the meeting has been "very useful" and it may well be that a new chapter in Anglo-Irish relations is about to begin'. In the North, the press led with the story of the return to their families of Ulstermen held as prisoners of war ('Belfast grandmothers dance a jig as Korea men come home'). Readers were told that Churchill had now flown off to the South of France for a short holiday, but were given no hint of the fact that his last Prime Ministerial engagement before leaving had been to have lunch with de Valera.[51]

Churchill's eightieth birthday was noticed at length in the Irish press, though even here the Irish response was fairly conditional. There was plenty of coverage of the 'tributes to Sir Winston', the Irish Ambassador called personally to convey his Government's best wishes, and there were in the *Irish Times* appreciative reviews of such celebratory volumes as Sir James Marchant's *Winston Churchill: Servant of Crown and Commonwealth* and *The Wit of Winston Churchill*, even if in both cases the reviewers kept well off the subject of Ireland. The *Irish Times* also carried its own article, 'Sir Winston Churchill, The Living Legend', but when listing unofficial 'Irish tributes to Sir Winston' was forced to draw them mainly from Ulster. The only unofficial tribute quoted from the South was in fact from the Dublin Branch of the British Legion, which may be assumed to have been fairly untypical of Irish opinion as a whole. Other Irish papers printed equally extended repertories of tributes, but presented them as England's celebration of Churchill rather than something in which Ireland was much involved. Even when recording world tributes, for example from the United States or Australia, there was little sense that this was a world to which Ireland itself belonged. Much the same happened on the occasion of such later rites of passage as Churchill's 1955 retirement from the premiership, his 1958 golden wedding, and his retirement from the Commons in 1964. Lesser events like his triumphant visit to Washington in 1959 and his honorary citizenship of the United States in 1963 went largely unreported in Eire, though given predictable attention by press and politicians in the North.[52]

Churchill was, wrote the *Belfast Telegraph* in 1954, not only 'the greatest Englishman of our times' and 'the man of the twentieth century', but also 'the expression of our national character' (the word 'our' here having, as it was meant to, a particular force). Once he had retired, he was awarded the first ever Ulster gallantry medal in modern times, made as a replica of the one awarded to Major Rogers after the Battle of the Boyne. This last award was presented to Churchill by the Northern Ireland Prime Minister, as part of ceremonials to mark the award to him at the same time of the freedoms of the cities of Belfast and Londonderry (the medallion allowing the whole of Ulster's population to claim a share in honouring him, not just people from the two cities). Churchill had told Lord Moran in 1953 that 'they'd give me a great reception if I went to Dublin' (a somewhat dubious idea), but for this ceremonial he did not in fact even visit Belfast, the various Ulster delegations calling on him at the City of London's Mansion House. The actual regalia were, however, carefully customised to celebrate loyalism as much as Churchill himself, Londonderry for example giving him his freedom scroll in a casket that had on its lid a replica of 'roaring Meg', the cannon that had kept the Catholics at bay during the siege of 1689. Churchill made an appropriate speech, celebrating as he did on every possible post-war occasion the war record of Northern Ireland, and Ulster's leaders thanked him for being their staunch supporter as well as Britain's in times of storm and stress.[53]

It was, however, impossible to maintain the South's detachment in the second half of January 1965, between Churchill's final stroke and his funeral. For a week, Irish newspapers gave their readers daily bulletins on Churchill's fight for life, mostly on the front pages, though at lesser length and less prominently displayed than was the case with newspapers in London, New York, Toronto or Sydney. After he died the Monday editions of the dailies went to town in reporting a major news story. The *Irish Independent*, for example, led on 25 January with a 'Britain in Mourning' story, and also carried on the front page a story about plans for a state funeral, printed de Valera's tribute, and reported that 'the Holy Father is deeply grieved' by Churchill's death. On inside pages, there was a full-page obituary, a page of photographs covering Churchill's long career, most of a page of his best-known phrases, and a page of tributes from around the world. This was certainly generous, and was replicated in scale in many other papers, but it was also subtly undermined by several points within that extensive coverage. First, the front page also carried the story that the RTE television studios in Dublin had had to be surrounded by the Garda on the previous evening when the announcement that it would broadcast an hour-long tribute to Churchill was followed immediately by protests and a telephoned bomb-threat. The offices of the company that had made the film had had red paint thrown over their windows. Second, the obituary covered in generous tone all of Churchill's career, except for his relations with Ireland, while a second column on this subject was considerably more critical, concluding with de Valera's 1945 broadcast rebuke to Churchill. The page of photographs did not show Churchill with any Irishmen, so distancing the country itself from its celebration of the man. There was, for example, no reprinting of that 1953 handshake with de Valera, nor, rather less surprisingly, was there any photograph of Churchill with Michael Collins in 1921.[54]

In all of this, the tone of Irish reaction was largely set by de Valera himself, now President rather than Taoiseach and well over eighty years old, but still highly influential. As Foreign Minister Aiken told Tim Pat Coogan, several years after de Valera moved up to the presidency, 'we are only carrying on his work'. It was de Valera's tribute to Churchill that now went forth officially from Ireland, not one from the Government of Sean Lemass (who sent only a personal, unpublished message to Churchill's widow). De Valera's own *Irish Press* indeed headed a front-page story in its edition on Churchill's death with the words, 'President Sends His Sympathy', as if this was the most significant part of the day's news. In the light of the apparent thawing of their personal relations since 1952, and the warm message that de Valera had sent on Churchill's ninetieth birthday only two months earlier, that tribute was remarkably unforgiving: 'Sir Winston Churchill was a great Englishman, one of the greatest of his time, a tower of strength to his own people and to their allies round the world. For this he will be acclaimed throughout the world.' His first sentence was carefully worded so as not to include Ireland or say anything about Irish opinion. The second was terse and not particularly about Ireland either. But even this grudging start was warm by comparison with what followed.

> But we in Ireland had to regard Sir Winston over a long period as a dangerous adversary. The fact that he did not violate our neutrality during the war must always stand to his credit, though he indicated that, in certain circumstances, he was prepared to do so. In this connection, I think I cannot do better than repeat a passage from a broadcast I made at the end of the war.

There followed two paragraphs from that 1945 broadcast which now made up half of de Valera's entire tribute to Churchill in 1965, and a final perfunctory message of sympathy to Clementine Churchill.[55]

Over the week between Churchill's death and the state funeral, this highly conditional response continued, extremely untypical of the press around the free world. The *Irish Times* kept up its reporting of the funeral plans, and concentrated some attention on how Ireland ought to take part in it, but no story at all was carried by most Irish papers on most days of that week. It was noted, though, that flags of foreign embassies in Dublin were flying at half-mast, but not on Government buildings. There would be no official Government mourning processes for Churchill in Ireland, and the Irish Government would be represented at the funeral not by de Valera or Lemass, but by the Foreign Minister Frank Aiken. It was pointed out that this was normal practice for the Irish Government, though since de Valera had personally attended President Kennedy's funeral in 1963 it was clearly a normal practice that could be changed on appropriate occasions, and the British press was distinctly unimpressed by the lack of priority given to the funeral by the Irish. Aiken was in many ways a hopelessly inappropriate chief mourner for Churchill: he had been a leading figure in the IRA during the 1919–21 wars, and had toured Irish communities in the USA during the Second World War in the hope of destabilising the presidency of Churchill's great ally Franklin Roosevelt, a tour in which he had been billed with his IRA rank as 'General Aiken'. The wartime editor of the *Irish Times* had observed that Aiken was 'well known for his anti-British feelings'. Fortunately the British press knew too little Irish history to make such connections, which might have caused it to get really excited.

The same refusal to treat Churchill's funeral as anything out of the ordinary (exactly the opposite of the response in Canada, for example, where the Government specifically decided to go beyond normal mourning practices to denote an extraordinary man's death) was to be seen in other ways too in Dublin. When the Scandinavian manager responsible for running RTE began to make plans to carry the funeral itself live and at full length, as his colleagues all across Europe were doing, he was quietly reminded that this was not the way in which the Irish Government wanted this event covered. His plans were quickly scrapped, Ireland alone among the Eurovision countries did not take a live transmission from London, and RTE viewers saw only an edited report of the funeral on the Saturday-evening news bulletin. The hapless television executives now had to report that they had been offered live transmission, 'but had decided not to accept it. They were of the opinion that the extended news bulletin, with a filmed report, would give adequate coverage.' The American Embassy in Dublin reported back to Washington that the Irish Government's intention was only to do what was 'barely correct', since it had not forgotten Churchill's role in the Partition Treaty of 1921 or his 'vendetta' against de Valera over Irish neutrality in the war. The Irish, a Government source explained to the Ambassador, would 'make no attempt to join the masses in paying tribute'.[56]

Not everyone in Ireland was prepared to take this approach lying down, but, as in the celebration of VE Day in 1945, the minority status of those who tried to fight back only emphasised the solidarity of the majority. James Dillon, former leader of Fine Gael, voiced a far warmer tribute to Churchill than did the President, quoting Churchill's 1945 statement of gratitude to the British people for their wartime support as expressing what Ireland *ought* now to be saying to Churchill: 'when Nazism and Communism combined in 1939 to destroy freedom, his was the leadership that preserved it'. Memorial services were held in St Patrick's (Anglican) Cathedral, Dublin, attended by the British Ambassador and most of the diplomatic corps but by no Government representative, and in the chapel of Trinity College (in which Protestant establishment the Irish Catholic hierarchy had recently reminded its flock that enrolment was in itself a sin, unless the Church had expressly agreed in advance). In Limerick, the Anglican Bishop argued in his memorial address that Churchill 'had never had any ill feeling for Ireland. We in this country must not be aloof or ungrateful, nor should we shame ourselves with a half-hearted tribute ... Churchill saved Ireland from invasion which would have been evil.'

Above all the *Irish Times* provided a vocal mouthpiece for such minority views. The paper had conceded on the day it printed Churchill's obituary that he had had 'what, in all fairness, may best be described as an unhappy relationship with this country', and had mourned his passing in relatively defensive terms. A series of articles on 'Churchill and Ireland', for example, terminated in 1921, and took obvious pleasure in recounting the story of Churchill being 'booed out' of Belfast in 1912. Nevertheless, once it became clear how limited official recognition of Churchill's death was to be, the paper became sharply critical, and to judge from letters printed in its correspondence columns it was reflecting its readers' opinions in doing so. One correspondent even raked up the issue of de Valera's condolences to Hitler's successors in 1945 as a point of comparison. The paper lamented the tone of de Valera's tribute, and regretted the sending only of Aiken to the funeral, for 'it would be better if the Taoiseach were to attend' (even the *Irish Times* presumably saw no point in suggesting that de Valera went in person). If Chancellor Erhard of Germany could set aside memories of the RAF's destruction of German cities in 1943–5 under Churchill's orders and attend his funeral, and President de Gaulle could set aside battles of the past, then surely Ireland should be equally magnanimous. It pointed out how many people – and of what high rank – were coming to London from the rest of the world, and how handsomely Northern Ireland would be represented, and pointedly contrasted this with Ireland's insultingly low-level representation. It noted tellingly that even Ian Smith of

Rhodesia was going to be there, despite currently being at complete loggerheads with Britain. Finally, it took issue with the decision not to broadcast the funeral live, so as to give Irish people the chance to mourn personally when their Government had refused to do so adequately on their behalf, and again published a sheaf of letters in support of its view.

None of this protesting had the faintest impact on Government policy or the rest of the country, and it is notable that no other Irish paper seems even to have carried the story that some sections of Irish opinion were critical of the policy of the Government and the RTE, so effective was the self-censorship of matters Churchillian that had continued ever since actual wartime censorship ended in 1945. On the day of the funeral itself, the *Irish Times* reminded its readers that most of them could anyway watch the funeral on either the BBC or Ulster Television, and gave full details of how to tune into their programmes. Two days later, it manifestly took a good deal of pleasure from reporting that traffic in Dublin had been unusually light during the hours of the BBC's live funeral transmission, and that shops had reported only light trading, as customers stayed at home to watch the programme for themselves. Meanwhile, the British Embassy had received many visitors asking to sign its condolence book.[57]

None of this means of course that the Irish Government did not represent majority opinion in the country, for many people would clearly have watched the funeral transmission as a formidable piece of pageantry and the first live outside broadcast of its type that had ever been offered to them on any occasion at all. It does, though, suggest that resistance to the commemoration of Churchill may not have been as widespread as the Government feared. But it was the Government's extremely low-key response in 1965 that set the scene for the future. By 1974, even the *Irish Times* let the centenary of Churchill's birth pass without comment, being preoccupied rather with the bombing of Birmingham by the IRA. There was no Churchill commemorative stamp or coin, there is no statue of Churchill in Dublin as there is in most European capital cities, and the authorities in Irish cities have apparently felt no desire to name buildings or streets after him either.[58]

If, as the British Ambassador in Dublin despairingly cabled back to London after Churchill's 1945 broadcast, 'phrases make history here', his many unwise words about Ireland had seemingly blotted out in the collective Irish memory much of his active career that was far more

positive for Ireland. But, whereas for many of his admirers around the
world Churchill personified a certain sort of Britishness, that was clearly
not seen in a positive light by a nation struggling to be free of its past
as a British colony and of the historical legacy of partition that this still
entailed throughout the twentieth century. It is hard to disagree with
Mary Bromage's blunt assessment that while Churchill's view of Ireland
was principled even when governed by tactical flexibility,

> the principle from which he never wavered in his approach to
> the Irish Question was simply what was good for England . . .
> This, in the course of his career, proved to be a different matter
> from what was good for Empire, for world order or, of course,
> for Ireland.

As a result of this, he and de Valera moved on essentially parallel
courses, each acting in stubborn defence of his own country's interests,
but whereas de Valera had by the 1940s grasped this point, recognised
Churchill as 'a great war minister' – and even conceded that if he had
been an Englishman he would probably have voted for Churchill in
1945 – Churchill never did, largely because he had never accepted that
the best interests of England and Ireland were different in the first
place.[59] In this, as in so many other attitudes, he was imprisoned for
life in the late-Victorian world in which he had grown up – ironically,
in Dublin. Just how little the mature Churchill understood his reputation
among the Celtic peoples is underlined by a remarkable statement that he
made to his doctor in September 1945. Despite his robust and unashamed
defence of the rights of Ulster, Churchill 'spoke of Ireland', and
announced that 'he thought if he had gone on [as Prime Minister] he
would have been able to bring her back into the fold. Anyway, as far
as he was concerned, there would always be a candle burning in the
window for the wandering daughter.' This romantic fantasy was generally contrasted with a tough realism about partition. As he told Anthony
Montague Browne near the end of his life, he had always had a 'soft
spot for the [Southern] Irish people', but the people of Ulster were 'our
flesh and bone'.[60]

6

'The Father of Europe'?:
Churchill and the Europeans

THOUGH THE MAIN FOCUS of Churchill's international activities
after 1945 was with the English-speaking peoples, and though he frequently said that the fostering of closer relations between Britain and
America was the issue closest to his heart, the 'three circles' concept of
British international policy which he did so much to popularise also
encompassed Britain's role as a European power. If only for the reason
of ease of access in that pre-jet age, he visited Europe far more than he
crossed the oceans to other continents, and he was conscious of British
and European cultures being closely related over centuries past. He
could on occasion speak most movingly on such matters, as when he
evoked at Fulton the ancient European capitals of the East, now lost
from sight behind his 'iron curtain', or when at Zurich he urged a
rapprochement between France and Germany to heal the wounds within
the European family which had both caused and been deepened by the
two world wars. In all this, his concept of Europe was wide and flexible
– he also looked forward at Zurich to the day when Russia too could
enter a united Europe, an aspiration with which the actual framers of
European integration would not come to terms until the 1990s. Finally,
he won in 1958 the Charlemagne Prize for his services to the cause of
uniting 'Europe'. Because of his Zurich call for a 'United States of
Europe' in 1946, his subsequent sponsorship of the United Europe campaign, and his influential role at the European congresses of the late
1940s, he is widely regarded within the post-war European institutions
as one of the founding fathers. In the Palais de l'Europe in Strasbourg,
not only is his bust prominently displayed among the heroes of the first

Churchill's Ark
Rand Daily Mail, March 1947

generation, but there are also on display photographs of him speaking at key meetings and socialising with the leaders of the other European nations. It is only fair to add at once that all of this presents a rather one-sided picture, and that he is more celebrated as an ancestor in the loose, inter-governmental Council of Europe than in the integrationist, supranational European Union. Indeed, in the deeply contentious British internal debate on 'Europe' in the 1990s, Churchill was claimed as an ally by both sides, the supporters of European union largely basing their claims on his words between 1945 and 1951, the Eurosceptics on his later deeds in office. In much the same way, even in the 1950s and 1960s, though Robert Menzies of Australia thought him to be far too much of a European to have any real sympathy with the British Commonwealth, Charles de Gaulle thought him too pro-American to commit Britain to France or to Europe. In both cases, it all depends where you look for your evidence.

This chapter will analyse Winston Churchill's post-war impact on the various European countries, before attempting to answer the vexed question of how good a 'European' he ever was. It is necessary to begin by explaining why he was able to have the impact that he did. He held after all no pre-war ministerial post which involved much contact with European politicians after 1922, and while he continued to visit European countries in the 1930s (including Germany, where he narrowly missed meeting Adolf Hitler), it was as a private citizen on holiday, not as a national representative carrying on official business and therefore being photographed and reported locally. Though international agencies carried his 1930s speeches on foreign policy as news items in their own right, it was naturally rather hit and miss whether and how much they were actually reported in the European press. He had contracts to write regularly for the *Evening Standard* in London and for *Collier's* in the USA, but it was again all rather haphazard as to whether they would translate and sell on his articles to other outlets.

All of this changed dramatically in 1937 when an initially reluctant Churchill signed, at Austen Chamberlain's suggestion, a deal with Emery Reves, the proprietor of the Paris-based Co-operation Press Agency. Reves was a Hungarian Jew, already exiled and ruined because of the Nazi takeover in Germany, and he would lose everything once again when leaving Paris in 1940. He was both an ardent anti-fascist and an extremely talented salesman, and when Churchill finally agreed to use his agency services he was able to market Churchill's newspaper columns all over the world and make a fortune for both of them. Though Reves made him so much money, Churchill often treated him with appalling condescension, ignoring letters, stalling decisions, and then, when he finally made up his mind, expecting Reves to drop everything he was doing for other clients and rush to his side. In 1946, he demanded, after months of silence, that Reves not only fly the same day from Paris to London – it was already afternoon on a foggy day – but then continue on the next day by sea to America for an extended period. When Reves pointed out that neither the flight nor a transatlantic crossing on the maiden voyage of the *Queen Elizabeth* would be easy to arrange at short notice, Churchill made a few calls to well-placed friends at the Paris Embassy and Cunard and brushed aside his objections. But even Churchill could not lift the fog, and as a result Reves only just got to Southampton before his boat sailed. When he met in the ship's bar Lord Camrose, whom he was supposed to be assisting in selling the serial rights to Churchill's war memoirs in North America, it transpired that Churchill had not even remembered to tell Camrose that he was coming. (One contemporary noted that this was all part of Churchill's eighteenth-century, aristocratic manner, it being traditional to have a tame Jew on hand to look after business affairs.) Reves recognised that in his world of communications Churchill was a star product who just had to be taken as he was, and he was in any case motivated politically in his desire to have Churchill's writings against appeasement read throughout the world. After Reves' success in exploiting the market value of his war memoirs, particularly in relation to their newspaper serialisation, Churchill and Reves became friends too, and Churchill spent many weeks in the 1950s at Reves' villa in the South of France. Even then the relationship could be imperilled by Reves' suspicion that Churchill took him for granted.[1]

What matters here is the sheer success of Reves in getting Churchill into the newspapers of free Europe. The *Evening Standard* had worked with four European newspapers (all in France or the Benelux countries) in circulating Churchill's columns, and had produced a foreign income for Churchill of under £25 for each piece of writing. Within four months Reves had raised this to two dozen newspapers in eighteen countries and increased the gross income for each piece to almost a hundred pounds. Since the articles rolled off the production line about fortnightly, these new arrangements produced for Churchill a very substantial income indeed (even though Reves took a larger percentage than his previous agents) and helped him to surmount the 1937–9 financial crisis in his personal fortunes which almost necessitated the sale of Chartwell. More important historically, though, was the fact that when Churchill now wrote on such events as the 1938 Munich crisis, he was read all over Europe and the world. His 15 September 1938 column, 'Crisis', was carried by seventeen European papers and ten in the Empire (even this number understating the impact, because some outlets like the Dutch *Utrechtsch Nieuwesblad* syndicated his columns to ten more provincial papers). As Reves later put it, with pardonable pride, 'through my services he got on the front pages of the newspapers in twenty-five languages, with up to a fifteen, even a twenty million total circulation'. In the same period, Churchill's book of pre-war speeches, *Step by Step*, appeared not only in English, but also in French, German (in Holland), Italian, Swedish, Danish, Norwegian and Spanish. Reves was, wrote *The Times* in 1981, 'the idealist who sold Churchill to the world'.[2]

All of this had to come to an end in September 1939 when Churchill returned to office at the Admiralty, though the recovery of an official salary provided at least partial compensation for the loss of literary earnings. He could anyway now make news for himself as First Lord of the Admiralty, and from 1940 as Prime Minister, but such news would be reported and better understood in free Europe because of his much enhanced name-recognition there after all Reves' spadework in the previous two years. From 1940 onwards, however, there was not much left of free Europe with uncensored newspapers to report his doings, and the medium consequently had to change. From 1940 it was BBC radio that carried Churchill's message around Europe, rebroadcasting his war speeches for those among the local elites who spoke English, but also translating and summarising his words for the rest of its overseas audience.

For English-speakers in the Netherlands, his voice was as evocative as it was in Australia or the Far East, as indeed it was for a mass of ordinary French people who heard his single BBC broadcast in French. Paul Reynaud, writing in 1953, argued that 'all those who heard his broadcast to the French on October 21, 1940, retain an unforgettable memory of the deep emotion they felt when listening to it' Listening to the BBC, including Churchill's speeches as one of the main focuses in its presentation of Britain's war effort, was in itself an act of resistance for the occupied peoples, and required a good deal less risk than blowing up trains or collecting information. It could therefore involve far more of the local populations than those actively engaged in the actual resistance movements. When Churchill was celebrated around Western Europe after 1945, the speeches of ministers, mayors and vice chancellors invariably contained some reference to their pleasure in now hearing his voice in person, a familiar voice from years of radio listening, and even when his voice was not specifically mentioned there was always the citation of his war speeches as indispensable words of hope in years past. For example, Professor Mohr of the University of Oslo proclaimed in 1948 that Churchill would:

> stand not only as the spokesman, but as the personification of your people, its history and its noblest traditions. Your inspiring words, to which we listened with beating hearts, not only gave us courage and confidence, but also lit a feeling of obligation and the burning desire to do our duty in the gigantic fight for everything that makes life worthwhile.

When the assembled academic community cheered these words, Churchill responded by both waving his academic cap and giving his famous V-sign.

The Danes clearly had the same thought in mind, for he was greeted in Copenhagen by the Danish Radio Symphony Orchestra playing the first movement of Beethoven's fifth symphony (the 'Victory theme'), chosen because of its use on the wartime BBC to which they had secretly listened. When he visited Leyden in 1946, an unofficial part of his reception was the presentation of a cake by the students' club: this was, despite severe food shortages, 6 feet long, 4 feet wide and 2.5 feet deep, in the form of a model of the University building. Its walls were made of nougat, the towers of icing, and in the basements were tiny icing-sugar figures of students secretly listening to the BBC as they had done during the war. In Copenhagen in 1950, he also met the former members of a schoolboy Churchill Club, which had in wartime listened to his broadcasts and, inspired by them, carried out acts of anti-Nazi sabotage. In due course, his Nobel Prize citation, when he won the prize for Literature in 1953, made a point of including his war speeches as part of his literary output, words broadcast around Europe to keep hope alive. In some cases, for example the Netherlands, this wartime impact would then be reinforced by the return in 1944–5 of ministers of governments in exile and their monarchs, all people who had got to know Churchill personally during their sojourns in Britain since 1940, and who now praised him to the skies during peace celebrations in their own countries. For all these reasons, Churchill had by 1945 achieved a giant stature across the whole of Western Europe, though, as we shall see, the actual nature of the individual national responses varied greatly.[3]

His fame was then cemented through multitudes of post-war publications, not least his own war memoirs. With the help of Emery Reves, these six volumes appeared in all the significant Western European languages, were serialised in major newspapers throughout Europe as well as in the English-speaking countries, and apparently read avidly there too. Sometimes, indeed, the timing was particularly apt in reminding readers what it was in Churchill's life they were meant to be celebrating: in the same week of 1950 in which he was received in triumph in Copenhagen, the Danish papers began the serialisation of volume four, *The Hinge of Fate*. He was equally fortunate in the translation into other languages of the various adulatory books on Churchill that first appeared in English after 1945. The biography by the American Robert Lewis Taylor, for example, was translated into Swedish, Spanish, Hebrew and Norwegian within a year of its first appearance in the United States. But plenty of books on Churchill originated in other languages too. In addition to three books on Churchill that appeared in Spanish but were published in Cuba, Chile and Uruguay, the British Library and the New York Public Library contain between them thirty more books dating from the period 1945–55 for which the original language was not English and the place of publication in continental Europe: seven of these were in French, four in Swedish, four in Dutch, three in each of Norwegian, Spanish and German (one of them published in Switzerland), two each in Italian and Czech, one in Portuguese. Given the Churchill legend at the time, the mood of these books was predictably supportive, and if not all were purely hagiographical in tone, none seems to have taken a critical line either. A further seventeen books on Churchill first appeared in European languages between 1955 and 1970, five of them now in German and four in Italian as wartime hostilities receded from immediate memory.[4]

FRANCE

The European country that Churchill had visited most often over his long life, the one with which he felt the closest affinity, was France; he had probably already crossed the Channel a hundred times when he went to France as First Lord of the Admiralty in 1939. And though his command of French was to say the least idiosyncratic, even to the point of deliberate self-parody ('Prenez garde. Je vais parler français!'), he had a reasonable working knowledge of the language, certainly more than he had of any other tongue except English. He was proud of his close association with three generations of French political leaders, from his arrival on the scene of European defence politics during the Entente's preparations for the Great War, when he had first visited France ministerially to witness military manoeuvres in 1907, through to the diplomacy of the Cold War in the 1950s. Paris's *Le Soir* had been one of the first and most loyal outlets for his 1930s newspaper columns, Georges Clemenceau was a politician he particularly admired and had written about as the epitome of war leadership in his *Great Contemporaries*, while in the later 1940s he could count on former French premiers like Edouard Herriot and Paul Reynaud as personal friends. In the last two decades of his life he spent several weeks of each year on the Riviera, painting and soaking up the sun.

The relationship was close then, and Churchill may even be claimed as one of the architects of French recovery of great-power status in the period after 1945, but it was far from unproblematic, not least because of Churchill's tempestuous personal relations with Charles de Gaulle. During the 1930s, Churchill had envisaged a coming war in which Britain's alliance with France would be the lynchpin of its own security, as it had been in 1914–18. Part of his despair over Munich in 1938 stemmed from his awareness that the British Government's actions had weakened French confidence in its own main ally, and it is clear that Churchill had not the faintest expectation that France might collapse in a future war as it quickly did in 1940. As the French army retreated across the north-east of France in May–June 1940, Churchill was regularly in the country, trying to harry its government into action, urging it not to despair and promising British aid – much as he did with more success in Washington in December 1941. Recalling those days in June 1945, Edouard Herriot said that Churchill had 'cried like a child' when he could not persuade France to fight on, but added:

> If at that time, discouraged, he too had capitulated instead of gritting his teeth and pulling himself together in a gesture of energy, what would we be at this moment? We should not be here today, all united together among friends: there would be the Gestapo instead. We must remain faithful to this old friendship, because the British are a people who love justice and freedom, and perhaps who love liberty more than we do. The British fought for right and liberty. Many died on the battlefields of France. We must not forget that – ever.

Even after the evacuation from Dunkirk, Churchill was determined that British troops return to France further west and keep up a continental war alongside the French.[5]

Churchill even offered France a permanent political union with Britain during this stressful time. In putting forward this extraordinary proposal, he sought to show how committed Britain was to France's defence, but if accepted Anglo-French Union would also have allowed a legally recognised French government to continue the war from Britain or North Africa, after metropolitan France was occupied (with crucial consequences for control of the French fleet and French overseas colonies). This was just what did occur in Norway and the Netherlands, and Churchill's own vow to continue the war from the Empire if the British Isles were occupied was of the same character. Nevertheless, he needed some persuading when the plan was first put to him by Jean Monnet (as did de Gaulle), he took no action to transfer the RAF's remaining reserves to France as Monnet had also demanded, and he certainly did not intervene in his 'action this day' mode to ensure that the Foreign Office processed the relevant documents quickly, the weekend being sacrosanct for the FO even in June 1940. The wording of his appeal was also a touch insensitive. He told Premier Reynaud that 'if England won the war France would be restored to her dignity and greatness', a prospect that a French cabinet was no more likely to find reassuring than did Australians when they heard that Churchill had said that it did not matter if Australia itself was conquered by the Japanese, since this could easily be reversed after the war was won elsewhere. Delays contributed to the failure of the scheme, but in the desperate, defeatist mood of France in June 1940 no such encouragement had much chance of success anyway.

Churchill had therefore to be content to receive de Gaulle in London, not as head of a French government in exile but as the ministerial and military leader of a group of Frenchmen who had individually repudiated their Government's decision to surrender, a very different thing. Just how far the surrender of France had changed things from what might have been in 1940 was made brutally clear when Churchill was asked in the Commons late in the war if the offer of union with France still stood now that liberated France might discuss it again. His reply was a curt 'No, sir.' (He was indeed by this time talking more about common citizenship with the United States than with France.) Four years later a suspicious French Assembly, the deputies' memories reawakened by reading Churchill's war memoirs on 1940, debated that original offer of Anglo-French union in 1940: Churchill's own words, 'Rarely has so generous a proposal encountered such a hostile reception,' could after all hardly be ignored in France. Few of the Assembly's members had a good word for the idea, either as to its seriousness at the time or as to its being an incident that could teach anything for the present and the future.[6]

Not the least of Churchill's extraordinary contributions in summer 1940 was the mental agility with which he rethought all his own previous convictions and for the first time imagined how Britain could fight on after France had surrendered. The first consequence of this for France itself was the ruthless action taken in the Mediterranean by the Royal Navy to neutralise the French fleet, a policy that went well enough in Egypt but which in the Algerian ports caused considerable loss of French sailors' lives. This naturally caused an outcry in France, especially after the generosity of Churchill's language towards France only days earlier. Thereafter his wartime relationship with France was less difficult. As in other countries his later broadcast speeches – especially his 1940 broadcast in French, beginning 'C'est moi, Churchill, qui vous parle . . .' – were much listened to and the resistance movements at least in the north of France had their supplies, organisation, instructions and encouragement from Britain, not least because of the presence there of de Gaulle's Free French forces, themselves armed and financed by Britain. Though the much quoted Churchillian remark that, of all the crosses that he had to bear in wartime, 'the heaviest was the [Gaullist] Cross of Lorraine', is very likely apocryphal, its fame as a saying derives from the certainty that he thought along those lines, even if he never actually said it.

De Gaulle was an extremely difficult ally to deal with, not only because he had an elevated sense of his personal importance (way above what he and the Free French forces actually counted for in the global conflict of 1940–3), but also because he saw himself as the true government of France, even if nobody else did, and therefore claimed rights he could not be given, and resented the inevitable slights (for example, the denying after the Casablanca Conference of his right to attend summit meetings of Allied leaders along with the 'big three'). De Gaulle must surely also have been appalled by Churchill's routine massacring of the French language. Churchill generally just translated the English words and paid no attention whatsoever to syntax or subtlety. The young Harold Wilson witnessed his explanation of why he could not release to de Gaulle French gold held in the Bank of England: 'Mon cher Général, quand je me trouve en face de la Vieille Dame de Threadneedle Street, alors je suis tout à fait impotent.' In the circumstances Churchill was remarkably understanding, far more so than Roosevelt – and Roosevelt was safely in Washington and therefore isolated from de Gaulle's

Daily Mail, 27 April 1959

worst behaviour. It was Churchill's British Government that stood up for de Gaulle as the Free French leader recognised by the Allies, when the Americans wanted to ditch him in 1942 in favour of the far more dubious Admiral Darlan. And if (as has been claimed but not yet proved either way) Darlan's subsequent assassination was connived in by the British, then they committed an act from which de Gaulle was bound to be the main beneficiary. Once D-Day had taken place, British forces in France made little effort to stop de Gaulle simply setting up his own civil government as the Allied lines advanced across France, and in due course Churchill was happy to arrange for Paris to appear to be liberated by his Free French forces, and for de Gaulle himself to take a prominent part in the process. Jean Monnet has argued that de Gaulle's emergence as France's leader in 1944–5 owed much to his own abilities, but was also due 'in part to powerful support from outside, in the form of Churchill's loyal and stubborn friendship'.[7]

All of this was in any case consistent with British foreign policy towards Europe as the war drew to a close, centring as it did on the aim of building up France as a potential ally for the future, especially if the Russians were to go on moving west and the Americans to go home. The Francophile Anthony Eden may have helped to press this policy on Churchill on behalf of the Foreign Office, but he did not dissent from it. In September 1943, Churchill himself declared, 'I regard the restoration of France . . . as a sacred duty . . . It is one of the most enduring interests of Britain in Europe that there should be a strong France.' At Yalta, as Harry Hopkins reported to Roosevelt, Churchill and Eden 'fought like tigers for France'.[8] Without such British advocacy, France would not have been given its own zone of occupation in defeated Germany in the teeth of Russian resistance, and was unlikely to have been awarded a permanent seat in the Security Council of the new United Nations organisation either. After all, in the aftermath of defeat, devastation, a four-year occupation, and a liberation that had done further damage to life and property, France was in no position to make good its own claim to great-power status in 1945. If de Gaulle's sensitivities had already been outraged by his treatment when resident in Britain, and national pride dented by the fact that France had been mainly liberated by 'les Anglo-Saxons', then the awareness that British patronage had helped to restore France's international role too would hardly have helped. Having been kept out of the post-war economic planning at Dumbarton Oaks and of the political summit at Yalta, it was indeed far from clear that the French would even accept the role which Churchill had persuaded Roosevelt to offer them.[9]

Once having performed this act of self-interested charity to France, however, Churchill spent the rest of his active political career trying to escape from its consequences. When the Americans excluded Britain from the ANZUS pact, for example, he was extremely unimpressed on being told that the inclusion of Britain must also open the door to France as the other great colonial power in the region. And, when seeking at regular intervals summit conferences with the USA after he returned to office in 1951, he was outraged by the American suggestion that any meeting to co-ordinate Western policies towards Russia should include France (and possibly Germany too by 1953) as well as Britain. Wherever possible, he scornfully refused to include 'the bloody Frogs' in his plans, and at Bermuda in 1953 was delighted that the illness of the French premier Laniel meant that he missed most of the meetings. Churchill, immersed in a novel by C. S. Forester on the Napoleonic Wars called *Death to the French*, then managed to get himself photographed by the press with the book in his hand and the title clearly visible. The conference over, he persuaded Lord Moran to administer the appropriate dosage to Laniel, so that he would remain 'heavily drugged' throughout the flight home, and Churchill would thereby be spared the boredom of having to speak French. In part this reflected some real worries about the political stability of Fourth Republic France in the early post-war years, especially when in 1946 the Communists seemed to be on the rise there (exactly the outcome he had sought to avoid when backing de Gaulle and the Gaullist resistance in 1944–5).

There was, though, an inherent contradiction between Churchill's desire to see France rise again as an *available* ally in Europe (arguably indeed this involved his whole policy on European recovery) and his core aim that Britain should remain America's sole partner in determining the Western world order – a contradiction easy to see from the viewpoint of Washington and Paris, but apparently invisible from Chartwell and Chequers. When he had delivered his 'iron curtain' speech, with its demand for an Anglo-American special relationship to police the world, he received an immediate request for clarification from his old cabinet colleague Duff Cooper, by then British Ambassador in Paris. Cooper reported that many Frenchmen were worried that Churchill 'had given up France as a lost country which could no longer be of assistance to anyone', and that his hopes 'were centred solely on the United States'. Frenchmen who did entertain such worries would not have been much reassured by Churchill's reply, which regretted that France had 'fallen again into political fatuity' and hoped that the Communists would not win the impending election – in which case he would consider them 'ruined for ever', though he trusted 'that even a Communist France will not debar me from Monte Carlo'. He concluded with the hope 'that France will shape her destiny in harmony with the two great Western democracies', but even that patronising view did not envisage France ever actually *becoming* one of the great Western democracies, alongside Britain and America. De Gaulle's own memoirs record Churchill saying to him that if ever Britain had to choose between France and the open seas he would choose the ocean. This is once again a Churchillian saying whose accuracy has been challenged, but there is not too much doubt that it represented his thoughts if never his words.[10]

The war memoirs did not, however, only raise French sensitivities over the issue of the offer of Anglo-French Union. Despite deletions from the French edition of material likely to be thought insulting, the French army in particular was not happy with Churchill's account of 1940. As Reves mischievously put it to Churchill in 1949, 'it seems that your Memoirs have aroused the aggressive spirit of the French generals which was so lacking in 1939. Perhaps it was a mistake not to publish this second volume at the start of the war.' All of this contributed to Churchill's continuously prickly relations with de Gaulle, which proved the backdrop to one of the wickedest jokes of his final years. When consulted by the War Office on plans being made for his funeral, he asked for changes from previous versions of the route to be taken by the funeral procession, so that it would now entrain at Waterloo Station rather than Paddington. Asked why he wanted to make such a change, the railway links between Paddington and Oxfordshire being so much easier, he replied with a twinkle in his eye that he expected de Gaulle to outlive him, and hoped that on the day of his funeral the French President would be forced to remember the Battle of Waterloo. But there are places around the world where de Gaulle has had the last laugh, for example in the wax museum in Prague, where the figures of Churchill and de Gaulle stand side by side, each lifesize, and it is there-fore impossible to look at Churchill without being aware of the great, overshadowing presence of de Gaulle. Ironically, Churchill had told Monnet, when he first met de Gaulle in 1940, 'He is a man of my stature.' On the same occasion, de Gaulle, who like Churchill preferred to pay compliments with an autobiographical slant, said of Churchill that 'he is made for grandiose tasks'. During his active career after 1945, however, Churchill did not often have to deal politically with de Gaulle, since the General was out of office until after his own retirement, and de Gaulle did not anyway bear personal – as opposed to political – grudges. As soon as he returned as French President in 1958, he made sure that Churchill was awarded the Cross of the Liberation, which he had through some oversight missed out on a decade earlier when it was given to Eisenhower. When Churchill died, he delivered one of the loftiest and most eloquent tributes to the man, put bygones behind him, and attended the funeral in person. De Gaulle, after all, was the last one likely to miss a chance to celebrate a truly great man, and to point out from the evidence of Churchill's career that great men could change the course of history. Talking to Lord Gladwyn, the former British

Ambassador in Paris, de Gaulle confided that he had been 'profoundly impressed' with the funeral and much moved.[11]

The fact that Churchill's failure to receive the Cross of the Liberation in the 1940s was indeed an oversight rather than an intended snub is shown clearly enough in the showers of other French honours that came his way as soon as the war was over – indeed from the moment that France was liberated. Even before the end of 1944, a Parisian publisher had issued biographies of all the Allied leaders, but with interestingly varied titles. De Gaulle was 'soldat et politique' and Roosevelt 'La Dictature de la liberté', but Churchill's biography was called *Winston Churchill, ou l'Ami de France*. Written by a prominent Molière scholar and theologian, Jacques Arnavon, it took an extremely upbeat view of Churchill's life and significance. The foreword hailed the gigantic achievement of Churchill, who, in the greatest revolution in the annals of humanity, had saved the world from tyranny. It concluded that what Frenchmen would remember is that 'at the most critical time' Churchill had emerged as unrelentingly energetic and faithful to truth. 'France salutes in Winston Churchill a genius and a friend. She knows he believes in her, and she believes she must worthily return his trust, despite her martyrdom and misery, in the immense work of regeneration and recovery.'

A few French towns immediately decided to rename a street in his honour, for example at Brive-la-Gaillarde, or later took the decision to commemorate a visit at this time, as at Caen, where a bridge (previously the Pont l'Abbatoirs!) was renamed in 1953 to remind its citizens of his incognito visit to Normandy in 1944, when he had crossed the bridge in person. A visit to Paris in November 1944 was a great success, not least because Churchill was able to make use at the Quai d'Orsay of a gold bath prepared for Hermann Goering – and to take delight in the fact that Eden had as Foreign Secretary only a silver one. The French War Office had somehow found and displayed a bust of the Duke of Marlborough, so Churchill was also greeted by his great ancestor, and he repaid the compliment by laying a wreath before the statue of Clemenceau and respectfully visiting the tomb of Napoleon. The streets were packed, he took the salute at a huge military parade, and, as Duff Cooper noted, 'whenever there was a pause, there were large cries of "Churchill" from all over the crowd'. As early as January 1945 he was made a member of the Académie Française, and in the same month a French translation of his war speeches was published. In his last weeks as Prime Minister in 1945 he was actively speaking about the need for a revived France to play a full part in European affairs, and, when his general election defeat became clear, one of the most outspoken critics of his removal from office was the French General Weygand. In November 1945, on a visit to Paris, he received the gold medal of the Académie in person, attended a banquet in his honour, lunched with de Gaulle and was cheered through the streets.[12]

Though French politicians and newspapers were critical of what he had to say at Fulton in March 1946 and lukewarm about his proposals at Zurich in September, the honours continued to flow. A special tribute to Churchill's war leadership was incorporated in a report by the foreign affairs committee of the French Assembly in July 1946 and in December he was awarded the Médaille Militaire, France's equivalent of the Victoria Cross. At the presentation ceremony in the following month, the ancient practice whereby persons of high rank were actually given their medal by an uncommissioned soldier who already held the award was given a special twist for Churchill, who received his from Premier Ramadier, a war veteran who had received his own MM while serving as a sergeant in 1914. (Churchill was wearing for the occasion the splendid dress uniform of a colonel of Hussars, much as he had earlier upstaged Clemenceau by turning up to another French dinner in the red-striped trousers and plumed hat of an Elder Brother of Trinity House. Asked to explain all this finery, he replied that he was 'un Frère Ainé de la Trinité' – the Trinity's elder brother. 'Ah, quelle belle situation!' responded the Frenchman.) After lunch with the premier, Churchill dined with the President. Walking from the British Embassy to the Elysée Palace, he was cheered and clapped all the way, his new medal prominent on the lapel of his evening dress.[13]

Later visits allowed other French cities to see and cheer him too, Bordeaux in 1948, Cannes, Metz and Strasbourg in 1949, Nancy in 1950, among many others, and in each of these cases he was made a freeman of the city too. His expectations of such visits are shown clearly enough by the fact that, when Churchill found that Strasbourg was celebrating a public holiday on the day of his visit in 1949, he was 'rather put out' (as Harold Macmillan noted in his diary) when told that it was actually for the Feast of the Annunciation and not just in his honour. He became president of the Anglo-French Friendship Society in 1950 and was thereafter regularly re-elected (a post specifically commemorated by Angoulême in naming a new boulevard after him in 1976 on the proposal of the society). In that capacity he had planned to greet the French President when he landed at Dover on an official visit in 1950 until political business made it impossible (but a press release was issued lest it seem like a snub to France). In similar vein he sent as Prime Minister an extravagant message to France on the fiftieth anniversary of the Entente Cordiale in 1954, and a personal message to veterans of the Free French forces when they gathered for a commemorative reunion in 1953. Though his war memoirs dealt with sensitive issues like the French surrender in 1940 and the subsequent naval attacks on French warships, and a few reviewers were critical of the way in which he had presented the story, their publication also provided the opportunity for veteran French politicians like Herriot and Reynaud to endorse their accuracy and urge Frenchmen to read the books for themselves.[14]

As the freedoms suggest, though, Churchill's legend in France was recognised not only by the political class in Paris, but all across the land. There was a cluster of such commemorations on the Riviera where even after 1955 he was a regular visitor: Cap d'Ail made him its honorary *maire* and gave him a sash of office to prove it, Roquebrune awarded its freedom, a large monument was unveiled on the Riviera in 1967 and a bust in Monte Carlo in 1969. There was indeed a new burst of namings of streets after Churchill following his death, including the Avenue Winston Churchill in Paris, a viaduct in Strasbourg (now guarded at one end by a block of flats named Residences le Winston) and a Pont Churchill in Lyons.[15]

By the end of the century, thoroughfares named after Churchill existed all across France, many clustered in the war zones of the eastern frontier (Arras, Laon, Lille, Sainte-Dizier) and the Normandy area (Bayeux, Caen, Le Havre, Le Mans) as well as the Riviera, but a visitor is just as likely to encounter a Boulevard Winston Churchill, a Place Churchill or an Avenue Sir Winston Churchill in the west (Nantes, Rennes), the Massif Central (Clermont-Ferrand, Limoges), the Loire Valley (Tours, Angoulême) or the south-east (Toulon). To be sure, they are far outnumbered by streets named after modern French statesmen like Clemenceau and Poincaré, and even by the omnipresent Boulevards du President Wilson of 1919, but they are about as common as those named after the charismatic President Kennedy in the 1960s. In the case of Rennes in Brittany, Churchill and Kennedy were actually commemorated at the same council meeting as a result of a single proposal by the

Maire. Certainly no other foreigners are encountered so often on French street signs.[16]

What then was the point of all these namings? Sometimes, there was administrative necessity to push it along, as when Charleville-Mezières was created from five previous municipalities and sought to avoid confusion where it had more than one street with the same name by renaming one of them, hence the Place Carnot in Charleville became Place Winston-Churchill. Even here, though, the memory of Churchill just after his death was clearly a motive too, and this was usually quite explicit. The Maire of Limoges, for instance, informed his council that he had sent the British Ambassador condolences from the Limousins as soon as Churchill's death was announced. He also urged that, as an act of 'hommage public', the town should name a street in honour of Churchill so that the name of the man who so largely contributed to saving the liberty of humanity in the Second World War would remain known to all future generations. For Lille, where Churchill had personally witnessed as Minister of Munitions the liberation parade in 1918 as well as contributing more directly to the city's second liberation in 1944, he was simply 'one of the heroes of this century' and the Maire's citation averred that French men and women would never forget the indomitable courage of Churchill and the British people in 1940–1, without which they, the Lillois, could not have recovered their freedom. The citation put forward by the socialist Maire of Le Havre, after recounting earlier phases of Churchill's career, noted that during the most sombre hours of the war he had been 'in the eyes of the world the last bastion of resistance to the forces of the Axis'. Sometimes the commemoration was given a more specifically local focus, generally from towns in the war zones. Laon noted the need to render homage to 'a great British statesman' precisely because it had suffered so much in the four years of occupation, 1940–4, and given so many of its own children to the war in which Churchill had played such a 'predominant role'. Tours had a different local slant. It recalled the visit of Churchill to the city in June 1940, when for three days Tours had actually been 'the capital of France' after the Government fled from Paris and before it moved on to Bordeaux, and cited approvingly Churchill's account in his war memoirs of meeting de Gaulle there, thus neatly linking two men of destiny with its own place in history.[17]

Such memorialising did not fade in the 1960s when most of these streets were renamed. The centre of Paris had had an Avenue Winston Churchill (formerly named after Alexander III of Russia) since 1966 too, but no statue until Jacques Chirac became President of the Republic. Though deeply devoted to the memory of Churchill's old adversary de Gaulle (whom London had belatedly honoured with a statue only in 1993), and to the maintenance of a Gaullist tradition in French politics, Chirac personally ensured that Paris should like most European capitals have a statue of Winston Churchill, duly inaugurated in the presence of both himself and Queen Elizabeth in 1998. Edward VII, as the promoter of the 1904 Entente Cordiale, was the only previous Briton to be so honoured in Paris. Though Paul Reynaud's claim in 1953, that Churchill was 'of all men now living . . . incontestably the most generally popular in France', was somewhat over the top, the Maire of Saint-Vigor le Grand near Caen could maintain even in 2001 that 'avant et depuis le Débarquement des forces alliées en Normandie le 06 Juin 1944 qui nous a tous liberé du joug nazi, la mémoire de Sir Winston Churchill reste et restera éternellement gravée dans notre esprit et celui des nos descendants'.[18]

THE LOW COUNTRIES

In the case of Belgium, Luxembourg and the Netherlands, admiration for Churchill and all that he stood for was uncomplicatedly warm. These were after all places with a pro-British tradition anyway, and in Belgium's case also grateful for Britain's sacrifices in 1914–18. At the start of that war he had sought personally to galvanise the defence of Antwerp against the Germans and then for some months in 1915–16 had commanded a battalion in the trenches at 'Plugstreet' in Belgian Flanders. (It was perhaps significant that when the Dutch honoured him in 1948, even their bands played 'It's a long way to Tipperary', though the country had been neutral in 1914–18.) All three countries continued to receive Churchill's newspaper articles right through until the outbreak of war and his return to ministerial office in 1939. Already in 1937, soon after Emery Reves began marketing the product, Churchill's political columns were being carried by *Le Soir* in Brussels, by the *Luxemburger Zeitung*, by Rotterdam's *Nieuwe Rotterdamsche Courant* and Amsterdam's *Algemeen Handelsblad* (as well as papers in many smaller Dutch towns).[19]

Many of those who read the Churchillian warnings about appeasement between 1937 and 1939 would have seen them as all too prophetic when their own three inoffensive countries – threatening nobody and part of no alliance system – became in 1940 the casualties of appeasement's failure. Even Ireland's Prime Minister de Valera, rarely to be heard voicing criticisms of German policy, was outspoken in his denunciation of these undeclared invasions of the neutral Benelux countries, foreseeing in their fate the future destiny of Ireland were Britain and France to fall too. Thereafter, with resistance in the Low Countries directed and supplied from London (and not much affected by the different agendas pursued by Communists within the resistance movements of Italy and southern France), with the BBC overseas broadcasts easy to tune into for receivers so near to the United Kingdom, with their governments in exile in London and (in the Netherlands case) their royal family in Britain for the duration too, citizens of these occupied countries naturally looked to Britain and its leader for any hope of future liberation. In due course, since their armies were on the left of the Allied advance from Normandy to the Rhine in 1944–5, British and Canadian troops rather than Americans mainly liberated Belgium and the Netherlands. Montgomery's armies suffered additional casualties in trying to liberate the Dutch too quickly at Arnhem, while the hinge between the British and American armies was the point in Luxembourg that the Germans exploited in the Ardennes offensive of winter 1944–5. In the final months of the war, with the Benelux countries now behind the Allied lines, Churchill visited them several times as he criss-crossed Europe between conferences with Allied leaders and visits to Montgomery's armies. When spotted by the local population – these visits not being advertised in advance for security reasons – there were spontaneous demonstrations of affection. At a dinner at the Mansion House in November 1944, Churchill hailed the presence of the Burgomaster of Brussels as 'living proof' of the Allies' success in liberating free peoples, and both the event and the speech were given even greater prominence in the Belgian press. Shortly afterwards he attended a celebratory lunch in his honour at the Belgian Embassy in London, and when visiting Antwerp in 1946 he greeted the Burgomaster as 'an old friend' who had also spent the war years in London. When Dutch civilians were accidentally killed by RAF raids on German rocket sites, Churchill was highly critical, not only because the raids had missed their targets but also because they had caused such anguish to 'a friendly people'.[20]

With the war over and Churchill soon out of office, the statements of gratitude could become more planned, more formal and more elaborate. Even before he left office in July 1945, he had been offered the freedom of Antwerp in recognition of the 'moral support' he had given to the Belgian and Dutch people and of his wartime leadership of the Allies. During an official visit in the following November he was formally installed as an Antwerp freeman 'in the presence of the Antwerp school community', and became a freeman of Brussels too. Over that same week in Belgium, he was awarded an honorary degree, a generous gift of diamonds and a fine tapestry (the latter ending up on loan to the Victoria and Albert Museum). He was made an associate of the Belgian Academy and addressed the Belgian Parliament, of which he was made an honorary life member. 'The Belgian people', reported the *Daily Telegraph*, 'must be the cheerleaders of Europe.'

> Sometimes this lung power was concentrated on a single figure. Sometimes the lungs just let out an indescribable roar, sometimes they said 'Vive Churchill!' But more often they said 'Church-heel! Church-heel! Church-heel!'

A girl student told Churchill that his broadcasts had made her and her friends all want to learn English (a desire possibly reinforced by his recent Brussels address in French), while university students greeted him with the 'V for Victory' theme from Beethoven's fifth symphony, already almost a personal anthem on foreign trips. A recently discovered new plant from the Belgian Congo was officially declared to be the 'Sodum Churchillianum', and for good measure Churchill's daughter was commemorated too in a new dahlia to be called 'Mary Churchill'. This visit, his first foreign trip on public business after he went into opposition, largely set the pattern for later visits to other countries as each strove to outdo their predecessors in adulation. It also set another, less satisfactory precedent. Speaking in Brussels, Churchill had talked about 'a United States of Europe' emerging in the near future, but he had also told the Belgians that:

> The affairs of Great Britain and the British Commonwealth and Empire are becoming ever more closely interwoven with those of the United States, and that an underlying unity of thought and conviction increasingly pervades the English-speaking world.

In other words, Churchill's fatal ambiguity on 'Europe' was already in place in November 1945.[21]

Gifts continued to flow in, such as a cigar box made of malachite and ivory sent from the Belgian Congo in April 1946, presented on the initiative of the Minister for the Colonies. In August he was back again for another week in Brussels, being given lunch by the Prince Regent and being awarded the Order of Leopold. It was later announced that Churchill had been given special permission actually to wear the award, a privilege not normally granted to foreigners.[22] He was back again in October 1948 and in February 1949, Brussels being already one of the crossroads of the movement towards European integration. On the latter occasion there were demonstrations against Churchill's support for the Cold War and for European unity by the Belgian Communists, at the instigation of their *Drapeau Rouge* newspaper, but the small number of boos (and a mere twenty arrests) only indicated the weakness of their opposition when compared to the huge crowds that turned out to cheer. Churchill of all people was not likely to be upset by small groups of fanatics shouting such slogans as 'Hitler also wanted to unite Europe.' As Prime Minister after 1951, he maintained friendly relations with Paul-Henri Spaak, the dominant Belgian political figure of the age, and sent special condolences in 1953 when Belgium was devastated by floods. Spaak recalled in his memoirs that Churchill's career had taught him many things, not least in his reaction to electoral defeat in 1945, when he had shown wisdom but never resignation: 'one had only to hear him speak of that cruel shock, and the revenge he would wreak to know the two sentiments should never be confused'. He continued to visit Churchill whenever in London, 'to pay him my respects and show him my friendship. I saw the old lion when he was tired, but I never saw him without being moved. To the very end I tried to show him that, like so many others, I had not forgotten what we owed him.'[23]

Churchill had already taken special care in the way in which his war memoirs treated the Belgians' surrender in 1940, coming as it did at a critical juncture for British troops still engaged in battle at Dunkirk and expecting that the Belgians would keep up fighting for a little longer and so give the defenders of Dunkirk more time to evacuate.[24] However, even the care with which he had worded his account did not (and probably could not) entirely satisfy the Belgians, and especially those conscious of the honour of King Leopold, who had personally taken the decision to surrender. Churchill had suggested to Reves that he might write a short introduction to the French translation of the volume covering 1940, so as to offer 'words for them appreciative of the French Army and soothing offence given both to French and Belgian military circles'. He was nevertheless in receipt of 'an aggressive and disagreeable letter' from the distinguished historian Henri Pirenne, acting on behalf of King Leopold, who had been deeply upset by Churchill's attempt to soothe him. The King's secretary, Baron Carton de Wiart, also wrote to Churchill, asking him to repudiate the statement he had made in the Commons on 4 June 1940, indicating that Belgium had surrendered unexpectedly and 'without prior consultation with its allies', a statement reprinted in his memoirs. This Churchill declined to do, though he had actually known of the likely Belgian surrender in 1940 (through a message from the Belgian King to George VI) several days before it happened. The British King now connived at Churchill's little deception and continued to do so in other ways too, for example by denying King Leopold an invitation to the wedding of the future Queen Elizabeth II. Churchill merely reminded de Wiart that 'at the time I rendered the most complete homage to the Belgian army', and that he had said nothing since to criticise in any way 'the value and honour of the Belgian army and its commanders'. In view of the political crisis then going on in Belgium, leading up to a referendum on the future of the monarchy, the special preface was then withdrawn from further French editions of the book, since it seemed only to have drawn attention to an inescapably contentious problem. All of this demonstrates clearly enough the extent to which the fine-tuning of Churchill's war memoirs was indeed a matter of post-war political statecraft, but it also shows that even such national leaders as King Leopold cared deeply what Churchill said about them, in view of the large numbers of Belgian citizens who were reading and being influenced by his words.[25]

None of this had a lasting effect on Churchill's admirers in Belgium. Antwerp, Brussels, Dinant and Liège all named streets after him, some immediately after the war ended in 1945, others when he died in 1965 (Antwerp also then renamed a Churchilldok after him, a commemorative plaque being unveiled shortly afterwards by Queen Elizabeth II). His statue was erected in Brussels' Avenue Churchill in 1967, unveiled in the presence of Belgium's Prince Albert and Britain's Princess Margaret by Paul-Henri Spaak with a glowing tribute to Churchill. He was a man who had:

> par son courage, son obstination, sa confiance en lui-même et dans la peuple qu'il représentait, a été l'élément décisif de la résistance au mal et de la défaite de celui-ci. L'éloge que l'on peut faire de lui se résume en une seule phrase très courte mais lourde de signification: sans lui l'avenir aurait été différent ... Churchill fût notre leader à tous. L'immortalité que nous lui conférons en érigeant cette statue qui bravera le temps et empechera l'oubli, c'est aussi celle de la glorieuse aventure que nous avons vécue.

In due course there was also a Churchill statue erected in 1973 in Luxembourg, where there was already a Place Churchill too, unveiled in similar terms and with an equivalent assertion of Churchill's lasting significance to the Grand Duchy and its inhabitants. He had been awarded the freedom of Luxembourg city in 1946, following a banquet given by the Chamber of Commerce.[26]

In the case of the Netherlands, things were less complicated, for the royal family was closer to Churchill and had nothing to fear from what he might write about them in his war memoirs. In addition to defending Dutch civilians against stray RAF bombs in the last years of the war, he was also active in ensuring that relief supplies got through. A first official thank-you came in November 1945 when he visited Queen Wilhelmina and was given the originals of several letters of his great ancestor the Duke of Marlborough to the Dutch Estates, gifts sensitively chosen to appeal both to his familial piety and to his historical interests, but also presumably of considerable monetary value. Six months later, he was fêted in the Netherlands much as he had already been fêted in Belgium. The Queen took an active part in the proceedings, accompanying him around the country as if he himself was visiting royalty. He received an honorary degree from the ancient university of Leyden, addressed the States General (the Dutch Parliament), received the gold medal of Solstdijk, and was made an honorary member of Rotterdam City Council, among many other miscellaneous honours, the Rotterdam citation referring to his exceptional services in defence of democracy and in the liberation of the Netherlands. (The council seat in which he sat during the ceremony still carries a small plaque to celebrate the historic moment when it bore the great man's posterior.) In due course, as in Belgium, he was given special permission to wear his Dutch awards outside the country, notably the insignia of the Knight Grand Cross, Netherlands Lion. Dutch enthusiasm was demonstrated in what the *Daily Mail* called 'five miles of cheering crowds' in Amsterdam, and in a much photographed stroll in the Solstdijk Park in which his only companions were the young Dutch princesses, Wilhelmina's grand-children. When he left in a Dutch airliner, Prince Bernhard personally piloted an escorting plane as far as the border. In 1948 Churchill enjoyed a second week of Dutch triumphs, residing at the Solstdijk Palace itself when in The Hague for the European Movement's congress, and the following year he received the Grotius Medal for his defence of the rule of law during the Second World War. In 1950, he was again lunching with the Dutch Queen, though this time in London. Rotterdam installed a Churchill bust in its City Hall on his eightieth birthday in 1954, and in 1955 the Dutch Parliament commissioned a portrait of Churchill by the Dutch artist Max Nauta to hang on the walls of a new reception room. Churchill gave Nauta four sittings at Chartwell to facilitate the portrait, and the painting was duly displayed in London before going to The Hague. At a reception at the Dutch Embassy, Nauta not only praised Churchill's own paintings but also took pride in the number of Dutch painters whose work hung on the walls of Chartwell, so bringing his subject just a little closer to the place where the portrait would in future be hung. The Dutch were clearly very anxious to own a piece of Winston. Churchill remained anxious to reciprocate such awards and compliments, for example responding to the award of the Grotius Medal with the assertion:

> He had been deeply touched by the kindness with which he had always been treated by the Dutch people. Queen Juliana was the reigning sovereign of a State which had played so fine a part not only in the history of Europe, but in the cause of freedom.

This concern continued long after retirement, as in his sending a message of respect for the Dutch war dead, on the twentieth anniversary of the 1940 invasion of the Netherlands in May 1960. And the Dutch continued to pay their respects too: The Hague has a Winston-Churchillplein outside its Congress Centre, commemorating his

important role there in 1948, but the sign also identifies Churchill as
the leader of Britain and the West in the Second World War. Rotterdam
too has a Churchillplein, renamed to honour him shortly after he died.
Amsterdam's Churchilllaan intersects appropriately enough with Vic-
toryplein, thus associating him in perpetuity with memories of Dutch
liberation in 1944–5, but that broad thoroughfare contains, somewhat
oddly, a statue not of Churchill but of his great adversary in Indian
policy, Mahatma Gandhi. What the shade of Winston Churchill thought
when that 'half-naked fakir' was erected in stone and bronze in the
middle of *his* street in a great European city was fortunately inaudible
to the human ear.[27]

SCANDINAVIA

For the Danes and Norwegians, the wartime story was much as it was
for the Belgians and the Dutch, small nations already aware of Churchill
through newspaper outlets in Oslo, Bergen, Stavanger and Copenhagen.[28] In the war they could once again receive the BBC without
undue difficulty, and mount resistance movements that were run from
London, though through not being on the way to Berlin they were
liberated very late and not visited by Churchill or other British leaders
until long after the war had ended. But Churchill was careful to send
Norway a personal message in May 1945, the country's first independence
day that could be celebrated since 1939 happily coinciding with the
month of liberation and the end of the war. There were then early plans
for Churchill to visit Norway in 1946, but these had to be cancelled
because of threats that the small but active Norwegian Communist Party
would disrupt proceedings as a protest against Churchill's 'iron curtain'
speech at Fulton. The King and Government were not prepared to do
more than postpone the celebrations, which duly took place on a Churchill visit to Oslo in May 1949, by which stage Norway's adhesion to
NATO had rather settled the foreign policy issue anyway. During that
visit Churchill stayed with King Haakon at the Palace, and otherwise
conformed to what was now more or less a set pattern: he received
an honorary degree from Oslo University, addressed the Norwegian
Parliament, and drove through Oslo to receive the city's homage, duly
delivered by large cheering crowds who made up in vehemence for the
fact that they had had to wait three years for their chance. There were

crowds all the way from the airport to greet Churchill's arrival, and fifteen miles of Norwegians cheered him on a motorcade tour after a civic lunch. The *New York Times* reported:

A conquering hero's welcome greeted Winston Churchill ... The party drove seven miles in the King's car through streets thronged with cheering crowds. Many wept with emotion. Others gave the 'V' sign and shouted, 'We shall never forget you.' In the harbour, boats and tugs formed up in the 'V' formation.

The honorary-degree citation praised him as 'the man who made history, wrote history and lived history ... the world's greatest torch-bearer during the dark ages of war'. Finally, a Norwegian whaling-ship owner was so moved by the emotions engendered by Churchill's presence that he gave 200,000 crowns to endow a British Institute at Oslo University in memory of the debt that Norwegians owed to Churchill. In 1976, following a decision made in Churchill's centenary year 1974, the Norwegians installed a statue of him in Oslo to commemorate his visit to the city in 1949.[13]

Denmark was equally fulsome in its gratitude. Early in the war, schoolboy members of the Danish resistance had also formed those clandestine Churchill Clubs and, though the military effect of their exploits was probably small, the psychological impact was considerable. With Denmark's liberation necessarily delayed by the failure of the Allies to win the war in 1944, Churchill had made a special BBC broadcast in January 1945 to the Danish resistance movement, thanking them for their sacrifices and urging them to greater efforts in the months to come. He was awarded the Danish Liberty Medal in 1946, lunched with the King in London in 1949, and accepted an honorary degree from the University of Copenhagen in May 1950. This last gesture seems to have prompted King Frederick to invite Churchill to Copenhagen as his personal guest, so that he could receive the degree and other honours, a visit that took place in October. In addition to the degree (for the ceremony of which he wore his Danish Liberty Medal), Churchill was given a gala dinner by the city and a banquet by the King, reciprocating by hosting a reception at the British Embassy. (Though he was still of course only the leader of the Opposition he acted on such occasions as if he was a head of government and expected to be treated like one by

British legations abroad.) He was also awarded the Order of the Ele-
phant, Denmark's highest honour, the only other contemporary holders
being Montgomery, Eisenhower and Niels Bohr, and laid a wreath at
the Danish Resistance Memorial.

The crowds in the streets of Copenhagen were, if anything, even
more vociferous than they had been in the earlier visits to other capitals.
They were estimated by the police as the largest the city had ever seen,
and were headlined by the *Daily Telegraph* as 'Mr Churchill welcomed
by 100,000 Danes', cheering and shouting 'We want Winnie' outside
the Town Hall where he was due to address them from the balcony.
When the speech ended, and after a Danish resistance leader had hailed
Churchill as 'our great leader in our common fight', the crowd sang
'For He's a Jolly Good Fellow' (so incidentally demonstrating the language skills that had made Churchill's wartime broadcasts directly
accessible in Denmark). In his speech, the University's dean hailed 'that
land which has given us a Shakespeare, a Milton, a Faraday, a Darwin;
that England which gave us a Churchill when we needed him, has
our love and admiration for ever'. Once again there were attempts to
commemorate the visit with something permanent and useful – in
addition, that is, to the books published in each country, reprinting the
relevant citations and speeches. In Denmark's case this took the form
of a public subscription to set up a travelling scholarship fund, so that
British students could study in Copenhagen, and considerable sums of
money were collected. Since grants were made from capital rather than
income, it ran out towards the end of the 1950s, but many British
students had benefited from the Danes' warm memories of Churchill
in the meantime.[30]

Again, the links seemed to last. Churchill was attending Embassy
lunches with the Norwegians when the King passed through London in
1949, and on other occasions later, and though it seems not to have
been the custom to honour foreigners in the naming of streets, Oslo
acquired a Churchill statue in 1976, following a decision taken around
the time of the centenary of his birth. For the Danes, Churchill agreed
to become the patron of a series of publications of Danish medieval
texts (a rare foray into the history of the non-English-speaking peoples),
kept in touch with the Danish royal family whenever they visited
London, and received an additional gift of a set of Hans Christian
Andersen china in 1954. Copenhagen still has a Churchill Park near the

waterfront within which was installed in 1954 a bust of Churchill with an appropriate legend. When it was unveiled, an American journalist rhapsodised – if with an unfortunate choice of words, given the notorious flatness of the country – over 'bonfires blazing on every hill in Denmark'. Fifty years after his visit to Copenhagen, his daughter Lady Soames opened there a 'Remember Winston Churchill' exhibition in 2000, following an earlier one opened by Robert Hardy in 1994. The opening was attended by members of the wartime resistance and a former Danish Prime Minister, and the exhibition was so successful that other cities in Denmark were soon asking for it to appear there too.[31]

Further east in Scandinavia, relations were necessarily more distant. Though both Sweden and Finland had been on the circulation list for Churchill press articles in the 1930s, through such outlets as Stockholm's *Dagens Nyheter* and Helsinki's *Helsingin Sanomat*, it had been hard to keep such outlets open as German pressure on small neutral countries mounted in 1938–9. Finland was then a German ally during the war and an enforced Soviet dependency during the Cold War, while Sweden opted for neutrality in both contests. There is not much sign that Churchill paid further attention to Finland, and he clearly gave Sweden a low priority. When welcomed to Norway, he was presented with a small silver replica of a Viking ship, in what was by chance the same month in which the Swedes reaffirmed that their neutrality would continue into the Cold War. Churchill roused the Norwegians to laughter with a response which praised the Vikings as 'certainly not well grounded in the principles of neutrality'. This was also a palpable dig at Norway's Communists who were by then preaching neutrality and also boycotting the ceremonies in his honour.

In 1953, when the Swedish Academy awarded him a Nobel Prize, it was an honour that he greatly valued. It was very remunerative too: as Winston wrote to Clementine, '£12,000 free of tax, not bad!' But he added rather less cheerfully, 'I think we shall have to go to Stockholm in December & stay with the King and Queen there.' To his secretary, he made it clear that being one of several prize-winners in different categories was not sufficient either. He told him 'with provocative humour' that he was 'not going to stand up there with those chemists' and with Albert Schweitzer (referred to dismissively by Churchill as 'a catch-'em alive-o' – he had won the Peace Prize). In the event, Churchill did not feel obliged to receive the prize in person (nor did Schweitzer in fact), though by then he was of course a hard-pressed Prime Minister of almost eighty, in only indifferent health and off to a conference in Bermuda. Yet only a few months earlier he had been positively eager to go to Stockholm when Eisenhower had suggested holding a summit conference there. It was thus Churchill's wife and daughter who were fêted by King Gustav rather than Winston himself. Clementine accepted the prize on Winston's behalf and read his acceptance speech, a courteous and duly grateful text, but one that necessarily did not include the sort of paragraph on shared wartime sacrifices for the freedom of the world that cropped up in any such speech made in Oslo or Antwerp. The Swedes were simply not part of the club of nations that had accepted Churchill's moral lead in the Second World War, an exclusion that was marked in 1965 by the British Government's decision to award two places for official mourners to each country that had been a British wartime ally, but only one to countries that had then been hostile – or neutral. The Danes and Norwegians were thus each given two seats in St Paul's Cathedral for Churchill's funeral, the Swedes only one. This was noted and somewhat resented in Stockholm, as American diplomats reported back to Washington, for, as some Swedes carefully pointed out, neither Denmark nor Norway had actually chosen to join the Allied side in the war, they had merely found themselves there when Germany invaded them. It was almost as if Sweden was retrospectively half wishing for itself a different past, so that it could be enrolled in the Churchill fan club as a full member.[32]

SWITZERLAND

Though neutral in all the conflicts of the twentieth century, the Swiss were able to enjoy a rapport with Churchill that was very different from the distancing of Churchill from Sweden – partly no doubt because Switzerland was one of his holiday destinations and conveniently on the way to others, while Sweden was not. When in September 1946 Churchill visited Switzerland for three weeks of rest, recuperation and painting, he found that it had perforce become an official visit because the Swiss themselves had made it one. He was greeted with a warmth quite comparable to his reception in countries that had recently been occupied by the Nazis and which felt that in part at least they owed their liberation to his efforts. It is therefore highly significant that the illuminated address presented to him by the University of Zurich expressed the Swiss people's admiration for the British people and their war leader, 'to whose steadfastness in war the Swiss people owed their own freedom'. When the holiday part of his trip ended, Churchill visited the Geneva agency of the International Red Cross, which had dealt with the interests of prisoners of war for the previous six years, so demonstrating in effect the practical value of friendly neutrals to belligerent powers (something he rarely conceded in the cases of Sweden or Ireland). Several lunches were given in his honour, and though he had expressed the wish that there be no official appointments except the lecture he was booked to deliver at the University of Zurich (and hence was zealously guarded by the Swiss police when at home) he had only to set foot outside for impromptu demonstrations of affection to be unleashed. He was given an official lunch by the Swiss federal council in Bern, following a night in which he was accommodated at the Château de Lohn, the Swiss equivalent of Chequers (again a remarkable privilege for a visiting Opposition leader). When seen in the streets of the federal capital, as the American Ambassador reported, 'the people of Bern gave Mr Churchill a most enthusiastic reception. Their tribute was spontaneous and very flattering. Most unusual for so undemonstrative a population.'

When he finally reached Zurich to deliver his big speech on the future of Europe, once again large crowds gathered and bunches of flowers were thrown at his car as he drove to the University. In contrast to the sceptical response of Europe's governments, when Churchill ended the speech with the ringing words 'Let Europe arise', the assembled faculty and students, and those listening outside the hall to loudspeakers, though they had listened to most of the speech in an attentive silence, now all rose at once and cheered. Churchill had already had on that day a civic reception and a crowd in the Münsterhof which was (or so at least the correspondent of *The Times* was assured) 'the largest mass of people yet seen in Zurich'. The Bern cantonal council duly published under its own auspices a commemorative volume in which the speeches delivered on this visit were reprinted in English, French and German. The memory of this single post-war visit, in this case not butressed by the post-war diplomatic co-operation in NATO that reinforced his links with other European countries, clearly meant a great deal to some Swiss people, and when Churchill died a fund was launched to commemorate it with a Churchill memorial, a text carved into a massive granite slab above Lake Thun. Even wartime neutrality in Churchill's finest hour was, it seems, no obstacle to joining the bandwagon of adulation.[33]

SOUTHERN EUROPE

In the case of those neutrals with regimes on the far right, Spain and Portugal, there was a readiness to celebrate Churchill, but held back in this case by reticence on his part. He had tried to avoid taking sides in the Spanish Civil War, but if forced to make a choice would probably have preferred victory by the (fascist) Nationalists to a win for the Republicans, especially when by 1937–8 the Republican side was dominated by the Spanish Communists and substantially under the influence of the Soviet Union. What he really wanted was a compromise peace that would restore liberal democracy, and this was just not on offer. Towards the end, as it became clear that a Franco government could be as subservient to Hitler and Mussolini as a Republican government would be to Stalin, he opted for a Republican victory, but by then the Nationalists were going to win anyway. When he became Prime Minister in 1940, he sent Sir Samuel Hoare to Madrid as Ambassador in the hope of persuading Franco at least to remain neutral. This he succeeded in doing (with vital consequences for the safety of Gibraltar, and hence of the British positions in the Mediterranean), though the substantial counter-influence of Germany ensured that Spain was a relatively hostile neutral: Churchill himself regarded Spain as a 'non-belligerent' rather than an actual neutral. By 1945, then, Churchill had an ambivalent view of Franco's Spain. Writing in January of that year, he admitted that 'Spanish policy did not oppose us at two critical moments of the war, namely, at the time of the collapse of France in 1940 [the time of Italy's entry into the war] and at the moment of the Anglo-American invasion of North Africa in 1942 . . .' But he was careful to add, 'I also remember that throughout the war German influence in Spain has constantly been permitted to embarrass the war effort of Great Britain and her allies,' and that Spanish troops had actually taken part with Germany against Russia on the eastern front.[34]

By that stage, though, the reference to Russia was little more than a debating point, for his growing perception of a future Russian/

Communist threat as the war drew to a close was leading him to identify right-wing forces like the Greek monarchists and the Iberian peninsula's fascist regimes as potential allies in the next round of conflict. He was therefore strongly opposed to suggestions, whether from Russia or from the British left, that the Allies should use the dominant position that they had gained in 1945 to remove from power Franco in Madrid and Salazar in Lisbon. How clear this was to Spain itself is indicated in the support for him in books that the Franco regime allowed to be published, and in the dismay expressed in Spanish newspapers (themselves under strict censorship) at the British election result that forced Churchill out of office in July 1945. In his war memoirs, Churchill allowed himself an ironic tribute to the slippery way in which Franco had managed to avoid being drawn into the war by his fellow fascist dictators. 'It is fashionable at the present time to dwell on the vices of General Franco, and I am therefore glad to place on record this testimony to the duplicity and ingratitude of his dealings with Hitler and Mussolini.'[35]

Thereafter, as the Cold War set in and Churchill emerged as one of its prophets, there was a convergence of Churchill's international policy with that of Franco: Spain was one of the countries which quickly and warmly endorsed his 'iron curtain' speech in 1946, and the regime permitted Spanish publication and serialisation of his war memoirs. On the basis of balance-of-power policies, which he had explicitly applied to Spain during its civil war period and which were now reinforced by anti-Communism, Churchill became a supporter of thawing out the freezing isolation in which Franco had been placed by the international community in 1945, of Spanish participation in the United Nations and NATO. For its part the Spanish regime continued to praise Churchill at every opportunity and allowed the publication in Madrid of favour- able books on Churchill's life. Churchill himself, however, was simply practising the *Realpolitik* of finding friends among his enemy's enemies (as he had done even with Russian Communism in 1941–5) and never came near to endorsing Franco's regime and its ideology. Asked for his view of Franco in 1946, Churchill replied, 'if I were a Spaniard I would not wish to live under his government', but went straight on to argue that this was a matter for Spaniards alone, and that other countries should not stir up more disorder there when the country was just beginning to recover from the stresses of 1936–9. Though Clementine Churchill convalesced from an illness in Spain in 1951, Winston never visited the country after 1935. Had he done so, he would have received what would no doubt have been the cheers of the Spanish people – whether spontaneous or orchestrated is another matter – but such an event never occurred, and a press story that he would visit Portugal in 1946 was equally wide of the mark. When he died, the Spanish Government issued a warm tribute to his life and work, though naturally concentrating its attention more on what had happened since 1945, which was to that regime the real 'finest hour' of Winston Churchill.[36]

Italy presented different problems again, for Italians had both fought against the Allies in 1940–3 in an officially declared war and fought with the Allies when Mussolini was reinstalled by the Nazis in 1943 – an ambiguity brought out by the many Italian war memorials which identify two separate wars in these years. Churchill was not inclined easily to forgive the first or to give much credit for the second. This approach embroiled him in controversy even before the war ended. Speaking off the cuff during a visit to British troops in Naples in January 1945, he argued that Italy would have to 'work its passage' back into the international community, and that it did not matter much if this was an extended process, since Italy was of only marginal importance to the defence of the West. This was unwise, to say the least, but it was also a poor reflection of Churchill's own considered views, for he was in fact extremely anxious to see a non-Communist Italy alongside Greece and Spain in order to bolster Britain's position as a Mediterranean power. However, it probably did reflect his real opinion of what the Italians could contribute to anybody's defence, including their own. (He had after all pointed out with wicked wit, when deflecting a Commons attack on him after Mussolini declared war in 1940, that it was only fair that Germany should have Italy as an ally, for Britain had already had its turn with that burden in 1916–18.) His Naples remarks were widely reported and caused outrage among Italians in the democratic parties that Mussolini had suppressed, Nenni's socialists being particularly vociferous. Churchill then issued statements in 'clarification' of his published remarks and claimed to have been misquoted. The Italian authorities declared themselves entirely satisfied, but the incident seems not to have been quickly forgotten.

Further wounding remarks about Italy as the war drew to a close can only have compounded the grievance, and, though he briefly visited Italy in the summer of 1945 to recover from the strains of the previous five years, this was only a personal visit to make use of Alexander's private villa on Lake Como. Italian children gathered to watch him paint, and he was generally received with a welcome by 'the country people', but his letters home do not indicate too much personal sympathy on his own part. Churchill's limited confidence in the Italians in 1945 was indicated clearly enough by the fact that he was being guarded by a detachment of two dozen armed British soldiers. When he visited the Italian riviera near Genoa, he had to abandon the painting of a scene of war damage when a hostile crowd gathered, booing and shaking fists. His reflection that he would have reacted in much the same way if Hitler had turned up to paint bomb damage in London after the war was fair enough in itself, but also showed that he still regarded Italy as a conquered enemy rather than a recent ally.[37]

Over time, as it became clear that Italy would not go Communist, relations warmed. He met and was happy to work with Italian delegates at European conventions, usually Christian Democrats with strong links to Britain's ally the United States, though he cannot have been amused to be celebrated as one of five *Padri della Patria* alongside De Gasperi in 1949, given that the book dignified Salazar and Franco with the same title. As he moved back towards ministerial office in 1950–1, things became more cordial – at least on an individual basis – and when the Italian premier and Foreign Minister visited London in March 1951 they called on Churchill and then entertained him at the Italian Embassy. When he retired as Prime Minister in 1955 it was to Sicily that the Churchills went for a holiday in the spring sunshine. But it was still less than wholehearted warmth, and as late as 1958 the Italian Communists were attacking Churchill for his role in the Cold War. When he died in 1965, the Italian Government ensured that it played a full part in the funeral along with the rest of the international community, but no special memorialising seems to have taken place in Italy itself. There is no statue of Churchill or an equivalent memorial in Italy; Rome has a small Piazzale Churchill in a decidedly non-prominent position, but no other Italian city appears to have followed the example.[38]

Greece too had ambivalent views, not least because Churchill's decision to use British troops against the Greek left in the last year of the war had firmly allied him with one side in a deeply divided political nation. Since the monarchists won that battle, with the help of the British troops, Churchill was made a freeman of Athens in February

1945 and had an Athenian street named after him in the following month. Nine years later, however, with Churchill again Prime Minister and reluctant to intervene to back Greek aspirations over Cyprus, that street was returned to its former name and the Churchill association blotted out. A later discussion about renaming it again produced a lively and characteristic correspondence from the readership of *The Times* on the vexed (but hardly significant) issue of how actually to render Churchill's name phonetically into modern Greek, but no further action in Athens. When he died, the Greeks like the Italians joined the rest of Western Europe in carrying the Eurovision coverage of the funeral and sent an appropriate team of mourners to the funeral itself, but did not make any special local efforts. Even the extreme left joined in tributes in the Greek Parliament, where the Communist leader remarked that 'in spite of our past differences, we acknowledge him as the leader of the anti-fascist crusade which led the allies to victory in the last war'. The removal of Stalin from the pantheon of Communist heroes by 1965 had apparently left Churchill with an unchallengeable claim to that particular title all across Europe.[39]

Entirely predictably, the fiercely loyal British colonies of Gibraltar and Malta were the only parts of the Mediterranean that fully entered into the memorialising of Churchill's greatness. He did not visit Gibraltar, probably to avoid antagonising Spain, but he was in Malta in February 1945 and was received with acclamation as he hailed the story of the island's defence in the prolonged siege of 1941–2, a story he also recounted with evident pleasure in his war memoirs. In 1954, as his eightieth birthday approached, the Maltese Government commissioned a Churchill bust to commemorate his association with the islands and their own proud war record.[40]

GERMANY

If Italy was a difficult case, then Germany was of course even more so. Churchill had been but a rare visitor, knew little of German culture and did not even attempt to learn the language (remarking just before the Great War, 'I'll never learn that beastly language, until the Kaiser marches on London'). Despite the two world wars, he was certainly no virulent anti-German over his long political career, and tried to maintain a clear distinction between the wickedness of the Nazis and the rest of the German people whose culpability was more debatable. With this distinction in mind, he had vehemently opposed the Americans' Morgenthau Plan for the post-war de-industrialisation of Germany, he had been incensed by Stalin's suggestion at Tehran that the Allies should after occupying Germany shoot fifty thousand Germans out of hand, and was not much more impressed by the Americans' demand for unconditional surrender by Germany as the only basis for ending the war. There were, however, also occasions towards the end of the war when Churchill seemed less aware of the distinction. He vowed in early 1945 that Germany's use of the indiscriminate flying bombs would never be forgotten by the British people, and in April that year he seemed to assert collective German responsibility for the concentration camps by then being opened up. More often, he simply argued that he could see 'no alternative to the acceptance of Germany back into the family of Europe', though he sometimes added that there would be a need for Germany like Italy to 'work her passage' back by good behaviour first.[41]

In speeches about the future of Germany, and in a broadcast to Germany itself at the end of the war, he promised that while war criminals would be ruthlessly hunted down and dealt with, Germany as a whole would be fairly treated. In this readiness to practise his own maxim of 'in victory, magnanimity', he was some considerable way ahead of much of British public opinion. A few examples will suffice. First, when Churchill supported the admission of West Germany to the post-war European conventions he was bitterly attacked by such MPs as the future Labour cabinet Minister Richard Crossman, in terms close to pure racism:

A policy towards Germany based on romantic chivalry was mere sentiment. Any policy towards Germany had to be based on long-term knowledge of what the danger was. These romantic somersaults after the bombing to destruction of German cities, this offer to shake hands, was a fine piece of cricket field psychology, but the Germans never believed in cricket, only in conquering Europe.

Hugh Dalton was not much more forthcoming, regarding Churchill's attempts to bring Germany back into the community of nations as a betrayal of all that Britain had fought for in the war. For his own part, Dalton, on the way to a function where Germans were to be present, sang to a friend, 'We'll gouge out their eyes! We'll stamp on their bellies! We'll tear out their livers!' Second, when in 1950 the new West German Government allowed the singing of the traditional German national anthem, with its assertion that Germany should be 'over all', Churchill scoffed at the scaremongers, pointing out that 'Rule Britannia' might reasonably be thought equally provocative to foreigners, but that such national songs had great internal value and need not be taken literally by foreigners. (Alas, Churchill was not quite so generous to South Africa. He intervened to prevent its national anthem from being played in London at a reception associated with the Coronation in 1953, with the words, 'I will not have this Boer hymn!') His generous description of Konrad Adenauer as 'the greatest German Chancellor since Bismarck' drew a withering reproof from A. J. P. Taylor, rarely a Churchill critic as we have seen. This 'only indicated how little Churchill understood of the German experience', for Adenauer was a Catholic from the Rhineland, 'for whom the unity of Western Europe came first', while Bismarck was a Prussian Junker who wanted Germany actually to run Europe. The reproof may have been apt historically, but the exchange also showed how far Taylor was imprisoned in the history that they both studied, while Churchill was not. Finally, when he lunched with Chancellor Adenauer in 1951, there were protest demonstrations outside – protests that Churchill brushed aside.

When Labour MPs tried to prevent the visit to Britain in 1953 of the German General Speidel, Rommel's former Chief of Staff, he was equally dismissive, paying warm tribute to Rommel as an anti-Nazi as well as a great general. So brave did this appear that he even received a telegram of thanks from the Afrika Korps veterans' club. If Labour's alternative line was pursued, then, Churchill argued,

> there would be no peace possible between those two great branches of the human family. Such keeping alive of hatred was one of the worst injuries that could be done to the peace of the world, and any popularity gained thereby was a shame to the Member who attempted to gather it . . .

Nor was this only a debating stance for public occasions. In 1954 he was arguing to Lord Moran that 'if millions of people in one country learn to hate millions in another, trouble is bound to come. This fellow Aneurin Bevan is deliberately stirring up anger and passion by bringing up Germany's aims in the war. It is very wrong.' Such generous feelings were not, however, always warmly reciprocated, for despite Churchill being applauded by the admirers of Field Marshal Rommel, Germans were unexpectedly slow to buy Churchill's war memoirs. Emery Reves had optimistically hoped that Germany would be one of the best markets in Europe, but in 1951 he reported that the most recent volume had sold only five thousand copies and that serial publication in the newspapers had generated 'hundreds of letters of protest and caused a serious drop in circulation'.[42]

Churchill's own post-war view of Germany was grandiloquently set out at Columbia University in New York in 1946, when he said that 'in my heart there is no abiding hatred for any great race on earth' and argued that there must be 'no pariah nations'. His generous view of Germany was also expressed in a number of other messages of greater directness, for example when the Ruhr valley was seriously flooded in 1954. The irony of that last occasion was that the floods had provided a British film studio with the chance to send a camera plane over to photograph footage of the flooded Ruhr, to be incorporated in the forthcoming *Dam Busters* film. Even as Churchill lamented the loss of life in these 1954 floods, the film-makers were preparing to re-enact the floods of 1943, to which Churchill's RAF had made such a contribution, for a film which Churchill loved when it was released in 1955.[43]

Nevertheless, generosity was powerfully reinforced by the desire to reinstate a strong Germany in the Western community as a barrier to Soviet expansion. In November 1954, Churchill told his constituents in Woodford that even in 1945 he had instructed Montgomery to stockpile the German army's weapons as they were surrendered, but to keep them ready for reissue in case German troops had to be used at once as part of the defence of the West. There was a furore in the press, Montgomery denied ever receiving such an order, and a search of the files indicated that Churchill had in fact never sent it, so that he had to apologise in some embarrassment, a gaffe that undoubtedly helped those cabinet colleagues that wanted him now to retire. But it is inconceivable that Churchill would have made such a claim unless he had at least known that it reflected his thinking in 1945, even if those thoughts had never been acted on. He was therefore quite open to the actual rearmament of Germany when the issue came up in the early 1950s, certainly more so than either the French or the British Labour Party, and he struck up from the beginning a good working relationship with Konrad Adenauer when he became Chancellor of the new West Germany, as well as socialising happily enough with the German delegates at European meetings. By 1954 he was exchanging gifts, birthday greetings and messages of mutual admiration with Adenauer, something that continued after his retirement and which therefore presumably meant more to both of them than the need to work together as heads of government. Adenauer was given a Churchill painting, and Adenauer in turn presented Churchill with an engraving of Bonn under siege by his ancestor Marlborough. The German Chancellor felt that his own prestige was raised by his association with Churchill, and when he died his funeral was modelled on Churchill's own. On Churchill's eightieth birthday, Adenauer's message spoke of Germany's deep admiration for Churchill, and when Churchill died Adenauer spoke both for Germany and for himself, for 'through all these years Churchill showed me only friendship and amiability'.[44]

What Churchill seems to have been strangely reluctant to do, though, was actually to visit Germany himself. Adenauer kept urging him to come, but Churchill either never responded to those particular paragraphs within his messages or agreed that a visit would be a good idea but then never arranged one. (He did, however rehearse for the journalist Malcolm Muggeridge the speech he would give if he went to Cologne, where he expected 'to address a huge gathering, perhaps 30,000, and he believed he would receive a great ovation'.) An imaginative idea that Adenauer and Churchill should meet together with their respective grandchildren as an act of international reconciliation came to nothing. Nor did Churchill respond positively when invited to visit Blindheim in Bavaria, to celebrate the 250th anniversary of his famous ancestor's victory at 'Blenheim', though he had visited it in the 1930s when researching his biography of Marlborough and accepted in 1949 a gift from the village, given 'out of regard for Mr Churchill and the people of Britain'. Possibly Churchill feared for his reception in a Germany still recovering from the ravages of British bombing, but more likely he feared to get ahead of other people's prejudices at home. As he lunched with Adenauer in Downing Street in 1951, there were three hundred demonstrators chanting their slogans of hatred outside, though such restraints did not deter him from posing with the German Chancellor on the doorstep as they shook hands. When he did finally agree to go to Germany in order to accept in 1956 the Charlemagne Prize at Aachen, he was roundly criticised by representatives of German refugees who had fled from the Nazis to Britain, and once again by some of the British left too. Churchill himself approached that particular visit with some trepidation, considering at one time pulling out of the engagement altogether and uncertain about the topic for his speech. He managed to cover his tracks somewhat by visiting his old regiment on the same trip, and so was photographed in circumstances which emphasised his association with the war effort of 1940–5 as well as with post-war forgiveness. Despite an attack from a local paper which compared Churchill to Hitler, his welcome in Aachen was warm enough, there was only a small (German) protest meeting, and the elaborate security precautions turned out not to have been needed. From Aachen he went on to Bonn to visit Adenauer, but most of his six-day visit was taken up with meeting British troops rather than German civilians. It was only a few weeks later that he returned to the country for a second time, to watch one of his horses run at Düsseldorf, and was fêted by the local Jockey Club – some things rise entirely above politics – though he was once again criticised by German anti-Nazi refugees. Thereafter he travelled less and less, and when in Europe tended to go straight to the French Riviera, so he did not apparently visit Germany again.[45]

When Churchill died, the German Chancellor – by then the pro-British Ludwig Erhard – issued a generous message of condolence, and attended his funeral in person. The Federal Government also held its own memorial service for Churchill in Bonn, at which the elderly Adenauer was one of the mourners. Its sternest critic could not have faulted the German Government in the way it acted in January 1965, while the German television audience joined the rest of Europe in watching the ceremonials of 30 January in very large numbers. When Erhard spoke to Harold Wilson during his visit to London for the funeral, 'he spoke of the high esteem in which Churchill was held in Germany and of his European ideas and vision', it presumably being easier to view Churchill positively for events which began in 1946 than for those which ended in 1945. But there were some limits to post-war Germany's accommodation with Churchill: there is no Churchill statue or memorial in Bonn – or in Berlin, come to that – the plan to stage an exhibition of his paintings in Aachen in 1956 seems to have fallen through, and there is apparently no German city that has named a street after him. There are in fact very few German city streets named after foreigners of any kind, but a few like Hamburg honoured John Kennedy in this way after his Presidential visit and his assertion of support for the divided country (an honour for which he did not even have to proclaim 'Ich bin ein Hamburger'). When Churchill visited Aachen in 1956, the German crowds were mainly silent, rather (as Churchill's doctor noted) 'as Londoners received Bulganin and Khrushchev'. In the early post-war years such reservations in German adherence to the rest of the world's Churchill worship were no doubt all the greater. The *Sydney Morning Herald*, for instance, reported in 1949 a German opinion poll in which Churchill came second as the 'greatest politician of the past' (he would certainly not have liked the 'of the past' at this stage of his career) and presented it as an example of his ability to inspire affection even among recent enemies. Unfortunately, the detail of the story showed that, while Churchill had indeed attracted 773 votes, he was not far ahead of Adolf Hitler with 575 – and miles behind Bismarck who had scored over four thousand.[46]

EASTERN EUROPE

Before 1939, readers of Eastern European newspapers would have had as good a chance of reading Churchill's words in translation as would readers in the West: in summer 1938 they were being syndicated to Warsaw, Krakow, Prague, Budapest, Bucharest, Belgrade, Kaunas, Tallinn and Riga, though by spring 1939 the twin pressures from Hitler and Stalin had already closed off most such outlets.[47] In wartime he had rarely given Eastern Europe a high priority in his thinking, but, as the war drew to a close and the Red Army marched into the area, it was disputes over Poland that made Churchill into the earliest of the cold warriors. Not only was Poland the main cause of deteriorating relations with Stalin in 1944–5, with the 'London Poles' being denied the chance to return in triumph under British patronage (as, say, the Norwegian government in exile was preparing to do), but their soldiers and airmen who had fought with Britain could not even be returned safely to their own country. Churchill therefore guaranteed British citizenship to the free Poles who had fought with Britain – for example as members of Polish fighter squadrons during the Battle of Britain and as paratroops at Arnhem. In the post-war years he continued to associate himself with their cause. In 1947 he suggested that these Polish veterans be called up and used to garrison Germany and so free 180,000 British men for the labour shortage in the economy. It is not clear how the Germans would have reacted to this plan for their defence, but these right-wing Poles would presumably have given a good account of themselves against the Red Army in combat, had the plan ever been carried out. In 1949 Churchill was attending a veterans' reception in memory of General Sikorski. In much the same way, he not only lamented the loss of the eastern half of the European family in the Fulton speech, but missed few opportunities in the years that followed to draw attention to the anti-democratic pressures on those countries from Russia. Most of all he lamented the fate of democracy in Czechoslovakia, where a plan to commemorate his own war services by naming a street after him in Prague was abandoned in 1947 as just too controversial in the face of the developing Cold War. His plan to visit Prague after the war and receive there an honorary degree had to be abandoned for the same reasons, but the Czech specialist and writer Robert Bruce Lockhart deeply regretted this, noting in his diary that Churchill 'is a hero to the Czechs' and might have done 'much to correct the ultra pro-Russian bias' there. Churchill paid an eloquent tribute to Jan Masaryk on his death in 1948, refusing to accept that it had been accidental, and returned to the fray repeatedly in the months that followed. Nor was the defence of the Czechs as obvious a cause as it would seem in retrospect: when he lamented in 1949 that the Czechs had become 'a mere pawn' in the Russian empire, he was heckled by Labour MPs with cries of 'Rubbish!' But Czechoslovakia was not his only concern in the region: in 1950 he sent a supportive message to refugees from the Baltic states which would have been seen as equally provocative in Moscow.[48]

He was indeed from this point onwards treated as an enemy by the Russians, and under their influence by their puppet regimes in Eastern Europe too. In June 1947, for example, the Rumanian regime banned all mention of his name in the media, and in 1951 he was viciously abused on Hungarian radio, while the Russians themselves lost few opportunities to denounce him as a warmonger on radio, in newspapers and even in feature films. *Secret Mission*, a Russian film of 1950, depicted Churchill trying to make a separate peace with Hitler in January 1945, to free the Nazis to counter-attack Russia, and looking forward to a world war against Communism, 'which may not be so hard to start but may cost the lives of half the world's population before it is ended'. This monstrous perversion of recent history opened simultaneously in twenty-five Moscow cinemas, later won the coveted Stalin Prize, and was then shown all over Eastern Europe. Given the prominence and indeed growing fame of Churchill around the world, he remained important enough to receive the personal attention of the Russian leaders themselves. Vishinsky attacked him in 1952 and Gromyko (with the aid of highly selective misquotations) in 1951. Interestingly, the attacks by Gromyko at a Paris conference were mainly refuted by the French rather than the British delegates.[49]

Though Churchill was from 1950 the leading Western exponent of a peacemaking summit to wind down Cold War tensions, Russia's Stalinist leaders seem initially to have been sufficiently the prisoners of their own propaganda to convince themselves that this must be insincere, given his earlier bloodcurdling warnings about Russian expansionism. After Stalin died and the Cold War did gradually thaw, if discontinuously, his successors found it difficult to pursue a consistent line towards Churchill. His eightieth birthday in 1954 did not prompt a Russian response at all, and though there were appreciative comments on Russian radio when he reached eighty-five in 1959, repeated when he retired from the Commons in 1964, he was attacked in the Russian media in 1962, and again after his ninetieth birthday in 1964, when he was once more depicted as a warmonger: *Izvestia* argued that 'to him, author of the Fulton speech, belong the unworthy laurels of one of the main organisers of the Cold War'. When he died, though, the Russian media was mainly respectful, as were other Communist regimes like the Polish and Czech: *Rude Pravo* in Prague even daringly maintained that Churchill's 'greatness lies in that he was able, at certain periods of his life, to see beyond his own class'. A high-ranking Russian delegation came to the funeral to pay respects, and the breach seemed to have been healed at last, as witnessed by the appearance in Moscow of a reasonably fair biography of Churchill in Russian as early as 1967. But Russian television did not carry the funeral ceremonials live, as even many of the other Eastern European countries did, and there were occasional lapses, as when in 1966 *Pravda* argued of Churchill's Fulton speech that it had 'legalised the sad role of the junior partner of the United States. That was the beginning of the sale of England.'[50]

Such grudging and erratic acknowledgement, achieved anyway only after a couple of generations, did not remotely compare with the broad enthusiasm for Churchill that was allowed to develop in the West, and the continuation of the satellite regimes until the collapse of the Soviet Empire some forty-five years after the end of the Second World War ensured that there was no formal memorialising of Churchill in Eastern Europe. By the time that freedom limpingly returned in the 1990s, memories of the Second World War and Churchill's part in it were not uppermost in the minds of the new democratic regimes. No Churchill street was ceremonially unveiled in Moscow, no plaque and no statue, and the same is true of other former Communist states – but with one clear and interesting exception. Almost immediately after the 'velvet revolution', the Winston Churchill Square that had proved too controversial in 1947 was put in place in the central area of Prague. When Margaret Thatcher visited the city soon after its liberation from the Eastern bloc, she made much the same connection as many Czechs were making: 'we failed you in 1938, when a disastrous policy of appeasement allowed Hitler to extinguish your independence. Churchill was quick to repudiate the Munich Agreement . . .' At about the same time a Churchill bust appeared, close to the British Embassy and just below Prague Castle in the new town. The bust was offered at cost by the Czech-born sculptor Franta Belsky and paid for by three large companies. It bears as an inscription in Czech the four-line 'theme' of Churchill's war memoirs ('In war resolution; in defeat, defiance; in victory, magnanimity; in peace, goodwill'): Belsky had already sculpted other Churchill busts and statues in the West, and had indeed been inspired to do so partly through memory of Churchill having sent a ship specially to collect volunteer Czech soldiers when France collapsed in 1940, so saving them from near-certain death at the hands of the Nazis. By the end of the decade this bust had been joined on the streets of Prague by a full-scale statue, placed in Namesty Winston Churchill after a public subscription, and on the initiative of Václav Havel, the President of the Republic. This was a life-size copy of the statue that stands in London's Parliament Square. Having experienced some years with a hundred-foot statue of Stalin dominating part of the Prague skyline, Czechs like Václav Havel would understandably prefer Churchill no more than life-size. Prague thus became – if belatedly – the only place in the world except London to have more than one celebratory representation of Churchill on permanent display in its streets. The betrayal of their country at

Munich as a prime symbol of Churchill's battle against appeasement in the 1930s makes him a natural object of veneration for the Czechs, while his support for Masaryk and his vocal opposition to the subornation of Czech democracy in 1948 provided a reinforcing argument of considerable weight. But these were factors that could not be expected to have the same impact in Vienna, Budapest or Warsaw, where the political experience both of the 1930s and of the later 1940s had been so different. At the end of the century, a Café-Bar Churchill opened around the corner from the Prague square named after Churchill. This was obviously a marketing ploy not unlike that favoured by similar bars in Edinburgh and Manchester (and hence it prominently advertises the sale of 'Churchill cigars'), but it also shows which parts of Churchill's life still resonate in the Czech capital. The bar has nine photographs of Churchill on display, seven of which show Churchill on his own and all of which date from 1940 or later. There is also one of Churchill with the uniformed Eisenhower of 1944–5, reminding visitors of his war and Cold War record. But the photograph that catches the eye when first entering the bar shows Churchill with – of all people – Neville Chamberlain, and hence evokes at once the memory of 'Munich'. It is no doubt meant to.[51]

BUT WAS CHURCHILL A 'EUROPEAN'?

Celebration of Churchill there certainly was, then, right across Europe, but does he qualify as an ancestor of the narrower European 'project' that has produced the European Union as an economic and political power bloc? Or can he, in other words, be convicted of the charge he himself laid against the Attlee Government when attacking in 1948 its lukewarmness on European unity: 'We must beware of those about whom Bismarck said, "When they say they agree with something in principle, they mean that they have no intention of carrying it out in practice."' Or was he, as Hugo Young has averred, not only 'the last begetter of British greatness', but 'also the prime exponent of British ambiguity'?[52]

In this we need to be careful not to apply to Churchill in the 1940s and 1950s tests of Europeanness that almost every politician of the age would have failed, so rapidly did the concept of 'Europe' advance over the next half-century. We must also be careful to note the changes in his views over time, and especially in the context of changes over the same timescale in the international scene. It was after all one of Churchill's enduring political characteristics that he constantly shifted tactically as events dictated different paths to the same objective. The trick in analysing his moves is therefore usually to find the consistent principle and then to see how necessity forced him to chop and change tactically in order to come nearer to its achievement. In this case it is not hard to work out: Churchill said repeatedly in his last active decade that his overriding objectives (continued from wartime) were British security and, linked with it, the Anglo-American alliance. In that context his apparent shifts and changes on 'Europe' become more comprehensible. Even before such post-war developments became clear, however, the lack of depth in his commitment to European co-operation was obvious enough to insiders: though he talked in the early years of the war about the desirability of a 'Council of Europe' when it ended, when in 1944 it became necessary to plan practically for the post-war world he raised strong objections to the same concepts. He was also so flexible in his thinking about what 'Europe' actually meant that his cogitations about post-war European co-operation were indistinguishable from vague hopes of world government.[53]

As the war ended, Churchill utterly failed to get from Roosevelt any assurance of permanent American commitment to the defence of Western Europe, and indeed in the last year of the war Roosevelt had shown rather that he saw himself as standing *between* Churchill and Stalin rather than alongside Britain and against Russia. Though Harry Truman would take a very different line, as a new President in April 1945 he was not likely to shift policy at once, not least since he largely inherited Roosevelt's cabinet, including such pro-Russian figures as Henry Wallace. American forces were therefore progressively withdrawn from Europe in the year after the war. It was in this dangerous atmosphere that Churchill promoted the recovery of France's great-power status and envisaged the rapid return of Germany to the European family of nations, though he was careful also to reject de Gaulle's offer of a binding Anglo-French alliance lest it encourage the Americans to think that they were not needed for European defence. But, for the first months of peacetime, neither Germany nor France offered much hope of being a reliable ally soon, and France certainly did not wish to be allied to Germany anyway. So the model of a European collaboration within which Franco-German enmity could be submerged was a natural one, and also offered the only available means by which the smaller nations could be collectively mobilised too. In these desperate months, Churchill's dreams of European unity went a good deal further than they were ever to be allowed to do later. In an article he wrote for *Collier's*, for example, his first column for the American press since 1939, he speculated on the possibility of European stamps, currency and customs regulations. Even more strikingly, he used in the article the word 'we' to make it clear that Britain would be a full partner in such arrangements. Forty years later, when European monetary integration was wrecking John Major's Government, the *Independent* mischievously ran a front-page story with the headline 'Top Tory comes out for the Euro', and only when readers turned to page 2 did it make clear that this was Churchill. As it pointed out, 'his federalist thinking is well known, but his support for a common currency was not'.[54]

Though he appealed at Fulton in March 1946, at about the same time as the *Collier's* article was appearing in the United States, for an Anglo-American military alliance, he also argued there that regional security pacts were no challenge to the United Nations, and might in fact be the best way of ensuring that world opinion had the means of enforcing its views. The special relationship was one such regional arrangement, but a European combination for defending West Germany against Russia was just such another. By the time he spoke again on the subject, at Zurich in September, the American position had hardened considerably and the trend was moving back towards greater rather than less military commitment to Europe, for example in the sending of heavy naval units to the Mediterranean. But the permanence and weight of such new American commitments was still far from assured. At Zurich, therefore, he had the trickier task of promoting his European option without making it appear as an alternative to the special relationship or the need for American forces in Europe. He thus went much further in the European direction, stating in advance that his now open advocacy of Franco-German collaboration would shock his listeners (and readers of the speech in the newspapers), as indeed it did at least in France. In the frenzied reaction to his call for a 'United States of Europe' it was much less noticed that he had subtly modified the position that Britain would play in his grand new scheme of things. Though the idea of a United States of Europe dated back to proposals by Aristide

Briand in the 1920s, this was surely a choice of words by Churchill as much for American readers as for Europeans. Now there was no unambiguous 'we' in his plans for 'Europe', and a close reading of what he actually did say indicates that Britain would like America to be an outside sponsor of the new United States of Europe, not a fully paid-up member. Presumably to deflect charges that this was all hostile to Russia and provocative cold-warmongering, he looked forward in the speech to a time when Russia could join the new European combination. How far this was merely window-dressing was visible even at the other end of the world: an Australian newspaper pointed out that, whereas Churchill did not rule out Russia joining, in fact if Russia joined there would be no need for a European combination in the first place, since it was all about resisting Russian expansion.

He was anxious that Commonwealth countries should not misunderstand his European initiative as being in any way inimical to the Commonwealth and Britain's independent role. In 1947 he urged the Dominions to welcome his moves to bring Germany into a 'United Europe', for they had no reason not to be 'with Britain in our cause. They felt that Britain was geographically and historically part of Europe, and they themselves had an inheritance in Europe. The youth of the Dominions twice in living memory had died in wars brought about by European discord, in the prevention of which they were powerless.' Note that while Britain was asserted to be geographically and historically in Europe, no mention was made of either politics or economics. In the same way, at Zurich, he had argued mysteriously that 'the English-speaking world would be apart from this', but at the same time that somehow it would be 'closely connected'. Or as he had argued in an article on a United States of Europe even in 1930, 'we have our own dream and our own task. We are *with* Europe but not *of* it. We are linked but not comprised.'[55]

Why was this not obvious at the time? In part it was because Churchill was by no means the only European political leader using words like 'unity', 'federation' and 'union' in a way that was to say the least ambiguous. In any case, those words could not then have the specificity that they attained when actual European institutions were created in the next generation. In part, too, ambiguity continued because nobody in Britain was likely to call Churchill's bluff. Labour was if anything even less committed to 'Europe' than the Conservatives, the

Liberals hardly even existed as a separate party in the decade 1945–55, and the Conservatives were content to use the issue until 1951 as a way of attacking the Attlee Government. As Richard Crossman noted in his diary soon after Churchill returned to office in 1951, Labour 'was not able to berate [Churchill] for going back on his leadership of the European Movement, for the simple reason that Labour has been wholly isolationist itself'. Privately, though, most Tories too knew well enough that they did not agree with what Churchill was saying about Europe. When Australia's Robert Menzies visited in 1948 and talked to many senior Tories including Eden, Salisbury and Swinton, as well as Churchill himself, he was relieved to hear that Churchill's campaign for a united Europe was no threat whatsoever to the Commonwealth. Lord Swinton told him that a recent meeting at the Conservative College then housed on his Yorkshire estate had shown that the party's rank-and-file activists were utterly indifferent, if not actually hostile, to Churchill's views on Europe. He also claimed, as Menzies recorded in his diary, that Churchill's plans were 'regarded as quite unreal by all Conservatives save Winston, only "out of office" politicians are participating, as usual building from the roof down ... The "complete scheme on paper" boys are mostly unreal and mostly careerists anyhow.' This was highly significant, for as Churchill himself was about that time reminding Jean Monnet when congratulated on his war services, 'Just remember this. Everything I did I was able to do because I was Leader of the Conservative Party.' Swinton very probably counted Harold Macmillan, David Maxwell Fyfe and Duncan Sandys among those 'careerists', but the active involvement of his son-in-law Sandys was also one of the factors that convinced Europeans that Churchill meant business.

That apart, though, why did the genuine European integrationists on the continent fail to spot Churchill's fatal ambiguities on their pet subject? Some claim with hindsight to have done so at the time, as did Jean Monnet, but if so he certainly did not say so. Paul-Henri Spaak's later view is persuasive enough, if a touch over-kind to Churchill because of his own warm admiration for the man. For Spaak, Churchill's 'beautiful' Zurich speech 'caused a considerable stir', because 'he still enjoyed tremendous prestige and undeniable authority throughout the democratic world'. Ambiguity remained for Spaak himself, until in the 1950s Churchill himself refused to consider British involvement in the European Coal and Steel Community. That uncertainty continued mainly because:

For a number of years after his Zurich speech nobody asked him exactly what was on his mind when he made it. People were only too glad of his backing for a great cause. The ambivalence of the speech suited everyone, and it was therefore unjust to Churchill when people later took him to task for his attitude.

However, even Spaak had to add that 'he was perhaps wrong not to have clarified his position when the time was right and to have allowed people to believe that there was a powerful movement in Britain ready to press for that country's integration with continental Europe'. If British politicians all had their different reasons for keeping quiet, and continental integrationists reasons even to welcome his ambiguity, Churchill himself simply must have known that people were drawing the wrong conclusions from what he had said. He not only did not disillusion them, but actually encouraged illusions by the keenness of his association with the integrationists in the later 1940s. Having addressed a cheering crowd of twenty thousand in the Place Kléber in Strasbourg in 1949, when the Council of Europe was inaugurated, he threw himself into the work of the Council. Harold Macmillan noted in his diary that 'he is entertaining very freely – Americans, French, Belgians, Dutch, Italians – all who can be flattered or cajoled'. He also reported in a letter home that Churchill 'certainly took more trouble to listen to the debates than I have ever known him to do in the House of Commons. He walked about, chatted to each representative, went into the smoking room, and generally took a lot of trouble to win the sympathetic affection of his new parliamentary colleagues.' It is hardly surprising then that the assembled European parliamentarians concluded that he shared their hopes and dreams, especially when he appealed at the same meetings for 'the growth of the united sentiment of Europeanism'.[56]

And so the pattern continued. As the Americans moved towards the Truman Doctrine, the Marshall Plan, the Berlin airlift and the formation of NATO in 1947–9, it became clear that British security could now realistically depend more on the special relationship than on European allies. There was of course no need to make such an explicit choice, for Europeans made up most of the member states in NATO, and collaborated to benefit from Marshall Aid too. Since Americans expected such European collaborations as part of the price of American military and economic aid, it was necessary to continue to behave as though these were also part of Britain's objectives, and points could even be scored off the Attlee Government for its refusal to attend officially the European congress at Strasbourg. This is not to suggest that Churchill had no motive other than the cynical for his endorsement of European unity after 1947, for the time and energy that he devoted to the United Europe movement and to meetings abroad would indicate otherwise. But these were initiatives that pointed forward to the broadly collaborationist Council of Europe, of which Churchill is quite rightly regarded as a founding influence. They did not even pretend to commit either Churchill or Britain to economic and military co-operation in a European army (on which subject he was privately absolutely scathing) or supranational bodies for economic and political integration of the sort that began to emerge in the 1950s.[57]

In the Conservative election manifestos of 1950 and 1951 he said very little about all this, and a great deal about the Empire and Imperial economic development, a concentration reflected in his election speeches and campaigning. The 1950 manifesto promised that he would 'labour for a United Europe' but, since this would include 'in course of time those unhappy countries still behind the Iron Curtain', it was a pretty safe promise in terms of its chances of early achievement. In office after 1951 he was less openly antagonistic to the European project than his Foreign Secretary Anthony Eden, who famously remarked, 'We know in our bones that we cannot be part of this.' Churchill did, though, tell his cabinet in a very early Prime Ministerial paper that 'I have never thought that Britain ... should ... become an integral part of a European Federation, and have never given the slightest support to the idea.' Instead of describing three equal circles of British influence, he now placed the Commonwealth and Empire first, the 'fraternal association' of the English-speaking world second, and – in third place – 'United Europe, to which we are a separate closely and specially related ally'. His European admirers would have been devastated had they been able to read so blatant (and so ahistorical) a dissociation of Churchill from his own recent past. He therefore did little or nothing in practice to promote Britain's part in it during the crucial, formative years of a European community. He quietly obstructed the idea of a European Defence Community, quietly because Americans favoured the idea, and rejoiced when it failed in the French Assembly. He had no wish for Britain to take part in the coal and steel community that was the actual

'Nonsense, Madam – all babies look like me'
Herblock in *The Washington Post*

progenitor of the EEC, while the real focus of his international involvement in the years 1951–5 was always the desire for a three-power summit
from which the other European countries would be deliberately excluded
– and very damagingly so in Germany's case, since such a summit might
well decide the future of the country without hearing the views of its
Government. The 1955 Conservative manifesto, issued by Eden after
Churchill's retirement but reflecting policy developed over his four years
as peacetime Prime Minister, referred frequently to the American alliance and more than once to 'Western European Union', but not at all
to what was by then already happening in the gestation of a European
community.[58]

Speaking to the former independent MP Sir Stephen King-Hall,
Churchill later argued that he had wanted to commit Britain to 'Europe'
when Prime Minister after 1951, but that 'my party was too strong for
me'. Though Eden would certainly have opposed such an initiative and
others would have supported him, Churchill's claim would be more
convincing if there was any evidence that he had actually tried to achieve
something different from what actually happened. When at the time
real pro-Europeans like his friend Violet Bonham Carter urged Churchill
to give such a lead, he responded 'civilly, but no more', as his political
secretary later noted. 'WSC said he had quite enough over which to
fall out with Anthony Eden, without adding an issue that was not of

urgent importance . . . and he was unwilling to receive delegations on the subject.' Yet it was in those years when Britain's leaders thought that Europe was 'not of urgent importance' that the country missed the European bus. But then punctuality had never been Churchill's forte: he regularly joked that, being a sporting man, he like to give a train a chance to get away uncaught. There were certainly those like Macmillan and Maxwell Fyfe, not to mention his own son-in-law Duncan Sandys, who would have responded if given a lead (though their own record as 'pro-Europeans' in 1945–55 was far less sound than they were later to claim). There was anyway no such Churchillian lead.[59]

When Britain finally did seek membership of the European Community in the early 1960s, Churchill had long retired, but an indiscretion by his old friend Montgomery nevertheless embroiled him in the debate. Having talked to Churchill, Monty announced to journalists that Churchill shared his own strongly Eurosceptic opinions. It is hard to know whether to take this at face value, for Montgomery was quite capable of taking a refusal to argue with him for full-hearted agreement with his views. Churchill was by then very old and frail anyway, but the Macmillan Government took it all very seriously. Churchill, who had refused ever to dissociate himself from any policy pursued by his Tory successors in office, was persuaded to publish a letter to his constituency association (written in fact by the highly Eurosceptic Anthony Montague Browne), a refutation of the views attributed to him by Montgomery, and so rescue Macmillan from some real embarrassment. Reprinted in full in the party's *Weekly Newsletter*, so that all party activists could read it, Churchill's statement stressed that he was supportive of Britain's application to the EEC, 'not because I think we shall be able to join, but because there appears to be no other way to find out exactly whether the conditions of membership are acceptable'. He then added, in an ominous tone that would have encouraged the anti-Marketeers in the party rather than the Government, that no sacrifice of Commonwealth interests in the negotiations for EEC entry 'could be agreed', a position which almost guaranteed his opposition to any deal that might be struck in Brussels. Most crucially though, he reworked his own recent past to dissociate himself from the 'Europe' now on the agenda.

In a speech in Zurich in 1946, I urged the creation of the European family and I am sometimes given credit for stimulat-

ing the ideals of European unity which led to the formation of
the Economic and the other two communities. But we have
another role which we cannot abdicate, that of leader of the
Commonwealth and of our partners in the European Free Trade
Association. In my conception, I never contemplated the dimin-
ution of the Commonwealth.[60]

The empty assurances that the British Government was even then
unavailingly giving to the Australians, and Britain's European negotiator
Edward Heath to the Dominions' High Commissioners in London,
that the EEC was all about economics and would make no significant
difference to the political role of the Commonwealth, shows just how
justified such fears were.

In its very first issue in October 1962, *Private Eye* (already practising
the principle of getting a joke out of running together two contemporary
stories that was to serve it well in the years to come) mixed up the
de-Stalinisation of Russia with Britain's debate on the EEC. Under the
headline 'Churchill cult next for party axe', and noting that Premier
Macmillan had 'already relegated many who rose to power in the Churchill era to minor diplomatic and industrial posts', it reminded readers
that Churchill 'was largely responsible for the Party's old anti-European
policy, and the recent switch in the Party line on this issue has confused
and embarrassed Party members'.[61] Even in the real world, though,
Churchill's public statement fell well short of a ringing endorsement of
the European Economic Community which Britain was now seeking to
join, and was far more compatible with the looser associations which
Churchill himself had actually promoted both in opposition and in
office. A 'pro-European' in 1946 had thus become a 'Eurosceptic' in
1962 (though the actual word had yet to be invented). This was not
because of changes in his own views, rather more that the 'project' had
moved beyond the point where he could offer his support. Is it too
fanciful to suggest that in this, as in so much else, Churchill was decades
ahead of opinion on the British right?

What remains most striking, however, after this lengthy reiteration
of the extremely high regard with which both Churchill and Britain
itself were held across Europe after 1945, is, as Professor M. R. D. Foot
has put it, the recklessness with which such a national asset was wasted
by British Governments over the next two decades. Whatever role Britain

ZURICH, 1946   ZURICH, 1996

The Times, 19 September 1996

might have sought to play after 1945, Churchill had ensured that the ball was at our feet, though somehow neither he nor his successors were ever able to run with it. This was a failure of foreign policy that could well come to weigh heavily in the historical scales of judgement.[62]

PART THREE

7

'An English-Speaking Union
in my own Person':
Churchill the American

WHEN INTRODUCING THE YOUNG WINSTON CHURCHILL to speak in New York in 1900, during the lecture tour that followed his escape from South Africa with a price on his head, Mark Twain proclaimed: 'Behold the perfect man,' one who combined a father's British ancestry and tradition with a mother's American democratic values. And when addressing the US Congress shortly after Pearl Harbor in 1941, Churchill himself drew attention to his parentage and evoked laughter and applause with his claim that if he had only had an American father and a British mother, instead of the other way round, he might well have got to Congress 'on my own'. When later in his career a Labour MP taunted him in the Commons with being 'a Yankee mongrel', he delighted in the phrase, and irritated his critic even more by treating it as if it were a tribute.[1]

In the post-war years, a formidable Churchill legend grew up in the United States, which seemed almost to claim Churchill as America's own, even while acknowledging at the same time that he remained quintessentially English. The process of Churchill's secular canonisation in the United States owed much to those who had personal experience of Churchill's wartime leadership, or had family and personal connections, and the names of Averell Harriman, Dwight Eisenhower, Dean Acheson, Kay Halle, Ed Murrow and others in one or other of those categories will arise again and again in this chapter. Such Anglophile Americans shared – sometimes quite explicitly – Churchill's own belief in the essential unity of the English-speaking peoples, but they were also able to use Churchill's name and standing in post-war America as a tool with which to resist the powerful isolationist and Asia lobbies, and instead to commit America to support democracy in Europe as its prime overseas objective. Needless to say, the British Government was always happy enough to play its part in the building up of the image of 'the greatest living Englishman' in America. Churchill's personal participation in the process was motivated by a subtler package of ideas, but at heart it reflected a belief that he could be a personal channel through which the leadership of the forces of freedom in the world would pass from Britain to the United States – a process about which he had an absolute conviction but understandably mixed feelings. As we have seen, Churchill was prepared in 1946 even to say privately that he wished he had been born an American.[2] More often he used his own ambiguous national status in order to conceal the passing on of the torch, for he was, as he once told Adlai Stevenson, 'an English-speaking union in my own person'. His final testament was equally ambiguous: among the many stipulations that he made about his state funeral in 1965 was that American and British flags should fly side by side along the route of the procession, and that the music for the service should include the 'Battle Hymn of the Republic' as well as 'Land of Hope and Glory'. The *Washington Post* noted indeed that the 'Anglo-US theme' had dominated the day.[3]

The process did not of course start from nowhere when Churchill retired in 1955. As his career ebbed and flowed in the forty years between the two events described at the start of this chapter, Churchill himself was already conscious of the advantages that dual parentage had given him, and was a frequent and well-rewarded speaker on the United States lecture circuits, a regular contributor to American magazines and newspapers, and a friend of such prominent Americans as Bernard Baruch, William Randolph Hearst and Henry Luce.[4] He had some of his happiest moments – being photographed like a gangster, with a tommy-gun – and some of his blackest moments – being knocked down and almost killed in a New York street – in the USA.[5] Once he left the army in 1900, Churchill the great imperialist spent more of his time in the anti-colonial USA than in the British Empire. Economics had something to do with this preference. Churchill enjoyed an epicurean lifestyle that kept him constantly short of money, for, as his friend Lord

Birkenhead once pointed out, he was easily satisfied – the best was always acceptable. The *Sydney Morning Herald* ironically juxtaposed in January 1952 a downbeat account of 'Britain's Economic Crisis – Worst since War' with the tale of Churchill's transatlantic voyage on the *Queen Mary*, when he had dined on oysters on every day but one, 'when caviar was substituted'.

Something of the cost of entertaining Churchill is conveyed by the special provisions laid on by Pan Am when Churchill's party joined the airline for a single transatlantic flight in 1961: the list of stores over and above the usual first-class complement included two bottles of cognac, seven bottles of 'good wine', and two pounds of stilton cheese. While Britain provided opportunities for Churchill to make money out of his original career as a journalist and writer, the size of the North American media and publishing markets ensured that the pickings were always better there.[6] Churchill's strategy for avoiding penury also included regular holidays at other people's expense; the knowledge that Baruch, Luce and others would (and could afford to) allow him to stay rent-free in exotic but private West Indian and Mediterranean locations as well as in New York, sometimes for periods of weeks and with a substantial party of relatives and staff, must have simplified things considerably. Churchill was quite unashamed about such an attitude to life, defiantly telling his private secretary in the 1950s that 'it is no bad thing to attach a restaurant car to your train when you are starting on a journey of unknown duration'. Montague Browne also recounts the story of Churchill receiving a draft letter to a generous friend which concluded with the words 'I am most grateful . . .' He struck out these words and substituted 'I am indeed obliged . . .', giving as his reason, 'I am not most grateful under £500.' Montague Browne's conclusion, that 'this was a jest, I trust and believe', seems less than *absolutely* confident.[7]

But Churchill's fascination with the United States was informed by other motives too; as a young man he seems to have imbibed some of the pan-Anglo-Saxonism that was popular around 1900 in both Washington and London, and may well have drawn the phrase 'English-speaking peoples' from that Rooseveltian source.[8] Interestingly, though, while Theodore Roosevelt and Cecil Rhodes had prophesied the inevitable unity of the 'English-speaking people', Churchill almost invariably spoke and wrote of the 'English-speaking people*s*', a far more slippery concept that implied continuing diversity and independence within the grand scheme of things. There was always a strong Anglo-Americanism at the core of his thinking, only briefly interupted by the poor relations between Britain and the US Government in the later 1920s.[9]

All of this is brought out strongly by Churchill's association from its foundation in 1918 with the English-Speaking Union (E-SU), of which he was chairman and then honorary deputy president until his death. This was the brainchild of Sir Evelyn Wrench, a Northcliffe journalist and press executive and a strong Empire man who had in 1910 founded the Overseas Club (later the Overseas League) as a kind of 'grown up Boy Scouts' which would 'draw together in the bonds of comradeship the peoples now living under the folds of the British flag'. Wrench also recognised, like many of the pan-Anglo-Saxonists of the Edwardian period, that the United States was crucial to the attainment of his idea. He later wrote of how a 1904 visit to Canada (when he was just twenty-two) had inspired him with this vision of 'the romance of Empire', much as Churchill had been inspired on visits to North America at the same age. 'In future, always at the back of my mind was the haunting knowledge of this dual problem. How were we to organise the far-flung sections of the British Empire to greatest mutual advantage and, at the same time, how best to promote understanding between the two sections of the English-speaking race?' Henceforth he had lived 'to promote the cause of English-Speaking unity'. By 1911, Wrench had met Churchill and was friendly with others like Beaverbrook who shared their 'romantic vision'. Great War service, partly with Beaverbrook in the Ministry of Information in 1918, when he was in effective charge of British propaganda in the USA and the Dominions, gave wrench contacts all round the world, and it was in alliance with the American Ambassador to Britain, Walter Hines Page, that he launched the English-Speaking Union at a dinner in June 1918.

One of the first acts of the new organisation's steering committee was to invite Churchill to be a founding vice president, an honour soon also conferred on Franklin Roosevelt – which suggests considerable foresight on Wrench's part in 1918. As he told the visiting President Woodrow Wilson in 1919, his objective was now – note the subtle widening of the pre-war aim – 'to draw together in bonds of comradeship the English-Speaking peoples of the world'. At the E-SU's initial peacetime event in 1919, the first of its annual banquets to celebrate George Washington's birthday, Churchill was in the chair, and he was then invited to chair the Union itself, but was presumably too busy with ministerial duties to accept. In 1921 he did take over the E-SU's British Empire chairmanship for four years, in succession to Wrench himself and Lord Reading (Britain's wartime Ambassador in Washington). Churchill was thus from the start the most important British politician to be associated with the new body, and was prepared to make time to chair it in a period when he was both at the start and at the end a cabinet Minister. He was for example a warm supporter of the plan organised by Wrench to present the University of Oxford with £20,000 of Lord Rothermere's money to endow a chair in American history.[10]

Thereafter, the E-SU became a supporters' club for Churchill as well as a propagandist in both the Commonwealth and the United States for the cause he most believed in. By the time of his death, it had some eighty thousand members in about 160 branches, half in the United States, half in the Commonwealth (of which in turn half were in Britain), and premises in London, and in several cities of the United States, Canada and Australia. In 1964, it used the premières in most parts of the British Commonwealth of Jack Le Vien's film on Churchill, *The Finest Hours*, to fundraise for its educational and exchange schemes, schemes which Wrench had launched to ensure closer 'personal contact' between English-speakers around the world, underpinning its work in creating libraries and organising lectures. Initially, those selected for travel were to be 'private individuals, professors, preachers and sportsmen', but later teachers, politicians and students became the priority groups, because of their capacity to influence others. At the London première in the Royal Festival Hall, three thousand people paid up to fifteen guineas each, with a distinguished attendance from the social and political elite serenaded by the band of the Blues, and escorted on and off the premises by the Irish Guards.

The Union noted that the showing of *The Finest Hours* would have a directly educational as well as fundraising potential, so closely did Churchill's actual life match the organisation's objectives. Those dual objectives were neatly brought together when Prince Philip as the president of the Commonwealth E-SU handed over to the American Railroad Museum in 1968 two old pieces of British rolling stock: one had been part of Churchill's funeral train in 1965, while the other had been used by Eisenhower between D-Day and the end of the war in 1945. It was also caught well by the 1964 ceremony in which the Australian chairman of the Commonwealth E-SU, Lord Baillieu, presented a bust of Churchill for display in the American E-SU's headquarters in New York. In the course of his speech he remarked that:

> Wherever the qualities of courage, resolution, nobility of character, steadfastness of purpose are ranked among men, then Sir Winston's fame will be assured of an imperishable place ... [Churchill] knew the cornerstone of any enduring system of world peace and security was the British–American working partnership.

When Churchill died, it was the E-SU that initiated the movements that led on to the Churchill Memorial Trusts in Britain, Australia, New Zealand and the United States, and the British headquarters in London initiated an annual Churchill banquet from 1966, and then an annual Churchill lecture from the centenary year, 1974, to ensure that his memory stayed alive. By the end of the century, its speakers had included Presidents Ford and Reagan, Henry Kissinger, Alexander Haig and Warren Burger, Averell Harriman and Katharine Graham. From Britain and Europe speakers had included Churchill's son-in-law Christopher Soames, the Princess Royal, Ralf Dahrendorf and Mary Robinson.[11]

As he aged, there was also for Churchill a strong consciousness that he had a special role to play as a mediator between the increasingly strained international position of his father's country and the rising but as yet unacknowledged potential of his mother's. It was one of Churchill's keenest beliefs as another war came over the horizon in the 1930s that Britain's only real security lay in an Anglo-American military alliance. His decision to write after 1934 a multi-volume *History of the English-Speaking Peoples*, with a strongly Anglo-American theme, was motivated not only by the size of the American book market at a time of particular stringency in Churchill's finances, but also by the chance to use his history as a personal act of foreign policy. He explained to his historian–assistant Maurice Ashley in 1939, as the *History* neared completion:

> the theme is emerging of the growth of freedom and law, of the rights of the individual, of the subordination of the State to the fundamental and moral conceptions of an ever-

comprehending community. Of these ideas the English-speaking peoples were the authors, then the trustees, and must now become the armed champions.

Just in case it was not obvious, he added, 'All of this of course has a current application,' but it was not only a theme for Churchill the historian. In the same year, he cited as the common Anglo-American inheritance Magna Carta, Habeas Corpus, the Petition of Right, trial by jury, common law and parliamentary democracy. It was but a small step from this to add to the list the American Declaration of Independence (from *Britain*) and the Gettysburg Address, and his wartime Government frequently did so, for example in the propaganda documentaries *Words for Battle* (in which Laurence Olivier orated as both Churchill and Lincoln), and *Come the Four Corners* (in which the Hungarian-born Leslie Howard included such sources in his evocation of the English-speaking inheritance).

In 1935, Churchill had already argued to the American readers of *Collier's* magazine that the UK and the USA should pool their air and naval forces, and use these, along with 'the whole of their influence and money power', to deter aggression and protect its victims. 'Everyone', he admitted, 'can see the arguments against the English-Speaking Peoples becoming the policemen of the world. The only thing that can be said on the other side is that if they did so none of us would ever live to see another war...' Apart from the rhetorical device involving the ironical use here of 'only', a device much like his frequent claim that democracy was the worst system of government in the world, 'except for all the others', the words used suggest two points for comment. First, he was consciously rejecting Bonar Law's 1922 assertion that 'we cannot alone act as the policeman of the world', made at the point at which the post-war settlement of 1919 began visibly to unravel, but suggesting a partnership that would share the burden. Second, Churchill was offering in the days of the League of Nations, and well before the Anglo-American alliance of 1941–5, something strikingly similar to the suggestion made at Fulton in 1946, that even if the new United Nations were to become a world court, then the English-speaking peoples would have to act as its sheriffs.[12] That theme strengthened in the post-war years, with especial care being taken to entrench it in his war memoirs, sometimes through a rather cavalier rewriting of the past. So, for example, he built up Anthony Eden's resignation from the Foreign Office in 1938 as the moment when Neville Chamberlain rashly threw away the offer of an American alliance to deter Hitlerian aggression, adding the dramatically autobiographical recollection that this was the only night in the appeasement period in which he lay awake with worry. At the time, though, he understood that President Roosevelt was offering only a conference unlikely to lead to anything worth having, thought that Eden had resigned on the wrong issue, and quickly demonstrated his own continuing support for Chamberlain.

When the Second World War provided him with the premiership in 1940, Churchill pursued an American alliance with single-minded determination, and believed in its inevitability even when there was virtually no justification. He also directed much of his Government's energy to the task of winning over American domestic opinion. It was indeed his belief that America simply *must* join Britain's fight against fascism that he gave as his main justification for Britain continuing to fight in 1940–1. In a secret session in the Commons on 20 June 1940, for example, Churchill argued that nothing would stir the Americans like fighting actually taking place in England (a sobering thought for his hearers, no doubt), but that, once Roosevelt had been re-elected in the autumn's Presidential election, 'the whole English-Speaking world' would soon be 'in the line together'. His secondary justification for fighting on, belief that the Nazi economy would soon collapse of its own accord, was equally difficult to sustain with evidence. This is most certainly not to suggest that Churchill was wrong to argue for a continued war in 1940–1, merely that when pressed for grounds to justify a decision that was as much instinctive as calculated, he fell back on the inevitability of American assistance – which was actually a long time in coming and which, but for events beyond his control, might well not have come at all. It was, as David Reynolds has persuasively concluded, a case of the right policy pursued for the wrong reasons.[13]

The end of this difficult period came when Pearl Harbor and Hitler's reckless declaration of war on the United States enabled Churchill at last to believe in the inevitability of Britain emerging from the war on the winning side (a conclusion that he had *not* drawn from the entry of the Soviet Union into the war seven months earlier). It is notable that while Churchill's war memoirs speak of his having had a rare sleepless night in 1938 over Eden's resignation, they also record the fact that he slept exceptionally well when the news of Pearl Harbor in 1941 brought about the American alliance he had so long sought.

By then, a mass of Americans who in 1939 can hardly have heard of Churchill, and who certainly had not had a very positive image of what he stood for, had had their perceptions transformed. The process had been encouraged by the British propaganda campaign in North America, and by Churchill's own radio speeches rebroadcast to the United States as news material in 1940–1. The British Ambassador Lord Lothian, for example, cabled in July 1940 that 'there is universal admiration here for Winston and the spirit of the country'. The war correspondent Drew Middleton saw clear personal evidence of this when he returned to his family in Orange, New Jersey. As Nicholas Cull recounts it,

> Although never previously Anglophile, they now lay under the Prime Minister's spell. Churchill's appearance on the radio plunged his welcome-home dinner into silence. No one spoke until the speech was finished. An old uncle broke the silence, 'What a great man.' The others echoed, 'What a great people.'

When the speeches were published in the United States in spring 1941, the relatively anodyne title of the British edition, *Into Battle*, had been changed to *Blood, Sweat and Tears*, a choice indicating the expectation that his broadcast phrases were already well known in America. It became a best-seller, with over sixty thousand copies printed, and the book was then reissued in the Book of the Month Club and attracted very positive reviews. The *Saturday Review of Literature* for example concluded that 'if British democracy wins the war, Winston Churchill will rank with Abraham Lincoln in the annals of freedom'. Cecil Driver in the *Yale Review* praised Churchill's oratory as 'majestic' and considered the book as exemplary both in the use of prose and for insights into Churchill's personality, but decided that the speeches also amounted to more:

> Churchill's speeches have themselves become major events in the war. His great appeals – particularly those of last Summer – have steadied the nerves and steeled the will of his people in their supreme ordeal. His own tenacity has both reflected and invigorated that of the whole British Commonwealth. More

than that, there is in these pages a patriotism which burns at such intensity that it has transcended the boundaries of a state until it has become the beacon of the western way of life.

This was a powerful response from a country still to be neutral for another half-year. When *Time* magazine made Churchill its 'man of the year' for 1940, it did so with the invocation, 'there are no neutral hearts, Winston Churchill, except those that have stopped beating'. The effect of such responses to Churchill is also indicated, as Jonathan Sikorsky has suggested, by the award to him in June 1941 of an honorary doctorate by Rochester University, the first he received in the United States. Not the least significant part of this decision was the fact that the presentation was made by the University's president, a Quaker and former iso-lationist.[14]

There was also encouragement given to the idea of Churchill the statesman by the Roosevelt Administration in such events as the Atlantic Charter of 1941, and by the spontaneous building up of Churchill as a war hero by American correspondents who were sharing Britain's Blitz war in London. Ed Murrow, for example, told his CBS audience in May 1940 that Churchill now became Prime Minister 'with the tremendous advantage of being the man who was right' before the war, and con-cluded at the end of 1940 that Churchill's arrival in the premiership had been the most important event of the year. So valued was Murrow in this intermediary role that Churchill offered him the post of Director-General of the BBC, but, despite Felix Frankfurter urging him to accept and thereby create a marvellous means of strengthening Anglo-American relations after the war, he turned it down on the ground that it would produce too great a conflict of loyalties. The fact that Churchill did not see such a conflict as existing is of course interesting in itself.[15]

It was nevertheless a slow process at the top, for when he first returned to office in 1939 Washington insiders perceived him not as Britain's national saviour but as an old man who both drank too much and was too right-wing to fit in with the priorities of the New Dealers, an interpretation sedulously promoted by the American Ambassador in London, Joseph Kennedy. Churchill was just not, as Kennedy put it, 'on our team'. Though Churchill later made much of the fact that he was from September 1939 in intimate contact with Roosevelt, over the eight months that he was at the Admiralty, he received only three

messages from the President, mainly brief, compared to eight of Churchill's own messages that went the other way. Only after his first broadcasts as Prime Minister did perceptions of both Churchill and Britain's
chances in the war begin to change in America, and only when Roosevelt
began in the winter of 1940–1 to receive upbeat accounts of Churchill
from trusted emissaries in London like Harry Hopkins and Averell
Harriman did he begin to be seen as a truly great leader. In the same
period came the end to the running down of Churchill by Kennedy
when he was replaced as American Ambassador in London. The new
man, Gilbert Winant, Churchill was careful to cultivate with regular
invitations to weekends at Chequers, even though he did not find him
conversationally very interesting. He was handled personally by the
Prime Minister, rather than through the Foreign Office, with positive
effects on ambassadorial reports made during 1941 to Roosevelt. Churchill was by then a big enough figure in America for Warner Brothers
to buy the film rights to his youthful autobiography, *My Early Life*, for
the princely sum of £7,500. His visit to Washington in December 1941
completed the process, for he breezed into a capital city reeling from the
unexpected Japanese attack, and impressed Administration members,
pressmen and military figures who met him with his belligerence, with
his urging to get back on to the offensive by all possible means, and
with his irrepressible personality. His press conference was marked by
spontaneous cheering, reported by *Newsweek* as unprecedented in the
history of Presidential meetings with the press, and his address to Congress achieved a similar response. *Time* observed that it was 'not so
much the speech as the personality that put it over', and it was also
noted that Churchill's V-sign was then picked up and replicated by
American leaders too, so far had he imprinted his own mood on the
occasion. *Life* concluded that 'Churchill sold Washington on the war
and on Britain. And he sold Washington on himself.'[16]

From this point on, American writers as much as British ones
collaborated in the build-up of Churchill's image and reputation, with
no holds barred. In Britain, as we have seen, the ideological framework
of a 'people's war' militated against hero-worship while it lasted, but in
the United States there was no reason to limit the burgeoning admiration
for Churchill as the embodiment of an ally. American film-makers went
more overboard on Churchill as the far-sighted prophet of war than the
British media did. Frank Capra's 'Why We Fight' series of documentaries

swallowed whole Churchill's rhetorical account of what should have been done to avoid war in the 1930s, and made many complimentary remarks about Churchill in the process. The first film, *Prelude to War*, having ended with the Nazi destruction of Poland and therefore needing a morale-boosting climax, actually concluded with a Churchill speech closing with the reassuring 'All will be well,' though it had been delivered on a quite different occasion. His words then led straight into a Hollywood chorus intoning 'Onward Christian Soldiers'. The second film, *The Nazis Strike*, celebrated Churchill-led British resistance after Dunkirk and reminded viewers that he had 'tried for years to warn the world against Germany'. The fourth film, *The Battle of Britain*, made the dubious assertion that the British people had themselves chosen Churchill as their leader (when they had in fact had no say in the matter), and ended with the narrator (Walter Huston) claiming that Churchill had spoken for the world as well as for Britain in his 'Never in the field of human conflict' tribute to the RAF's fighter pilots. No wonder Churchill so liked the films. When shown in Britain, the series was preceded by a short film of Churchill himself in which he argued somewhat disingenuously that he had never fully grasped the master-narrative of the 1930s until seeing Capra's film *Prelude to War*, but that he now thought Capra had got it just about right. The feature film *Mission to Moscow* (directed by Michael Curtiz for Warner Brothers in 1943, and apparently made at the express wish of the Roosevelt Administration) was based on Joseph Davies's ambassadorial memoirs covering his time in Moscow. Like the book, the film portrayed Churchill as a lone but vindicated critic of appeasement, and if he hated (as he did) the heavy, wooden performance of himself in the film, Churchill can hardly have disliked the message. When they covered such topics at all, British films were much more indirect. Quite how good Davies's own judgement was, however, may be deduced from his remark about Canada's Mackenzie King, that 'History will recognise him as a truly great man'. Not yet, it hasn't.[17]

In 1943, Churchill was thought such a big figure in the United States that he was used to spearhead the third drive for war loans, being photographed – as always in the right costume for the performance, in this case a white suit for the Washington summer – buying the first hundred-dollar bond from the Secretary of the Treasury. How far down all this promotion of the Churchill cult had percolated may be seen in

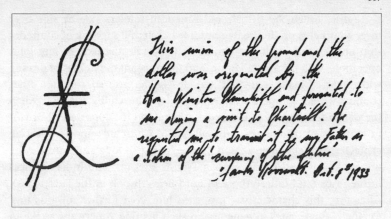

Union of the pound and the dollar
From Kay Halle, *Irrepressible Churchill*

a child's essay quoted in the *New York Times Magazine* a month earlier: 'Mr Churchill is a very busy man. He never seems to be in the place we think he is. He smokes a lot of cigars. I wonder where he gets them. He annoys the enemy a lot by holding up two fingers and by calling them Narzies . . .' An American would thus have concluded by 1945, from what he had read and seen in America about Winston Churchill, that Churchill was a formidable figure in both peace and war, and a staunch and reliable friend of the United States. Even in 1940 when America was neutral Churchill had made bows in its direction in his major war speeches: in the 'finest hour' speech of 18 June, he carefully inserted the words 'including the United States of America' into the paragraph which predicted 'a new dark age' for the world if Britain's war effort were to fail. Since Pearl Harbor, though, Churchill had even more deliberately built this up with direct appeals to American opinion in his speeches, knowing that they would also be heard in America itself, notably in quoting lines by Longfellow with which Americans would be more familiar than his British audience, and later the Arthur Hugh Clough lines culminating in the invocation, 'Westward, look, the land is bright'. Among the wartime 'thinking aloud' proposals that Churchill made in the pursuit of his objective were a common Anglo-American citizenship, a single Anglo-American currency, and even the adoption of a common core vocabulary of Basic English – though these were all ideas that aroused little interest in Washington.[18]

Battles fought by British and American soldiers side by side over three continents undoubtedly reinforced Churchill's feeling of comradeship and kinship with the United States, while the lack of any joint operations with the Soviet Union, and the constant difficulties of dealing with Stalin, Chiang Kai-shek and de Gaulle ensured that no other country would compete with America for Churchill's affection when the war ended. Loyalty to comrades in arms and to supporters of Britain in its times of trouble was after all one of Churchill's most endearing characteristics, the main reason that he fought so long and hard for the unpopular interests of the Russian Tsarists after 1917 and Indian princes in the 1930s (and indeed those of Lord Beaverbrook in the later 1940s). After 1945 this characteristic propelled him even further towards love for the United States in general and such fighting Americans as Ike in particular.

Churchill's loss of office in the post-war British election was received with some bewilderment in the American press, and presumably also by ordinary Americans who pondered on the question, but American papers did not shirk the possibility that Churchill had actually been consciously rejected by the British electorate. The *Boston Globe* reported the story under the headline 'Churchill out, Laborite Attlee in', while the *Chicago Tribune* had 'Attlee on Job as Premier, Laborites Rule Britain'. The Boston paper was fairly typical in offering an unflattering front-page photograph of Churchill with the stark caption 'Out at 70. At least nine members of his cabinet and two members of his family defeated', and almost all papers recorded the large vote against Churchill himself and for an unknown independent in his Woodford constituency. Asking rhetorically 'why did it happen?' the *Globe* came up with three explanations, none of them flattering to Churchill. First, 'country wants New Deal in domestic affairs and does not trust Conservatives to put through reforms'; second, 'dissatisfaction with Tory foreign policy toward Greece, Italy, Spain and Russia' (in other words with Churchill's *current* policy, not with Chamberlain's in the 1930s); third, 'the Churchill type of campaign' at the election. It assured its readers that there would be no discontinuity in British policy at the Potsdam Conference now that Attlee had replaced Churchill, but it also anticipated closer Anglo-American ties since Harry Truman would be closer in spirit to Attlee than to the reactionary Churchill, offered a positive account of Major Attlee himself as a 'soldier–statesman', and even printed a column predicting that 'Labor victory will make Britain No. 1 world influence'.

But not everyone was so optimistic. The more anti-Communist, isolationist *Chicago Tribune* had a cartoon depicting Stalin gloating over the British election results, and another in which Attlee corrects Churchill's pro-American 'Westward the course of Empire takes its way!' rhetoric to read 'Leftward . . .' Some, like the *Los Angeles Times*, were yet more downbeat, since 'for the time being the government of the ablest Briton of the generation has been voted out of office'. Almost without exception, though, the American papers, and the American politicians they reported in giving reactions to the British election result, agreed that the British had not – could not have – rejected Churchill's war services.[19] As the *New York Daily News* put it, 'Churchill, 99 chances to 1, will go down in history as the greatest Englishman of his time, and one of the greatest Englishmen of all time. They can't take that away from him.' The *San Francisco Chronicle* showed in cartoon form Churchill's footsteps in 'the sands of time', while the *Washington Post* asserted that 'what he has done binds Mr Churchill to eternal fame'. The *Philadelphia Inquirer*, though welcoming Labour's win, nevertheless concluded simply that 'there can be no dispute regarding Winston Churchill's inestimable services to Great Britain and the allied cause when Britain stood like a rock against the forces of aggression . . .' Churchill's greatness was not doubted, but it was all now in the past, and the British electorate had quite rightly voted for the future.[20]

But whatever that defeat did to Churchill's standing in Britain, it did not apparently lower it in America, and when the news was announced that Churchill would visit the United States early in 1946 he was besieged with invitations to speak. Asking him to go on from Fulton to his own home town of Abilene, Kansas, or at least to visit him in Washington, General Eisenhower explained that the knowledge that Churchill was staying with him would add to his prestige among his military colleagues – a rather remarkable admission for a supreme allied commander to make in his hour of triumph, though he later offered a similar sort of homage by stealing Churchill's V-sign as an electioneering tool in his successful campaign for the presidency in 1952.[21] The number and persistence of such invitations, the huge number of people who vainly sought tickets to hear him speak, and the size and warmth of the crowds that turned out to greet him when he spoke in Fulton, Missouri (with Truman in tow), and Colonial Williamsburg, Virginia (alongside

Ike), are all evidence of the breadth of support for what Churchill was by then deemed to stand for by ordinary Americans. So many presents were showered on him by Americans during that first post-war transatlantic visit that it required a van as well as cars to convey the Churchill party back from Southampton to Chartwell on his return.[22]

American reaction to Churchill's 'sinews of peace' speech at Fulton has been discussed in Chapter Four; in many areas of the Eastern United States newspaper columnists and editors supported his views, and even those newspapers further west that rejected his prescription of a military alliance against Russia accepted his diagnosis of a Russian threat. Even those like Eisenhower, who at that time disagreed entirely with Churchill's view of Russia, did not allow the Fulton speech to lessen their respect and admiration for the man – indeed his courage in making such a speech in the isolationist Mid-West could be a cause for additional admiration even from those who disagreed with what he said.[23] The Truman Doctrine, Marshall Aid and NATO could all then be read as having been called for by Churchill in Fulton, and he himself rarely missed an opportunity to point this out: only seven months after Fulton, he was gloating over the fact that, if he now said the same thing, nobody would even notice, so completely had his stance become that of the governments of the West.

For the rest of his Opposition period, Churchill's words and actions – including his procession around Europe picking up honorary citizenships, prizes and other honours – were widely reported in the United States, and on the occasions of his visits to America his views and his presence were again widely sought. He was warmly received when he spoke at MIT in 1949, and intended to come to the University of Pennsylvania to make a similar oration in 1950. On each occasion, Churchill visited the President and senior members of the Administration and spent time with the Washington Press Club. It can have done no harm to Churchill's American reputation to be equally popular with Truman, Acheson and Harriman on the one hand, and with their Republican critics on the other, men who saw Churchill as the sort of cold warrior that they too could admire in the heyday of McCarthy. He was always careful to back both sides. When Truman won so surprisingly in 1948, Churchill told him that it had been his business, 'as a foreigner, or half a foreigner, to keep out of American politics', but that now the election was over he rejoiced in the renewal of his 'comradeship' with the Democratic Party; when the Republican Eisenhower won in 1952, Churchill was equally fulsome in expressing his pleasure. Ike was not taken in, minuting on the letter in which Churchill expressed his joy that Eisenhower had defeated Adlai Stevenson for the presidency, 'Did we know that Mr Churchill was a Republican?' He was perfectly correct to suspect Churchill's truthfulness here, for, over the very same weekend as he wrote to Eisenhower, Churchill was saying to Jock Colville about Ike's election, 'For your private ear, I am greatly disturbed. I think this makes war much more probable.'[24]

Both his reputation and the memory of what he had achieved as a war leader were reinforced by the enthusistic American reception of his war memoirs. They sold well, both in the original Houghton, Mifflin hardback edition (which remained in print for almost forty years) and when issued by the Book of the Month Club, and they were read by a much wider audience when serialised in *Life* magazine. The reviews were by no means all positive – some found his rolling paragraphs and sonorous sentences overblown and one or two thought that the inclusion of so many documents made the books dull, but few doubted either the historic nature of the achievement that the books described or their essential truth. J. R. Neumann in the *New Republic*, for example, concluded of *The Gathering Storm* that 'the book gives complete, meticulously documented proof of Churchill's prescient and resolute role' during the appeasement years. A. O. McCormick in the *New York Times* noted that 'few books belong in the category of great events, in the sense that the epoch they depict will always live as they saw it', but decided that 'this book is one of them'. J. H. Jackson, in the *San Francisco Chronicle*, thought it 'a once in a generation kind of book', and Vincent Sheean in the *New York Herald Tribune* 'one of those solid masterpieces, brilliant but durable, which cannot be surpassed'. Even those who were more guarded, like W. B. Willcox in the *Yale Review*, had to concede the book's 'power, as one of the outstanding documents of our time', and though he found it 'far from definitive and occasionally biased', he recognised that Churchill's centrality to the issues he was describing gave him a unique claim to write about them: 'Only Roosevelt might have written a comparable work. Since he did not, this one will remain unique in the literature of the war.'[25]

The second volume, *Their Finest Hour*, was if anything even better received, describing as it did the period of 1940–1 when most Americans had first become aware of Churchill's greatness. Now even the professionals joined in the chorus of praise. Preston Slosson in the *American Historical Review* thought that the book had 'a double value. Firstly, an epic story has been told in epic fashion ... Secondly, as the head of affairs, Churchill naturally knew many details of the war better than anyone else, and his narrative will confirm, check or correct the histories of lesser men.' Drew Middleton in the *New York Times*, concluding that 'this is history' (which is more than Churchill himself ever claimed), argued that now for the first time ordinary Americans who had not been in London in 1940 would be able to understand the magnitude of his achievement. Keith Hutchison in the *Nation* had certainly absorbed and accepted Churchill's key message, for to him the book showed Churchill as the executive man of action as well as the inspiration of the British people. As evidence of the man of action, he cited the reprinted Churchillian minutes used in 1940 to:

> suggest, prod, question, inspire and when necessary direct ...
> Because the British people had faith in themselves, their darkest
> hour became their finest. And in Winston Churchill they found
> not only the leader they deserved but a chronicler worthy of
> their deeds.[26]

The tone of that last extract, published in the same week as both Churchill's belligerent speech at MIT and the signing of the NATO treaty in New York, indicates how far the Cold War mentality of the time helped to ensure that the message of the first two volumes was well received, with their argument on the need for preparedness, standing up to dictators, and courage in the 'darkest hour'. Such a link did a great deal to build up the idea of Churchill's exceptional gifts as a leader, particularly when it is borne in mind that Churchill, it was widely believed in America, had been equally alone in 1945–6 in perceiving the need to stand up to Stalin. It would be wearisome to go through reviews of the later volumes, and to a large extent unnecessary: they generally received cooler notices, if only because the material they covered was in any case less exciting to Americans. But few reviews were actually hostile, so positive had been the impact of the early volumes in establishing the authority of the series, and in any case the final volume, *Triumph and Tragedy*, prompted renewed assertions of Churchill's uniquely prophetic powers, contrasted on the American right with the 'blindness' of Roosevelt and Truman.

As Britain's 1950 election neared, the Truman Administration distanced itself from the still partisan Churchill so as to be seen to be even-handed, and kept its distance when that election produced a close result and the likelihood of another contest. The American press, by now heavily under the influence of the Cold War and McCarthyism and far less likely to be sympathetic to a British Labour government, was generally disappointed by Churchill's failure to win in 1950. Papers that had given a guarded welcome to British 'Laborites' taking power in 1945, seeing in it the dawn of a British New Deal, lamented the re-election of the same British 'Socialists' in 1950. So when Churchill returned as Prime Minister for a final term in 1951, joy was more or less unconfined, the only regret being that he did not have a bigger majority. The *Chicago Tribune* exulted with 'three strikes and you're out for socialism in the British Empire', now that Britain had followed the example of Australia and New Zealand in throwing out Labour governments, while the *Los Angeles Times* cartoonist went for bowling language with 'Ten Strike!' (the 'ten' in 10 Downing Street being made up of Churchill's cigar rampant and his round hat). The *San Francisco Chronicle* headed its story 'IT'S CHURCHILL', with the subhead 'But Majority Likely to be Small'. London crowds were said to have mobbed Churchill as he returned to Downing Street, flattering photographs were printed, and the 'Britain ends six years of socialism' angle was clearly seen as extremely positive. One caption, under a benign, beaming Churchill photograph, was 'a smiling "Winnie" (1951) proved the old adage wrong – beaten champions DO come back'. The *Boston Globe*, as pro-Attlee as anyone in America had been in 1945, now accepted that Churchill's return would bring a more 'rugged' government, 'greater insistence upon the British view', and 'a firm line'. American papers could even claim that the return of the seventy-six-year-old Churchill would add 'vigour' to British policy, so completely had they lost faith in the British left as part of their Cold War mentality.

At the elite level, fears that Churchill was past it – or simply *passé* – were more serious, and the routine monitoring of his health by American officials was not reassuring. Even in 1952, the State Department advised Truman that 'although still robust and vigorous at seventy-seven, [Churchill] is hard of hearing and prone to fall asleep, circumstances which have considerably lessened his effectiveness in the House in recent years'. By 1954, and far more seriously, the American Ambassador was reporting Churchill's lapse in the House in which he had given away nuclear information in order to score a party point, causing many to doubt his judgement. Meeting Churchill after an interval in 1951, Eisenhower noted how far he had aged, and failed to move on with world events. 'Frankly', he noted in his diary,

> I believe that, subconsciously, my great friend is trying to relive the days of his greatest glory . . . To my mind he simply will not think in terms of today but only of the war years . . . My regretful opinion is that the prime minister no longer absorbs new ideas; exhortation and appeals to the emotions and senti- ments still have some effect on him – exposition does not.

A few weeks later, he reiterated that 'he is quite definitely showing the effects of the passing years'. Much as he held 'Winston in my personal affection' and admired 'his past accomplishments and leadership', Ike wished that he would 'turn the leadership of the British Conservative Party to a younger man'.[27]

In office, Churchill's predilection for another sort of mission to Moscow, to wind down the Cold War, gave both the Truman and Eisenhower teams some difficult moments, but on the occasion of their meetings there was invariably personal warmth and much nostalgic revisiting of the wartime alliance for which the name 'Churchill' stood. Truman and Eisenhower yielded nothing to each other in their admir- ation for the old boy as he approached his ninth decade, and if Eisen- hower was a shade more likely to allow his personal feelings to influence actual policy discussions with the Prime Minister, then he also had in Dulles one of the few American leaders of the period who was able to resist the Churchill charm (Churchill reacted to this by lampooning him as 'Dull, Duller, Dullest . . .'). Truman, a shade more businesslike in keeping Churchill to the point, was backed by Dean Acheson as Secretary of State, a man who had an open veneration for Churchill. This is not to suggest that Acheson simply rolled over and let Churchill walk over him – far from it. In early 1952 he took a very tough line with Churchill over a speech that Churchill deviously planned to make in the Commons, but in such an affectionate way that they ended the dispute as even closer friends and with Churchill slyly admitting to his trick. Acheson himself wrote later that by 1946 his feelings for Churchill were 'not very different from that combination of deep respect, veneration and affection, warm but not intimate, which a loyal but sophisticated Catholic might have for the Pope'. Eschewing such fine distinctions, J. L. Harper has concluded simply that 'if Anglo-Saxon brotherhood was Acheson's basic creed, Churchill was his Pontiff'.[28]

However, it was Churchill's final retirement in 1955 that opened the way for the apotheosis, for it both removed any sense that American admiration of Churchill was somehow 'taking sides' against the British Labour Party, and at the same time prevented policy issues from arising on which Churchill and the American Government need argue in public. Finally, Churchill's retirement just after his eightieth birthday relieved the United States of having to support as leader of a key ally a man whose mental faculties were increasingly suspect, and whose judgement on sensitive issues could cause embarrassment. Once he had retired his increasing frailness contributed to the veneration, and occasional reports of his continued good health and his still-functioning appetites became evidence of his uniqueness and his undiminished zest for life. In 1957, Churchill lunched with the American Ambassador in London and the Chairman of the Senate Foreign Relations Committee, Senator Green; emerging from the meeting, Green told reporters that Churchill was still in excellent health and full of vitality, though since he himself was ninety and Churchill a mere eighty-three, his standards may have been a little suspect.[29] From 1954–5, then, the celebratory process went ahead without limitation of any sort, and occasional attempts to check it with suggestions that enough was enough, or that dangerous precedents were being set, were swept aside by the growing tide of opinion which argued that Churchill was unique and should be celebrated in every way possible while time yet allowed.

His eightieth birthday in 1954 and retirement in 1955 each prompted prominent stories about Churchill's greatness in the press and tributes from American politicians. The *Boston Globe*, for example, offered a prominent 'Britain Hails Churchill at 80' story, reprinting tributes in full, and added what was virtually a premature obituary, a full-page account in words and photographs of Churchill's career to date. Columns by Robert Sherwood argued that Churchill had 'forged victory from every defeat', seeing him as 'half-American and All English'. In April 1955, the *New York Daily News* filled its front page with a retirement photograph, headlined 'Winnie bows to age', and both printed in full Eisenhower's tribute to Churchill and gave its own in an editorial. His retirement prompted the feeling that the end of such a career should be marked by the conferring of appropriate American honours, and these spontaneously arose across the country from various groups. In June 1955, Churchill became the first non-American to receive the Freedom Award from Freedom House in New York City (the main home of his Jerome ancestors); in due course, the British Ambassador received the commemorative plaque on Churchill's behalf, presented by Churchill's closest American friend Bernard Baruch. By the end of the year Churchill had also been honoured by the New York Board of Trade. New York City had honoured Churchill too by way of marking his mother's birthplace in Brooklyn, which was for a time a museum. Since May 1952, Number 426 Henry Street has borne a plaque which records it as Jenny Jerome's birthplace, but also makes it clear that it is being marked only because she was the mother of Winston Churchill, 'a staunch friend of the United States . . . to evidence the esteem in which her son is held by the people of this country'. The only problem is that the plaque is mounted on the wrong house, for although the Jerome family had indeed lived there in the past, in January 1850 when she was born they were at 197 Amity Street nearby. This presumably means that the earth removed from the grounds of Jenny Jerome's 'birthplace' in Brooklyn, so as to be mixed symbolically with earth from Chartwell within the plinth of the Washington statue of Churchill, was also from the wrong place.[30]

There was obvious symbolism in the collection of funds by the Lions Club of Atlantic City, New Jersey, to purchase a new lion cub for him since they had read in the the newspapers that Churchill's pet lion had died in its pen at London Zoo.[31] Churchill also became the first recipient of the Colonial Williamsburg award, Virginia, the idea presumably having arisen from his 1946 visit; the announcement spoke of Churchill as 'the richest and most versatile personality of our times'. Was there, though, some contradiction in a place that symbolised America's anti-colonial war against Britain honouring the great imperialist Churchill? Not so, argued the biographer of Thomas Jefferson, Dumas Malone, for 'the greatest Englishman of our times' shared the 'undying belief in human freedom and the dignity of the individual which was manifest in the greatest of these historic Virginians'. And in any case

Churchill could trace his ancestry back to Americans who had fought *against* the redcoats of King George, which was what entitled him to his membership of the Society of Cincinnati. He could also trace his ancestry back to the redcoats themselves, but that made a less satisfactory story for the occasion.[32]

The allegation that his ancestry and his Britishness made it impossible for him to properly identify with democratic Americans was not new in 1955, and whenever it surfaced Churchill was quick to repudiate its implications. In September 1949, for example, when he was in Boston to address the MIT, he was attacked in the US Senate by the isolationist Senator Langer: 'the same Winston Churchill who brags that he is half-American, took up arms for Spain and fought against the US and did all he could to defeat us'. This absurd misrepresentation was easily refuted, but Churchill took considerable trouble to do so, cabling the friendlier Senator Connally to point out that he had not even been in North America during the 1898 Spanish–American War, which Langer had confused with the 1895 Spanish–Cuban War, when Churchill had anyway been a war correspondent rather than a soldier. Connally duly read Churchill's cable into the Congressional Record, but by then it had already been released to the press and printed all over the world. Churchill then gained additional publicity when the Boston police laid on extra security precautions to ensure his safety. Nor was he slow to accuse his American critics themselves of unAmerican behaviour, a gibe that he directed at former Vice President Henry Wallace in 1947 (in addition to labelling Wallace a 'crypto-Communist'). And he was certainly unabashed and unembarrassed about his appeal to American patriotism. It was noted in 1949 that when the American national anthem was played at his meeting in Boston he joined in with enthusiasm. The vigour of his singing was noticed by the audience, which 'gradually hushed'. Eventually, 'alone among the 15,000 present in the vast arena, he sang the concluding bars of the anthem', and so hymned single-handedly the home of the brave and the land of the free. These too were stories that travelled the world.[33]

Americans were by no means the only people honouring Churchill as his life drew to a close. Americans could read in their papers that in Canada he had become Grand Seigneur of the Hudson's Bay Company and at Aachen been awarded the Charlemagne Prize. When the town of Harrow made him an honorary citizen, US Senator Mike Mansfield was for some reason in attendance to claim that Churchill was 'not just a citizen of Britain but of the world'. In much the same way, the American Bar Association made Churchill their guest of honour when meeting in London: Chief Justice Earl Warren thought Churchill had proved to be the key figure in ensuring that the rule of law triumphed over brute force, while the Association president argued that Churchill was 'an Englishman to the marrow of his bones but the cherished property of all the free world'. The six hundred assembled American lawyers turned the dinner into 'an outpouring of respect and affection for Sir Winston', giving him an ovation when he entered, cheering every time his name was mentioned, and cheering 'wildly' when he left.[34]

However, not content with claiming their share of the world's property in Sir Winston, many well-placed Americans were also already arguing that Congress should do something to establish their own country's proprietary rights in the man. The first suggestion of making Churchill an American citizen in some way seems to have arisen even while Truman was President, but he was told that the law prevented it and let the matter drop.[35] In 1955, Eisenhower put forward the same suggestion, but was again told by the State Department that the legal situation prevented it, and that even if possible it would be a bad precedent; the letter saying all this from Dulles to Eisenhower was extraordinarily curt.[36] The idea also surfaced in the press in 1955, as a suggestion from a New Yorker who had himself emigrated from Britain in 1923. When it was taken up by Senator Smathers of Florida, the opponents now had to give their reasons in public. The State Department argued that there were no precedents (since the usually quoted case of the Marquis Lafayette was in fact different),[37] and that any proposal for Churchill would raise 'many troublesome and embarrassing questions'. The Immigration and Naturalization Service, even more negatively, argued that the concept of 'honorary citizenship' was simply an impossible one to make viable within the Constitution, while full citizenship would require Churchill 'to forswear his allegiance to every foreign state' and pay US income tax.[38]

Balked of their objective, some supporters of a Churchill citizenship then settled for a lesser honour for Churchill. Smathers proposed a resolution expressing 'high appreciation of the outstanding contribution of Sir Winston Churchill to the cause of freedom and world peace', which duly passed the Senate unanimously and was presented to Churchill on an embossed scroll. Eisenhower was persuaded to back Nelson Rockefeller's idea of a special medallion to be given to Churchill after a joint resolution of Congress. When shown the draft resolution, Ike struck out as the key words in the citation 'for valor', and replaced them with 'for courageous leadership'. In his message to Congress recommending the honour, the President referred to Churchill as 'a good friend of this country', and suggested that his retirement provided the moment 'at which this Government might appropriately recognise the vast debt that the present generation of mankind owes to him'. The emphasis was on 'the entire world, including the United States' as beneficiary of Churchill's war leadership, a view that was unlikely to satisfy those who wanted a specifically American tribute. However, in the private letter that accompanied the actual medallion, Ike wrote to Churchill in different terms: this time the emphasis was on 'the English-speaking peoples', with 'the entire world' thrown in as an afterthought, and he cited 'millions of my countrymen' as joining in the tribute. The medallion, on which Churchill's likeness was based on a painting of him done by Eisenhower himself, was presented in London by Ambassador Aldrich on Churchill's eighty-first birthday.[39]

Others were not so easily put off, and the idea of making Churchill a US citizen kept surfacing throughout 1956–9, on one occasion attracting a broadcast on CBS radio by Eric Sevareid (another former wartime correspondent who had met Churchill in London) and a powerful supporting speech from Senator John Kennedy of Massachusetts, which would be of great significance later.[40] The main reason that the idea did not get anywhere at this stage, apart from the continued obstruction by the Administration which Eisenhower would not override, was that Churchill let it be known, quietly but firmly, that he could not accept such an honour. In the immediate aftermath of the 1956 Suez Crisis, which had built up such strongly anti-American feelings in Britain that 120 Tory MPs signed a motion deploring American foreign policy, he clearly felt that he would antagonise some British people by accepting an American citizenship. But that did not in any way diminish Churchill's view of what the future must hold. Meeting Harold Macmillan immediately after he became Prime Minister in 1957, Churchill urged him to work to repair the breach with Washington and accept 'that we have got to face the years ahead with our American friends – as friends and not become satellites or subservient to them. We must become good partners.'[41] This was advice that Macmillan was very ready to take, for he too had mixed Anglo-American parentage and a strong sense of shared, transatlantic loyalty. Of course the gradually circulating knowledge that Churchill had felt that he had to refuse citizenship (even when it had never in fact been offered to him) because of the poor state of Anglo-American relations merely ensured that the supporters of the idea redoubled their efforts, if only to show that the breach with Britain had been healed. But this would take time, and Churchill could at least be built up in other ways while they waited.

The ideological project that lay behind the idea of Churchill as an American citizen was given quite a boost in the later 1950s by the publication and massive readership of Churchill's *History of the English-Speaking Peoples*, and particularly of volumes three (on early America and the American Revolution), and four (which dwelt at length on the American Civil War, but with an evenhandedness that enabled Churchill to memorialise Lee as much as Lincoln). Nash Burger felt that Churchill fully understood American history, as only an insider would do, and had shown 'a keen understanding of the forces that worked to produce our system of government'. The title of the books, each volume of which remained a best-seller for weeks in the United States, did much to widen the use of the key phrase behind Churchill's concept, and reviewers frequently noted (in the case of Americans, with some satisfaction) that, beyond Britain and the USA, Churchill had not much to say about the other places where English was spoken. His account of the American Revolution in the third volume was welcomed in the *Philadelphia Inquirer* as 'superb history ... His picture of the British attitude toward that struggle should give many an American reader a new concept of the atmosphere in which it was fought'. It was 'a history, not simply of Britain, but of her numerous offspring who have left their mark in language, tradition, culture and law, from Hudson's Bay to Ceylon, from New Zealand to the Channel Isles', a family of British offspring which, though it was not stated in the review by name, clearly included the United States. Reviewing the same volume for the *San Francisco Chronicle*, the future Defence Secretary Caspar Weinberger reported that 'the majestic, massive, vigorous and thoroughly delightful history of England [sic] that Mr Churchill has been writing so magnificently rolls on here into familiar centuries for American readers'. Six months later, he welcomed the final volume with even greater enthusi-

asm, and demonstrated that he had fully understood the political point
that Churchill had been making by writing the books in the first place.
This was 'a masterly tale of the governments of England and America,
the problems they faced, their struggles for survival against opposition
forces seeking to become governments, and above all the development
of the close relationship between the two great democracies which
together twice saved the free world, many years after Mr Churchill's
history ends'.[42]

Churchill the writer was then followed into a place of special eminence by Churchill the painter, and in this case the impresario was the
President himself. Eisenhower's painter's interest and his own Mid-
Western roots came together to produce the first ever retrospective of
Winston Churchill art, a travelling exhibition that opened in Kansas
City in January 1958, and then visited several other city galleries including
the Smithsonian and the Metropolitan Museum of Art. First, Ike wrote
to Churchill to recommend to him 'two of my very good friends', one
of whom, Joyce Hall, was owner of the Hallmark Cards company, one
of the largest employers in Kansas City, and also much involved with
the city's Nelson Art Gallery. Hallmark had used Churchill paintings
on their cards and they apparently sold well: in 1961, the company
donated £1,200 to the Churchill College Appeal, representing half a
year's profit on such cards, and in 1964, the Hallmark Gallery in New
York City was hoping to open with another Churchill exhibition. Ike
wrote that a Churchill exhibition would:

> not only attract a good deal of attention among all the people
> here interested in painting; but I am certain it would serve in
> a very definite way to strengthen the friendship between our
> two countries. I am not sure that you realise the tremendous
> affection that the American people feel for you. It is a very
> tangible part of the lives of most Americans; in great numbers
> they would welcome the chance to see your paintings and, in
> so doing, pay personal tribute to you. The tour would create a
> wave of goodwill across our country . . .

It would have taken a far more modest man than Churchill ever
was to resist such blandishments, and, in accepting the suggestion, he
expressed the hope that an exhibition would indeed 'make a contribution
to our theme' – the unity of the English-speaking peoples. He tied

Eisenhower into public endorsement of the project by getting him to write the foreword to the exhibition catalogue, but also offered him the choice of one of the thirty paintings on show to keep as his own.[43] A few months later, Eisenhower wrote that 'all America is looking forward to the visit of the Queen' in 1958, and asked whether Churchill might come too, and thus attend the launch of his exhibition. Churchill, no doubt remembering 1946 and feeling that another trip to Missouri would be unduly taxing, enthusiastically agreed to come to the exhibition when it reached Washington, but then illness prevented him from travelling to America at all in 1958.[44]

It must be said that not everyone was quite so sure that a Churchill art show was anything but a 'public relations stunt' – as in a sense it was, since it had for Eisenhower a political as much as a cultural purpose. Several museums turned down the exhibition when offered it, some of them in a roundly insulting manner. The assistant director of the Pittsburgh Carnegie Institute, for example, remarked, 'I understand that Churchill is a terrific bricklayer too, but nobody is exhibiting bricks this season.' In due course, art galleries would be all too happy to exhibit piles of bricks, but this was still the conservative 1950s and it was Pittsburgh. Cincinnati's Art Museum was just as cutting: 'This is "Churchill Art", not just art. Our interest, as a museum should be, is in art, not history.' The prestigious Chicago Art Institute was another that refused, saying tartly that 'We have certain professional standards . . .', but in this case the outcry from within the city was so great that the director was out of office within a week, somewhat unconvincingly claiming that his move to a smaller upstate gallery had been decided much earlier. Those galleries that had signed up for the show were naturally equally vociferous in support of their own judgements, usually arguing on artistic grounds, but frequently conceding that the case for the defence was at least half political. Kansas City's Nelson Art Gallery pointed out that they were 'representing another side of one of the greatest personalities of our time', while the director of Manhattan's Metropolitan Museum of Art took the straightforwardly political line: 'Think how eager we would be to see the paintings of Alfred the Great were they to be discovered tomorrow.' The story was widely reported throughout North America and the Commonwealth, not least in places like Melbourne where the exhibition would go next.[45]

It is interesting to note that all the places that refused to join in the celebration of Churchill the artist were in the traditionally isolationist Mid-West (and Kansas City's support for it is easily explained by the involvement of Hall and Eisenhower), while almost all of the places where the show was seen had no such tradition. While Churchill's art had long been respectable enough to earn his paintings the right of exhibition in London even without the prestige added by his name, they were not exactly at the cutting edge of modern manners in painting. Indeed, Churchill's painting – like Churchill's writing – was so generally accessible partly because it was done after 1945 in a language of two generations earlier. Having viewed the exhibition in Kansas City, Harry Truman (no mean aesthetic judge in fact, though he rarely allowed this to appear in public) was heard to declare, 'Damn well done! You can at least tell what he painted, and that is more than you can say about many of these modern painters.'[46]

The exhibition was a great success: Eisenhower's catalogue introduction praised Churchill to the skies and drew particular attention to the fact that Churchill 'has often described himself, especially during the fateful war years when our respective countries were comrades-in-arms, as "half-American"'.[47] He also sent a special message of commendation for the opening ceremony, and wrote regularly to Churchill to tell him how it was going: in February 1958 he reported that in Kansas City his paintings were 'drawing unprecedented numbers' and getting the sort of attention in Eastern papers that was most unusual for any arts event west of the Mississippi. In April he reported that in Washington forty thousand people had attended on the first Sunday showing, six times the normal number.[48] In October, with London's Royal Academy now at last showing his collected paintings once they had been seen in Australia and New Zealand as well as Canada and the USA, Churchill wrote to Ike that 'you have gained for me a worldwide reputation as a painter'. Two years later, Churchill paintings were auctioned for a considerable sum as a part of World Refugee Year, such was indeed that 'worldwide reputation'.[49]

No doubt many who attended these exhibitions of Churchill's art were more interested in the man than the canvases, but interest there certainly was. But the Churchill retrospective of 1958 proved to be only the prelude in idolatry to the great man's final official visit to the United States, another event engineered by Eisenhower. Although illness prevented this from taking place in 1958, Ike was determined to bring it off in 1959 if possible, and so was Churchill, despite his still fragile health. In May 1959, Churchill spent a week in the USA, half in New York (partly spent privately on a visit to Baruch, partly on a much trumpeted visit to a distant American relative)[50] and half in Washington. The latter part included an afternoon outing to Ike's Gettysburg farm, during which they drove over the battlefield on Ike's electric golf cart, a means of transport that both acknowledged Churchill's failing mobility and ensured that the press could not hear their conversation. Eisenhower had recently been deeply embarrassed when showing the self-invited Monty over the battlefield, since his guest had audibly scorned the generalship of *both* sides in 1863, insults delightedly reported by the American press. The American press covered every part of Churchill's trip at great length, giving voluminous details of his hats, clothes, food, cigars and so on, and the occasion also triggered adulatory editorials and columns. When Churchill entered the Oval Office and found a framed photograph of Montgomery on Eisenhower's office wall, he delighted his hosts by glowering at it for several seconds and then disbelievingly shrugged his shoulders with characteristic eloquence.[51]

There was no doubting official America's welcome to Churchill. When, on arrival in New York, an officious customs man pushed through the crowd and insisted on personally examining Churchill's baggage, he was simply lifted off the ground by the shoulders by two secret service men who had been hovering near by and unceremoniously removed from the scene, 'his feet pedalling furiously'. Unofficial America had also clearly taken Churchill to its heart by then, as Anthony Montague Browne had noticed on a recent trip to Monte Carlo. As Churchill awaited his car outside the casino, up rushed Frank Sinatra, 'wrung him by the hand' and announced, 'I've wanted to do that for twenty years.' (Churchill's response was to demand, 'Who the hell was that?' and was none the wiser when he was told.) At dinner in the White House, Eisenhower dwelt lovingly on his long friendship with Churchill, but focussed his remarks on a wartime occasion on which an American officer had quoted the line, 'Shoot if you must this old grey head'; Churchill had immediately recited the entire poem from which the line came, 'so all of us agreed that he was a little bit more American than we were'. That poem, 'Barbara Frietchie', was in fact one of Churchill's favourite turns put on for Americans. Eleanor Roosevelt, advising the new President in 1945, had told Harry Truman that 'if you talk to him about books, and let him quote to you from his marvellous memory, everything on earth from Barbara Frietchie to the Nonsense Rhymes and Greek Tragedy, you will find him easier to deal with on political subjects'. Churchill, replying to Eisenhower, welcomed the presence of 'so many of the most distinguished figures of the United States of America' and urged that 'it is in close and increasing fellowship, the brotherhood of English-speaking peoples, that we must work'. At the airport before he left, he reiterated the same message, that all would be well, 'as long as the United States and Great Britain are united, bound together'. This was virtually the same message that he had used to Ike in 1953, when he said that 'my hope for the future is founded on the increasing unity of the English-Speaking Peoples. If that holds, all holds. If that fails no one can be sure of what will happen.'[52] The week led to some great disappointments for those who had been angling for invitations to one or more of the events: when Secretary Benson was excluded from an outing with Churchill to see azaleas in the arboretum he was 'crushed'. Eisenhower's personal secretary, Ann Whitman, concluded her note on the week's events with the reflection that 'to see Sir Winston is to look upon history – history that is heroic and great', a fairly typical reaction to meeting the great man at this late stage of his life.[53]

The only sour note in May 1959 was the way in which the Churchill visit became sucked into the Truman–Eisenhower feud, with each seemingly trying to claim a closer friendship with Churchill than the other could manage. In retirement, Truman was quite a good hater, and sometimes with good cause: when Westminster College tried to get him to persuade President Nixon to attend the dedication of their Churchill Memorial in 1969, his old friend Harry Vaughan reported that 'ever since the campaign of 1952 when Mr Nixon said that "20 years under Roosevelt and Truman were 20 years of Treason", Dick and HST have not been in perfect rapport'. But Truman, like Eisenhower, was still a great admirer of Churchill, and had lunched with him at Chartwell on his only peacetime visit to England, in 1956. When the Trumans had a private showing of the Churchill exhibition in Kansas City, Bess Truman pulled off a nice bit of one-upmanship: 'Someone asked Mrs Truman if she would like to take any of the paintings home with her [as Eisenhower was being allowed to do]. "No," she replied, "We already have one".'[54] Truman was therefore unlikely to accept any invitation to Eisenhower's

White House, having never forgiven him for his failure to disown Joseph McCarthy's attack on General Marshall in 1952. But the invitation itself came impossibly late and clashed with plans for Truman's own seventy-fifth birthday party in New York, which he unavailingly sought to get Churchill to attend, using Averell Harriman as a go-between. Eisenhower then remarked pointedly on the fact that many of those attending the dinner had cancelled other important commitments in order to come, a reference which the press assumed to be directed at Truman, who felt obliged to write twice to Churchill to explain his absence.[55]

Despite this unfortunate clash (and Churchill anyway kept himself well above the fray),[56] there is no doubting the impact that the Churchill visit made, not least because many could see that it would never be repeated. Press reports reiterated the fact that the Washington and New York streets had been full of people, both adults and children.[57] At the end of May, Ike was still able to write to Churchill that 'stories are still appearing in some of our magazines about your visit to this country. America of course claims at least half of you as her very own.'[58]

Nineteen fifty-nine was the last occasion on which Churchill made a planned visit to the United States, though when bad weather cancelled a transatlantic flight and forced him to make an overnight stop in New York on his way back from a cruise in April 1961, it caused quite a flap at the White House. Although Churchill had to turn down President Kennedy's offer to jet him to an informal meeting in Washington, both he and Kennedy told the press how much they had appreciated the opportunity to speak to each other on the telephone (it would appear that only Churchill's secretary Anthony Montague Brown did in fact speak to Kennedy). The limousine he used was laid on by the New York Chamber of Commerce, flying together the British and the American flags to symbolise his unique status. Three hundred 'plain Americans' managed to make it to the airport, despite the complete lack of publicity, and one New Yorker was quoted as having brought her six-year-old son so that he could see 'one of the greatest men who ever lived'. The sad epilogue to the near-miss meeting with Kennedy was the message sent back to Churchill by Emery Reves in 1963, that the President was 'longing' to have a Churchill painting to hang in the White House, for he was one of Churchill's 'truly great admirers'. Churchill was considering sending him one when Kennedy was assassinated.[59]

Relations were also reinforced by Randolph Churchill's rumbustious friendship with the Kennedys – his two cables of congratulation after the Cuban missile crisis reading, 'It's a great day for the Irish!' and 'Well done. It's bloody marvellous.' At least these short telegrams did not produce the reaction of Arthur Schlesinger to a Randolph Churchill letter three months later: 'God knows what he's talking about in the second paragraph!' The friendship was perhaps a mixed blessing for Anglo-American relations: Schlesinger reported to Kennedy in 1963 that, 'regarding no sacrifice too great in the cause of the Special Relationship, I sat up drinking with Randolph Churchill until two o'clock this morning . . .'. But Churchill the younger remained close enough to the Kennedys to be their choice as JFK's official biographer until his own early death terminated the idea. Their desire to have the same biographer for Churchill and JFK was indeed the sincerest form of flattery.[60]

By 1962, the question of the honorary citizenship was again being actively propounded, this time in a new context, for now both the President and his close advisers were willing to do something to bring it about. John Kennedy had seen Churchill in action in London in 1938–9, and the question of Churchill as a war leader was one of the subjects with which he had an early disagreement with his ambassador father. As a voracious reader of recent history, he was a lifelong admirer of Churchill the writer as well as Churchill the statesman. In 1961 he claimed to have read all of Churchill's books, he had gone back to Hansard to read up Churchill's less well-known speeches, and in the month of his Inauguration as President was trying to track down a particular reference to the Akond of Swat that he had long ago seen in Churchill's *The River War*. The focus of the citation that Kennedy produced for the honorary citizenship ceremony in 1963 was on Churchill the wordspinner, declaring that 'he mobilised the English language and sent it into battle'. Though much quoted later as a Kennedy original, this was in fact an unacknowledged quotation from Churchill's Nobel Prize citation of 1953, but a lively argument then arose as to its origin; Eric Sevareid on CBS attributed it to Ed Murrow, but it seems in fact to have been first used during the war by the British journalist Beverly Nichols.[61]

The two catalysts that set the ball rolling again were the persistence of Kay Halle, who had been fighting an unrelenting campaign for the honorary citizenship for years, and the arrival of Kennedy at the White House. Kennedy was the less committed of the two; he always had to remember the Irish hostility to Churchill that still affected a few

Democratic Party supporters, not least in his native Boston, and protest letters did come in, one of them from a 'Mr Joseph Kennedy', though it seems unlikely to have been *the* Joseph Kennedy who was by then incapacitated with a stroke. JFK was increasingly at loggerheads with Congress as his presidency went on, and was not keen to take on an unnecessary legislative battle; and any salutation of one of the great names of the past jarred with the President's wish to present his Administration as youthful and forward-looking. It is significant that the speech delivered at the actual honorary citizenship ceremony was criticised as one of the worst of his presidency, for he had been drawn into a pastiche of Churchill's own rhetoric, rather than using his own, fresher way with words: Murray Kempton wrote that 'Mr Kennedy's language has been displaced in time, not forward but back.' Kennedy could therefore on occasion seem lukewarm, or at least understandably preoccupied with higher priorities, but his support was there when really needed. In January 1963, a note from Schlesinger to Kennedy's press secretary warned him that a reporter would shortly ask Kennedy for his views on the citizenship proposal. After reciting the latest supportive legal advice, in part achieved precisely because the White House was now bludgeoning State and Justice into co-operation, he concluded that 'I hope the President will give the idea strong support.' Kennedy obliged, and this boosted the campaign when it most mattered.[62]

Kay Halle had no such doubts and no higher priorities, and she was well placed to take advantage of the situation created by Democrat control of both Houses of Congress and of the White House. She had conceived the idea during her first visit to Chartwell in 1931, hearing Churchill's conversation 'laced with allusions to his American ancestry'. As an American correspondent in wartime London she had established many friendships with people in the British establishment and media, and was well known to the Churchill family. As 'the Cleveland Department Store heiress' she had independent means, and as a professional writer and a tireless Democrat Party worker who had been a long-term friend of the Kennedy clan and an early supporter of JFK's Presidential campaign, she had all the right connections – in Washington, out in the Mid-West and in the American media. Her contribution to the Kennedy Inauguration had been to organise the statement of support for Kennedy signed by dozens of prominent people in the arts world which helped to create the 'Camelot' image of the new White House, and it was when calling on Kennedy to be thanked for this little task that she had her opportunity. When Kennedy asked politely if there was any favour he could do her in return, she reminded him that he was on record as a supporter of an honorary citizenship for Churchill and asked him now to give it Presidential support. This was in effect Kay Halle calling in a campaign debt, and Kennedy duly promised to see what he could do. From this point, despite delays and misgivings, it became and remained an Administration-backed proposal.[63]

Nevertheless, it still would not have got anywhere without a skilfully co-ordinated campaign in which Halle was able to pull all the appropriate levers. Her friendship with Schlesinger, a great Churchill admirer himself and Special Assistant in the Kennedy White House, was clearly one important link, but only one of many that this extremely well-connected campaigner made use of. When needing legal advice, she was able to consult (both of them on first-name terms) John Foster QC MP, Recorder of Oxford and formerly a diplomat at the British Embassy in Washington, and in the United States Felix Frankfurter, a Justice of the Supreme Court and one of the most respected jurists of the time. When she needed the public backing of the surviving ex-Presidents, she found mutual friends through whom to approach Truman, Eisenhower and even Herbert Hoover, and all three obliged by supporting publicly Churchill becoming an honorary citizen. The problem was, as the *Manchester Guardian* had written when the issue had last been debated in 1959 (though delighted to learn that Halle was descended from the founder of their city's famous orchestra), that almost everyone liked the idea, 'if only the dangers of precedent can be avoided'. In February 1962, a year after her conversation with Kennedy in Inauguration week, Halle wrote to enquire what the White House was doing about it, reminding them that JFK had said 'he thought it a terrific idea', but that it must be done soon, 'so the old boy will still be able to take in the honour'; at this time she also recruited Vice President Johnson as a supporter, using Walter Lippmann as a contact. After a first stalling reply, Kennedy himself replied that 'it appears to be unconstitutional and for that reason would be unwise. One of the Navy ships however is going to be named after him.'[64]

Balked in her attempt to get the President to father the proposal, Halle went back to her roots. Reinspired by a visit to Chartwell, she wrote a trenchant article in July for the Cleveland *Plain Dealer*, setting

out the full case for an honorary citizenship; the editor then secured its
syndication coast to coast, and circulated on Halle's behalf to all Ohio's
Senators and Representatives his view that this was 'a piece of unfinished
War Effort, the cap sheaf, the final recognition of a man to whom we
undoubtedly owe our hides today . . . This to me furnishes a marvellous
opportunity to build some unusual international public relations, and
the cost almost nothing.' Within a few days, Senator Stephen Young of
Ohio had a bill before the Senate and was reporting many letters of
support and none against – 'this is quite unusual'. Among those who
volunteered their support was Rep. James Roosevelt, FDR's son, Senator
Barry Goldwater, and the influential Senator William Fulbright, Chairman of the Foreign Relations Committee. Fulbright felt unable to go
public with his views, though, 'in view of the neo-isolationism which
lies just below the surface in some parts of this nation', including Arkansas where he faced re-election later in the year. The whole issue
was clearly being viewed as symbolic of more than just an honour to
Churchill.[65] One clever attempt to outflank the 'neo-isolationists', and
to build an even stronger Anglo-American bridge, was Halle's proposal
that Britain should make Eisenhower an honorary citizen at the same
time as Churchill was honoured in the USA. This had to be abandoned
when it became clear that left-wing Labour MPs would oppose the idea
in Britain, and thus make it counter-productive; even the editor of the
Tory-inclined *Evening Standard* advised caution, as Ike was 'still quite
a controversial figure politically'.[66] Late in August, Schlesinger felt that
the main proposal would not come off, 'despite the newspapers', which
had lobbied hard for its adoption, and in September even supporters
recognised that they would have to postpone action until the next session
of Congress.[67]

The Churchill family, kept pretty well informed of what was going
on, carefully avoided taking any part in the campaign – 'Surely it should
come as a surprise?' wrote Randolph Churchill to 'Dearest Kay' Halle,
on 26 October 1962. The occasional leak can have done no harm, though,
as when it was reported that Sir Winston was known to be 'moved' by
the proposal, views conveyed confidentially to the Chairman of the
House Judiciary Committee through Britain's Washington Embassy, but
also given publicity in the *Washington Post*.[68]

By January 1963, the situation had been transformed; persistent
lobbying had lined up far more supporters in Congress, while State and

Justice had been persuaded to reverse their earlier view, and the Budget Office had signified support. Several American states – reacting no doubt to the press debate of the previous summer – were debating bills that would bypass Congress and make Churchill a citizen of Tennessee, Nebraska, Ohio, West Virginia, Maryland and New Hampshire among others, a pretty good cross-section of the Union between them. Among those who came out publicly in support at this stage were Lyndon Johnson and Hubert Humphrey.[69]

In January 1963, with Congress now debating bills at the start of the session when they had time enough to pass them, Schlesinger urged Halle to return to Washington 'to pull all the threads together'. She had already signified the strategy for 1963 in a letter published, with strong editorial support, in the Washington Post. The idea now was to meet head-on the hostility of what Time called 'the worrywarts' in Congress who feared 'that the honour might later be passed out like green stamps'. She asserted that 'some might consider this setting a precedent. If it were anyone else the point could be argued. Sir Winston is a precedent.' Along the same lines, Halle argued to Time magazine's Roy Larsen, 'all I can say is if ever again anyone of the magnitude and credentials of Sir Winston swims into our ken, then let's give him the same honour'. The effectiveness of this line of argument may have been suggested by the reasoning that had been going on within State, for as an assistant secretary had told the Vice President when explaining the Department's change of mind, 'there is only one Churchill per century'.[70]

The problem now was 'apathy', getting Congress actually to act on a proposal that almost all members supported, and this was achieved by stepping up the pressure. Ohio's Rep. Frances Bolton, sponsor of one of the House bills under consideration, was one of many who urged people to write in with their views to the Chairman of the Judiciary Committee, while Halle continued to work the press. She had especially valuable support from the Washington Post – picking up a line from Churchill himself, Halle later told the Post that it had 'provided the roar' for the campaign. She did not neglect the foreign policy case as well as the arguments for the honour as such, reminding Time that, after de Gaulle's veto had excluded Britain from the EEC, the honorary citizenship 'would certainly buck up Britain and the Commonwealth at a moment they badly need it'. (That assumption that the Commonwealth was as devastated as Britain by its failure to enter the Common

Market – when actually some member states were hugely relieved – suggests a very Churchillian assumption that Britain and its Dominions had no really separate interests and identities.) One of the most telling inputs to the debate was a scathing, Congress-bashing radio broadcast by Bill Leonard on CBS, characteristic of much of the exasperation now being expressed in the media. Despite his fabled tenacity,

> not even Sir Winston may have the stamina to survive the heavy footed crawl at which the Congress of the United States is going about the task of making Winston Churchill an honorary citizen ... Indeed it took us less time – if somewhat more effort – to help Mr Churchill settle his quarrel with the Third Reich than it is taking Congress to act ...

He reminded listeners that in 1959 Kennedy, 'who had more influence on the Hill in those days than he currently enjoys', had urged Congress to 'race' back and pass a resolution, but experience in the three Congresses since had shown that 'the red tape is mightier than the noble sentiment'. The problem was the lack of precedent, 'and that makes most lawyers super-cautious, very nervous and very slow. Sir Winston can be thankful that the United States acted somewhat more swiftly in aiding Britain's wartime Prime Minister in his hour of darkest trial than it has in honoring him in his twilight.'[71]

Under such pressure, and indeed subjected to such general scorn, the opponents in Congress melted away and the momentum behind the idea became unstoppable. The Immigration and Nationality sub-committee now completed its tedious business and recommended acceptance, allowing the House Judiciary Committee unanimously to back both the idea and Kay Halle's argument in its support; they reported that they had endorsed the bill, 'well aware of its unprecedented nature'. The full House voted acceptance by 377 votes to 21. Only three Representatives actually spoke against the bill, all of them concentrating on the argument as to precedents, while supporters like James Roosevelt argued the same point in reverse: 'rarely in the history of civilisation has there appeared a man of the stature of Winston Churchill'. Those Congressmen who had been in the minority were often given a rough handling back home, the *Des Moines Register* for example regretting the stain on Iowa's good name caused by the 'bad manners' of those who had voted with the noes. In the Senate, passage was even easier, for a much larger proportion of the legislators had committed themselves in advance as sponsors of one bill or another; on 2 April, the Senate approved the proposal without a vote, but wrote in Senator Everett Dirksen's stipulation that 'since the Constitution of the United States allows for no titles of nobility . . . the record ought to show that, here, he will be Mr Winston Churchill'. The title was also carefully stated to be one that would not pass to Churchill's heirs. This sophistry neatly allowed Sir Winston to remain entirely British and aristocratic, while Mr Churchill became an American and a democrat. Cartoonists and columnists had a fine old time with the Jacobin concept of 'Citizen Churchill', but always in affectionate tones.[72]

Those who knew something of the inside story also knew where congratulations should be directed: *Newsday* wrote that it was 'all thanks to that blonde', while Sir Isaiah Berlin cabled Halle from Britain, 'Attagirl Well Done Love Isaiah'. In 1967, Kay Halle became an Officer of the Order of the British Empire, so considerable were thought to be her efforts on behalf of British interests in the United States, and when the English-Speaking Union honoured her in 1971, the host for the evening was the British Ambassador. The more public responses were positive too: the *Richmond Times Dispatch* thought Churchill 'the greatest living member of the human race', while the *Boston Record* said like many that 'the honour is ours. Welcome Winnie. It's always been difficult to think of him as anything but American anyway.' The *Philadelphia Inquirer* was sure that:

> this signal honor has the approval of most Americans. Certainly
> to any who recall his wonderful services to a beleaguered world,
> as well as to his own country, during the Second World War,
> welcoming this doughty 88-year-old warrior, son of an Ameri-
> can Mother, to our ranks is a shining honour to ourselves.

The *Christian Science Monitor* felt that it was less a matter of honouring a foreigner than of 'bringing an American home', while the caricaturist of the Cleveland *Plain Dealer* drew Winston with an Uncle Sam hat (with a Mad Hatter label in the band, reading 'Honorary Citizen of the United States'), and the caption 'On you it looks good'. Curiously, this last cartoon, by Pulitzer prizewinner Ed Kueckes, also showed Churchill in the act of giving his 'V for Victory' sign with two fingers raised, but with the hand facing backwards rather than palm-forward, so that

ON YOU IT LOOKS GOOD.

Cleveland (Ohio) *Plain Dealer*, 9 April 1963

it became to British eyes an extremely rude gesture rather than an heroic one; even more curiously, the International Churchill Society later adopted the same drawing for an early fundraising campaign. To be fair, Churchill too occasionally used the V-sign in the same way, and one such photograph had been included in 1945 in an anthology of Churchill pictures, with the cheeky caption 'and so ended the year 1941'.[73]

The President lost no time in signing the bill, sending the pen he had used to Sir Winston to add to his collection of memorabilia, and a ceremony was quickly arranged for 9 April 1963 in the White House rose garden so that the honorary citizenship could be formally conferred. Britain's part in this American ceremony was emphasised by such tactful expedients as invitations sent to the entire (British) National Theatre Company then playing in Washington, so that the very English Sir John Gielgud and Sir Ralph Richardson were both there to see Mr Churchill made an American. The ceremony was performed, at the BBC's suggestion, at prime viewing time in Britain and broadcast live over the new Telstar satellite link; it was also shown live in six other countries as well as Britain and the USA, and surprisingly these included Hungary and Czechoslovakia. There was some danger that the new technology would distract attention from the event itself – the *Daily Telegraph* enthused over the 'good steady picture for 13 minutes' and printed on its front page next day a photograph of the television picture itself – but it did allow Churchill, unfit by then to cross the Atlantic, to be a live spectator. Randolph Churchill travelled over to Washington to receive the honour on his father's behalf, and collected the official honorary citizenship documents and passport which the State Department had invented over the previous couple of days. The speech that he read was fulsome and appropriately grateful, the summation of much that Churchill had been saying since 1940.

> I am, as you know, half American by blood, and the story of my association with that mighty and benevolent nation goes back nearly ninety years to the day of my father's marriage. In this century of storm and tragedy, I contemplate with high satisfaction the constant factor of the interwoven and upward progress of our peoples . . . Mr President, your action illumin-ates the theme of unity of the English-speaking peoples to which I have devoted a large part of my life.

But the speech also contained a belligerent paragraph rejecting the argument that Britain 'should now be relegated to a tame and minor role in the world'. This was generally taken as a hit at Dean Acheson, who had recently irritated many Britons with his observation that Britain had lost an empire but not yet found a role. Acheson delightedly thought that the barbs were aimed at him: 'Yes, wasn't it a heck of a note? The first act of our first honorary citizen is to attack a former Secretary of State!' Schlesinger was not at all sure whether the actual author of the speech was Winston or Randolph, for Winston was generally better mannered on the big occasion than this speech made him appear (it was actually written by Anthony Montague Browne). But such doubts were not aired in public, and the offending paragraph was taken as evidence that the old fire was still alight, and therefore that the honour had come in time for the old man to appreciate its meaning. The *Daily Sketch* noted happily that the first act of Churchill himself after watching

Bloody Yank
Chicago Sun Times, *c.* 9 April 1963

the ceremony had been to light a cigar while the *Daily Telegraph*'s cartoonist had the Statue of Liberty holding one aloft.[74]

At this point, it might well have been felt that enough really had been done, and, when asked at a press conference whether he also favoured a statue of Churchill in Washington, the President said that he did not – at some point all of this must stop; the *Washington Evening Star* diplomatically reported that he probably did not know that such a statue was already being planned by the English-Speaking Union, specifically to repay the debt felt to be owed by the erection of FDR's likeness in Grosvenor Square, London, the money having been raised by the Pilgrims Trust. Kennedy did agree that month to become with Harry Truman honorary co-chairman of the Churchill Memorial planned for Fulton.[75]

Of course not all Americans were equally enthusiastic about Churchill, and some indeed maintained a spirited hostility throughout. These were almost entirely Americans of Irish extraction, linked with the Catholic Church, East Coast trades unions and Irish community newspapers in Boston and New York, but, in view of the centrality of such groups to at least the Democratic vote in several states, they could not be ignored (Harry Truman, when President, joined the Friendly Sons of St Patrick himself, making sure to be a member in a marginal state). Nevertheless, tracking the bile-driven coverage of Churchill in such press outlets only confirms how far outside the American mainstream they were – more hostile to Churchill on Irish grounds even than the Irish who had remained in Ireland, and considerably more hostile than Irish Australians. The *Gaelic American* is a case in point, though the fact that as a Catholic paper it was as hostile to Communism as it was to Churchill led it into some strange contortions. In the week in which Berlin fell in 1945, it was mainly reporting a rally to demand a united Ireland ('The Creator made Ireland a geographic entity') and action to prevent the flooding of the American market with cheap British goods at the cost of American workers' jobs (some chance, in the relative economic conditions of May 1945!) An editorial attributed Victory in Europe entirely to the American army, and so discounted both the British and the Russians. When it reported Churchill's ill-judged attack on de Valera in his Victory broadcast, it was under the headline 'Ireland is Dragooned', so evoking memories of Oliver Cromwell and the slaughters of Drogheda and Wexford. Churchill's behaviour was compared unfavourably with that of Michael Quill ('Mike the Bronx Pedlar'), a politician in the New York Irish community who had had the temerity to criticise de Valera's visit to the German Legation in Dublin to offer condolences on the death of Hitler (something that the *Gaelic American* had not actually reported itself). In the following weeks, it printed in full de Valera's 'calm, scholarly reply' to Churchill, following up by quoting the endorsement of de Valera by the *Jesuit Weekly* and the *Labour Leader*. It then took particular delight in printing a refutation of Churchill's attack on Irish neutrality by London's *Sunday Times*, which had pointed out how much help Ireland had given to the Allies (something that once again the *Gaelic American* had not previously revealed, so wedded was it to de Valera's neutrality policy).[76]

When Churchill lost office in the 1945 general election, the paper did not even deign to mention the fact, its only British news that week being the story of a telegram sent to Attlee from Cork, attacking Irish partition. In March 1946, when most American newspapers were busy debating Churchill's 'iron curtain' speech, the *Gaelic American* was happy to join in with his anti-Communism by attacking the State Department ('cluttered up with Fellow Travellers ever since the New Deal') for its hostility to Franco, but its only reference to Churchill himself that month was to report a Catholic priest denouncing New York's award of a gold medal to him, for Churchill was 'one of Ireland's greatest enemies'. Meanwhile it remained robustly opposed to all forms of post-war American aid to Britain, its account of the 1946 loan head-lined 'Credit Men Say England Welches on Debts'.[77]

Back in 1912, Churchill had argued in a speech in Belfast, when supporting Irish home rule, that 'the Irishmen overseas . . . are now the most serious obstacles to Anglo-American friendship'. Insofar as Churchill had himself come to embody that friendship, they were also the most serious obstacles to his international fame.[78] When he returned to power as Prime Minister in 1951, the only British news carried by the *Gaelic American* that week was headlined 'Compromise be damned, Welsh patriots say No to England's Empire' – and amazingly this story from the rather minority-fare *Welsh Republican* newspaper was deemed the main world news story. Its claim a week later, that Wales was 'clamoring for its full freedom', was strangely at odds with the fact that Welsh Nationalist candidates had come nowhere near to winning a single seat at the recent general election. An editorial dismissed Churchill as the organiser of Black and Tan terrorism in 1919–21, and a man now coming to Washington to demand a couple of billion dollars more of America's money. 'If Prime Minister Churchill is coming to America for more money, he should come with clean hands. Or better still, stay at home.' Similar sentiments were sometimes to be found in the letters columns of more mainstream papers, almost invariably in New York and Boston, and usually from correspondents with Irish names. In the week of Churchill's first visit as Prime Minister in 1952, the *Boston Globe* printed Martin Morgan's letter arguing that 'Winston ("There'll always be an England") Churchill has once again returned to do his bit toward increasing the already staggering American tax rate . . .' How far all this hatred had taken leave even of Irish realities was indicated in 1953, when de Valera for the first time met Churchill, at Downing Street – and found that they got on surprisingly well. The *Gaelic American* naturally failed even to report this news, preferring to print an editorial on the 150th anniversary of the hanging of Robert Emmet by the British.[79]

And so it went on. While other American newspapers celebrated Churchill's birthday in 1954 and his retirement in 1955, the *Irish World and American Industrial Liberator* (as the *Gaelic American* had now become) ignored both events, reporting instead criticisms by Irish Americans of the Unionist Government in Northern Ireland on the first occasion, and a cable from the Ancient Order of Hibernians urging Churchill to end Irish partition on the other. His later visits were completely ignored, but when a bill to make him an honorary US citizen seemed likely to pass, there was an indignant editorial headed 'Honorary Citizen for What?'

> Winston Churchill came to this country, not to help the United States but to take all he could get for his native England – our boys and our money – many of our boys lost their lives and are now buried in foreign lands, while others are maimed and in hospitals throughout our land.

Having got this off his chest, the editor returned to the more congenial task of celebrating an anniversary of what 'the Wexford men ... the heroes on the hill' had achieved during the rising of 1798. When Churchill lay dying, the paper ignored the fact, and when he died the only tribute printed was the double-edged one from Eamon de Valera. The editor was moved to add a week later an unforgiving editorial of his own on 'the Churchill enigma'. Over the past few weeks,

> the Churchill image was flashed before our eyes and dinned into our ears via Television and radio. He was hailed as THE MAN OF THE CENTURY by the commentators, with all his virtues extolled and his many failures glossed over. There was little or no comment made about the disaster he caused at the Dardanelles in World War I, nor the fact that World War II could have ended sooner than it did (and thousands of American and British lives saved) but for Churchill's determination to hold on to his almost limitless power ...

He was duly lambasted as a British imperialist, duper of America, fair-weather friend of Russia who reversed his course as soon as he could, and – despite his early support for Irish home rule – an apostle of 'Orange fanaticism'. Above all he was 'one of Ireland's bitterest adversaries', the author through the Black and Tans of 'the most tragic chapters of Irish history'. Irish Americans were certainly involved too in a number of the regular (but anonymous) death threats received and logged by the FBI each time Churchill visited the United States after 1941; one from Ohio in 1952 announced that 'that cynical old British beast has got to die ... the Irish patriots should have shot and killed him years ago'.[80]

There was, to say the least, an air of sheer desperation about all this, though the editor and his most partisan readers no doubt believed it all to be the absolute truth. That desperation no doubt derived, as the opening paragraph indicated, from awareness that very few Americans actually shared such views, and that they were to be found by then nowhere else in the media.

The Fulton project and the Washington statue were to be the main focuses of America's physical commemoration of Churchill over the rest of the 1960s, but neither had been brought to fruition before the events surrounding Churchill's death and funeral had shed a remarkable light into the depths of what Americans felt about their new fellow citizen. In the meantime, honours continued to flow in from voluntary groups: among many others, a Churchill Freedom Foundation was founded in Nebraska, the State of Kentucky commissioned him as a Kentucky colonel (which entitled him to a five-gallon barrel of bourbon each year), and the Congress of American Indians marked his supposed Iroquois blood by naming him 'Chief Leader of Men'.[81] From the day when his stroke was reported on 16 January 1965, through the lengthy final illness, death, funeral preparations and state funeral on the 30th, major American papers kept Churchill on the front page for a full fortnight; most published at least one special supplement when he died, and the more Anglophile then produced a second adulatory supplement about the funeral too.[82]

Churchill was thus by the time of his death 'that great American', as Lyndon Johnson was by 1965 calling him, and a useful superlative to apply to America's friends and supporters around the world. More broadly, Churchill had acquired in the United States the status of the greatest man of the century. *Time* magazine, which had already made him 'man of the year' for 1940 and 'man of the half-century' in 1950, brought out a funeral edition in which the cover bore simply his portrait and the legend 'Giant of the Century'. *National Geographic* sold five million copies of its own Churchill funeral edition, and broke new technological ground by giving away with it a record of excerpts from the funeral service, linked by a remarkably over-the-top tribute to Churchill by David Brinkley. Having unintentionally messed up American representation at Churchill's funeral, Johnson decided to name America's highest mountain after him as a sort of reparation. Unfortunately, the peak in question, a twenty-thousand-foot mountain in the Alaska range in the state of Alaska, was already named Mount McKinley after a former US President. The Alaska state legislature identified another and hitherto unnamed mountain in the Wrangell range, 'appropriate in grandeur' for the honouring of Churchill, but Johnson would not back off, since anything less than the highest peak would not now do. As a result Alaska gained a new 'Mount Churchill' and Mount McKinley itself had its twin summits renamed the 'Churchill Peaks'. Only the best would do. In 1968, when the Overseas Press Club of New York polled 3,500 international pressmen, Churchill was voted 'the one individual who has made the greatest mark for good upon our times'; Franklin Roosevelt came second, Truman tenth and Eisenhower twelfth, among this mainly American elite group. Three years later, after interviewing seventy current and former heads of state, a Gallup poll found that Abraham Lincoln could still beat Churchill for the title of 'most admired person in history', but that Churchill came second, ahead of Gandhi (which would no doubt have given Winston particular pleasure), Shakespeare and Socrates.[83]

8

'The Lynchpin of the English-Speaking Peoples': Churchill and Canada

WITHIN CHURCHILL'S BROAD APPEAL to the English-speaking peoples of the world after 1945, and the overall response that was both wide and deep, there is a good case for arguing that Canada occupied a position of special prominence. This was partly because Canada itself had a place of special affection in Churchill's heart, but also because regular visits, extensive personal friendships and years of practical co-operation after 1940 all helped to reinforce – and to make more lasting – the Churchill message to Canada, in a way that proved more problematic in the other British Dominions.

Canadians did not have many reasons to bear personal grudges against Churchill for his role in the Great War, as Australians and New Zealanders were said to have done over Gallipoli, and there were indeed prominent Canadians like the Conservative George Drew who could say proudly that they had first met Churchill while serving together on the western front in 1916. That he had even then made an impact on such men is evidenced by the depth of their recollections. Drew recalled in 1964, 'I well remember the costume that he wore' when he encountered Churchill at a cavalry officers' reception near Ploegsteert nearly half a century earlier: 'he had a trench coat with the fur outside, a French helmet about three sizes too small, and [a] shepherd's stock'. Churchill had in 1915 been much impressed by the Canadian officer universally known as 'Foghorn Macdonald', impressed by both his 'ornate profanity and deafening voice', and he had generally referred to the man at his later meetings with Drew. It was perhaps not entirely coincidental that this reminiscence was shared with Georges Vanier, then Canada's Governor-General, himself a veteran of the same trench war, and another great Churchill admirer.[1] For Drew's successor as Conservative leader, the Canadian Prime Minister John Diefenbaker, actually meeting Churchill had come much later, but he was proud to have seen him in action as early as 1916, in the British House of Commons, standing there in a soldier's uniform attacking the Asquith Government's mismanagement of the war from the soldier's viewpoint – and (though Churchill himself certainly could not have known it for another quarter-century) making himself a lifelong hero to a young Canadian in the public gallery.

There were however Second World War events, notably the Dieppe raid and the heavy casualties arising from mismanagement of the Normandy campaign of 1944, which could well have been a problem for Churchill's reputation in Canada.[2] That they were not is indicated clearly enough by the fact that the Royal Canadian Legion of veterans took an active part in memorialising Churchill after 1965, responding positively to the Churchill image much as did those veterans of the earlier war, Drew and Vanier. The breadth of Churchill's admiring contacts in Canada by the 1960s is shown by the fact that Canada's official party in London for the Churchill funeral in January 1965 numbered eleven, surely the largest from any overseas country at an event for which tickets were exceedingly hard to come by. Canada's official party included the Prime Minister and leader of the Opposition and their wives, two other Ministers, the Speakers of both the Canadian House and the Senate, the cabinet Secretary, the Vice Chief of the Defence Staff, and the president of the Royal Canadian Legion. In addition to these official mourners, there were eleven more Canadians seated in St Paul's Cathedral for the service, as personal guests of the Churchill family, including Drew and Joseph Smallwood, the premier of Newfoundland.[3] While some European countries like Sweden were allowed to send only one mourner – and even France sent only three – Canada had managed to be represented by twenty-two, so hugely overshadowing both in quality and in quantity the team from the United States, and adding to President Johnson's domestic difficulties.[4]

Churchill's personal connection with Canada had begun long before he met Canadians at 'Plugstreet' in 1915–16, indeed even before his own parliamentary career began with entry into the House of Commons in 1901. When he visited North America in the aftermath of his escape from Boer captivity, Canada was an important part of the lecture tour from which he hoped to raise enough money to launch himself into politics. Though he did not actually make the money he expected, largely because his North American agent ('a vulgar Yankee impresario') had the better of the terms of the contract, actual audiences were large and sometimes noisy. When speaking in the United States, he met heckling from pro-Boers and, what was worse, patronising remarks about his presence from anti-colonials. But, as he later wrote in *My Early Life*, 'all this quiet tolerance changed when we crossed the Canadian border. Here again were present the enthusiastic throngs to which I had accustomed myself at home.' The takings at the door for Churchill's lecture in Toronto were about £450, a very large sum for the time (Churchill's entire profit from eight weeks of lecturing was £1,600); he himself reported to his mother that he had had 'magnificent audiences in Montreal, Ottawa & Toronto and had a great success with them'. He spent Christmas 1900 in Government House, Ottawa, and then went on into the west, hearing the news of Queen Victoria's death in January 1901 in Winnipeg, and thereby witnessing that 'great and solemn event' in a place 'far away among the snows – fourteen hundred miles from any British town of importance'. (He meant Toronto.) He was enraptured both by the spread of civilisation represented in the speed with which cities like Winnipeg had arisen from nothing and by the obvious economic potential for the future, writing to his mother on 22 January:

> Fancy, my dear Mama, twenty years ago, there were only a few mud huts and tents, and last night, a magnificent audience of men in evening dress and ladies half out of it, filled a fine opera house and we took $1,150 at the door. At the back of the town there is a huge wheat field, nine hundred and eighty miles long and two hundred and thirty miles broad. One day, this will feed the whole of the British Isles. I called them 'Great Britain's bread spot' at which they purred. They are furiously British and a visit to them is most exhilarating!

So encouraged was Churchill by what he had seen in Canada that he made a bet with an American for a hundred pounds, against the proposition that at least a quarter of Canada, Australia or India would have seceded from the British Crown within ten years.[5] Churchill clearly loved this first encounter with Canada, but by this stage Canada had also achieved what was surely another Churchill first, when the Government of Prince Edward Island (even further from 'any British town of importance') had named a rural post office 'Churchill', in honour of his escape from the Boers. When a settlement gathered around the post office, it was duly also called Churchill, though the fact that the town placed its church on a hill may have helped to keep the name alive in the succeeding years of Churchill's relative obscurity.[6] Canada's remotest and smallest Atlantic province thus inaugurated the first of many Churchill namings in the Dominion, and when Churchill himself died, the citizens of Churchill, PEI, were duly reported to be marking the event with a special degree of solemnity.[7]

From 1900, Churchill was a frequent visitor to Canada, most notably on the lengthy coast-to-coast tour that he made in 1929. Winston's regular letters home to Clementine enthused about Canada as a 'vast lush country', and he noted on 15 August (by which stage he had reached only Ottawa on his journey westwards) that 'the immense size and progress of this country impresses itself upon one more every day . . . The sentimental feeling towards England is wonderful. The United States are stretching their tentacles out in all directions, but the Canadian National Spirit and personality is becoming so powerful and self-contained that I do not think we need fear the future.'[8] During the trip, Churchill was royally entertained by Prime Ministers, Governors and the Governor-General, as well as by the Canadian Pacific Railway, which provided a palatial railroad car,[9] facilitated his stay in some of the best hotels in the world, and even loaned him a stenographer to help on his current writing projects. He met lots of prominent Canadians and some not so prominent: a British ex-sergeant, for example, who had encountered him last at the Battle of Omdurman in 1898 and who now presented him with a box of cigars, which rather suggests that Churchill's personal tastes were also fairly well known, in this case in Ottawa. He spoke in most of the Canadian cities, including places in the west that he had not reached before, and saw all the major sights – among them Niagara Falls, bears, Lake Louise and Banff National Park in the Rockies, and 'the beautiful and luxuriant Pacific Coast'. He reported on 27 August from Banff that 'I have been wonderfully received in Canada. Never in my whole life have I been welcomed with so much genuine interest &

admiration as throughout this vast country. All parties and classes have mingled in the welcome . . . I am profoundly touched.' Finally, he experienced Victoria on Vancouver Island, where he addressed 'an enormous luncheon, 700 or 800 men, the cream of Victoria', and thoroughly enjoyed himself in 'the most English of all Canadian towns'.[10] Though he spent only a month in Canada, and then almost twice as long in the United States, it was clearly the revelation of Canada's size, variety, warmth and loyalty to the Englishness that Churchill so prized when he found it among colonials that stuck in his mind. At that point, out of office and out of sympathy with his party, and with his career at a low ebb, he even contemplated selling up in England and emigrating to the Empire; it was to Canada that he proposed to go.[11] He wrote to Clementine Churchill from Banff, on 27 August 1929,

> I am greatly attracted to this country. Immense developments are going forward. There are fortunes to be made in many directions. The tide is flowing strongly. I have made up my mind that if N[eville] Ch[amberlain] is made leader of the C[onservative] P[arty] or anyone else of that kind, I clear out of politics & see if I cannot make you & the kittens a little more comfortable before I die. Only one goal still attracts me [the premiership], & if that were barred I sh[oul]d quit the dreary fields for pastures new. As Daniel Peggoty says, 'There's mighty lands beyond the seas'.[12]

It is perhaps significant that by 1946, with the wartime experience of working with the mighty forces of the USA behind him, and now far more popular there than in his earlier life, Churchill was rather declaring that the only place with an unbounded future, the only place in which a young man would wish to be born, was the United States. In 1921, the competition for dominance within the English-speaking world was already in his mind, if couched in terms of friendly rivalry. Addressing the theme of 'the great dominions', he told the Empire Parliamentary Association that 'if we try to stand by ourselves, we could never meet our great sister nation, who speaks our language, who are our kith and kin, across the Atlantic, on those terms of perfect equality'. No wonder that Mackenzie King always suspected Churchill of wanting to remove some of Canada's independence through a scheme of Imperial Federation, a united states of the British Empire which would have greater bargaining power in Washington. By the 1920s, though, Churchill was seen by Canadians in London as one of the British politicians especially sympathetic to their country and in tune with their aspirations, hence his invitation to address, in 1929 and again in 1939, annual dinners of the Canadian Club in London, high-profile occasions at the Savoy Hotel. On each occasion he argued the special place of Canada as 'the centre of the English-speaking world', linking Britain and the United States. He had also acquired by then a fortuitous personal link with Canada, for his country house, Chartwell, was just outside the Kentish village of Westerham, the birthplace of General James Wolfe, whose victory and death in battle in 1759 had secured Canada for Britain. In 1927, Churchill was speaking, also at the Savoy, to the Wolfe Society bicentenary dinner, and though he was usually careful to link the memory of Wolfe with the French general Montcalm, the loser in 1759, and so make an appropriate bow in the direction of French-speaking Canada too, his hearers cannot have had much doubt where his sympathies actually lay.[13]

Later visits only reinforced that affection, though on these occasions he got no further than the most populous areas of the Canadian east (and, in the earlier 1941 visit, to Placentia Bay off Newfoundland, which was not even in Canada, since Newfoundland was not yet part of the federation). Three times in wartime he visited Canada, by now as Britain's heroic leader in the fight against Hitler and with his voice and personality universally known from the BBC radio rebroadcasts of his speeches to North America in 1940–1. Arriving in Ottawa in December 1941, hot from the triumph in Washington that followed Pearl Harbor and America's entry into the war, he managed to top even his own speech to the US Congress with a similar address to the two Houses of the Canadian Parliament, a speech also broadcast live throughout Canada and then immediately published by Ottawa. Most of that speech was a sober account of the progress of the war, not pleasant hearing for those worried about the fate of Canadian soldiers in Hong Kong and Singapore, but it was enlivened by the 'some chicken, some neck' joke about French defeatism in 1940. If this was a pointed appeal to French Canadians, the question 'What kind of a people do they think we are?' delighted especially the Anglo-Canadians who had no doubt that *they* were still part of one British people. He was also careful to identify Canada's special role in what would now inevitably be a mainly

Anglo-American war effort, speaking of Canada as 'the lynchpin' of the alliance, a magnet that would draw both Britain and the United States to itself in military co-operation and so bind the triangle of North Atlantic maritime democracies closer together. This was a neat concept in itself, and a phrase that stuck in the mind, being much quoted in after-dinner speeches in Canada in the years after the war.[14]

The 1941 visit was brief, and limited to Ottawa's federal parliamentarians, though the response of citizens in the Canadian capital to their brief sightings of Churchill suggests a considerable degree of public warmth too.[15] On two later wartime visits, associated with the Quebec conferences of 1943 and 1944, proceedings were more relaxed. Churchill offered to drive through the streets of Montreal, Quebec and Toronto with Prime Minister Mackenzie King, 'as I have done in London', he visited Niagara Falls for the third time (where he told a foolishly enquiring journalist that the Falls looked to him much as they had in 1929 – 'the main principle remains the same'), and he was seen by large crowds on all these occasions, as well as meeting more Canadians in politics and the upper reaches of society.[16] His secretary John Martin noted of a train journey from Halifax to Quebec in 1943, 'crowds gather wherever we stop, and wave and cheer the PM and return his V sign'.[17] On the 1944 trip, another secretary recorded of Churchill's arrival in Halifax, 'Great cheers and cameras clicking. We boarded a ... train. PM stood on the observation platform and joined the crowd in singing "God Save the King" and "Oh Canada". As so often on such occasions, he was deeply moved.' Seven days later, when Churchill left Quebec, a quite different crowd gathered around his train and sang 'Auld Lang Syne'. When with Mackenzie King, Churchill 'kept explaining what a great joy it was to them [the Churchill family] to see Canada'.[18] That popular enthusiasm at stations and in the streets on all these wartime occasions was clear evidence of the esteem in which Churchill was held, so much so that Mackenzie King took care to accompany the Churchill motorcade and share in the plaudits. When a loyal Liberal MP expressed his pleasure that King and Churchill were now so much at one that they were simultaneously using Churchill's famous V-sign to the crowds, the Tory John Diefenbaker responded that they might both use the sign but their 'Vs' stood for different things. With Churchill 'V' meant victory, for King it meant votes.[19]

Churchill's loss of office in the 1945 general election seemed from the viewpoint of Canada quite inexplicable. The *Toronto Globe* recognised tough-mindedly that the results were partly a repudiation of Churchill as well as of his party, and did not expect him to be back:

> The mandate was all too clear. He who had proved one of the greatest wartime leaders this fighting country has had in its long history wasn't wanted for peace. A few hundred people who had been waiting with idle curiosity outside 10 Downing Street saw the familiar burly figure with the inevitable cigar, stump out of the gates and into his automobile at 7 o'clock this evening. The car drove him to Buckingham Palace. There even fewer people waited. They saw Winston Churchill for the last time as Prime Minister.

Even this paper editorialised, however, that Churchill's defeat was 'a world loss', for 'Prime Minister Churchill was not the sole possession of the United Kingdom in these critical days', and it published a 'dropping the pilot' cartoon in which an elector is making Churchill walk the plank to oblivion and saying, 'Thanks a lot, Winnie. Hope you don't mind popping off ... You remind me too much of war!' The paper went on also to report the gist of London newspapers' analysis of the election, that it did not involve any lack of gratitude to Churchill for his service in the war.[20] The *Vancouver Sun* too was uncompromising in reporting Churchill's defeat as a personal one (noting the large vote against him at Woodford), emphasising the simultaneous political fall of his relations and of cronies like Bracken (blaming the defeat indeed largely on bad advice from Bracken and Beaverbrook). It also published an editorial ('End of the Churchill Era') and what amounted to Churchill's political obituary, concluding that although he had 'undoubtedly ... saved the Empire' in 1940, he could now have unlimited time to spend on his memoirs.[21] More pro-Conservative papers were more partisan in their reading of the results, seeing Churchill's defeat as mainly the rejection of his party rather than of himself, while the *Calgary Herald* (noting that 'His work is done. He has been told to go') reported a groundswell of opinion building up in Canada for the unemployed Churchill now to be made Governor-General.[22]

Whenever Churchill visited the United States after the war, the news prompted suggestions that he should also take in Canada as part of the trip, in 1946 and again in 1949, but on neither occasion was he able and

For Victory in Peace
Toronto Globe & Mail, 7 March 1946

willing to do so.[23] The 'iron curtain' speech that he made at Fulton, calling for resolute action to resist Soviet expansion, was (as shown in Chapter Four) made with considerable Canadian Government connivance behind the scenes, and was more immediately welcomed in Canada than in some parts of the United States, possibly because it coincided with the trial of a Soviet spy ring that had penetrated to the heart of the Canadian Government, hence indicating to Canadians that the threat was not just in Eastern Europe. 'It takes Churchill to tell them, said a Calgary policeman today, and this was fairly typical of Calgary comment.'[24] His subsequent great foreign policy speeches of the late 1940s, at Zurich and Strasbourg for example, were less noticed by the Canadian papers, partly no doubt because they were more directed towards Europe than to the Atlantic alliance and global affairs. But there is not much doubt that readers of the Canadian press would have had Churchill's name fairly continuously in their minds while he was in opposition, for example through the reviews of the earlier volumes of his war memoirs in 1948–9, fixing for readers of both the books themselves and of their reviews the idea of Churchill as the ignored prophet of the 1930s and the inspiration of 1940. The *Toronto Globe*, noting that in *The Gathering Storm* Churchill had pulled no punches, heaping 'sweeping blame [for the war's outbreak] on everyone else, except Anthony Eden', went on to conclude that his argument against the appeasers 'seems generally sound'.[25]

Canadians were therefore mentally prepared to welcome Churchill's return to office in 1951, and they certainly seem to have done so. Louis St Laurent, as Prime Minister, wrote to congratulate Churchill and to offer all possible co-operation, though he was careful to commiserate with equal warmth with Attlee on his defeat.[26] Canada's Conservatives had no such inhibitions. George Drew had cabled Churchill on 19 October, a week before polling day in Britain, 'our thoughts and prayers are with you in this last week of campaign, which means almost as much to Canada as to you. Confidently hope that a week from today you will again be Prime Minister of Great Britain. We can then rejoice for what it means to Britain and also to us in our restored faith in future of British partnership.' A week later, with a Tory win now in the bag, he cabled more succinctly: 'This is the finest hour for many a long year.'[27] Conservative newspapers were equally fulsome, the *Toronto Telegram* for example heading its story 'Winnie Wins Last Prize. Given Working Majority. Socialist Regime Ended'. The editorial now interpreted the Conservative Party victory as a highly personal one for Churchill, for 'to his own efforts and popularity much of its success may be attributed'. In place of 'dropping the pilot,' the naval theme was continued with a cartoon showing Churchill taking the helm from Attlee, with the words, 'Well, Clem, the owners want me to take over.' The naval involvement of Churchill with Canada went back to 1911–14, and in the maritime provinces in particular it was always harped on: in 1951, the message in Halifax was simply 'Winnie is Back', an affectionate parody of the Admiralty's 'Winston is back' telegram to the Fleet of 1939, when he was reappointed First Lord. The *Toronto Globe*, which had reported in 1950 that opinion in Ottawa (if mainly among Conservatives) had been disappointed by Churchill's failure to regain office at

An historic signal goes through the Fleet
Halifax Chronicle-Herald (Canada), 27 October 1951

that year's election, now thought that 'most Canadians will be pleased
and reassured by the British election results . . . They will be reassured
because their future, like that of every free nation, depends upon
Britain's economic health, her military strength and her political wisdom. With Mr Churchill again Prime Minister, there is real hope that
Britain will regain her ancient place among the nations.' Here a cartoon
portrayed Churchill as 'The Old Master', rolling up his sleeves and

getting out his paintbrushes to touch up 'Britain's sombre picture'. This was a straightforward parody of David Low's famous wartime cartoon, except that the original showed Churchill accompanied by ministers and ordinary people – whereas now he was alone in the position of mastership.[28]

Churchill's return to the British premiership in 1951 was also the prelude to an almost immediate official visit to North America, mainly so that he could explore his ideas on winding down the Cold War with the Americans. In the Canadian Parliament, the news provoked an immediate demand that Churchill be persuaded to come to Canada too, and address Parliament as in 1941, but the Conservatives also demanded that Parliament stay in session rather than adjourning as planned in early 1952, so that 'the greatest living statesman . . . the greatest parliamentarian under our parliamentary system' could speak to Canadians from a background so like his own Westminster. Prime Minister St Laurent confirmed that he had already sent an invitation, but eventually announced that Churchill would make only one speech in Ottawa, at a parliamentarians' dinner rather than actually in Parliament. But normal conventions would be suspended for such a special occasion at least to the extent that the dinner would include 'the lady Members, although the dinner would otherwise be a dinner for men only'.[29]

Churchill duly came to Ottawa in January 1952, met the Canadian cabinet in private session, responded to a generous introduction from St Laurent, and made another warm appeal to the Canadian people in his own broadcast speech. It was noted in the press that the dinner was 'as rigidly exclusive a gathering as the capital, noted for its respect for protocol, has seen for a long time', but 'the exclusiveness of the dinner . . . took nothing away from its enthusiasm. The 300-odd guests . . . applauded and cheered the British statesman time and again throughout his half-hour broadcast speech. At its conclusion, led by the Governor-General Lord Alexander, and Prime Minister St Laurent, the gathering stood up and cheered.' Perhaps the enthusiasm of those present owed something to the fact that Churchill had told both the cabinet and a later press conference that Britain was going to ask for no further economic aid from Canada – though one correspondent was so moved by the speech that he urged St Laurent to give Britain half of Canada's annual surplus anyway. More likely it was Churchill's 'references to the Commonwealth tie and the rise of the "Atlantic community" [which] stirred the hearts and minds of his audience', a response replicated editorially throughout the Canadian press. And, once again, glimpses of Churchill in the streets of Ottawa prompted cheering crowds and singing: 'on the street he was engulfed by a crowd which, like the one inside the station, seemed to want nothing more than to show him they thought him a swell guy.[30] The varied and sometimes extraordinarily visceral responses that a Churchill speech could produce were vividly revealed in St Laurent's subsequent postbag. J. B. Eaton wrote from Chicago to urge, 'Please help 150,000,000 American people to get relief from the British – ship the British Stalin from your country to London. We mean the windbag Churchill.' Rather more typical was T. J. Alexander, writing from Toronto to complain that when 'our beloved Winnie' was in Ottawa, 'Oh Canada' was played instead of 'God Save the King', which real patriots thought needlessly insulting to the distinguished visitor. A somewhat muddled correspondent from Kent wrote that 'we love you Canadian people all, and conveying this message from England: God Save the King, and God Bless us All, and Canada "the Maypole Leaf" [sic] for ever'. The mental image of scarlet-coated Mounties dancing round maypoles while singing 'God Save the King' is in itself quite irresistible as sheer ignorant enthusiasm for Empire.[31]

There may have been rather more to the symbolism of ceremonial music than appeared at first sight, for Lester Pearson recalled an earlier meeting at which Churchill had complained to him (as Canada's External Affairs Minister) that the Royal Canadian Navy had abandoned the regular playing of 'Rule Britannia' on shipboard. Once back in Ottawa, Pearson forgot that he had promised to look into this and see if he could get the decision reversed, but realised with horror when Churchill's 1952 visit was planned that he was all too likely to be asked what had been done. Astutely, he ensured that when Churchill stepped from his car to be greeted by the Canadian cabinet, a band immediately struck up 'Rule Britannia'. Churchill beamed appreciatively, and (Pearson thought) assumed that he had got his way. If he did indeed think that at the time, then he was in for a shock, for press reports said that Churchill had in 1952 given the Canadian cabinet a hard time over the same question ('Winnie gives 'em Heck' was one headline) and secured a promise that the Canadian sailors would play 'Rule Britannia' at least when British naval officers came on board.[32] Whether there was any such dispute or not, when Parliament itself reassembled after the

Queen's Speech in February 1952, there were still warm feelings about Churchill's recent visit. Edmund George, proposing the loyal address and reviewing the past year in Canadian politics as was conventional on these occasions, cited Churchill's visit as the highlight of the year, but revisited too the reason for his fame among Canadians: 'Mr Churchill is no stranger to Canada and it was a pleasure to welcome him back. In those dark days during the Second World War he became far more than Prime Minister of Great Britain. For all of us his voice was the symbol of human freedom. He had become the symbol of the unconquerable spirit of free men and women faced with terrible danger.'[33]

The overall Canadian view of Churchill as a world statesman in this period is also given weight in the *Official Record* of ordinary debates in the House of Commons. No session between 1945 and 1955 went by without Churchill being quoted as a fount of wisdom by more than one Canadian MP, in debates on the Gold Standard, on the decision to found the United Nations Organisation, on atomic deterrence, on NATO, on the Korean War, and on defence expenditure – among many topics.[34] He was much cited as an autodidact by supporters of a proposal for a Canadian National Library in 1952 (which shows among other things a fairly close acquaintanceship with *My Early Life*). Drew rhapsodised over Churchill's reading in India in the 1890s which had made him 'perhaps the greatest writer of this day in the English tongue, perhaps the greatest writer of English apart from Shakespeare' (and this was well *before* Churchill won the Nobel Prize for Literature). He went on to argue that Churchill was seen,

> not only as the greatest historian of our day, but as a man whose every act has been inspired by the confidence that has come from the record of history throughout the years. I like to think that at the time when all the arithmetic of war made it clear that there was no reason for Britain to survive in the Spring of 1940, it was knowledge gained from the pages of history, which was in Churchill's mind, that right has given might in the years that have passed, that gave him courage and spirit to give leadership to the whole free world in those dangerous days.[35]

That Drew was far from alone among Canadians in seeing the improving moral to be drawn from Churchill's career as inseparable from his writings is confirmed by the activities of many Canadian memorialists of Churchill to create, endow and extend a series of Churchill collections in university libraries (for example in Toronto and in Calgary), centres for the study of his life based around his own books.

Those books were already surprisingly well known (not least by Drew himself, who was able to point out in 1952 that such phrases as 'blood, sweat and tears' (sic) were not originals by Churchill, but quotations that demonstrated his knowledge of the literature of the past – in this case John Donne and Lord Byron, though very few British people would have known it). Churchill himself was quoted in the Canadian Commons from his wartime and post-war speeches, from the war memoirs as they began to appear from 1948, from *My Early Life*, from *Great Contemporaries* (notably for that book's violent attack on Communism as a creed), and even from the relatively obscure *The Aftermath*, all of which suggests considerable breadth of collective knowledge of Churchill the writer as well as a desire simply to use his name for effect. He was cited by the Opposition Conservatives as a believer in the need for close parliamentary scrutiny of government (suggesting that he had both 'parliamentary experience' and 'information in regard to defence' which was 'superior to Canadian ministers'), and by Liberal Ministers as a supporter of détente in foreign policy. Lester Pearson indeed made a point of citing Churchill whenever he was winding up a debate on external affairs, defending his own support for détente with such remarks as 'it will not, I think, be argued in this House that Mr Churchill is a man likely to truckle to or appease aggressors'. Pearson was happy to cite Churchill as 'a much greater authority on foreign affairs than I, than any of us possibly', but only of course when Churchill's views could be quoted in defence of Canadian foreign policy, as they often could be. It was undeniably effective to quote such words and then add, 'those words, Mr Speaker, were written by one who has never been considered naïve, soft or indeed especially meek'. Canadian antiseparatists could also quote appositely his offer of Anglo-French Union in 1940 and his war memoirs' conclusion that it would be vital in future 'to weave Gaul and Teuton so closely together' that disputes would become unthinkable, a message that might apply to Canada even more than to Europe.[36]

There were indeed Canadian politicians who seem to have kept useful little files of Churchill extracts just in case they needed them on some future occasion, so valuable was his name as a talisman.[37] So often was Churchill quoted that quoting him became in itself something of cliché that was remarked upon: James Macdonnell introduced one such quotation in 1953 with the words, 'as on so many occasions, Churchill has something to say' (in this case on the fact that you could come back from an election defeat). Quoting Churchill could even provoke irritation: Ernest Hansell was moved to point out in 1953 that 'the Hon. Member for Kootenay brings in the name of Churchill as if everybody is going to step up and say "Hurrah, hurrah!" Mr Churchill can be wrong.' Likewise, the maverick Quebec MP Jean-François Pouliot seemed thoroughly to enjoy quoting Churchill in every inappropriate context, for example bringing up his 'iron curtain' speech when in 1953 his admirers were citing his support for détente, though here the main object seems to have been to wind up and generally antagonise Churchill's more pompous admirers, for Pouliot himself was a Conservative who also admired Churchill and quoted him approvingly when it suited him.[38]

When, following his 1953 stroke, Churchill suddenly announced in 1954 another diplomatic visit to Washington, Canadians again expected to be included, though the omens were by then not good. Canada's High Commissioner in London, passing on to his Government the apologies of the Commonwealth Relations Office for the sudden announcement of the Churchill trip (the CRO had not informed Ottawa mainly because the PM had not informed the CRO), reminded St Laurent that Churchill would be unlikely to extend what was already going to be a long trip for an octogenarian: 'he is very old and pretty frail, and the journey to Washington on which he has set his heart will tax him pretty severely'. Canada was advised to make do with Anthony Eden instead.[39] Nevertheless, St Laurent did press on with his invitation, and Churchill did come to Ottawa, though he declined to make a public speech or to appear at anything other than private meetings. He attended an official lunch hosted by the British High Commissioner in Ottawa and a dinner party hosted by St Laurent himself, as well as private meetings with the Prime Minister and his cabinet, and with larger groups of MPs. In the end, Churchill did make a very short radio broadcast and Eden made one for CBC television, but the final dinner had to be cut short so that the British party could fly back to New York in order to sail at midnight on the *Queen Elizabeth*.

This time, much of the comment on Churchill was valedictory and autumnal, it being recognised that he was unlikely to visit Canada again (at least not as an active political leader), and there was much defiant comment on how well he appeared to have recovered his health. Crowds were again large and enthusiastic. Just how high a standard was expected by Canadians came out when there was subsequent, hostile press comment on the informality of the arrangements – actually in accordance with Churchill's own wishes. St Laurent had to defend himself from charges that he had insultingly dined Churchill in a hotel rather than in his official residence, pointing out that it had never been intended for large gatherings, while the Governor-General had to remind critics that his own residence was undergoing such extensive reconstruction at the time of Churchill's unforeseen visit that he himself was sleeping when in Ottawa in a railway car. The criticisms indicated how strongly many Canadians felt that only the best would do for 'the greatest living Englishman'.[40]

Unsurprisingly, Churchill's eightieth birthday only a few months later was much noticed in Canada. On 29 November, the *Edmonton Journal*, for example, told its readers, 'Entire United Kingdom Ready to Mark Churchill's Birthday'; his health would be drunk in pubs and bars all across the land, parliamentarians would gather to present a memorial from both Houses, and a cheque for a million pounds from the birthday appeal (to which many Canadians had contributed) would be handed over. Emotionally, it was noted that Churchill's day would begin with a cup of tea made from 'two spoonfuls in an envelope with a little sugar', sent to him by a pensioner as 'the only present I can afford', a gift said to have moved him greatly. By the following day, the story was not of the UK, but 'Whole World Pays Churchill Homage as "Old Warrior" Marks 80th Birthday', with a large front-page photograph of the man himself, 'already a history-book figure'. This homage, even from his bitterest political enemies, was proof of the 'largely spontaneous' outburst of affection, evidence (as an editorial put it) of 'the unique place which Churchill occupies in the hearts of the British nation, and indeed of the English-speaking peoples everywhere'. That final dual-formulation would not include French Canadians, but would incorporate both British-stock Canadians in Manitoba who thought themselves part of the 'British nation' anyway and first-nation Canadians who also spoke English.[41]

Churchill did not manage to visit Canada again after 1954, though he accepted the freedom of Toronto in 1958 (Mayor Nathan Phillips having obligingly created the honour specially for Churchill – it had not existed before in the city).[42] Churchill hoped to come to Toronto to receive the honour personally, but his health did not permit, though there were brief hopes that he might again add on a short visit to his Washington–New York trip of 1959. By this stage, the High Commissioner's 1954 advice was more nearly correct and there was no real chance that Churchill would by then extend a punishing schedule. When he retired from the premiership in 1955, though, the Canadian House of Commons passed a fulsome motion of tribute and greetings to Churchill, with the support of all the parties. St Laurent spoke of '80 years of restless activity' and remarked that 'few figures in history have compressed so many careers in a single life span'. He went on to quote Churchill's statement that he had only 'given the roar' of the 'nation and race dwelling all round the globe' in 1940, but rejected it too: Churchill had done far more than that and anyway 'we all agree that his "roar" was one of the greatest and most memorable sounds ever to come from a human throat'.

Drew for the Conservatives was if anything even more positive about Churchill, but also more melancholy: 'I think that most of us here today have an uneasy feeling that the end of a great period of parliamentary history has now appeared before our eyes.' Churchill had for fifteen years been 'the authentic leader of the free world', and for Drew a key factor (illustrated by his 'some chicken, some neck' joke in Ottawa in 1941) had been his ability 'to convey his meaning in simple colloquial terms of the people . . . terms which appealed to people everywhere, because the words he used were understood in every language whatever it might be'. Nevertheless, Drew recognised, in appreciative references to Churchill's reputation in the USA and in the Commonwealth, that it was the English-speaking peoples to whom Churchill had appealed in their own language that were the heart of Churchill's worldwide constituency. He was 'the greatest statesman of all time, and I am confident that history will declare that fact', but Drew was also keen to place his war leadership in 1940–5 merely on a par with his 'contribution to the unity of the western world' from 1946 onwards. 'I think it will be found that his immense prestige brought together nations which seemed then to be drawing apart,' which made him now 'the elder statesman not only of Britain but of all the free nations'.[43]

This was fulsome stuff, but by no means the end of the story, for on subsequent Churchill birthdays equally complimentary things were said in the Canadian Commons, and whenever Churchill's health was reported to be at risk messages of condolence were dispatched, on all these occasions Churchill's replies being carefully read into the record by the Speaker. In 1960 for example, for Churchill's eighty-sixth birthday, Prime Minister Diefenbaker referred glowingly to 'the world's most revered statesman and the most distinguished member of Canada's Privy Council', a man 'already immortal in his own lifetime'. On such occasions, the party leaders seemed to falling over themselves to claim closeness with Churchill, as if some of his greatness might therefore rub off on them; in 1962, Diefenbaker referred to the time when he had last met Churchill, and Pearson responded that he too had had a long association with Churchill, 'like the Prime Minister'.[44]

When in due course Churchill retired from the Commons in 1964, there were again extravagant tributes to 'a many sided genius, the Renaissance man 400 years after the Renaissance' (Pearson), while Diefenbaker remarked that 'one often hears it said that it must have been wonderful to live in some other age, in the golden age of the past. We who have lived in the lifetime of Sir Winston Churchill could not ask for more.' By now, then, merely to have been alive in the twentieth century was to share in Churchill's glory, though party politics were still just beneath the surface. Having heard the leader of the Ralliement Créditiste argue that Churchill devoted all his life to two great principles, the British Empire and democracy, and had only one shortcoming, 'that he was a Conservative all his life', the historian Pearson immediately intervened ('in the interests of historical accuracy') to remind the House that 'Sir Winston Churchill, like the present Leader of the Opposition [Harold Wilson], was at one time a Liberal'. Diefenbaker immediately responded by reminding 'the right hon. Prime Minister that he was at one time a Conservative'. When the leader of the Créditistes asked 'whether Sir Winston Churchill was at one time a member of the Social Credit party', Pearson responded loftily that even Churchill's 'ambition did not reach those heights'. For all the obvious lightheartedness of the exchange, it is clear that everyone present wanted a piece of Churchill to call their own.[45]

Such sentiments might well have taken something of a knock, in Canada as elsewhere in the Commonwealth, from Churchill's own

History of the English-Speaking Peoples, when its four volumes were published between 1956 and 1958. The first two volumes caused no particular difficulty, since they covered the medieval and early modern periods, though even then it was noted that Churchill had little to say about the early British discovery voyages across the Atlantic. With volume three on the eighteenth century, it became clear to reviewers that Churchill was really writing about 'the contribution of the English nation to the spawning of the English-Speaking nations' in a series of books that were 'a eulogistic account of the part which England and not the English people, or peoples, has played in world history'. With volume four on the nineteenth century, the issue became very plain, for Canada received only six pages (much the same as the seven for Australia) which were unceremoniously yoked to five on South Africa under the title 'The migration of the peoples'; there were 170 pages on Britain and over a hundred on the United States. Faced with this devastating neglect of their own country in a book which might well have accorded it some prominence, given its title, Canadian reviewers offered the book as a whole a guarded welcome and then ignored altogether what Churchill had said (or not said) about Canada. *Canadian Forum* thought it Churchill's 'least memorable work' and predicted that it would be quickly forgotten once 'the book merchants have stopped peddling it around the countryside'. Churchill's publisher in Canada wrote to him to say that though 'some Canadian critics have deplored the fact that you did not devote more space to Canada', it had in general been 'extremely well received'. It had indeed prompted the Mayor of Toronto to renew requests through the publisher for Churchill to visit once more. 'I think you might like to know that the Mayor literally plans to turn Toronto upside down should you ever make the trip. He states that he would make it the most memorable day in the history of Toronto.' By 1958, though, Churchill was planning no more such trips.[46]

Canadians in the provinces of Ontario and Quebec could, however, take advantage of Churchill's travelling art exhibition, which appeared in galleries in Toronto and Montreal in 1958 as part of the North American tour that began in Kansas City. In keeping with the gravity of the occasion, Prime Minister Diefenbaker contributed a foreword to the exhibition catalogue for Toronto (though he seems to have had to be reminded by his secretary actually to go and see the paintings himself, if indeed he ever did). St Laurent in 1955, and in due course Diefenbaker and Pearson too, were all lined up well ahead of the time to provide the BBC and CBC with an obituary statement on Churchill for whenever his death should occur.

Diefenbaker was also co-operating personally to fulfil requests for the provision of suitable Canadian ingredients (such as maple syrup) for Churchill's eighty-fourth birthday cake, and sending Canada's heartiest good wishes to the Churchills on their Golden Wedding in the same year. And general expectations remained high too: one correspondent in 1959 urged Diefenbaker to make sure that the eighty-four-year-old Churchill headed the West's delegation to the coming summit conference, while another had suggested in 1958 that the Canadian Government propose that Churchill be a made a freeman of the entire Commonwealth.[47] It was then suggested that Churchill be made an honorary citizen of Canada, mirroring the decision taken by the USA in 1963, though since he was already a member of the Canadian Privy Council such a step proved to be unnecessary – he already possessed more Canadian rights than most Canadians enjoyed themselves. That Churchill himself saw this as a signal honour to him personally was demonstrated in constant references to it in his Canadian speeches and his correspondence with Canadians: when St Laurent congratulated him on his return to office in 1951, his reply began, 'As you know I have the honour to be a Canadian Privy Councillor . . .' And it was probably the fact that he was also clerk to the Privy Council that enabled Canada's cabinet secretary to go Churchill's funeral in 1965.[48]

Churchill's final illness, death and funeral were widely reported in the Canadian press. The story remained on the front pages of the major papers from the news of his illness on 16 January 1965 until his funeral had been fully reported on 2 February. Initially these accounts were of his long struggle for life, with medical bulletins printed alongside photographs of family members and of the respectful crowds gathered in Hyde Park Gate. Then when he died the papers printed lengthy, eulogistic obituaries, generally spread over several pages and accompanied by at least a page of Churchill photographs. For a further week there was news of the lying-in-state, of arrangements for Canadians to sign books of condolence, of arrangements for the state funeral and of the way in which most Canadian towns and cities were arranging their own memorial services in the weeks to come. There was much pride in the fact that the Telstar satellite, with its tracking station in Nova Scotia, would make Halifax the nerve centre for all the North American live television broadcasts of the funeral service itself (rather less pride in the fact that broadcasters in the area had accidentally broadcast Churchill's obituary before he died). Finally, there were lengthy accounts of the funeral itself, followed by warm editorial welcomes for a Churchill Memorial Trust to be launched in Canada. Any Canadians who read newspapers regularly in that winter fortnight of 1965 would have had no doubt that Churchill had been the man of the century, a great supporter of both freedom and parliamentary democracy, and a good friend of Canada: the *Moncton Times* editorialised when he died that 'if the British Empire and Commonwealth should last for a thousand years, men will still say "this was their finest citizen"'. If any dissenting voices were raised against this flood-tide of eulogising, they were certainly not reported, while the number and tone of supportive editorials, cartoons, appreciations of 'Winnie's' life and significance, reported tributes to Churchill by federal, provincial and local politicians – and news in general – were absolutely overwhelming. As the *Halifax Chronicle-Herald*'s headline informed Haligonians on 2 February, 'Churchill slips into History: A Hero Gone to Rest'.[49]

What was Churchill's real relationship with the various Canadian leaders who made such warm remarks about him in public on every possible occasion from 1940 onwards? Relations were clearly most tricky with Mackenzie King, always ready to detect an intended slight to himself in any Canadian tribute to Churchill and deeply suspicious of Churchill's imperial politics as likely to lead to Canada's subordination in a British-dominated and more centralised Commonwealth. In any case, they had certainly not hit it off personally when they first met in Canada in 1900, and Churchill had had to apologise to King for making 'a frightful ass' of himself, when they next met in London; asked who he wished to meet on that trip, King had replied, 'anybody but Churchill. I've met him and he's the last man I want to see.' King may also have had after 1940 a guilt complex over his unflinching support for Neville Chamberlain and appeasement in the 1930s, much as Canada's later Governor-General Vincent Massey had, for as High Commissioner in London he had also been a committed appeaser.[50] John Diefenbaker thought that 'neither liked the other. Churchill disliked [King's] political opportunism. King envied the popularity of Churchill,' while, when talking to Diefenbaker in 1941, King had exploded, 'Churchill, Churchill!

'We shall not see his like again'
Halifax Herald (Canada), 25 January 1965

When did he ever bleed for Canada?' That was the later and uncorrobor-
ated reminiscence of a fairly embittered opponent (and one who was
said to quote Churchill so often in the Commons partly because he
knew that it would upset King), but the view that King never entirely
trusted or warmed to Churchill was confirmed by Lester Pearson too;

the envy of Churchill can in any case be seen easily enough between the lines in King's own published diary.[51]

The point emerges clearly from a vicious little spat that King had in 1947 with the organisers of a monument to Allied wartime co-operation, erected on the US–Canadian border at Niagara Falls. King was horrified to discover not only that the carillon bells being hung by the Niagara Falls bridge corporation were dedicated only 'to God's glory and in grateful memory of our nations' leaders, Winston Spencer Churchill and Franklin Delano Roosevelt', but that the company was asking for Canadian tax exemption on their investment. This implied that Churchill was Canada's leader, and King (who had after all been Prime Minister for over twenty years, and had a reasonable claim to be the Commonwealth's senior premier) was nowhere, a point underlined by the fact that the bell labelled 'Churchill' was the largest on the carillon. King immediately suspected plots and a 'campaign against me'. He probably even saw Churchill's hand behind it, for he diagnosed the cause of the problem as his own refusal to bring Canadian Conservatives into a national government to fight the war in 1941, as Churchill as well as the Canadian Tories themselves had urged him to do. King was relieved to know that George Drew (then Prime Minister of Ontario) had not been directly involved, but found that he had nevertheless 'countenanced' the memorial. At one point, Liberal supporters of King were even planning to have the bells melted down, so incensed were they at the implied insult to their leader. But in due course it was agreed to take the bells down and remove from them their insulting inscriptions, news that was received by Conservatives in the House with stony faces. King's diary account concluded, 'I regarded the whole business as a comedy of errors,' which was far from his own view before it had been resolved in his favour, when he had been more inclined to see it as a tragedy of ingratitude like King Lear. The company appears not to have got its tax back.[52]

Despite such deep and divisive suspicions, at the practical level Churchill and King co-operated both harmoniously and with considerable mutual trust, a fact brought out well by the role that King played in the evolution of Churchill's 'iron curtain' speech. Even in the autumn of 1945, when King was in London, Churchill had outlined his plans for the speech at Fulton in March 1946, telling King far more than he told either the British Government or his own Conservative colleagues;

King reciprocated with confidential information on Canada's own intentions with regard to the Soviet Union, also swearing Churchill to silence. King's diary makes all this clear, but so do letters in the Churchill papers. As King left, Churchill said flatteringly to him, in reference to the coming Canadian elections:

> other men are as children in the leadership of the party as compared to yourself. You have shown understanding and capacity to lead that other men have not got, or words to that effect. He used the expression that he hoped that God would bless me. No words could have been kinder than his as we parted. It was the sweetest side of his nature throughout – a really beautiful side. One cannot help loving him when that side of his nature is to the fore.

Mackenzie King thus went home and sent to Churchill a copy of the Ogdensburg Agreement of 1941 between Canada and the United States, suggesting that this would make a suitable model on which Churchill could base his proposal of a more extended permanent co-operation between the USA and the Commonwealth, and Churchill duly built the speech around exactly that idea. At the last minute, though, just before he set off to deliver his speech in Fulton, Churchill asked King to come to Washington to see him and go over his speech in detail. Such a visit could not be private, and might even seem to the press to be related to the spy trial in Ottawa and hence cause a political panic. It seems equally clear that while he was prepared to offer private advice, King (like Truman and his team) did not want any advance association in public with what Churchill was going to say. He therefore pleaded unbreakable engagements in Ottawa and asked Churchill to show the speech instead to Lester Pearson, then the Canadian Ambassador in Washington. Pearson duly went over it on Canada's behalf, removed factual errors and toned down the intended demand for a military alliance to less provocative wording, after which King again spoke to Churchill on the telephone and confirmed his agreement, as he did again when he had heard the actual speech broadcast (though characteristically King also felt – and noted in his diary – a pang of jealousy when Churchill got all the credit for the speech that he had had such a hand in framing). All of this suggests a remarkably close degree of trust between two experienced politicians, even if it also relied at least in part on Churchill's skill in stroking King's self-absorbed ego.[53]

Things were much more relaxed with King's successor Louis St Laurent, who was careful to behave correctly towards Churchill and not to seem to favour him over the British Labour Party, but who nevertheless greeted him with uncomplicated warmth whenever they met in Ottawa or in London, and prompted a similar response from Churchill. St Laurent lunched with Churchill when in London for the Coronation in 1953, an honour not accorded to all visiting premiers, and again when there in 1954, while Churchill, having discovered that St Laurent's birthday would occur during his 1954 visit, had a birthday cake made for him by the Dorchester Hotel and proposed his health personally. Being less temperamental and less self-regarding than King, St Laurent was happy to regard Churchill as the senior figure in the Commonwealth – he had after all become a prime minister long before St Laurent, as well as heading a bigger country. He noted that despite being 'deaf and old' at his final Commonwealth Conference, Churchill was still able to impose his personality on the assembled premiers. By the 1950s, there were in any case no dangers of Churchill centralising the Commonwealth, in the way that a more combined war effort might conceivably have allowed him to do in 1941–2 (or at least so King thought when he declined to join the Imperial war cabinet suggested by the Australians). St Laurent's tribute to Churchill when he retired has already been quoted, but he was equally gracious when introducing Churchill to speak in Ottawa in 1952 and 1954, and there is no reason to suppose any insincerity on his part. He was even prepared to accept without protest Churchill's poaching of Canada's Governor-General, Alexander, to join his new cabinet in 1951, giving St Laurent a difficult and unnecessary problem to solve, just as he was ready to put up with the subsequent inadvertent leak of the news in London before the Canadian Government and press had been prepared for it. As St Laurent put it in 1952, for him too, 'Mr Churchill, in those dark days [of 1940], had become far more than the Prime Minister of one country'. He continued to assert Churchill's *international* importance in all his later tributes, and hence his centrality to Canadians' lives too.[54]

Lester Pearson on the other hand seems to have respected Churchill as a leader and to have been able to make the appropriate noises at ceremonial moments (he was after all a career diplomat), and yet to have remained detached from Churchill and never quite to have fallen under his spell. If he had such a hero, it was probably Lloyd George, whom he had come to admire greatly while a student at Oxford. As a young man working at Canada's High Commission in London, Pearson had been repelled by Churchill's behaviour during the 1936 Abdication Crisis, which he thought irresponsible and self-serving. He recognised, though, by the time of Munich in 1938 that Churchill was offering an important lead, and by 1940 he was writing admiringly of the 'clear and heartening effect of Churchill' and of Churchill as 'John Bull incarnate'. As a diplomat now in Washington, he had Churchill sign his copy of the 1940 destroyers-for-bases deal, but soon felt that Churchill's direct line to Roosevelt had marginalised Canada (before the USA entered the war, Canada had had an important intermediary role). As External Affairs Minister after the war, Pearson co-operated with Churchill as required, but his simply 'forgetting' to raise the question of 'Rule Britannia' in Ottawa on Churchill's behalf suggests that their minds did not exactly meet. This was more than confirmed when Pearson met the New Zealand Foreign Secretary Fred Doidge, incidentally one of Churchill's greatest admirers in the world; hearing Doidge describe New Zealand as 'a daughter in her mother's house but mistress in her own', Pearson was appalled to hear sentiments that 'so echoed Victorian times'. It was precisely that lack of identification with imperial symbols and Victorian language that separated Pearson intellectually from Churchill and which led him into his difficult but ultimately successful crusade as Prime Minister for a new Canadian flag in place of the red ensign, a move that Churchill presumably deplored as much, if not as vocally, as did the Canadian Conservatives. Pearson was not above using Churchill's name in debate, as has been indicated above, and as Prime Minister he acquiesced when 'according to Liberal political analysts' a photograph of himself with Churchill 'produced the most positive responses among Canadians polled', and so used it in his electioneering. But he was also Prime Minister when Canada allowed to pass by the moment for planning and instituting a proper national memorial to Sir Winston in the mid-1960s. As we shall see, it just did not seem to be for Pearson the high priority that it was for Bob Menzies in Australia or for Keith Holyoake in New Zealand.[55]

Canada's Conservatives felt no such detachment from Churchill, for not only did he embody a view of the Commonwealth closer to their own than to that of Canadian Liberals, and of Canada's continuing

English inheritance which was also more popular on the Canadian right than elsewhere, but he also led from 1940 to 1955 the British party with which Canadian Tories instinctively sympathised and wanted to see in power in Westminster. Despite his need to stay on good terms with the Liberals when in power in Ottawa, there is not much doubt that Churchill shared the same sense of instinctive alliance with the Canadian Conservatives, as he did with the New Zealand National Party. When Diefenbaker returned the Conservatives to power in 1957, their first post-war government, he was almost immediately required to go to London for a Commonwealth Prime Ministers' Conference. Entertained to lunch by the Churchills at Hyde Park Gate, he was told by Clementine Churchill that Churchill had been so excited that he had 'danced' when he had been told that the Conservatives had won the Canadian election. Churchill's own demeanour seemed to confirm this, and when Diefenbaker asked why the British were so interested in what had happened at the Canadian polls, Churchill replied, 'Interested? Why shouldn't they be? It's the most important event since the end of the war.' Their friendship survived even Churchill's discovery that Diefenbaker did not drink brandy (he was relieved to know that 'Dief' was not a prohibitionist, but would scarcely have been appeased by Mrs Diefenbaker's assurance that her husband did occasionally take a small sherry). He visited the Churchills on each later visit to London, even as late as 1963 (by which time Churchill was receiving very few visitors), and he constantly referred to their meetings when talking about Churchill, as he often did. He sent to Churchill copies of books about himself when first published in North America, sent copies of books about Churchill to others as thank-you presents, for example to the Menzies, after they had entertained him in Australia, he kept Colonial Williamsburg's 1946 tribute to Churchill in his office bookcase, and he displayed a signed photograph of himself with Churchill on his office wall. Ironically, that photograph was impulsively but generously given away to Dalton Camp, another great Churchill admirer among the Canadian Conservatives, just before Camp arranged the coup which unseated Diefenbaker as Conservative leader. Diefenbaker was actually at Churchill's funeral for 'four crowded days' while Camp was organising the party executive meeting that would begin his downfall, and when he had been overthrown Diefenbaker immediately compared himself to Churchill in the wilderness from his party in the 1930s.

As he became older and increasingly embittered, his identification with Churchill was a continuing reassurance to him. He planned his own state funeral in considerable detail (taking as its title 'Operation Hope Not', the same code used for the Churchill funeral). He thus ensured that as for Churchill there would be military bands (playing in fact in the Ottawa cathedral two of the same hymns used at St Paul's in 1965), that there would be a long funeral cortège by train (in his case thousands of miles back to Saskatchewan, rather than Churchill's fifty-mile final ride to Oxfordshire), and a simple stone slab over his grave, which bore only his name and dates – just as had been done for Churchill in Bladon churchyard. It is not difficult to see why contemporaries thought that Diefenbaker was actually obsessed by Churchill, and his long, defiant campaign to resist Pearson's new Canadian flag, bereft of British symbols and tradition, was compared both by himself and by others to one of Churchill's own crusades against the fashionable opinions of the time.[56] As Diefenbaker regularly reminded his audiences, when larding his speeches with Churchill quotations, he had been devoted to Churchill ever since seeing him in parliamentary action in 1916, and especially since seeing him again from the gallery of the British House of Commons, denouncing appeasement in 1936, immediately after Diefenbaker had himself been repelled by witnessing the Nazi regime at the Berlin Olympics. As he reminded the Canadian Commons in 1955, 'yes, he [Churchill] was right then, and others were wrong'. He was therefore committed to Churchill even during his wilderness years, and subsequent events merely reinforced a lifelong tendency towards hero-worship of a great man and (as befitted such a long-time member of the Canadian Commons) a great parliamentarian too. As Diefenbaker put it in his 1964 tribute, 'In all his greatness, sir, what stands out is that he was always a House of Commons man ... We are here as Canadians in the parliament of this country, believing in freedom and knowing what Churchill's contribution has been.'[57]

George Drew was, however, Churchill's most effective admirer in Canadian federal politics, and, quite apart from his early meeting with Churchill in 1916, his lengthy subsequent career certainly fitted him for that role; he was a long-term provincial premier in Ontario, the heart of English Canada, federal Conservative Party leader from 1948 to 1956 when Churchill was in his post-war prime, and High Commissioner in London, 1957–63, during Churchill's declining years. He thus had both the experience and the contacts that made him the natural choice to chair the Canadian branch of the Winston Churchill Memorial Trust when one was proposed in 1964, a post that he accepted with alacrity. As is shown above, Drew's admiration for Churchill was both profound and partisan – his political files for the 1948–56 period included not only clippings and extracts from Churchill speeches, but also quite a few policy documents from the British Conservative Party. He was clearly extremely well read in Churchill's career and writings, and not as likely as Diefenbaker to misattribute to Churchill any good story about Britain and its leaders. He too met and thoroughly enjoyed the company of Churchill on all possible occasions, collected the books, stamps and memorabilia, and treasured in particular a photograph of himself and Churchill outside his Upper Brook Street, London, official residence, a photograph of which multiple copies were made, signed and distributed to friends. As with Churchill's many admirers around the world, Drew gave rather more than he got back, and his allegiance was purchased in a seller's market. When, in December 1951, he cabled fervent Christmas greetings to Churchill, having already congratulated him both on his birthday and on his return to office only a few weeks earlier, he does not seem to have received a reply (for he would certainly have kept it if he had); and when in November 1952 he again sent birthday congratulations and hopes 'for long years of health and vigor to carry on your great work on behalf of the Empire and all mankind', he received a fairly cool ten-word reply that hardly indicated personal attention to his message by Churchill himself. When Churchill reached the age of eighty in 1954, Drew cabled, 'May I say how deeply I shall always treasure your friendship during the eventful years in which you have placed all mankind for ever in your debt?' It is unlikely that any other Commonwealth politician other than Bob Menzies and Jan Smuts would have been able to claim 'friendship' with Churchill so confidently, and it certainly demonstrates a different tone in the relationship to that claimed by Diefenbaker or any of Canada's leading Liberals.[58]

Drew, like Diefenbaker but most unlike Pearson, had a defiantly unchanging view of Britain and the Commonwealth, as was indicated by the valedictory articles when he retired as High Commissioner in London: the *Toronto Telegraph* noted that he had been sent to London precisely because he was 'a man who combines wholehearted love of Canada with admiration for the British heritage and tradition', while the *Vancouver Sun*, 'conceding that in some respects he may be old-fashioned', nevertheless thought that 'he believes devoutly in the British connection and the greatness of the Commonwealth'. It is not therefore at all surprising that Drew was shocked and horrified by Britain's 1962 application to join the European Economic Community. He argued that Britain's signature of the Treaty of Rome would mean 'the end of the Commonwealth', and strongly resented the smokescreen briefings being given to the Commonwealth High Commissioners in London by Edward Heath on behalf of the British Government, to the effect that it was 'all economic' and need have no effect on Britain's international political arrangements. With the benefit of hindsight, Drew emerges from the argument with considerably more credit than Heath, but it seems very likely that Drew was also much closer than Heath to Churchill's private views on the EEC in 1962, as indicated by Monty's typically outrageous breach of the confidentiality of a private conversation with him. Drew was careful to explain that he and Canada had no problems with 'Churchill's Council of Europe idea', or even with the European Free Trade Area, but felt both threatened and abandoned by British interest in the protectionist EEC.[59]

In April 1964, with Drew now back from London, Prime Minister Pearson invited him to chair the proposed Memorial Trust in Canada, in view both of his previous experience of educational exchanges in the Commonwealth and of 'your personal closeness to Sir Winston'. Drew was certainly excited by the idea, seeing as did many other Churchill admirers around the world that travelling educational scholarships in the Commonwealth and the USA of the type that the Trust would facilitate would be a 'form of memorial [which] is the very best which could possibly have been planned to perpetuate the memory of a man who had such unbounded faith in the Commonwealth'.[60] He therefore began to contact a possible fundraising team, and Canada joined with other Commonwealth countries and the USA in announcing in London two days after Churchill's funeral their participation in an international appeal for funds for travelling Churchill scholarships. The *Edmonton Journal* was typical in welcoming both the fact that Canada was standing with Australia, New Zealand, the United Kingdom and the USA in the appeal, and the form that it would take in travelling scholarships. Drew was now publicly named as chairman, the press response was positive (both as to the idea and as to his suitability for the task), and a few donations rolled in at once in response to the news. The problem was that nothing had actually yet been done to prepare for this in Canada, whereas in all the other countries concerned committees were in place with separate teams to tackle different types of donors, tax implications had been thoroughly researched, and literature was already apparently in draft. The other countries were all therefore able to seize the moment in 1965 when admiration for Churchill was at its absolute height and rake in a lot of money to endow permanent scholarship schemes, but Canada was not.

The reason for the initial delay was twofold. First, Drew was well aware that failure to straighten out the tax difficulties in advance had seriously hampered Canadian fundraising for Churchill College a couple of years earlier (the problem being that tax exemptions on donations were not easy to arrange when the money would be spent outside the country – in this case, apparently by an international committee). Despite the enthusiasm of Diefenbaker, the Federal Government had no real leverage since it had no direct responsibility for education, while most of the provincial premiers decided that they had higher priorities for educational funds than a college in Cambridge. So Canada's most important contribution to Churchill College was probably the fine wood with which the dining hall is floored and panelled. Second, Drew was trying to cope with his wife's serious illness throughout 1964 and moving back and forth between Canada and Italy, so that mail was forever going missing or taking a long time to catch up, and the tax issues on which everything else was waiting never got straightened out. This difficulty was compounded by the fact that within a few weeks of Churchill's death Drew's wife died, and then he himself was ill for a long period through to late 1965. He had the melancholy task of fielding letters about the Trust throughout the year, explaining to possible donors and enquirers about scholarships that everything had been delayed by his personal circumstances but that it would all get going soon. By autumn 1965, he was well aware that he was really not going to able to do the job properly, and tried to resign, only for Prime Minister Pearson to keep passing the buck back to him by asking him to find his own successor. Several imploring letters were therefore sent out by Drew to well-qualified and well-connected potential chairmen. Each turned him down, sometimes after further delays, and usually because they were already heavily involved in running appeals for some other good educational cause.

Herein perhaps lay the fundamental reason why it all proved more difficult in Canada than elsewhere. Higher education was in the mid-1960s undergoing rapid expansion in Canada, but whereas the similar expansion in Britain was taxation-funded, much of it in Canada rested on public subscriptions; the same page of the *Toronto Globe and Mail* that first announced the Churchill Fellowships scheme also reported the actual launch of a $15 million appeal for York University. Belatedly, at the end of 1965, the Federal Government offered a pump-priming grant (which had been in place in Australia, New Zealand and Britain nearly two years earlier), and this briefly raised Drew's hopes. He gamely argued that Churchill's fame would last for years, and that an appeal could therefore be as effective in 1966 or 1967 as in 1965, but the truth was that the moment had already passed. It is not clear exactly when and by whom the whole idea was dropped, but no proper appeal was ever launched and no Memorial Trust or Fellowships were therefore ever endowed. George Drew desperately wanted it to succeed but just could not do it at the time it had to be done, and Lester Pearson was all in favour of it in principle but did not want the problem actually back on his own desk. The Governor-General meanwhile was mainly telling them both that he was happy to be patron of the scheme but could not be expected to do anything more than allow his name to be used.[61]

However, if the Canadian national Government did not exactly cover itself in glory in memorialising Churchill in 1965, provincial, local and private initiatives more than made up for the deficit. All across Canada, there remain today Churchill namings to commemorate the veneration with which he was held in the period in which he died; Edmonton, the capital of Alberta, was for example quick to start a debate, in the week of the funeral, on an appropriate street to be renamed in Churchill's honour, leading in due course to its central Churchill Square.[62] In Ontario, the heart of English sentiment in Canada for two centuries, more than sixty streets, boulevards and roads are named after Churchill, as are eight schools and colleges, and there is a sprinkling of similar namings in the Atlantic provinces and out west. St John's, the capital of Newfoundland, also has a Churchill Square. There are also Winston Churchill parks (for example in Toronto), Churchill retirement residences (in Edmonton), Churchill apartments (in Victoria, BC), and Churchill cigar stores (in Vancouver and several other cities), many of the last sporting paintings or cartoon drawings of the man in their windows or on their signboards. If 'Churchill' is predictably less likely to occur in the province of Quebec, there are still about twenty cases of Rue Winston Churchill or their equivalent in the Montreal area.

More significantly, perhaps, there were several successful attempts to match Churchill's stature with major natural phenomena. The Churchill Peak in British Columbia (almost ten thousand feet high) was named in 1944, part of a Battle of Britain Range of mountains, but the Churchill Range (325 square kilometres of the Rocky Mountains in Alberta) was given its name in 1965, following his funeral. Most substantially of all, the major river in Labrador, previously known as the Hamilton, became the Churchill river in 1965, as a direct result of the warmth of feeling for Churchill on the day of his funeral in the heart of Prime Minister Smallwood of Newfoundland. The major thousand-foot waterfall on the river thus also became the Churchill Falls, a name that would be much bandied about later, for in 1967 work began to make it the site of one of Canada's biggest hydro-electricity projects. There is now also a settlement of Churchill Falls around the plant. Here at least Churchill had had some direct input into the place destined to be named after him, for as Prime Minister in 1953 he had received Smallwood, decided that the hydro-electric scheme was 'a grand imperial idea – and I don't mean imperialist!', and helped along the process of creating a London consortium to raise the capital. He even apparently promised to take ten thousand shares in the scheme himself. The renaming of the Churchill Falls in 1965 did however indicate some of the problems with such initiatives, much as the attempt to rebrand Alaska's Mount McKinley after Churchill was doing at the time. Joey Smallwood had the actual idea in London and announced it without consulting anyone back home, where there was a strong institutional prejudice against giving up well-known existing names (what, after all, was wrong with 'Hamilton'? asked the *Cape Breton Post*). Smallwood managed to tough it out and get his way, and the new name caught on. 'Churchill' had been less successful in the war years, when there was an attempt to substitute his name for the township of Swastika, Ontario: the inhabitants decided that the name they had had for nearly forty years – derived from a shape on a lady's charm bracelet rather than a Nazi symbol – was quite good enough, and in this case the patriots had to retreat.[63]

One patriot who did not back off when facing stiff opposition, taking his cue from Churchill himself, was Henry Jackman, a Toronto lawyer and architect who wanted a proper physical memorial to Churchill to be placed in the capital of Ontario. He began by aiming high, urging that a forty-foot-tall Churchill head be placed on the Toronto waterfront, much like Mount Rushmore, and offering as an alternative an equally large pair of revolving fingers making Churchill's V-sign, and offering to find $100,000 personally so that a scheme of this type could be adopted. (Critics noted that, if the fingers revolved, they would offer a rude gesture as often as a patriotic one.) The architect deputed by the Mayor to negotiate with Jackman later recalled just how difficult this could be, for 'he would turn up at meetings armed with a tape recorder and play Churchill's speeches. Try arguing down the immensity of Jackman's ideas with Churchill's voice in the background calling for greater and greater sacrifice and more heroic effort.' Eventually there was convergence between Jackman's undoubted generosity and his enthusiasm for Churchill on the one hand and the nervousness of the city fathers lest something rather tasteless should get through and actually damage Churchill's fame and standing. The compromise was to erect a conventional statue of Churchill, and indeed a very fine one, unveiled in October 1977, and substantially funded by Jackman himself, though the plaque mounted on the plinth also acknowledged the support of a committee of citizens. The placing of the statue was another compromise, with its supporters wanting it outside the provincial legislature and its opponents seeking to place it in Churchill Park, outside the city centre altogether. It was eventually placed outside the City Hall, appropriately enough since the city had actually agreed to it, and in Nathan Phillips Square (itself named after the admirer who had made Churchill a freeman). It was, though, less satisfactory in view of the modernistic architecture which serves as the backdrop to a traditional bronze statue. Not resting content with this (and Jackman had already got Delhi's unwanted equestrian statue of Edward VII moved to Toronto's Queen's Park), he immediately started on other cities. By February 1979 it was reported that Halifax had now agreed to a statue to be erected later that year and that he was (now aged seventy-nine) moving on to try his luck with Edmonton. If 'never surrender' was a favourite Churchill motto in his old age, the same might well have been said of at least one of his Canadian admirers.[64]

Finally, Canadians have done a great deal practically to keep Churchill's memory alive – and began to do this formally before anyone else.

Here the lead came from the west, for the first annual memorial dinner to Churchill was held in April 1965 in Edmonton and addressed by Lord Montgomery of Alamein. The initial purpose was twofold, to, 'keep alive the memory of the late Sir Winston in the minds of those who were blessed to live in his time', and to raise money to finance a scholarship for a tenth-grade high-school student, following a competition to find the best essay on Churchill in the province's schools. Edmonton's Churchill Society had been founded in January 1964, in preparation for Churchill's ninetieth birthday later that year, and in the expectation that post-humous memorialising could not now be long delayed.[65] That initial dinner was a great success, and by the end of the 1960s it was being replicated annually, not only in Edmonton but also in Calgary and Vancouver; indeed the fact that parallel dinners were taking place in all the three major western cities was probably crucial to their success, for this enabled the cost of flying out a British VIP to address the dinners to be shared between more than one group of diners. In 1967 the speaker was Alexander, followed by R. A. Butler in 1968, Alec Douglas-Home in 1969 and General Mark Clark in 1970. Sir Ian Jacob, Alan Lennox-Boyd, Sir Colin Coote and Sir Fitzroy Maclean were among those who visited and spoke in the 1970s. By 1993, the dinners had been addressed by nine former British cabinet ministers, Churchill intimates like Jock Colville, Anthony Montague Browne, Ian Jacob and Lord Mountbatten and leading British historians like Robert Blake, Robert Rhodes James and Michael Howard.

The dinners were social occasions of the first order, with an all-male company of five hundred arrayed in white tie and tails, wearing decorations: Calgary's top table in 1969 included the provincial premier and leader of the Opposition, the Bishop of Calgary, three judges and a justice of the supreme court, newspaper editors and the Speaker of the Alberta House, together with a former Canadian minister of defence. The proceeds of that dinner were given to the University of Calgary for the creation of a Churchill collection in its library. The evening's formality, and especially the men-only rule, began during the 1970s to attract some barbed comments in the press, but even this was in the tone of affectionate banter, for the 'Winnie Dinner' was by then a prized institution. So strict was the men-only rule that Mary Soames, accompanying her husband Christopher who was the chief guest in 1979, had to dine in a side-room, even though she was the chief living relative of the man whose 'heroic memory' was being toasted in the main hall. Thereafter the event moved a little, first with girl-students allowed into the dinner when they had won a prize in the essay competition and with Mary Soames herself becoming the first woman speaker to address the dinner in 1982 (she was also the Society's patron). Women were allowed to join by that year and the Society itself chose a woman president in 1986. The linking together of different forms of memorialising Sir Winston was aptly brought out when the Society awarded prizes at its 1973 dinner to students of Sir Winston Churchill High School, which had won its sponsored debating competition.[66]

Similar initiatives were also taking place elsewhere in Canada by the 1970s, and at the end of the century Toronto had two separate groups in existence to commemorate Churchill, the Other Club of Ontario (in effect the local chapter of the International Churchill Society and the Churchill Center, but named after one of Churchill's own favourite social gatherings in London) and the Churchill Society for the Advancement of Parliamentary Democracy, which had been co-founded in 1982 by an academic who had sought unavailingly to get the Federal Government to launch an appeal for Churchill College in 1962, and which has sponsored among other things a Churchill collection in a Churchill Room in the University of Toronto's library and also holds annual dinners (addressed in 1999 and 2000 by Professors David Dilks and John Lukacs). It was also a Canadian, John Plumpton, who helped in the development of the International Churchill Society itself, by urging its transformation from a bunch of enthusiastic stamp-collectors in California into a group of Churchill enthusiasts with far wider interests, and all across the English-speaking world. At the end of 'Churchill's century', the ICS itself was probably stronger in Canada, in terms either of members per head of population or of the regularity with which 'the heroic memory' is toasted and the man himself remembered, than in either Britain or the United States, and was in any case a long way ahead of Australia or New Zealand.[67]

It may be as well therefore to conclude by asking why this was – what was it that ensured that Churchill's reputation and standing went deeper and proved to be less transient than in the superficially similar circumstances of the British Dominions of the southern hemisphere? Clearly the continuation of strong affection for Britain itself among many English-speaking Canadians has a part to play in explaining the lasting impact of the man who seemed to embody Britishness. The very centrality of national and linguistic issues to the Canadian political scene would have facilitated this. It was probably no coincidence then that when George Drew had typed up and filed for use in a future speech an apposite quotation from Shakespeare's *King John* ('This England never did, nor never shall, lie at the proud foot of a conqueror . . .'), he filed it not under S for Shakespeare, or indeed under E for England, but in his file of Churchill clippings, though the great man seems never to have used the line himself. Canadians were always anxious to claim Churchill as more than just Britain's leader, but 'Churchill equals England' was clearly a central assumption in their minds.[68]

Nevertheless, much the same could be said of Australia or New Zealand, so something more substantial was at work in Canada. Part of the explanation lies in Churchill's personal connections with individual Canadians and with the whole geographical extent of the country; when he died in 1965, the Vancouver suburb of New Westminster was able to remind itself not only that its very name reflected the scene of Churchill's greatest triumphs but that he had actually been in the area in 1929, visited the cathedral and addressed the Canadian Club, and so claim a part of his history for itself. The citizens of Edmonton, likewise, were reminded that Churchill had visited in 1929, that the *Journal*'s columnist had actually met and spoken to him, and that he had predicted a great future for the Canadian west in his speech in the city thirty-six years earlier.[69] Beyond that range of personal contacts over two-thirds of a century (which meant among other things that he did not have to rely for the promotion of his image in Canada on the dubious medium of his very greatest Canadian friend, Lord Beaverbrook), there was the regularity of his visits, and the centrality of Canada itself to his post-war vision of a special relationship between the Commonwealth and the United States. British and American historians have tended to underestimate Canada's role in the international politics of 1945–55, coming as it did between periods when the direct Washington–London axis was central to both countries' international diplomacy. The invisible hand of Mackenzie King and Lester Pearson in Churchill's Fulton speech of 1946 has already been cited, but there is a good case to be made too for Canada's centrality to the way in which the United Nations was shaped in 1945, and especially for the emergence of NATO, where John English sees Canada's diplomacy as 'catalytic'.[70]

Churchill understood all of this, as he argued rhetorically time and again, in referring to Canada's 'lynchpin' position (which he could hardly have claimed of Australia, say), and what is more he welcomed it. Back in 1940, when the USA was no part of any alliance, he had cabled Mackenzie King to say that he was 'deeply interested' in the Ogdensburg Defence Agreement that linked Canada with the United States, in 1946 he had accepted the advice of King and Pearson that for tactical reasons to do with American public opinion he should limit his demand to a similar defensive link between the USA and the whole Commonwealth, but in NATO he got just what he had always wanted, a standing military alliance of which many European countries were members, but of which Britain, the USA and Canada were the central components. NATO would very likely have come into being without Canada, but it is nevertheless clear that its emergence was made much easier by the presence of a third party friendly to both Britain and America – as Churchill himself invariably pointed out. In the early 1950s, when Churchill sought to use the security generated by NATO's very existence as a strong platform from which he could seek détente with Russia, and so antagonised Eisenhower's more hawkish Administration in Washington, once again Canada helped to oil the wheels and limit the damage.[71]

Practical and mutually advantageous co-operation – on a triangular basis – thus underlined and reinforced rhetoric, and even at the time the significance of this was evident. Louis St Laurent, for example, spoke in 1952 of the value *to Canada* of Churchill's Anglo-American parentage: 'we acknowledge that no man living has done more than you have to bring about an association of hearts and minds between your father's native land and your mother's native land', from which Canada would also be the beneficiary. Shortly afterwards, a backbencher put that same argument in a slightly different but complementary way: 'In Canada, our first concern outside of our boundaries is for the closest and most friendly relations between Canada and the United States. We acknowledge with gratitude that no living man has done more than he to bring this about.' Canadians were also fond of quoting Churchill's favourite 'lynchpin' description of Canada's own part in the process of Western convergence, most forcefully in Churchillian words quoted by James Macdonnell in the Canadian Commons in 1954:

The long unguarded frontier, the habits and intercourse of daily life, the fruitful and profitable connections of business, the sympathies and even the antipathies of honest neighbourliness, make Canada the binder-together of the English-Speaking People. She is a magnet exercising a double attraction, drawing both Great Britain and the United States towards herself, and thus drawing them closer to each other. She is the only surviving bond which stretches from Europe across the Atlantic Ocean. In fact, no state, no country, no band of men, can more truly be described as the lynchpin of world peace and progress.[72]

Flattering to Canadians, yes, but not so far as to lose touch with the practical political realities of the decade of Churchill's post-war maturity, and in any case such words were merely the logical conclusion of what Churchill himself had been saying in Canada and to Canadians ever since 1900.

Perhaps there was something very specific to the national character in Canadians' reaction to Churchill too, a quality of admiration teased out by the columnist Charles Lynch for the *Edmonton Journal* – but then widely reprinted in other papers, which suggests that their editors found its argument persuasive. 'Winston Churchill', he began,

was our greatest hero, and I think he was fond of us too. I am speaking about Canadians, who are so suspicious of hero figures that we have none of the home-brew variety, though we are trying to create some posthumously to serve for our centennial year. Lacking heroes of our own, we accepted Churchill ... as one of us. He was an authentic Canadian hero – he became and will remain part of our native story.

Since Canadians were inherently suspicious of their leaders, but felt like everyone else the need to admire somebody, Churchill was just sufficiently distant (but because of his regular visits sufficiently familiar at the same time) to fit the bill perfectly. As a result, 'we were, and remain, uncritical of Churchill, reserving a special place for him in our affection and esteem'. The choice of the last three words was significant, for it certainly does seem that affection as well as esteem was important in Canadian views of Churchill. Hence the universal Canadian use of 'Winnie' in both personal and newspaper accounts of his visits, an appellation which was uncommon in Australia and would have seemed disrespectful in New Zealand. Lynch concluded his account with a personal reminiscence of Churchill's 1945 visit to Canadian troops in Germany, a reminiscence characteristic of this presentation of the great man as a lovable rogue. Knowing Churchill's tastes, the Canadian officers had laid on a plentiful supply of drink, only for the teetotal Montgomery to notice a tray full of bottles and at once move his briefing into another room, but not before Churchill had seen for himself what lay behind the quickly slammed door. As a result, his temper deteriorated steadily as the day wore on, and 'by lunchtime, in the Reichwald forest, he was like a bear'. The Corps Commander, General Simmons, solved the problem by radioing ahead to the units to be visited in the afternoon, instructing each unit to provide their guest with appropriate stimulants (served in a tea mug so as not to arouse Monty's suspicions). As a result, 'the rest of the day passed swimmingly'. Lynch concluded of this event, which he had witnessed first-hand as a war correspondent, 'I think the day did wonders for Churchill's regard for Canadian initiative.' That type of story, which it would not be difficult to retell in a quite different tone of voice – as the childish and self-indulgent behaviour of a man who really ought to have known better – was invariably presented instead as evidence of Churchill's outsize personality and irresistible charm. The sort of nods and winks that were involved on the day, in Anglo-Canadian collusion to hoodwink the austere Montgomery, were no doubt exactly what did help to add affection to esteem in all Churchill's brushes with Canadians over half a century. But Lynch was also able to record that when Churchill first drove up to the Canadian headquarters on that day in 1945, disembarking from an armoured car and jauntily giving his V-sign, Canadian soldiers, 'who were notoriously suspicious of politicians', had no such inhibitions about surrounding and cheering Churchill.[73] Whatever the reasons, the breadth of affection was obviously very great.

Canada was a place, then, where Churchill felt that he was in touch with an unbounded future of promise, but among people who took pride in their English inheritance. He felt the same sense of future promise in the United States, but in Canada he was also surrounded by people who spoke to him of loyalty to the King and of their affection for Britain.[74] They also sang to him and cheered him personally as the very embodiment of Britain during his later years. No wonder that there was a meeting of minds and affections, or that it was one that lasted. This is brought out nicely in the wartime exchange that took place between Churchill and Bob Morrison, part of a Canadian detachment detailed to guard Chartwell. Seeing Churchill approach, Morrison saluted, and their exchange continued as follows:

WSC: Why didn't you challenge me, Canada?

BM: I know who you are.

WSC: Oh, how do you know me?

BM: By your cigar, bald head, double chin, short neck, and fat belly, sir.

WSC: But, don't forget that the Germans have bald men with short necks and fat bellies who smoke cigars.

BM: You're right, sir, but they would do up the bottom button of their vests.[75]

9

'The Brightest Gem in the British Crown': Churchill in New Zealand[1]

IN HIS POST-WAR APPEALS for the unity of the English-speaking peoples, as at Fulton (where, as we have seen, his thinking appears to have been at least influenced by Mackenzie King and Lester Pearson of Canada), Churchill believed that he was acting not just for Britain but on behalf of the British Empire and Commonwealth as a whole.[2] And since he saw no alternative to a British-led grouping, he continued to put it that way round: when offered a draft Conservative Party statement on Commonwealth and Empire policy in 1949, he crossed out the title and amended it to read 'Empire and Commonwealth'.[3] His preference was easy enough to detect from the Commonwealth end too: the New Zealand Prime Minister Keith Holyoake spoke in 1965 of Churchill's belief in the Empire and Commonwealth, but conceded that Churchill was well known to be 'fonder' of the former than of the latter.[4] Churchill had of course never actually been to New Zealand, just as he never visited Australia, Singapore or Hong Kong; nor did he ever go either to South Africa or to India after he left the army in 1900. During his sixty-three years in Parliament, the great 'man of Empire' visited only East African colonies (in 1908, as Colonial Under Secretary), Egypt and the Mediterranean (in wartime), the West Indies (for holidays), Bermuda (for a 1953 conference) and Canada (frequently, if often on the way to or from the USA, or as a base on which to meet American Presidents on non-American territory). It seems worth asking then how Churchill and his international fame were viewed from the most distant foothold of the English-speaking peoples, where hardly anyone had any personal experience of him on which to base their opinions. How was he viewed in New Zealand, and how was that image itself constructed in the 'Britain of the South'?

New Zealand's relations with Churchill up to 1945 had not exactly been unproblematic, and in popular histories that troubled legacy still survives: after 1918, he was forever associated in the Kiwi memory with the tragedy of Gallipoli. New Zealand's Churchill problem was then reinforced during the Second World War: he was criticised for wasting the lives and freedom of New Zealand soldiers in a doomed fight to defend Crete in 1941; he was reluctant to send New Zealand troops back from the Mediterranean to defend their homes and families when the Japanese danger loomed in 1942; and he was said to have forced the New Zealanders into another costly (and arguably unnecessary) battle for Monte Cassino in the Italian campaign of 1943. Writing as recently as 1988, Tom Brooking could depict Churchill as responsible for the disasters of Gallipoli, for causing 'the unnecessary slaughter of New Zealanders' on Crete, and for provoking further bloodshed by being impatient for an attack at Cassino.[5] Nevertheless, it seems clear that in New Zealand there was less hostility to Churchill over these incidents than there was in Australia on comparable grounds. The New Zealand Government in fact agreed to leave the 2nd New Zealand Division in the Mediterranean in 1942, at Churchill's urgent request, and to accept US Marines as their defenders instead (so accelerating a drift from the British into the US orbit of which Churchill himself then strongly disapproved). The Australians insisted on bringing their boys home, so prompting some of Churchill's choicest remarks of the entire war period, but the New Zealand Government even collaborated with Churchill on the drafting of his formal request for the retention of the troops, so as to ensure that he got the right answer when it was debated in Parliament in Wellington.[6]

New Zealand was of course over two thousand miles further from the Japanese threat than was Australia (and New Zealand was not bombed by the Japanese like Darwin in Northern Australia). This may in itself explain the different reactions in Canberra and Wellington, but it also seems at least possible that New Zealanders' hostility to Churchill as a military leader had never been so pronounced in the first place, possibly because New Zealand itself had lacked the large Irish component among its original migrant population which contributed so signally to suspicion of Churchill both in Australia and in parts of the United States; being more English than the other British Dominions, in other words, as a self-conscious 'Britain of the South', New Zealand reacted to Churchill more as the British themselves were doing.[7] This is given some credence by the fact that when the New Zealand Labour Government launched a series of auctions for the war effort in 1942, exactly the period of disagreement over war policy and only a year after Crete, it chose to call them 'Churchill auctions'. Donors provided plenty of goods and bidders plenty of money, so that the fundraising was highly successful, which rather suggests that Churchill's name was not much of an obstacle.[8] On the political right there was an even warmer regard for Churchill, though later bathed in a glow of rose-tinted nostalgia. As the National Party Prime Minister Keith Holyoake recalled in 1964, speaking of the 'shared memories' of wartime: 'I think we all felt during that tremendous time in history that so long as the heart of this great man continued to beat and Big Ben continued to toll the hours, the heart of Empire and the free world was still beating and the world was safe for democracy.'[9] Note how Churchill and Big Ben go together in this reminiscence, Churchill in effect incarnating Britishness – which was very probably his problem with the Boston, and the Sydney, Irish too.

When the war ended in victory, New Zealanders were indeed so respectful of Churchill (and no doubt also used to conformity after years of wartime controls) that most of them heeded their Government's instruction and did not even start the celebrations of VE Day until Churchill on the BBC had told them officially that the war was over.[10] Churchill seems to have recognised the distinction between the Australian and New Zealand positions that emerged in 1942: when both countries later accepted the Americans' insistence that Britain be excluded from participation in their ANZUS tripartite defence pact of 1951, he told his cabinet that 'he greatly regretted the Australian acquiescence in the attempt of the United States to usurp our special position in relation to Australia and New Zealand' (apparently not feeling the same hostility to New Zealand on the ground that it was Australia that had sold the pass).[11] It was at about this time that he also gave the visiting New Zealand deputy Prime Minister the greatest pleasure of his life when he declared that, since India had become a republic, it was his view that

New Zealand was now 'the brightest gem in the British crown'.[12] It is unlikely that he ever repeated this remark in the presence of Bob Menzies, but the distinction was nevertheless a real one in his mind, and it is significant that the lifelong Cavalier Churchill saw it as the Crown's role in the Commonwealth to be the glue that held the gems together.

Over the next twenty years, New Zealand politicians and pressmen played a full part in celebrating Churchill's burgeoning fame. When he lost power in July 1945, the New Zealand press was absolutely baffled, and for the most part reported the story as Churchill's defeat rather than British Labour's victory. The Wellington-based *Dominion*'s editorial was headed simply 'Mr Churchill's defeat', while the *New Zealand Herald* wrote that 'in this historic hour in the political history of Great Britain', the 'first thoughts of millions of people in the British Empire will be for Mr Churchill'. Even when describing the result in party political terms, the Christchurch *Press* assured its readers that 'Mr Churchill's defeat, incidental to that of his party, diminishes his stature as a national leader by not a hairsbreadth; nor does it signify, or bring, any decline in the British people's gratitude to him or regard for him.'[13] Well, maybe so, but the subsequent claim that 'he has taken his dismissal, as he took office, without thought for himself', was several miles wide of the mark and indicative more of wishful thinking than of inside information.

Within days, Sidney Holland, leader of the National Party Opposition, was urging the New Zealand Labour Government to bring Churchill to New Zealand as an official guest, 'so as to enable the people of New Zealand to express to him their profound admiration of, and grateful thanks for, the inspiring leadership he gave to our Empire during those critical years when everything we held dear was in danger'. When the Labour Government's spokesman replied coolly that Churchill knew he had a standing invitation anyway, Holland urged that it be renewed in the recent 'ultimate circumstances', only to be rebuffed; Labour in Wellington clearly did not wish to do anything to undermine Labour at Westminster. Only a few weeks later, New Zealand MPs debated a proposal to take up a subscription for a statue of 'this great Englishman, the greatest Englishman of all time', to be placed in the grounds of the Parliament House in Wellington, which had it gone ahead would have been the first Churchill statue to be erected anywhere in the world. It was notable that the supporters of the statue project included the Returned Servicemen's Association, which suggests that rancour over Gallipoli and Crete was not all that has been claimed. National Party MPs kept up the attack over a series of debates, the lead taken by Fred Doidge, a former Beaverbrook press manager who had known Churchill well when he lived in London. E. P. Aderman MP (National, New Plymouth) was still arguing the case for a Churchill memorial in 1947, hoping by then for a 'New Zealand room' in the rebuilt (Westminster) House of Commons, 'right in the heart of the Empire', to be dedicated to the memory of Churchill's 'very unique and distinguished services . . . as leader during World War II'.[14]

The vocabulary of such speeches indicated just how far the New Zealand right at least, in seeking to honour a 'great Englishman', thought of themselves as still sharing in Churchill's English nationality. It is not then very surprising that Doidge, as Minister of External Affairs in 1949–51, greatly regretted having excluded Britain from the ANZUS pact. When he was appointed High Commissioner in London in 1951, the US State Department privately described him as 'more English than an Englishman', as a man whose loyalty to the Crown was 'almost a religion', and as 'one of the last of the "Empire Citizens"'. As High Commissioner, he was thought to have persuaded Prime Minister Holland to make the long and arduous journey to London to demonstrate New Zealand's loyalty at Elizabeth II's Coronation in 1953. Given these predilections, it is not surprising that Doidge got on so well with Winston Churchill, nor that Churchill paid him such a warm tribute (most fully reported in Beaverbrook's *Daily Express*, naturally) when he died in London, still High Commissioner, in 1954.[15]

In opposition during the late 1940s, Churchill continued to get a good press at the other side of the world, notably for such speeches as the one delivered at Fulton,[16] and his war memoirs were enthusiastically reviewed there. Nor is it surprising then that his return to office in 1951 was greeted with considerable warmth, tempered only by disappointment that he did not have a bigger Commons majority; the *New Zealand Herald* wrote that despite that disappointment the election had produced 'one outstanding gain. It has brought back to the world stage a statesman with clear ideas about what he hopes to do and resolute to protect British interests.' *The Dominion* reported that London streets had been filled with crowds chanting 'We want Churchill', signs of a 'surge of new hope in the Mother Country', which was to say the least a rather partial account of reactions to his election with fewer actual votes than Labour.[17]

With such a start, even the spat over the ANZUS pact did not damage Churchill's warm regard in the New Zealand press, and, so far as the press is a guide, more widely with the New Zealand public too. So for example, when New Zealand Ministers visited London in 1952 to discuss trade between the two countries, the *Otago Daily Times* (Dunedin) reported the close personal interest that Britain's Prime Minister was taking in the Dominion's affairs, adding to its story accounts of New Zealanders' conversations with Churchill and the presentation to them of signed copies of his books; in 1953 it reported the presentation to Churchill of a specially made cigar cabinet by disabled New Zealand war veterans (more old soldiers who bore no grudges), and in 1954 it reported the birthday congratulations sent to Churchill by the Mayor of Dunedin and Churchill's message of thanks for such warmhearted good wishes on his birthday.[18]

That eightieth birthday in 1954 was, however, celebrated more widely than just in Dunedin. *The Press* for example devoted thirty column inches on 30 November to preparations for the birthday celebrations under the headline 'Spontaneous Toast is "Sir Winston"' and the sub-head 'Place among the Immortals in his own Lifetime'. On the following day, the London celebrations were given forty-five column inches, together with a photograph of the specially commissioned Graham Sutherland portrait which was to have so short a life in the Churchill household. The English eye is naturally drawn to an equally prominent story on the same page about an 'Uphill fight by England' to avoid an innings defeat in the Brisbane Test match; the paper cheekily reported the MCC's telegram to Churchill saying 'We could do with your eighty not out, sir.' On another page, *The Press* reported New Zealand's official congratulations to Churchill in which Prime Minister Holland sent an oil painting of a New Zealand landscape, urged him to come and see the country for himself, and celebrated the Churchill achievements in somewhat over-the-top language even by the standards of that special day. New Zealanders were also being urged, by both their Government and their newspapers, to contribute to the Churchill birthday appeal which in due course helped to launch Churchill College in Cambridge. The *New Zealand Herald* noted the extreme disappointment of many who had made out their appeal cheques to Churchill himself, hoping that he would have to endorse them for transfer to the Appeal fund, and so net them a Churchill autograph when their cheques were eventually returned by their banks; the banks had however scuppered this clever wheeze by agreeing to accept a rubber stamp endorsement for the fund, since there were simply too many cheques for the great man to sign (he was after all still Prime Minister *and* in poor health after his 1953 stroke).[19]

Only five months later, it all had to be done again when Churchill bowed out of office for the last time, *The Dominion* heading its extensive coverage with the words 'Giant among Statesmen Defeated Only by Advancing Years'. Taking their cue from Parliament, all the newspapers devoted a page or more to Churchill's retirement, a review of his career, photo-spreads and generalised adulation. In the House of Representatives, Prime Minister Holland moved a resolution recording Parliament's 'deep appreciation' of Churchill's 'service to the Commonwealth', citing him as a 'continuing inspiration not only to the Commonwealth but to the world'. Churchill, he argued, had like John Bull typified Britain, England and Englishness the world over; he would never retire 'from the special place he holds in the hearts and affections of the British people around the world. We British people are indeed grateful that we have been given such a man.' He reminded the House that no such resolution about a British Prime Minister had ever been proposed before in Wellington, and in due course suggested that the House should further abandon precedent by standing and passing his motion by acclamation. Walter Nash for the Labour Party had a little harmless fun, reminding Government MPs that Churchill was not the sole possession of one New Zealand party, that Churchill himself had in fact belonged to many parties in his time, and that his early life had been rather 'eventful' (something of which Nash had personal memories since he had lived in Birmingham until 1909). Having had his fun, though, Nash associated Labour with the resolution and led his MPs to join in the standing ovation for Churchill that duly followed.[20]

Nor did Churchill's retirement end the process of celebration. In 1958, the House of Representatives, with Nash now Prime Minister and Keith Holyoake leader of the National Party, passed another motion, welcoming the gift of a Churchill portrait to hang in the Parliament House itself. Nash called Churchill 'the greatest man of his age if not of all time in the English-speaking world', and Holyoake thought the hanging of his portrait in 'this replica of the House of Commons at Westminster' was an appropriate tribute to 'the greatest Commoner of our time if not of all time'. Later in the same year, an exhibition of Churchill's own paintings was viewed by large crowds in each of the four New Zealand cities that it visited, with Nash opening the show in Wellington in person. New Zealand received this first-ever exhibition of Churchill art about six months after the USA, but a year before it was shown in London. And so it went on: in 1962 the House was passing a resolution of condolence when Churchill broke his leg, and in 1964 the most fulsome of all such resolutions was prompted by Churchill's retirement from the Commons. On each occasion, Churchill's messages of thanks were duly read into the parliamentary record by the Speaker, as if New Zealand legislators were reluctant to miss even a drop of his interest in their country. And those replies were also suitably flattering: in 1964 Churchill assured his loyal subjects in Wellington that 'I will never forget the staunch friendship and unswerving courage of our brothers and comrades in arms in New Zealand.'[21]

On each of these occasions, the New Zealand press gave plenty of coverage to the stories, reiterating every time the cause of the celebrations in Churchill's war service to the Empire and to freedom worldwide. They also filled in between these events with reports of Churchill's health, his foreign travel, awards and holidays, his books when published, and such events as his Golden Wedding in 1958. Although many of these reports were syndicated, either through the New Zealand Press Association or by reprinting stories from Australian papers, there were invariably attempts to link them directly to the New Zealand people, for example when the views of New Zealand tourists in London could be quoted in association with a Churchill birthday party. And Churchill himself – or at least his staff – was scrupulous in sending appropriate responses to any messages of goodwill, such as the note sent from Chartwell to the students of the King Edward Technical College in Dunedin after they had sent birthday greetings in 1959. That handwritten note was not only framed to hang on the College's walls, but was also reproduced on the front pages of various newspapers, though it said in fact virtually nothing except 'thank you'.[22]

All of this set the stage for Churchill's death and funeral in January 1965, a prolonged process since two weeks passed between the first reports of his illness and the actual day of the funeral – followed in

New Zealand's case by another period of waiting before the BBC film of the funeral could be flown to Wellington and re-edited for transmission on New Zealand television. (In the northern hemisphere satellites and cables by then allowed instantaneous transmission of such events; the Telstar satellite had indeed been first used to allow Churchill himself and the British in general to watch live the Washington ceremony making him an honorary American citizen in 1963.) For two whole weeks, then, all the main New Zealand papers kept the Churchill story on their front pages. The *Otago Daily Times* filled its entire front page with just Churchill's portrait, name and dates when he actually died, and most of the others gave him equally prominent billing.

There seems to be no reason to doubt that New Zealanders in general were caught up in all of this in the same way as the British and North Americans. Once again there were interviews with New Zealanders in London taking part in the process – a tourist joining the vigil outside Churchill's house as he was dying, for example, reported names of New Zealanders who had signed the condolence book in London, a naval officer who would be in the procession, and extensive coverage of those from the Dominion who were taking part in the actual funeral, notably the Archdeacon of St Pauls and an air commodore (both of whom must have been gratified but amazed by the sudden interest taken in them by their countrymen). Likewise, the many picture supplements included not only some of the most famous from Churchill's life but also many taken with New Zealand soldiers like Bernard Freyberg. There seems to have been a considerable popular response too. Parliament and many other local bodies – such as the Whangerei Magistrates' Court – adjourned in respect when the death was reported. New Zealanders observed a two-minute silence on the actual funeral day, during which trains stopped wherever they happened to be, and traffic halted in the city streets, while race meetings and Test match cricket were rescheduled to avoid the day altogether. An official national memorial service was held in the cathedral in Wellington, but many other cities and towns followed suit, and churches, chapels and synagogues were apparently well filled – and not only by the *pakeha*, white New Zealanders: an Anglican Maori congregation in Rotorua paid the especial tribute of singing a hymn normally used as a lament only at Maori funerals.[23] The scale of the popular response can also be seen in the fact that when the British High Commission provided condolence books for signature only in Wellington and Christchurch, it was rapidly reminded that this just would not do. Shortly afterwards, places to sign were also made available in Auckland and Dunedin, and hundreds queued up to add their names to the list in all four cities.[24]

It seems clear, then, that New Zealanders at every level of society wanted to feel involved in the funeral process, and there may be a clue to their motivation in the way in which the press reported the event as a very English one. British and American commentators too were stressing both the Englishness of the occasion and the symbolic nature of Churchill's death as a punctuation mark, denoting the end of Britain as a major force in the world. Given that New Zealand had recently entered into a crisis of identity, occasioned by Britain's first application to join the European Economic Community in 1961,[25] it is not surprising that the 1965 celebrations of Churchill's Englishness reawakened by his death and funeral occasioned similar reflections there. It had been as customary for New Zealand journalists as for Americans to mark Churchill birthdays and honours by making trips 'down in the murky East End of London' for suitable quotations that were then printed in a sort of stage-cockney dialect, but when Churchill died they surpassed themselves. A New Zealand Press Association report, appropriately enough compiled in Churchill Road, Canning Town, was printed in part in every major paper, and at length in the New Zealand Herald, so anxious were they to stress their part in Churchill's Englishness for a last time.

'He was the last of the tough Englishmen,' Joe Stanley was reported as saying; 'I cried when I heard the news,' said eighty-three-year-old Lucy Harvey. 'That's straight up [a subtitle for readers in Auckland here conveying the fact that "straight up" was cockney for "It's the truth"]. I'd have gone in his place. I tell you I would. "A great man?" Why, he was the greatest that ever breathed air.' In case these might seem to be the views only of working-class Tories, Bert Parkins was quoted next: 'It wasn't his politics. I'm Labour Party and a working man and he was a toff, but he had guts ... Politics apart he had guts. He was real English.' Tom Stanley then added the necessary historical perspective: 'You can say that again, mate. If it wasn't for old Winnie, we'd be having a crooked cross [subtitle for Aucklanders: a swastika] here, and that's right, dead right, guv.' Henry Skerritt agreed: 'He gave us Churchill Road. It's not much of a life, but it's life, and it's a damned sight better than a Nazi salute.'[26] Now, leaving aside subversive doubts as to whether anyone except taxi-drivers ever spoke in such a manner, and our natural suspicion that the whole thing was made up on a rainy day by a cynical journalist in a pub, without going anywhere near the East End, the decision to print yards of such stuff when Churchill died does still seem to convey the idea that at least someone in New Zealand saw Churchill, New Zealand and Englishness as inextricably intertwined, with the latter two rather less likely to cohere when the first could no longer mediate between them. This is given further credence by the extraordinary decision of the *Herald*'s editor to place on his front page when Churchill died an account of Winston proclaiming that the educational failings of boys or girls in such matters as Latin and mathematics ought to be treated generously, but that any child who failed to learn English should be whipped, 'and whipped hard'. The concept of the 'English-speaking peoples' had a lot to do with Churchill's image in New Zealand. The Prime Minister himself argued that, through Churchill's funeral, 'in our small way we felt and shared something of the reflected glory of this great Englishman'.[27]

In any case, the view that New Zealanders still wanted to link themselves to the name of Churchill in 1965 is given powerful reinforcement by the fundraising for the Winston Churchill Memorial Trust. The initiative was actually launched by Prime Minister Holyoake when in London for the funeral, to which he had made the longest journey of any of those attending, it still taking three days of travel to get from Wellington to London in 1965. The announcement was given a very favourable response by politicians and press in New Zealand, many of them picking up on the idea of an international trust to support goodwill travel by ordinary people as embodying Churchill's idea of the English-speaking peoples. Wellington's fund all the same evolved rapidly into a specifically New Zealand enterprise with its beneficiaries restricted to New Zealand nationals, rather than forming part of a grander international project as at first envisaged (and no further New Zealand money seems to have gone on to Churchill College, for example, as Alexander had hoped).[28]

Money, however, was raised on a grand scale, especially following a generous start-up cheque for £10,000 from the Auckland Savings Bank and £50,000 from the Government, while Holyoake also cunningly encouraged citizen donations by making gifts of up to £25 tax-deductible. As in Australia, the Returned Servicemen's Association weighed in heavily with support and activities, which is yet more evidence that veterans had no hard feelings about Churchill's war record. Interestingly, it was the New Zealand Labour movement that was least enthusiastic, some trades councils like Wellington's refusing to take any part in the scheme at all, even though the Labour Party officially supported it, so perhaps Tonypandy was still more of a problem for Churchill's reputation than Gallipoli? Banks and businesses paid up, as did the major city councils, and thousands of ordinary people. Within a week, £100,000 had been pledged, and this rose to £150,000 after another month. Progress then rather stalled, and although no official target had been given it seems likely that a quarter of a million pounds had been the unofficial aim (a very large sum indeed for New Zealand in 1965). The appeal was due to end in March, but after further appeals and house-to-house collections it went on into the summer, by which time the fund stood at just over £230,000, though with more to come from covenanted bequests already arranged.[29]

Such a sum provided adequate resources with which to launch the Trust, producing enough interest on its capital to support about fifteen travelling scholarships a year (rather more, relative to population, than was achieved either in Britain or in the USA, but less than Australia). Legislation to put the Trust on a permanent footing was passed during the 1965 Session, with the full support of all parties. The bill provided for beneficiaries to be limited to New Zealand citizens, who should engage in travel for the benefit of their trade or occupation *in* New Zealand, or for the advancement of the Commonwealth 'as a beneficial influence in world affairs'. The Trust would be an independent body, though it would be administered by the Department of Internal Affairs, and care was taken to ensure that its initial membership included a good balance of political opinion. Speakers in favour of the bill were, however, careful to stress that the Trust had a dual purpose, both as a body which would prevent 'the mists of time from too darkly obscuring his memory', and as aiming to achieve tangible results for New Zealanders; they were, said Keith Holyoake, not just 'performing an act of piety'.[30] When assessing which of these two objectives was actually uppermost in legislators' minds, we may note that on the only other occasion on which the Trust was discussed at all in Parliament in its first five years it was because backbenchers were unsure whether New Zealand was getting value for money from the travel awards that had by then been made. In that short debate in 1968 the name of Sir Winston was never even mentioned.[31]

But Churchill's name was to live on in New Zealand in the name of the Trust and in its own attempts to remind its Fellows, and applicants for its Fellowships, of that dual purpose in its origins. Its literature, like that of its sister organisations in other countries, continues to remind readers that 'Sir Winston Churchill believed that world peace and greater international understanding could be promoted through ordinary people travelling to other countries and experiencing other cultures,' and its formal documents continue to bear his photographic portrait (in the Karsh of Ottawa 'angry lion' look). The great man of Empire might not be amused to learn that by the 1990s the Trust was sending as many of its travelling Fellows to countries outside as inside the Commonwealth, but he would have pleasurable feelings if he learned that half of all the New Zealand Churchill Fellows go to America and that over four-fifths of them are still visiting the English-speaking peoples.[32]

There are many other ways in which Churchill's name and face remain visible in contemporary New Zealand. The 1965 proposal to name a new city just south of Auckland after Churchill was not carried out (it became Clevedon instead), but very many streets and public buildings did attract the name, so that there are still about a hundred streets in New Zealand bearing Churchill's name, and many others with related names like 'Chartwell'. This process had started during the 1945 wave of post-war gratitude, hence the frequent proximity of a street named after Montgomery or Portal or Freyberg in the same housing development. There seems to have been a second wave of namings in the 1960s when retirement, death and burial brought Churchill's name back to the fore. This was apparently the basis of the Crofton Downs subdivision of Wellington, where a single suburb grouped around Churchill Drive also contains streets named after Winston, Randolph, Clementine, Sarah and Jerome, Chartwell, Chequers, Commons, Admiralty, Chancellor, Sandhurst, Cavalry, Tower (of London, presumably, but why?), Dundee and Woodford (which indicates that some real research went into this programme of naming). There is also a Chartwell school and a Churchill supermarket, and – apparently as an afterthought – a Thatcher Crescent.[33]

Auckland has a Churchill Club, and a Churchill Park (dedicated in 1945, though some of it was later sold off for housing, since 'even with the help of the name "Churchill", the trees did not thrive'.[34] In the Auckland suburbs there is a Churchill's Olde English Restaurant and a Churchill Takeaway. Hamilton has a Chartwell shopping mall; Rotorua has a Churchill Bar, Marlborough a Churchill Hospital Trust, Gisborne a Churchill Park, and Christchurch a hospital, a sheltered housing complex and a pub. Some of these have a drawing or cartoon of Churchill on their name-board, suggesting that his hat and bow tie still evoke visual recognition too.[35] Too much should not be made of all this of course, for there was a long tradition of naming New Zealand places after imperial heroes, as the cities of Wellington, Nelson and Napier all indicate clearly enough, and things may not always be what they seem anyway. The city of Blenheim in the Province of Marlborough owes its nomenclature to a family member long before Sir Winston, and it has in fact no memorial to Winston Churchill, while it is far from clear that the habit of using Chartwell as a New Zealand name owes anything to Winston Churchill at all: it may well be a corruption of the Charwell river near Kaikoura, itself presumably a corruption of Cherwell and therefore a much earlier English importation.[36] Moreover, the present inhabitants of a Churchill Street or School presumably have little knowledge of its origins anyway: that restaurant in the Auckland suburbs clearly uses his name and face merely as a peg on which to hang its half-timbered 'olde English' identity, rather than being a real act of homage now, while Wellington's Chartwell Drive School now specialises in teaching Japanese and has 'Chartwell' in Japanese as well as English on the board – which asserts its own Pacific identity. It was certainly never a priority of Churchill that the English-speaking peoples should be taught to speak Japanese.[37] All the same, the sheer extent of Churchill's name, across the length and breadth of both islands, and deriving entirely from the post-war years, does remain as striking evidence of what he quite recently meant to New Zealanders at large.

In other ways, too, there are indications that though New Zealanders, like Americans and Britons, memorialised Churchill fairly actively until the 1960s, as New Zealand's international path diverged from Britain's the relevance of Churchill as a link became less significant. The fine portrait of Churchill presented to the people of New Zealand in 1958, for example, the product of a private donation by a well-known philanthropist and admirer of Churchill, Sir John Robert MacKenzie, rather than of a public subscription, does not hang in a prominent place in the Parliament House and is not seen by the public when touring the building. Likewise, the British High Commission has a painting of 'Churchill on the way to Westminster' but it is placed in the residence 'in a non-prominent place' where it too would not be seen by visitors.[38] And in New Zealand, unlike Australia, Britain, Canada and the USA, no statue was ever erected in the capital city to provide a permanent reminder of attitudes that were clear and heartfelt in the 1945–65 period. When the idea was actively mooted in New Zealand in and after 1945, the Labour Government did not give it much support, but, despite the public endorsement of the idea by some of its MPs, neither did the National Party, and when its leader Sidney Holland received correspon- dence urging that he put himself at the head of a great national subscrip- tion, he replied that he simply did not have the time. 'No one is a greater admirer of Mr Churchill than I am,' wrote Holland, and in 1947 he put himself out considerably to entertain Churchill's son Randolph on a speech tour in New Zealand, but memorialising Winston sculp- turally was clearly never a high priority.[39]

Churchill's name has figured from time to time in the more recent historical debate, for example when a National Party television broadcast claimed in 1975 that its leader Robert Muldoon went a 'a little bit Mr Churchill's way', and the maverick politician Winston Peters has natur- ally – given his Christian name – tended to be seen as exhibiting some of Churchill's less desirable political traits, such as changing his party rather too often, but these are fairly superficial links; Muldoon's resem- blance to Churchill was no more than skin-deep, as was that of Margaret Thatcher or Ronald Reagan (who made the same claims, and rather more often), and since Peters' birth certificate spelled Winston with a 'y' rather than a 'i' this too may also be a false trail.[40]

In the 1990s, New Zealand's antique shops seemed to contain little of the memorabilia of Churchill – coins, stamps and toby jugs for instance – that is common in other English-speaking countries, and it does not now have a branch of the International Churchill Society, though one existed as recently as 1990. The intense admiration for Churchill that occasioned the events described above seems now to have faded into much lower-key memories of the man than exist in Canada, for example – a visual and political icon still, but not an active focus of loyalty or identity. As has been shown, Churchill's post-war fame in New Zealand was always closely linked with perceptions of New Zealand's own English heritage, and has not therefore survived the shift to an alternative Pacific region identity that the country has developed since Britain tilted its own international focus towards (if not yet quite into) 'Europe'.

But Churchill himself should not escape some of the responsibility for the relative transience of his impact on opinion in New Zealand, for such imperial outposts were always in practice secondary in his own order of priorities to the North Atlantic world and the special relationship. After all he never made it to New Zealand himself, despite the desperate insistence of New Zealand Governments that he should visit them. He can scarcely be blamed for not wanting to embark on such an arduous trip after he retired at the age of eighty in 1955 – Harold Macmillan in 1958 was the first British Premier ever to visit New Zealand – but there were extended longueurs during his earlier mature career, during the 1930s or in the later 1940s, when he was out of office and could easily have fitted in a visit to Australasia by sea had he really wanted to (as indeed his colleague Anthony Eden did in 1949). The tickertape reception of Field Marshal Montgomery when he visited Auckland shortly after the war, and the equally vigorous welcome given to Mountbatten and to Randolph Churchill when they visited soon afterwards, suggest that Winston Churchill would have been fêted across the length of both islands had he ever gone there, and such personal contacts as he could have made would no doubt have given his reputation there a much greater solidity. It rested in fact on a remarkably small base of personal contacts, friendship with Bernard Freyberg that went back to 1934 (but Freyberg anyway spent much of his later career in Britain),[41] the personal loyalty of Fred Doidge (who anyway died in 1954), and brief meetings with successive New Zealand political leaders when they were in London. There was in New Zealand no Menzies, no Smuts, no Eisenhower, prominent figures who could and did act as cheerleaders for Churchill in their own country.

The Labour leaders Peter Fraser and Walter Nash seemed best able to resist the Churchill charm, but then each of them had also begun their own political lives in the circles of the British left where Churchill was never popular. Fraser, during an important wartime visit to Britain in 1941, did much to help boost the British war effort through his speeches and visits to factories (especially in his native Scotland), but was insistent on portraying a 'people's war' for democracy rather than a nationalist battle led by the aristocratic Churchill. He hailed the coalition rather than the Prime Minister, and thoroughly enjoyed toasting the Soviet Union as the world's best hope against the Nazis, something over which Churchill had to grit his teeth.[42] When revisiting Inverness in 1948, he referred to Franklin Roosevelt as 'the greatest man of our day', a decidedly unconventional choice among the British of that time, and when commiserating with a Scottish socialist friend on British Labour's loss of seats in the 1950 general election, he added encouragingly, 'but at any rate the Tories did not win'.[43] As indicated above, Nash kept a similar distance, though he was more generous than Fraser in paying appropriately graceful tributes to Churchill on the big occasions, visiting him in London as late as 1961 (by which time their combined age was 166 and they could be forgiven for mellowing a little).[44]

By contrast, the very pro-British National Party leaders Sidney Holland and Keith Jacka Holyoake actually knew much less about Britain but had far less trouble falling for Churchill; it is hard to resist the view that in these two cases Churchill gained a great deal of goodwill in return for a very small investment of his time and energy. Holland first visited Britain at the end of the war, accompanied by Fred Doidge, in order to discuss future trading links. At the end of the tour, he made a broadcast to New Zealand about his trip, which described their 'thrill' in visiting the New Zealand troops in Italy, but he continued:

> Our thrills were not at an end, however, for we received an invitation to have lunch, with the one man I would not have missed seeing for worlds. Mr Churchill sent a car for us, and we drove to his [sic] famous home in the country at [sic] Chequers . . . Those happy hours will always remain a treasured memory and incidentally a most valuable experience. I gave Mr Churchill the messages so many people asked me to deliver before I left New Zealand. I told him there was nothing the people would like more than for him to pay us a visit. He said that he had always hoped and still hopes that such a visit may yet be possible. He certainly has a very warm spot in his heart for New Zealand.[45]

A few weeks later, commenting on the results of the British general election to a British Tory correspondent, Holland wrote with detachment and great perception about the failings of British Conservatism and its need to base itself more on the people, as his own party had done, but added, 'I just cannot understand ten thousand people voting against Churchill' in his own constituency.[46]

Holland was as good as his broadcast word in remembering his 1945 meeting with Churchill, referring back to it 'with pride and pleasure', and often.[47] But he was far from sure that Churchill would remember meeting *him*, and his letters to Churchill indicate that he was determined that it should indeed remain in their joint memory ('you may recall doing me the honour of having me to lunch . . .', 20 April 1948; 'May I recall our meeting in 1945 . . .', 1 December 1949). He was usually writing to Churchill to ask him to give up half an hour to meet a New Zealand dignitary who was visiting London, and Churchill seems usually to have agreed, but at little personal cost since this was at most an annual task.[48] There was in any case an easy meeting of minds, as was indicated when in 1948 the National Party was seeking an introductory paragraph from Churchill for its newspaper, *Freedom*. Holland assured Churchill that his party 'do not and will not forget your services to our Empire down the years', adding that 'in this distant outpost we feel very concerned at recent trends and attitudes towards our great Empire', notably the tendency to drop the word 'British' when substituting Commonwealth for Empire; the National Party sought rather to 'kindle the fires of patriotism and to re-awaken in the people the love of and loyalty to the British Empire'. Churchill, no doubt moved by such loyal sentiments right after his own heart, duly responded with a paragraph beginning, 'Far in distance but close to our hearts, New Zealand sets an example of love and loyalty to the British Empire . . .'[49] Such correspondence was triggered, however, almost entirely from the Holland end, with Churchill merely responding on cue, but he did add Holland to the list of those who received signed copies of his books. In 1952 he sent him a more unusual piece of memorabilia, a fine (coloured) example of one of Clement Attlee's celebrated doodles (which was also duly filed for posterity).[50]

On the face of it, Keith Holyoake ought to have been less of a pushover for the Churchill charm offensive, for 'Kiwi Keith' is popularly supposed to have been responsible as Prime Minister for promoting in the 1960s the reorientation of New Zealand's trade and loyalties away from Britain.[51] In fact, though, a single afternoon spent with Churchill in 1952, this time at Chartwell, had much the same effect on Holyoake that the 1945 meeting had had on Holland. He continued to refer back to it as the greatest event in his life for years afterwards, and his only biographer so far took the hint by introducing a series of rather improbable comparisons between Holyoake's career and Churchill's.[52] Holyoake's actual recollections of the meeting at Chartwell varied on different occasions (including confusion even as to which year it had occurred in), but he was absolutely constant in asserting that he had spent several hours alone with Churchill, that Churchill had shown him 'all his treasures', that he had 'talked about so many things that I did not have much to say', and that it would all live in his memory for ever.[53] Like Holland, Holyoake's loyalty to the Churchill charm was also cemented by the regular receipt of signed copies of the books as they came out, and through other memorabilia such as a Churchill cigar. These he counted among his most treasured possessions.[54] In this context, Holyoake's long trek to the funeral, his extravagant eulogies for Churchill in January 1965, and his sponsorship of the Memorial Trust, even while reorientating his foreign policy away from Britain, because British policy had made this necessary, all become easy to understand. Association with Churchill, right into the mid-1960s, was seen as conferring a touch of Churchill's greatness on his perceived 'friends', the recipients of his time and of his attention. For Robert Muldoon, ten years later and too young to have met Churchill, a much cruder claim had to be made.

If Churchill was operating in a buyer's market when purchasing the allegiance of Holland and Holyoake, he laid out little more of his capital when writing about New Zealand in those books that they so treasured. The war memoirs contain suitable passages in celebration of Kiwi valour and loyalty, and single out Freyberg for special praise as a commander, but (as in most other ways) they stick closely to the view of the war as seen from Churchill's own perspective. There is, for example, little to indicate an understanding of the problems caused for the Australasians by his insistence on putting the Middle East ahead of their own defence from Japanese invasion.[55]

More surprisingly, though (given its title), the History of the English-Speaking Peoples was equally centred on the Atlantic and the northern hemisphere. The structure of the work did not allow for any discussion of New Zealand in the first three volumes, which took the story up to the end of the eighteenth century, and those volumes were respectfully

'King Alfred . . . King Harold . . . Queen Elizabeth . . . William Pitt . . .'
Daily Express, 24 April 1956

received and reviewed in New Zealand.[56] (For those New Zealanders
who like Churchill himself saw their history before 1780 as inseparable
from British history, this emphasis on the British heritage was presumably no great problem.) When, however, Churchill reached the final
volume, on the period 1815–1914, New Zealand received only the most
perfunctory of mentions, a mere four pages tacked on to seven on
Australia, and placed immediately before a hundred pages on the United
States in the same period.[57] Nor were those pages written with any great
verve, or with much sign that Churchill rather than his research assistants
had put them together in the first place and worked over them in later
drafts. The material on New Zealand was drafted before the war, and
when Alan Hodge as Churchill's chief research assistant went over the
text to restart work on it in 1953, he reported that New Zealand already
had 'its measure' (though at that stage the text included nothing on
Australia). Subsequent amendments to the various succeeding drafts
were almost all in Hodge's or Denis Kelly's handwriting, the effect of
which was to *reduce* the section on New Zealand from its original 2500
words to the 1500 eventually published. It is notable that no specialist
in Imperial history seems to have been among the team of historians
who advised on the book (which is perhaps why at one stage the chapter
including New Zealand was to have been called 'The New Continent'),
and that nobody in New Zealand was put on the list of a hundred or

more friends and celebrities who would receive free, inscribed copies. The *Daily Mail's* reviewer, noting that Canada also received only six pages in the book, wondered 'why did Churchill forget Sir John?' (Mac-Donald, Canada's first Prime Minister, who was not even mentioned); but similar points might have been made about all the Dominions, whose under-emphasis in a book of that title was studied and insulting. Churchill manages to describe the formation of New Zealand without mentioning the key figures of George Grey, Julius Vogel or Richard Seddon. Arthur Bryant, writing in the *Sunday Times*, agreed with Clement Attlee's famous suggestion that the entire series should have been called 'Bits of history that interested me', and added that the four volumes were in fact merely a political and military history of Britain, to which had been added only 'a picture in miniature of the creation of the United States'.[58]

Even when describing events outside Australasia in which New Zealanders had played an active and loyal part, for example in the Boer War, there is no mention of the fact. It is not hard to see how a Churchill fully motivated to his task could have drawn a graphic picture of far-off but loyal New Zealand sending over six thousand soldiers to fight for the Motherland in South Africa (a larger proportion of its population than was sent by any other part of the Empire), of the gallantry and resource that its soldiers displayed, of the public subscriptions that paid for much of the military effort, and indeed of the impeccably Imperial sentiments with which New Zealand's premier received the news of the war in the first place, but all of these opportunities for Churchill's purplest prose were allowed to pass by.[59]

R. M. Burdon, when reviewing for New Zealand's *Listener* magazine volume three of the series, had drawn attention to Churchill's own preface in which he stated that he had concentrated on events that most interested him, which Burdon thought to be 'foreign policy, foreign wars and famous leaders'. If this was so – as it undeniably was – then the inescapable moral to be drawn from the final volume was that Churchill actually had little interest in New Zealand. It was, however, a conclusion that was far too painful for New Zealanders to draw, which presumably explains why the final volume seems to have scarcely received a review in the country.[60] This view, at the end of his career, was at least consistent with the position that he had taken up in his maiden parliamentary speech more than half a century earlier, in which he had indeed rhapsodised over the Boer War role of 'the humblest farmer in the most distant province' of the Empire, but in saying this had praised Canada and Australia and ignored New Zealand. Nor was this concentration on the North Atlantic new in the last phase of Churchill's career, when the *History* was published, for an analysis of speeches delivered over his entire career reveals the same focus of attention. The eight volumes of collected Churchill speeches contain four on Australia (only one of which was delivered after 1921), and none at all on New Zealand, but seventeen on Canada and forty-four on the United States (in each case spanning more than fifty years of his political career). The index to the eight volumes bears out this finding in the 'General Subject Guide', with twenty-three mentions of Australia and six of New Zealand, but thirty-eight references to Canada and literally hundreds to the USA. These are crude measurements, but the order of priorities that they reveal is absolutely unmistakable.[61]

Such indications of Churchill's *lack* of commitment to the British Imperial side of his English-speaking peoples bring us back to where we started. Between 1945 and 1965, there was a convergence of interest between Churchill and many New Zealanders, in the articulation of a continuing imperial dimension to New Zealand's life and international identity, and very real personal admiration by large numbers of New Zealanders for what Churchill the man had actually done between 1940 and 1945. Was there not, though, an element of delusion on both sides, brought to the surface by the shift of actual British international policy during the 1960s, but too recently and too painfully perhaps to limit the very real Kiwi celebration of all that Churchill stood for, for the last time, in 1965? This meant that there was therefore less reason for the permanent celebration of Churchill in New Zealand that has occurred in Canada and in the United States, where his post-war presence, his practical commitment to co-operation and the continuing convergence of foreign policies after 1965 combined to ensure that his posthumous reputation there rested on firmer ground. As the 'Britain of the South' ceased to define itself that way, the memory of 'the greatest living Englishman' seemingly had less purchase on its citizens' hearts and minds.

10

'Bad Stock': Churchill and Australia[1]

AT FIRST SIGHT, Churchill's post-war reputation in Australia is a bundle of irreconcilable paradoxes. He was in 1915 the principal author (if not quite the 'onlie begetter') of the ill-fated Gallipoli expedition which cost more than six thousand Australian lives and scarred the national consciousness for decades; in the Second World War he committed Australian troops to the doomed Greek and Crete campaigns of 1941, and he impugned their sticking-power and their martial valour over Tobruk and Singapore, and yet he was loved and honoured after 1945 by the principal Australian veterans' organisation, the Returned Servicemen's League. He was regularly at loggerheads with Australian governments of all parties from 1941 onwards, signally failing to place Australia's interests on a par with those of Britain, and in 1941–2 treated the young Robert Menzies quite brutally, yet most Australian politicians of that generation seem to have continued to admire him hugely, while Menzies became one of his greatest fans. Churchill never visited Australia, despite clamorous appeals for him to do so, and may indeed have doubted his reception had he come, having a low opinion both of Australia and of its leaders. Some Australian historians have argued like David Day that he 'betrayed' Australia, callously and quite deliberately, in the early years of the war, and yet his name continues to be honoured in the naming of Australian streets, parks and at least one school. While there was some opposition to the celebration of all things Churchillian in post-war Australia (more anyway, and more openly, than in any other English-speaking country except Ireland), Australia nevertheless fundraised more successfully than anywhere else for a permanent

Churchill memorial when he died in 1965, and its Winston Churchill Memorial Trust still flourishes, sending dozens of Australians abroad each year in Churchill's memory. In the closing decades of Churchill's century, Australians continued to use Churchill's words and his political legacy in ordinary political discourse, their leaders to express their admiration. As the century ended, Australia was indeed led by John Winston Howard, who had been named after the great man in 1939 and still talked in interviews of Churchill as his greatest political hero.

None of this began in 1945 or even in 1940, as mention of Gallipoli indicates. Australians began to celebrate the deeds of Winston Churchill before the Commonwealth itself came into existence, with widespread newspaper accounts of his escape from Boer captivity in 1900. Melbourne and Sydney had already named streets after his father Lord Randolph Churchill, and the celebratory tone of those reports in 1900 already indicated the way in which Winston would always be perceived, as an adventurous British patriot, most popular with the Australians for whom the British connection was a central thread of their own identity and least admired by such oppositional Australians as the Victorian Irish, some of whom were as sceptical of Britain's South African War as were the Irish back home. Churchill, for his part, first met Australian troops in South Africa in 1900 and was not impressed by either their discipline or their professionalism, probably never overcoming that initial impression that Australians were a rough lot. His continuing association with Imperial Britishness is indicated clearly enough with the naming of a few Churchill thoroughfares after him even before 1914, for example at Munster in Western Australia in 1913, during development of the Henderson naval base near Perth for the new Royal Australian Navy, while Churchill was First Lord of the Admiralty.[2]

Gallipoli and its aftermath apparently caused many Australians to question the Imperial connection and the leadership of the Empire by such scions of the British ruling class as Churchill, though this was never a simple response.[3] In the first place, the overall Australian reaction to Gallipoli was a double one, for in forging the country's very identity these battles had inevitably produced positive memories and national pride as well as the negative horror of lives wasted.[4] It would have been difficult to reject outright the author of the campaign that had produced such an ambiguous effect, and when Churchill's defence of his own actions was produced, in *The World Crisis*, it was respectfully received

and reviewed in Australia as elsewhere.[5] In December 1918, shortly after
the Armistice, Churchill himself paid eloquent tribute to 'the fame of
the Anzacs', in a speech to the Australia and New Zealand luncheon club
in London. Australasia had poured forth 'a stream of virile manhood,
unsurpassed among all the great contending nations', and had also
'produced from civilian elements that degree of military genius and
careful staff work without which bravery has so often failed to obtain
its objective'. The latter point was fairly easily decoded as an attack on
such career generals as Haig and on the staff work of the British army,
and would no doubt have gone down well among his listeners. Three
years later he was addressing the same audience, on Anzac Day itself,
in words that might have been heard at scores of similar commemorations all across Australia.

> The celebration of Anzac day has already taken a definite place
> in the British Empire, and our gathering is only one of many.
> These celebrations will continue as long as the British Empire
> endures, and as long as Australia and New Zealand are the
> home of a free, warlike race of British stock.

The mere fact that Churchill was chosen to address such a gathering
on such a day indicates clearly enough that he was not seen – at least
by Australians in London – as unacceptable. In any case, the main focus
of Australian rhetorical attacks on Britain during and after the Great
War was the stereotypical image of effete, selfish and weak-minded
aristocracy, which hardly matched Churchill's classless *un*gentlemanly
and red-blooded political style, and at the 1921 lunch he was careful to
portray himself as, like the Anzacs, a victim of Gallipoli rather than its
progenitor. Even such inter-war Australian polemics as *The Sporting
English: From Frontline to Bodyline* did not therefore single Churchill
out as a particular villain, and his entire indifference to cricket may at
least have saved him from getting involved in the nastier Anglo-
Australian disputes over bowling tactics in the 1930s. When Don Bradman finally recovered from the attack of peritonitis that almost killed
him at the end of the Australians' 1934 tour, Churchill was – most
improbably – on hand at Victoria Station to see him off on his journey
home. In fact that meeting on 18 December 1934 was fortuitous: Don
and Jessie Bradman were leaving on the boat train when Churchill was
also seeing off his wife for a four-month cruise. However, noting the

dense crowds who had indeed come to see Bradman off, Churchill asked the *Daily Mail* journalist Tom Clarke to introduce them. Clarke implausibly insisted to Bradman that Churchill was 'a keen cricket fan' who merely wanted to shake his hand. Though Bradman initially demurred ('I am only a cricketer . . . What are we going to talk about?'), he eventually agreed to pose with Churchill for a press photographer, a contrived photo-opportunity from which Churchill was the only beneficiary. Bradman would soon become a firm admirer of Churchill as a result of 1940, but mutual interest in cricket had nothing whatsoever to do with it.[6]

Churchill had, though, already established himself by the 1930s as an international political figure with a sharp profile down-under, if one of whom leading Australians were somewhat wary.[7] Australia's Great War Prime Minister Billy Hughes had a stock of Churchill stories from 1917–19 with which he was still regaling colleagues in the 1940s, while his own premiership had come to an undignified end in 1921 partly because his suspicious Country Party allies had not allowed him to go to an Imperial Conference in London, lest he be seduced by 'the most brilliant improvisations' of Lloyd George and Churchill into agreeing something contrary to Australia's interests.[8] Richard Nixon once defined one of the attributes of a great man as the ability to make an unforgettable impression at a first meeting,[9] and Churchill was able to do this with such prominent Australians as R. G. Casey who briefly served under him in the trenches in 1915 and dined with him as soon as he returned to London in 1924,[10] Earle Page who met him to co-ordinate Imperial financial policy after the return to the Gold Standard in 1925,[11] and S. M. Bruce when they met at an Imperial Conference in 1926. There were also several prominent Australian industrialists within Churchill's wide circle of international contacts, notably W. S. Robinson of the Zinc Company and Clive Baillieu of Broken Hill Proprietary.[12] Churchill was indeed the only British politician well enough known in Australia to be invited in 1933 as an official guest for the combined centenary celebrations of the State of Victoria and the City of Melbourne in the following year (the others officially invited were Malcolm Campbell, J. M. Barrie, Rudyard Kipling and the royal Countess of Athlone).[13] We should not perhaps make too much of the fact that he did not accept the invitation, for neither did any of the others on the initial list, the eventual British guests being the Duke of Gloucester, John Masefield

and Lord Milne.[14] It is, however, significant that when Clementine Churchill was to visit the East Indies and Australasia in 1934–5 Winston chose
not to go with her. Nothing would in fact have been better for Churchill's
career and reputation than to miss the final debates on the Government
of India Bill and his son's by-election candidacy as an independent
Conservative, events which estranged him from his party and kept him
out of office for the rest of the decade, while he could presumably
have progressed his *Marlborough* biography substantially during the
prolonged periods at sea, but there was never much chance that he
would have agreed to do so.[15] Clementine therefore came to Australia
early in 1935 without Winston, though Australian newspapers thought
both this and Randolph Churchill's by-election to be worth reporting.[16]
Over the next few years, Churchill's own political activities attracted a
good deal of attention in the Australian press too, notably his trenchant
speeches in favour of greater armaments and a more robust policy
towards Nazi Germany, despite his being on both counts well adrift
from the more pacific preferences of the Australian as well as the British
Governments.

In Churchill's finest hour in the second half of 1940, however,
Australians joined the rest of the Empire in developing a deep admiration
for him, fuelled above all by hearing his great radio speeches, rebroadcast
by the ABC, and from press reports mainly recycled from British and
American newspapers. Australians heard Churchill himself (or at least
thought that they had done so, though in a few cases it may have been
the actor Norman Shelley, who occasionally impersonated the Prime
Minister for overseas listeners),[17] and would generally have heard his
words personally before the local newspapers had reported them. Later
tributes to Churchill's war leadership invariably harked back in Australia
as elsewhere to the broadcasts of 1940, as part of Australia's own war.
A Sydney paper, for example, printed in August 1945 a reader's letter
arguing that 'all through the dark days of the war his broadcasts were
like a clarion call to the nation. What the Empire owes him we shall
never know in full.' When four years later Churchill attended the Alamein reunion, the same paper headlined its story, 'The voice they
knew'.[18] The centrality of Churchill to Australia's perception of its own
war effort is further underlined by the way in which his name and face
were used to recruit for Australia's armed forces and in the sale of
war bonds. Melbourne's big stores made photographs of Churchill the

centrepiece of window-displays for such patriotic purposes in 1940 and early 1941, and the displays were themselves then photographed by the city's newspapers. Australian papers were also keen to publish photographs of Churchill visiting Australian troops in the Middle East, the juxtaposition of lines of slouch-hats with Churchill's familiar pork-pie bowler providing a powerful symbol of Australians following his lead.[19] As an Australian biographer wrote in January 1941, 'the Empire should, and I think does, thank God for Mr Churchill'.[20]

This was all fine in the first months of Churchill's war premiership, until the spring of 1941, when the focus of the war was on the Battle of Britain and the Blitz, for during that period Australians could admire Britain and its leader unreservedly. Churchill seems indeed to have tried hard to maintain exactly that spirit of admiration, for when confronted by critical Australian emissaries one of his favourite ploys was to take them with him on a tour of bombed areas of Britain, as he did with both Menzies in 1941 and H. V. Evatt in 1942, so enabling them to witness at the same time both his own popularity and the fortitude of the British under fire. It no doubt also cheered the bombed civilians with reminders of allies across the sea.[21] Earle Page noted that, when in November 1941 he reiterated Australia's demand for better air provision for the defence of Singapore, Churchill whisked him off 'the same day' to inspect bomb damage in East Anglia.[22] Incensed by later Churchillian hints that Australia was not pulling its weight in the war, John Curtin tried the same trick, issuing jointly in his own name and that of General Douglas MacArthur an invitation to Churchill to visit Australia in 1942 and see for himself the hive of war activity. But Churchill was not to be drawn and asked Curtin to come to London instead.[23]

Once Australian troops were deployed in significant numbers in the Middle East, and especially as the threat of a Japanese war loomed during the second half of 1941, Australia's interests and Britain's were no longer quite the same, but neither could now instinctively imagine the world as the other naturally saw it. It is notable, for example, that while Churchill received news of Pearl Harbor in December 1941 with jubilation (because it meant that America was now a British ally and the war was therefore bound to be won in the end), Australians received it with something more like consternation (since it exposed their own country to attack and possible invasion by the Japanese – while the pick of their army was manning Tobruk rather than Darwin). Similarly, when

Churchill told Menzies insouciantly that Australia was bound to receive a bit of a 'mauling' until its allies could get there to help in its defence, he was no doubt thinking of the substantial mauling that Britain itself had received in 1940–1. Despite Menzies' own deep admiration for the British people's steadiness under fire, he could not be expected to receive Churchill's acceptance of a similar fate for Australia with the same equanimity. Australians urged the reinforcement of Singapore during autumn 1941, before Japan went to war, and indeed in the hope of deterring it from doing so, but Churchill merely promised immediate reinforcement as soon as war actually began in the east (and in the meantime used the troops where they were needed right then). Australia demanded that any Japanese invasion of Thailand should be treated as a *casus belli* by the British Empire, but Churchill refused to give such a promise, since he knew that he dared not move a step ahead of Roosevelt.[24]

In all of this, Churchill's views become much more understandable when it is remembered how completely he underestimated the Japanese, mainly because of racial assumptions that prevented him from grasping that Asians might ever defeat trained European armies in approximately equal numbers. As we have seen, on the very eve of Pearl Harbor, he confided to a journalist that if the Japanese did go to war, then they would 'fold up like the Italians. The Japs are the wops of the Far East.'[25] Australians were hardly exempt from the same racial assumptions, but they had also had half a century of worrying about the threat to their empty continent from Asia, and they were anyway just too near to Japan to be as confident as Churchill could afford to be: Britain's 'far east' was Australia's 'near north'. Of course, when war did come to the region in December 1941, it was the European colonies that folded up before Japan's headlong onslaught, rather than the Japanese themselves, and there proved to be no time to get troops there from other theatres of war in time to affect the outcome. It was thus Australian rather than Churchillian assumptions that seemed to have been vindicated, though limited bombing of one Australian city, Darwin, hardly constituted a 'mauling' comparable to what Britain experienced in 1940–1, and the invasion threat to Australia never materialised either, mainly because the Americans, whom Churchill had been above all else determined to draw into the Pacific war should it happen, were indeed there – *just* in time – to win the battles of the Coral Sea and Midway.

Whether all this amounts to a great Churchillian betrayal of Australia, as David Day has argued,[26] is more dubious, and so far Australian historians have not been persuaded that he has made out his case. For 'betrayal' would surely require proof that Churchill *knew* that he was wrong in his predictions about Japanese military capability, and (far more damagingly for his broader historical reputation as a military strategist) this just does not seem to have been the case. More likely there were simply misplaced assumptions and different perspectives imposed by geographical distance and diverging national interests. So, for example, when Churchill argued (probably anyway a case of his thinking aloud in a characteristically provocative manner) that were Australia to be invaded and conquered then it could easily be liberated later, when the real war had been won elsewhere, he was probably right. It is far harder to imagine a scenario in which Hitler could ever have been beaten if Britain had once surrendered, for the task of re-invading Europe from the other side of the Atlantic and without air cover would surely have proved impossible. But, whatever the logic, it was hardly to be expected that Australians would view it that way, or indeed that Churchill himself would have done so, had roles been reversed and he had been sitting in Canberra rather than London. And in all probability his failure ever to visit Australasia was a fatal inhibition to his ability to imagine what the world looked like from that perspective, either then or later, while Australians' wartime brusqueness in arguing their case led him to talk about the 'troublesome attitude of the colonies' (sic) and no doubt reinforced his conviction that not much better was to be expected from a people of such inferior racial stock, mostly derived from either Irish migrants or convicts,[27] much the same view of racial hierarchies indeed that had led him to write off the Japanese in the first place.

Churchill therefore had a series of wartime disputes with Australian governments, whether led by Menzies and Fadden[28] from the right or by Labor's Curtin from the left, and from 1941 onwards he was constantly harried by Australian special representatives in London, Menzies himself, Page, Casey and Evatt. Casey, a sympathiser who nevertheless noted in 1942 that Churchill 'gets more like Henry VIII every year', was defiantly told by the Prime Minister, 'you can't kick me around the room. I'm not kickable.'[29] They disputed over the deployment of Australian troops in the Middle East and to Crete, a period of rest for the Australians garrisoning Tobruk, the reinforcement of Singapore, the return of troops from the Middle East to defend Australia (when Churchill first refused to find shipping and then redirected the Australians to Burma without even consulting Canberra), and the dispatch of fighters and bombers to enable the RAAF to play its part in Australia's defence. Churchill was deeply hurt by Curtin's grand declaration that henceforth Australia would look to America rather than Britain for its defence (as indeed was Roosevelt, who saw it as close to treason to America's most important ally, though it was the logical consequence of his own 'Europe first' policy for the war), and did not scruple to threaten use of his friendship with Roosevelt to undermine Curtin's standing with his new defender. Exchanges of views by cable sometimes became extremely sharp – even though Churchill's staff usually persuaded him to tone down his initial belligerence. In the case of Churchill's precipitate appointment of the Australian Casey to a ministerial post in his Government, after inadequate time to prepare the ground in Canberra, he confounded his mistake by telling Curtin that he would like Menzies to succeed Casey as Australian representative in Washington, which was none of his business and, thought Casey, 'a dreadful blunder'.[30]

These last confrontational exchanges were promptly published by Curtin, and on another occasion he offered trenchant views on Churchill's running of the war in a signed article in the Melbourne press. On the other side, the BBC's damaging (and false) story that Curtin was during the war crisis of January 1942 taking a holiday could only have been broadcast with the approval of the British censors, and in this case probably the prior knowledge of Downing Street.[31] Though assailed by Australians of all parties, Churchill seems indeed to have entertained a particular dislike for Curtin: Labor's Evatt accused him to the British Labour minister Stafford Cripps of praising Menzies in a speech, 'solely to make political play with our Prime Minister'.[32] (Evatt also made sure that Cripps, Churchill's rival in British war leadership in 1942, knew exactly how critical Menzies was of Churchill when talking to Australians – he had described Churchill as 'suffering from a dictatorship complex which approached megalomania' – which rather suggests that the party-politicking was going on in both directions.) When Evatt himself in due course persuaded Churchill to send back some Spitfire squadrons to the Australian theatre of war, he first theatrically accepted Evatt's case by overruling his air advisers in Evatt's presence, and then covertly made sure that the fighters did not actually return until after the pending Australian election, in case they helped Curtin to win. As Brendan Bracken said of Evatt, 'He came, he saw, and Churchill conquered.'[33] In fact Curtin won re-election easily, as Churchill should have expected if his Australian intelligence had been better. Being seen though to have publicly antagonised Curtin, who after his early death in 1945 became (as W. J. Hudson put it) 'a secular saint' in post-war Australia, can have done little good for Churchill's standing there, despite Sir Paul Hasluck's later demolition of much of the pro-Curtin, anti-Churchill case. In this context it is not entirely surprising that Australian Labor took a positive view of Churchill's own defeat in the British post-war general election, the *Canberra Times* headlining its story 'Labor glee at Canberra'. In some quarters, such a view of Churchill never faded, though it became increasingly rare actually to express it. When Sydney's *Bulletin* printed an unusually restrained Churchill obituary in 1965, it nevertheless upset one reader, who wrote to complain that:

Churchill is not an Australian hero and most Australians know that he declared us expendable. He retained the RAAF in England; he wanted to deploy Australian troops in Burma. In short he cared nothing for Australia as long as England's interests were being looked after. Let France and West Germany honour him, but let us honour the men who looked after this country.

The writer came, ironically, from Concord, NSW, but it was probably far from coincidental that he bore the Irish name John O'Leary.[34]

More generally, Australians like the rest of the world were simply surprised by Churchill's landslide electoral defeat, but the Australian press perhaps reflected Churchill's now ambivalent reputation there in reporting the news relatively coolly, the only notes of alarm being aroused by reported concern in Washington and jubilation in India. The overall mood was much like that of Richard Casey, who wrote in his diary, 'Thumping win for Labour who have clear majority over all other parties. At least 9 Conservative ministers beaten. The people of the UK know their own minds.'[35] Even Australian papers on the right reported Labour's victory in Britain without undue alarm, as well they might when their own country had a popular Labor government which openly identified itself with Attlee's triumph (the ALP held a rally in

Sydney to celebrate the British election result).[36] Quite a few papers prominently reported the defeat of Churchill's family and such friends as Bracken among the Conservative casualties, and the large vote for an independent standing against Churchill himself, so at least hinting that the result was partly a reaction against Churchill himself. But most of them editorialised in a quite contrary direction, writing elegiacally that the result reflected no rejection of Churchill in person, or any lack of gratitude for his war service. The *Canberra Times*, for example, argued that 'nothing can alter the place that he has earned in the hearts of his people or the history of his race. He has suffered political casualty in the contest which mattered least' (which is certainly not what Churchill himself thought at the time).[37]

Almost all editors wrote such columns and news reports in the tone reserved for political obituaries, and it is clear that no Australian commentators envisaged the seventy-year-old Churchill ever returning to power. Cartoons and editorials on the theme of 'dropping the pilot' – first applied to Bismarck's departure from office and now reapplied to Churchill, on whom the naval cap fitted more appositely – involved both a confirmation of the man's stature and achievement and an assumption of finality. The Hobart *Mercury*, for example, argued that 'despite the temporary blow to his prestige, it may be better that he should leave office at the height of his fame, his historic task done, rather than risk loss of reputation in the hurly-burly of party politics' (Churchill would not have agreed with that either).[38] One or two put all of this more brutally: Brisbane's *Courier-Mail*, having captioned a (very small) photograph of Churchill on the front page with the single word 'Rejected', added an editorial in which the theme was 'Goodbye, good luck and farewell'. The *Sydney Morning Herald*, guessing at the offer of a peerage that would shortly come Churchill's way, urged him to retire from the Commons and write his memoirs, since his party needed a fresh start under a different leader.[39]

Within days, however, it was clear that Churchill would not bow out gracefully, since news of his rejection of a dukedom and the Garter was in all the Australian papers. It was also clear that Churchill would continue to divide Australians on party lines, for on 2 August, less than a week after the British election results, Arthur Fadden for the Liberal–Country Party Opposition proposed in the House of Representatives that Australia should formally thank Churchill for his war services to the Empire. Ben Chifley, leading the Labor Government since Curtin's death, refused to allow standing orders to be suspended to allow such a motion to be debated, arguing that Members would need time to think about it, and adding when challenged that it all 'seemed to have political implications'. He noted that, 'from time to time', Curtin and other ministers had expressed 'their warm admiration of the war work done by Mr Churchill as Britain's war leader' (a somewhat selective account of the previous four years) 'but whether this House should carry a motion about a matter which concerns another country is a matter to which I would like to give some thought'. If it had not been political so far, it certainly became so after this ungenerous response. Critics in Parliament and the press pointed out that the British Labour Party had served under Churchill in a National Government in the period to be covered by any congratulatory motion, and that Chifley had indeed already sent a fulsome telegram of congratulations to Attlee after he had beaten Churchill out of office. Chifley's claim that he had congratulated Attlee as the leader of a party, while refusing to congratulate Churchill in his separate capacity as head of the Australian Government, did not convince many that he too was not acting 'politically'.[40]

Churchill himself was the same week telling his doctor that 'they want me to go to Australia and New Zealand, but I haven't the heart or strength or life for it'. The *Sydney Morning Herald* nevertheless editorialised scathingly ('A Little Matter of Honour') against Chifley, arguing that his attitude was spiteful and demeaning for a national leader, and many other papers took the same line, printing angry letters from readers to reinforce the point. None of this appears to have impressed Chifley in the least, for the following year, in approving speeches on Britain's war effort, he did not even mention Churchill. He was no doubt reinforced in his hostility by Churchill's own attacks on Australian Labor's nationalisation plans and the regular quoting of Churchill's anti-socialist speeches by Australian Liberals.[41]

The divisive nature of Churchill's name and image in Australian party politics had no equivalent in New Zealand, Canada or the United States. In all of these places, though the right naturally celebrated his achievements more than the left, all parties strove to associate themselves with his fame. In Britain of course he was at least as polarising a figure as he was in Australia. Ironically, however, it was from that fiasco of early August 1945 that Churchill's standing in Australia began its recovery, for

448 MAN OF THE CENTURY

his supporters redoubled their efforts, probably sensing a stick with which to beat their own Government. When Parliament reconvened on 29 August, the gloves came off. Chifley's speech reviewing the war as a whole paid tribute to the leaders of the Allied cause by mentioning with equal warmth Churchill, Attlee, Roosevelt, Truman and Curtin, but this was far from satisfying the Opposition.

Emboldened by Menzies' eloquent support for Churchill as Australia's war leader as well as Britain's, Fadden too now referred to Churchill as leading 'the British Commonwealth of Nations' through the war, and paid tribute to his services 'to the British Empire, and indeed to civilisation'. He also twisted the knife by pointing out that both Attlee and New Zealand's Labour Prime Minister Peter Fraser had made generous remarks about Churchill in their speeches on the end of the war, suggesting that Australian Labor was uniquely spiteful in refusing to do the same.[42] If Chifley ever contemplated changing his mind, this sally made it impossible for him to do so, and the matter then dropped – except that a year later Harold Holt reminded the House that Chifley had asked for time to think about Fadden's original motion, and enquired sardonically how long it would be before he was ready to come forward with the results of his cognitive processes. This gave Fadden the chance to read his motion for a third time, with even more extravagant rhetoric in its support, though this doubtless also owed something to Churchill's growing international recovery of prestige after his Fulton speech: Churchill was now 'the greatest man which the British Empire has produced during the last century, perhaps the greatest indeed who has ever served civilisation'. A Melbourne paper wrote that 'to dodge the payment of this well-earned tribute would be a piece of pettiness and bad grace which we hope our legislators would not deliberately commit'. But the Government again took refuge in procedural devices and made no substantive response.[43]

Three years later the refusal to thank Churchill formally for his war leadership was still rankling: in a debate in which a Labour Member had blamed Churchill and Roosevelt for the spread of Communism throughout Europe, because of the deal made at Yalta, the Liberal Member L. W. Hamilton rounded on the ALP with memories of their lack of generosity in earlier debates: 'Any honourable member who would ridicule Mr Churchill in this Parliament ought to hang his head in shame, and the members of a Government which countenances such utterances ought to be ashamed of themselves.' Liberals could also use Churchill aggressively as well as defensively in this party-political manner, as when their New South Wales State Council cabled Churchill in 1947 to express the hope 'that once again under your leadership Britain will have the courage to cut the socialist cancer which is sapping her heart, lowering her living standards and destroying her prestige'. This message was clearly at least as much a commentary on Australian as on British politics.[44]

Thwarted by Labor's majority, the Opposition could do no more, though their failure to pass – or even to resubmit for debate – Fadden's 1945 motion when they won power in 1949 does rather suggest that Chifley had been right to argue that it was all 'political'. In the meantime, they could only pay tributes to Churchill in other ways. In Western Australia, where Labor was not the majority party, the Legislative Council passed in September 1945 a motion of thanks to Churchill for 'his leadership of the British nation during its long struggle against aggression' and 'for the example that he has shown to every citizen of the British Empire, and, in fact, of the world'. The terms of the debate make it quite clear that supporters of the motion considered Australians to be included still in 'the British nation', as well as in the Empire and the world. Churchill's accession to the Admiralty in 1911 had been, it was argued, 'a turning point in the history of our race', and the debate was also replete with appreciative citations of Cecil Rhodes, Kitchener, Kipling and Pitt. The motion passed without a vote, even though the ministerial respondent to the debate had repeatedly needled Labor with references to Attlee giving Churchill 'the credit that he deserved', and even by saying that Churchill had 'galvanised' Australia's war effort. He had also scaled down the contribution of Curtin.[45]

Western Australia was also the source of one of Churchill's most treasured gifts, the black swans that adorned the lake at Chartwell, though since the Kentish foxes regularly helped themselves to a free meal, they had to be equally regularly reinforced with new gifts of the same type, initially from Melbourne Zoo, and finally by a donation from Menzies himself.[46] Churchill never failed to point them out to his many visitors, and on at least one occasion startled lunchtime guests by insisting that they all rush down the slope to the lake, banging pots and pans to scare away invading 'Narsies' (an intrusion by Canada geese). He also received from the Australia Stockowners' Association a

'Wot, stay in the same cage as that wild man, not me!'
Daily Worker, 3 May 1949

pair of South Australian white kangaroos. These had to be housed at London Zoo, along with the lion cub presented to him by American admirers from New Jersey and the platypus apparently presented to him by Evatt, but there were evocative pictures from time to time in the Australian press of Churchill visiting the zoo to feed his kangaroos personally – the male naturally having been christened 'Digger'. Head-lines included 'Churchill visits his pet 'roo', and 'Mr Churchill Meets Digger, a Dinkum Australian'.[47] Other gifts sent to Churchill as tribute from his Australian admirers included a rare map from Marlborough's time, a portrait of Marlborough himself, a shillelagh said to have belonged to his mother's family, and an antique cigar-cutter. And when it was necessary to rename a species of apple originally called Winter King because the name proved to have been already used elsewhere, 'Winston' was chosen because the apple in question would 'withstand any storm'. The rest of the catalogue description (which says much of Churchill's image in 1949) included the words 'Very thick skin. Remains firm until the end of the season ... Wonderful keeper and late bloomer'.[48]

Churchill's life was indeed very regularly reported while he was out of office between 1945 and 1951, including not only his speeches, honours and foreign trips, but also his illnesses, his liking for large meals, his

love of publicity (on his own terms – his refusal to be photographed
while swimming was also reported), and his household pets.[49] Even the
ups and downs of the life of the American lion sent to Churchill were
charted, it being noted for example that London Zoo had turned down
the idea of having its portrait painted. This would have been a good
use of its funds only if it was important 'zoologically', rather than merely
'politically', but perhaps Churchill could paint it himself.[50] It is notable
that, while the American gift of a lion drew on obvious Churchillian
and British symbolism, all of Australia's animal gifts were native species.
It is rather as if the determination behind them was to link him more
closely to Australia than simply to celebrate his achievements.(One Melbourne paper even thought it worthy of report that New Zealand had
decided *not* to send Churchill a Kiwi bird.)[51] Nothing bears out this
more directly than the anxiety of Australians to persuade Churchill
actually to go to their country, a hope that was endlessly reiterated
between 1945 and the later 1950s, despite plenty of evidence that he may
never have intended to make the trip.

Stories that Churchill would now visit Australia began to circulate
soon after VE Day and the British election campaign, it being assumed
that he would wish to see the Pacific war theatre for himself.[52] But
they were widespread only when his election defeat provided him with
enforced leisure and the chance to recuperate from the physical effects
of five years of war leadership in a climate warmer than Europe could
offer during the approaching northern winter. At this stage in summer
and early autumn 1945, Churchill may indeed have been contemplating
a lengthy holiday in the south, though for the senior Conservative Party
sources in London cited in support the wish was probably father to the
thought too.[53] However, once he accepted in early November Harry
Truman's invitation to deliver a lecture in Missouri in the following
March, he was able to plan a visit to Florida and Cuba for the warm
weather in January–March, with the added bonus of a political opportunity too, a speech platform from which he could relaunch his flagging
career as an international statesman. This weighing of alternatives in
autumn 1945 set the pattern for the next fifteen years, with Churchill
regularly saying that he would like to come to Australasia when his other
commitments allowed, but actually going instead to North America. It
was all a matter of priorities, for Anthony Eden, who had already visited
in 1925, made time to revisit Australia and New Zealand in 1949, and

returned for a third time in 1957 – but Eden was less enamoured of the Americans and more a true Empire man than Churchill had ever been. The low priority that Australia had in Churchill's plans was in any case indicated by the range of other places that he visited, all faithfully reported in the Australian press: in the early post-war years, Australians could read of his reception and honouring in Belgium, Denmark, France, Germany, Italy, Morocco, the Netherlands, Norway, Switzerland and the West Indies, as well as in the United States and Canada.[54] Some even among his admirers drew the conclusion of Robert Gilmore, who entitled a 1953 column, datelined London, 'You won't drag Churchill to Australia': British Ministers came to Australia when policy discussions required it – Duncan Sandys to discuss the Woomera nuclear-test site, for example – but those who were close to British Conservatives knew that, 'despite all the talk about "the Empire", there is no great enthusiasm for those Dominions which stem from proletarian colonisation'. This is strikingly close to the memory of Menzies' daughter, that her father had once resignedly remarked that 'those people never come here', but it was not a remark that he would have made publicly. When Sandys came again in 1961 in an effort to persuade Australians to support Britain's application to enter the EEC, he 'managed to irritate almost every Australian in sight' (as a civil servant put it), but Menzies merely told Churchill how much they had enjoyed having his son-in-law to stay with them.[55]

More often, though, such was the admiration for Churchill that the blame for this was placed not on Churchill himself but on Australian governments which, it was alleged, had not invited him with sufficient warmth and persistence. It is probable that Churchill's reluctance to come to Australia owed at least something to the fear that his welcome there would not be warm or unanimous – a fear that would not have applied elsewhere. The ecstatic welcomes for Montgomery, Mountbatten and Randolph Churchill suggest otherwise, and Churchill's admirers invariably assured him (and each other) that he should entertain no such doubt. Letters began to appear in the press early in August 1945, and were in many cases endorsed editorially. 'Face to face he should be told what he meant to us; and face to face we should have the inspiration of his spirit and his words.' Victorians would welcome Churchill when he came to 'this remote but important part of the Empire', added State Premier Dunstan.

The people of Australia realised the great debt of gratitude they owed him for his inspiring leadership in the dark days when other Empires crumbled beneath the might of the German military machine. A visit from Mr Churchill would further strengthen the ties of fellowship between the people of Australia and the homeland, and would enable this great statesman to see for himself the wonderful potentialities of this country. He could be assured of a right royal welcome.[56]

Visits by Montgomery and others reawakened public demands for a Churchill visit ('We've seen Monty; now for Mr Churchill'). Monty paid a warm tribute to Churchill while meeting Australian war veterans in Melbourne in 1947, but was well aware that what they really wanted was a sight of the man himself: 'I am glad you feel the same about Winston Churchill as I do. We could never have won the war without his inspired leadership. I shall certainly give him the message that he must come out here. If he says he can't come then I'll come back again myself and bring him with me [cheers].' There were even hopes that the Queen's successful visit in 1954 and Churchill's retirement from active politics soon afterwards would remove the stumbling blocks. It was all as if Australian admirers just could not bring themselves to accept that he simply did not want to come.[57]

In the Commonwealth Parliament, Chifley was asked in September 1945 if Churchill had been officially invited. Though he responded woodenly that Curtin's wartime invitation to Churchill still stood, he also agreed to consider the matter further. A week later, Senator Brand remarked that 'it is pleasing to hear . . . that Mr Winston Churchill will visit Australia shortly. The people of Australia are anxious to see and hear the inspired head of the nation which stood alone against Nazi Germany in the first eighteen months of the war.' For admirers like Brand, as this shows, Australia (which after all went to war on Britain's side in 1939) was still part of 'the British nation', and Churchill had been its wartime head. That was certainly the view of Senator McLachlan, who argued in the same month that:

in all our history, I do not think we have had a leader who so inspired his people as Mr Churchill did in the dark days of 1940–41. Whilst we deplore the fact that this great statesman no longer holds the reins of leadership in the Mother of

Parliaments, we realise that we are a democratic people, and that in democratic countries the will of the people is supreme. We can only hope that Mr Churchill's successors will realise that they are charged with the responsibility of framing a policy not only for the United Kingdom, but also one to guide an Empire on which the sun never sets.[58]

In summer 1946, following Chifley's invitation to Clement Attlee to visit Australia, the Opposition were quick to suggest once more that only partisanship was denying Churchill a similar welcome. Menzies craftily put his own question about a possible Churchill visit 'on behalf of certain sporting bodies which had intimated to me their desire to be associated with an invitation to him'. Chifley once again bent before the wind, responding that since sports clubs had approached him too (so presumably making it seem less 'political' – though Churchill was hardly likely to be interested in a visit to the Lawn Tennis Association of Australia) he would formally renew the invitation by writing to Churchill himself. He did so in gracious but cool terms, concluding that 'a reply from you that some such arrangement would be agreeable to you and Mrs Churchill would give great pleasure to all Australians'. Two years later, pressed again in the House, this time by a Member speaking on behalf of the town of Ararat in Victoria, an exasperated Chifley replied that Churchill had invariably said that he was currently too busy with politics and writing, but that he would always be welcome if he chose to come. This type of defence invariably produced counter-attacks that entirely missed the point, as in a 1948 letter to a Sydney paper regretting that Churchill should 'have to' lead a political party. Rather, he should be a 'Prime Minister Emeritus', free to tour the Empire and receive its 'homage'. Yet it was Churchill himself who had indignantly refused to retire from party politics and be exhibited 'like a prize bull'.[59] Finally in the Commonwealth Parliament, once the right was back in power in both countries in 1951, E. J. Eggins urged Menzies to invite Churchill again, 'so that the people of this country may pay a personal tribute to him for the great service that he rendered during the war years', a visit that would be especially appropriate now that, 'following the lead of Australia and New Zealand, the United Kingdom has removed a socialist administration from office'. Party point-scoring was not overlooked by the ALP either, the very next question producing a Labor demand for an early Commonwealth Conference, 'now that that great Empire-builder, Mr Winston Churchill, has been returned to power'.[60]

Thwarted in the Federal Parliament while Labor held power (or so they believed), the Australian right turned elsewhere for the means to promote a Churchill visit. In Western Australia, the Assembly heard in August 1945 a demand that Churchill be entertained there, and a month later the same thing happened in the Victorian State Assembly, a member urging that if Churchill did indeed come, 'I trust we shall let ourselves go.'[61] Letters to the press urged that Melbourne take the lead, and the Lord Mayor duly convened a public meeting to test opinion on an official invitation to Churchill, but was forestalled by the state premier issuing an invitation anyway. Churchill should come for 'as long as possible', and would be assured of 'a warm welcome from the Victorian people'.[62] The Lord Mayor was enquiring again in mid-1947, producing from Churchill the reply that he would like to come 'if it were possible', but pleading that 'parliamentary duties and the urgent pressure of affairs' ruled it out for the present. Churchill's birthday two months later provided State Premier Hollway with the opportunity to tack a renewed invitation on to birthday congratulations. When Churchill sent back thanks for the good wishes but ignored the invitation, Hollway announced optimistically that this must mean that the invitation was under serious consideration in London. It didn't, it wasn't, and no more was ever heard of it.[63]

Nevertheless, Churchill's standing in Australia continued to rise in the post-war years, if once again in a more politically partisan way than in the other Dominions. This derived in part from his emergence as an early prophet of the Cold War. It seems, for example, extremely likely that his nomination in 1946 as a life member of the Returned Servicemen's League (despite Gallipoli and Crete, as critics pointed out in letters to the press) owed a good deal to that organisation's increasingly anti-Communist crusading in the months after his own 'iron curtain' speech.[64] That speech at Fulton was reported in full in almost all the Australian newspapers, and his call for resistance to Russia by the English-speaking peoples was endorsed editorially almost as widely. Adelaide's *Advertiser* wrote of 'a voice to heed', and reminded readers of Churchill's foresight in the 1930s; in Perth, the *West Australian* praised such 'plain speaking' and welcomed his call for closer unity between

the USA and the Commonwealth; the *Sydney Morning Herald* welcomed
a clarion-call for the forces of democracy. The mixed American reaction
to the speech was, however, also widely reported, and it was only when
Stalin attacked the speech as that of a 'warmonger' and American
opinion came round to supporting it that enthusiastic unanimity was
also established in the Australian press.[65]

Even then, there was no such unanimity among the politicians.
Menzies, noting on the very day of Churchill's speech that the Australian
House of Representatives was debating the attempt by Australian Communists to dictate through the trade unions policy towards Indonesia,
announced that Churchill had spoken for Australia. His Labor critics
immediately pointed out that neither Churchill nor Menzies himself
had that right while there was a Labor Government in Canberra. Chifley
simply refused to comment on the speech when first made, much as
Attlee was doing in London at the time, and even in speeches on foreign
policy made in the following summer he stressed the role of the United
Nations rather than Churchill's English-Speaking peoples. In Parliament,
during a debate on the army estimates, the Liberal Thomas White drew
attention to Churchill's speech on the day on which it was first reported,
and immediately stirred up a party battle: Eddie Ward interjected to
remind Members that Churchill was 'an old Tory', and White riposted
that if so he was 'an old Tory who worked with Stalin', from whom
Labor drew its inspiration. Churchill himself once remarked to Menzies
that 'you Australians do conduct your politics with a fine 18th-century
robustness', and this was certainly true of the parliamentary citations
of Churchill over the next few years. Supporters from the right drew
attention to his record from the 1930s and his overall image as a defence
and foreign policy specialist, while Labor critics denounced him as both
an appeaser in the past (of Russia, at Yalta) and a warmonger now.[66]

Within this broadly partisan reaction, there were two events when
Churchill's increasing support on the Australian right, itself a growing
force in the country in this period, was vulnerable, first when in October
1946 his call at Zurich for a 'United States of Europe' seemed to undermine the Commonwealth, and second when he precipitately urged
British people not to emigrate to Australia but to stay and 'fight socialism' at home. The Zurich speech was widely reported, if not quite so
widely as his earlier one in Missouri, but Australian admirers seem to
have been all too ready to accept the view that Britain would be an

external sponsor of such a European union rather than a core member (though the widespread reporting of French opposition to his ideas may have indicated that there was also some relief that it could not immediately go ahead). The Melbourne *Herald* concluded happily enough that 'it would be over-simplifying history to expect Europe to achieve in a generation or so the working unity of the British Commonwealth'. Hobart's *Mercury* noted perceptively that this was really all part of Churchill's Cold War rallying of Europe, and that it anyway contained a contradiction in respect of Russia: 'Mr Churchill said that if Russia came in all will be well. It might be retorted that if Russia came in all would be unnecessary.'[67] After this, Churchill's association with the idea of a United Europe rarely seems to have ruffled Australian feathers. The *Sydney Morning Herald* argued in 1947 that there was no reason for the Dominions not to be 'with Britain in this cause' of reincorporating Germany into the community of European nations, for 'Britain was geographically part of Europe, and they themselves had an inheritance in Europe. The youth of the Dominions twice in living memory had died in wars brought about by European discord, in the prevention of which they had been powerless.' A later editorial was even more complacent, when it argued that little harm could come from an idea backed by 'the Empire's two greatest living statesmen', Churchill and Smuts.[68]

Churchill's brief foray into the sensitive area of Anglo-Australian migration was one of his less sensible pronouncements, motivated entirely by domestic anti-socialist campaigning, but threatening in principle the expansion of Australia's population from British stock to which all Australian parties were committed. For the Labor Government, Arthur Calwell issued only a dignified and non-partisan rebuke, while quickly extending his search for migrants to other parts of Europe. From the right few politicians could be found to make any comment at all. Calwell claimed in his memoirs that Churchill had 'really submarined some of our efforts' to get British migrants, but it seems unlikely that the brief disagreement had much impact at all in any but the shortest of runs. It was in any case an uncharacteristic attitude for Churchill to adopt, and a temporary one. Far more typical was his observation reported in 1949: 'Do not suppose that half a century from now you will not see 70 or 80 millions of Britons spread around the world, and united in defence of our traditions . . .'[69]

A third dispute, again entirely of Churchill's making, involved the exclusion of Britain from the ANZUS treaty signed by Australia, New Zealand and the United States. The Attlee Government, giving a higher priority to economics over prestige than did Churchill, had not wanted to play a part, though it would probably have preferred the talks to fail rather than succeed and then exclude Britain from participation. Churchill, returning to office at exactly this juncture, promptly blamed Australia for Britain's exclusion. It had actually been the USA that wanted a dance for only three partners, arguing that, if Britain were admitted to a Pacific security arrangement, it would be necessary to invite France and the Netherlands too, and perhaps Thailand, an argument that did not impress Churchill, for he did not see Britain as being on a par with 'the bloody Frogs' on this or any other issue. He therefore pressed hard for a change of mind, and won over New Zealand but not Australia. His blaming of Australia may thus have become right in the end, since the USA could not easily have resisted both of its partners if they had demanded the same thing strongly enough – Menzies did ask for some form of British 'association' with ANZUS but does not seem to have been too upset when the Americans turned him down. Not only did Churchill press Menzies hard to ask again, despite Menzies pointing out that 'the real answers could not be given in public', but he then went on pressing and would not take no for an answer, until in 1954 the South-East Asian Treaty Organisation provided just such a wider body for regional security, and by general agreement. Meanwhile Britain, apparently unconscious of any irony, had opposed an Australian request for association with NATO. This seems to argue the extent to which the Cold War was a binding force between Churchill and the Australians only when viewed globally, but that when the British and Australians viewed even the Cold War regionally, then separate interests predominated in their mind, just as they had done in 1941–2. Fortunately, there were few such regional issues to dispute about in the twenty years after 1945; less fortunately, there were plenty from the mid-1960s onwards, after which the countries drifted steadily apart.[70]

Such narrow areas of disagreement pale into insignificance when placed alongside the burgeoning fame of Churchill in Australia after 1945, part of the worldwide recovery of prestige that he achieved in the decade after his 1945 defeat. Nothing was more important here than a special Australian edition of his war memoirs. When serialised in the Herald group of newspapers, and hence reaching large readerships in all the main cities, Churchill's views about the recent past saturated the market. Each volume appeared in daily instalments for a period of at least five weeks, seven weeks (or *thirty-five* weekday issues of the papers, not many fewer excepts than the forty-two that were published in Britain) for the crucial first volume that established his credentials as a uniquely far-sighted opponent of appeasement in the 1930s. How widely they were read can be seen from all sorts of evidence, not least from the number of people who wrote to the papers to offer comments on details. This readership no doubt also encouraged mass purchase of the books themselves when they then appeared, at which point 'booksellers reported one of the heaviest demands in the history of the trade', the Australian press having already told readers that the books had sold out almost immediately in the United Kingdom. Apparently other Churchill titles such as *My Early Life* and *Great Contemporaries* experienced a renewed resurgence of interest in Australian bookshops too. In due course, from 1956 through to 1958, all four volumes of Churchill's *History of the English-Speaking Peoples* were also serialised for weeks on end, much as the war memoirs had been.[71]

No practising politician before or since can have had such prolonged (and favourable) exposure even in his own country as Churchill derived from his war memoirs, but in his case exposure on that grand scale was literally global. There was, to be sure, some price to be paid for all this, mainly because Churchill had been pretty careless in respect of Australian sensitivities when completing his text. He thus included opinions and documents that would quite certainly have been excised if their equivalent had ever been in a draft relating to either Britain or the United States. In Australia, as in France and Belgium therefore, the appearance of the books prompted hostile as well as favourable debate, refutations and ripostes as well as eulogies, and some of these were at a high level of government. (It would only be fair to add that there were also reviews of fawning credulity, including one in the religious column of the Melbourne *Herald*, where the clergyman–writer concluded that reading *The Gathering Storm* would prove to any reader the existence of a divine providence.) In 1948, the Liberal politician and distinguished ex-soldier Wilfrid Kent-Hughes called for an apology from Churchill for his derogatory remarks about the calibre of Australian troops. An item of Churchill's correspondence with Curtin led to questions in the Senate when published in the papers in March 1949. The volume covering 1941 revealed Churchill's 'word quarrel' with Menzies over Dakar (exactly the sort of event which would have been cut out of the book if the argument had been with Eisenhower), so that Menzies had to issue a quick press release in which he denied that their personal relations had ever been bad, while revelations of Menzies' proposal of an Imperial war cabinet led to calls for an enquiry into what he had been up to. Only a few days later, it was Evatt who was publicly dissociating himself from Churchill's account. More generally, Curtin's admirers found Churchill's account of their relationship singularly hard to accept. Arthur Fadden, however, waited until he wrote his memoirs to point out the critical fact that Churchill's war memoirs 'misinterpreted' his own activities over Tobruk, mainly because, 'while quoting from his own messages, he did not reveal the contents of those from Australia'. This was of course true of Churchill's books as a whole, but only in the case of Australia and Ireland had 'his own messages' been so consistently rude.[72]

In 1943, Churchill was clearly thinking of Australia when he spoke openly in cabinet of 'the troublesome attitudes of the colonies', given his relative carefulness over Canada and South Africa, while, thought David Day, 'New Zealand's deference to Whitehall only encouraged him in his Victorian ways.' This was very much what Ben Chifley thought at the time, upset as he was by Churchill's 'outmoded notions of the status and role of the Dominions'. Even the Liberal Percy Spender had to lecture Churchill in the United States on his use of 'Empire' rather than 'Commonwealth', making him 'annoyed' and 'pugnacious' in the process. In this, though, Churchill may actually have been more in touch with Australian opinion than were his Australian critics: even in 1951, an opinion poll showed that 80 per cent of Australians wished to remain in the Empire, the vast majority preferring indeed the concept of Empire to the looser and more novel idea of a British Commonwealth. His choosing not to come to Australia was though the key piece of evidence of his view of the country. It seems unlikely that he ever actually decided never to visit, as has been claimed by Ann Moyal, largely on the unreliable evidence of Beaverbrook's claim to speak for both of them. More likely, he simply failed to give it a high enough priority in the 1930s or the late 1940s, and then as he aged it became just too difficult for a man over eighty to contemplate. (Elizabeth II was after all in 1954 the first reigning monarch ever to visit Australia, Harold Macmillan in 1958

Queen Elizabeth II and President Jacques Chirac bow in homage to
the Churchill statue in Paris, 1999.

Churchill busts and statues (clockwise
from top left) in the Palais de l'Europe,
Strasbourg; Washington DC;
Canberra, Australia (awaiting a new
coat of bronze paint after being
re-located in 2001); and outside the
British embassy in Prague.

ABOVE Twin statues of Winston and Clementine Churchill, in Kansas City, and BELOW of Churchill with Franklin Roosevelt in Bond Street, London.

ABOVE Down-under comes to London: Churchill with New Zealand soldiers in Downing Street, 1941.

BELOW Feeding his kangaroo at London Zoo, 1947.

ABOVE Churchill the painter: at work on a landscape beside Lake Geneva, 1946.

BELOW The studio at Chartwell.

LEFT Commemorative Churchill streets in Arras, France; Perth, Western Australia; Prague, Czech Republic; Adelaide, South Australia; Pimlico, London; suburb of Brisbane, Queensland; Canning Town, London; The Hague and Amsterdam, the Netherlands; Strasbourg, France; and Hobart, Tasmania.

ABOVE Trading on the Churchill name in New Zealand: Christchurch, Auckland and Rotorua.

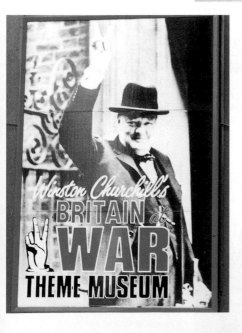

SIR WINSTON CHURCHILL
1874 - 1965

This statue, by William McVey (1902-1995), was erected in 1966 by public subscription, on the initiative of the English Speaking Union. One foot stands on United States soil, one on British Embassy grounds; a symbol of Churchill's Anglo-American descent, and of the Alliance he did so much to forge, in war and in peace.

GREATER LONDON COUNCIL
SIR WINSTON CHURCHILL, K.G.
1874 - 1965
Prime Minister
lived and died here

THIS PORCH IS GIVEN IN MEMORY OF

WINSTON CHURCHILL

WHOSE FAITH AND FAMILY BESTRODE THE SEA, LINKING MEN ON EITHER SIDE IN LIBERTY

TO WHOM WE OWE "THAT GLEAMING FLASH OF RESOLVE WHICH LIFTS THE HEARTS OF MEN AND NATIONS, AND SPRINGS FROM THE SPIRITUAL FOUNDATIONS OF HUMAN LIFE ITSELF"

World Broadcast
4·27·41

Churchill inscriptions (clockwise from top left) in Washington DC (Pennsylvania Avenue and the National Cathedral), Westminster, Southwark and Hyde Park Gate, London.

Winston Churchill's BRITAIN at WAR THEME MUSEUM

CABINET WAR ROOMS

Adults	£5.80
Children (0 - 15 years)	FREE
Students	£4.20
Senior Citizens (60 years and over)	£4.20

Reduced admission charges for groups of 10 or more

Churchill
The War Years

A special exhibition on Churchill's leadership in World War II

Churchill commemorated (clockwise from top left) in a cigar shop, Vancouver, Canada; a gift shop in London; a school in Queensland; a park in Toronto, Canada; and a hospital in Christchurch, New Zealand.

the first serving British Prime Minister to do so.) But the effect of not coming was to deny himself a chance to imbibe something of the Australian spirit at first hand and so avoid giving needless offence by his words and deeds.

Nothing brings this out more clearly than the treatment of Australia in his *History of the English-Speaking Peoples* published in 1958, and his casual treatment of the Returned Servicemen's League a decade earlier. The first three volumes of the *History of the English-Speaking Peoples* had been well enough received in Australia and seem to have sold well, but since they went up only to 1815 they did not need to deal with Australia itself; Richard Casey was fairly typical in thinking that their deficiencies in content and balance were more than compensated by Churchill's 'remarkable command of words and of thought'. In the final volume, however, on the nineteenth century, his lack of interest was clear for all to see, for Australia was allotted just seven pages in a chapter on 'The Migration of the Peoples II' (it also covered New Zealand – Canada and South Africa being even more uneasily yoked together in 'The Migration of the Peoples I'). A mere 22 pages out of 300 were thus given to all four Dominions added together, compared to 170 on Britain and 104 on the United States. Though this was supposed to be about 'the English-speaking peoples', his own order of priorities could not have been made clearer, and when he came to the book's denouement in the Boer War he scarcely even mentioned Kipling's men from the 'Younger Countries' who had done so much to win it for Britain, by sending their 'men who could shoot and ride'. The volume's title, *The Great Democracies*, was a phrase that Churchill had often used as a shorthand for Britain and the USA, and thus excluded the Dominions from the book's remit – so perhaps they should have been grateful to get a mention at all. The book was hardly noticed in Australian newspapers' pages of book reviews, and was ignored altogether by more serious magazines, and even admiring newspapers reported that it had had some bad reviews in Britain. Most revealingly of all, when the volume was serialised in the Herald newspapers, the chapter on Australia and New Zealand (in which Australians might have been expected to take the greatest interest) was simply excluded from the chosen highlights. His admirers in the *Herald*'s management presumably felt that printing what he had to say, barely the equivalent of a single broadsheet page, and written with none of his usual verve (if indeed he did write it himself, which seems doubtful), would do nothing for his reputation. So they simply suppressed it. There was no Australian edition of the books, as there had been for the war memoirs, though there were separate editions for both Canada and the United States.[73]

However, even this cavalier treatment of Australia pales by comparison with Churchill's lack of interest when the Returned Servicemen's League tried to honour him with life membership. This had been decided, on the proposal of the Victoria branch, by the RSL's first post-war conference, and all branches were then circularised in March 1946, inviting suggestions of a 'token truly representative of Australia and of the League for forwarding and presentation to Mr Winston Churchill as a token of the League's admiration and appreciation, and in recognition of the services rendered by him to the Empire'. Tasmania immediately suggested that Churchill be urged to come to Australia to receive this signal honour in person. Victoria's suggestion that he be given a large cigar box in 'specially selected Australian fiddleback' wood, mounted with a replica RSL badge, seems to have been the one chosen (the branch had also urged that Churchill be given 'a Diggers' welcome' when he visited). After a long delay, Churchill replied through a secretary (the letter apparently being sent by sea rather than airmail) that he was happy to accept the offer but could at present make no promises to visit. The League immediately wrote back to ensure that, 'when Mr Churchill finds it convenient to visit Australia', they would be given plenty of notice, so as to arrange a fitting welcome, a request that produced only a 'your request has been noted' reply, after another two months had passed (and saying 'if' rather than 'when' about any Churchill visit).

The federal executive of the RSL, presumably made restive by such offhand treatment, suggested in February 1947 that since there would be an Empire-wide conference of veterans' organisations in London in the following July, an RSL deputation might wait on Churchill then and give him his honour personally. Once again there was a five-week delay while the reply came by sea, and then a secretary thanked the RSL for offering life membership and accepted it on Churchill's behalf (Churchill's staff had obviously forgotten that they had already done this some months earlier, and cannot even have properly read the latest RSL letter), but declined to add an appointment for the RSL to Churchill's crowded summer diary. At this point the RSL, which was after all easily the largest voluntary group in Australia and was treated with considerable deference by all Australian governments, became very restive indeed. The secretary enlisted the aid of the British Legion, ex-Prime Minister Bruce (now in London) and the Australian High Commissioner: 'Quite possibly neither Mr Churchill nor Mr Curtis [the secretary] has any idea of the numerical strength (375,000) of the league nor of the important part it has played in the national life of Australia since its inception in 1916 ... Awaiting your valued advice at your earliest convenience.' Even this did not manage a date in July, but Churchill did agree to see a small number of RSL representatives at his London home in the following November. This further delay meant that the RSL's national leadership would not be in London and so would miss the occasion, which in turn led to a spat between the High Commission and the Agent-General of Victoria (himself a veteran) as to who would make the presentation. Eventually, all was smoothed over, and Churchill was given his present and badge on 13 November. He then had the quite amazing nerve to complain that they had not laid on a reporter to take down his impromptu remarks and issue them as a press release. He does not seem to have been in too good a mood altogether, to judge from his unsmiling countenance when photographs were being taken, but he was (noted one present who had been pressed into the role of stenographer):

> visibly affected by the presentation. He replied at considerable
> length and in words that left no doubt about his recognition
> of the part played by the ex-servicemen and women of Australia
> in two wars and his appreciation of the very great honour
> which had been conferred on him by the League ... Finally Mr
> Churchill proposed that he would wear the badge and that he
> would have framed the Life Membership certificate.

The words quoted above derive from a letter sent off immediately to the RSL headquarters in Canberra. When the actual notes of speeches made on the day arrived too, the RSL might not have been quite so pleased to see that Churchill had also referred in his speech to 'the anxiety he had felt and the efforts he made for the protection of Australia when Japan was running riot in the Pacific', not quite most Australians' memory of his order of priorities in 1942. The note of his speech was not however published in Australia, either in the RSL's own magazines and annual reports or in its press release, and there was certainly no mention of just how difficult it had been to get Churchill's attention so as to give him the award in the first place. Rather, the ceremony was reported in a glow of appreciative verbiage, claiming that it showed just how much Australia meant to Winston Churchill, a rather inexact reflection of the facts of the case. '"Some think my age is against such a long trip, but Australia is the one country I want to see", he said. Tears welled up in Mr Churchill's eyes and his head quivered emotionally as the badge was pinned on . . ."[74]

Such insensitivities can have had little impact against the tide of Churchill's own words that rolled ceaselessly towards the reading public, particularly when they were covered up by his admirers, as the RSL had done. When added to the equally ceaseless diet of news about his present life and lifestyle – the sort of blanket coverage that ensured that even a short Churchill holiday generated half a dozen different news stories and a couple of pictures – it is hardly surprising that he was by the mid-1950s regarded in Australia, as he was elsewhere, as a uniquely great historical figure. When he spoke at MIT in Boston in 1949, the Melbourne *Herald* noted that radio and television hook-ups had, as was now usual, ensured that he would speak to 'a world audience', a remarkable feat for a politician still out of office.[75]

Churchill's political recovery was thus reported a good deal more favourably than his 1945 eclipse, and indeed was now being reported on terms that Churchill himself might have chosen. It was noteworthy for example that most Australian papers, while reporting in neutral tones the victory of 'Labour' in Britain in 1945, celebrated the setback to British 'socialism' in 1950, so far had the political terms of trade shifted in Churchill's favour as the Cold War got going. Chifley and Evatt both sent to Attlee encouraging messages on his narrow majority in 1950, but were then rebuked by Prime Minister Menzies for doing so: 'Great Britain, as an economic and political power in the world, is vital to us in Australia. We don't pretend to be neutral in our thinking regarding the British election. I would have confined it to thinking, but for the fact that my principal political opponents here have openly intervened on behalf of the British Labour Party.' There followed a blistering attack on Labour/Labor, reported under the headline 'Mr Menzies declares against socialists here and in the UK'. The fact was, though, that Churchill had lost again, and to some this meant that the seventy-six-year-old would now have to retire – for the good of the anti-socialist cause itself. The *Sydney Morning Herald*, for example, after writing in extravagant praise of his war services, came to the conclusion that 'his great work lies behind him, and in a different sphere. The younger generation might well be more responsive to a leader whose mind was more closely attuned to their own.' Menzies had thought much the same when recording in his diary in 1948 the view of the fifth Lord Salisbury, that 'Winston was once vewy pwogwessive but it was a vewy long time ago!'[76]

Fortunately for Churchill's wish to return as Prime Minister, the 1950 result was so close that another election could not be long delayed, and he was therefore able to fight off demands that he retire. (It would of course never have occurred to him as a possibility that he himself might be an obstacle to the causes he believed in.) When in 1951 his party inched its way back into office and he therefore became Prime Minister for a second time, there was a chorus of acclamation in Australia. The *Canberra Times* was no doubt reflecting the dominance of the Australian right in the Commonwealth's capital in welcoming back 'the ageing but still magnificent Mr Churchill'. But it was fairly typical of Australian newspapers in arguing that 'within the British Empire the disappearance of socialist governments may pave the way to a more closely knit and effective organisation', a process in which Churchill would be 'a rallying voice' towards the restoration of Britain's 'authoritative place in world affairs'. The Brisbane *Courier-Mail* hailed 'the grand old man of Empire', expecting him to inject a new vigour into restoring the enterprise and the prestige 'that are the heritage of Old England'. The Melbourne *Herald* thought that nobody would begrudge Churchill another term and, like most of the papers, wrote as if the whole of Britain were rejoicing at the election and its result. Australians would indeed have had to look very hard to find any reference to the fact that Labour had got more votes than the Conservatives in the 1951 poll, or that most working-class constituencies had stubbornly resisted the Conservative recovery. The *Mercury* was also in line with the other papers in supporting Churchill's demand for a summit conference, remarking that 'the idea of striking quickly and directly at the core of the problem is typically Churchillian'.[77] Robert Menzies, this time unprovoked by Labor opponents, who had gone strangely quiet about Britain, reverted to thinking about the British election result rather than making political capital out of it, but he made sure that Churchill at least was privy to those thoughts:

> It is one of our conventions that we in Australia take no hand in your politics. But I must tell you personally how much I congratulate you on a victory which expresses faith in yourself and a continuing belief in the superb destiny and duty of the British Empire. Pray accept my affectionate regards and the assurance of my full cooperation in the common task.[78]

But if Menzies was the Dean of Churchill Studies in Australia from the 1950s, he did no more than head a faculty that was self-generated and self-sustaining. As Churchill moved through the various rites of passage that characterised his last dozen years, he was almost unanimously celebrated in Australia, as in the rest of the English-speaking world. Menzies was by no means the only man to keep silent about his reservations in this time, so that Churchill as a polariser of Australian party politics gradually gave way to Churchill as an idol of the whole Australian elite – if never quite of the whole Australian people. This was first marked in the eightieth-birthday celebrations on 30 November 1954, coinciding with the appeal for a Churchill birthday fund worldwide, the fund from which Churchill College was initially endowed. The *Sydney Morning Herald* was reporting the progress of this fund for several weeks before Churchill's actual birthday. Australians were carefully informed that all donors to the appeal would receive a (facsimile) letter of thanks from Churchill himself, while the names of donors would be placed in a book of honour, with copies in the public libraries of every contributing country, the High Commissioners helping to co-ordinate these arrangements. On 18 November, curious rumours of Churchill's death swept through Melbourne, 'hundreds of Canberra people telephoned Melbourne newspapers to check the rumour', and all the radio stations broadcast hourly denials.[79] By 27 November, Menzies was being asked in the House of Representatives if he planned to congratulate Churchill officially, and replied that he would send a telegram 'on behalf of all of us', a constituency that extended considerably further than his congratulations on Churchill's knighthood of the Garter in the previous year, sent only on behalf of 'my colleagues and I' in the Government. In the event he went even further, cabling congratulations on behalf of 'all Australians'.

The Legislative Assembly of South Australia witnessed a similar exchange on 30 November: when a Member asked that the premier send good wishes to Churchill, Sir Thomas Playford replied that he had already 'taken it upon himself' to congratulate Churchill, 'on behalf of the Government and People of this State', thanking him for 'his achievements and record in the interests of the British Commonwealth and the rest of the free world'. Perhaps anticipating that this still might not pass without adverse comment from the ALP, he stressed that it was a non-political matter, since Churchill had been an 'inspiration not only to the British people but to the whole of the free world'. His insertion, twice, of 'free' before 'world' rather gave away the Cold War origins of Churchill's increased popularity on the Australian right, but he need not have feared, for no adverse comment was offered. In New South Wales, the Legislative Assembly passed without opposition a formal motion of thanks to Churchill, on the proposition of ALP Premier Cahill ('He has proved himself one of the world's great workers . . .'). Perhaps encouraged by such evidence of Churchill's broadened appeal, all newspapers now really let themselves go, some by hailing Churchill on the actual day of his birthday, and all of them on 1 December in extravagant reports of the ceremonies held in London to mark the day, and in printing tributes to Churchill. On the same day, the ABC showed a half-hour celebratory documentary on Churchill's life. The *Sydney Morning Herald* devoted half its front page to a story headlined 'Triumph for Churchill: Londoners Mob Sir Winston on his Eightieth Birthday', and gave over a third of an inside page ('Free World Pays Tribute to Great Leader') to tributes from the British and American press and from leaders of half a dozen other countries. Much the same tone characterised the *Argus* ('World Joins in Salute to his Day'), the *Advertiser* ('London Honours Churchill: Coronation Scenes Re-Created'), the *Mercury* ('Churchill, Statesman and Prophet, 80 Today'), the *West Australian* ('World Statesmen Pay Tribute to Churchill'), the *Courier-Mail* ('London Mobs Churchill in 80th Year: Crowds Sing "Happy Birthday"'), and the *Canberra Times* ('The Great Man is Eighty'). The reasoning behind all that generalised adulation was to be found in the *Mercury*'s editorial ('Man of Destiny') which argued that 'as long as the British race and its institutions survive it will be remembered that they survived only because of the peculiar genius of Churchill', and concluded:

The world can afford to forget everything about Churchill except
that at that hour history was changed so that men still enjoy
the freedoms it took centuries to win. As Sir Winston Churchill
today reaches the eminence of 80 years the British Commonwealth, and indeed the free world, may well unite in thanks for
the life and spirit of a great figure.

By 1954 then, the basis on which Churchill was to be celebrated for
the rest of his life was fully and firmly established: his services in 1940
and at the onset of the Cold War now blotted out all his other acknowledged faults. His larger-than-life persona was also widely noted in these
celebrations, and indeed in the assiduous reporting of the fate of the
Graham Sutherland portrait given to him on that birthday: 'Banished
to storage', reported the Melbourne *Herald* in January, 'still unframed',
noted the *Sydney Morning Herald*, the following August. Nevertheless,
even now, Australia's celebration of Churchill was a touch less assured
than elsewhere, for it was admiration that was being expressed rather
than affection, and there was still little claim of any shared ownership
of the man and his achievements. Australians, for example, seem hardly
ever to have routinely referred to 'Winnie', and few Australians could
be brought out to share with readers their personal memories of the
man, since so few had ever actually met him. As we have seen, it was
much the same in New Zealand, but very different in Canada, where
he had by then been a real (if occasional) presence for more than half
a century.[80]

The fact that Churchill was eighty when he was so celebrated in
November 1954 lent a valedictory tone to many of the newspaper
appraisals, but his retirement as Prime Minister only a few months later
provided the occasion to consolidate in more yards of newsprint the
reputation now generally conceded to him. This time politicians had
no doubts about the appropriateness of formal resolutions, knowing
that they would pass without embarrassing opposition: the Victoria State
Assembly so resolved, when Sir Thomas Maltby, who had like Richard
Casey known Churchill ever since meeting him in France in 1915, urged
the state premier to 'do no less than others have done' in wishing
Churchill well on his retirement. The British press was on strike in April
1955, so on this occasion Australian papers could not use their normal
device of reprinting tributes from London, but they had no difficulty

in recycling the material from the previous November. The *Canberra Times* reported the retirement of 'the greatest Englishman of them all'; the *West Australian* headlined its story 'All the Free World Hails the Old Lion'; the *Courier-Mail* editorialised on 'A Great Man', and recalled wonderingly that many had thought he should retire in 1945 (conveniently forgetting that the *Courier-Mail* itself had said just this at the time); the *Sydney Morning Herald* led pages of tributes with one from Menzies, in which he suggested that it was 'useless to ransack the English language for superlatives to describe Sir Winston Churchill. The simple fact was that this world leader was in a true sense a great man, and probably the greatest of our time.' Richard Casey merely told his diary that he had 'Listened to the BBC description of Winston's resignation – one is inclined to call it abdication'. The overall tone was thus more like a memorial service than a funeral, celebratory and positive for the most part, downbeat only so far as it was recognised that Churchill himself had not really wanted to step down, but that even he could not for ever defy time and age. 'Winston, tearful, leaves Number Ten', reported the Melbourne *Herald*.[81]

It might have been expected that, with Churchill now finally retired, the process would have ended, but all the papers continued to mark almost every episode of his remaining decade with stories, and to notice especially his birthdays, honours, books, anniversaries and illnesses. In the year after his retirement, for example, news of Churchill's doings was on the pages of the *Sydney Morning Herald* about once a fortnight, and though this degree of coverage was not maintained by the early 1960s, such major events as his Golden Wedding anniversary in 1958, his formal visit to America in 1959 and the honorary citizenship awarded by the US Congress in 1963 each produced a clutch of stories. These stories and his continuing self-indulgence as he edged towards ninety did allow for a more affectionate tone to predominate than in the past, it being noticed for example that Golden Wedding presents included 'a massive chocolate cigar, a crate of champagne and a gigantic bottle of cognac'.[82]

For Australians, however, the most important Churchill episode of the period after his retirement was a non-political one, the seven-city tour of his one-man art exhibition in 1958. Churchill's interest in painting had begun in 1915 but developed to the point where his canvases were exhibited (anonymously at first) only in the post-war years.

Australians were told by their newspapers about this from the first, there being a regular diet of stories about the number of paintings he had completed on various holidays, their exhibition, sale and the prices they fetched, his book *Painting as a Pastime*, the 'fat cheque' he received when his paintings appeared on American Christmas cards, and his election as an Honorary Academician.

Menzies had not only been shown the studio at Chartwell in 1948 but had in 1955 acquired a Churchill painting of his own, a privilege reserved for more intimate friends and major world leaders. This was indeed one of Churchill's very best paintings, *Sailing Boats in Harbour at Antibes*, and one with which Churchill had actually been unwilling to part when Menzies chose it off the wall of his study at Chartwell. His objection, that it was one of his best pictures, was neatly countered by Christopher Soames' tactful observation that he could hardly give the Australian Prime Minister one of his *worst*, and Menzies bore it triumphantly away. On his return to Canberra ('I have always wanted one of Sir Winston's pictures. The gift has been one of the greatest delights of my visit to London . . .'), the painting was hung for the public to see in the King's Hall of the Parliament House, and then offered for exhibition in other galleries. It was later acquired by the Australian Government, and at the end of the century, appropriately enough, the painting was in the (new) Parliament House, hanging on the wall of Prime Minister John Winston Howard's office.[83]

However, when in 1957 Menzies heard that a Churchill 'retrospective' was to be mounted in North America, under the joint patronage of President Eisenhower and Joyce Hall of Hallmark Cards, he determined to make sure that Australia was included, and wrote directly to Churchill to persuade him to allow this, offering sponsorship by the Commonwealth Government. The exhibition thus went on an English-speaking world (rather than just an American) tour, and Australia and New Zealand each saw 'the first exhibition of his paintings' before Londoners were given the chance to do so. Like Eisenhower in the USA, Menzies contributed a personal foreword to the catalogue used for Australian galleries, but he also contributed his own Churchill painting (with a catalogue note, acknowledging its loan 'from his private collection', which made him sound like an art patron on the scale of Getty or Guggenheim), and it also adorned the cover of the Australian catalogue in a fine colour reproduction. In his foreword, Menzies actually

BAD STOCK': CHURCHILL AND AUSTRALIA

said very little about Churchill as a painter, on which he was less qualified
to write than Eisenhower. (Churchill's eclectic style of painting, which
led the Royal Academy on occasion to hang his works in its 'mad
gallery', would anyway not always have been to Menzies' famously conservative taste in art, a subject on which he had sometimes been at odds
with the Australian arts community.) He therefore restricted himself to
enthusing about the many-sidedness of Churchill's talent, and to arguing
that the most interesting thing about the pictures was simply that Churchill had painted them. The Chicago Institute of Art had refused to find
space for the exhibition on the ground that it was only of political
interest, not artistic (and the Australian press had crowed when its
director had then resigned during the outcry that followed in the USA),
but Menzies was effectively saying that the political importance of the
man was exactly what made the paintings worth seeing.

> The pictures represent the spare-time hobby and relaxation of
> the busiest and most weighty man of his period. Scores of
> thousands of men and women have seen and will see them.
> They will remember and enjoy them as paintings. But, if they
> are like me, they will stand near them and say to themselves,
> 'He stood just like this, and his hand put that pigment on that
> canvas. It is as if I stood near him and watched him!' The
> greatest privilege in life is to meet and know and talk with an
> immortal. Failing that, it is a great and warming thing to live
> in his age, to hear his words and to see his work.

Churchill himself wrote to thank Menzies for 'the very kind things
you say . . . and . . . the characteristically graceful way in which you say
them', and added that he would very much like to see Menzies again
soon. When would he be coming to London? However symbolic a
presence was offered by his paintings, the real thing was only to be
encountered by Australians if they flew halfway round the world.[84]

It is not too fanciful to argue, then, that the importance of the art
exhibition of 1958 was precisely as a substitute for the real presence of
Churchill, who was clearly now never going to visit, but whose creative
art could be both a symbol of his greatness and an almost transcendental
presence, much as his broadcast words had been in 1940. The exhibition
opened in the Parliament House in Canberra in August 1958, and then
went on in turn to all the major public galleries of Sydney, Brisbane,

Melbourne, Hobart, Adelaide and Perth, before moving on to New Zealand. The *Advertiser* sent its art critic to New York in March 1958, to give its readers a preview of the exhibition heading to Adelaide later in the year, and then supported his positive response with half a page of photographs ('World copyright of these pictures reserved for Sir Winston Churchill'). The *Canberra Times* also gave considerable publicity before the showing opened, and then reported at length speeches made at the opening ceremony by Menzies and by the Governor-General, Sir William Slim. Menzies was keen to point out that 'the paintings showed real ability, and would not be out of place in any art exhibition', but Slim took almost the same line as Menzies' catalogue foreword. Churchill was multi-talented, and excelled at everything he did. The paintings expressed the man, not so much 'by the perfection or technical skill, but by the robust and at times rugged simplicity of his greatness'. For 'here on these walls are paintings from the hand of the most famous Englishman of our time. As an artist he has inevitably put into them something of himself, and as they are studied, you will, I feel sure, feel a real contact with greatness.'

The King's Hall was crowded for that opening ceremony, 'all seating was filled and crowds gathered around the entrances', and reports indicated that it continued to be crowded for twelve hours a day over the next week. This set the pattern, with heavy attendances reported wherever the exhibition was shown, and on occasion opening hours extended to cope with the crowds. And while the *Sydney Morning Herald*'s anonymous art critic was decidedly sniffy about the paintings ('a jumble of clichés . . . there are hundreds of our more provincial amateurs who paint as well'), the paper's news reports were all about the crowds flocking to see them and the 'house full' signs used to prevent the gallery becoming dangerously overcrowded. It does not of course take a very high proportion of a city's population to fill an art gallery for a week, but the popular response to thirty-six of Churchill's paintings in 1958 does nonetheless indicate the extent of interest in the man that was widespread in all the state capitals as well as in Canberra. In this, Australia's response exactly replicated that in North America and New Zealand.[85]

It replicated too in the way in which during the quarter-century after 1945 the name of Churchill was applied to thoroughfares and other sites. Not though with statues, for no original Churchill statue was erected in Australia and none seems ever to have been proposed. This probably reflects no more than the tendency in that generation for Australians to commemorate more through non-representational and useful memorials than physical likenesses[86] – the prolific statuary of Melbourne and Sydney almost all dating from a much earlier time. The Winston Churchill Memorial Trust was exactly such a useful way of honouring a past hero, though it also acquired early in its life a copy of the Churchill statue first erected in London's Parliament Square, and this has stood prominently outside its Canberra headquarters ever since. The Commonwealth Government also acquired soon after Churchill's death one of the limited edition of Oscar Nemon's bust of Churchill, which was exhibited for many years in the King's Hall of the (old) Parliament building. It was later placed in storage, presumably because both the new Parliament building and the National Portrait Gallery that occupies part of the old one display the likenesses only of Australians, monarchs and governors. (Churchill's portrait appears in the National Portrait Gallery of Washington DC because he was an honorary citizen of the United States, but it has no equivalent claim on the Australian one.) The Trust's headquarters was naturally called Churchill House, as was the Sydney building of the British Empire Union from the late 1940s, following fundraising of £400,000 in honour of Churchill's services to the Empire during the war. In much the same way, Australian and other overseas servicemen in London had socialised at the Churchill Club, which continued to operate into the post-war years and with which the RSL was actively liaising in 1946. It was also in the immediate post-war years, given the regularity with which Churchill's face was to be seen in Australian papers, that a large outcrop standing beside the Sturt highway was dubbed Churchill Rock, its outline bearing an uncanny resemblance to his profile, with hat, chin, nose and cigar. The Warrumbungles in New South Wales soon acquired another Churchill Rock, named for the same reason.[87]

As has been shown, the process of naming streets after Churchill had begun even before the Great War, but it was during and after the 1939–45 war that this became a widespread practice. For the most part this was done not by renaming existing streets but by attaching Churchill's name to new thoroughfares. As nearby and intersecting streets in the same areas indicate, this mainly came in two phases, the late 1940s when war memories were uppermost, and in the 1960s and 1970s when Churchill was more personally commemorated. Churchill National Park in Victoria manages actually to date from both periods, being first created in 1940–1 and then relaunched with Churchill's name just after his 1965 funeral. Hence the Churchill Crescent (with its Churchill Reserve) of Narelian Vale, Sydney, with streets named Montgomery, Tobruk and Alamein, as well as Churchill and Winston, clearly dates from the 1940s, as does the Churchill Street of Forbes, NSW, connecting as it does with Attlee Street, and the Churchill Road of Mafra, Victoria, where Churchill is close to Montgomery, Roosevelt and MacArthur. The number of places at which Churchill and Tobruk intersect across the length and breadth of Australia is indeed a sign of how far his wartime disputes with the Australian Government had vanished so soon from the popular memory, however important they may have seemed to biographers of Curtin and later historians.

Occasionally Churchill still figures by name in a positive tidal wave of war nostalgia, as in Golden Beach on Queensland's Sunshine Coast, where streets are named after Churchill, Haig, Monash, Montgomery, Birdwood, Wavell, Cunningham, French and Kitchener – and, somewhat incongruously, Drake. Inland at Palmwoods, Churchill Street passes the Commonwealth War Graves Commission's cemetery for the dead of 1942–5. Other juxtapositions were celebratory in a less ambiguous manner, as where the Churchill Drive at Mooroolburla, Melbourne, intersects with Statesman Crescent. The 1960s namings generally place Churchill alone, with no contiguous war references, and frequently indeed double the homage by placing the Churchill name alongside a Downing Street, or a Winston Court. Visiting the town of Churchill, Victoria (for which, see below) in 1965, the *Bulletin*'s columnist 'Batman' noted that it had Heesom Crescent, McInnes Crescent and Howard Avenue. 'One would have thought at the very least we would have had Montgomery of Alamein Court, Field Marshall Alan Brooke Close and Lord Alexander of Tunis Boulevard.' In fact such namings would by then (as his tone implied) have been well out of date, for Montgomery's fame had already evaporated while Churchill's had deepened. Mackay, Queensland, seems to be almost unique in Australia in following a common American practice, whereby Churchill becomes merely part of a group of miscellaneous British associations: in Mackay, Churchill is surrounded by Dickens, Raleigh and Tudor, among others, as well as by Downing and Marlborough.[88]

It is not easy to deconstruct such namings, and it would take a lifetime of research into local authority archives and the records of speculative builders to do so properly. But some points do clearly emerge. First, the sheer number of namings and their geographical spread. The Sydney metropolitan area has eighteen Churchill thorough-fares and two Churchill reserves, rural New South Wales another four-teen; Melbourne has twenty-eight and the rest of Victoria another twenty; Brisbane has eleven and there are fourteen in the rest of Queens-land. Smaller but still significant numbers in the other states would reflect both smaller populations and a slower rate of suburban growth (and hence of new streets needing names) since the 1960s. Overall though, there are about 150 Australian thoroughfares named Churchill spread across cities, suburbs and country areas in every state and terri-tory. This denotes at the least a widespread acquiescence by planners and legislators in these processes of recognition, even if most of the actual residents affected found that their street had gained such a name before they first moved in. Comparisons can also be instructive, for Western Australia seems to be the only state with more streets named after Menzies than Churchill (in most areas Menzies has so far attracted only half as many namings) and nowhere do either Curtin or Chifley get near to beating Churchill in this particular poll of popularity. Sir John Monash and Sir Donald Bradman are apparently the only twen-tieth-century Australians consistently to outshine Churchill on the street signs, but both were very special types of hero in a country which rarely celebrates its 'tall poppies', and neither was a politician in a land which consistently takes a rather cynical view of its rulers. Churchill was thus honoured more than any Australian politician has been.

It is noticeable in this context that there is no statue or Churchill Street at all in either Hong Kong or Singapore (where Churchill's post-war fame suffered considerably from the prevailing sense of betrayal by his Government over the Japanese occupation – a much greater 'betrayal' indeed than even David Day has ever claimed for Australia). Since both were British colonies for decades after 1945, the colonial authorities must have felt nervous of provoking hostility by commemorating Churchill there. There was no such problem in Singapore, however, about honouring Mountbatten, who was seen as the liberator, or even General Percival, who had commanded during the siege and helpfully ignored Churchill's instruction to lay the city waste before surrendering to the Japanese. Long after independence, there are still Mountbatten and

Percival Streets in Singapore. Across the Pacific, Fiji was (like Tonga and Australia) never occupied by Japan, and Churchill's name can be and still is honoured there. The city of Leutoka, for example, has a Churchill Park in which, inappropriate as it may seem, Rugby League is avidly played and watched.

Not every Australian Churchill Street was of course named after *Winston* Churchill (though the proximity of a Winston Way or a block of flats named Winston proves just how many were, certainly over a hundred). A surprising number in the inner cities commemorated his father, as in both Adelaide and Melbourne, and a few no doubt recalled more local worthies or even the builder himself. Churchill Island on the Victorian coast was named after a minor British government official who was a friend of the early settler Lieutenant Grant, as the *Cambridge Dictionary of Australian Places* records, while Churchill Creek and Churchill Reef were also probably namings of a similar antiquity. The *Cambridge Dictionary*'s uncertainty about the Churchill subdivision of Ipswich in the Brisbane metropolitan area of Queensland, 'presumably' named after Britain's wartime leader, is understandable enough.[89] It had actually been named in the late 1800s after Queensland's Churchill shire dating from 1845 – far too early even to be named after Lord Randolph. It cannot have had anything at all to do with Winston, and nor would the Churchill state school which opened there in 1923. In the post-war years, however, as his fame in Australia spread, the local authority seems to have decided to adopt him anyway, naming contiguous streets not only after Churchill, but also after Winston, Leonard *and* Spencer. The school now has as its motto 'No Success without Endurance', a Churchillian theme which can scarcely be coincidental. This was clearly no mere acquiescence, but a deliberate act of homage, and seems likely to have been typical. Adelaide city's Churchill Street was a nineteenth-century naming, but when the Churchill Memorial Appeal took place in 1965, it was conspicuous by its generosity, enabling the local paper to head its report 'Street Was Loyal'.[90]

Homage to Churchill indicated in namings did not necessarily go very deep, and was usually cost-free anyway. This is brought out by the sorry story of the Victorian Government's decision to name after him a new town which was to be constructed as a satellite community for the Hazelwood power plant in the La Trobe Valley. It had been intended to call the town Hazelwood too, but in the euphoric mood surrounding

Churchill's funeral, Churchill was chosen instead. When the news broke, the area erupted in outrage, demanding that Hazelwood be the name because of its local associations – it had been named after the daughter of an early settler, a girl called Hazel. The lead was taken by a farmer called Tom Lawless, an RAAF veteran who held office in the local branch of the RSL, and who only a few weeks earlier had been patriotically collecting money for the Churchill Memorial Trust. There was thus no hostility to Churchill himself in the 'Don't Change to Churchill' campaign, merely a reluctance to sacrifice a traditional local association for a distant one, as was demonstrated by the campaigners' suggestion that the town of Hazelwood have a Churchill Square at its centre. The State Housing Minister (whose idea the renaming had all been, though he was not now admitting it) promptly called the local campaigning 'the greatest possible insult to the name of a great wartime leader', and reminded the shire council that it had been 'most enthusiastic' about the idea when he first consulted them. The postmaster patiently explained that having two Hazelwoods in close proximity would be an administrative disaster, but the authorities were unable to stop the campaign's progress.

Although at that time only three hundred people lived in the area (over sixteen thousand lived in the valley as a whole, however), a petition bearing 1100 names was sent to the state government, the local football team reversed its decision to switch its own name from Hazelwood to Churchill, and the shire council which had already approved the name change back-pedalled furiously and demanded time to think again. The state cabinet had to visit the La Trobe Valley to appease local opinion, and waited impatiently while the shire kept deferring a decision. In the end nerves held, the shire voted by six votes to five to reaffirm the name change, and the switch to Churchill was implemented. But there was still plenty of discontent, and one citizen at least felt strongly enough to deface the new town sign with gunshots. This was presumably not Lawless, who was scrupulously lawful in all his doings. He had after all been at pains to point out that democratic self-government was exactly what Churchill himself had become so famous for defending. When the shire's duly elected council stood firm, he reluctantly accepted the decision, and although other protesters vowed to fight on and sent further deputations to Melbourne, the shire, the state government and (more importantly) the local paper all decided that this issue could now safely be ignored. Churchill, Victoria did not, however, grow into the showpiece town of over fifty thousand people that had been envisaged in 1965, having by the end of the century only a tenth of that number and a location dwarfed by the power station where most of them worked.

Indicating that this was not simply a local phenomenon in the Gippsland region of Victoria, in much the same period a similar dispute was being played out in Sydney's north-western suburbs, when it was decided to develop a suburb called Winston Hills from the areas previously known as Old Toongabbie and Model Farm, so removing indigenous as well as settler associations. Here again there was local opposition, though nowhere near as vociferous as in Victoria, but once again the authorities forced it through. In this case, the British political connections of the honorand were all too clearly spelled out, for Winston Hills now has not only a Churchill Drive, but also roads named after eleven other British Prime Ministers from Robert Peel to Harold Wilson. Presumably in deference to Churchill's posthumous preferences, Neville Chamberlain is one of those omitted (though Stanley Baldwin does make it into this particular first eleven).[91]

Such disputes, involving even the partial rejection of Churchill, were extremely untypical of Australia by the 1960s. More characteristic of attitudes was the tally of political autobiographers who paid homage to Churchill in their texts and dutifully printed at least one picture of him in their books (preferably when he was talking to *them*). Biographers played the same game on behalf of their subjects. Sir Earle Page, for example, never one of nature's deferentials, actually dedicated his autobiography 'by special permission' to Winston Churchill, 'whose courage and indomitable will inspired and saved the free world', and then added a grovelling thanks to Churchill for the right to print these compliments and to quote from his own 1942 diary which described their conversations. The process of mutual admiration was completed in a foreword by Beaverbrook which noted Page's important role in the war cabinet in 1942 and argued that he was 'completely Australian in his approach ... and yet distinctively imperial in outlook'. W. S. Robinson's book had a similar approach and might well have had a similar dedication had he lived to see it through the press. Arthur Fadden adopted a rather different literary strategy, quoting an exchange in which he had compared one of Churchill's cigars to 'a log of Queensland cedar', after which they enjoyed 'a couple of drinks together' and Churchill gave

him a signed copy of his war memoirs. All of this made Fadden himself
seem very much on terms of equality with the great man and was
probably included for exactly that reason. Nor were such tributes to
greatness limited to the Australian right. Evatt was a man whom Churchill disliked so much that he could hardly bear to be in the same room
with him, but Evatt himself thought that they had actually had a close
relationship. He was frequently to be heard paying tributes to Churchill's
greatness, as in 1953 when as ALP leader he argued that Churchill was
a greater man than either Lloyd George or Pitt (for the Australian left
was also trapped within the Imperial world for the purposes of making
such odorous comparisons). His successor Arthur Calwell was equally
generous, reprinting in full in his memoirs the funeral tribute to Churchill that he had paid in 1965.[92]

It is not surprising then that the next political generation, people
who could claim no personal connection with Churchill, nevertheless
continued to make obeisance, whether they were on the right or the
left. As an Oxford student, Malcolm Fraser was already offering his
tutor the view that Winston Churchill was the best sort of Conservative
leader, 'a radical determined to destroy evil', and when a mature politician he continued to quote Churchill fairly regularly. One of his biographers goes so far as to compare Fraser with Churchill, in that each
had had a privileged but neglected childhood, so toughening them up
for later life. Billy Snedden was another Churchill-quoter, for example
in support of Australia's stand in Vietnam. On the other side of the
House, Gough Whitlam explained his own failure to foresee dismissal
by the Governor-General as comparable to Churchill's blindness over
the unpreparedness of Singapore in 1942, while a Whitlam biographer
thought that their careers showed several similarities, including both
narcissistic qualities and a degree of fertility in policy-making that
required them to be kept under constant restraint by less imaginative
colleagues. Paul Keating, despite emerging from Sydney's Bankstown,
an Irish community where Churchill was not widely admired and for
whom a more natural hero would have been Jack Lang, had already
read Churchill's *The World Crisis* by the time he was fourteen.

> I was absolutely excited by Churchill's life. He is the reason
> why I am in public life. He had all the things. He had a lot of
> warts, and problems, and he had a lot of views I wouldn't

subscribe to. But the general horsepower, the depth of view,
the willingness to take decisions. He was an adventurer about
the right things. And I like the sort of swash-buckling style.

When Sir Geoffrey Howe visited Australia in 1990, Keating revealed
at a reception that he had just read the second volume of William Manchester's life of Churchill and was again full of enthusiasm for Churchill
as a result. John Howard was also present and later recalled that Keating
'was every bit the sort of budding Anglophile, certainly as far as Winston
is concerned. And I thought, "This bloke must have some good in him".'[93]

Howard himself has been the contemporary Australian political
leader most associated with Churchill's legacy, not least because his
middle name Winston was itself an act of homage to Churchill by his
parents (he thus shares his Christian names, if little else, with John
Winston Lennon, another baptismal victim of parental Churchillo-
philia). In Howard's case, parental devotion to Churchill was very real,
for (as a biographer puts it), 'he was conceived soon after the Munich
agreement' of 1938, and born in July 1939 when Churchill himself was
still in the political wilderness, his father being a strong opponent of
appeasement and a 'keen supporter of Winston Churchill'. Such a label
could well have been inhibiting to an aspirant conservative minister:
once he became a federal front-bencher, columnists and critics tended
invariably to use his threefold name rather than just calling him John
Howard as before, and in tones that indicated that Howard was pre-
sumptuous in the extreme to compare himself with Churchill. But
Howard has been unrepentant in his own stated admiration for Churchill. It was noted in 1995 that 'his heroes today are the same as in his
youth, Churchill, Menzies and Mountbatten', he has had Churchill's
painting rehung in his Prime Ministerial office, and in 2001 he was
telling a journalist that Churchill was still his main hero: 'I regard
Winston Churchill as the figure of the century, because he more than
any other person turned the tide against the greatest threat to humanity
of the century.' It was equally significant that once he had quoted these
words, the *Australian Financial Review*'s Tony Walker felt compelled to
add on his own account, 'Difficult to argue with that! Cometh the hour,
cometh the man ...'[94] Contemporary Australians therefore find many
different, and to an extent contradictory, things to admire in Churchill
– Fraser likes his aristocratic radicalism, Keating his sheer bravado,

Howard his ability to battle through adversity. In this, they are each of them seeing a Churchill more than a little like themselves, but each clearly draws considerable comfort from also being a little like Churchill.

John Howard was not likely ever to have switched his allegiance, but it can only have been reinforced by the accident that placed him in London at the time of Churchill's death and funeral, the final act of the drama to which his reluctant retirement from the Commons in the previous summer had provided a prologue. Australian legislators frequently referred to Churchill as 'a great Commoner', to his importance in saving representative government in 1940–5, and to their own heritage from the 'Mother of Parliaments' with which Churchill was so closely identified. His final appearance in the British Commons in July 1964 was therefore bound to be seen as an historic occasion. The *Mercury* registered the single discordant note about Churchill's lifetime achievement at the end of his political life, reporting the arrest of a protester outside his London home for having shouted out that Churchill was a traitor ('Communism and coloured immigration are the fruits of our victory. Winston Churchill is the biggest war criminal unhung'). It was also happy to note that he had needed to be arrested for his own safety, such was the mood of the crowd around him, and that he certainly deserved his conviction and fine for using insulting words, 'likely to lead to a breach of the peace'. There were no such embarrassments in Australia, where Churchill (like Curtin) had become 'a secular saint' – even if the two were still not to be mentioned in the same breath. In both New South Wales and South Australia the state legislatures passed appropriate resolutions, while in the Federal Parliament the Senate unanimously recorded 'its appreciation of his unsurpassed and splendid contribution to parliamentary democracy, and of the inspired leadership and tenacity of purpose which he brought to the free world in the period of its greatest danger'. Party politics was not perhaps quite absent from all this, even though now invisible, for when Menzies sent to Churchill a copy of the similar resolution passed by the House of Representatives, he enclosed a copy of his own speech delivered in proposing the motion, but made no reference to Arthur Calwell's speech in seconding it.[95] Association with – and especially intimate friendship with – Churchill seemed to carry a share of his greatness and was thus for restricted application only.

None of this would have adequately prepared the Australian public for January and February 1965. Churchill's final illness was reported in Australia on 18 January, his death on 25 January, and his funeral on 1 February. During that fortnight, the story was on the front page of all the newspapers every day, while the emotional level at which it was described and analysed gradually strengthened, as the case of the *West Australian* demonstrates. Its first story, headlined 'Churchill's hold on life weakens', accepted as unsurprising the early death of a failing ninety-year-old. Gradually, however, his week-long fight for life after a major stroke became in itself both a matter of interest and a metaphor for his life of strife (when he died the *Mercury*'s headline was 'Old Warrior Loses his Last Great Battle'), while photographs of his family, his doctors and other visitors to his bedside provided ways of varying the angle of the story. It also became clear that in London itself something very special was seen to be taking place, reflected in the large but silent crowds that assembled each day. There was also an increasing awareness in the paper's coverage that this was not just a matter for the English, but almost a case in which the whole free world was holding its breath. On 25 January, the *West Australian* led its front page with the story 'Churchill Dies: No Pain at End', accompanied by a large photograph of Churchill in the 1950s, unsmiling but resolute. An editorial hailed him as 'unquestionably the greatest Englishman in history' and concluded that there would 'in the winnowing processes of history . . . always be a place for Churchill the national leader, Churchill the inspiration and architect of freedom's victory, Churchill the world statesman, and Churchill the man'. The rest of the editorial page consisted of an obituary ('Great Free World Leader') and a syndicated cartoon from London, on the theme of the ninety ages of man. This showed the elderly Churchill surrounded by many other Churchills – MP, author, bricklayer, artist, racegoer, polo-player and so on. Looking at a bottle of champagne, he is saying, 'Ah, 1874 – a good year.' Reinforcing the same message, the paper also reprinted Low's wartime drawing of Churchill as 'The Head Man', striding in to chair a Chiefs of Staff committee, with all the other members again being himself in different uniforms. There was a selection of the most famous Churchill quotations, a column appreciating his role as a war leader, a whole page of Churchill photographs from the young MP of 1904 to the Garter knight of 1953, and many paragraphs of tributes paid by the Queen, the Pope and two archbishops, the heads of government in Britain, France, the USA, Australia, New Zealand,

Canada, Malaysia, West Germany, Taiwan and Yugoslavia. Very little else was reported that day in the Australian press, and since they had had a week to prepare while Churchill was dying, this was a well-prepared and well-thought-out process. It is therefore perhaps of some significance that, although Churchill's link with England, the Empire, the world and the free world is variously celebrated, and Australia is naturally included in several of these categories, there was no real attempt in Australia to claim any special relationship with Churchill as was being claimed for their countries by the American and Canadian press. Churchill had both gained and lost stature since the mid-1950s, for he was now perceived to be the greatest of all Englishmen and the greatest man in the world, but much less often to be the leader of a British race among which Australians included themselves.[96]

Over the following week, the story was less prominently reported, but became significantly more localised and Australian in focus. While leading on 26 January with the headline 'UK begins week of tribute to Churchill', the *West Australian* also gave considerable attention to Menzies' assessment of Churchill and reported the flying of flags at half-mast in Perth. It also printed a reader's letter hailing Churchill as 'the greatest executive personality of all time'. On the following day, further tributes from around Australia and the world and news of the funeral plans in London ran alongside the leaked reports of Australia's memorial appeal. On the 28th, pictures of Churchill's lying-in-state and of prominent mourners headed by Harold Wilson were balanced by details of memorial services to be held in Perth on the funeral day, in both Anglican and Roman Catholic cathedrals. On the 29th, the story of long queues to view Churchill's coffin was matched by the report of a Churchill stamp to be issued in Australia. On the 30th, photographs of London's mile-long queue were accompanied by news that Menzies would be an official pall-bearer, and a reminder that Churchill had so valued Perth's black swans. And alongside this Anglo-Australian sequence on the news pages ran readers' letters in which actual meetings of Churchill and Australians were described. One such letter from Geoff Burgoyne recalled a luncheon addressed by Churchill at Hever Castle in 1946, during the Empire Economic Conference. Introducing himself after lunch as 'Burgoyne, of Perth, Western Australia', he was gratified to hear Churchill respond, 'Oh, I have two of your black swans, a gift from your city . . .' Even letter-writers who were free from imperial nostalgia could find a positive Australian angle in Churchill's death: W. H. Lawson accepted that Britain's Empire had now gone the way of Rome's, but argued that 'the greatest tribute we can pay to the great national leader who has left us is to bring his inspiration and example to bear in our work for this young country of Australia'. On 1 February, the *West Australian* gave heavy verbal and photographic coverage to the funeral service, the cortège by boat and train towards interment at Bladon, and the queues that were now forming there. But it also highlighted Menzies' funeral broadcast on the BBC, announced the times at which the ABC would show films of the funeral in Australia, and described Perth's own memorial services – packed in the Anglican cathedral, only a 'small' congregation for the separate Catholic service.[97]

This systematic change of tone in reporting between Churchill's death and funeral (so turning his passing into a story in which Australians could feel a personal interest) was reflected in all the other papers too, as indeed was the general character of reporting and editorial comment over the entire fortnight.[98] Some of this uniformity of approach no doubt reflected their dependence on Reuters and other agency services, especially the Australian Associated Press, but since the Australian press was shortly to be so expertly managed in the interests of the Memorial Trust appeal, it seems not unlikely that such behind-the-scenes management had in fact already swung into action before the appeal was even launched. It seems equally likely that, if such management was indeed taking place, it was pushing at an open door, for Australian writers appear to have shared in the world's wish to claim a bit of Churchill for themselves and their country during that emotional time. Those few in the elite who had really become close to Churchill were in considerable demand for their memories. Menzies was initially at sea when Churchill fell ill, taking a recuperative cruise across the Pacific, and then on his way to London pursued by his funeral clothes and decorations from Canberra, so that he was a fairly limited presence in the Australian press. He was mainly reported through written appreciations that had been drafted weeks earlier and were now issued by Deputy Prime Minister McEwen on his behalf in Canberra, but he was of course doing his bit by playing such a leading part in London, as both the senior Commonwealth Prime Minister ('in point of time', he emphasised) and an intimate friend of the deceased. Richard Casey was thus pressed into extremely active service before flying to London to attend the funeral himself. On the very day on which Churchill's stroke was reported, he gave appreciations for Channel 10 and the *Australian*, 'to be used if he dies', on the following day he wrote twelve hundred words on Churchill for the Melbourne *Herald*, supplementing the story with his own photograph of himself with Churchill, and the next day he made television recordings for both Channel 7 and the BBC.[99]

The irresistible pull that Churchill's death and funeral exerted is demonstrated most strongly in the pages of the *Australian*, launched by Rupert Murdoch only a few months earlier to be Australia's first 'national' newspaper – national both in the geographical spread of its coverage and readership and in the ending of the Anglocentrism that still characterised such rivals as the *Sydney Morning Herald*, which in that generation still routinely appointed Britons like Angus Maude to its editorial chair. Initially, the *Australian* was cooler than the other papers in reporting Churchill's passing and the funeral plans, a stance that was reinforced by the use of Britain's *Guardian* as the source of reprinted stories rather than the *Daily Telegraph*'s pieces taken by the Herald group. On his death however, this paper too was drawn into the emotional whirlpool and the desire to link the story ever more closely with its readers, for example by printing on 25 January a whole page of Commonwealth tributes. But 'Commonwealth' in this case denoted not the international organisation but the whole of Australia, every state's leader being quoted, and for good measure several Opposition and RSL leaders too. On 1 February it issued a Churchill Souvenir Edition with two pages of funeral pictures, and had already re-emphasised the breadth of Australian memorialising by reporting memorial services in every state capital (each one attended by the Governor and a federal minister), together with many other services in churches, chapels and synagogues.[100]

The degree of official patronage for such memorials and the sometimes eccentric messages conveyed in the less official ones is brought out by what took place in Adelaide. The cathedral was packed with a thousand people, including not only the State Governor and Premier, the Federal Army Minister, Chief Justice and heads of state departments, but also the city council, the consular corps, the heads of the armed services and the judiciary. The Bishop of Adelaide led the service, but was supported by the Roman Catholic Archbishop, and by the state leaders of the Lutheran, Evangelical Lutheran, Presbyterian, Baptist, Church of Christ and Greek Orthodox Churches. The Bishop valiantly managed to trace through Churchill's agnostic career 'essentially the Christian tradition'. He was at least nearer to a truth that Churchill himself would have recognised than the Congregational pastor who at his own church's service began well but got into deep water when trying to apply the lessons of Churchill's life to Australia's future:

> Never before has it been given to a man to be so mourned by all men. And never before has it been given to one man to have been so admired, honored and loved by his fellows in his lifetime. Australians need the great Churchill qualities, including patriotism and the spirit of adventure and service, to meet the challenge of this land, with its vast outback, and to lead South-East Asia from within.

There was in these services much celebration of Churchill's 'irrepressible personality' and belligerence, aspects that Australians had not always found so attractive in the past. Tasmania's official order of service included not only the hymn 'Soldiers, Who are Christ's Below' but also 'Fight the Good Fight', a martial theme which Churchill would have much appreciated. The Dean's address made no attempt to claim that Churchill had exhibited Christian virtues, resting its argument rather on his individuality and his leadership skills, and concluding that 'when the situation demanded it, God provided the man'. Tasmania does, though, offer a further example of the range of church memorials as well as the quality of attendance in Hobart's cathedral, for the same issue of the *Mercury* reported well-attended services on the same day in Launceston, Devonport and Birnie. Simply by going in such numbers to Saturday services all around the country, Australian Christians (and indeed Australian Jews on the following day too) showed, as the newspaper coverage did, the breadth of Churchill's standing in Australia when he died. The showing of the BBC's ninety-minute film of Churchill's funeral on three different Australian channels on 1 February, at noon, 1.30 and 8.30 respectively, indicated the same assumptions in the network managers' decisions too.[101]

The collective Australian response to Menzies' bold pledge that Australians would raise a million pounds in a single day for a national Churchill Memorial was the plainest evidence of both the breadth and depth of Churchill's fame in Australia, and for this we must first understand Menzies' own complicated relations with the great man.

11

Robert Menzies, Worldwide Leader of the Churchill Appreciation Society

ROBERT MENZIES' RELATIONSHIP WITH CHURCHILL, like that of Australia as a whole, was paradoxical. He did not at first take to him, and he was harshly treated by Churchill when they first collaborated during the war cabinet meetings of 1941. Churchill seems not to have had a particularly high regard for the Australian Prime Minister and was thereafter slow to change his mind. For his part, Menzies did not become especially close to Churchill until some years after the war, but they then developed a warm and affectionate friendship that extended to their respective families, as well as a fraternal political association as the senior Commonwealth premiers of the 1950s. Finally, as Churchill aged, Menzies emerged as the English-speaking world's prime defender of the Churchill legend, although he still harboured reservations about Churchill's actual policies and even about matters on which others never doubted his greatness. When Churchill died in 1965, Menzies delivered one of the most highly regarded eulogies, broadcast by the BBC during its coverage of the Churchill funeral and published soon afterwards as *Menzies on Churchill*. This was widely hailed as evidence that the Churchillian role as the world's leading English-language orator had fallen to Menzies. That status was then confirmed by Menzies' appointment as Churchill's direct successor (on the Queen's personal recommendation) as Lord Warden of the Cinque Ports in Kent.

More unofficial confirmations came in invitations to Menzies to preside at the inaugurations of various Churchill memorials, including the Churchill statue on the village green in Westerham near Chartwell. He was also invited during the later 1960s (but could not accept) to take part in the unveiling of the Churchill statue in Washington DC, and to speak at such early Churchill gatherings as the annual Churchill banquet in Calgary, Alberta. He did speak in 1968 at the golden jubilee banquet of the English-Speaking Union of the Commonwealth, another cause close to both Menzies' heart and Churchill's. These last were a clear enough indication that Menzies' close link with Churchill was perceived in the United States and the Commonwealth as well as in the United Kingdom and Australia. His two volumes of autobiography each made Churchill a central character – far too central in the view of many reviewers – but his brilliant championing of the Winston Churchill Memorial Trust in Australia itself made it the most successful of all the fundraising memorials that followed Churchill's death, despite the fact that Australia contained more citizens who were actively hostile to the Churchill legend than any other developed country except Ireland. The story of Menzies' relationship with both Churchill the man and Churchill the legend is therefore an instructive one as we seek to understand what it was that ensured Churchill's worldwide and lasting fame.

Robert Menzies fell in love with all things British during his first visit to London in 1935 but was decidely underwhelmed by the experience of watching Churchill in action in the Commons.[1] 'The idol has feet of clay,' Menzies noted sadly in his diary (though even this implies that Churchill was already an idol of some sort, and Menzies conceded that 'I had no delusions of grandeur in his presence'). Sir John Bunting thought that what had attracted Menzies to Churchill from afar – as it also attracted him to F. E. Smith – was his 'capacity to enjoy life boisterously'.[2] What initially let Churchill down in Menzies' eyes was his habit of reading all his speeches, even when they were merely lighthearted after-dinner remarks, which the natural orator Menzies would never have done, even before his years of experience at the bar. Moreover, he observed acidly that in terms of their content Churchill's speeches were 'a constant repetition of "I told you so", and first class men don't usually indulge in this luxury. If a first-rater has once said an important thing, he doesn't need to remind people that he's said it.'[3] Closer acquaintance extended this initial disapproval to a more generalised lack of respect for Churchill's politics and manner, Menzies coming to the conclusion that Churchill was fatally self-indulgent and undisciplined both in body and in mind, a view in which he was no doubt confirmed by meeting so many of Churchill's British contemporaries during the same trip, men who had reached the same conclusion after years of observation.

Menzies certainly admired Baldwin more than Churchill, both for his speaking style and for his foreign policy. When in early 1940 – by which time Menzies was Australian Prime Minister – Churchill began to be talked about as Neville Chamberlain's successor, Menzies was far from supportive of the idea, agreeing with Bruce, then Australian High Commissioner in London, that Churchill was far too excitable and unreliable for the position of war leader, and he helped Chamberlain to stop Churchill's 'ill-considered stunt' to mine Norwegian waters.[4] Menzies told Bruce, 'I am convinced that Winston is a menace. He is a publicity seeker, he stirs up hazards in a world already seething with them, and he is lacking in judgement.'[5] For his part, Churchill seems not to have expressed recorded views on Menzies at that time, but it is unlikely that he was impressed by one who was at least as blind as Chamberlain to the real nature of Nazi Germany. His rough handling of Menzies in 1941 may indeed owe quite a lot to his reluctance to take lessons in war leadership from an all too-recent appeaser. This had more than a little in common with attacks on Menzies back home, where his leadership was more often identified with Chamberlainite weakness than with Churchillian strength, even by Australian Labor which had few reasons to admire Churchill.[6] Even when celebrating Churchill's war leadership in 1954, Menzies acknowledged that:

> Winston Churchill had for many years been a controversial figure in Australia. Not known in person, he was in turn thought of as brilliant, unstable, brave, indiscreet, born to be a minority leader. So recently as in 1939, he was, so it was said, a spent force.

He did not of course by then acknowledge that this had been his own view at the time.[7]

It has been powerfully argued that Menzies' 1941 visit to Britain with its cabinet-room clashes with Churchill was a pivotal moment in his career and in the development of his political psychology, forcing him at last to become his own man with a more Australian-centred political identity.[8] Such interpretations do not appear to give sufficient weight either to the reservations about Churchill that he had been expressing for the previous six years or to the continued admiration that he felt for him even after their bitterest disputes. There was certainly an epic clash of wills, for Menzies had been a dominant figure in his own cabinet, but nevertheless expected it to be a real forum for debate, while Churchill's war cabinet seemed to him to be a hopelessly unbusinesslike place where nobody stood up to the Prime Minister as he rambled on about one obsession or other. When he tried to confront Churchill, for example over the necessity of adequate air cover for Australian troops in Greece, reassurances were given but not carried out, and his position was undermined by apparent agreement between the generals on the spot of which he knew nothing (and of which, in some cases, the Australian military in the Middle East knew nothing either). The phrase, 'He came, he saw, and Churchill conquered', might have been as appropriately applied to Menzies as to Evatt, except that Menzies had his own friends in the British establishment who urged him on in his demand for more businesslike methods of government, and he had too much willpower to permit silent acquiescence.

The breach was not even limited to matters of concern solely to Australia, for Menzies was arguing for an Imperial war cabinet in which all the Dominions would be directly consulted on strategy. He may even have had aspirations to head such a cabinet himself, though few historians have accepted David Day's view that Menzies aimed to topple Churchill altogether.[9] They also clashed over Ireland, where Menzies decided, against Churchill's wishes, to undertake a personal mission to de Valera in the hope of bringing Ireland into the war – Churchill told him bluntly that if he visited that 'murderer and perjurer' it would not be with the backing of the British Government.[10] The Irish mission failed anyway, while efforts to create an Imperial war cabinet foundered on the indifference of the other Dominions: New Zealand was as ever uncomplicatedly loyal to the London-centred view of Empire, South Africa's Prime Minister Smuts told Menzies that the Dominions should mind their own business and let Churchill run the war, and Canada's Mackenzie King thought that an Imperial war cabinet had dangerous overtones of Imperial federation about it, and would not agree to the idea unless it met as often in the Dominions as in London – a hopelessly impractical way to run a war.[11] All of which perhaps explains why Menzies needed de Valera as an inside ally who would certainly not have been supine nor have deferred so much to Churchill – and indeed why Churchill was not at all keen on the idea.

Menzies was perhaps bound to lose in these battles with Churchill, but he was nevertheless deeply upset by the experience, not least because the failure of his London mission was a contributory reason for his own downfall as Prime Minister shortly after he returned home. Nevertheless, even in this time of personal crisis and deep disillusion, Menzies continued to pay generous tributes to Churchill: in a cable to Arthur Fadden in March 1941, for example, he wrote that Churchill's 'experience since becoming prime minister has obviously ripened his judgement' (so reversing his greatest earlier doubt about the man) 'and he combines in a unique way most remarkable fighting and driving qualities with an exceptional mastery of the details of both plans and equipment'; in his diary at about that time he recorded that 'Churchill grows on me.'[12] By and large, more negative views came to predominate over the positive as his sojourn in London continued, but his final appraisal of the man was a remarkably balanced one, one indeed that it would be difficult to fault with the advantages of hindsight, every negative set against a positive – for example: 'Is a superb dinner table talker . . . but never listens to anybody else if he can help it.'[13]

When he returned home, Menzies described Churchill to the press as 'a great fighting leader', and once in opposition continued often to take Churchill's side against Australia's Labour Government in the fierce quarrels that followed, a stance that did very little for his standing in his own country at the time. In all of this Menzies acted with considerably more generosity than did Churchill, who may have been at least a little jealous of the success of Menzies' radio broadcasts on the BBC (published as To the People of Britain and quickly selling five thousand copies); he had after all driven J. B. Priestley off the airwaves in the previous year. When Menzies in December 1941 cabled Churchill fulsome – and expensive – congratulations on his birthday ('You may rely on us all. My own small association with you is a proud memory and an inspiration for the future. Warmest personal regards'), Churchill sent only three words in reply ('Thankyou so much').[14] Churchill was in any case informed about Menzies bad-mouthing him and his management of the war, for example when an indiscreet interview with a war correspondent was intercepted by the censors after the reporter filed his story,[15] but he may well not have seen the equivalent tributes that Menzies paid him more privately. Whatever the cause, Churchill ruthlessly blocked all Menzies' efforts to get himself a proper job in the war effort after he ceased to be Australia's Prime Minister: he stymied his appointment as Allied supremo in Singapore when Duff Cooper suggested it, he refused to have him as a minister in his own Government, and then insultingly appointed Casey instead (Casey being Menzies' main rival of his own generation among Australian Liberals), and, by blunderingly suggesting it himself, he ensured that Menzies would not be sent to Washington either.

Some of this was soon available in print for Australians to read for themselves, but Churchill's war memoirs were far from being the only area in which Churchill displayed his insensitivity to Menzies' interests and feelings. When, for example, he cabled to commiserate with Menzies for losing office in 1941, he wrote as follows: 'I went through a similar experience when I was removed from the Admiralty when I could have given the ANZACs a fair chance of victory at the Dardanelles.' When it is recalled just how many setbacks there had been in Churchill's career before 1939, his decision to cite his resignation over Gallipoli (and in this flagrantly ahistorical manner, never mind the reference to 'the Dardanelles', a name which no Australian would have used) was a quite extraordinary comparison to throw in the face of an Australian. Gallipoli had after all been an acknowledged military disaster, and nothing remotely comparable could be blamed on Menzies even by his severest critic. But, even as their paths converged in the 1950s, Churchill continued to ignore the thin ice in their relationship. If David Day is even partly right in his view that Menzies had tried to enter British politics and topple Churchill in 1941, then Anthony Montague Browne's account of their meeting some ten years later suggests a similar insensitivity, perhaps even a mischievous readiness to wound: 'WSC set out with apparent seriousness to persuade Menzies to leave Australia, enter the House of Commons immediately, and soon succeed the incumbent as Prime Minister.' Likewise, all too often in the later 1950s, he would write to ask when Menzies was next coming to London – but then list in the same letter his own extensive international travel plans to other places.[16]

When Menzies wrote directly to Churchill to ask for some useful war work in 1942, the latter replied that he was doing more good for the war effort by staying in Australia – where he was not now even the leader of the Opposition and had no power to achieve anything at all.[17] In the circumstances, and with his career at its lowest ebb, Menzies' continuing admiration for Churchill takes some explaining, but it was undoubtedly there. When Churchill lost the 1945 general election, Menzies (his daughter remembers) was 'devastated', strong evidence of the sincerity of what he wrote to Churchill at the time: 'This political blast will leave the pages of your personal history unruffled. Personally, I shall always feel pride in having been privileged to serve for a while beside you.' Though Churchill received thousands of such messages, this was one which he read with pleasure and to which he quickly replied, cabling that he was 'delighted to receive your lively telegram. I always look back to our adventure in Britain.'[18] Since 'adventure' was one of the most positive autobiographical words that Churchill used in such messages – after 1946, his messages to Harry Truman rarely failed to mention their 'adventure' together in Missouri – it seems that Churchill had least now admitted Menzies to the club of his cronies from the recent war.

Menzies' view at this stage was extremely positive – in public as well as in private. He urged the House of Representatives formally to thank Churchill for his war leadership, recalling that it had already passed such motions of thanks to John Curtin and Franklin Roosevelt (though on their deaths in each case) and urged a similar motion about Churchill, 'the chief architect of victory'. He also went much further than other MPs had done, since Arthur Fadden's original motion had spoken only of Churchill as 'Britain's war leader', by expressly associating Churchill with Australia's own war:

> If ever in human history one man, by undaunted courage, matchless moral force, and unsurpassed eloquence, altered the course of history, it was Churchill. I believe that he has, and will continue to have, the love and gratitude of every good Australian now living in this country, or to live in it for centuries to come.

Over the next few years while both men were in opposition, Menzies continued to endorse Churchill's views, hailing his Fulton speech as Churchill speaking for Australia as well as Britain, explaining that nothing in Churchill's Zurich call for a United States of Europe need upset Australia or the Commonwealth, and quickly explaining away allegations that he and Churchill had quarrelled in 1941 when the relevant volume of Churchill's war memoirs came out. Menzies showed though that there was parallel thinking here, as well as one-sided endorsement, for in reacting to the 'iron curtain' speech he highlighted and accepted Churchill's underlying argument that:

the case for close and abiding associations between the English-Speaking Peoples is that, by natural evolution from a large common racial and traditional stock, they possess a common love of individual freedom, a common language, a common religious outlook, common political institutions and a similar educational development, which offers solid foundations for a special association which will mean a building of reality into the United Nations organisation itself.

This was almost exactly the way in which Churchill himself was describing his aims during his American visit, though there had clearly been no prior consultation between them, as Churchill had had with Canada's political leaders. Menzies was also from 1945 onwards always happy to introduce Churchill's name into debates in Canberra, on such domestic matters as public ownership as well as on international affairs, and this was in part the reason that Churchill remained so contentious a figure in Australian party politics.

There remained, though, a great gap between them – in effect the thirteen thousand miles of distance which prevented the personal warmth which Churchill evoked from such American leaders as Eisenhower and Truman, a warmth that had arisen simply because he was able to meet them relatively often. It will therefore be as well to trace the process of Menzies' and Churchill's convergence from its shaky start in 1941. As has been seen, Menzies emerged from their 1941 disputes without deep grudges, but Churchill's impressions of Menzies had been rather more negative. Though they did not fall out as completely as has sometimes been alleged, there was certainly a lack of warmth. Churchill preferred to do business with Menzies' rival Richard Casey, who might well have seemed more likely to become Australia's Prime Minister than Menzies, while Menzies expected Churchill to retire anyway – indeed thought that he should – and had plenty of other British patrons. (He noted in 1948 that Churchill's wish to avenge his 1945 electoral defeat was 'natural, but unfortunate'.) Churchill personally allowed Casey to reject the peerage that would normally have gone with the Governorship of Bengal in 1944, so that he would be freer to re-enter Australian Liberal politics: 'one had jealously to protect one's political usefulness'. When Casey did in due course re-enter the House of Representatives in 1949, a cable from Churchill was among the congratulations he received.[19]

There is no evidence that Churchill sent a similar message of goodwill to Menzies (who had after all just won the election and become Prime Minister!) Correspondence between Churchill and Menzies in the late 1940s was invariably initiated by Menzies, and Churchill's replies were usually brief and formal. Distance between them was also indicated clearly enough by their mutual use of the 'Dear Mr Churchill' and 'Dear Mr Menzies' style of address.

All the same, the passage of time and the disappearance of issues that had divided them in 1941, together with the fact that each was now projecting himself as an anti-socialist crusader both at home and internationally, must have reduced the size of the gap. For Menzies, the crucial point seems to have been his London visit of 1948. Though he made calls and arranged social engagements with his usual enthusiasm as soon as he arrived, and included both Attlee and Eden (and many other Conservative leaders) among his early conversations, he had no contact with Churchill until an accidental meeting at a royal garden party, where (to judge from his diary) they had little to say to each other. From his other contacts, Menzies received plenty of evidence of Churchill's erratic current form as a party leader, and decided that the Conservatives would never prosper until he stepped down: 'This is terrible but true,' he confided to his diary.[20]

Then, on the following day, *four weeks* after he had arrived in London, he spent several hours with Churchill at Chartwell and had his first prolonged conversation with the great man for seven years. Churchill laid on the full Chartwell charm offensive, showing Menzies his paintings, the garden wall that he had built in his wilderness years, the operations room from which he was producing his war memoirs (no doubt with a few glimpses of classified documents to add a little spice to the occasion). Though Menzies could not have known it, this was a standard procedure for Churchill with important guests. Walter Graebner of *Time* magazine had an almost identical experience in the same period, with equal effect on his lasting view of Churchill's greatness. Even occasional tourists peering through the Chartwell gates could be invited in and treated to a tour of the premises when Churchill was feeling bored, a treat he gave to some visiting US sailors in 1949.[21]

Menzies found Churchill 'in the old siren suit and a baggy waterproof coat and a cigar, supervising the building of a rockery'. (That image of Churchill *wearing* a cigar, as he wore his famous siren suit, is remarkably perceptive.) He was surprised to find that 'the old man looks no older, but has mellowed marvellously. Conversation is now a two-way affair, vastly cheerful, friendly and informative.' He decided that 'only Boswell could do justice to it anyhow', but tried to capture the essence of Churchill's flow of conversation in three pages of his diary. During these exchanges, Churchill told him that his next published volume of war memoirs would cover their wartime collaboration, including their disagreement over Dakar: 'He asked for, and I cheerfully gave permission to quote our cabled exchanges,' something Menzies would regret when he came to read the book, since Churchill would as usual mainly quote his own words and ignore Menzies' replies. But Churchill did reassure Menzies that 'European Union is not, in his opinion, inconsistent with British Empire. He draws me a diagram at the dinner table . . . How he loves a graphic touch like this.' The diagram in question, duly copied into Menzies' diary from the napkin on which Churchill had drawn it, was one of Churchill's favourites, the 'three circles' concept of British international policy. The three circles intersected only in London (and in this case he actually drew the British Isles within the intersected area, for 'the one sector common to the three is, in shape, roughly like the British Isles'), the three areas being 'B[ritish] E[mpire]', 'United Europe' and 'English-Speaking World'. This was subtly different from the usual version. Churchill's third circle was more often the 'special relationship' of Britain and the USA (the Dominions thus coming under the Commonwealth or, in Churchill's preferred form, 'Empire'), but here the Dominions came under 'English-Speaking World', and 'British Empire' would consist only of Britain and the colonies. Whether the change was a deliberate one of Churchill's, or simply a matter of Menzies misinterpreting a point of detail, is impossible to prove, but it had the significant effect of recognising that Australia also had a direct relationship with the USA (not just through Britain) and is therefore far more likely to have proved attractive to Menzies than the usual version.[22]

Whatever the meaning of the graphics and the semantics, Menzies had clearly now fallen under Churchill's spell, as so many did after prolonged exposure to his post-war charms. He had however done so to a large extent because Churchill had 'mellowed marvellously', so that he could now take part in a real exchange of views, a matter of importance to Menzies who certainly thought that his views on world affairs were worth hearing. It is perhaps no accident that one of the Churchill-

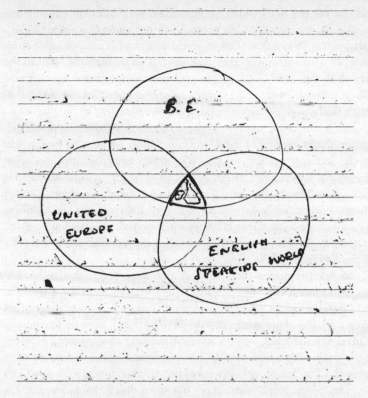

'The Three Circles of British Power': Menzies Diary

and-Menzies photographs that Menzies seems to have liked most, and used to illustrate his writings on the subject of their relationship, shows them relaxing together in the garden of Number Ten – but with Churchill apparently listening as Menzies speaks. By 1948 then, the gap had narrowed considerably: Churchill cabled to wish Menzies 'God speed' when he left, his letters now began 'My dear Menzies' and his cables were signed 'Winston'. When Menzies sought to use Cold War tensions as a political weapon during the 1949 election campaign, he was happy to quote from Churchill speeches on the subject to indicate both that he saw Churchill as a man of special authority and that they were of the same mind. Menzies' return as Prime Minister in 1949 then confirmed that he rather than Casey was the Australian Liberal to reckon with for the rest of Churchill's political life, and Churchill's own return to office in 1951 completed the process, for they could now – the ANZUS pact apart – be political allies in world affairs with much to gain from each other's cooperation. They thus moved on by the early 1950s to the 'My dear Bob' and 'Dear Winston' basis of real friendship. Richard Casey, however, remained a sort of spectre at their feast of friendship. Since Casey was unhappy working under Menzies, he in 1951 asked Churchill if he could take him back into the *British* Government instead, and no doubt endeared himself to Churchill by telling him that Britain should indeed be added to ANZUS. When Churchill died, Menzies' deputy put forward to Menzies only with apparent trepidation the idea that Casey should be Australia's second official mourner. Though Menzies immediately agreed to this, Casey then wrote an extensive account of the funeral into his diary without once mentioning Menzies' presence in London or his BBC broadcast that was to most people one of the highlights of the day.[23]

Menzies remained then, through the 1950s to the end of his life, the visible leader of Churchill's supporters' club in Australia, a friend of the Churchill family as well as of Winston, and a tireless defender of his reputation and of the lessons that ought to be drawn from his life. In 1955, Wilfrid Kent-Hughes, by then a junior minister in the Liberal Government, when with a journalist on an overseas visit made indiscreet references to Churchill being no friend of the Australian people: 'I think he's the grand old man of British history, but his trouble is that he's never been able to see East of Suez.' The inevitable story broke while Menzies himself was visiting Churchill in London – actually 'drinking his whisky' when the BBC broadcast the news, it was claimed – but he ensured on his return that Kent-Hughes was relegated to the back benches. This was only the last of several indiscretions, but one that could not be overlooked.[24]

Menzies also worked hard at the personal friendship and was ingenious at writing in ways that would arouse a spark of interest in Churchill as he aged. So, for example, when Lord Cherwell, Churchill's 'Prof', visited Australia in 1953, an anxious secretary asked if the Prime Minister would wish to entertain him. A press clipping indicated that Cherwell was a 'sad-faced ... bachelor, non-smoker and vegetarian', and the secretary added that 'the only thing it does not say is that he [also] does not drink', but added helpfully that Sir Stephen Holmes was keen to entertain him as a fellow scientist. The gregarious Menzies minuted briskly, 'In that case, let Holmes have him!' But when Cherwell died in 1957 it was to Churchill rather than to Cherwell's family that Menzies sent a most sensitive letter of condolence, knowing how much Churchill would be grieving: 'Please understand how many of us there are who, when they heard of his death, thought instantly of you and sent unspoken messages of sympathy for you.'[25]

Menzies never missed dispatching congratulations on a Churchill birthday, and if on occasion the memory at work was his secretary's rather than his own he invariably came up with a turn of phrase that suggested personal thought. In 1959, Churchill's eighty-fifth, it was 'This is a historic day. We are all with you in spirit and affection,' which prompted (as few of the sackfuls of congratulations did by this stage), an immediate and personal reply: 'Thankyou so much for your telegram, dear Bob. Winston.' In 1963 when he was fighting for his political life in a close election, Menzies nevertheless found time to cable: 'Today is a most interesting day – your birthday, St Andrew's Day, and my trial by the electors. I hope that I come out of my battle one-tenth as well as you have come out of yours – battles which we remember and for which we always have you in our minds and in our hearts.' On Churchill's ninetieth and last birthday, Menzies wrote, 'Immortals do not need birthday anniversaries, but in spite of this two mere mortals send you their love today and always, Bob and Pat Menzies.'[26]

Beyond all this, Churchill and Menzies sent each other 'get well soon' messages when either was ill, they met and enjoyed each other's memories whenever Menzies was in London, they exchanged presents of books and paintings, Menzies was an avid collector (and filer) of Churchill stories and cartoons from the press, and they found in the Suez Crisis, in the development of the Commonwealth and in Britain's drift into 'Europe' under Macmillan issues on which they were naturally in harmony. Menzies' attempt to mediate during the Suez Crisis of 1956 was not one of the happier aspects of his international career, but its most bizarre moment came when he first met Colonel Nasser. In the hope of breaking the ice and establishing a rapport with the Egyptian leader, he asked if he had ever met Churchill. Nasser said that he had not, but that he was a great admirer, and this gave Menzies all the encouragement he needed to tell his favourite stories to a new audience. When the crisis erupted into war, however, Menzies proved one of Britain's few supporters among world leaders, unwilling as he was to disbelieve Eden's false promises, and Churchill (who had been more ambivalent during the actual crisis) wrote to thank him for his 'two magnificent speeches'.[27]

The convergence of their opinions over the Commonwealth, as it developed during the 1950s from an amiable white man's club into a turbulent debating forum on colonial policy, owed nothing to political correctness on either side. Neither Menzies nor Churchill approved of the behaviour of India's leader Nehru at Commonwealth Conferences, neither wanted South Africa pressurised over racial policy at the risk of its departure from the club (Menzies indeed foreseeing that his 'white Australia' policy might place him next in line), and neither admired the anti-colonial posturings of Ghana's Kwame Nkrumah. Churchill for example told his doctor in 1955 that the Commonwealth Conference had been 'a hell of a business ... not at all like the old gatherings of the Dominions'. When Menzies missed meeting Churchill during his 1961 visit to London, he wrote to say how much he had regretted their not being able to discuss the damaging impact on the Dominions of Britain's application to join the EEC, on which he had perhaps hoped to enlist Churchill's support at a critical time for Australia, just as it was about to be deserted by Britain. But he concluded: 'You must feel just as puzzled as I am about some of the modern developments in the Commonwealth. Perhaps we are paying too great a price for the doubtful advantage of retaining some countries in nominal membership?' Churchill rarely sent long replies to letters by this stage, but in this case was clearly much exercised by what Menzies had said about Nkrumah's pro-Soviet and anti-democratic tendencies ('in substance, a dictatorship'). Not only did he reply at length to express his entire agreement with what Menzies had written ('I feel as unhappy as you do ...'), but enclosed for Menzies' personal information a letter that he had recently sent to Macmillan, demanding that the Queen's projected visit to Ghana be cancelled, lest it be used to bolster an anti-British regime. No doubt Ghana would leave the Commonwealth, but 'I am not convinced that would be a great loss.' In 1948, Menzies and Churchill had allied to resist the replacement of 'Empire' by 'Commonwealth', and the dropping of the word 'British' from the organisation's title, as suggested at a Commonwealth Conference overwhelmingly attended by Prime Ministers from the left in their respective countries. By 1967, though, had he still been alive, Churchill would have been unlikely to dissent from the view that Menzies expressed in 1961, that 'the "Winds of Change" are blowing a little too strongly', or from his 1967 Ditchley Foundation Lecture which argued that the Commonwealth 'is no longer British'.[28]

Menzies on the other hand remained defiantly British in his own sense of personal identity, and the fact that such an Anglophile was his main source of information about Australia can only have increased Churchill's lack of grasp about what was actually happening there. For, even while Menzies remained Prime Minister, the two countries' paths continued to diverge, and his own lack of effort to get Britain into the ANZUS pact after Churchill demanded it in 1951 suggests that Menzies was at least pragmatically complicit in the process. Paul Hasluck argued in 1980 that 'Menzies was thoroughly Australian. He loved things British and he enjoyed the company of the cultivated British, but in his frank admiration of another country he never ceased to be himself or lost his own identity as an Australian.' There seems no reason to doubt this testimony from one who knew him well, except that Menzies and many other Australians of his generation would surely have argued at least until the 1960s that it was possible to be British and Australian without derogation from either identity. Menzies himself often went further, in the same way that Churchill himself did, in arguing the wider identity of the English-speaking peoples, as he explicitly did when lecturing in Virginia after his retirement: 'we are the same kinds of people'. His very invitation to speak in Virginia was of course evidence of the sort of thing that he was claiming and of his own status as its advocate. Viewed from the perspective of Britain itself, however, as Menzies visited annually, made gracefully loyalist speeches and received honours and awards – more freedoms and honorary degrees indeed even than Churchill acquired – and was invariably photographed at a cricket match, it was the Anglophilia of Menzies that stood out rather than his Anglophonism. And since no alternative vision of Australianness was so regularly on display in London (this being before the days even of Clive James, Germaine Greer and Barry Humphries), it was all too easy for the British to draw the false conclusion that this was the Australian identity. It was noted, for example, that Menzies had been 'very warmly acknowledged' by British cinema audiences when he appeared on newsreels of the Coronation, and that he spoke lovingly of 'his London' (meaning Churchill's) but then added in an emotional tone, 'our London', during his 1965 funeral broadcast.[29]

Menzies' most important contribution to the debate about the Churchill legend came in a signed chapter that he contributed in 1954 to a volume presented in homage to Churchill on his eightieth birthday, *Winston Churchill: Servant of Crown and Commonwealth*. When Sir James Marchant first asked him to contribute, he let him know (as editors do on such occasions) how many other important figures had agreed to take part – T. S. Eliot, Harry Truman, Lord Halifax – none of whom ever produced their chapters of course. Menzies responded enthusiastically that 'I am honoured to have been asked and am happy to contribute.' He needed to be reminded from time to time actually to produce his own text, but he did so in time, and it was included in Cassell's published volume. It was hailed as one of the best pieces of writing in the book, one of the few chapters that adopted the elevated tone that Churchill himself would have chosen for such an occasion, and so was thought to be particularly fitting. Since Menzies' allotted task was to write on Churchill and the Commonwealth, he was in fact the only one of the team of eighteen contributors dealing directly with half of the area claimed by the title of the book. When it appeared, Churchill duly wrote to thank him profusely: 'what you say is gratifying indeed'. But, in order to write such a thing, Churchill must either not have read Menzies' chapter first, or have agreed with its highly unconventional presentation of his attitude to the Commonwealth. The first is a good deal more likely than the second.[30]

Menzies paid plenty of tributes to Churchill's many qualities in his ten pages. He was 'the Englishman, *par excellence*, full of perfection and imperfection, at all times human and understandable, yet rising to great issues with an almost divine power and character and authority'. He was also now 'the acknowledged leader of a great Commonwealth of Nations', a position he had acquired not through rational processes (such rational processes would indeed be unEnglish anyway), but by undeniable personal enterprise and achievement. As Menzies got to his real theme, however, it all became more negative. Churchill was no Joseph Chamberlain, no economic unifier of Empire, and was not really any sort of imperial man at heart, for 'he is much too European for that. No man can serve two masters.' (Menzies might profitably have remembered this when accepting Churchill's easy assurances that a united Europe was not inconsistent with the Empire.) No, he could not devote his energies to Europe's balance of power and at the same time 'stand in spirit among the factories of Australia or the green farms of New Zealand, or breathe the "spicy breezes that blow o'er Ceylon's Isle"'. Churchill 'wore his Empire with a difference'. There followed a defensive paragraph in which Menzies asserted that this was just a personal view, for 'a cat may look at a king', and was anyway secondary to Churchill's achievement in leading the Empire in 1940.

On thousands of Australian farms, in factory and counting house throughout a dozen nations, he became, almost overnight, the man of destiny and familiar friend, the voice of courage and defiance, the common spokesman and inspirer of the British people, clear across the world.

All this was, Menzies acknowledged, to state the platitudinous, and he thus contented himself for the rest of his chapter in drawing four conclusions from Churchill's life. Churchill had faith in himself; he knew 'his own people' and spoke in 'accents of the English' (note, though, that Menzies considered himself a Scot and usually used 'British' when Australians were to be included in the concept, and in other places he replaced 'the people of England' of an early draft with 'the British people' in the final version); he had 'a rich and chuckling and sometimes impish sense of humour'; finally, 'he loved and loves his job'. The chapter concluded with a résumé of 'those subtle and human elements which enabled him to turn defeat into victory, and which made him, in great areas of the British Commonwealth which he had never seen, a pillar of fire by night and of cloud by day'. In all this fine Gibbonian rhetoric – which Churchill doubtless loved if and when he ever read it – it was easy to miss the fact that Menzies had only said two things about Churchill and the Commonwealth, which was supposed to be his theme: first that he placed Empire second to Europe, and second that he had never seen much of it for himself and could not therefore grasp its 'spirit'.[31]

Menzies was perhaps conscious of the negative way in which his tribute might be read, for he toned down from the original draft some of the sharper barbs: 'He has never been identified with great Empire economic policies', for example, became 'He has not been particularly identified with . . .', and a second positive reference to Joseph Chamberlain as a unifier of Empire was removed altogether. The replacement of 'the golden beaches' by 'the factories of Australia', however, may have been a subtle move in the other direction, for Churchill himself seems never to have grasped that post-war Australia aspired economically to be something more than just a purveyor of food to the British market. As late as 1950 he had been saying in Edwardian tones that 'our brothers in their spacious food lands must feel that they have an assured market in the Mother Country'. In 1952, Menzies had found when visiting him in London that he was reluctant to devote his limited mental energy to a trade agreement of the sort that Australia now needed, and Churchill was then affronted when Australia imposed import restrictions of its own, without discrimination in favour of British goods. By contrast, Menzies, who had consistently opposed the 1932 Ottawa agreements on Commonwealth trade, argued when Prime Minister, as John Howard has put it, 'that the need for Australia to develop its own manufacturing base demanded greater understanding than Britain was prepared to extend'. Despite its elevated tone, therefore, Menzies' account of Churchill and the Commonwealth was suffused with darker hues when read in an Australian accent, and it was only his tactful application of the blinding light of 1940 that prevented this from being obvious. Sir Evelyn Wrench, who contributed the equivalent chapter on Churchill and the Empire to a rival tributary volume of essays, made a much better fist of it, though he too had to resort to praising Churchill as war leader in order to achieve the appropriate tone of celebration.[32]

When invited to pay later tributes, as he so frequently was, Menzies concentrated on the war years and on Churchill's personal qualities, and avoided the issue of his relations with Australia and his view of the Commonwealth – as he did for example in his books *Afternoon Light* and *The Measure of the Years*, though Churchill is a major figure in both. As that 1954 essay suggested, then, Menzies retained serious reservations about Churchill even while greatly enjoying his friendship and praising him to the skies. He was critical of Churchill staying on so long as Prime Minister while his health and vitality waned, and may well have retired himself earlier than was necessary in order to avoid making a similar mistake. Nor did he ever change his initial opinion that Churchill was inferior to him as a public speaker or his view that Churchill was less effective in domestic politics. Sometimes these reservations – and his refusal to suppress them – could get him into real difficulties in public. When in 1974 he spoke at a ceremony at which he was given a leather-bound set of Churchill's complete works, an event that must have produced almost his final word on Churchill, he got into quite a tangle. He began by routinely referring to Churchill's 'genius', then corrected himself by adding 'not as a speaker – he was never an impromptu or extemporaneous speaker – he preferred on the whole to dictate, and to correct, and to read . . .' Perhaps sensing that this was not quite what the occasion demanded, he then corrected his self-correction by asserting that 'he did it all so magnificently that one would never know'. Getting back on track, he continued, 'but, as a writer, I think he has no superior in this century', the 'but' undermining all his efforts to sound positive about Churchill as a speaker. It was much easier when he moved on to discuss Churchill the war leader and then to recall him as a 'friend – an intimate friend – debating things with him, getting a chuckle out of life . . . a privilege I shall always remember. Nothing greater ever happened in my life to me.'[33]

It was perhaps inevitable that the collisions and even the co-operations of two such powerful personalities should generate bruises and jealousies as well as a warm mutual regard, but there is not the faintest reason to doubt the sincerity of Menzies' final remark quoted above. It no doubt gave him some real satisfaction to be hailed as Churchill's heir when the great man died in 1965. His speech on the outbreak of war in 1939 had been hailed as 'Churchillian', and he was thought in 1941 to be the only radio broadcaster in the Commonwealth able to mobilise the language as Churchill had done. When Churchill died, Menzies' contribution to his funeral was itself compared to Churchill's use of language and he was freely compared to Churchill himself by Harold Wilson (no doubt in this case seeking similar assurances in return), a hint taken by Menzies' biographers such as Percy Joske. He was much in demand for duties such as unveiling statues and speaking at Churchill commemorations and dinners. When nominated by the Queen to succeed Churchill as Lord Warden of the Cinque Ports, the appointment therefore seemed extremely fitting to the British, if faintly ridiculous to many Australians. (It was characteristic of both men that Churchill loved the uniform that went with the job but hardly ever went near the Cinque Ports after being inaugurated, while Menzies hated the dressing-up but was extremely attentive to his duties – though he lived at the other side of the world and Churchill only at the other end of Kent.)[34]

Menzies had been irritated in the extreme when, during a Common-wealth Prime Ministers' meeting, Harold Macmillan had been briefly called away and had handed over the chairmanship to Nehru rather than to Menzies himself. (Nehru was senior in the sense that he had been continuously in office for longer than Menzies, but Menzies had become a Commonwealth Prime Minister for the first time years earlier than Nehru. The real issue was of course not longevity but the ending of the 'white man's club'.) Now in 1965, though, Nehru was dead and Menzies still Australian Prime Minister, unchallenged for the role of senior Commonwealth statesman by Canada's Lester Pearson or New Zealand's Keith Holyoake. Menzies thus appeared – and was reported – as the senior Commonwealth figure and a pall-bearer at Churchill's funeral. Its importance to him is indicated well enough in the many boxes of papers and press-cuttings about the event which were kept for posterity, but it was the broadcast that he made as Churchill's coffin was leaving St Paul's Cathedral that set the seal on his association with the event. Much as Dwight Eisenhower returned home to a chorus of praise in the USA for his similar broadcast, Menzies received a shower of congratulatory mail. The Anzac Association of Women assured him that he was 'the top orator of the Commonwealth'. Anthony Eden thought it 'just perfect in sincerity and balance'. Viscount Monckton wrote that 'the very mantle of Churchill seemed to fall on you . . .' And Lord Normanbrook, 'writing as one old friend of Winston to another', felt that 'you said, so simply, and so plainly from the heart, so many of the things which we were all feeling about him at this time – and which we shall continue to talk about as long as we live'. Since Dame Pattie Menzies had been obliged to remain in her seat in St Paul's while Menzies was broadcasting from the crypt, she had missed her husband's triumph; the ABC considerately sent her a film of the service so that she could enjoy it at leisure.[35]

Success in occasional oratory is usually ephemeral, but in this case Menzies had a second triumph. When Churchill's publisher Cassell's decided later in 1965 to reissue the Menzies speech in book form – four pages only of text, but sumptuously bound – Menzies himself received half the five hundred volumes printed and gave them to friends at the Christmas season. (Cassell's gave the rest away to their own favoured customers.) They went out to most prominent Australians (the distribution list including both the war historian C. E. W. Bean and the cricketer Don Bradman, as well as political leaders) and to leaders in other countries, an eclectic list that in the United States included Hubert

Humphrey and Averell Harriman as well as President Johnson, in Britain Colin Cowdrey and Prince Philip. This distribution produced another flood of appreciative mail for Menzies, more considered and less emotional than at the time of the funeral, and in some cases probably less sincere too. Bradman sent thanks for 'that wonderful contribution of yours on WSC . . . It will always adorn my library as a reminder of two great men.' Lyndon Johnson, thanking his 'old and dear friend' Menzies, sent the most over-the-top acknowledgement: 'I shall count this small volume among those assets I cherish and hold dear to me . . . May God grant you long life. Your wisdom and your eloquency [sic] are part of the free world's heritage and they need to be given freely to those of us who are inspired by them.' Such fulsomeness was no doubt connected to Menzies' recent decision to commit Australian soldiers to support America in Vietnam – a decision of which Churchill himself would hardly have approved, given his resistance to a similar request from the French in 1954. But the Australian High Commissioner in Nairobi may well have sent the most welcome response. 'For some years you have been the best speaker in the English language, and those in future who wish to exemplify your gift will turn to this speech.' It must be said that even reading the speech long after the event suggests that such sentiments were by no means out of place.[36]

Menzies' own commitment to Churchill was, however, demonstrated to more lasting effect during 1965, in his heading the campaign for a Winston Churchill Memorial Trust. Plans had been under way for some years to establish a permanent but useful memorial to Churchill in the United States, Britain, Canada and New Zealand, a project coordinated internationally by the English-Speaking Union and in developing which Australia's Clive Baillieu (chairman of the Commonwealth's English-Speaking Union) had taken a leading part. During the period after Churchill retired, fundraising in his honour had mainly centred on Churchill College, and in this both America and the Dominions had already been involved (including gifts in kind, such as timber for the dining hall). By 1959, though, thanks to a million-pound grant from the Ford Foundation, the College's appeal for £3.3 million was almost completed and there was room to plan for further Churchill memorials. The scheme proposed by the president of the American E-SU, Arthur Houghton, was for international student-exchange scholarships, initially on the Anglo-American basis that Churchill had approved in July 1958, but later extended with Baillieu's enthusiastic agreement to encompass the Dominions too. The model for the scheme was the Rhodes scholarships, themselves set up in 1902 to promote better awareness of other English-speaking peoples among young people, but the beneficiaries of the new scheme would not be in full-time education (other schemes, including Churchill College itself, being deemed to have dealt with this), but would be representative, ordinary citizens. With Churchill visibly ageing, much active planning took place, and a 'Project C' was worked out and agreed in principle by the end of 1960, with Menzies already involved personally and pledging the full support of the Australian Government.[37]

When Churchill broke his leg while on holiday in France in October 1962 and real fears were expressed as to how much longer he would live, the intensity of planning accelerated, but only in Australia was there enough energy put into this process for a complete fundraising scheme ready to be implemented as soon as he died ('X day', in the fundraisers' planning jargon). Menzies was among a number of Commonwealth figures who had not been impressed by the methods adopted either in the Churchill College appeal or in the subsequent appeal to launch Kennedy scholarships – the latter having been so unsuccessful that the British Government had had to step in and top up the volunteers' efforts with a large grant from public funds. He was determined that Churchill's name should not be connected with a 'second rate appeal', and told Baillieu bluntly that he would not be personally associated as chairman with any scheme that was not professionally managed. It was therefore decided to approach as the Australian appeal's director William Kilpatrick, a fundraiser of proven worth since he had only recently headed Australia's national heart foundation appeal (many of whose state organisers now found themselves working for the Churchill scheme themselves). Kilpatrick was a man of independent means (describing himself as 'a Collins Street farmer', roughly the equivalent of a Wall Street rancher to an American) and with a strong commitment to public service. He was already heavily committed, but replied to Menzies that 'a Prime Minister's wish would be his command and he would do it'. Menzies therefore also now agreed to act as the appeal's sponsor and president, though with the leaders of the ALP and the Country Party as his deputies, and the Governor-General as patron, so preserving its non-political status, and planning was rapidly undertaken during the last couple of years of Churchill's life.[38]

A large number of eminent people were involved in this planning process, as sub-committees worked out schemes for awarding scholarships, the best ways to approach business, state governments and the trades unions for help, and the actual mechanics of collecting, banking and counting small donations. The state premiers and leaders of opposition were each appointed to shadow positions to head appeals in their own states, together with the lord mayors of the capital cities lest their noses be put out of joint, all of these receiving letters from Menzies to thank them for agreeing to join the team, and when an office-holder or a state government changed new sheaves of letters were dispatched from Canberra to keep the machine as representative as possible. But the key element of the master plan was Kilpatrick's own idea. In Australia, the appeal would be launched as soon as possible after Churchill's funeral had taken place, it would run for less than a month, and it would aim at a published target of over a million pounds, most of it to be collected on a single day. None of the other countries involved was so bold – and none was so successful. The million-pound target was to be broken down into separate published targets for each state and territory, and then into smaller units for each region, country area and group of suburbs (these smaller targets never being published). There were also internal targets for business and for anticipated contributions from the Commonwealth and state governments, all of which had been sounded out and had made provisional decisions before the appeal was launched, but these would be rolled up into the overall state targets, so encouraging a healthy degree of competition.

Since, in the case of public companies at least, this would have required board-level discussion (and in cabinets too), the secrecy with which all this planning was achieved was quite remarkable. The same is true of preparations for the collection of small sums from the general public, which the RSL undertook to organise across the entire country, and planning for which must therefore have involved at least the office-holders in all its two thousand sub-branches. Yet the acceptance of secrecy was such that the extensive minutes of its federal executive make no mention at all of the RSL's connection to any appeal until it was over. The RSL may indeed have had its own reasons for wanting a success like this, for it was under serious attack. A controversial play,

The One Day of the Year, ALP attacks from left-wingers like Jim Cairns, and an adverse ABC documentary had collectively tarnished its image during the early 1960s, its critics depicting it (in the succinct words of its own historians) as 'outdated, introverted, drink-sodden and militaristic'.

> It was thus on the lookout for a chance to restore its reputation for public service, and when the appeal was successfully concluded, the RSL's President told his executive that more than anything else this effort of the League's ... will reflect great credit on the Returned Servicemen's League. Not only has the RSL been thus associated with commemorating the name of our [sic] greatest wartime leader, but we have been the instrument by which a remarkable system of scholarships available to Australians of every walk of life has been established in perpetuity ... I would suggest to you that this is a classic example of the type of work the League can undertake in the years ahead, projects of a broad national kind.

Not only did the RSL banish memories of Gallipoli and Greece from its collective memory (as one or two letters to the press pointed out), it also forgot Churchill's cavalier treatment of the organisation itself in 1946–7. Security was effective, and no press leak took place until after Churchill had died anyway, only a few days before the formal launch took place.

Success in this field may have owed quite a lot to the work of the appeal's state publicity officers. These were all powerful media professionals whose names were not published in any of the torrent of press releases that poured out during February 1965 (they had been listed for those with a 'need to know' in the appeal's publicity manual, a substantial bound volume completed in May 1964). For South Australia press management was undertaken by the managing director of Adelaide's *Advertiser*, the state's biggest newspaper; for New South Wales it was the general manager of the Fairfax newspaper group, and for Victoria the advertising manager of the Myer's chain of department stores. The manual also contained lists of supportive press contacts for every town; letterheads, press advertisements, posters and leaflets already designed and ready for use; plans to get free poster sites on every train, tram and railway station; slides to be shown to cinema audiences; procedures for the direct mailing of a million letters to individual Australians; plans to link Churchill's memory to service in Australia's wars, and so justify the use of the army and navy to support the appeal; and plans for a commemorative Churchill stamp (which the postmaster-general had already agreed to in advance). In the circumstances, Kilpatrick's warning in the following November (after hearing privately of Churchill's failing health) that the organisation should now be brought to 'concert pitch' seems to have been erring well on the side of caution.[39]

In the last week of January 1965, there were a few last-minutes tunings and some first-night nerves, but Menzies cabled from London to swing the plans into action. On the first working day after Churchill's funeral, 1 February 1965, he thus held with other Commonwealth leaders a press conference in London at which the international appeal, Australia's million-pound target and the single collection day were all formally announced, and at which he was as usual adjudged to have made the best speech in Churchill's memory. That statement was already in the hands of the Australian press, which therefore announced the appeal (and in every case gave editorial endorsement too) on the next day, after they had deluged their readers with photographs of the funeral pageantry in London. The momentum was not allowed to slip by even a fraction, and the fact that 'door-knock day' would be as soon as 28 February enabled it to be maintained until the appeal was over. Most papers carried reports of the local progress of the appeal two or three times a week until about the 20th, generally identifying each of their stories with the appeal's logo-drawing of Churchill's two-fingered 'V for Victory' salute, but in the final week it reached every issue of almost every paper.

In part this was probably effective press management by those invisible state publicity officers, but it was also no doubt due to the plethora of actual news stories generated during Australia's 'Churchill Week'. Television and radio carried over those last few days recorded broadcasts by Menzies, Calwell and Governor-General Lord De L'Isle, and in several states from their governors and other such prominent citizens as the chief justice too. There were also professionally made advertisements for the appeal shown between programmes. Interim information about government and industrial contributions built up a sense that big money was already rolling in, and readers were reminded that Fellowship awards were guaranteed to every state, but that more would go to the states that contributed most. The armed forces were also now unleashed to add some razzmatazz on the summer streets (the headline 'Gay Parades before the Door Knock' *not* foreshadowing Pride week). Sydney witnessed its biggest military parade since 1945, with the visiting Prince Philip helpfully on hand to take the salute, the RAAF arranged fly-pasts in most cities, and the RAN held 'navy days' with visitors looking over their ships in the ports. Police and army bands gave public concerts, invariably including a Churchill march specially written by an admirer in New South Wales (but presumably not its nauseatingly sentimental words).

Not everyone liked this hype, some indeed pointing out that it was tasteless in the extreme to use TV jingles in a memorial to a great man who had only just been buried, and almost equally bad to have Churchill appeal posters in shop windows, surrounded by refrigerators and washing machines. Only the independently minded *Australian* provided a platform for such rejections of the modern world, its own columnist John Olsen detecting 'the sick hands of the men in grey flannel suits using their grey flannel heads to equate Churchill with some fleeting idol of the new pop culture. They are putting him not on the top of Mount Olympus but on the top of a mountain of coke bottles and electric guitars.' Shirley Venn from South Yarra, in a letter to the *Australian*, worried – if with some irony – that that slick PR campaign might even be counter-productive:

> Only three more days to D for Donation Day, so the radio and TV stations remind us. The public have already reacted to the trite, sentimental and thoroughly distasteful campaign, and I'm now afraid that the reaction will cause many to withhold a generous donation to a good cause. Will every Australian please join with me and give to the Churchill Appeal, and give all you can afford, for if the appeal is not successful on the first day we will have to bear the utterly ghastly publicity campaign all over again. So please give – not so the world can remember, but so we can forget.

On the same day, another reader invited the appeal's 'zealous and patriotic organisers' to raise £5 million in the next year in memory of Curtin. 'After all, if £1,000,000 is to be raised to honour in perpetuity the name of a man who (to put it kindly) somewhat jeopardised the safety of our country by declaring us expendable during the Second World War, surely £5,000,000 seems little enough to honour the name of the man who did all in his power to preserve our country . . .'[40]

This last letter was representative of the few voices raised in direct opposition to the honouring of Churchill in 1965, but it was largely limited to a few corners of the ALP and to Catholics, for all of whom Curtin and the oppositional Australianness for which his memory stood was a higher priority. The Labor MP Allan Fraser, for example, was neither a left-winger nor a regular critic of the British connection (he had for example suggested in the late 1940s that a stone from the bombed-out British House of Commons be brought to Australia to perpetuate the link between Canberra and the birthplace of parliamentary democracy). But he was a maverick figure who was no stranger to controversy – Menzies had once blisteringly rounded on him and described Fraser's attack on his Government as being delivered 'with all that intolerable self-righteousness that characterises the honourable Member for Eden-Monaro' – and one of the few politicians to 'step outside the British embrace' in the debate on the EEC. Fraser now publicly criticised the Churchill appeal as inappropriate for a country pursuing a course separate from Britain's, and promoted by 'high-pressure brain-washing techniques' verging on 'mind-conditioning'.

In Broken Hill, New South Wales, a company town in which the ALP and the trades unions were practically synonymous, there was an acrimonious split. The local ALP decided, despite the national and state ALP backing for it, not to support the appeal, as a result of which few volunteer collectors could be found and little money was collected. Interestingly, across the state in Newcastle, an equally industrial city but with a less turbulent recent record in Labor and trades union politics, the local ALP followed the official party line, backed the appeal and helped to raise a great deal of money. In this they would have been aided considerably by the fact that the local *Herald* newspaper ran no fewer than forty-two supportive stories during the twenty-five days of the appeal. It was reported that when the Broken Hill city council decided to stick to supporting the appeal, and so defy the local party to which most of its members belonged, 'some aldermen bitterly attacked the late Sir Winston Churchill'. One claimed that he had 'no sympathy whatever for the common man', that he had 'died a millionaire' and so should provide the money for his own memorial, and that he had been 'the most bitter anti-Labour and anti-Australian man who ever lived'. The RSL was said to be 'dismayed' by the tone of the debate ('Where is our national pride?'). The town's honour was, however, saved by even bigger contributions from the mining companies and from the RSL sub-branch's own funds. Of the £15,000 raised in Broken Hill, £12,000 came from industry and only £1600 from doorstep contributions, but this did not prevent the appeal's local publicity officer from crowing: 'if I may quote Liberace, we have been so upset that we have cried all the way to the bank'.[41]

Allan Fraser and the Broken Hill ALP were conspicuous mainly because hardly anybody else from the left joined them in what the *Bulletin* called 'the class-war opposition because Churchill was a conservative'. Since about a quarter of Australians were Catholics in the 1960s, however, criticism by their Church could have been far more serious. In fact, most of the Catholic hierarchy had taken part in memorial services either in their own cathedrals (as in Melbourne) or ecumenically, and they now preserved a diplomatic silence. It was left to the Catholic press to open up the debate, and in view of the hornet's nest that was then stirred up the bishops must have congratulated themselves on their silence. The main focus of attack was the Melbourne archdiocesan weekly paper, the *Advocate*, though other Catholic papers like the *Tribune* joined in rather less trenchantly. The *Advocate* got off on the wrong foot by printing Churchill's obituary in its columns on 21 January, some days after his stroke but several days before he died – a perfectly understandable mistake for a weekly paper with early deadlines, but a rather tactless one, especially when the tone was fairly critical. It began well, praising his war leadership and his oratory, but then devoted rather more space to 'some deficiencies', before concluding with a prayer for the peace of his soul, 'at the end of his long life of active service to the land he loved so well' (a form of words that definitely did not include Australia). A week later, the front page reported tributes ('The Pope and Church Leaders Grieve at Churchill's Death'), but once again in mixed tones: Archbishop Simonds had said that it was Churchill's 'obstinacy' that saved Western civilisation in 1940, and called him a 'great leader of English public life'. Later issues drew attention to the grieving of British Catholics, but also recalled the way in which Churchill's Government had failed in 1944 to fulfil his pledge on religious education ('that compromise by Anglicans and Nonconformists which allowed a watered-down type of Christianity to be taught in state schools'). Much greater space was allotted to Earnon de Valera's Irish tribute, a poisonous brew of all Churchill's least representative statements on Irish nationalism. The prominence given to de Valera in the *Advocate* indeed says much about the ethnic composition of its readership, as does its story the same month on Roger Casement's bones being repatriated and the full page devoted to 'The Shamrock, Ireland's National Emblem'. The Dublin and London columnists, however, also drew attention to the fact that several of Churchill's relatives were Catholics and that he had worked with such Catholics as Marshal Foch and de Gaulle (the latter a fairly desperate choice for a Churchill intimate), as if Australian Catholics too needed reassurance that they had a share of ownership in him. Oddly, it was the *Advocate*'s German columnist who provided the strongest tribute to Churchill, quoting liberally from an article in the German press by Golo Mann, though ending on the argument that Churchill had been 'the "last Roman"', the embodiment of a tradition which has passed away'.[42]

This mixed bag of reactions was nothing compared to the editorial published by the *Advocate* on 18 February, 'Australia and the Churchill Legend'. Claiming that 'we feel impelled to echo the strong objections voiced by Mr Allan Fraser', it rejected the 'high-pressure brainwashing technique' adopted by the Churchill appeal, identifying it as an approach which was 'part and parcel of a British pattern of thought and emotion which is highly undesirable, because it is inconsistent with the development of a true Australian national feeling, in which all our citizens can be united whatever their origin'.

> If it is necessary to be 'loyal to Britain' in a special way to be a 'good Australian', there are millions of our European and Irish-born citizens who cannot hope to 'make the grade'; while the evil of a colonial nostalgia, which can blur the public vision regarding the facts of power and the need of independent Australian policy-making, should be clear to all sensible people. Whatever honour we pay to Churchill, therefore, as well as other valiant defenders of the free world in our time, let us recognise that this country cannot live on other people's legends . . .

Hinting at John Curtin but not mentioning him by name, the writer concluded that 'they may not be of Churchillian stature, but they are our own, and they loved and served our country as he did not'.

In the Anglophile press, this polemic was immediately denounced as almost treasonable (which rather made the writer's point), but even among the *Advocate*'s own readership there was no consensus of support. A week later it printed a short letter supporting its stance from 'a Protestant and [an] Australian, more so than the promoters of this Trust', and clearly a staunch ALP supporter: 'They were strangely absent when Ben Chifley died. No trust for him, of course, the answer is, he was Australian.' But it also printed a thoughtful letter from an Irish-born Catholic, arguing not only that it was perfectly reasonable for the British-stock Protestant majority of Australians to celebrate Churchill if they wished, but also that the 'new Australians' from Eastern and Southern Europe had special reasons to thank Churchill. While most Australians had hardly heard a shot fired in anger, they had 'been through a hell on earth that lasted for about five years, so they have a far sharper vision of what Sir Winston saved them from than we have'. A third letter enquired bluntly how 'the parochial and insular views you have expressed can come from a responsible newspaper. I thank God that these views in this ecumenical age are not the official ones of the Catholic Church but . . . an expression of opinion of Irish-type thinking that used to be prevalent thirty to forty years ago.' The paper made no official reply to these letters, but printed two more in later weeks, one a priest's powerful and persuasive rejection of the editorial as 'a retrograde step towards the petulant rivalries of earlier times'. Pointing out that all great men had acquired exaggerated legends, including Melbourne's recently deceased Archbishop Mannix, he came to the heart of the matter:

> You make the whole campaign seem like some British plot to subvert Australia, and make the insulting implication that those who support it are perhaps being disloyal to their country. Loyalty and enthusiasm to Britain are no more disloyal or provocative of illusion than loyalty and affection towards Ireland or towards His Holiness . . . You say that you are not motivated by any sense of 'hostility towards Britain'. I am afraid that few will believe you. I only hope that Victorian Catholics will treat your editorial with the contempt that it regrettably deserves and give generously to the Churchill Memorial Fund.

That letter, however, was not even published until the appeal was over, as was the final letter in support of the paper, from an English migrant who argued that Churchill had been 'pre-eminently an Englishman'. 'Given his background and his training, his earlier years, it is difficult to see how he could have viewed the British Empire as other than as an extension of England; and Australia, most distant part of it, as the least important . . .' As we have seen, this view of Churchill was not far from Menzies' own, but it was not an opinion being expressed in 1965 by anyone but the few critics of the appeal.[43]

As this debate in the columns of the *Advocate* demonstrates, Churchill's reputation in Australia continued to be a means by which different groups of Australians expressed their own sense of identity – whether 'British' or 'Australian'. There is, however, plenty of anecdotal evidence that the *Advocate*'s critics were right to see a difference between Irish Catholics within the Australian population and the newer Catholic arrivals from Italy and Eastern Europe, people who had their own desire to idolise Churchill, and for reasons that had nothing to do with his Britishness. Many collectors reported that they received their biggest contributions from such recent arrivals, people who had been anti-fascist in the 1940s but listened to Churchill on their wartime radios even while in Axis or Axis-occupied countries.[44] The *Morwell Advertiser* noted this tendency among Eastern Europeans in the La Trobe Valley, and it may well have been their pro-Churchill views that blocked the 'Don't Change to Churchill' campaign there a few weeks later – a campaign, ironically, led by Australians of British stock. Sydney's *Bulletin* claimed in March that there had been significant opposition from new Australians, because of Churchill's sell-out to Stalin at Yalta, and that, in suburbs where they were strongest, 'the contributions were derisively small'. These were of course about the poorest of all Australians, apart from Aboriginals (whose presence in the country was totally ignored by all reporters of the appeal). They may well not yet have had links to the various community organisations that were doing most of the collecting, so their suburbs would have been least well organised for the appeal anyway, but there is no evidence apart from a few lines in the *Bulletin* to support the claim that they were inherently hostile, and plenty to suggest the contrary.[45]

There was in any case a non-Catholic majority, and for these, and especially perhaps for Anglicans, the Churchill appeal was indeed a way of celebrating their Britishness. Brian Fletcher has demonstrated how into the 1960s the Church of England 'helped to keep alive in Australia that facet of nationalism which was associated with being British'.[46] There are still indeed Australian Anglicans of the older generations who defiantly define themselves as 'Church of *England*' rather than 'Anglican' or 'Episcopalian'. Even among Catholics, critics were few and far between, or at least kept their heads down to avoid the flak. The appeal's organisers could indeed 'cry all the way to the bank', for the outcome exceeded their hopes by a wide margin and Clementine Churchill wrote at once to Menzies to say 'How wonderful Australia is, and how wonderful you are, as without you to lead and guide I don't think this splendid result could have been achieved.'[47] Instead of the million pounds aimed at, the appeal eventually netted £2,312,749, and every state and territory easily exceeded its target. The Commonwealth and state governments had given £210,000 of this, and business contributions had produced over a million, but some two-thirds of a million pounds had been contributed during the 28 February nationwide door-knock. Since the Commonwealth Government's £75,000 and the large business donations were credited back to the states in proportion to their targets, the final figures were expressed entirely by state, and allow some limited analysis.

State	Target (A)£	Sum collected (A)£	Percentage overshoot
New South Wales	410,000	723,840	76.5
Victoria	360,000	683,624	89.9
Queensland	90,000	214,327	138.1
South Australia	80,000	367,594	359.5
Western Australia	60,000	123,221	105.4
Tasmania	35,000	116,062	231.6
Canberra	10,000	22,541	125.4
Northern Territory	5,000	17,535	250.7
Papua New Guinea	5,000	44,005	1366.8
AUSTRALIA	1,053,000 [sic]	2,312,749	119.6

The original targets were devised according to population and relative wealth, though no doubt adjusted to take account of Kilpatrick's experience of earlier fundraising appeals. The territories' figures tell us little, since the original targets were fairly notional, and there was presumably little in the way of industrial contributions from Canberra, little else from Papua New Guinea. But the relative performance of the six states looks more interesting, for whatever the yardstick the same states performed best. Whether compared to their shares of the national population, or to the size of their economies, South Australia, Tasmania and Victoria contributed the most, Queensland, Western Australia and New South Wales the least. In part this difference no doubt represented the proportion of populations in rural areas where collecting was more difficult and resistance perhaps higher (despite the collectors' valiant resort to old-fashioned pedal radios to canvass the outback). In part, though, the pattern defies expectations, for Western Australia had the highest proportion of recent British migrants and might therefore have been expected to respond generously, given the nature of the recent press debates. The Catholic populations especially of New South Wales and Victoria were no obstacle to fundraising successfully in both states, but in Victoria where the Church had been more hostile the population gave more generously – perhaps there were now more non-Irish in the Catholic community than the press had grasped, or perhaps the *Advocate* had merely managed to stir up the Protestants to give more. The general predominance of the south-east may indeed reflect no more than the heartland of Menzies' Liberal Party, whose contacts (in the press, but also in the wider community, such as RSL branches) were so important a part of the appeal.

The amount of money raised allowed the Australian Winston Churchill Memorial Trust to be launched successfully a few weeks later, with Menzies as its national president (Calwell and McEwen remaining deputies), Kilpatrick its national chairman. Its first annual report and many others over the next decade recognised Menzies' crucial role by printing a photograph of Menzies and Churchill conversing together as friends. A particular favourite was the one of Menzies and Churchill seated together in the garden of Ten Downing Street, with Menzies talking and Churchill listening benignly. Income from the invested sums, only part of which was regarded as spendable if the capital sum was not to be eroded by inflation, allowed forty-nine travelling scholarships in the first year, selected from twelve hundred applicants. These forty-nine Churchill Fellows were distributed among the states roughly in proportion to their contributions to the funds (selection mainly being done at state level), and contained ten women, many from the country districts, and an age-range from nineteen to fifty-five. Shrewd investment of the capital sum (part of it from the 1970s until 2001 in a Canberra headquarters in which space was let to other charities so as to produce further income) has enabled the scheme to continue to prosper and to produce a similar number of Fellows each year. It has now enabled about two thousand Australians to visit other countries in pursuit of their trade or profession, a high proportion of them going to Britain or the United States (a pattern of which Churchill would no doubt have strongly approved).[48]

The Trust's primary aim, as indicated in its articles of association, was 'by the award of Memorial Fellowships to be known as "Churchill Fellowships" to perpetuate and honour the memory of Sir Winston Churchill'. Menzies, foreseeing that revisionist historians would soon seek to blacken Churchill's name when those who had known him well were no longer around to defend it (he had even discouragingly told Churchill himself that this would happen), was determined that this would be 'a perpetual trust'. At the initial London press conference, Menzies had recalled with pleasure the number of young people who had seen Churchill's lying-in-state in Westminster, much as in Australia the RSL noted with equal pleasure the enthusiasm of its younger collectors who had knocked on so many doors: 'We call them long-haired, unkempt, irresponsible, irreverent and undisciplined, but give them a job to do, and they show results,' reported Western Australia's appeals co-ordinator, his statement fondly recalled fifteen years later in a branch history. Menzies went on to argue that:

men are easily forgotten and the names of even the greatest may suffer some kind of eclipse for a while, but it is vital that this man should never be forgotten. It is vital that his spirit, touched with immortality as it was, should continue to be immortal, a living thing, a continuing presence among many generations to come in countries which speak the English language – a language in which he, by the miracle of science, was able to address so many scores of millions of people during the war, touching them, inspiring them, driving pessimism underground. None of us who lived through all this could ever forget it. I think we have a great task here to see that it is never forgotten.

A 'continuous debt' could be met only by a continuous repayment, and this demanded not a monument, but a living body. 'In 200 years there will be Churchill Fellows, men and women of all sorts of colours, all sorts of religious beliefs, all sorts of experience ... thousands of them, as time goes by, who will carry this great name, this proud name, and who will think it a matter of honour to think of him and to perpetuate his memory.' This has always been at the heart of what Australia's Memorial Trust has done: Churchill's statue stands outside its office, his words are quoted at its meetings, and his photograph adorns its literature.[49]

There was, though, a secondary purpose to the Trust, which was the sheer usefulness of the scholarship system itself – this is apparently why so many eminent Australian academics sat on its committees in the early years – and this has since perhaps become of even greater significance. If, as Donald Horne noted at this time, 'pro-British, imperialistic, jingoist feeling [was] dying with the older generation', it would be natural for Australians to find more to admire in the useful side of the Churchill Trust as years passed than in its commemorative aspect. The initial idea had been for an international trust to cover the whole of the Commonwealth and the USA, with an international committee to control the resources raised collectively in the various countries, an idea partly intended to facilitate the transfer of scholarship funds from the richer countries to those 'in deficit', in effect from Britain, the United States and the Dominions to Britain's remaining colonies. Although this plan was being developed by the Australian Clive Baillieu, any such commitment was strenuously opposed by Kilpatrick and his fellow organisers in Australia, backed when required by Menzies himself. There would be legal difficulties, since the tax-free status of donations, conceded in advance by the Commonwealth Government, was a key factor in getting people to give, and money thus raised could not be spent outside the country or by a body that was not itself Australian. But the main argument was simply, as Kilpatrick put it in 1964, that 'Australians being Australians wish to have almost complete autonomy.' He did concede that, if this was granted, a voluntary scheme might well be set up later to deal with 'emergent nations', but little progress had been made on this when Churchill died.

The Australians then went ahead with their appeal, while the other countries only began properly then to plan their own efforts, which meant that in Britain and in New Zealand the appeals were less successful (per head of population), in the United States efforts were largely diverted to other Churchillian causes, and in Canada an appeal never happened at all. When in February 1965 Baillieu again floated his earlier idea, Kilpatrick was able to flatten him with the argument that Australia's appeal had already been launched on the basis of an autonomous Australian trust and could not now be changed. As that appeal gathered momentum during February 1965, its propaganda tended to stress more and more the value of the Trust to ordinary Australians, as Kilpatrick successfully urged Menzies to do in his final television broadcast, and as Calwell then did without prompting. Tasmania's Governor carefully pointed out that it was a chance 'on the one hand' to set up a 'living memorial' to Churchill, and on the other to establish 'something of the greatest value for this and succeeding generations'. It was, urged the state's Chief Justice, 'no mere monument to the past' for which he was soliciting funds.

This tactic may have been partly intended to deflect the criticisms discussed above, but it does also mean that we have no way of telling how many Australians gave money simply because it was a good cause, irrespective of its connection to Churchill. The two arguments for contributing became hopelessly confused as the campaign went on, as in a column in Perth's *Daily News* by Kirwan Ward: 'it seems to me that there are two campaigns on at the moment. One is the Sir Winston Churchill Memorial Fund, and the other is the knock-Churchill movement. The remedy for the knockers is simple enough: if you did not like Churchill, and if you do not want to help Australian children to get scholarships, then you did not have to give. This wouldn't have hurt Churchill in life and it certainly won't hurt him in death.' Opponents were being branded simultaneously as unpatriotic, ungrateful, petty and ungenerous to Australia's future generations. Once the Trust was fully in being in Australia, it became the model on which the other trusts were then based, so that each became effectively autonomous, and the relative lack of success of fundraising elsewhere no doubt made the Australians even more reluctant to pool resources internationally. There were thus fraternal exchanges of information and occasional visits, and Menzies was given a medallion by the British Trust, 'as a token of respect for our overseas brothers in enterprise', but no effective international body ever emerged, and no Australian resources were offered to 'emergent nations'. Apart from Menzies' personal presence at meetings and unveilings abroad, then, Australia's remarkably generous memorialising of Churchill would be carried out by, with and for the benefit of Australians alone.[50]

Timing was clearly crucial in all of this. The February 1965 appeal came ten years after the eightieth-birthday Churchill collection to which many Australians had already contributed, and so was not too soon; it also came just before Australia's Vietnam War and Britain's reiterated and ultimately successful applications to join 'Europe' marked their divergent paths in a way that was impossible to ignore; and it came before there was any chance of the presence of Churchill himself fading from the forefront of memory after his death and funeral. The appeal's success may well therefore have owed at least something to Australians' awareness that this would be 'one last rally' for all that Churchill had stood for in the Anglo-Australian identity. Or, as Arthur Calwell put the same viewpoint in his memoirs, Australians knew well that the Churchill funeral was also the obsequies of the British Empire, delayed for so long only because of Churchill's long life. The Churchill–Menzies relationship was thus, in death as in life, a means by which the Anglo-Australian relationship was mediated. The 1965 appeal was also a rather conditional tribute to the great man, organised on the strict understanding that Australian interests should take first place and never be sacrificed to some cloudy notion of the English-speaking peoples, a collectivity that Menzies was happy enough to advocate but which did not blind him to its limitations as a basis for Australian foreign policy. Since Churchill's own commitment to Australia and to Australian participation in such a grand scheme of things had been in its turn highly conditional, there was indeed a neat symmetry in the outcome.[51]

PART FOUR

12

The Man of the Century – and of the Next?

DURING, THE 1960S AND ESPECIALLY AFTER his death in 1965, it was widely predicted that the Churchill myth would now be subject to a more iconoclastic scrutiny, a scrutiny which would be bound to lower his reputation – would in effect cut him down to size.[1] Yet Kingsley Amis, writing in 1964 that 'the time for debunking Winston Churchill is not yet', also warned that 'when it comes it will not succeed as easily as with other great personages'. Why not? Because, as Lawrence Malkin put it three years later, this 'giant of a man had faults as memorable as his triumphs were historic. But his personality still casts such a brilliant light that history cannot yet see into the shadows.' Lord Moran asked even in 1957, only twelve years after the end of the war, 'Why hasn't the legend been defaced?' The reply from Oliver Franks was simply that 'Nothing but a colossal blunder would have undone the work of those five years of war leadership' in creating the legend in the first place, and (unlike the years before 1939, we might think) there had been no colossal post-war Churchill blunder. Malkin thought in 1967 that Churchill 'would remain in popular estimation, for years to come, "in the uncontradicted judgement of even the radical historian A. J. P. Taylor, "the saviour of his country"'. Three years later, the *Times Literary Supplement* noted that 'all great men become due sooner or later for debunking by lesser men. But Churchill still seems to be a case apart. Others abide our question; he is free. Our assessment of him is still virtually unchanged from what it was ten or twenty years ago.' In 1983, that Taylor phrase remained for Peter Hennessy both the summary of Churchill's standing in more recent historiography and the explanation of the still-lively market in Churchill memorabilia.[2]

The first attempts to cut Churchill down to size fared little better than Alanbrooke's diaries had done in 1957. The highly provocative first in the field was Goronwy Rees, when he attempted a comprehensive revisionist view of Churchill in *Encounter* in 1965. Rees came to the conclusion that Churchill's great war services – themselves less great than had been thought before adjusting the claims of the war memoirs with reference to Alanbrooke – were anyway but one episode in a long career of only mixed success. The reply by A. L. Rowse, also in *Encounter*, was called 'Churchill considered historically' (which is just what it was not). It was in fact a viciously polemical whitewash in which the 'lifelong socialist' Rowse attempted to justify even Churchill's colonialist views on India and his blood-curdling belligerence during the General Strike. Over and above his devotion to Churchill, Rowse must really have enjoyed this particular piece of literary in-fighting, for Rees had earlier organised the younger fellows to block his election as Warden of All Souls. Even years later Rowse was writing dismissively that Rees 'would never have made a historian', that he had been the *Partie Führer* of the anti-Rowse faction in the College, and describing with evident pleasure Rees' disappointing time at the University of Wales. After Rees organised the blocking group at All Souls, Rowse, 'being a good Celt . . . never forgave it or them' – when Rees revisited Oxford Rowse even refused to speak to him. In this, as in some other cases too no doubt, Churchill was merely the ground on which academics who already hated each other paraded their animosities.[3]

The first seriously researched revisionist account, however, was from Robert Rhodes James, who had some personal animus against Churchill, as a relative had been killed at Gallipoli. His *Churchill: A Study in Failure, 1900–1939* (1970) was therefore cannily shaped, for its title would enrage the true believers in Churchill's lifelong genius, while its chronological remit meant that he did not have to tackle the years of the 'finest hour' and after the war. He composed a defensive preface, disclaiming any attempt at a 'serious and fundamental revaluation of such a remarkable personality so shortly after his death'. His aim would be the lesser one of explaining why Churchill's career, 'after so successful a beginning', then lapsed 'so drastically; and why did it require a desperate national crisis to restore his fortunes?' What he did *not* believe was the explanation conveniently offered by Lloyd George – convenient because it explained his own twenty years in the wilderness after 1922 as well as Churchill's in the 1930s, though Churchill himself had in *The Gathering Storm* come close to endorsing Lloyd George's version of events. Lloyd George had argued that such things were the consequence of 'the distrust and trepidation with which mediocrity views genius at close quarters'. However, in this same period, in which the first attempts to rescue the reputations of the appeasing Prime Ministers Baldwin and Chamberlain appeared, Rhodes James placed Churchill back into the real political world of pre-1939, rather than regarding the era simply as one in which 'giants' had been out of office during 'the rule of the pygmies', as viewed through the distorting lens of 1940 in such works as C. L. Mowat's influential *Britain between the Wars*. In this attempt he substantially succeeded, and, though some reviewers were critical of his temerity, a more realistic and balanced assessment of Churchill in his first forty years in politics began to be made, somewhere between the over-critical tone of most books published before 1939 and the excessively adulatory ones that came after 1945. Over Antwerp, the Dardanelles and the General Strike, and other such incidents in Churchill's first career, Rhodes James came to the measured view that he deserved at least some of the blame that had stuck to him over the years, while over India he decided that Churchill's had been a 'lamentable struggle' from which it was 'impossible to extract anything of advantage' to the man. The Abdication Crisis had been a 'major catastrophe', since it had limited Churchill's effectiveness on other issues that really mattered. For, though the book had noted Churchill's 'inconsistencies and failures of diagnosis' in the anti-appeasement campaign of 1933–9, yet he had 'persevered with a theme and a warning' on rearmament, and 'he was right'. Rhodes James' conclusion was a fairly stark one: had Churchill's career come to an end in 1938 or 1939, it would have had to be concluded that he had 'failed', and failed because his wonderful oratorical gifts and his formidable power for administrative work were not matched by the capacity to inspire trust – almost exactly what Wallace Germains had concluded in *The Tragedy of Winston Churchill* in 1931. Rhodes James had achieved this judgement without touching on the war years at all, a period in respect of which he had a profound and lasting admiration for Churchill. There was in fact, as at least one reviewer noticed, a mismatch between the book's title and its content, for it was not 'an exercise in de-bunking

... On the contrary it is a study of marvellous resilience and courage in recovering from setbacks.' As a result Rhodes James was able to remain a historian acceptable to Churchill's admirers, the editor of his complete speeches in 1974, a speaker at Churchill banquets in Canada and deliverer of a Churchill lecture at Fulton. Perhaps wisely, he resisted the temptation to write a second volume on Churchill as a 'Study in Success' after 1939, for the scepticism he had applied to the earlier period would not have been universally welcome. At the end of his life, he remained both proud of his reputation as one of the first to restore reality to writing about Churchill and sharply critical of anyone who questioned Churchill's role in the war.[4]

Though billed in the United States as *Churchill Revised* (1969), *Churchill: Four Faces and the Man* (its English title) had no such elevated ambition. This was a rather curious book, with no editor and five contributors, each of considerable weight, and has been generally catalogued by librarians as authored by 'A. J. P. Taylor at al.', simply because his essay appeared first. H. D. Ziman in the *Daily Telegraph* thought that these were a group of cooler and more distant admirers of Churchill than the authors of *Action This Day* (for which see below). Taylor wrote on Churchill the statesman, Rhodes James on Churchill the politician (and inevitably in an unedited book this meant that they traversed some of the same ground). Though neither said much that was either new or consistently critical, Taylor wrote a quirky account of an aristocratic politician who 'never understood the effect that he had on others', and who long outlived the political values that he had inherited in the 1890s, but who came good in 1940 because those values were suddenly – if surprisingly – fashionable and in demand. As Ziman summarised it, Taylor offered up Churchill as 'an erratic individual, drawn forward by ambition and self-confidence' to his meeting with destiny in 1940, but 'the strategy of the war was his' and the victory was therefore also his. Rhodes James outlined the account then about to appear in his book-length study of Churchill's 'failure' before 1939, but, though he also added glowing passages on Churchill as war leader, suggested that he had actually left 'no message and no vision to the new rising generation today'.

To an older generation for whom the war was the most vivid experience of their lives, this cold-blooded attitude appears incomprehensible and even blasphemous. But they forget that, for some forty years, Churchill was to his contemporaries as unreal, as remote, and as irrelevant a personality as he now appears to the young men and women who were unborn when the war ended.

Jack Plumb wrote an elegant essay which seriously undermined Churchill's credentials as a historian (but mainly with reference to his writing on events before 1939) and Basil Liddell Hart a polemical one on Churchill as strategist, taking the opportunity to pillory his own least favourite strategists and generals as well as to praise Churchill. These were the four faces of Churchill, but most reviewers concentrated their attention on the final essay, 'the man' himself, a psychological investigation of Churchill's character by the psychiatrist Anthony Storr. Working almost entirely from secondary sources – and, said critical reviewers, attempting the impossible, since he had never even met his 'patient' – Storr built up a fascinating version of what had driven Churchill to such determination over a long career, the influence of parental neglect, his mood-swings and his 'black dog' depressions. Some reviewers hailed this as a breakthrough in the understanding of a great man, others saw it as a prying into a world that ought to be left private. But both camps seemed uncomfortable with an essay that 'explained' Churchill's career in such a deterministic manner, reducing that formidable willpower which was at the heart of Churchill's historical significance to a psychological over-compensation, and challenging indeed the very idea of conscious human control over the great historical events which Churchill's later career had hitherto seemed to prove. Hence, for Storr, 'in 1940, Churchill became the hero that he had always dreamed of being. It was his finest hour.' Britain needed just such a figure in that 'dark time . . . a man who could dream dreams of victory when all seemed lost. Winston Churchill was such a man,' but his 'dynamic force' came from 'the romantic world of fantasy in which he had his true being'.[5]

Storr's view of Churchill strongly influenced all later accounts, sometimes dangerously so in the more inexpert hands: Kenneth Morgan, for example, wrote punningly of William Manchester's *The Last Lion* biography of Churchill that he had blundered into a new form of an old historical fallacy, 'Post Spock, ergo propter Spock'. One of the people most interested in Storr's perceptive view of Churchill was his fellow contributor A. J P. Taylor, even though confessing that he really thought that people were 'born with their dispositions, not shaped by lack or excess of parental love during childhood'. He dined with Storr, to see whether the same insights could be applied to Beaverbrook, whose biography he was then writing. Unfortunately, having described in great detail Beaverbrook's extraordinary character, Taylor drew from Storr the confident assertion that Beaverbrook must therefore have been a neglected only child. Taylor knew well that he wasn't, and the conversation abruptly terminated his interest in psychology as a method of understanding people in history. His regular quoting, though, of one of Churchill's remarks about his wartime government, 'All I wanted was compliance with my views after reasonable discussion,' may very well tell us more about his own psychology than it does about Churchill's.[6]

Storr might have foreseen the distaste which critics would display for the laying bare of Churchill's inner life – whether he got it right or not, and irrespective of how plausible it seemed to be. For he had already witnessed the outrage that had greeted the publication in 1966 of Lord Moran's diaries, one of his own chief sources of information on Churchill's medical and psychological state. Moran had been Churchill's doctor for the last quarter-century of his life and had on occasion seen his patient often and at very close hand. It was therefore easy to represent the publication of so many of his patient's intimate medical details only a year after his death as a form of professional betrayal, even as a breach of the Hippocratic oath sworn by all doctors at the start of their careers. Randolph Churchill told *The Lancet* even before the book came out that Moran was creating 'a bad precedent which none should follow'. Both Clementine and Randolph Churchill encouraged the British Medical Association to censure Moran for ethical misconduct, and Moran was duly censured, though not expelled altogether as the family had hoped. He was, however, required to resign from the Other Club, of which Winston Churchill had been a founder member and stalwart, and to which he had introduced Moran himself. As John Colville acidly wrote even as late as 1981, 'It is a convention generally accepted that professional men do not write about their clients and customers any more than priests reveal the secrets of the confessional.' That Moran, a former President of the Royal College of Physicians and one of the leaders of his profession, should now do this was seen as a great issue of ethics, and he was therefore denounced not only by reviewers but also in numerous letters to *The Times*, by admirers of Churchill and by other doctors. Randolph Churchill asked 'for my father' simply that he be treated to the same courtesy as any patient would expect from their GP, while Mary Soames fumed that 'Lord Moran has done an outrageous thing in complete breach of a doctor's ethics.'

With the greater detachment that came from not being either part of the family or a friend of Churchill's, Cyril Connolly could see that 'Lord Moran's devotion to Sir Winston shines through everything he writes.' Robert Blake thought that it was 'a unique portrait', which would be read for at least fifty years, and the *Guardian* reviewer concluded that it was a 'literary masterpiece'. Happy that they had a book-selling controversy on their hands, the book's paperback publisher printed all these views on the cover, and then for good measure added the Hippocratic oath itself. The *Times Literary Supplement* produced a hostile but fair review of the book which may be seen as representing the middle ground: the advance serial publication in a Sunday paper had done Moran less than justice, for (as in the case of Alanbrooke in 1957) the extracts published had been 'more sensational than the whole', the family were justified in their concerns, and various people quoted in the book, such as Lord Normanbrook, had already disclaimed words that Moran alleged that they had said. However, despite its limitations, the book would be a useful historical source, and would offer historians considerable insights into Churchill's last quarter-century. Two years later, Harold Macmillan finally put the story to bed with a characteristically cynical publisher's reflection on the ethics of printing such a personal memoir. Speaking about Moran's diaries at a book launch of his own in New York, he said that he could 'imagine how Winston would have reacted to that book'.

> He would ask Moran how much he got for it. If he said £2000, Churchill would say that it was a violation of the hippocratic oath. But if he said eighty thousand quid, Winston would say that he should have got a hundred thousand. He admired anyone who could get money out of the press.

Macmillan then added, rather in keeping with Moran's picture of the ageing Churchill (which his own experience would have confirmed), that all his comments should be judged by the fact that 'I have reached the age of indiscretion.'[7]

Moran's account certainly presented an unheroic Churchill, and over the entire period that Rhodes James left untouched in his *Study in Failure* book, for in the Moran diaries Churchill appears as a pill-popping hypochondriac, petty and jealous with colleagues, maudlin about his own declining powers, and quite outrageously lazy when in office as Prime Minister after 1951. But it also presents a warm and plausible human being, full of life and vitality (if decreasingly so as he moved through his eighties – but that likewise was all too plausible), and herein lay the real danger in the book. If Moran was offering an accurate and persuasive picture of the man in general, then many of the assiduously cultivated myths about the older Churchill – the resignation with which he accepted defeat in 1945, the readiness with which he laid down power in 1955, and the continuing vitality of the man even as he got very old, to give but three examples – would be undermined, perhaps wrecked for ever. Defenders of Churchill therefore seized on the ethical weakness of Moran's position as a publisher of medical secrets and mounted a fairly vicious counter-attack. He had further opened himself to such attacks by turning down Clementine Churchill's request that he not publish the diaries, and then refusing even to show her the proofs in advance of publication. He could also be portrayed as self-seeking, for example in his pursuit of a peerage (and later of a viscountcy that he never got) and in his sometimes spiteful attacks on other prominent physicians, and in asking Churchill to make him Minister of Health, for which he had no political qualifications whatsoever, though to be fair to Moran the same lack did not deter Churchill from making Alexander his Minister of Defence.

It was pointed out that certain facts in the book could not actually be correct – as must always be true in a long diary, written in haste late in the evenings – and it was then gently hinted that Moran might in fact have written some of it rather later than the dates of individual entries suggested. The logic of such attacks is hard to work out, but they were possibly intended to suggest that Moran was antedating Churchill's physical decline by writing about it with more hindsight than his dating indicated. Then it was pointed out that doctors only generally saw their patients when they were ill (or thought they were, in the elderly Churchill's case), and that the days on which Churchill saw Moran were therefore untypical of the whole period. From this it was easy to argue that he had usually been fitter for work, less agitated and not so querulous as Moran had suggested. This last point was well made, and needs to be taken into account in any use of Moran's book as evidence of the pace of Churchill's overall physical decline, though we have no better source from a medically qualified observer, and indeed have no remotely equivalent source at all for most major political figures. Hence Moran rarely saw Churchill at all in the years 1940 and 1941, when he was usually fit and well, and these were the key years of his contribution to the war, though he then saw him more often once his health deteriorated. What that attacking argument could not do was to explain away specific remarks that Churchill made to Moran on particular days, apparently written down then or soon afterwards, nor his overall view of the position in the later years. More valid was the allegation that Moran was a better physician than a historian, as a result of which the linking passages between edited diary extracts were bound to present even good evidence in a false light. He was for example at pains to argue that in the last months of the war Churchill's declining physical powers limited his ability to control the onset of the Cold War, because he could not impose his views on Roosevelt – a very different version of events from Churchill's own. In fact it was Roosevelt who was dying in those months during and after Yalta, rather than Churchill. As more evidence later emerged, from official government papers for example under the thirty-year rule, and with more unguarded memoirs from other Churchill intimates and contemporaries appearing as time passed, Lord Moran's overall picture of Churchill has come to be seen as pretty close to the mark. At the time, though, it was all too often portrayed as a tainted source from an ethically challenged professional man who did not know his own limitations, and who came (partly indeed through close association with Churchill) to have delusions of grandeur about his role and his judgement. The armour-plate of Churchill's defenders had held out.[8]

Nevertheless, there was plainly a need for a counter-attack, and this came in the form of a book of essays by several of Churchill's wartime staffers, under the title *Action This Day*. Lord Normanbrook, who appears to have been the motivating force behind the book, argued that 'we cannot accept [Moran's] assessment as it stands. We believe that in some respects it is incorrect and in others incomplete and on both counts misleading.' The tone was set clearly enough by the editor, Sir John Wheeler-Bennett, who could 'not resist the temptation to pay my own tribute to Sir Winston', in the 1930s 'a tower of strength and a comfort' to those who had then understood the coming horror of 'a fresh outbreak of the *furor teutonicus*' (not for Wheeler-Bennett Churchill's doctrine of magnanimity in victory then). In 1940, Churchill was 'the Lord of the event', for 'the man and his hour had met'. He was also careful to point out (even though 'it goes without saying') that:

> the recorded observations of those whose intimacy with Sir Winston was so regular and so close must of necessity rank higher in historical value and content than those of others who saw him only sporadically and then only at moments of emergency, transience or ill-health.

He added that Clementine Churchill had been consulted and given her approval of the book being written.

These were all palpable hits at Moran, and each of the writers duly took the hint, if indeed they needed a hint. Lord Bridges and Lord Normanbrook wrote from the perspective of the Cabinet Office, having been Churchill's Cabinet Secretaries in 1940–5 and 1951–5 respectively; John Colville, Leslie Rowan and John Martin wrote as Churchill's private secretaries; General Sir Ian Jacob represented the military, having been Ismay's senior assistant in the military wing of the war cabinet secretariat. Collectively therefore they were well equipped to correct Moran's perspective as an observer of Churchill, for they had indeed been closer to him for more of the time – except in the period after 1955 when Moran's representation of physical decline could not be refuted, and they were (as the approving *TLS* reviewer insisted) 'all men of great distinction . . . and men of great authority in their own right'. Apart from Wheeler-Bennett himself, however, they were no more historians than Moran had been, and so their desire finally to set the record straight was no more likely to succeed than had his own. Few notes of criticism were permitted to intrude on the traditional picture, and in some cases this involved not just putting a favourable spin on events but departures from the strict truth. Normanbrook for example was not saying privately in 1951–5 what he now said in print about Churchill's capacity for high office during his second term as Prime Minister, and he certainly knew better than to argue that Churchill's final resignation in 1955 was not forced on him by colleagues, or that 'when the time came, he went with dignity'. All the same, the very fact that Moran had published ensured that a rounder picture of Churchill's working habits was now possible, and Jacob in particular put on the record here a more balanced picture of Churchill's eccentric working habits as wartime premier than had been admitted by most of the hostile reviewers of the Alanbrooke diaries eleven years earlier. Nor could these writers dispute Moran's clinical judgements, and hence there was more acknowledgement than previously of Churchill's unpredictable moods, and in Wheeler-Bennett's introduction even a reference to Churchill's 'black depressions'.

This book, then, counter-balanced Moran's by erring too far on the other side, but this at least allowed historians to begin to form a balanced judgement of Churchill the man and his way of working. Thereafter 'the Churchillians', as Colville now dubbed the inner circle of admirers and close associates, continued to publish similar accounts, for example in a book of wartime memoirs by John Martin and three books by Colville himself. It was notable, though, that when Colville came in the 1980s to publish his own diary (having written in 1976 that 'I shall not publish it'), he devoted over six hundred pages to the war years and only about eighty to the four years of Churchill's second premiership, when presumably a fuller reprint from his later diary might well have seemed to confirm some of Lord Moran's gloomier strictures on Churchill's inability to concentrate and general unfitness for office after his second stroke in 1953. There is no doubting the real and overriding respect and affection for Churchill the man that his close associates demonstrated in all these books, and the clear evidence of his ability to inspire such lifelong devotion is indeed a historical fact of supreme importance, but it also makes them rather suspect witnesses when it comes to wider historical judgements.[9]

In any case, such an emerging balance in the judgement of Churchill's historical role had hardly got going before the Churchill centenary of 1974 produced another orgy of general celebrations, exhibitions, memorials and memorabilia which was not exactly marked by any general wish to treat him as an ordinary historical figure. The centenary was, however, the occasion for some mega-publishing events which made available a great deal of Churchill material on which later studies could rely. His complete speeches were published in eight large volumes, and though this edition had its weaknesses (not being for example actually complete), it made available at least in good libraries a mass of Churchill's spoken words, particularly from before and after the war, which had previously tended to be lost in the endless anthologising of his famous orations of 1940 and 1941. In due course an abridged version of about a thousand pages appeared (the complete edition having run to almost nine thousand pages), again giving a representation of Churchill the speaker over the whole sixty years of his public life. Similarly, a complete edition of Churchill's own books and writings appeared as another centenary event, appropriately enough in the 'Library of Imperial History'. Once again, the selection of some of the editions from which to anthologise the whole man's output was subject to some criticism, but this not only made generally available the rather rare early Churchill books, but also carefully reprinted four volumes of Churchill's essays, many of which had never been collected in book form before. A rival set of Churchill's 'Major Works' also appeared in 1974, running to a mere twenty-five volumes, produced by Diner's Club on subscription. The very act of publishing in the centenary year eight volumes of 'complete' speeches, four volumes of 'complete' essays and a twenty-two-volume set of the other complete works was of course yet another assertion of Churchill's gigantic historical status, for nothing like it had ever been done for any other British politician – or could have been, for none of them had said and written so much.[10]

The same was true of the official biography, already half finished by the centenary. This was again on a scale that in itself exalted Churchill by comparison with rivals. It has dwarfed the four-volume official lives of both Gladstone and Disraeli, and beside it the standard two-volume Victorian biographies of the type that Winston himself had written of his father seemed mere pamphlets. Churchill had accepted that an official life should be written, but had not wished it to appear in his lifetime, and had dithered somewhat over its authorship. His son Randolph was desperately keen to have the job, and when his biography of *Lord Derby, King of Lancashire* appeared to general acclaim in 1960, Winston gradually accommodated himself to the idea that his tempestuous son should write his biography, just as he himself had written his own father's in 1906. Randolph, who had been offered £450 to write his father's life thirty years earlier, when Winston had rapidly persuaded him out of the idea, determined that it should be a 'Great Biography', and 'great' here clearly implied size as well as quality. This was to be a book which would be a national as well as a publishing event, much as Winston Churchill's own major works had been.[11]

THE MAN OF THE CENTURY - AND OF THE NEXT?   539

In 1961 Randolph set to work with a will, quickly establishing the legal and serialisation rights, access to the necessary papers, moving over a million documents into a special strong-room built into his house in Suffolk, and assembling the team who would work with him on the project, once again much as Churchill had worked on such books as his war memoirs. Among those early recruits was Michael Wolff, who in 1974 edited Churchill's collected essays during a brief but unsuccessful foray into Heathite Conservative politics, and Martin Gilbert who would complete the biography after Randolph's early death, aged only fifty-seven. It was in defence of the biography that *Private Eye* was successfully sued in 1963, after it had published a nasty little piece suggesting that Randolph intended merely to whitewash Churchill with a fabricated assembly of unrepresentative facts, but no real progress could be made until Churchill died in 1965. Thereafter, though, those early preparations ensured that things moved fast, with the first of five projected volumes appearing in 1966, and a second, carrying the story up to 1914, in 1967. Reviews were generally warm, for, though one or two carping critics suggested that Randolph had merely acquired the task by inheritance, most saw the book's real value and these early volumes sold extremely well (as the evidence of their ubiquity in second-hand bookshops demonstrates to this day). So successful had Randolph been in combining the efforts of a first-rate professional research team with the command of the language that he had inherited from Winston, and which he knew well that he too must use in such a task, that the books were most effective. When Victor Feske said that 'Churchill never forgot that he wrote principally for the educated layman and that such a reader expected more than dull accuracy alone,' he was actually talking about Winston, but it could equally be said of Randolph. Nor had he, despite *Private Eye*'s predictions, been afraid to criticise or to reveal his father's weaker points – notably in this early period his precocious egocentricity and over-confidence. The policy adopted had been that 'he shall be his own biographer' – a phrase borrowed from J. G. Lockhart, when he was writing the life of Sir Walter Scott. Through Winston's own words, for example in letters to his mother, his less attractive side had been allowed to emerge alongside the impressive trajectory of a young man achieving great things at an enviably early age.[12]

The *TLS* gave each of the first two volumes front-page coverage, as 'an event full of promise of a monumental accomplishment', much as it had greeted Winston Churchill's own post-war books. 'Apart from a few asides,' it noted, 'the man is left to tell his own story,' though it also pointed out that the actual selection of Churchill's own documents required an important if hidden editorial hand at work. The first documentary volumes – for Randolph had decided that the biography could be both readable and comprehensive if he separated off the bulk of the documents into parallel volumes – were hailed as 'outstanding', giving 'great pleasure', and with 'excellent editing'. Likewise the second volume of the 'long-paced biography' itself was further praised as 'vivid and readable'. So impressive were the reviews of these early volumes, and so great was the momentum that had been established towards the completion of the project, that Randolph was discussing with the Kennedy family writing next the official life of President Kennedy, but then in June 1968 Randolph Churchill died. Martin Gilbert had withdrawn from the team on health grounds, but was now able to return and become the writer of the remaining volumes, a project to which he had by 2002 devoted thirty-five years. He had by 2001 published in the official biography sixteen books, plus various other spin-off volumes on Churchill and a host of essays and published lectures.

This change of director was bound to produce some loss of momentum, and there was anyway work to complete in seeing through the press the documentary companion volumes for 1901–14. The next actual volume of the main text did not therefore appear until 1971, and thereafter they came out at irregular intervals until 1988, with the documentary collections following on. Since these companion volumes have so far reached only the early 1940s, over two decades of Churchill's life remain to be chronicled in this way. As all this suggests, the change of writer from a gifted amateur backed by professionals to a writer who is a supreme professional himself had another effect too. A biography which had started out as a five-volume assault on the general public abruptly shifted to become instead a longer series of books likely to be bought only by historians, libraries and Churchill enthusiasts. The *TLS* noted the change at once by giving volume three inside-page reviews notable more for respect than enthusiasm, while the *English Historical Review*, a professional journal which had ignored Randolph Churchill's first two volumes, now reviewed Gilbert's later ones. Gilbert was, thought *TLS*'s anonymous reviewer, a 'worthy successor' to Randolph Churchill, and he had crafted a 'classical tragedy' from Churchill's first major setback, but 'interestingly enough' he was 'more partisan than the hero's son', and stylistically he was 'rather less racy'. 'His list of sources is staggering in its comprehensiveness. He has visited the ground both in Gallipoli and in Flanders. He has ferreted out with extraordinary pains many obscure witnesses of great events'. What it did *not* say though – as it had said of Randolph's volumes – was that it was also a rattling good read for the layman.

In the *American Historical Review* Samuel Hurwitz had welcomed Randolph's volumes, even though noting that they were 'filial rather than detached'. For volume three, Raymond Callahan thought in the same journal that Gilbert had failed to confront the specific criticisms of Churchill made by such recent writers as Arthur Marder, and decided that he had made a major but not definitive contribution to the historiography of the Dardanelles. In *History*, Henry Pelling reported that Gilbert had introduced 'a considerable slowing of the tempo of the work as Randolph envisaged it'. He praised Gilbert for printing lots of documents which enabled the reader to make up his own mind, but then rather undercut this by reminding readers that 'this is an official biography, and Churchill is obviously Mr Gilbert's hero . . .' These sorts of review set the tone for coverage of the rest of the series, though there was naturally a more upbeat feel when the story reached Churchill's accession to the premiership and the summer of 1940.[13]

Gilbert's first volume indicated the reality of the change clearly enough, for in it he covered only the twenty-nine months between the start of the Great War and the end of 1916. This was a formidable academic achievement which ruthlessly destroyed myths through the deployment of hard evidence, and covered the key period of Churchill's life when all that early promise seemed to have been blasted by the fiasco of the Dardanelles. But at over eight hundred pages, almost a page for every day of Churchill's life in these years, it was certainly not a book for the general reader. Gilbert had also abandoned the over-arching themes and sub-titles which Randolph had attached to the earlier volumes: the second volume's sub-title *Young Statesman, 1901–1914*, was followed simply by the third volume's austere *1914–1916*. This practice of Gilbert's, followed until the story reached 1939, after which the last three became *Finest Hour, 1939–1941*, *Road to Victory, 1941–1945*, and *Never Despair, 1945–1965*, was indicative of a truly significant shift of gear when he took over the project. Gilbert followed Randolph

Churchill's policy of letting Churchill be his own biographer, but he was rather more reluctant than Randolph to offer comment of his own, either in adding his own words or through leaving out editorially many of Churchill's either. Any biographer must mainly represent his subject and his subject's view of his career, but few would be content to leave it at that and so eschew an editorial intervention from time to time. Gilbert, though, has clearly seen this as simply not his role. Hence, when the final volume ends and Churchill is duly dead and buried, there is merely one more page on the subject of death and bereavement, and no attempt at all to sum up Winston Churchill, his significance, his strengths and his weaknesses. Exactly the same is true of the single-volume life of Churchill that Gilbert published soon after completing the main project.[14]

Churchill's own view of himself is thus unmediated – and to a great extent uncriticised – by a man who, perhaps inevitably, came over thirty years of exposure to that remarkable personality to be one of his very greatest admirers. The unevenness of the chronological coverage also contributed to this biography being rather more the case for the defence than an authoritative final verdict. Well over half of Gilbert's six volumes are devoted to the exciting story of Churchill as the happy warrior during two world wars, rather less to the remaining forty years of his life after 1914. Even if the ten years of Churchill's retirement after 1955 are left out of the calculation, Gilbert's six volumes devote on average more than 350 pages a year to the two world wars (again almost a page for every day of Churchill's life), but under a hundred pages a year to the thirty years of peacetime. As a result, the not very impressive story of his second premiership in the 1950s gets a mere 475 pages of the final volume, while in volume four almost as many pages are devoted to Churchill's twenty months at the Colonial Office in 1921–2, a period of no special significance in either his life or the office. While some eras of Churchill's life are extraordinarily over-exposed, others are barely touched on. Churchill was for example leader of the Conservative Party for fifteen years, 1940–55, but in none of the three volumes that cover those years does this side of his life – without which he could not have returned to office as Prime Minister and would hardly have been so listened to internationally either – get more than a passing mention.

All this was brought out in 1983 in an extremely perceptive review of the sixth (and first Second World War) volume of the official biography by Stephen Koss; by now even such pivotal new volumes in the series were down to a third of an inside page of the *TLS*. Noting that 'like the mighty Mississippi . . . the official biography of Sir Winston Churchill rolls on', he found this to be 'the most satisfying instalment so far' and was full of praise for Gilbert's exemplary scholarship and detachment. Nevertheless, Koss was not very happy with the style of the biography or the way it had been constructed even in a volume that was its own finest hour. Lockhart's dictum that 'he shall be his own biographer' sounded fine, but 'implies a certain illogicality as well as a self-conscious inhibition. Living men may write autobiographies, not biographies. Dead men can do neither.' Gilbert's detachment was therefore a problem in itself, and 'one wishes that he had seen fit to intervene more emphatically between Churchill and the emotive issues of his career'. He provided lots of documents which enabled readers to make up their own minds on the big issues, and so could not fairly be accused of being over-partisan, but:

> Controversies are delineated, but seldom evaluated. Instead the author provides a day-by-day, sometimes hour-by-hour chronology The sources, skilfully assembled, are expected – and indeed required – to speak for themselves. With regard to the fall of France, for example, they do so eloquently. Often, however, they echo, contradict or speak past each other. The effect, curiously enough, is to dissipate the dramatic tension.

Often, 'the reader, unassisted, may find it difficult to reach conclusions', and Koss then listed about ten major questions on 1939–41 on which the book offered evidence for an answer but no actual answer. It would not do simply to accept, as Churchill himself did when writing on the bombardment of the French navy in 1940 after the Vichy surrender, that judgement should be left 'to the world and to history', if one was oneself a historian rather than just the willing pen of Churchill himself, acting as his own biographer. Finally, Koss questioned the scale itself of this 'mighty Mississippi' of a biography.

> The welter of information, at times more overwhelming than instructive, might have been alleviated by fewer and shorter extracts from published works, particularly Churchill's own retrospective accounts. Likewise, certain letters of congratulation

and commendation might have been consigned to the 'Companion' volumes . . . If Churchill had a fault, ventured Colonel . . . Ian Jacob, 'it was to go into too much detail'. With due respect, the same must be said about his official biographer, whose achievement awaits proper appraisal at its conclusion.

When Gilbert produced the eighth and final volume five years later, though, it most certainly did not conclude with a 'proper appraisal' of Churchill, and in view of the scale of the task few reviewers attempted a 'proper appraisal' of the eight volumes of biography either. There can indeed have been few reviewers anywhere in the world who had actually read right through the eight fat volumes and so qualified themselves to appraise the project properly.[15]

It is very difficult to work on Churchill in any way at all and not be overwhelmed by the man, his achievements and his personality – especially in war. On balance, Churchill's official biography was probably the greatest feat of sustained scholarship brought off by any single historian working in Britain in the last third of the twentieth century, and Gilbert's knighthood for services to history was more than well merited. In the end, though, a project that is too large for reading by all but the dedicated few, but necessarily also selectively incomplete (since the length and range of the Churchill career and the size and scale of the Churchill papers makes completeness impossible, at least in book form), invites an uncomfortable question: 'What was it all *for*?' The official biography had by 2002 been in progress for forty years. At the present rate of publication of documentary volumes, if his biographers ever finish the task it will have taken about as long to chronicle his active political career as it took Churchill himself to live it. We can be forgiven for suspecting that the advocate of 'action this day' might by now have got more than a little impatient with the rate of progress. But the sheer scale and longevity of the official biography has reinforced once again the very idea of Churchill's greatness. As in so much else relating to Churchill's career, there has never been anything like it in Britain, and it is impossible to believe that it will ever be done again.

The influence of the official biography has largely then been at second hand, as other historians have used its great treasures of narrative, anecdote, insight and documentary back-up, and so passed on to many who have certainly not read the eight volumes (let alone the documentary companions) the gist of Churchill's life. Henry Pelling attempted such a task at considerable length but in a single volume as early as 1974, but seems not to have had either the writing skills to make him a natural biographer or the sympathy with his subject to make any lasting impact with his book. Dozens of writers have followed him into the field since. What appeared to be the most likely contender for the title of the most admired interpretative biography of Churchill was that begun by William Manchester with *The Last Lion* (1983), but this too succumbed to Gilbert's tendencies – over-concentration on the heroic periods of Churchill's life and writing at excessive length because Churchill seems so giant a figure. Despite its enormous length when covering only the period of Churchill's life up to 1932, Manchester's *The Last Lion* devoted a mere thirty-two pages to the five years that Churchill spent at the Treasury in 1924–9, while the whole of the second volume, *The Caged Lion* (1988), was given over to the six years 1932–8, the period of his campaign against appeasement. Manchester thus lost velocity once he moved into the 1930s, and it seems unlikely that his biography will be completed.

Meanwhile, the most important recent insights on Churchill arise from smaller studies, often in collections of conference papers, and three such volumes have appeared since 1993, from Churchill College, from the University of Texas, and from the Royal Historical Society. Roy Jenkins in 2001, writing at length but within one polished and most readable volume, and with the additional insight of a man who had held some of the same posts that Churchill himself occupied, did bring it off, though, and it seems likely that this will remain the authoritative single text for years to come. This brought Jenkins too into the ranks of the 'New Churchillians'; in March 2002 he delivered the Crosby Kemper lecture at the Churchill Memorial in Fulton, Missouri, and addressed the English-Speaking Union in London. However, Manchester and Jenkins, like most of the other lesser (or at least shorter) writers, have based their work heavily on Gilbert's blazing of the broad avenues through the undergrowth. Some good short Churchill lives have also appeared for example from Norman Rose, Geoffrey Best and Keith Robbins. They have rarely challenged Gilbert's – or should one say Churchill's? – view of what was and what was not important in Churchill's life, and they like most other writers have been reluctant to go beyond Gilbert's selections of documents for their sources. What is most striking of all, though, is just how many books on Churchill continue to flow from the presses. When Frederick Woods compiled a fairly exhaustive list in Churchill's centenary year, 1974, he counted 248 books about or substantially about Churchill, half of which had come out since his retirement in 1955. By the end of the century the figure had about doubled again, and major libraries in Britain and the United States each had at least two or three hundred Churchill books in their catalogues.[16]

Long before the centenary in any case, the memory of Churchill had ceased to depend only on words – whether in books, or in gramophone recordings of his speeches. Films and television programmes had added their necessarily simplified messages to the common stock of memory, but so had the iconography of visual representation. Given the alleged 'quintessential Englishness' of Churchill, and the Dickensian lifestyle that he led, it was not surprising that he was widely commemorated by toby jugs. The first such representation dates from 1927, but it was in the war years that the idea really took off, ten separate designs coming on to the market between 1941 and 1945, some of these (like Royal Doulton's) remaining available for many years afterwards. The prevailing style of these may be seen in the pair produced by Burgess and Leigh, one of which depicts Churchill as John Bull while the other has him making the V-sign. Another appeared in 1953, marking Churchill's second premiership (a jug changing hands at sales for about £1600 at the start of the twenty-first century), but four more versions were marketed as late as 1987–90, the climax of the Thatcher years and the period during which the cabinet war rooms were opened in homage to Churchill's war leadership, and in which 'Winston Churchill's Britain at War Experience' first opened in the railway arches under London Bridge station (and was soon voted 'London's top tourist attraction'). Five more then appeared in the 1990s, including a fiftieth anniversary of VE Day jug in 1995, with both a British bulldog and an American bald eagle, selling even when new for a far from modest £147. By the end of the century, at least twenty-two different Churchill toby jugs had been issued – compared to two each of Baldwin, Chamberlain, Lloyd George and Monty, or one each for Asquith, Beatty, Cripps, French, Jellicoe, Kitchener, MacDonald, Margaret Thatcher and John Major. Among figures from before the twentieth century, Henry VIII (five different jugs) was the most prominent, but Bluff King Hal's total was utterly dwarfed by Churchill's two dozen. It is not easy to establish production numbers for these articles, but in a competitive market it is at least safe to conclude that such a plethora of Churchill memorabilia would not have come out without a public keen and willing to buy it. Individual designs have not varied greatly, with much repetition of Churchill with a bulldog, in military or naval uniform, and usually with a cigar and an expression made to resemble Karsh's 'angry lion' portrait of 1941. The war and his role as war leader was clearly the dominant theme.[17]

It would be tedious to trace here the commemoration of Churchill in other types of memorabilia, the more recent of them aimed directly at a fairly restricted collectors' market. These can in any case be fairly exhaustively investigated in Ronald Smith's *Churchill: Images of Greatness*, but a few points may be made about the mass of ashtrays, plates, mugs, figurines, miniature busts and other types of Churchilliana. They have been saturated with the same images of Churchill's war as have the toby jugs, with military uniforms, flags, bulldogs, Spitfires and other weapons of the 1940s. Churchill's actual portrayal continues the same theme, with V-sign, cigar, hat, bow tie, siren suit and so on. All of this tends to narrow the commemoration of the man to six of his sixty years in British public life. There are also a number of projections of the same Churchill image in museums, for example in the Hastings Embroidery commissioned to commemorate the 900th anniversary of the Battle of Hastings, the 'Overlord Tapestry' in Portsmouth's D-Day Museum, and in a mosaic floor representing 'The Modern Virtues' in London's National Gallery. He is likewise to be found, in some very strange company indeed (including both Gerry Adams and David Trimble), as an exhibit in the recently opened National Museum of Liberty in Philadelphia, just a block away from Independence Hall and the Liberty Bell. Most of the major portrait galleries in the Western world have his portrait (notably including the extremely fine Douglas Chandor portrait in Washington DC, one of the best ever taken from life by an artist), as have many parliaments and legislatures. Britain's National Portrait Gallery contains not only a painting but also one of the limited number of copies of Jacob Epstein's Churchill bust (perhaps the best of all), others being at Churchill College, the Imperial War Museum and the Queen Elizabeth II Conference Centre. Churchill is similarly on show in the waxworks of Madam Tussaud's in London (where he had progressively aged over his career after being first installed in 1909, but where he is now back at the age that he was in the 1940s), in Amsterdam, in Copenhagen and in Prague. As well as Churchill statues in Paris, the Benelux countries, Scandinavia and the Czech Republic, there is one in Australia, three in Canada, at least four in the United States and about a dozen in Britain.[18]

A rather wider international public across the world was also buying and using Churchill stamps. By the end of the century, 126 different postal authorities had issued Churchill stamps, in some cases many times over. Even when we exclude temporary postal systems allowed only during the 1971 British postal strike, and offshore islands making local issues only (Davaar island in Campbelltown loch, Argyllshire, having issued no fewer than sixteen Churchill stamps between 1965 and 1974), there remain about a hundred sovereign states and British colonies on the list. A few of these go back to wartime, and not always in obvious places – the South American republic of Colombia for example, not even an ally, issued a Churchill stamp in 1945 as part of a set with Roosevelt and Stalin. The great concentration of Churchill issues came, however, in the eighteen months after his death, not least because a single and rather fine design was used across such remaining British colonies as Aden, Basutoland, the Falklands and Hong Kong.

This deployed both the Karsh portrait and the Blitz image of St Paul's Cathedral surrounded by searchlights in the night sky. But commemoration of Churchill at that time was by no means confined to the Commonwealth or the English-speaking countries, for there were also Churchill stamps issued in 1965 or shortly afterwards in Brazil, Ecuador, Germany (as part of a set commemorating Adenauer), Liberia, Paraguay, Upper Volta and Venezuela. There was then a further concentration of Churchill issues in the year of his centenary, 1974, and again across the whole world (including the Cameroons, Congo Brazzaville, Dominica and Nicaragua).

Thereafter there has been no obvious pattern, except for a bunching of Churchill issues as during the 1990s the many fiftieth anniversaries of the Second World War rolled by. The Marshall Islands, for example, put Churchill's face on a war-related stamp in every year from 1990 to 1995. Russia issued its first Churchill stamp in 1989 as the Cold War was finally wound down, and produced another in 1995 to celebrate VE Day's fiftieth anniversary. There was some tendency to dwell on Churchill the painter in stamp issues, either by using his paintings in the design or by offering pictures of him actually painting them (Brunei,

1973). Others linked the stamp design with a visible local image of the man, the Nemon bust actually in Monte Carlo used by Monaco in 1974 or its own statue used by Luxembourg in the same year. Many though used and reused the Karsh portrait (as did the initial British stamps of 1965), and these were just part of the dominant theme, a heroic image and a link with the war. Later issues drew on Churchill's established fame and iconography to celebrate something that was more local, as did the Channel Isles in celebrating liberation anniversaries in 1970 and 1995; the Cayman Islands celebrated the Queen Mother's ninetieth birthday in 1990 by putting her alongside Churchill on a stamp. Others reiterated Churchill's association with America, as did Liberia when hailing the centenary of the Statue of Liberty with a Churchill stamp in 1987, and Burundi by putting Churchill on a stamp with the US Capitol for background in 1967.

No doubt many of these were issued for low commercial motives rather than in homage to anyone or anything – the fact that so many of the Churchill stamps came from third-world countries desperate for hard currency undoubtedly suggests this, while there has not yet been a Churchill stamp from France or Italy or anywhere in Scandinavia, and only one each from Australia and Canada (both in 1965). It was no doubt a similar mixture of homage and commercial judgement that led the National Trust to use Churchill as one of the designs for its own anniversary stamp issues in 1995, a shrewd judgement too, given the numbers of visitors who annually make the trip to the National Trust's Chartwell. Nevertheless, there was clearly a market for such issues, and, as in the case of the toby jugs, it would be hard to find any other twentieth-century politician anywhere in the world who has had anything like this degree of philatelic exposure. Churchill stamps were anyway collected partly for the man as well as for the philately, and it was a group of stamp enthusiasts who first began the organisation that has evolved into the International Churchill Society. But, whatever the motivation, hundreds of millions of correspondents the world over have been reminded at regular intervals over a third of a century that Churchill was one of the great men of the age, and, because of the icons of the Second World War that usually surrounded him on their letters, they were also reminded just why this was. The Cook Islands set of Churchill stamps of 1974 make this point clearly enough, but it could be replicated many times over. That set of six commemorative stamps showed Churchill with Blenheim (ancestry), at Chartwell (family man, memories of the wilderness years), at Buckingham Palace (VE Day), with St Paul's (the Blitz), with the Houses of Parliament (democracy) and making his 'V for Victory' sign (war leader). Not just a set of stamps, then, but a set of values too.[19]

Churchill was undoubtedly seen as representing enduring values in the memorialising of him that went on in the United States, for the uproar in America over representation at the Churchill funeral in 1965 indicated the breadth of admiration for Churchill there, and reinforced the determination of those Americans planning permanent memorials on US soil. The Fulton Memorial was the less controversial of the two, and had Presidential backing throughout: Kennedy welcomed the original idea of bringing a bombed-out Wren church from London to the Mid-West, which clearly appealed to his sense of history. He told the President of Westminster College that 'it will tie together powerful events – the 17th century, 1940 and the blitz, the Iron Curtain address, and the extraordinary and powerful influence on the free world of Sir Winston Churchill's public service'. In the more prosaic language of minute-takers, the College resolved to set up 'a monument to the ideals of international co-operation, particularly among the English-Speaking nations, as suggested by Mr Churchill in his "Iron Curtain" speech'. Within that package it would literally set in stone the kinship alliance of Britain and the United States. That was precisely the objective aimed at by the originator of the idea, James H. Williams, who was both a Westminster College trustee and a stalwart of the English-Speaking Union, and the E-SU's branches in St Louis and Kansas City were active in helping to raise the necessary cash.

The London church in question, St Mary Aldermanbury, had been John Milton's parish church (not to mention that of the notorious Judge Jeffreys of the 1688 Bloody Assizes), and probably a place of worship used by William Shakespeare – certainly by the two actors who published his First Folio, both of whom were buried there. This made the building a part of the cultural inheritance of Anglo-Saxon Americans as well as Londoners (and hence was much touted in fundraising literature), but the decision to leave some of the 'fire scars' of 1941 intact in the reconstructed building was a conscious decision to commemorate 'the English people's suffering in their finest hour'. By the time that the project got started Kennedy was dead, but several donations to the Churchill

Memorial were made in his memory. Lyndon Johnson then gave a powerful impetus to the fundraising appeal for $1.5 million, and a few days later Harry Truman turned the first sod of the project in Fulton, with the British Ambassador in attendance. The *New York Times* continued to give supportive coverage as the project went ahead, not least because the rebuilding of a London church in Missouri made for eye-catching photographs. No opportunity was missed to remind readers that the Memorial was 'a symbol of Sir Winston's resistance to tyranny, and the anti-totalitarian ties he helped to forge among the English-speaking nations'. The Memorial's location, close to the recently completed Interstate 70, linked together a heritage trail which also took in the memorials to Thomas Jefferson, Harry Truman and Dwight Eisenhower (in St Louis, Independence and Abilene respectively), so that even while the building was going up the project was already attracting some ten thousand visitors a year, despite being a hundred miles from the nearest centre of population.[20]

Collecting the huge sum of money involved was by no means easy, but by 1967 over a million dollars had been raised. A boost was given at a $100-a-plate dinner at the New York Hilton; Eisenhower was honorary chairman of the dinner committee, and the president of McGraw-Hill (one of Churchill's US publishers) co-chairman, together with Henry Luce, Averell Harriman and David Bruce, while Douglas Fairbanks Jr (a quite different sort of Anglo-American) was toastmaster. The programme included a dramatic reading of the Fulton speech by Rod Steiger, a toast to Churchill by Walter Cronkite, and an address by the British Foreign Office Minister Lord Caradon. The Churchill message was also kept alive by the Green Lecture in Fulton, the lecture series which had been raised to fame by Churchill himself in 1946, and which thereafter often had a lecture with Churchill as its theme, or a lecturer who would talk about Churchill from personal experience. In 1969, it was Lord Mountbatten, who like Eisenhower had been a supreme allied commander in the war and thus embodied Churchill's 'theme' of Anglo-American unity, and he duly propounded that theme in his speech. From 1979, this was reinforced by a second endowed lecture at Fulton, the Crosby Kemper Lecture, which was devoted to Churchill's memory; early lecturers included Sir John Colville, Martin Gilbert and Sir William Deakin. Other avenues could be exploited too by such a well-connected group of enthusiasts. When the United States issued a commemorative

Churchill stamp in May 1965, a group of friendly US Senators arranged for the launch of the first-day cover to be in Fulton, and considerable press coverage for the Appeal was generated in the process. In May 1969, the Memorial was formally dedicated, and the group started out on the less glamorous and far more difficult task of raising funds for an endowment; the first effort was a letter over the signature of Walter Cronkite, but apparently more successful in bringing in Churchill memorabilia for exhibition than in raising cash.[21]

Part of the problem, already in the 1960s, was the range of Churchill memorials being planned, each of which was effectively seeking to raise money from the same sympathisers. From the start, it had been heavy going to collect the cash for a statue in Washington, and here the erection of an original work of art – under the fierce scrutiny of capital-city attention – also raised aesthetic and political questions that could be ignored by the reconstructors of Sir Christopher Wren's work in Missouri. Again, the patient prodding and diplomatic spadework of Kay Halle helped bring off the scheme. Halle was instrumental in getting the commission for the statue awarded to Bill McVey, a fellow Cleve-lander who had already executed heroic statues of Davy Crockett and Jim Bowie, and the reliefs on the San Jacinto monument in Texas. When she privately showed McVey's model for a Churchill statue, several of the E-SU Committee, including Adlai Stevenson and Averell Harriman, were reportedly 'thunderstruck'. The actual design of the figure was only part of the story, for the key achievement was its placement outside the British Embassy. Churchill's statue would stand on a mixture of British and American earth within the stone plinth (the British earth coming from Chartwell, the American from the alleged Jerome home in Brooklyn). The design adopted by McVey was of a 'walking statue', which allowed Churchill's forward foot to be on the sidewalk (and thus in Washington DC) while his back foot was in the Embassy precinct (and thus on British soil, legally as well as symbolically). Churchill thus bestrode the Atlantic, but the unintended consequence of a walking statue with the right hand upraised in a victory salute, was that, when placed at the edge of Massachusetts Avenue, it seemed to prosaic observers as if Sir Winston was hailing a cab.

The selection of McVey ensured that a heroic Churchill without modernist overtones would be produced, and hence there was no risk of it being unacceptable to the family, as Graham Sutherland's 1954 portrait had been, or as controversial as the Woodford statue of Churchill. It also provided a lever for raising money from the banks in Ohio, just as the highly controversial decision to give the bronze Churchill a cigar opened up the way for an appeal to US cigar manufacturers to contribute too – though this brought in only $187, compared to $2550 raised by the E-SU branch in Indianapolis, the largest single contributor. But the battle within the English-Speaking Union over whether the statue should include a cigar was bitter and prolonged. Halle successfully argued that Churchill himself had positively wanted a cigar to be one of his most public associations, but politically correct critics responded that it would set a bad example to future generations and trivialise the great man's memory. The British House of Commons, considering the same issue at the same time, ducked the question by noting that smoking was not allowed in the lobbies of the Palace of Westminster – even by statues – and so did not include one. This produced a scathing, if not very poetic, rebuke from a correspondent to the *Yorkshire Post*:

> Aesthetics was not offered – blood, toil, and sweat, and tears
> Were all that Churchill proffered, in Britain's darkest years.
> It heartened all, the free cigar, throughout that bitter war –
> The hand that made the V-sign, held also a cigar.
> Drop his cigar? Have at you! What can this nonsense be?
> As well de-torch the statue, that stands for Liberty!

A Washington DC benefit performance of Jack Le Vien's film *The Finest Hours* in 1964 also brought in a good deal of cash, with post-film receptions laid on by the British, Australian. Canadian and New Zealand embassies, a rare example of 'English-speaking peoples' being taken literally. In 1965 the main event was a ball at the British Embassy, attended by three hundred people, paying a hundred dollars each, while two years earlier it had been an Embassy garden party. Despite claims that money for the statue had been raised as 'a spontaneous tribute from thousands of Americans across the nation', it is pretty clear that it would never have been erected at all without the continuous backing of the British Embassy and the repeated generosity of America's Anglophile and internationalist elite. It is notable that, at precisely this time, many of the same people were signing up on Averell Harriman's subscription list for $17,000 to buy an Epstein bust of Churchill for display inside the White House. Other donors on this list of seventeen of what the First Lady called Churchill's 'friends and fellow warriors' included Eisenhower, Ed Murrow, General Omar Bradley and four former American ambassadors to Britain.[22]

The implications of memorialising Churchill in the minds of the key American Churchillians, around the time of his death, may be deduced from the speeches at the statue's 1966 unveiling and from the nature of the ceremony itself. The three speakers were Lauris Norstad (president of the English-Speaking Union but formerly Supreme Allied Commander of NATO – as Ike had once been), Dean Rusk (again representing LBJ, though with remarks drafted by Kay Halle), and Randolph Churchill on behalf of the family. Each of them paid homage to Churchill's Fulton 'dream' of a closer relationship between Britain and America, the 'Battle Hymn of the Republic' was sung as a Churchill favourite, reference was made to the recent British memorial to John Kennedy at Runnymede (which with its evocation of Magna Carta was itself an appeal to the common heritage) and much emphasis was given to the symbolic placement of the Churchill statue with a foot in both camps – a transatlantic bridge in miniature. Music was provided by the Marines band, the Bishop of Washington offered a blessing, and the nearby Washington cathedral provided an 'English peal' of bells to celebrate the dedication of the statue. Shortly afterwards the cathedral itself added a Churchill porch, with another dedicatory plaque of its own. The only anticipated problem, the unpredictable presence of Randolph Churchill, could not be avoided, though the E-SU's British director-general confided that 'we are hoping for a persistent, non-lethal but completely debilitating attack of flu to befall a certain inhabitant of East Bergholt from about the 6th to the 13th of April'. In the event, Randolph was on his best behaviour, and did not cause the stir that he had done when accepting his father's honorary citizenship three years earlier.[23]

The statue's plinth also contained a time capsule, together with a letter to be opened by 'Mr President of the future', on 9 April 2063, the centenary of Churchill's honorary citizenship of the USA, when he would find 'striking evidence of the admiration and respect in which this great Anglo-American was held by countless Americans of this age'. The capsule contained lists of the contributors to the statue fund, along with copies of television film of Churchill's life and his funeral, and microfilmed copies of his books. The future President would learn from opening the capsule that:

Sir Winston was more than one of the great figures of history. He was also a living symbol not only of Anglo-American comradeship but also of indomitable courage against overwhelming odds . . . With Sir Winston we believe that in the comradeship of the English-Speaking peoples will always lie the greatest hopes for the peace and welfare of mankind.[24]

Part of the financial problem with the statue arose from the fact that it was only half of what the English-Speaking Union planned to do, for, like Westminster College in Fulton, they had long-term plans for commemoration as well as a structure to erect. Alongside the statue, there was to be a memorial fund to provide for Winston Churchill scholarships, and this had been a key factor in getting the thirty thousand ordinary members in E-SU branches all over the country to fundraise for a scheme run by the Washington branch's elite. The E-SU was keen to associate Eisenhower with this programme, and, although Ike made a policy as an ex-President of the United States of never linking himself directly with any appeals for funds, he had always supported 'efforts over the years to achieve even greater solidarity between peoples of the English Speaking nations' (as he told John Kennedy in 1963). He gave the E-SU a share of the royalties he received when *National Geographic* used him as a consultant for its coverage of Churchill's funeral, and helped to arrange in 1964 an honorary Columbia University degree for Evelyn Wrench (the E-SU's founder). When he had accepted the largely formal post of president of the E-SU in 1963, he had thought it 'a happy expression of [my] devotion to the cause of Commonwealth–American understanding'. In order to manage a large endowment appeal and to process applications for scholarships, the E-SU had to make a substantial change in its way of working in 1965, including the setting up of a staffed, permanent office. Ike also agreed to do his bit for Anglo-American relations by serving as patron of a 1964 tour by the Royal Shakespeare Company, and regretted not being able to attend an E-SU benefit performance of *My Fair Lady*. This was a remarkably clever choice for such a gathering of the English-speakers – despite George Bernard Shaw's reference to the fact that 'in America they haven't spoken it for years' surviving into the song lyrics.[25]

Alongside the English-Speaking Union – and to an extent competing with it – was the Winston Churchill Memorial Fund, which set up a

Churchill Foundation, under the general patronage of Harry Truman, with the main purpose of supporting Churchill College in Cambridge, and of creating Churchill scholarships. The E-SU and the Foundation agreed in 1965 that their common objective was 'designed to add strength and wisdom to the people of our own country as well as to strengthen the ties which bind the United Kingdom and the United States together'. For a time they collaborated on fundraising, but parted company in 1968 because they had different priorities. The retirement of Carl Gilbert from his position with the Gilette Company, which had provided the Foundation with office space and administrative support, prompted some hard thinking, and not until Lew Douglas (another former Ambassador in London) took over in 1970 did the momentum resume. Again the British Embassy could be extremely helpful. It co-ordinated plans to ensure that a visit by Princess Margaret would help the appeal in 1965, and bore the travel costs of the Duke and Duchess of Kent to a fundraising première of *Young Winston* in 1972 (and thereby helped to raise $60,000 for the cause).[26]

Tentative negotiations for a merger between the Fulton Memorial and the Churchill Foundation petered out in 1972, with the Foundation continuing to insist that its role was to back the English memorial, Churchill College. The various American Churchill memorials therefore continued in their separate existences, but all survived, despite an initial struggle to raise the money required; the Foundation has now supported Churchill College with very substantial sums of money, the E-SU has funded a very large number of Churchill scholars for 'promising young Americans to travel and study in the Commonwealth', and the Fulton Memorial provides a bonanza for those seeking the display of Churchilliana in America's heartland.[27]

The end of this first phase of memorialising, but by no means the end of memorialising itself, came with the 1974 centenary of Churchill's birth. This produced a new spate of books about Churchill, an outpouring of commemorative items and stamps, a special television version of Churchill's war memoirs with Richard Burton in the main role, package tours to Churchill sites in England offered by the recently formed British Airways which apparently attracted plenty of American customers, an exhibition of Churchill material at the National Portrait Gallery in Washington (paralleling a London exhibition at Somerset House), and a commemorative Churchill dinner, also in Washington. That centenary dinner was sponsored jointly by the British Embassy and the Woodrow Wilson Center, with the chief speakers being Sir Christopher Soames and Secretary of State Henry Kissinger. Four buglers from Sir Winston's regiment of the 1890s announced dinner with a fanfare, several surviving American military leaders of the Second World War attended, and the menu was suitable to even the great man's own epicurean tastes. As the *New York Times* editorialised:

> The tributes, whether in print or on screen, bring it all back with a rush: that voice, rolling, volleying, thundering, drawing richly on the richest language of all, hurling defiance at Hitler and the 'Naahzies', summoning his countrymen from defeat and despair to their 'finest hour'; lifting around the world the hearts of free men and those struggling to be free ... How difficult it will be on this day to evaluate his contribution to the human race without mawkishness and sentimentality; how easy in centennial tributes to permit the legend to obscure the real man.

But despite its determination to paint Churchill, warts and all, and its reminder that 'he was often defeated, he was often wrong', the paper reacted with violent hostility to the attack on Churchill's good name by Richard Burton in that same centennial month. Despite even the best of intentions, it *was* still too soon to disentangle the legend from the man.[28]

In any case, by the time that Westminster College and the E-SU had got their memorials established, and a wider world was confirming its admiration for Churchill through the 1974 centenary, a more permanent form of memorialising was under way, the supporters' club that eventually became the International Churchill Society. Such efforts originated in a 1965 memorial banquet in Alberta, Canada, which soon became an annual event, the earliest speakers being Mountbatten, Earl Alexander of Tunis, Lord Butler of Saffron Walden and Sir Alec Douglas-Home, but the similar national groups that sprang up in different countries soon federated into a genuinely international body, with the largest component of both members and financial input contributed by the United States.[29]

In the meantime, the main nationwide commemoration of Churchill in Britain after his death was the Winston Churchill Memorial Trust.

This had been planned as part of a worldwide effort initiated by the English-Speaking Union and suggested originally by an American member, Edward Houghton, after a similar scheme that the E-SU itself had run for five years with a grant from the Ford Foundation had run out of money in 1961. Talks about linking such a scheme went back to the early 1950s, and had been actively pursued since 1958, the promoters of the idea subsequently seeking and getting Churchill's agreement that this would be a very acceptable form of international memorial.[30]

Despite great goodwill all round, it had proved impossible to harmonise the interests (not to mention the tax laws) of the different countries involved. Hence, though they were all announced on the same day in London, each national collection then became in effect separate and independent, and each trust that came into existence after fundraising looked after a single country. The British appeal was launched at that joint meeting on 1 February 1965, the day after Churchill's funeral, by Earl Alexander of Tunis, 'Churchill's favourite general' (as Jock Colville has put it). Alex announced that though Churchill had now gone to his rest and would be mourned, 'we must do more than that. We must honour his memory by showing our gratitude to him, for he did more to uphold the great freedom under which we live than any other in our time.' Churchill had greatly valued travel as a means of broadening the mind and reducing international misunderstandings, and so with Clementine Churchill's agreement, the Winston Churchill Memorial Trust would use money raised in memory of Winston to allow a 'chance in a lifetime' travel opportunity to people of any age or walk of life. As finally constituted, the Trust aimed therefore to perpetuate Churchill's name, 'by creating a fund to further the cause of education throughout the world, and in particular the English-speaking countries'.

That last bow in the direction of the English-speaking peoples was no doubt in part a relic of the original intention to create a federal scheme for them alone, but it also ensured that the scheme would fit even more closely with Churchill's own preferences. He had always had a mid-Victorian's Cobdenite belief in the civilising influence of travel and trade in the promotion of good feelings between nations, and had therefore correctly predicted that trade and travel between them might well do as much as war and diplomacy – preferably more – in bringing down the iron curtain. But he had also invariably seen the English-speaking peoples as the focus of his world and his aspirations. In May

1938, writing on 'the unity of English-speaking peoples', he had urged the promotion of travel by ordinary people, so that 'personal contact' could reinforce the influences of trade, communal self-interest and the 'willingness to consult' at governmental level. He would thus have been delighted to know that, at the end of the century, the British and the Americans visited each other's country, telephoned and faxed each other, and exchanged emails, in greater numbers than either Britons or Americans did any of these things with any other country. This was indeed the type of 'special relationship' of which he dreamed, and it was an aim built from the start into the work of the WCMT.[31]

The chief agency intended for fundraising was to be local authorities, and so in addition to the ten thousand appeal letters sent out to industry, two thousand were also dispatched to every local council in the United Kingdom. The E-SU had already 'charged' its members to assist in the planned house-to-house collection, as had the Women's Voluntary Service, the Boy Scouts, the British Legion and the Earl Haig Fund for Scotland. The letters and the rest of the appeal letter were given their Churchillian focus (and their reminder of the war) by the use of the 1941 Karsh photograph of Churchill, by which Karsh himself contributed generously to the appeal by waiving his royalties. Most of the fundraising was scheduled for a 'Churchill month', beginning on 28 February, though in practice not all local councils and their committee timetables were able to accommodate so short a timescale and the appeal therefore ran on until July. By then a total of £2.75 million had come in, including £350,000 from the British Government; actually the Government gave half a million pounds, but £150,000 was earmarked for the completion of Churchill College, Cambridge, not otherwise a beneficiary of the main appeal. The £2.4 million raised from non-governmental sources in Britain was a very substantial sum for the time, though well short of the target of £5 million. The overall total did not come near to matching the equivalent Australian appeal (in terms of the relative population sizes of the countries), but a higher proportion came from the public, less from public authorities out of the proceeds of taxation. The Queen abandoned the usual Palace refusal to get involved in charitable appeals and became the Trust's patron, while the Lord Mayor of London was equally innovative in appearing in person at the Baltic Exchange, the Stock Exchange and Lloyd's to ask for cash. The Trust itself included both Churchill friends and contacts (Lord Normanbrook) and others from the great and the good in the British elite (Lord Cromer, Sir Edward Boyle, Sir Reginald Benson). Likewise, the Council of the Trust which would have the duty of actually running things was chaired successively by Lord De L'Isle (a former Minister in Churchill's Government), Terence O'Neill (by then the ex-Prime Minister of Northern Ireland) and Anthony Montague Browne (Churchill's private secretary after retirement). Early Council members included Lord Byers (Liberal), Sir William Deakin (the historian, who had worked for Churchill), Sir Stanley Matthews (footballer), Sir Paul Chambers (industrialist), Sir William Penney (scientist) and Shirley Williams (Labour MP).[32]

The response to 1965's appeal varied considerably, indicating some continuing reservations about Churchill in parts of Britain even in the moment of his greatest and most unquestioned international fame. British banks announced that they would not make any charge for processing appeal donations, or for servicing special bank accounts set up by local authorities to contain the funds, and Alexander was reporting by 16 February a 'moving response'. But there was also some real opposition developing, almost entirely on the left, but very occasionally caused by the upsetting of local interests in an appeal for a national body. The Labour Mayor of Harwich refused to have anything to do with it, deploring the fact that there had been no memorial fund for Nye Bevan and that his own council had recently refused to back collections for the Freedom from Hunger Fund. *The Times* was able to reassure its readers, on the same page that contained the Harwich story, with the news that the International Publishing Corporation had agreed to give £25,000 to the appeal. In Lancashire a branch of the National Union of Mineworkers sent off over two thousand letters to Labour councils and trades union branches, urging them to refuse to take part; it saw the WCMT as 'a mendacious cadging orgy with the sole benefit of winning support for the Tories'. Conversely, industry and commerce rallied magnificently to the cause, the City and the West End boroughs of Chelsea, Holborn, Marylebone and Westminster between them raising almost half a million pounds, over a fifth of the entire national collection from non-governmental sources. In Jersey, there was a nasty little local dispute between the official appeal and one launched by a local newspaper, and the appeal committee eventually resigned en masse. Embarrassingly it was revealed that Churchill's own constituency of Wanstead and Woodford had not collected very much for the appeal (though it had only recently raised a large sum for his statue) and that nearby Ilford (recently merged with Wanstead and Woodford in the London Borough of Redbridge, but indignantly refusing to allow the new authority to be called Churchill) had by 25 March raised only £700 towards its target of £11,000. It is only fair to add that after an embarrassing delay, both parts of Redbridge exceeded their target, as did almost every other part of Britain where Churchill had had a personal connection. There was little hostility to Churchill in such places, but a good deal of apathy about fundraising in his memory.[33]

By July, when the appeal drew towards its close, 384 local authorities had exceeded the targets, but this also meant that about five times as many of them had not. The complete list of local totals carried in the national press did not give the targets for each authority, but they did indicate which ones had exceeded their target as well as giving the amount raised in each case, and this in itself showed an interesting pattern. No Welsh local authority in the urban areas had exceeded its target, and almost all the rural ones that had collected well were in constituencies represented by Conservative MPs, either on the English border or in resorts like Llandudno on the north coast. The entire county of Carmarthenshire had raised only £162, and there was a similar pattern in the mining valleys of Monmouthshire and Glamorgan. Protestant Ulster, on the other hand, had done the appeal proud, with Belfast alone raising over £13,000, while (despite those local disputes) the appeal in the Channel Isles eventually raised £14,562. In Scotland, too, with its positive response to Churchill generally, the appeal had done well, though Dundee's £2000 contrasted with over £70,000 collectively raised by Aberdeen, Edinburgh and Glasgow, and suggested that old battles with Churchill had still not been forgotten there either. The Scottish branches of the E-SU were particularly active, proudly noting that Aberdeen had been the first big city to reach its target, that Glasgow came second after London and Edinburgh third in actual totals, and that overall the 'Scottish percentage return had been the best in Britain'. More generally, in both England and in Scotland the appeal had done better in areas where the Conservative vote was strongest, not because it was a party stunt as the Lancashire miners contended, but because the more conservative (and Conservative) areas had autonomously responded more positively to the Churchill legend for years past, as well as in 1965. Nowhere did a local authority in a mining area exceed its

target (the £4 raised in the single-industry Yorkshire pit village of Dod-
worth being one of the lowest recorded by any council anywhere).
Almost every council in the rural North Riding of Yorkshire exceeded
its target, as did the rural parts of Somerset, Suffolk, Worcestershire
and Kent. If Churchill was the 'quintessential Englishman' of the world
of country cottages and thatched roofs, as Americans liked to think,
that was indeed the part of Britain – Ulster and Scotland apart – which
responded most generously to the appeal in his honour.[34]

The money was raised, though, and the total was easily enough to
run the proposed scheme. The first advertisement inviting applications
appeared in January 1966, three thousand applications were received,
and after the determinedly 'unbureaucratic' selection process insisted
on by the first director-general, Admiral Morice Greig, sixty-six awards
were announced, the first Churchill Fellow leaving for the United States
in June. Thereafter, the Trust settled into an annual routine of advertisement, selection and provision of support for its Fellows, using its annual
selection process as a means of raising its profile through the national
and local media, and encouraging returning Fellows to give it more
publicity in the process of making known the results of their travels
within their local or work communities (a condition of awards being
that Fellows shared the benefits of their travel in this way). From 1969,
there were enough returned Fellows to make possible the setting up of
regional associations of Churchill Fellows, and there were also by the
1970s newsletters and biannual awards ceremonies with Churchill med-
allions formally presented by such people as the Queen Mother, the
Prince of Wales and members of the Churchill family. By 1974 the Trust
had outgrown its initial association with the English-Speaking Union
(which had initially provided administrative back-up and support) and
moved to its own freehold premises in Kensington. It mounted only one
more early appeal, during Churchill's centenary year, which netted
£400,000, half for the WCMT and half for Churchill College. Shrewd
investment of the initial capital and the addition to capital of a proportion
of each year's interest did nevertheless ensure a steady growth in both
capital and income, and this in turn allowed an increase to a hundred in
the number of Fellowships awarded every year. By 1983, the Trust's initial
capital had more than doubled to £6.6 million, while by the mid-1990s the
figure was over £16 million, and the Trust had processed ninety thousand
applications and awarded over three thousand Fellowships.[35]

By the 1980s, this was a smoothly organised annual exercise, with the publicity alone generating each year some twelve thousand letters, fifty thousand posters and two hundred thousand leaflets, though by then almost a fifth of those who applied had actually heard of the scheme by word of mouth, many of these no doubt from former Fellows. By then, too, the length of Fellowships had fallen to about six weeks each, so allowing the Trust to continue to provide full costs of the travel itself, subsistence while abroad and some kitting-out expenses for visits to more remote areas. By then, the number of applicants had settled down to about 2,500 a year, and the number of awards at about a hundred. Two-thirds of Fellows were between twenty and thirty-nine (a group more strongly represented among Fellows than among all applicants, and a testimony to the Trust's determination to provide a once in a lifetime chance, but remaining faithful too to its initial decision that the travel concerned must be outside any formal academic framework).[36]

A detailed survey of the Trust's work in the early 1980s shows pretty clearly how far it had by then achieved its (and Churchill's) objectives. Eighty-nine per cent of Fellows responded that travel allowed by their Fellowship had fully achieved its purposes; 98 per cent thought that the travel did achieve for them 'a better understanding of the lives and work of people in other countries'; 79 per cent had maintained since returning to the UK contacts with people abroad that they had met while Fellows. Eighty-two per cent said that their Fellowship made them more effective in their careers, and 96 per cent that they had also been able to pass on benefits of their travel to others. Fellows over the first seventeen years had been disproportionately drawn from professional occupations and from the South of England, but manual workers (especially in rural areas) were still well represented, and so were local government and other clerical workers. Most interestingly, 51 per cent of all Fellows had visited Canada and the United States and an additional 5 per cent had gone to Australia and New Zealand, while only 29 per cent had travelled to Europe – so Europe was visited by only about half as many Fellows as went to the English-speaking countries. This could suggest no more than the fact that 'chance of a lifetime' travel necessarily privileged more distant countries, since European travel had become much easier. However, the proportion visiting Europe as Fellows had risen sharply in the early 1970s, peaking in about 1973 (when Britain joined the European

Economic Community), and then reverted to the previous pattern of a two-to-one preference for the English-speaking world. This was no doubt an outcome of which Churchill would thoroughly have approved, but it may of course have owed as much to the British reluctance to learn foreign languages as to anything political. The scheme had substantially outgrown its Churchillian origins, though the Karsh photograph continued to adorn WCMT publications, and still does. It was noticeable, for example, that the 1983 survey of past Fellows contained no question about Churchill, his career or his legacy. But the Trust has not neglected its own origins: each new Fellow in the 1990s was given a video on the life and significance of Winston Churchill, and awards ceremonies continued to be attended by the Churchill family and held in London's Guildhall, in front of the Churchill statue. There is nevertheless, as in the parallel schemes in Australia and New Zealand, a sense that the Trust would now be able to continue as a well-organised and successful charity without any Churchill link at all.[37]

In a broader sense, too, Churchill's name has been kept before the public through a process of word-association and namings. Unlike some other parts of the English-speaking world, the British have never gone in a big way for naming their male children after politicians (as opposed to royalty or film and pop stars), and there are not many Winstons to be found even among the baby-boomers of the late 1940s, when Churchill's fame was at its height. The few that did acquire his name – like John Winston Lennon when christened in Liverpool – probably did so as invisible and unheard second names, but are hardly likely to have led such resolutely unChurchillian lives as John Lennon. Denis Winston Healey, another well-known figure who did not parade his middle name, was named after Churchill as early as 1917, for Churchill had been for many years an idol of his Irish father, who was a lover of lost causes – Churchill being then in the doghouse after the Dardanelles episode. Later in his career Healey's middle name gave rise to a good deal of 'ribald comment' in Labour Party circles. Men named Winston in Britain today are far more likely to be of West Indian descent than British-born baby-boomers or retired Labour politicians, and this did indeed represent an act of homage to Churchill. Thousands of West Indians served in the British forces during the Second World War, and it was a sign of the admiration then still felt for the 'mother country' that on return home many of those servicemen married and called their first-born son

Winston in honour of Britain and the Empire's war leader. In due course, many of the families migrated to Britain and brought the name back to its place of origin, though the migration itself was a process of which Churchill himself did not approve, labelling these 1950s black arrivals as 'Hottentots', much as the third Lord Salisbury had done in the 1880s. Back in the West Indies, the 'roots' phenomenon and the consequent rediscovery of African names that had been removed from use during the slave period ended in the 1970s the popular practice of using Winston.[38]

If Britain did not have many white men called Winston, it did acquire other forms of commemoration by name. Churchill College in Cambridge is the most important single such commemoration of the Churchill name, and has, in addition to the fine record for science and engineering that it was created to attain, also become from 1973 a centre for Churchill studies. With the Churchill papers housed there after their controversial purchase by the state with proceeds from the National Lottery, the personal papers of Churchill admirers like Margaret Thatcher followed them as if drawn by a magnet, and so did those of many other contemporary politicians like Neil Kinnock and Enoch Powell. The Churchill Archives Centre at the College has therefore become easily the most important location at which to research into British politics since the 1940s, at least from the surviving records of politicians themselves. The College also keeps alive the memory of its Churchillian foundation, as the only Oxbridge College named for a twentieth-century figure who was not also a major benefactor, with an annual dinner and a programme of academic events and conferences on Churchill's life and times.

At a lower educational level, there are in England about a dozen Winston Churchill Schools, not perhaps as many as might be expected, though there has never been in Britain the same active tradition as in America of naming schools after national (as opposed to local) politicians, and the few Churchill Schools are more than exist to honour any other national politician. There is, however, a much livelier tradition of naming public houses after national political and military heroes, which has produced about twenty Churchill pubs and bars. Some of these, as in Churchill, Somerset, honour the family which gave the village its name, but were chosen all the same after Winston Churchill's finest hour. Others are in places with specific associations with Winston

Churchill, at Debden in Essex (which he used to represent in the Commons), at Ide Hill near Chartwell in Kent, and in Kensington near his London home. But there are three or four in Lancashire, a couple in Lincolnshire, and others spread all across England, indicating clearly enough the national nature of this type of remembrance. As in smaller forms of memorabilia, almost all the illustrations on pub signs locate Churchill in heroic stance, and almost all depict him at the age he was in the 1940s.[39]

Beyond the pubs, there remain Churchill streets, avenues and closes all across England.[40] These are more to be found in the Tory-voting South and the suburbs than in some of the larger industrial cities, but what is most noticeable is the sheer number and their geographical spread across practically every county, town and region. That larger number in the South and the suburbs may well be no more than a reflection of the fact that these are the areas in which new streets have mainly been built since the 1960s, for even in areas that were keen to honour Churchill there has sometimes been resistance to giving up an existing name to use his instead. In Liverpool in 1955, for example, local residents went to court and won an injunction against the city council to prevent it renaming Walton Hall Avenue as Winston Churchill Avenue, but only on the ground of unnecessary cost and with loud protests of their respect for Churchill ('No one adores Sir Winston Churchill more than I, and were it a new road it would be an excellent idea . . .'). A number of towns sought to turn town-planning schemes to advantage here, with a Winston Churchill thoroughfare as a sort of inner ring road, by-passing the town centre in traffic management schemes, as in both Salisbury and Basingstoke. Some English Churchill Streets are too old to have been named after Winston, and the association of the name with a nearby Salisbury, Gladstone or Beaconsfield clearly indicates a nineteenth-century naming in honour of Lord Randolph, as in Altrincham, Houghton-le-Spring and Newcastle-upon-Tyne. More often, though, Churchill is either used alone or in combination with other names that show plainly enough that it was Winston Churchill who was in mind. There are for example many English housing estates where several streets bear the name of different Prime Ministers (as in Dudley, which also has a Churchill shopping centre). In these cases, there is invariably one named after Churchill, whereas Attlee or Lloyd George or Macmillan are all optional extras, and Baldwin and Chamberlain are hardly ever to be seen. More often the groupings specifically commemorate the Second World War, by placing Churchill Road alongside Victory Crescent (Cheadle), or by surrounding Churchill with his ministerial or military colleagues of the time. Culcheth (Lancashire) has Churchill Avenue near to streets named after Beaverbrook, Attlee, Bevin and Eden; Walsall has Churchill with Cripps, Attlee and Bevin; Catshill (West Midlands) has Churchill with Montgomery, Alexander and Bracken, Lutterworth (Leicestershire) with Tedder and Cunningham, Oakham (Rutland) with Alexander and Mountbatten. Hilton (Derbyshire) has a plethora of D-Day namings, Churchill being surrounded by Montgomery, Normandy, Pegasus, Utah and Mulberry. Often Churchill is close to a street named after Roosevelt, but Chatham (Kent) seems to be unique in retaining a street named after Stalin too (though this *is* a rather small one, when compared to the longer thoroughfares honouring Churchill and FDR). Sometimes the support for heroes is more undifferentiated: Churchill is near to both John F. Kennedy and Lansbury in Tipton, West Midlands, and to a Botham Drive in Chadderton, Lancashire. Most often of all in estate names Churchill is accompanied by other direct acts of homage, with streets named Downing, Winston, Spencer, Chartwell and the like. Both local councils and speculative builders have thus contrived to keep his name in view in some two hundred English streets.[41]

As the spread of Churchill pub names suggests, low commercial motives have not been entirely absent from such acts of homage, and the guardians of Churchill's good name have sometimes striven unavailingly to prevent this. There were for example a couple of night clubs in London named Churchill's and Winston's, despite strong family disapproval of the fact that they denoted a side of his life – drinking and gambling – which was not part of the officially approved story. One of them solved the problem by losing its licence in 1952. Churchill himself refused to allow his name to be used by Charles Clore for the new Hilton hotel at Hyde Park Corner, and while he lived such bans were possible, if more on moral than legal grounds. In 1969, though, a prestigious Churchill Hotel did open in Portman Square, complete with a fine Churchill bust in the foyer. In Manchester the Portland Hotel named its main restaurant Churchill's, in memory of his long association with the city. Neither survives though: the Churchill Hotel failed financially and Churchill's restaurant has been rebranded and renamed by

Thistle Hotels as A Touch of Rhodes, in honour not of a wartime operation in the Eastern Mediterranean but of the television chef who redesigned its menu. Lower down the market, the same fate overtook the Winston Churchill public house in Cambridge, across the road from the College of that name, when it was turned into a McDonald's fast-food outlet.

But there remain many commercial operations that have annexed Churchill's name, most obviously in places with strong Churchill links like Woodford (a butcher's shop, among many others) and Westerham (an art gallery). Note the way in which even these types of links also celebrate known aspects of his lifestyle. Likewise, in New York, the only bookshop wholly devoted to Churchill's works, Chartwell Books, is proud to remind users that it is situated 'just a few blocks' from the place where Churchill was almost killed in a traffic accident in 1931. In January 2001, the owner was commemorating the centenary of Churchill's arrival in the House of Commons with a talk by Martin Gilbert. In the West End of London, the largest chain of souvenir shops is called Churchill Gifts and its shop windows are emblazoned with his face and his profile. Inside, however, there is nothing whatsoever on sale to represent the face and figure of Churchill himself, among masses of guardsmen, pillar boxes, red double-decker buses, bulldogs and images of Big Ben. His name represents England, and is perhaps intended also to suggest the quality of the goods on sale, but the actual person is absent.

Nationally too the commercial use of Churchill's name has tended to be for purposes of reassurance and to convey a sense of solidity, for example with a firm that sells helpful devices to be used in the home by the elderly (and advertised on television by Dame Thora Hird, herself a veteran of the Second World War, at least in its films). Most prominent at present is Churchill Insurance, with its bulldog mascot called Churchill, which has a gravelly, sub-Churchillian manner of speaking in television advertisements. Few of those who watch the adverts are likely to know that the company was launched in 1989 as a subsidiary of the Swiss company Winterthur (now part of Credit Suisse), and the name Churchill chosen 'because it embodies so many of its attributes: Britishness, trust, strength and perseverance'. They might well feel though that there is a very Churchillian 'action this day' quality in a company that has in only thirteen years built up to a base of almost three million customers and a turnover of over a billion pounds a year.

Nor are many people likely to remember the unsuccessful 1988 effort to turn Churchill's life into a West End musical, *Winnie*, though it ran for a few weeks and gave Robert Hardy a unique chance to play on stage the role that he had by then made so very much his own on television, before closing with losses of about £1.5 million. But the name Churchill remains a universal reference point for excellence that requires no further explanation. The television cook Delia Smith, who had herself recently achieved the rare honour of a personal entry in the Oxford English Dictionary (and who would therefore need no additional badges of distinction anyway) was dubbed by *The Times* 'the Winston Churchill of the kitchen', in a story replete with puns which depended entirely on readers recognising the Churchill originals. She had for example won the television ratings war but was 'losing the peas', after offering a diet of 'blood, toil and sweets . . .' And, incidentally, what the British electorate had done to Churchill in 1945, turned into the lingo of Blairite Britain, was to make him 'have a big, long rest and just chill out a little bit'. This was, and was no doubt meant to be, English up with which he would not have put.[42]

In more serious efforts to keep Churchill's memory alive, the key international player has certainly been the International Churchill Society (ICS). This emerged from disparate local groupings in three countries and only gradually got going as an effective body, but is now strongly supported, especially in North America, and well connected with both the British and American establishments. Initially, alongside the annual banquets held in the Canadian west, the chief focus of interest in Britain and the United States was in Churchill stamp-collecting, but these scattered enthusiasts were co-ordinated and given a sense of identity through a magazine, *Finest Hour*, edited by two Churchill enthusiasts, Dalton Newfield in California and Richard Langworth in New England. Both the magazine and the members took a wider interest in Churchill than was required for philately, and established early connections with the Churchill family and with others among Churchill's friends and contemporaries. Reconstituted formally as the International Churchill Society in 1971, it secured Lord Mountbatten as its patron until his assassination by the IRA in 1979; Churchill's daughter Mary Soames became patron in 1986.

Nevertheless, as the flow of Churchill stamps slowed down after the peak years of his funeral and centenary, the organisation appeared to have run its course. *Finest Hour* ceased to appear in 1975, and, though assets remained in the bank earning interest for future use, the only real activity for a few years was once again Churchill stamp enthusiasts and Canadian dinners. Then in 1981 Langworth restarted *Finest Hour* and the organisation really began to take off. By 1989, membership and activity were sufficiently widespread to require sub-division into separate national Churchill societies for Britain, Canada and the United States, the last two latterly also having regional chapters and branches with considerable autonomy. There was for a time an Australian branch, too, evoking from four countries the Churchillian 'English-speaking peoples' concept. In 1997, the American branch was renamed the Churchill Center, and devoted itself to fundraising for a large endowment to ensure a permanent commitment to memorialising Churchill when the generation of ICS founders retires. Many prominent Americans have been happy to associate themselves with this activity, including for example among its honorary members Secretary of State Colin Powell and former Defense Secretary Caspar Weinberger. British honorary members include Margaret Thatcher.[43]

The ICS held its first international conference in Fulton, Missouri, in 1983, with just four people present, but the following year in Toronto there were about thirty, and speakers included Martin Gilbert and the American Ambassador to Canada, Paul Robinson. By 1986, a Boston conference billed Caspar Weinberger as speaker and a hundred people were attending. The following year the conference at Dallas attracted sufficient media attention to be lampooned in *New Republic*, but in 1988 at Bretton Woods the speakers included Alistair Cooke and the Governor of New Hampshire. Nineteen-eighty-eight was also the first time in which academics, not necessarily all Churchill enthusiasts, played a part in Churchill conferences, the ICS 'providing the forum' for academic research into Churchill and for the reporting and publishing of findings, just as *Finest Hour* had long been seriously reviewing and discussing books in the field. Following this initiative, the Churchill Center then constituted a board of academic advisers drawn from all three countries, and has both published their contributions to ICS conferences and set up and published the findings of separate academic conferences. The 1996 Missouri conference timed to coincide with the fiftieth anniversary of Churchill's 'iron curtain' speech generated therefore a volume of essays on *Churchill's 'Iron Curtain' Speech Fifty Years Later* from an

American university press. ICS also tries to keep Churchill's own publications in print, and has managed to rescue from oblivion extremely rare ones such as his India speeches by sponsoring new editions. Its website puts much Churchill material on easy access and receives an astonishingly large number of visits from countries all over the world, while it receives about four hundred requests a year from schools for copies of its Churchill poster – the Karsh photograph and Churchill's words 'Study history'. It has since 1983 arranged Churchill visits for enthusiasts, for example a tour of places of Churchillian significance in South Africa, and tries to site its conferences to coincide with Churchill themes and anniversaries. In 2003 it plans to be in Bermuda to mark the fiftieth anniversary of Churchill's visit for the conference of 1953. There will now indeed be Churchill fiftieth and hundredth anniversaries to be celebrated for much of the next century, so there is no reason why the pace should slacken.

In all of this the ICS has been anxious to foster study of Churchill's life and significance, in the round, rather than simply providing further evidence for the man's admirers. In the same way, *Finest Hour* (now an impressive and professional-looking journal with plenty of solid content) has not been afraid of rocking the boat either, for example in publishing a rather critical account of the 1981 *Wilderness Years* television series on Churchill in the 1930s. ICS does nevertheless also provide a platform for the assertion of his special qualities and for the celebration of his memory, and criticism of *The Wilderness Years* has not prevented it also from welcoming the actor Robert Hardy (who played Churchill in the series) to its conferences and publishing a fascinating account from him of the difficulties of creating an acted Churchill. Through its website, its publications, its fostering of academic research and its programmes of seminars for students, it has thus done much to keep the flame alive. In 1995 the ICS Conference in Boston had as speakers, among others, Lady Soames, Arthur Schlesinger and William Buckley, and in 1996 in Sussex participants included Sir Martin Gilbert, Lady Soames and Churchill's granddaughter Celia Sandys. By the end of the century it had well over 2,500 members worldwide, the largest proportion in the United States, but the British and Canadian branches were also flourishing. The British had then the largest membership it had yet achieved, while the ICS's international president was a Canadian, John Plumpton. At San Diego in 2001, Sir Martin Gilbert dubbed the members of ICS 'the New Churchillians', and it seems likely that this accolade will continue to be used – though in fairness the concept ought to include such other enthusiasts as the organisers of the Churchill Memorial at Fulton. Just as 'the Churchillians', to use John Colville's phrase and the title of one of his books, were Churchill's first generation of wartime colleagues and associates, those who had devoted themselves after 1945 to keeping his memory bright – by no mean uncritically, as we have seen, but with dedication and enthusiasm – so 'the New Churchillians' enter on the same task for the new century.[44]

Alongside the reiteration of Churchill's importance by these 'New Churchillians', his name has remained permanently alive in the political debate as a consequence of individual politicians who sought either to praise his legacy for its own sake or to compare themselves and their colleagues in some way to the great man. The first to attempt this on a large scale in Britain was Harold Wilson, despite the tendency of critics to portray it as typical of his 'Yorkshire Walter Mitty' fantasies. This was something done from the very start of his premiership in *Private Eye*'s 'Mrs Wilson's Diary' column, as in '. . . I said as much to Harold as we were getting into bed, but he did not hear me, as he was practising his Winston Churchill face in the wardrobe mirror'.[45]

Wilson had a family connection to Churchill, for his uncle had been his constituency chairman and his father had been his deputy agent when he was a Manchester MP in 1906–8, and he had been 'regaled with stories about it as a child'. Self-comparisons with Churchill were then Wilson's stock in trade, and his less discriminating biographers have frequently kept up the act. When he became Opposition leader in 1963, there was a remarkable burst of media interest, 'greater than in any new premier or party leader since Churchill', while after his second election victory in 1966, he 'fill[ed] the political stage more completely than any premier since Churchill', as even Ben Pimlott has put it. So euphoric was Labour when he brought the party back into office after thirteen years in 'the wilderness' (in itself a phrase with a very Churchillian flavour), that he was thought at the 1964 party conference to have become (as the journalist Ernest Kay put it) 'Bevan and Churchill rolled into one. It was indeed his finest hour.'

Wilson's speeches after 1963 have been claimed to have had a 'Churchillian ring', his installation of a personal scientific adviser in Downing Street was compared to Churchill's use of Lord Cherwell, while two of the fifteen addresses personally selected for inclusion in a book of speeches covering his first year in office were about Churchill himself. Like others from this period, he invoked Churchill's memory in many ways. He often used Churchill's phrases (something he had been doing since the late 1940s, initially to infuriate the man himself in the Commons), and he was especially fond of appealing to the 'Dunkirk spirit' summoned up by Churchill in 1940, but applied by Wilson to the economic conditions of 1964–5. Wilson had as recently as 1961 'deprecated – perhaps rightly, perhaps wrongly – in crisis after crisis, appeals to the Dunkirk spirit as an answer to our problems', for what Britain actually needed was not 'a brief period of inspired improvisation' of the sort that Churchill had achieved in the war, but 'a very long, hard period of reorganisation and rededication'. Once he was Prime Minister, such reservations quickly vanished and his cabinet even formally approved a 'spirit of Dunkirk' campaign of ministerial speeches. As Wilson argued at Brighton in December 1964, 'after Dunkirk' in 1940 '[we] so mobilised our talent and untapped strength that apparent defeat was turned into a great victory. I believe that the spirit of Dunkirk will once again carry us through . . .' He considered crossing the Atlantic in that month in a warship, 'as Churchill had done in the war', and his meeting with Rhodesia's Ian Smith on HMS *Tiger* was compared by friendly journalists to Churchill's 1941 meeting with Franklin Roosevelt on HMS *Prince of Wales* in Newfoundland.[46]

Wilson's implied claim to be Britain's new Churchill received public endorsement from President Lyndon Johnson, no less, though this was more an act of American foreign policy than a considered judgement – Johnson was after all at just this time dubbing South Vietnam's leader 'the Winston Churchill of Asia'. This is brought out by what happened when relations then cooled between the Wilson Government and the Johnson Administration, to a large extent because of Harold Wilson's distinctly Churchillian refusal to allow Britain to become involved in Vietnam. Wilson had chiefly resisted the sending of British troops to Vietnam on the ground that Britain's Malaysian garrisons were already doing their bit in the region in the stand-off with Communism. When therefore British troops were to be withdrawn from East of Suez in 1967, and Wilson had to go to Washington to explain himself, the Johnson Administration imposed on him two remarkably petty sanctions. First, as Wilson's plane touched down, he had to listen to an American military

'The artist and his model'
Daily Telegraph, 1 August 1966

band playing 'The Road to Mandalay', the song from which the phrase
'East of Suez' originally derived. Second, the State Department formally
decided that it would no longer make favourable comparisons between
Harold Wilson and Winston Churchill, as it had been assiduously doing
for the previous three years.

For a Prime Minister who still regularly appealed to 'the Dunkirk
spirit' and who had in 1966 asked British electors to 'give us the tools
to finish the job', this must have been deeply wounding. It seems pretty
clear that American diplomats had sensed just how best to flatter Wilson
in 1964 and then used the same method in reverse three years later. But
Wilson was in no way deterred from his fantasies by such setbacks.
When planning his final retirement in 1975–6 he studied the Churchill
parallels very closely: he would get a knighthood, host a dinner for the
Queen in Downing Street and then devote his retirement years to writing. Once he had stepped down from office he would also appropriate
'the Churchill seat' in the House of Commons, the first in the front
row, below the gangway on the Government side, from which to deliver
stern warnings on great international issues. This last ambition tended
to come unstuck, for Labour MPs unimpressed by such matters as his

final, dubious honours list tended to refuse to vacate the seat when he wanted to occupy it.[47]

There is on the face of it something equally Walter Mitty-like about a story that Margaret Thatcher tells in her memoirs. When visiting a fortune-teller at a Conservative fête, as candidate for Dartford in 1950, she was told, 'You will be great – great as Churchill.' Though she remembers that this 'struck me as quite ridiculous', she nevertheless recalled it forty-five years later and included it in the book. It was Margaret Thatcher who would indeed most generally invite and receive comparison with Churchill. Even by the time of that fortune-telling session she was already both wearing a silver lapel pin of Churchill's profile and routinely referring to him in her speeches as 'Winston'. Each of them headed the Conservative Party for fifteen years, each was Prime Minister for about ten, and each managed a degree of domination over their ministerial colleagues that nobody in between had even attempted, let alone achieved. It was possible to detect similarities too in the desperate circumstances that each inherited when they took control. As Alan Clark, soon to be a true Thatcher devotee, noted in his diary on the thirty-fifth anniversary of Churchill's appointment as Prime Minister, only a few weeks after her election to the Tory leadership and when she was still finding her feet, 'What is to be the outcome of the terrible decline of the country – the total absence of leadership and inspiration in the Conservative Party? In 1939 [sic] at least we had Fighter Command and Winston.'

Thatcher herself was certainly never afraid to quote the great man or to refer back to his achievements, arguing for example in 1975 that 'the Tory answer is, as Sir Winston Churchill defined it, "to set the people free"'. Like Harold Wilson, she also adopted Churchill's two-finger 'V for Victory' sign, but unfortunately (since she had not yet got Gordon Reece permanently on hand to coach her for public appearances) got it the wrong way round and appeared only to be making a rude gesture to the Labour Party. Her memoirs' account of the other end of her career as leader also invokes the Churchill comparison, as leaders struck down in their hour of triumph, in his case shortly after VE Day, in hers after the somewhat less obviously victorious episode of the poll-tax riots. At her first party conference as party leader, at Blackpool in 1975, she invoked Churchill's name almost in the first breath of her speech, describing him as 'a man called by destiny to raise the name of

Sunday Times, 2 October 1983

Britain to supreme heights in the history of the free world', a tribute that was also something of a declaration of intent. As she came under increasing attack for her economic policy, she spoke in 1984 of people mocking Churchill in the past, but declared that he had been right to ignore such mockery. She was even willing to praise – if not always to put into practice – Churchill's doctrine of magnanimity in victory. The collected edition of her speeches contains numerous such tributes; the comprehensive compact-disc collection of her complete speeches includes dozens.[48]

Nowhere was the Thatcher-as-Churchill formula more successful than in Ronald Reagan's Washington, where both Churchill and Thatcher were individually popular. Reagan had himself quoted Churchill in a television broadcast in support of Richard Nixon's California gubernatorial campaign in 1962, and quoted him again in his 1981 Inaugural speech, twice in his first State of the Union Address in 1982, and then at regular intervals right through to his final Presidential radio address to the American people in 1989 – that last a reference to Churchill as a lifelong admirer of the American people. He was also proud of his friendship with Thatcher and of the regular comparisons of their friendship to Churchill's wartime alliance with Franklin Roosevelt. 'No matter how often she returned,' as Hugo Young has put it, 'Americans never seemed to tire of extending to her a greeting couched in terms of wonderment that she was a woman, a *strong* little woman, a woman like no other English person since Winston Churchill.'

Soon after becoming Prime Minister, Thatcher was receiving in Washington the Winston Churchill Foundation Award, the citation announcing that 'like Winston Churchill she is known for her courage, conviction, determination and willpower. Like Churchill she thrives on adversity.' As Young adds resignedly, she addressed in 1985 a joint session of the US Congress, 'the first British prime minister to do so since, inevitably, Churchill'. It was equally inevitable that she would remind her listeners of the fact that Churchill had last performed the same feat by quoting his words on the former occasion, but in case they missed the point she presented a bronze statuette of Churchill to commemorate both their visits. Reagan was also fixed with Thatcher in the mind of American Churchillians when both were among the earliest recipients of the Winston Churchill Award by the Churchill Foundation; the other two honorands among the first four were Churchill's friend Averell Harriman and (somewhat less explicably) Ross Perot. Nor did this seem out of place, for Thatcher, Reagan and many of their respective cabinet colleagues were from what Reagan's Defense Secretary Caspar Weinberger has called the wartime generation which 'learned from Churchill ... that we had to look danger in the face, and we had to be prepared to meet it. In fact, only if we were prepared to fight for peace would we be able to have peace.' Such shared perceptions certainly helped Britain to secure American aid for a war against aggression in the South Atlantic in 1982, but it also helped to steel both regimes to see through the last difficult phase of the Cold War and then to reap the benefits that Churchill had also predicted in his Fulton speech of 1946. Years after her fall from office in 1990, Thatcher was still to be seen several times a year speaking to American and international audiences, and hardly a speech was made without an appropriate reference to Churchill, for example at Fulton in 1996 or at an International Herald Tribune Conference in Beijing later the same year. Churchill was invoked in other ways too, by the display of a 'powerful portrait' of the man, first in her Commons office as leader of the Opposition and later in the ante-chamber to the cabinet room in Downing Street, by the conscious decision to use Chequers as a weekend retreat during the Falklands War, and by copious references to him in her memoirs.[49]

It was of Margaret Thatcher's ministry that it was said that the cabinet resembled a tigress who had surrounded herself with hamsters, but this was also quite close to the way that Churchill's wartime

Government appeared to observers like Robert Menzies (in this respect they were like no other governments of the century). Samuel Finer decided in 1987 that 'she has impressed herself on government as nobody has done since the war years of Churchill'. Or, as Patrick Cosgrave put it, 'just as Churchill ran his government as an extension of his own personality, so was she determined to do'. In her first years in office, she practised 'an instinctive nationalism ... in which the memory of Churchill (at least the 1940 version) has been central. For, as a young woman in Grantham during the war, she was influenced by Churchill's leadership and she frequently refers to Winston.' Her economic guru Alan Walters predictably went rather further, telling *Now!* magazine that Thatcher was 'the only real Tory leader since Winston Churchill'. Likewise, the Thatcherite convert from the left Paul Johnson thought her 'the best man in the cabinet' and likened her performance in the Falklands War to the 'gigantic and leonine spirit' of Churchill. Some at least tried to resist this exclusive claim, though with varying degrees of credibility, Field Marshal Lord Bramall's extended comparison of Churchill with Michael Heseltine being among the more implausible.[50]

For Norman Lamont, Thatcher was 'the greatest leader of the Conservative Party since Winston Churchill', and he noted with pride that after the Gulf War John Major achieved a surge in popularity in the polls that could be matched only by Churchill's in 1940. He also recalled with pleasure Boris Yeltsin's high regard for Churchill, whose prophecy in the Fulton speech that Communism must eventually fall had (eventually) come to pass by the time that Yeltsin visited London. Major himself had fond memories of Churchill being praised at considerable length by German Chancellor (and historian) Helmut Kohl, who 'often spoke of him with great warmth', and himself found that one of the greatest thrills of a visit to the White House was sleeping in a bedroom in which Churchill had slept – which seems an odd distinction for a man to claim after living for seven years in Downing Street and at Chequers. Equally oddly, Margaret Thatcher had a similar feeling during a visit to Moscow, when Mikhail Gorbachev entertained her in the same mansion in which Stalin had dined with Churchill. It seems that the real spirit of Churchill, because he was seen by his Tory successors mainly as an international statesman – they had formally dissociated themselves from the domestic policies of his post-war Government anyway – could be encountered only when playing away from home.[51]

Churchill remained then a role model for an astonishingly wide range of international figures in the 1990s. Those who were heads of government and heads of state included not only Thatcher and Major in Britain, George Bush in America and John Howard in Australia, leaders respectively of the parties of the right in three of Churchill's English-speaking peoples, but also such diverse European figures as Jacques Chirac, Václav Havel, Helmut Kohl and Boris Yeltsin. There was nevertheless some likelihood that once that generation of leaders who had been heavily influenced both by the Second World War and the Cold War retired from politics (as most of them had already done by the end of the century), then so would the influence of Churchill's memory tend to fall away. In any case, all of those men and women were on the political right in their own countries, a position from which admiration for a political conservative and a heroic figure of the past was a fairly comfortable posture to adopt. Conversely, Bill Clinton made few rhetorical gestures towards Churchill in an eight-year presidency of the United States, being perhaps the first President since Herbert Hoover to neglect that duty, and did not turn up in Fulton for the fiftieth anniversary of Churchill's 'iron curtain' speech in 1996, despite an earlier intention to attend. Likewise, Tony Blair's assertion that his new Government would in 1997 mark a decisive break with previous British history – not to mention his total lack of historical awareness, quite unprecedented for a recent British Prime Minister – suggested that in Britain too the arrival of the new century would finally relegate Churchill to the historians' books. By the 1990s, Churchill's life and career was noticeably absent from the British national curriculum for the study of history in schools. Although for both GCSE and A-level students, taking history examinations at the age of sixteen and eighteen, there was plenty of opportunity to study Bismarck, Stalin, Hitler and Mussolini, hardly any would now encounter Churchill. If he is touched on at all, it is only fleetingly, for the Second World War is now mainly recalled as a 'people's war', not as an example of a nation responding to positive leadership. This writing of Churchill out of a prominent place in the history of Britain – even during his 'finest hour' – reached its lowest point when a commemorative VE Day video distributed by the Department for Education to all schools in 1995 gave Churchill a mere fourteen seconds out of thirty-five minutes on the Second World War.[52]

The view that Churchill was now old hat at the end of the century was given reinforcement in the fevered speculation on the question of who *Time* magazine would make its man of the twentieth century, a noisy process in which supporters of the rival contenders jostled and hustled the magazine in making cases for their respective favourite sons. In the event, although it had made Churchill 'man of the year' for 1940 and 'man of the half-century' for 1901–50, *Time* did indeed decline to name him 'man of the century', opting instead for Franklin Roosevelt, with Albert Einstein placed second and Churchill third. Since Roosevelt had been dead before 1950 when Churchill beat him for the half-century title, this clearly involved historical revisionism rather than any new events that had enhanced Roosevelt's record. The magazine decided in fact that Churchill's domestic and Imperial record – notably his opposition to Indian self-government and to women's suffrage – now put him behind Roosevelt. In effect, it was saying that with the Cold War over, it was safe to go back to the comfortable domesticities and progressive political preferences of the New Deal. Non-Americans tended to feel that this decision in any case indicated America's greater tendency in 1999 than half a century earlier to value only events within its own borders. A poll in *US News and World Report* in summer 2001 confirmed this perspective, since it found that most Americans could not name a single living political figure in the world that they truly admired. Those that did respond included only Jesus and Mother Teresa as non-Americans in their top ten heroes of all time, while Michael Jordan and John Wayne made it into the top ten alongside Kennedy, Lincoln and Martin Luther King. Conversely, Nelson Mandela, Winston Churchill and the Pope all failed to register. The main effect of *Time*'s decision was to prompt many other British and North American magazines, including *Newsweek*, the *Sunday Times*, the *Wall Street Journal*, the *Boston Globe*, the *Ottawa Citizen*, the *Winnipeg Free Press* and television's *Fox News* to declare that *Time* had got it wrong and that Churchill was the greater man. Even *Playboy* agreed, citing Churchill as one of the century's ten 'real men', an enviable title he shared with, among others, Harry S. Truman, Ernest Hemingway – and Frank Sinatra.

The conservative journalist Chris Matthews, a national figure after regular appearances on CNBC's *Hardball* programme of political commentary, delivered an address in Maryland called 'Winston Churchill, Man of the Century'. Matthews announced, 'I loved this guy,' and concluded, 'I don't give a damn who *Time* magazine picks as their man

of the century. I know who he really is.' In the United States, the debate
probably helped indeed to bring Churchill into the spotlight once more,
and gave his admirers the opportunity to go on to the offensive. Churchill's claims were endorsed by Governor George W. Bush, by Presidential hopeful John McCain, and by Senators Edward Kennedy and Jessie
Helms from the opposite ends of the political spectrum. Ever the party
loyalist, Al Gore endorsed Roosevelt. Richard Langworth, former president of the Churchill Center, was in any case able to mount on National
Public Radio a powerful case for Churchill's pre-eminence. Einstein had
himself argued that bad politics were more likely to bring the world to
grief than bad science, and hence had implicitly endorsed Churchill's
claims over his own, while Roosevelt's strengths were overwhelmingly
to do with the United States rather than the world as a whole. Churchill
on the other hand, if perhaps 'over-appreciated' in the United States in
his lifetime because he was always on his best behaviour when visiting,
had been the one indispensable man on which the victory of freedom
over totalitarianism had depended in the 1940s. Or, as Matthews put it,
'it was Churchill's refusal to deal with Hitler when everyone else in the
country had hoped to find a solution through diplomacy that gave the
world a chance to defeat the Nazi regime in World War II'. This was
also the view propounded by George Lukacs in his book *Five Days in
May* (1999), devoted to the British cabinet debates on the question of
discussing peace terms with Hitler shortly after Churchill became Prime
Minister. Ironically, the crucial vote in those debates turned out to have
been cast not by Labour Ministers nor by Churchill (who were always
against peace talks at that time but could not control the Commons),
or by Foreign Secretary Halifax (who favoured talks), but by Neville
Chamberlain (whose support for Churchill was essential if he was to
carry on in office). But it was far from clear that Chamberlain would
have taken the same view if he had been Prime Minister himself.[53]

Langworth's view that Churchill also remained a political standard
or role model for young people interested in public affairs had recently
been reinforced by students' reactions at a Stanford University seminar
on his *My Early Life*. It was equally underlined by a couple of books
published at the end of Churchill's century, books which drew similar
conclusions, and neither of which was by a British writer. These show
how far Churchill the political rhetorician, writer and career model has
been absorbed into the collective thinking in countries other than

Britain. In the United States, academics working on Churchill are likely to be political scientists studying his political thought, or business studies teachers looking at leadership models (a genre almost entirely absent from Britain), or literary experts working on his books. The more rigidly compartmentalised British academic world tends to ensure that only historians ever study Churchill now, and then largely to seek an understanding of his own era, rather than to provide us with lessons for our own. Christian Graf von Krockow published his *Churchill, Man of the Century* in Germany in 1999, in English translation in London in 2000. For this Professor of Politics brought up during the Hitler years, Churchill's life story provides an important lesson in the life and achievements of 'the exemplary counter-player of tyranny', for he was 'not only the man who blocked Hitler's way to "final victory" in the West, but also the strict anti-Communist for whom only half the job had been done in 1945'. Though a deeply conservative figure, he was also a man who looked both backwards and forwards, for 'in Churchill the modern and persevering are mixed with the outdated and outlived'. Above all, he warns, it is important to accept that Churchill was not infallible, for it was claims to infallibility by such men as Hitler or Stalin that he stood *imperfectly* against, with all his foibles, and this is the 'message' from Churchill's life that can 'lead us into the future and guard us against the temptations awaiting us there'. This is powerful and absolutely persuasive, but it is a message that is still being undermined by those who are determined to believe that Churchill could do no wrong.[54]

There follows a nicely balanced account of Churchill's life which would be highly recommendable to those who did not know much of the story or the background. Professor Graf von Krockow allows himself plenty of latitude to criticise Churchill, for example over his Indian campaign and over the Abdication in 1931–6. Nor does he treat even the campaign against appeasement with awe, noting that Churchill's 'hysterical' demand for armaments in the early 1930s would if implemented have equipped the RAF with planes that would have been redundant by 1940. More generally, 'if Churchill stood head and shoulders above his contemporaries, then he did so also with regard to the magnitude of his errors'. From a political scientist's perspective, he gives persuasive evidence of the ways in which Churchill's campaigns against the Bolsheviks, Indian independence and the Nazis were all influenced by his reading of Edmund Burke. Everything pales into insignificance, though, when Churchill's weaknesses are compared to the internal resources he mobilised in seeing the need to resist totalitarianism and in providing the inspiration in 1940 for freedom's battle. Stripped of much of its unnecessary and indefensible outworks Churchill's fame emerges all the more brightly from this going over, and he himself emerges as a greater man than he sometimes seems when the voice of criticism is stilled. 'Where else do we learn anything about historical greatness if not from a clash with a disaster no one else proves able to cope with?' What was important, and should never be forgotten, was that Churchill had grasped from history, as a conservative defender of liberty and law, that it was necessary to take an optimistic view of progress in order not to lose heart; that as 'a dyed-in-the-wool liberal' he grasped that democracies had a mission to defend and export their values; and that as a born, self-confessed and confident warrior he would not let anyone obstruct his fight for what was right, but did so with a distrust of uncontrolled generals that only a warrior dared to espouse. For Graf von Krockow, the lessons of Churchill's life are therefore about putting beliefs into action, and the need to believe that such ideas as law and liberty are worth defending in word and deed. At the end of the century, 'a blood-soaked era full of horror',

> our gratitude is owed to a the man who in the hour of need, of the triumph of tyranny, when everything appeared to be lost, seized the banner of freedom and carried it unwaveringly onwards to victory.[55]

The second book was by an American, Stephen Mansfield, and is entitled *Never Give In*, published in 1995 in a series called Leaders in Action. This pocket-sized volume seems at first sight to be a book-length version of the sort of framed exhortations to their executives beloved of American business corporations ('The leader of the pack is the one with the power to see most clearly,' accompanying a fine photograph of a pack of wolves). Though the series does indeed appeal to that type of market in civics courses and training for business leadership, it actually rises well above its genre and makes a powerful case for Churchill as a role model in leadership, at any level and in any country. Churchill's life is deconstructed into about fifty short chapters of about six hundred words, grouped into broader categories like 'Winston Churchill, the Character of Leadership' and 'Winston Churchill, the Pillars of Leadership'. Narrative is mainly avoided, though there is a chronology of Churchill's life for the reader's guidance, the aim rather being to draw powerful single lessons from individual moments and aspects of Churchill's career. For example, we are shown how Churchill dealt with criticism, and by implication how we ourselves can learn to deal with it, while a chapter on 'the wilderness' teaches the lesson of keeping going in adversity through the cultivation of self-belief. A section on 'Death' records the fortitude with which Churchill approached his final inescapable defeat, but concludes that 'by living the present in terms of the eternal, he achieved a greatness that death cannot destroy'.

It would be easy to parody such approaches to the study of Churchill, but it would be a mistake, for this particular work shows a good deal of insight and is the product of great familiarity with the official biography and other lengthy works. Nor should we underestimate the importance of the belief that it represents and passes on – if often uncritically. In the same year as the book first appeared, one of the speakers at the International Churchill Society Conference in Boston was coach Johnny Parker of the New England Patriots. Coach Parker showed himself to be a serious reader of Churchill's life, though a relatively recent convert, and had all the enthusiasms of the convert too ('In one man I found both my hero and the greatest personage this century has produced . . . Revisionist historians need not apply here'). His address took the form of a personal, almost religious, testimony from a man of obvious and deep sincerity, attesting to the fact that the memory of what Churchill had endured in 1940 had helped him through personal problems, and asserting that these inspirational lessons were among those that he passed on when his professional footballers were flagging after a difficult time in training. 'Thus, Winston Churchill, who only once saw a game of American football, continues to inspire at least one football team, and I suspect many others . . .' As the success of the Churchill Center in North America also shows, there is a world out yonder, of which the British are barely aware; some of it continues to take Winston Churchill warmly to its heart and receives continuing inspiration from his life and record. Such people were no doubt horrified by *Time* refusing to make Churchill 'man of the century', and Graf von Krockow is by no means the only writer to choose 'man of the century' as his title for a work on Churchill in conscious defiance of *Time*'s verdict.[56]

Just about a fortnight before the attack on the World Trade Center in 2001, Churchill's continuing appeal as an Anglo-American symbol was restated in the first visit of the USS *Winston S. Churchill* to Britain itself. This powerful modern destroyer was the first American warship ever to be named after a foreign leader – if indeed Churchill was a foreign leader after his 1963 honorary citizenship of the USA – though Britain had had between 1968 and 1991 a nuclear submarine called HMS *Churchill*. (Previously there had also been the sail-training ship *Sir Winston Churchill* in 1966, and from 1940 a lend–lease destroyer HMS *Churchill*, but the second was officially named after a place in Gloucestershire rather than the Prime Minister, a harmless deception that fooled nobody.) The USS *Churchill*'s launch in New England was the occasion of much rejoicing among the American 'Churchillians', who had intervened to ensure that the 'S' was correctly inserted into the vessel's official name, a late change that cost the American taxpayer thousands of dollars. As it entered Portsmouth harbour in August 2001 for the International Festival of the Sea, it was welcomed not only by the Royal Navy, but also by a Spitfire flying overhead to evoke memories of its eponymous hero's finest hour.[57]

Time's judgement in December 1999 would in any case surely have been significantly modified if it had made the decision only two years later, for the onset of the world's first international crisis of the new century in September 2001 brought Churchill, his words and his legacy right back into the limelight. Within hours of the bombing of the World Trade Center, readers of newspapers all round the world were being assured that President George W. Bush had a bust of Churchill in the Oval Office at the White House, recently presented by the British Ambassador, Churchill still apparently being a useful resource of British foreign policy in the USA. So it had been when Richard Langworth of the ICS was honoured with an honorary CBE in 1999, 'in recognition of his contribution to British–American relations through promoting the memory of Winston Churchill in the United States' (as the Ambassador's citation put it). George W. Bush was thus being inspired in 2001–2 by Winston's steely – or at least bronzey – gaze. Both he and Tony Blair were liberally quoting from the speeches of Winston Churchill in their own rhetorical efforts to rally the West against terrorism, and in preparing for his 2002 State of the Union address Bush was being urged to emulate Churchill's emotional appeal in Washington in 1941. Blair 'inevitably' now found himself addressing the US Congress in succession to Churchill and Thatcher, and Bush's newly close relationship with Blair was freely compared to the alliance of Churchill and Roosevelt.

Even closer to home, the Mayor of New York, Rudolph Giuliani, was also behaving in an overtly Churchillian manner. So much so indeed that a cartoon in a Texas paper showed a couple of New Yorkers admiring a photograph of Churchill while one says, 'They say he was a Giuliani-esque leader . . .' The *Washington Post* dubbed Giuliani 'Churchill in a Yankees cap', much as Churchill himself had once been called a 'Yankee Marlborough'. An external threat nationally and a desperate situation locally requiring the rallying of morale had politicians all across the Western world reaching back into their folk memories of Churchill in 1940–1 for a lesson in how to respond. With Americans reluctant to take to the air, and widespread additional delays in any case bedevilling all air travel, it might well have been that the planned conference of the International Churchill Society in San Diego only eight weeks after 11 September would have been thinly attended. Not a bit of it. Those 'New Churchillians' from Britain, Canada and the United States responded by turning out in one of the largest conference attendances the Society has had, the singing of the American anthem was even more fervent, and discussions of what Churchill could mean to us today were conducted with more intensity than ever, under the shadow of recent events.[58]

When *Time* in due course made 'the mayor of the world', Rudy Guiliani, its 'man of the year' for 2001, his profile in the magazine effectively conceded that it had short-changed Churchill in 1999, since it now placed the highest value on all those qualities for which Churchill had stood but which had in 1999 seemed less valuable than others more attributable to Roosevelt. Within minutes of the attacks on New York, Giuliani 'took to the airwaves to calm and reassure his people', and then spent the day 'making a few hundred rapid-fire decisions' about rescue and security operations, visiting 'the apocalyptic attack scene' and touring hospitals to comfort families. These were already the universally remembered images of Churchill in 1940–1 in London, but more was to come. When Giuliani finally got back to his temporary apartment and reached his bedroom, he picked out a previously unread book, Roy Jenkins' biography of Churchill, 'turned straight to the chapters on World War II and drank in the Prime Minister's words: "I have nothing to offer but blood, toil, tears and sweat"'. There was, thought *Time*'s reporter, 'a bright magic at work when one great leader reaches into the past and finds another waiting to guide him'. But this comparison had been not the journalist's but Giuliani's own, for he had been thinking of Churchill ever since the terror attack began and had consciously sought out Jenkins' book in order to drink deep at the Churchillian spring.

> I was so proud of the people I saw on the street. No chaos, but they were frightened and confused, and it seemed to me that they needed to hear from my heart where I thought we were going. I was trying to think, 'Where can I go for some comparison to this, some lessons about how to handle it?' So I started thinking about Churchill and the people of London during the Blitz in 1940, who had to keep up their spirit during this sustained bombing. It was a comforting thought.

Churchill had in 1940 mobilised history as a part of the war effort, offering an informed assurance that the British people had been here before and as a people had lived to tell the tale. So now Giuliani offered a historical analogy that was both tough and comforting to his listeners, and like Churchill in 1940 found that the crisis brought out the very best in him, emotional depths that had not often been on display. There was also, again like Churchill in 1940, a sudden upsurge in his poll ratings and in people's perceptions of his future potentialities, for Giuliani was after all in 2001 twelve years younger than Churchill had been in 1939. To complete the argument and tie together the threads, *Time* was even able to quote the author of the book that had so re-inspired Guiliani with the Churchill message. 'What Giuliani succeeds in doing', opined Roy Jenkins, 'is what Churchill succeeded in doing in the dreadful summer of 1940: he managed to create an illusion that we were bound to win.' Looking back two months later, Giuliani himself wondered how much of Churchill's bravado had in fact been bluff. 'A lot of it had to be bluff,' he concluded, but without in the least reducing his respect for the man who had bluffed so effectively and with such important historical consequences. Early in the following year he visited London to receive an honorary KBE, but made sure to visit the underground cabinet war rooms of 1939–45 ('the highlight of his afternoon'), the site of many of Churchill's wartime activities. Offered the chance to sit in Churchill's actual chair, he modestly declined, but noticed delightedly, 'Look, look, there is his cigar.' Referring disparagingly to the American fashion for smoking bans, he added, 'Churchill smoked cigars and nobody complained. That's why they won the war.' He was presumably referring not to Hitler being a vegetarian non-smoker, but rather to Churchill's refusal to compromise even on the little things, the confident self-indulgences that made Churchill – and Giuliani himself – into such an outsize personality.[59]

The World Trade Center attacks and the war in Afghanistan which swiftly followed were the occasion of another Churchillian consequence. As the worldwide coalition against terrorism came into being, it was the close relationship between Britain and the United States that provided its effective core, and it was the armed forces from those countries (if inevitably now with far more of them coming from the USA) that provided the cutting edge of the Allied war effort. Collective self-interest clearly played its part, as it had done so often in the past, but it was more than that on display in such impromptu demonstrations of unity as the changing of the guard at Buckingham Palace to the music of the Royal Marines band playing 'The Star-Spangled Banner'. In 2001, as Margaret Thatcher had found in 1982 and John Major in 1990–1, a threat to democratic values from a totalitarian power effortlessly fired up again the 'special relationship' of Britain and the United States which had functioned in every major war since 1917 and been the subject of so much of Churchill's rhetorical and diplomatic efforts – including the very invention of the phrase. Though British defence policy had been edging cautiously towards a more European framework since 1997, some-times to the undisguised alarm of highly placed Americans, when the chips were down the old partnership re-emerged, so much so that it was Britain's partners in the European Union that now began to display a certain amount of jealousy. Rudy Giuliani, as his names indicate, was no British-stock American as Dean Acheson had been, but he declared on his London visit that Britain was still America's best friend and ally in the world.

This was an order of priorities of which Churchill would have thoroughly approved, as indeed did Margaret Thatcher, who had in partnership with Ronald Reagan done so much to keep such thinking alive in the period since Churchill's death. Churchill may or may not actually have said to de Gaulle in wartime – there is only a single source for this one – that if Britain ever had to choose between Europe on the one hand and America and the open seas on the other, then it would

'We shall defend our island, whatever the cost may be, we shall negotiate on the beaches, we shall negotiate on the landing grounds, we shall negotiate in the fields and in the streets, we shall negotiate in the hills; we shall NEVER decide.'
Daily Telegraph, 23 April 1997

have to choose America. But the post-war policies that he actually pursued in office were certainly more consistent with that view than with the claims of such men as Edward Heath that Churchill had been a founder of 'Europe' – for example in celebrating as Prime Minister in 1971 the silver jubilee of Churchill's Zurich speech of 1946. Since his death Britain has inched unsteadily closer to repudiating such a strategic preference, but has never yet actually faced up to it in such stark terms. The choice perhaps remains to be made. Thatcher had thus, nearly twenty years earlier, executed an important task in honour of the memory of 'the great Winston', as she usually called him. By replacing Edward Heath as Conservative leader in 1975, she toppled the only post-war British premier who had seriously intended to give greater priority to Europe than to Britain's relationship with the United States, and who cited Churchill the 'European' as the ancestor of this intended reorientation of British policy. But from 1979 onwards Prime Minister Thatcher reasserted the unity of the English-speaking peoples as the core of British foreign policy, just as it had been the chief theme both of the post-war Churchill and of his American admirers. Replying to Ronald Reagan's toast to her at a White House dinner in 1981, she began with the words, 'You mentioned Churchill. We all do . . .'⁶⁰

NOTES

Preface

1 Christopher Thorne, *Allies of a Kind; The United States, Britain and the War against Japan* (London, 1978), 730. I am grateful to Paul Addison for this reference. Robert Self ed., *The Neville Chamberlain Diary Letters*, vol. 2: *The Reform Years, 1921–1927* (London, 2000), 65.

2 Malcolm MacDonald, *Titans and Others* (London, 1972), 124–5; *New York Times*, 14 Feb. 1964.

3 Winston Churchill, 'The Dream', in Michael Wolff ed., *Collected Essays of Winston Churchill* (London, 1974), vol. 4, 510.

4 Winston Churchill, *Their Finest Hour* (London, 1949), chapter 31, quoted in Christian Graf von Krockow, *Churchill, Man of the Century* (London, 2000), 175.

5 English-Speaking Union, *Ten Churchill Lectures* (London, 1998), 35.

CHAPTER 1: *'The Greatest Dying Englishman': Churchill's Death and Funeral*

1 A. L. Rowse, *Memories of Men and Events* (London, 1980), 12; *Illustrated London News*, 30 Jan. 1965.

2 Anthony Montague Browne, *Long Sunset: Memoirs of Winston Churchill's Last Private Secretary* (London, 1995), 302–3.

3 *New Statesman*, 22 Jan. 1965.

4 David Cannadine, 'Churchill and the British Monarchy', *Transactions of the Royal Historical Society*, 6th series, vol. 11, 269.

5 *Guardian*, 16 Jan. 1965.

6 *Guardian*, 18 Jan. 1965.

7 *Guardian*, 19 to 23 Jan. 1965, *Daily Express*, 19 Jan. 1965; Alec Cairncross, *A Treasury Diary: The Wilson Years, 1964–66* (London, 1997), 32.

8 *Guardian*, 19 Jan. 1965.

9 *Daily Express*, 20 Jan. 1965.

10 *Daily Express*, 25 Jan. 1965, *Guardian*, 25 Jan. 1965.

11 *Daily Express*, 26 to 28 Jan. 1965, *Guardian*, 25 to 30 Jan. 1965.

12 *Daily Express*, 25 Jan. 1965, *Sunday Times*, 31 Jan. 1965.

13 Hubert Humphrey autobiographical tapes, box 7, tape 2, Hubert Humphrey Papers, Minnesota Historical Society, St Paul, Minnesota. Stephen Barber, 'His Finest Hour: The Death and Funeral of Sir Winston Churchill', MA dissertation, Queen Mary and Westfield College, 1997. The files relating to the funeral 'Operation Hope Not' are in the Public Record Office, as PREM13/204.

14 Quoted in Barber, 'His Finest Hour', 8.

15 *Sunday Times*, 7 Feb. 1965.

16 *Guardian*, 25 Jan. and 1 Feb. 1965; *Daily Mail*, 25 Jan. 1965; *Keesing's Contemporary Archives* (1965), 20536, 20568; *Daily Telegraph*, 1 Feb. 1965.

17 Mark Amory ed., *The Letters of Evelyn Waugh* (London, 1980), 630.

18 Graham Payne and Sheridan Morley eds, *The Noël Coward Diaries* (London, 1982), 591; *Sunday Times*, 31 Jan. 1965.

19 *Observer*, 31 Jan. 1965; *New Statesman*, 29 Jan. and 5 Feb. 1965.

20 Janet Morgan ed., *The Diaries of a Cabinet Minister, Richard Crossman*, vol. 1: *Minister of Housing, 1964–66* (London, 1975), 145; Tony Benn, *Out of the Wilderness: Diaries 1963–67* (London, 1988), 213.

21 *Daily Mail*, 25, 26 and 30 Jan. 1965.

22 *Economist*, 23 and 30 Jan. 1965; *Spectator*, 29 Jan. 1965; *New Statesman*, 29 Jan. 1965.

23 *Guardian*, 25 Jan. 1965.

24 *Economist*, 23 Jan. 1965.

25 *The Times*, 1 Feb. 1965.

26 *New York Times*, 14 Apr. 1963, reprinting recent cartoons from the *Daily Mail* and

Daily Express; Washington Evening Star,
7 Oct. 1965.

27 *Daily Telegraph,* 17 Mar. 1963; Joe
Orton, *What the Butler Saw* (London,
1969), 91–2; John Lahr ed., *The Orton
Diaries* (London, 1986), entries of 11 and
27 July 1967; Garry O'Connor, *Ralph
Richardson* (London, 1982), 256.

28 *New York Times,* 9 and 26 May 1963;
Washington Evening Star, 9 May 1963.

29 State Department Papers, POL6, UK.

30 Alan Magahy, *Humphrey Gibbs:
Beleaguered Governor* (London, 1998),
93, 97, 125.

31 State Department Papers, POL6, UK.

32 Lord Moran, *Winston Churchill: The
Struggle for Survival, 1940–1965* (Sphere
Books edn, London, 1968), 428.

33 David Halberstam, *The Best and the
Brightest* (Ballantyne Books edn, New
York, 1992), 431, 531. See also documents
in the Lyndon B. Johnson Presidential
Papers, White House Name files, box
222, 'Churchill, Winston', and National
Security Files, Country file, UK, box
214, 'Churchill funeral', Johnson Library.

34 *New York Times,* 27 Jan. 1965.

35 Dwight D. Eisenhower Post-Presidential
Papers, Signature file 1965, box 21,
folders 1 to 3, and box 16, folder 3,
Augusta-Walter Reed Series, box 4,
Eisenhower Library; *New York Times,* 5
Feb. 1965; Jack Shuyler to Harry
Truman, 27 Jan. 1965, Harry S. Truman
Post-Presidential Papers, Name file, box
59, file 'Churchill, death of', Truman
Library.

36 Lyndon B. Johnson Presidential Papers,
White House Name files, box 222,
'Winston Churchill', and National
Security Files, Country file, UK, box
214, 'Churchill funeral', Johnson Library.

37 *Ibid.; New York Times,* 31 Jan. 1965.

38 *New York Times,* 2 Feb. 1965.

39 Carl Solberg, *Hubert Humphrey: A
Biography* (New York, 1984), 265–6;
Humphrey autobiographical tapes, box
7, tapes 1, 2 and 8, and set 3, tape 2,
Hubert Humphrey Papers, Minnesota
Historical Society, St Paul, Minnesota.

40 State Department Papers, POL6, UK.

41 Walter Millis ed., *The Forrestal Diaries*
(London, 1952), 63.

42 Humphrey autobiographical tapes, box
7, tapes 1, 2 and 8, and set 3, tape 2,
Hubert Humphrey Papers, Minnesota

Historical Society, St Paul, Minnesota;
New York Times, 31 Jan. and 5, 6 and
17 Feb. 1965; *Washington Star,* 1 Feb.
1965.

43 State Department Papers, POL6 UK
and CUL6 UK.

CHAPTER 2: *'Had This War
Not Come, Who Would Speak of
Winston Churchill?'*

1 Alec Cairncross, *The Wilson Years: A
Treasury Diary, 1964–66* (London, 1997),
35; Robert Rhodes James, *Churchill: A
Study in Failure, 1900–1939*
(Harmondsworth, 1973).

2 Robert Self ed., *The Austen Chamberlain
Diary Letters* (London, 1995), 159; Robert
Self ed., *The Neville Chamberlain Diary
Letters,* vol. 2: *The Reform Years,
1921–1927* (London, 2000), 65–6.

3 David Cannadine, 'Churchill and the
British Monarchy', *Transactions of the
Royal Historical Society,* 6th series, vol.
11, 254; Martin Gilbert, *Churchill: A
Photographic Portrait* (Harmondsworth,
1974), no. 96; Ann Moyal, *Breakfast with
Beaverbrook* (Sydney, 1995), 4; Lord
Moran, *Winston Churchill: The Struggle
for Survival, 1940–1965* (Sphere Books
edn, London, 1968), 674; Mark Bonham
Carter and Mark Pottle eds, *Lantern
Slides: The Diaries and Letters of Violet
Bonham Carter, 1906–1914* (London,
1996), 414.

4 'Saki', *76 Short Stories* (London, 1956),
194–205.

5 Bonham Carter and Pottle, *Lantern
Slides,* 146, 316; Violet Bonham Carter,
Winston Churchill as I Knew Him
(Weidenfeld & Nicolson edn, London,
1995), 15, 18, 232.

6 For Churchill and Ireland see Chapter
Five.

7 Winston Churchill, *The People's Rights*
(Cape edn, London, 1970), 133–6, 142.

8 Rhodes James, *Churchill,* 79–114, 132–60,
193–200, 206–11, 219–25, 253–6, 266–9,
273–5, 344–5, 366–7.

9 Kenneth Young ed., *The Diaries of Sir
Robert Bruce Lockhart, 1915–1938*
(London, 1973), 182; David Carlton,
'Churchill and the Two "Evil Empires"',
*Transactions of the Royal Historical
Society,* 6th series, vol. 11, 337–8, 342;
Daily Herald, 30 Mar. 1933.

10 Robin Prior, *Churchill's World Crisis as History* (London, 1983), unpaginated introduction.

11 P. Paneth, *The Prime Minister* (London, 1943), 47.

12 Bonham Carter, *Winston Churchill*, 331; Norman Rose, *The Cliveden Set* (Cape edn, London, 2000), 134; Nigel Nicolson ed., *Harold Nicolson: Diaries and Letters, 1930–39* (London, 1966), 314.

13 Joseph King, *The Political Gambler, being the record of Rt. Hon. Winston Churchill MP* (Glasgow, 1919).

14 W. L. Germains, *The Tragedy of Winston Churchill* (London, 1931), esp. pp. 276–9.

15 John Ramsden, *The Age of Balfour and Baldwin, 1902–1940* (London, 1978), 334, 350–1; David Reynolds, 'Churchill's Writing of History', *Transactions of the Royal Historical Society*, 6th series, vol. 11, 242; Young, *Bruce Lockhart Diaries, 1915–1938*, 361; Mary Soames ed., *Speaking for Themselves: The Personal Letters of Winston and Clementine Churchill* (London, 1998), 341.

16 R. H. Pilpel, *Churchill in America* (New York, 1976), 111–12, 123, 145.

17 David Dilks, *Three Visitors to Canada: Baldwin, Chamberlain and Churchill*, Canada House Lecture Series, no. 28, Canada House (London, 1985).

18 *Bartlett's Familiar Quotations* (New York, 12th edn 1937, 14th edn 1955, 15th edn 1968).

19 *Oxford Dictionary of Quotations* (Oxford, 1941, 1953, 1992).

20 Dominique Enright, *The Wicked Wit of Winston Churchill* (London, 2001), 48.

21 Martin Gilbert, *Winston S. Churchill*, vol. 5: *1922–1939* (London, 1976), 62; 'Ephesian', *Winston Churchill* (London, 1927), 269; Nigel Nicolson ed., *Harold Nicolson: Diaries and Letters, 1939–45* (London, 1967), 307; Tom Jones, *A Diary with Letters, 1931–1950* (London, 1954), 204.

22 Robert Pearce ed., *Patrick Gordon Walker: Political Diaries, 1932–71* (London, 1991), 89; Ben Pimlott, *Harold Wilson* (London, 1992), 72.

23 Paul Addison, 'The Three Careers of Winston Churchill', *Transactions of the Royal Historical Society*, 6th series, vol. 11, 195; Zita Crossman's notes on the Labour Conference, included in Angus Calder and Dorothy Sheridan eds, *Speak for Yourself: A Mass-Observation Anthology* (London, 1984), 194.

24 Reprinted in Winston S. Churchill, *Thoughts and Adventures* (London, 1932).

25 Robert Rhodes James ed., *Chips: The Diaries of Sir Henry Channon* (London, 1967), 146; Ramsden, *Age of Balfour and Baldwin*, 368–9.

26 Lord Hailsham, *The Fulton Speech, Fifteen Years After*, Green Lecture (Westminster College, Fulton, Missouri, 1961).

27 Graham Greene, *The Ministry of Fear* (Harmondsworth, 1973), quoted in Stephen Barber, 'His Finest Hour: The Death and Funeral of Sir Winston Churchill', MA dissertation, Queen Mary and Westfield College, 1997), 4.

28 John Lukacs, 'Three Days in London', *American Spectator*, Aug. 1979; William McVey, 'Most Sculptable Man', essay, enclosed with McVey to Kay Halle, 22 Apr. 1966, Kay Halle Papers, folder C46, Kennedy Library; Moran, *Churchill*, 652–3; *Finest Hour*, 106, 18–19.

29 Yousef Karsh, *Faces of Destiny* (London, 1947), 7, 40; Nicholas Cull, *Selling War: The British Propaganda Campaign against American Neutrality in World War II* (Oxford, 1995), 107; Ronald A. Smith, *Churchill: Images of Greatness* (London, n.d. but c.1995), 27; English-Speaking Union, Washington DC Branch, 'Churchill Statue' files, 'Sculptor, Bill McVey' file.

30 Calder and Sheridan, *Speak for Yourself*, 114; Andrew Roberts, *Eminent Churchillians* (London, 1994), 50.

31 See for example John Wheeler-Bennett ed., *Action This Day: Working with Churchill* (London, 1968).

32 W. M. James, *The Portsmouth Letters* (London, 1946), 15; Kenneth Young ed., *Diaries of Sir Robert Bruce Lockhart, 1939–1965* (London, 1980), 648; Patrick Cosgrave, *Thatcher: The First Term* (London, 1985), 170; Moran, *Churchill*, 318–19.

33 John Ramsden, *The Age of Churchill and Eden, 1940–1957* (London, 1995), chapter 1.

34 J. M. Lee, *The Churchill Coalition, 1940–45* (London, 1980), 23; Edward R. Murrow, *This is London* (London, 1941), 266; Kevin Jeffreys ed., *Labour and the*

Wartime Coalition: From the Diaries of James Chuter Ede, 1941–45 (London, 1987), 214.

35 *Tribune*, 21 Mar. 1958; Foot went on to observe that 'of course he is wrong about the English people. They don't always like being governed so much. However, since the people only make the rarest of intrusions into his *History of the English-Speaking Peoples*, the point hardly arises.'

36 Celia Sandys, *Churchill: Wanted Dead or Alive* (London, 1999), 145–6; most of the original dispatches are reprinted in Frederick Woods ed., *Young Winston's Wars* (London, 1972).

37 Kenneth Young, *Churchill and Beaverbrook* (London, 1966), 46–53.

38 Brian Gardner, *Churchill in his Time* (London, 1968), 127.

39 Pilpel, *Churchill in America*, 147–8.

40 Sir Evelyn Wrench, 'Churchill and the Empire', in Charles Eade ed., *Churchill by his Contemporaries* (London, 1953), 200; Nelson Mandela, *Long Walk to Freedom* (Abacus edn, London, 1995), 58; Margaret Hixon, *Salote* (Dunedin, New Zealand, 2000), 122.

41 Stuart Ball ed., *Parliament and Politics in the Age of Churchill and Attlee: The Headlam Diaries, 1935–51* (London, 1999), 286; Richard Dimbleby, 'Churchill the Broadcaster', in Eade, *Churchill*, 280–1.

42 Sir George Arthur, *Concerning W. S. Churchill* (London, 1940), 194; Martin Gilbert, *Winston S. Churchill*, vol. 6: *Finest Hour, 1939–1941* (London, 1983), 97.

43 Stephen Laird and Walter Graebner, *Hitler's Reich and Churchill's Britain* (London 1942), 44

44 Mollie Panter-Downes, *London War Notes 1939–45* (London, 1971), 70; George Beardmore, *Civilians at War: Journals, 1939–46* (Oxford, 1986), 66; *Portsmouth Evening News*, 12 Dec. 1950; Anthony Livsey ed., *Are We at War? Letters to The Times, 1939–45* (London, 1989), 164; Pamela Street, *Portrait of a Historian* (London, 1979), 47; Churchill's foreword to Pitt's speeches is reprinted in Michael Wolff ed., *Collected Essays of Sir Winston Churchill* (London, 1974), vol. 1, 492.

45 Nicolson, *Harold Nicolson's Diaries and Letters, 1939–45*, 97; David Wenden,

'Churchill, Radio and Cinema', in William Roger Louis and Robert Blake eds, *Churchill* (Oxford, 1993), 223–5.

46 N. R. Smith, *Outside Information* (Macmillan, 1941), 41; James Agate, *Ego 6* (London, 1944), 133; Introduction, *Oxford Dictionary of Quotations* (Oxford, 1941 edn); oddly enough, as Churchill's actual words were incorporated into later editions, this interesting reflection on his *use* of the quotation as such was deleted from the introduction.

47 Graham Cawthorne, *A Visitor's Guide to Winston Churchill* (London, 1974), unpaginated. Enright, *Wicked Wit*, 131.

48 Tom Harrisson, *Living through the Blitz* (London, 1976), 213–14; *Manchester Evening News*, 26 Apr. 1941; *Manchester City News*, 2 May 1941.

49 Gardner, *Churchill in his Time*, 91; Pilpel, *Churchill in America*, 157; Smith, *Churchill* 31.

50 'Churchill Remembered', *Transactions of the Royal Historical Society*, 6th series, vol. 11, 398, 404–5.

51 Somerset Maugham, *Strictly Personal* (London, 1942), 130; Gardner, *Churchill in his Time*, 108, 96.

52 *Spectator*, 31 Dec. 1943; Paul Addison, *The Road to 1945* (London, 1975), 167; Calder and Sheridan, *Speak for Yourself*, 230.

53 Wenden, 'Churchill, Radio and Cinema', 224.

54 Kevin Jefferys, *The Churchill Coalition and Wartime Politics, 1940–45* (Manchester, 1991), 18, 150–1.

55 Jefferys, *Churchill Coalition*, 53; Lee, *Churchill Coalition*, 24, 140; John Colville, *The Churchillians* (London, 1981), 43; Moran, *Churchill*, 335.

56 Jefferys, *Churchill Coalition*, 160; Gardner, *Churchill in his Time*, 181, 237; Calder and Sheridan, *Speak for Yourself*, 224; Susan A. Brewer, *To Win the Peace: British Propaganda in the United States during World War II* (London, 1997), 127–8.

57 Addison, *Road to 1945*, 251; Calder and Sheridan, *Speak for Yourself*, 211–18; Mark Pottle ed., *Champion Redoubtable: The Diaries and Letters of Violet Bonham Carter, 1914–1945* (London, 1998), 263.

58 Ramsden, *Age of Churchill and Eden*, chapter 2; Ian Mikardo, *Back-Bencher* (London, 1988), 84.

59 Gardner, *Churchill in his Time*, 218.
Churchill had already committed
himself to Collins in November 1944 for
'any book you might write on the
Second World War', in return for which
they had given up their film rights on
the still unpublished *History of the
English-Speaking Peoples* – to Sir
Alexander Korda! See Newman Flower
to Churchill, 5 Feb. 1954, Churchill
Papers, 4/26.

60 Panter-Downes, *London War Notes*,
376–7

61 *The Times*, 9 May 1945; Randolph S.
Churchill ed., *The Unwritten Alliance:
Winston Churchill Speeches, 1953–59*
(London, 1960), 201–3; Isaiah Berlin, *Mr
Churchill in 1940* (London, 1949), 26–7.

62 *New York Times*, 10 Jan. 1956; William
Manchester, *The Last Lion, 1874–1932*
(London, 1983) and *The Caged Lion,
1932–1940* (1988).

63 *The Public Papers and Addresses of
Franklin D. Roosevelt* (New York, 1941),
15 Mar. 1941.

64 Gardner, *Churchill in his Time*, 101;
Sunday Times, 27 Apr. and 30 Nov. 1941.

65 Winston Churchill, 'Mass Effects in
Modern Life', in *Thoughts and
Adventures*; Winston Churchill, *Great
Contemporaries* (London, 1959), 244–59.

66 S. G. Millin, *The Sound of the Trumpet*
(London, 1947), 80; Gardner, *Churchill
in his Time*, 207; Ball, *Headlam Diaries*,
287.

67 Ernest Barker, *Winston Churchill*
(London, 1945), 41.

68 J. B. Priestley, *Britain at War* (London,
1942), 20, 114; Anon, *The British People
at War* (London, 1943), 2, 126–7; *Victory
Parade*, 1946.

69 Robert Lewis Taylor, *Winston Churchill:
The Biography of a Great Man* (New
York, 1954), 365.

70 Moran, *Churchill*, 319; Nigel Nicolson
ed., *Harold Nicolson: Diaries and Letters
1945–60* (London, 1967), 36, 63, 65; Ben
Pimlott ed., *Political Diary of Hugh
Dalton, 1918–40, 1945–60* (London,
1986), 365; Charles Andrews, *Senior
Statesman with a Future* (Cambridge,
Massachusetts, 1957) 1; note by Charles
Murphy of Churchill's dinner with *Time*
staff, 13 Mar. 1966, Kay Halle Papers,
folder 43(1), Kennedy Library;
Washington Evening Star, 18 Nov. 1964.

CHAPTER 3: 'The Greatest
Living Englishman'

1 John Ramsden, *The Age of Churchill and
Eden, 1940–1957* (London, 1995), 327.

2 A. H. Booth, *The True Story of Winston
Churchill* (Chicago, 1958), 128.

3 Quoted in Emrys Hughes, *Winston
Churchill, British Bulldog* (New York,
1955), 328.

4 Neal Ferrier ed., *Churchill: The Man of
the Century* (London, 1955).

5 A. M. Gollin, *From Omdurman to VE
Day* (London, 1964), 45.

6 Alan Moorhead, *Winston Churchill*
(London, 1960), 126.

7 Robert Lewis Taylor, *Winston Churchill:
The Biography of a Great Man* (New
York, 1954), iv.

8 'Arrangements for the Funeral of Sir
Winston Churchill ("Operation Hope
Not"), a note by the Cabinet Office',
1965, Public Record Office, PREM 13/
204, first drawn to my attention by
Peter Hennessy.

9 I owe this information to Professor
Keith Middlemas who as a Clerk of the
House of Commons was involved in the
funeral arrangements.

10 Pauline Bloncourt, *An Old and a Young
Leader* (London, 1970), 92; *New York
Times*, 20 Apr. 1963.

11 Ronald A. Smith, *Winston Churchill:
Images of Greatness* (London, n.d. but
c.1995), 91.

12 Oliver Jensen, 'The Gettysburg Address
in Eisenhowese', in Dwight Macdonald
ed., *Parodies* (London, 1961), 447; A. L.
Rowse, 'Churchill's Place in History', in
Charles Eade ed., *Churchill by his
Contemporaries* (London, 1953), 507.

13 *New York Times*, 30 Nov. 1955.

14 *New York Times*, 6 Jan. 1952.

15 Leo Rosten, *People I Have Known or
Admired* (New York, 1970), 84. Diana
Coolidge, *Winston Churchill and the
Story of the Two World Wars* (Boston,
Massachusetts, 1960), introduction.

16 Bill Adler ed., *The Churchill Wit* (New
York, 1965), 18; Anthony Montague
Browne, *Long Sunset: The Memoirs of
Winston Churchill's Last Private Secretary*
(London, 1995), 238.

17 Woodrow Wyatt, *Distinguished for
Talent* (London, 1958), 194; James
Humes, *Churchill: Speaker of the Century*

(New York, 1980), 238. John Young, *Winston Churchill's Last Campaign: Britain and the Cold War, 1951–1955* (Oxford, 1996), 257.

18 Professor Colin Matthew to the author, 14 March 1997, recalling the view from the Stranger's Gallery in about 1962.

19 *Daily Telegraph*, 29 July 1964; Rosten, *People*, 84.

20 Sir James Marchant ed., *Winston Spencer Churchill: Servant of Crown and Commonwealth* (London, 1954), 75; Janet Morgan ed., *The Backbench Diaries of Richard Crossman* (London, 1981), 231; *Daily Telegraph*, 28 July 1964; Tony Benn, 'The Media and the Political Process', James Cameron Memorial Lecture, 2001, in Hugh Stephenson ed., *Media Voices* (London, 2001), 332.

21 Lord Boyd-Carpenter, quoted in BBC radio discussion, *Living with Churchill*, broadcast 12 Sept. 1988, BBC tape no. TLN930/89VQ9026, drawn to my attention by Peter Hennessy. Prime Ministers did not have a guaranteed, timed period for parliamentary questions until the 1960s.

22 Booth, *True Story*, 130.

23 Roy Jenkins, 'Churchill, the Government of 1951–1955', in William Roger Louis and Robert Blake eds, *Churchill* (New York, 1993), 493.

24 Morgan, *Crossman Backbench Diaries*, 373.

25 Hughes, *Churchill, British Bulldog*, 298–9.

26 *Ibid.*, 299.

27 *Ibid.*, 327–8; at Fulton, as usual suiting his dress to the occasion, Churchill actually made the great speech wearing his honorary Oxford DCL robes, which he had borrowed from the President of Princeton for the occasion, Humes, *Churchill*, 224. Montague Browne, *Long Sunset*, 173; Kay Halle's note of interview with Christopher Sykes, information from Frank Gilbey, Halle Papers, folder 62, Kennedy Library; Lord Moran, *Winston Churchill: The Struggle for Survival, 1940–1965* (London, 1968), 429.

28 Ivan de la Bere, *The Queen's Orders of Chivalry* (London, 1964), 70; Morgan, *Crossman Backbench Diaries*, 236.

29 Lewis Broad, *Winston Churchill* (New York, 1958), 587–8; David Cannadine, 'Churchill and the Monarchy',

Transactions of the Royal Historical Society, 6th series, vol. 11, 269; Moran, *Churchill*, 450.

30 Princess Bibescu, *Churchill, ou le courage* (Paris, 1956), 178.

31 Graham Cawthorne ed., *The Churchill Legend* (London, n.d. but c.1958), 82.

32 Broad, *Churchill*, 573.

33 Ferrier, *Churchill*, 87; Hulton Archive, image number HN3048, 30 Nov. 1954.

34 Mary Soames, *Clementine Churchill* (Boston, Massachusetts, 1979), 587–8.

35 Cawthorne, *Churchill Legend*, 83.

36 Edgar Black, *Winston Churchill* (Derby, Connecticut, 1961), 290–1.

37 Hughes, *Churchill, British Bulldog*, 329; Young, *Churchill's Last Campaign*, 256.

38 Randolph S. Churchill ed., *The Unwritten Alliance: Winston Churchill Speeches, 1953–1959* (Boston, Massachusetts, 1960), 201.

39 Will Yolen and K. S. Giniger, *Heroes for our Times* (Harrisburg, Pennsylvania, 1968), 3. There have been many different versions of this story told over the years, in one of which the small boy was Churchill's grandson Nicholas Soannes, and in some of which Churchill's final words were somewhat implausibly rendered as 'Now buzz off,' but the essence of Churchill's reply to the question was always the same.

40 Fred Urquhart ed., *WSC: A Cartoon Biography* (London, 1955), 175.

41 Mollie Keller, *Winston Churchill* (New York, 1984), 105; Smith, *Churchill*, 159.

42 Broad, *Churchill*, 534–5.

43 Emrys Hughes, *Winston Churchill in War and Peace* (London, 1950), 235.

44 Cawthorne, *Churchill Legend*, 86. The white-cliffs project was the spontaneous idea of a local Margate resident, but £50,000 was said to have been collected for the project before it was scrapped. Taylor, *Winston Churchill*, 389–90.

45 *The Times*, 23 Feb. and 7 and 14 Sept. 1945, 4 Aug. 1947, 2 June 1949, 24 July 1953, 19 May and 30 Sept. 1955; *Brighton Evening Argus*, 25 Jan. 1965.

46 *The Times*, 26 July 1945, 13 July, 15 Aug. and 29 Oct. 1946, 16 Aug. 1951.

47 *The Times*, 19 June, 5 July and 20 Aug. 1945, 10 June 1947, 29 Mar. and 17 Aug. 1948, 6 May 1954, 13 Jan. 1958.

48 *The Times,* 1 Nov. 1946, 6 Dec. 1947, 8 Apr. 1948, 17 Apr. 1951.
49 *The Times,* 17 Nov. 1945, 21 June 1948, 19 June and 13 Dec. 1950.
50 *The Times,* 14 Oct. and 1 Dec. 1945, 27 June 1946, 21 July and 19 Nov. 1948, 22 May 1950, 7 June 1952, 24 May 1955.
51 *The Times,* 1 May 1947, 19 Oct. 1953.
52 *The Times,* 26 Apr., 21 Oct. and 6 Nov. 1945, 15 Apr., 22 June, 25 July and 7 Nov. 1946, 18 Feb. 1948, 20 Mar. and 1 May 1951, 9 Dec. 1954.
53 *The Times,* 5 Sept. 1946; *Gazette and Herald,* Blackpool, 7, 9 and 23 Sept. and 5 Oct. 1946; *West Lancashire Evening Gazette,* 4 and 5 Oct. 1946.
54 *Brighton and Hove Herald,* 8 June 1946; *Brighton Evening Argus,* 25 Jan. 1965.
55 *West Sussex Gazette,* 26 Nov. 1964, 28 Jan. 1965.
56 *Portsmouth Evening News,* 1 Nov. 1948.
57 *Portsmouth Evening News,* 12 Dec. 1948.
58 *Portsmouth Evening News,* 30 Nov. 1954; *Hampshire Times,* 7 Apr. 1955; *West Sussex Gazette,* 28 Jan. 1965.
59 *Western Daily Press,* 21 Apr. 1945.
60 MSC 920/C, Churchill, Winston, file, Manchester Local History Library.
61 *Arrangements for the Ceremony for the Presentation of the Freedom of the City of Manchester to the Right Honourable Winston Spencer-Churchill* [sic], *OM, CH, FRS, MP,* Manchester Local History Library.
62 *Manchester Evening News,* 29 July 1943, 12 Nov. 1947; *Manchester Guardian,* 4 and 6 Dec. 1947.
63 *Manchester Guardian,* 8 Dec. 1947.
64 *Sheffield Telegraph,* 16 to 18 Apr. 1951.
65 *Birmingham Post,* 29 to 31 Oct. and 1 and 2 Nov. 1946.
66 *Yorkshire Post,* 27 and 28 Oct. 1953; Moran, *Churchill,* 513.
67 *Staffordshire Chronicle,* 1 Sept. 1945.
68 *Northern Echo,* 23 Apr. and 9 May 1947.
69 *Courier and Advertiser,* Dundee, 9 and 19 Oct. 1943; *The Times,* 9 and 19 Oct. 1943.
70 *Luton News and Bedfordshire Chronicle,* 29 Apr., 6, 13, 20 and 27 May and 1 July 1948.
71 *The Times,* 1 and 10 Apr. and 9 Dec. 1946, 29 Oct. 1952, 19 Feb. 1954, 1 Mar. 1955, 30 Nov. 1961.
72 *The Times,* 11 Nov. and 2 Dec. 1953, 5 Feb. 1954, 22 June and 24 Sept. 1955, 18 Jan. 1957, 3 May 1962, 7 Dec. 1963, 22 and 23 Oct. 1964, 23 Apr. and 3 Dec. 1966, 19 May 1967, 5 Apr. and 20 May 1968, 5 Aug. 1971.
73 *The Times,* 22 Jan., 6 and 7 Mar., 23 Apr. and 25 July 1958, 24 Jan., 14 Sept. and 2 Nov. 1959; *New York Daily News,* 6 Dec. 1958.
74 *The Times,* 29 Oct. 1965, 1 Feb. 1966, 16 to 31 May and 1 and 6 June 1968, 4 to 30 July 1969.
75 *The Times,* 15 June and 8 Dec. 1945, 12 Sept. 1947, 16 Nov. 1954, 9 Mar. 1955, 15 June 1962, 24 and 27 May, 23 July and 22 Oct. 1965, 2 and 12 Feb. and 14 Mar. 1966, 8 Apr. 1967, 21 May 1969, 8 May and 3 June 1970, 20 July 1971, 14 Jan. 1974.
76 Churchill, *Unwritten Alliance;* François Kersaudy, *Churchill and de Gaulle* (New York, 1983), 425.
77 'Diary, week of May 4, 1956', Dwight D. Eisenhower Presidential Papers, DDE diary series, box 41, Eisenhower Library.
78 Viscount Montgomery to General Eisenhower, 28 Oct. 1951, Dwight D. Eisenhower Pre-Presidential Papers, Name file, box 82, file 'Montgomery, 3', Eisenhower Library.
79 President Kennedy to Winston Churchill, 14 Aug. 1961, John F. Kennedy Presidential Papers, President's Office Special Correspondence, box 28, folder 1, Winston S. Churchill, 1961–63, Kennedy Library; Ben Tucker, *Winston Churchill: His Life in Pictures* (London, 1945, 1950, 1955).
80 Churchill, *Unwritten Alliance,* 201–3.
81 It is only fair to add that Churchill's refusal of a peerage seems also to have been occasioned by the desire to keep a route to the Commons open for his son Randolph, who still had parliamentary ambitions in the 1950s (for Churchill remembered all too well that he had in the 1890s himself briefly been heir to the dukedom of Marlborough and so threatened with the eclipse of his own ambitions in the Lower House); there was also the fact that the perpetually impecunious Churchill could not safely anticipate living the rest of his life in the style expected of a duke. Montague Browne, *Long Sunset,* 182.
82 Keller, *Churchill,* 110.
83 Sam and Beryl Epstein, *Winston*

Churchill, Lion of Britain (Champaign, Illinois, 1971), 167; *The Times*, 14 June 1983; *National Trust Magazine*, Spring 1999.

84 Isaiah Berlin, *Mr Churchill in 1940* (London, 1949); Taylor, *Churchill*, 401–2.

85 Berlin, *Mr Churchill*, 26–7.

86 *New York Times Magazine*, 1 Nov. 1964; *New York Times Book Review*, 29 Nov. 1964.

87 Michael Ignatieff, *Isaiah Berlin: A Life* (London, 1998), 170–1, 195–6.

88 *The Times*, 2 Apr. 1968; Andrew Roberts, *Eminent Churchillians* (London, 1994), 303.

89 A. L. Rowse, *The End of an Epoch* (London, 1947), 77–89; A. L. Rowse, *The Spirit of English History* (London, 1943), 8, 130, 132.

90 A. L. Rowse, 'My Acquaintance with Churchill', in his *Memories of Men and Women* (London, 1980), 1–25; Rowse to Churchill, 19 Apr. 1958, Churchill Papers, 4/67B.

91 David Cannadine, *G. M. Trevelyan: A Life in History* (London, 1992), 16, 18, 90, 130, 133, 135–6, 139; Rowse, *Memories of Men and Women*, 101.

92 Linda Colley, *Lewis Namier* (London, 1989), 40, 42; A. L. Rowse, *All Souls and Appeasement* (London, 1961), 116; Moran, *Churchill*, 354; *The Times*, 9 Mar. 1959.

93 A. L. Rowse, *Historians I Have Known* (London, 1995), 117; Rowse, *Friends and Contemporaries* (London, 1989), 102–3; A. L. Rowse, *Portraits and Views* (London, 1979), 67, 184–9; A. J. P. Taylor, *A Personal History* (Coronet edn London, 1984), 146–7.

94 Pamela Street, *Portrait of a Historian* (London, 1979), 110–11, 119; Rowse, *Friends and Contemporaries*, 104; Roberts, *Eminent Churchillians*, 287; Montague Browne, *Long Sunset*, 318.

95 Street, *Portrait of a Historian*, 120, 142, 194; Arthur Bryant, *Spirit of England* (London, 1982), 42, 233; Rowse, *Friends and Contemporaries*, 95, 104–5, 110.

96 Kathy Burk, *Troublemaker: The Life and History of A. J. P. Taylor* (London, 2000), 412.

97 Chris Wrigley ed., *A. J. P. Taylor: A Complete Annotated Bibliography* (Hassocks, Sussex, 1980), 57, 93, 163, 195,

226, 373, 471; Taylor, *Personal History*, 195, 198, 218; Robert Cole, *A. J. P. Taylor: The Traitor within the Gates* (London, 1993), 208–9; A. J. P. Taylor, *English History, 1914–1945* (Oxford, 1965), 4; Rowse, *Historians*, 132; Rowse, *Portraits and Views*, 198–200; A. J. P. Taylor, *The Origins of the Second World War* (Penguin edn, Harmondsworth, 1964), 17–18, 85, 343, 349.

98 Sir Arthur Salusbury McNalty, *The Three Churchills* (London, 1949), 266.

99 Alistair Cooke ed., *General Eisenhower on the Military Churchill* (New York, 1970), 85.

100 Hughes, *Churchill in War and Peace* and *Churchill, British Bulldog*.

101 R. L. Tames, *Winston Churchill: An Informal Study of Greatness* (New York, 1952), 3.

102 Berlin, *Mr Churchill*, 39.

103 H. Ausbel et al. eds *Some Modern Historians of Britain* (New York, 1951), 306–24.

104 Anthony Montague Browne, quoted in BBC radio, *Living with Churchill*.

105 Broad, *Churchill*, 552–3; Churchill did not choose to compare himself to the rather lesser figures like Pearl S. Buck who had also been recent recipients of the Nobel Prize for Literature. The lack of regard was mutual: Buck thought his Fulton speech of 1946 to be 'a catastrophe' and concluded nervously that 'we are nearer war tonight' as a result of what Churchill had said. Harbutt, 'Fulton Speech', 103. Hemingway was quoted in Geoffrey Bocca, *Winston Churchill*, supplement published by *Cosmopolitan*, 1960, 51.

106 Stephen Ambrose, 'Churchill and Eisenhower in the Second World War', in Louis and Blake, *Churchill*, 406.

107 Stewart, *Churchill as Speaker and Writer*, 69; The Times, *The Churchill Years* (London, 1965) 185.

108 Bibescu, *Churchill, ou le courage*, 171; David Green, *Sir Winston Churchill at Blenheim Palace* (Oxford, 1959), 27.

109 Peter Boyle ed., *The Churchill–Eisenhower Correspondence, 1953–1955* (Chapel Hill, North Carolina, 1990), 203; in 1953 Eisenhower was even attempting a painting of Churchill from a photograph supplied by the subject himself.

110 Walter Graebner, *My Dear Mr Churchill* (Boston, Massachusetts, 1965), chapter XIII.

111 *The Times*, 5, 7, 13, 18 and 31 Mar., 23 and 30 Apr. and 4 and 8 Aug. 1959.

112 Virginia Cowles, *Winston Churchill: The Man and the Era* (New York, 1953), 361.

113 Alan Farrell, *Sir Winston Churchill* (London, 1962), 121; John Colville, *The Churchillians* (London, 1981), 27.

114 Gerald Sparrow, *Winston Churchill: Man of the Century* (London, 1965).

115 John Colville, *The Fringes of Power: Downing Street Diaries, 1939–1955* (London, 1985), 653.

116 Taylor, *Churchill*, 368; Colin Coote ed., *Winston Churchill's Maxims and Reflections* (London, 1947); F. B. Czardomski, *The Eloquence of Winston Churchill* (New York, 1957).

117 Humes, *Churchill*, 238–9; Montague Browne, *Long Sunset*, 305; *New York Times*, 29 Apr. 1965 and 9 Apr. 1967; Smith, *Churchill*, 22.

118 Menzies diary, 12 Aug. 1948, Menzies Papers, series 13, box 397, National Library of Australia; Casey diary, 26 Jan. to 1 Feb. 1965, Casey Papers, series 4, box 31, National Library of Australia; Moran, *Churchill*, 314, 515–16, 550, 699.

119 Broad, *Churchill*, 526; Kenneth Young ed., *Diaries of Sir Robert Bruce Lockhart, 1939–1965* (London, 1980), 625; Manfred Weidhorn, *Churchill's Rhetoric and Political Discourse* (Lanham, Maryland, Exxon Education Foundation Series, vol. 17, 1987), 98.

120 Montague Browne, *Long Sunset*, 113.

121 Rosten, *People*, 109; *New York Times*, 11 Apr. 1957; Adler, *Churchill Wit*, 29.

122 Humes, *Churchill*, 248.

123 Malcolm Muggeridge, *Chronicles of Wasted Time*, vol. 1: *The Green Stick* (Fontana edn, London, 1975), 44; George Lichtheim, 'Winston Churchill, Sketch for a Portrait', *Midstream*, Winter 1959, 3.

124 Marchant ed., *Churchill*, 137; Churchill quoted in Gilbert, *Churchill: A Life*, 86.

125 Quoted in Hughes, *Churchill in War and Peace*, 226.

126 Ramsden, *Age of Churchill and Eden*, 219. His riding to hounds on the eve of his seventy-fourth birthday had a similar effect; Young, *Bruce Lockhart Diaries, 1939–65*, 719–20; Gilbert,

Churchill: A Life, 882. Robert Rhodes James, 'Churchill the Parliamentarian, Orator and Statesman', in Blake and Louis, *Churchill*, 517.

127 Sheridan Morley, *Robert, my Father* (Orion edn, London, 1994), 259.

128 Black, *Churchill*, 9.

129 Marchant, *Churchill*; the other authors included Lord Norwich, Leo Amery, Sir Robert Menzies, Gilbert Murray, Bernard Baruch, Lord Simon and Lord Cecil of Chelwood.

130 Cawthorne, *Churchill Legend*, 92.

131 Bloncourt, *Old and Young Leader*, 92.

132 Quoted in David Reynolds, *Rich Relations: The American Occupation of Britain, 1942–1945* (New York, 1995), 176.

133 Marchant, *Churchill*, 139; *New York Times*, 22 June 1955.

134 Dean Acheson, *Sketches from Life* (New York, 1959), 78–9.

135 Cowles, *Churchill*, vii.

136 Berlin, *Mr Churchill*, 39; James Marlow in the *Norfolk Ledger Star*, 8 April 1963. It was not only the Sutherland painting that upset Churchill, for in 1957 he was embroiled in a row with a fellow Academician who had exhibited a Churchill portrait that made him 'very annoyed'. *New York Times*, 4 May 1957.

137 Booth, *True Story*, 134.

138 Cowles, *Churchill*, 370; *New York Times Magazine*, 5 Apr. 1964.

139 Quoted in *The Williamsburg Award* (Williamsburg, Virginia), 1957.

140 Robin Fedden, *Churchill at Chartwell* (London, 1969), 5; Keller, *Churchill*, 105.

141 Graebner, *Mr Churchill*, 116.

142 'Dean Acheson's Intimate Recollections of Winston Churchill', *Saturday Evening Post*, 18 Mar. 1961, 23.

143 Reader's Digest, *Man of the Century: A Churchill Cavalcade* (Boston, Massachusetts, 1965), v.

144 Keller, *Churchill*, 112.

145 Winston Churchill, *Thoughts and Adventures* (Odhams edn London, 1947), 20.

146 Taylor, *Churchill*, 403; Robert Rhodes James ed., *Chips: The Diaries of Sir Henry Channon* (London, 1967), 180; *New York Times*, 13 Nov. 1964; Rowse, *End of an Epoch*, 82, 84.

147 Transcript of final meeting of Churchill and Truman, 18 Jan. 1952, Harry S.

Truman Presidential Papers, GF box 115, file 'Churchill, Winston, meeting with President Truman, January 1952, I', Truman Library. 'Diary, week of May 4, 1959', Dwight D. Eisenhower Presidential Papers, DDE Diary series, box 41, Eisenhower Library.

148 Coolidge, *Churchill*, 262; *New York Times*, 13 Apr. 1955.

149 Graebner, *Mr Churchill*, 117.

150 Charles E. Frank, *Six Franks Abroad* (New York, 1967), 83.

151 Paul Manning and Milton Bronner, *Mr England: The Life Story of Winston Churchill, the Fighting Briton* (Philadelphia, 1941).

152 A. L. Rowse, *The English Spirit* (London, 1944); *The West in English History* (London, 1949); *The Early Churchills* (New York, 1956); *The Churchills from Marlborough to the Present* (New York, 1958); *The Spirit of English History* 8, 130, 132.

153 Rowse, 'Churchill in History', 492–507.

154 Stephen Graubard, *Burke, Disraeli and Churchill: The Politics of Perseverance* (Cambridge, Massachusetts, 1961).

155 Aubrey de Selincourt, *Six Great Englishmen* (London, 1953), 214 and passim.

156 Donald McFarlan, *Four Great Leaders*, Background to Modern Africa series (London, 1954).

157 Rowse, 'Churchill in History', 502; Hughes, *Churchill, British Bulldog*, 280; Reader's Digest, *Man of the Century*, 272; A. L. Rowse, 'Ernest Bevin', in his *Memoirs and Glimpses* (London, 1986).

158 Rowse, *All Souls*, 113; Chris Cook and John Ramsden eds, *By-Elections in British Politics* (2nd edn London, 1997), 117.

159 Rowse, *Memories of Men and Women*, 2.

160 Stewart, *Churchill as Writer and Speaker*, v (anonymous introduction to British edition).

161 Geoffrey Bruun, in *New York Times Magazine*, 27 Apr. 1957; McNalty was quite open about such an aim, but it is best seen in D. S. McBirnie, *Winston Churchill, Conservative* (no publisher or date given, but American in origin and apparently shortly after 1965).

162 Quoted in the *English Historical Review*, CX, no. 438, Sept. 1995, 948; Montague

Browne, *Long Sunset*, 110, 163, 228; Margaret Mein, *Winston Churchill and Christian Fellowship* (Stockwell, Ilfracombe, 1992), 13, 26–8; Robert Rhodes James ed. *Winston S. Churchill: His Complete Speeches, 1897–1963* (London, 1974), speech of 14 Jan. 1928; Winston Churchill, *History of the English-Speaking Peoples*, vol. 2: *The New World* (London, 1956), 70, 123–4, 270.

163 Winston Churchill, *Never Give In*, an anthology with introduction by Dwight Eisenhower (Kansas City, Missouri, 1967); Joad quoted by James Marlow in the *Daily Mail*, Hagerstown, Maryland, 9 Apr. 1963.

164 *New York Times*, 5 May 1959, 1 Dec. 1960.

165 Booth, *True Story*, 132; Moran, *Churchill*, 703.

166 Norman McGowan, *My Years with Churchill* (New York, 1958), 88.

167 Cawthorne, *Churchill Legend*, 118–19; Montague Browne, *Long Sunset*, 121.

168 Acheson, *Sketches*, 83–4.

169 Statement sent by Eisenhower to New York World's Fair, 9 May 1965, Dwight D. Eisenhower Post-Presidential Papers, 1965 Principal File, folder 2, Eisenhower Library; David Dilks, *Sir Winston Churchill* (London, 1965), 88.

170 Dumas Malone in *New York Times Magazine*, 4 Dec. 1955; *New York Times Book Magazine*, 25 Nov. 1955.

171 'Sir Winston Churchill, Fifty Years On', speech by Rt Hon. Margaret Thatcher MP, 9 May 1990, British Information Services, Policy Statement, 28/90.

172 Graham Cawthorne, *A Visitor's Guide to Winston Churchill* (London, 1974); A. L. Rowse, *Heritage of Britain* (London, 1977), 111–12.

173 David Cannadine ed., *The Speeches of Winston Churchill* (London, 1990), 319; Lord and Lady Longford, 'Winston Churchill', in Lord Longford and Sir John Wheeler-Bennett eds, *The History Makers* (London, 1973), 169.

174 *Memorial Addresses in the US Congress*, House document 209 (Washington DC, US Government Printing Office, 1965), 62, 110, 117.

175 Marchant, *Churchill*, 1.

176 R. W. Thompson, *The Yankee Marlborough* (London, 1973), 8.

177 William Shakespeare, *Richard III*, Act

III, scene 1; *Punch* cartoon in W. L. Germains, *The Tragedy of Winston Churchill* (London, 1931), 224.

178 Winston Churchill, *Heroes of History* (no editor or place of publication given but USA, 1968).

179 See Nathan Miller, *Theodore Roosevelt* (New York, 1992), 325, 412, 511, 541; Gilbert, *Churchill: A Life*, 138, 395

180 Mark Bonham Carter and Mark Pottle eds, *Lantern Slides: The Diaries and Letters of Violet Bonham Carter 1904–1914* (London, 1996), 356. Jonathan Sikorsky, 'From British Cassandra to American Hero', in *Finest Hour*, 108, 30.

181 *Ibid.*, 393.

182 Longfords, 'Winston Churchill', 168.

CHAPTER 4: *'I Must Justify Myself before History'*: Fulton and the War Memoirs

1 Pamela Street, *Portrait of a Historian* (London, 1979), 133.

2 We have also seen how open he had already been about his intention to write the history of the events in which he had figured, to his own advantage.

3 In view of occasional comments on the paradox that Churchill should in March 1946 have become more famous for using the phrase 'iron curtain' which had allegedly originated from Josef Goebbels and/or the Nazi Minister of Finance, it may be as well to give the real background. 'Iron curtain' was first used by the Queen of Belgium to describe the division of her country by the German invasion of 1914, and was first applied to Russia by the British socialist Ethel Snowden. Churchill borrowed it to describe Russia after the 1917 Revolution in *The World Crisis*, and thus used it long before the Nazis. In 1944–5 it was fairly widely applied to Eastern Europe after the advance of the Red Army, by *The Times* in an editorial as well as by Germans. At that time Churchill also used it in a telegram to Truman and – in the version 'an iron fence' – he had even used it to Stalin face to face (and received the reply, 'All fairy stories!'). There is nothing surprising in Churchill in the 1940s giving new fame

to a well-worn phrase, for the same can be said of 'Blood, sweat and tears' and of 'Never . . . has so much been owed . . . to so many' which Churchill himself had been using pretty continuously ever since the Edwardian period. For the origins of the other phrases referred to above, see recent editions of *Bartlett's Familiar Quotations*.

4 Arthur Booth, *The True Story of Winston Churchill* (Chicago, 1958), 128; Booth was assigned to follow Churchill on his overseas travels by the Press Association.

5 John Ramsden, *'That Will Depend on Who Writes the History.' Winston Churchill as his own Historian*, Inaugural Lecture published by Queen Mary and Westfield College (London, 1997), also included in W. Roger Louis, *More Adventures with Britannia* (Austin, Texas, 1999).

6 See for example Melvyn P. Leffler, *The Specter of Communism: The United States and the Origins of the Cold War, 1917–1953* (New York, 1994), 52–3; Martin Walker, *The Cold War* (London, 1994), 37–9; and especially Fraser J. Harbutt, *The Iron Curtain: Churchill, America and the Origins of the Cold War* (Oxford, 1986).

7 As argued by Harbutt, *Iron Curtain*, 152 and *passim*.

8 Churchill's visit to the United States in January–March 1946 produced a dozen specific correspondence and speech files that have survived, as well as documents in many other areas of the collection, and even all this seems not to include most of the three thousand or so letters to him from ordinary American citizens.

9 William E. Parrish, *Westminster College: An Informal History* (Fulton, Missouri, 1971), 211.

10 Churchill to Truman, 29 Jan. 1946, Truman to Churchill, 2 Feb. 1946, Churchill Papers, at Churchill College, Cambridge [hereafter CP] 2/158; Churchill to Frank McCluer, 30 Jan. 1946, CP 2/230; analysis of speeches, Jan. 1945 to June 1947, 27 June 1947, CP 5/1; Charles Ross diary, 7 Mar. 1946, Truman Library.

11 Speech notes, Fulton speech, 5 Mar. 1946, CP 5/3; Churchill to Truman, 8 Nov. 1945, Churchill to Frank McCluer, 5 Feb. 1946, CP 2/230.

12 Churchill to Col. Clarke, 1 Jan. 1946, CP 2/225; Miss Sturdee to Charles Campbell, 2 Feb. 1946, CP 2/224; Miss Sturdee to Philip Clarke, 4 Feb. 1946, CP 2/224; Halifax to Churchill, 3 Feb. 1946, Hickleton Papers, 4/11 (microfilm at Churchill College); R. H. Pilpel, *Churchill in America* (New York, 1976), 216; Harbutt, *Iron Curtain*, 168; Parrish, *Westminster College*, 201.

13 Speech notes, Fulton, 5 Mar. 1946, City Banquet in New York, 15 Mar. 1946, CP 5/4.

14 Speech notes, House of Commons, 22 Oct. 1946, CP 5/1; speech notes, House of Commons, 7 Nov. 1946, CP 5/2; Martin Gilbert, *Winston S. Churchill.* vol. 8: *Never Despair, 1945–1965* (London, 1988), 161.

15 Gilbert, *Churchill*, vol. 8, 180; speech notes, House of Commons, 7 Nov. 1945, CP 5/2.

16 Speech notes, Brussels, 16 Nov. 1945, CP 5/2.

17 Speech notes, House of Commons, 13 Dec. 1945, CP 5/2; speech notes, Miami, 26 Feb. 1946, CP 5/4.

18 Account of Clark Clifford, Truman's Counsel, quoted in Gilbert, *Churchill*, vol. 8, 196. The story was broadly confirmed by Charles Ross, Truman's press secretary, and another of the poker-players of 1946, Charles Ross Diary, Truman Library.

19 Churchill to Truman, 29 Nov. 1945, CP 2/230.

20 F. H. Harbutt, 'The Fulton Speech and the Iran Crisis of 1946: A Turning Point in American Foreign Policy', PhD thesis, University of California, Berkeley, 1979; see also summaries of radio commentaries and press reactions sent to Churchill from the White House Press Office, 7 Mar. 1946, CP 2/29; W. A. White to Churchill, 9 Mar. 1946, CP 2/230. Harbutt argues that the readiness of most Americans to accept from Churchill that there was a problem in respect of the Soviet Union which had to be addressed meant that even those who initially rejected his prescription of an alliance were eventually drawn into that too, because there was no other policy on offer to deal with the problem that they now

acknowledged, a device that owed something to the cunning with which Churchill had made his two major propositions at Fulton (without ever formally linking them), but which was not spotted by the opponents of the speech until too late. Harbutt, *Iron Curtain*, 203.

21 The telegrams and many others are filed in CP 2/226. Mail analysis from Consul-General, 27 Mar. 1946, CP 2/229; National Maritime Union to Truman, copied to Churchill, 17 Mar. 1946, CP 2/226; Virginia Cowles, *Winston Churchill: The Man and the Era* (New York, 1953), 357; Pilpel, *Churchill in America*, 228.

22 Notes by Charles Murphy on Churchill's dinner with *Time* staff, 13 Mar. 1966, Halle Papers, folder 48(1), Kennedy Library.

23 Churchill's secretary to Charles Campbell, 24 Jan. 1946, CP 2/224; Miss Sturdee to Philip Hayden, Columbia University, 22 Feb. 1946, CP 2/225; mail analysis by British Consul, Miami, 12 Mar. 1946, CP 2/228; note on New York mail by British Consul-General, 27 Mar. 1946, CP 2/229; note on logistic arrangements for trip, 10 Jan. 1946, CP 2/229; and see Harbutt, *Iron Curtain*, 227.

24 Churchill to Halifax, 9 Dec. 1945, CP 2/227; Churchill to Duff Cooper, 7 Apr. 1946, CP 2/5; Washington Embassy to Churchill, 18 Feb. 1946, CP 2/225.

25 Churchill to Alfred Barnes, 14 Dec. 1946, CP 2/228; Miss Gillette to Burke Trend, 3 Dec. 1946, and attached correspondence, CP 1/41; Gilbert, *Churchill*, vol. 8, 173–4; Lord Moran, *Winston Churchill: The Struggle for Survival, 1940–1965* (Sphere Books edn, London, 1968), 339.

26 Sarah Oliver to Churchill, 1 Apr. 1946, CP 1/41; Harold Braham to Churchill, 12 Mar. 1946, CP 2/224.

27 Halifax to Churchill, 7 Mar. 1946, CP 2/225; Philip C. Clarke to Churchill, 4 Feb. 1946, CP 2/224; Churchill to Attlee, 29 May 1946, CP 2/4.

28 National Maritime Union to President Truman, 17 Mar. 1946, J. E. Mason to Churchill, 16 Mar. 1946, and 'A Texan', Ned Tankersley to Churchill, 15 Mar. 1946, CP 2/226.

29 *Sunday Pictorial*, 26 Jan. 1947; transcript

of broadcast enclosed with Randolph Churchill to Winston Churchill, 2 Nov. 1946, CP 1/41.

30 Churchill to Halifax, 9 Dec. 1945, CP 2/227; Churchill to Alfred Barnes, 14 Dec. 1946, CP 2/228.

31 Churchill to Truman, 8 Nov. 1945, Harry S. Truman Presidential Papers, General File, GF 115, 'Churchill, Winston', Truman Library; Harbutt, *Iron Curtain*, 171; Churchill to Attlee, 7 Mar. 1946, and Attlee to Churchill, 14 Mar. 1946, CP 2/4; Ben Pimlott ed., *Political Diary of Hugh Dalton, 1918–40, 1945–60* (London, 1986), 366.

32 Halifax to Churchill, 3 Dec. 1945, CP 2/227.

33 Halifax to Churchill, 8 Feb. 1946, CP 2/227; Halifax diary quoted in Harbutt, *Iron Curtain*, 162; Halifax to Churchill, 14 Mar. 1946, CP 2/6.

34 Halifax to Churchill, 16 Mar. 1946, CP 2/26.

35 Harbutt, *Iron Curtain*, 171–2; David McCullough, *Truman* (New York, 1992), 490.

36 *Ottawa Journal*, 5 Mar. 1946; J. N. Henderson to Churchill, 11 Apr. 1946, CP 2/3, Walker, *Cold War*, 43: Alan Bullock, *Ernest Bevin: Foreign Secretary, 1945–51* (London, 1983), 222, 225–6; John Charmley, *Churchill's Grand Alliance* (London, 1995), 226; Francis Williams ed., *A Prime Minister Remembers* (London, 1961), 162.

37 Gilbert, *Churchill*, vol. 8, 162; King to Churchill, 1 Mar. 1946, CP 2/7; Harbutt, *Iron Curtain*, 162; King to Churchill, 6 Mar. 1946, CP 2/228; King to Churchill, 14 Mar. 1946 (enclosing King to Attlee, 5 Mar. 1946), and King to Churchill, 16 Mar. 1946, CP 2/7.

38 Churchill to Eden, enclosing correspondence with Bevin, 12 Apr. 1946, CP 2/5; Attlee to Churchill, 9 Oct. 1946, CP 2/4; Harbutt, *Iron Curtain*, 211; John Ramsden, *The Age of Churchill and Eden, 1940–1957* (London, 1995), 196.

39 David Dutton, *Anthony Eden* (London, 1997), 319–20; Duff Cooper to Churchill, 2 Apr. 1946, CP 2/5; James Stuart to Churchill, 7 Mar. 1946, and Churchill to Halifax, 10 Apr. 1946, CP 2/6.

40 Churchill to Truman, 29 Jan. 1946, CP 2/158; General Eaker to Churchill, 28 Jan. 1946, CP 2/226; Churchill to

General Motors, 25 Jan. 1946, Churchill to Col. Clarke, 10 Dec. 1945, CP 2/225; Churchill to Truman, 14 Feb. 1946, CP 2/158; schedule for train journey, 4–7 Mar. 1946, CP 2/230.

41 Diary of Charles Ross, 7 Mar. 1946, Truman Library; Churchill to Truman, 7 Mar. 1946, CP 2/158; Pilpel, *Churchill in America*, 218.

42 Truman to Churchill, 27 Sept. 1949, CP 2/158; John Colville, *The Churchillians* (London, 1983), 102.

43 Speech notes for Fulton speech, 5 Mar. 1946, CP 5/4; the idea that the 'iron curtain' paragraph was added at the last minute has been popularly believed for years, but is impossible to prove from the speech file in the Churchill papers. It is given some credibility, though, from the fact that the paragraph was on its own (incomplete) page in the press release, and was not included at all in the advance copies issued to the Eastern press before Churchill left Washington. Some Eastern papers did not therefore include any reference to the speech's most famous passage in their first reports.

44 Speech notes and preparatory papers for House of Commons speech, 7 Nov. 1945, CP 5/2; Churchill to Truman, 8 Nov. 1945, CP 2/4; Harbutt, *Iron Curtain*, 161; Churchill to Attlee, 7 Mar. 1946, CP 2/4.

45 Churchill to Truman, 29 Nov. 1945, CP 2/230; Churchill to Truman, 29 Jan. 1946, CP 2/158; Henry Norweb to Truman, 7 Feb. 1946, Harry S. Truman Presidential Papers, General File, GF115, 'Churchill, Winston, 1945–46', Truman Library; Churchill to Attlee, 7 Mar. 1946, CP 2/4; diary of Charles Ross, 18 Mar. 1946, Truman Library; *News and Observer*, Raleigh, North Carolina, 20 Mar. 1946; Walter Isaacson and Evan Thomas, *The Wise Men* (London, 1986), 363.

46 Speech notes, General Assembly of Virginia, 8 Mar. 1946, CP 5/4; Victor Todd to Churchill, 15 Mar. 1946, CP 2/226.

47 Pilpel, *Churchill in America*, 221; Dean Acheson, *Sketches from Life* (New York, 1959), 62.

48 Harbutt, *Iron Curtain*, 199; James Forrestal to Churchill, 8 Mar. 1946, CP

2/26; Harriman to Churchill, 19 Mar. 1946, CP 2/227; Truman to Churchill, 12 Mar. 1946, CP 2/158; Churchill himself still used code on some occasions, signing confidential telegrams as 'Colonel Warden' as in the war years; Truman's notes for Fulton, 5 Mar. 1946, Harry S. Truman Presidential Papers, General File, GF box 115, 'Churchill, Winston, 1945–46', Truman Library; Walter Millis ed., *The Forrestal Diaries* (London, 1952), 151, 159.

49 Lewis Brown to Churchill, 19 Mar. 1946, CP 2/224; Max Gordon to Churchill, 16 Mar. 1946, CP 2/226; Mail analysis by New York Consul-General, 27 Mar. 1946, and Rockefeller to Churchill, 19 Mar. 1946, CP 2/229; Harbutt, *Iron Curtain*, 204.

50 Halifax to Churchill, 15 Apr. 1946, CP 2/6; Truman to Churchill, 14 Oct. 1947, CP 2/158.

51 Clarke to Churchill, 4 Apr. 1946, CP 2/225; Churchill to Attlee, 7 Mar. 1946, CP 2/4; Randolph S. Churchill ed., *The Sinews of Peace; Winston S. Churchill Post-War Speeches* (London, 1948), 93, 226; Harbutt, *Iron Curtain*, 181, 215; Lewis Brown to Churchill, 19 Mar. 1946, CP 2/224; for once Bevin was quite wrong about Churchill, saying of the Fulton speech that Churchill 'invariably said the right thing at the wrong time'. Harbutt, *Iron Curtain*, 222.

52 Moran, *Churchill*, 332; Clarke to Churchill, 4 Apr. 1946, CP 2/225; Harbutt, *Iron Curtain* 4; Gilbert, *Churchill*, vol. 8, 220.

53 Randolph Churchill ed., *In the Balance: Winston Churchill Speeches, 1949 and 1950* (Boston, Massachusetts, 1951), 49; *Life*, 14 Apr. 1947, *Daily Telegraph*, 15 Apr. 1947.

54 Churchill, *Sinews of Peace*, v; A. L. Rowse, 'Churchill's Place in History', in Charles Eade ed., *Churchill by his Contemporaries* (London, 1953), 504.

55 Quentin Reynolds, *Winston Churchill* (New York, 1963), 162.

56 Martin Gilbert, *Winston Churchill*, a Clarendon Biography for young people (London, 1966), 102.

57 Notes by Charles Murphy on Churchill's dinner with *Time* staff, 13 Mar. 1966, Halle Papers, folder 48(1), Kennedy Library.

58 David Cannadine ed., *The Speeches of Winston Churchill* (London, 1990), 397; A. G. S. Norris, *A Very Great Soul* (Edinburgh, 1957), 254.

59 J. G. Lockhart, *Winston Churchill* (London, 1951), 156.

60 Diana Coolidge, *Winston Churchill and the Story of Two World Wars* (Boston, Massachusetts, 1960), 266.

61 Among the better-written and more serious such books were David Dilks, *Sir Winston Churchill* (London, 1965), A. M. Gollin, *From Omdurman to VE Day* (London, 1964), and Gilbert, *Churchill* (the Clarendon Biography cited in note 56 above), all three books by real historians which were targeted at schoolchildren.

62 James Humes, *Churchill: Speaker of the Century* (New York, 1980), 242; Winston Churchill, *Great Contemporaries* (Fontana edn London, 1959), 63; Roland Quinault, 'Joseph Chamberlain, a Reassessment', in T. R. Gourvish and Alan O'Day, *Later Victorian Britain* (London, 1988), 69–71.

63 Ramsden, *Age of Churchill and Eden*, 101, 178

64 Richard Langworth, *A Connoisseur's Guide to the Books of Sir Winston Churchill* (London, 1998), 283–6, 294–7.

65 MacDonald, *Titans*, 89; Stewart, *Churchill as Speaker*, 101.

66 Stephen Graubard, *Burke, Disraeli and Churchill: The Politics of Perseverance* (Cambridge, Massachusetts, 1961), 219; *New York Times*, 18 Oct. 1955.

67 Quoted in Merrill D. Peterson, *Lincoln in American Memory* (New York, 1994), 116.

68 F. W. Deakin, *Churchill as Historian*, Churchill Memorial Lecture, Winston Churchill Foundation (Zurich, 1968), 18; Maurice Ashley, *Churchill as Historian* (New York, 1968), 159, 169; John Connell, *Winston Churchill*, British Council Writers and their Work series, no. 80 (London, 1956), 37; Moran, *Churchill*, 759–60; Kenneth Young ed., *Diaries of Sir Robert Bruce Lockhart, 1939–1965* (London, 1980), 675, 724; Pimlott, *Dalton Diary*, 437.

69 Peter Hennessy, *Muddling Through* (London, 1996), 191.

70 Winston Churchill to President Truman, 5 May 1948; Memorandum for the

President by Admiral Leahy, 11 May 1948, President Truman to Winston Churchill, 18 May 1948, Harry S. Truman Presidential Papers, GF box 115, file 'Churchill, Winston S., 1947–1950', Truman Library.

71 Winston Churchill to Harry S. Truman, 30 Mar. 1953, Harry S. Truman Post-Presidential papers, Name file, box 59, file 'Churchill, 1953–1956', Truman Library.

72 Winston Churchill to President Truman, 12 Feb. 1951, Harry S. Truman Presidential Papers, GF box 115, file 'Churchill, Winston S., 1951–1953', Truman Library.

73 'Dean Acheson's intimate recollections of Winston Churchill', *Saturday Evening Post*, 18 Mar. 1961; Princeton seminar file, box 39, transcript of meeting on 11–13 Dec. 1953, Dean Acheson Papers, Truman Library; Philip Williams ed., *Diary of Hugh Gaitskell, 1945–1956* (London, 1983), 310, 312.

74 Young, *Bruce Lockhart Diaries, 1939–1965*, 667; Winston Churchill to President Eisenhower, 18 Mar. 1955, Dwight D. Eisenhower Presidential Papers, International series, box 19, file 'Eisenhower–Churchill, Jan. 1955–Apr. 1955', Eisenhower Library.

75 Winston Churchill to General Eisenhower, 23 June 1962, Dwight D. Eisenhower Post-Presidential Papers, 1962 Principal file, box 31, Eisenhower Library.

76 Robin Prior, *Churchill's World Crisis as History* (London, 1983), chapter 13; David Reynolds, 'Churchill's Writing of History: Appeasement, Autobiography and *The Gathering Storm*', *Transactions of the Royal Historical Society*, 6th series, vol. 11, 225.

77 Martin Gilbert, *Winston Churchill and Emery Reves: Correspondence, 1937–64* (Austin, Texas, 1997), 317; John Colville, *The Fringes of Power: Downing Street Diaries, 1939–1955* (London, 1985), 658; Robert Eden, 'History as Post-war Statecraft in Churchill's War Memoirs', conference paper, Woodrow Wilson Center, Washington DC, 1996, to be published in J. W. Muller ed., *The Post-War Churchill*, forthcoming, title provisional.

78 Winston Churchill to President

Eisenhower, 9 April. 1953, Dwight D. Eisenhower Presidential Papers, International series, box 18, file 'Esenhower–Churchill, Jan. 1953–May 1953', Eisenhower Library; Winston Churchill to Harry S. Truman, 30 Mar. 1953, Harry S. Truman Post-Presidential Papers, Name file, box 59, file 'Churchill, 1953–1956', Truman Library.

79 William Hillman to Harry S. Truman, 18 May 1953, Harry S. Truman Post-Presidential Papers, Name file, box 59, file 'Churchill, 1953–1956', Truman Library.

80 Ramsden, *Age of Churchill and Eden*, 177.

81 Gilbert, *Churchill and Reves*, 298, 300–3; General Eisenhower to Winston Churchill, 16 Feb. 1949, Dwight D. Eisenhower Pre-Presidential Papers, Name series, box 22, file 'Churchill, 2', Eisenhower Library.

82 *Atlantic Monthly*, 1954, 23–32.

83 John Kenneth Galbraith, The Churchill Production', *Esquire*, 24 Oct. 1978, 34.

84 Winston Churchill to General Eisenhower, 22 Jan. 1946, Dwight D. Eisenhower Pre-Presidential Papers, Name series, box 22, file 'Churchill, 2', Eisenhower Library; Reynolds, 'Churchill's Writing of History', 221.

85 General Eisenhower to Viscount Montgomery, 3 Nov. 1948, Dwight D. Eisenhower Pre-Presidential Papers, Name series, box 82, file 'Montgomery, 6', Eisenhower Library.

86 Cowles, *Churchill*, 362; Langworth, *Connoisseur's Guide*, 258.

87 *New York Times*, 11 May 1959.

88 Ismay to Eisenhower, 11 Oct. 1951, Dwight D. Eisenhower Pre-Presidential Papers, Name series, box 60, file 'Ismay, 1', Eisenhower Library.

89 Frederick Woods, *Artillery of Words: The Writings of Sir Winston Churchill* (London, 1992), 139, 142.

90 Letter from David Clarke, formerly Director of the Conservative Research Department, to John Ramsden, 12 Oct. 1996; Moran, *Churchill*, 495, 642; Reynolds, 'Churchill's Writing of History', 245.

91 President Eisenhower to General Ismay, 25 Jan. 1958, Dwight D. Eisenhower Presidential Papers, Name series, box 19,

file 'Ismay, 2'; General Ismay to President Eisenhower, 4 Nov. 1960, Dwight D. Eisenhower Presidential Papers, Name series, box 19, file 'Ismay 3', Eisenhower Library; Colville, *Churchillians*, 125; Moran, *Churchill*, 777.

92 Lord Ismay to President Eisenhower, 30 Dec. 1960, Dwight D. Eisenhower Presidential Papers, box 19, file 'Ismay, 3', Eisenhower Library.

93 President Eisenhower to Winston Churchill, 25 Jan. 1954, Dwight D. Eisenhower Presidential Papers, International series, box 19, file 'Eisenhower–Churchill, Jan 1954–June 1954', Eisenhower Library (emphasis added in quotation).

94 Lord Ismay to President Eisenhower, 2 Dec. 1960, Dwight D. Eisenhower Presidential Papers, box 19, file 'Ismay, 3', Eisenhower Library.

95 Quoted in Norman Rose, *Churchill, the Unruly Giant* (New York, 1994), 55; Martin Gilbert, 'Winston Churchill and the Strain of Office, 1914–1915', in Hugh Cecil and Peter Liddle eds, *Facing Armageddon: The First World War Experienced* (London, 1996), 36; Colville, *Churchillians*, 70.

96 Booth, *True Story of Winston Churchill*, 135–6.

97 Langworth, *Connoisseur's Guide*, 254–82; Gilbert, *Churchill and Reves*, 18.

98 Reynolds, 'Churchill's Writing of History', 223.

99 *Ibid.*, 224.

100 Robert Blake, 'Winston Churchill as Historian', lecture given in 1990 and published by the University of Texas, but also included in W. Roger Louis ed., *Adventures with Britannia: Personalities, Politics and Culture in Britain* (Austin, Texas, 1995), 42.

101 *New York Times*, 17 July 1960, 27 Nov. 1960.

102 *The Times* and the *Daily Worker*, 30 Apr. 1964; *New York Times*, 11 Nov. 1964; *Washington Evening Star*, 24 Nov. 1964.

103 Jack Le Vien and John Lord, *The Valiant Years* (London, 1963), vii, 286.

104 *The Times*, 21 July 1971; 8 and 19 July 1972; Anthony Montague Browne, *Long Sunset: The Memoirs of Winston Churchill's Last Private Secretary*

(London, 1995), 236; Jim Golland, *Not Winston, Just William? Winston Churchill at Harrow School* (Harrow, 1988), 5, 25, 39.

105 Winston Churchill, 'Japan Guesses Wrong', *Collier's*, 30 July 1938; Churchill's 1941 remark was noted down by the usually reliable American journalist John Gunther. Quoted in Nigel Hamilton, *JFK: Reckless Youth* (New York, 1992), 453; it seems that, in view of their admiration for Churchill, neither Gunther nor Kennedy, nor Clare Booth Luce who also knew of the story, put it into print.

106 Dutton, *Eden*, 67; Reynolds, 'Churchill's Writing of History', 233, 236. I acknowledge the wider debt I owe to David Dutton and David Reynolds in respect of this section of my argument; Stuart Ball, 'Churchill and the Conservative Party', *Transactions of the Royal Historical Society*, 6th series, vol. 11, 316–17.

107 Reynolds, 'Churchill's Writing of History', 240; Prior, *Churchill's World Crisis*, *passim* but especially chapter 9; Montague Browne, *Long Sunset*, 131.

108 Richard Powers, 'Winston Churchill's Parliamentary Commentary on British Foreign Policy, 1935–1938', *Journal of Modern History*, vol. 26, 1954, 170–82; Winston Churchill, 'England's No-Man', *Collier's*, 14 Oct. 1937; John Ramsden, *The Age of Balfour and Baldwin, 1902–1940* (London, 1978), 368.

109 A. J. P. Taylor, 'Daddy, What was Winston Churchill?', *New York Times Magazine*, 28 Apr. 1974; D. C. Watt, *Personalities and Policies* (London, 1965); Woods, *Artillery of Words*, 142.

110 Eisenhower quoted in Arthur Schlesinger Jr, 'On the Inscrutability of History', *Atlantic Monthly*, 1967, 13; Maurice Vaisse, 'Churchill and France', in R. A. C. Parker ed., *Churchill; Studies in Statesmanship* (London, 1995), 165.

111 *Washington Star*, 7 Oct. 1965.

112 Truman's introduction to a reprint of Churchill's 'Sinews of Peace' speech, Halcyon Commonwealth Foundation, New York, 1965.

113 Hugh Sidey, *Time*, 25 Feb. 1980.

114 Emmet Tyrrell Jr in the *Washington*

Post, 14 Feb. 1983; *New York Times*, 5 Aug. and 28 Dec. 1983.

115 John Cole, *As It Seemed to Me: Political Memoirs* (Phoenix edn, London, 1996), 272.

116 Schlesinger, 'Inscrutability of History', 13.

117 Alex Danchev and Daniel Todman eds, *War Diaries, 1939–1945: Field Marshal Lord Alanbrooke* (London, 2001), xx–xxiii; Street, *Portrait*, 146–54; Arthur Bryant ed., *The Turn of the Tide: The Alanbrooke Diaries* (New York, 1957), ix; Moran, *Churchill*, 746–51; Gilbert, *Churchill*, vol. 8, 1232–3; Colville, *Churchillians*, 142–3.

118 David Cannadine, *G. M. Trevelyan; A Life in History* (London, 1992), 139; *Guardian*, 2 Nov. 1959; Andrew Roberts, *Eminent Churchillians* (London, 1994), 318.

119 Sir John Kennedy, *The Business of War* (London, 1957), 115, 233.

120 *New York Times*, 25 Sept. 1960; Robert Blake and William Roger Louis eds, *Churchill* (New York, 1993), 375.

121 Menzies to Churchill, 7 Nov. 1957, Churchill to Menzies, 14 Nov. 1957, Menzies Papers, series 1, folder 58, National Library of Australia; *Sydney Morning Herald*, 4 Nov. 1957.

122 *New York Times*, 16 Mar. 1963; Moran, *Churchill*, 748; *Sunday Telegraph*, 1 Mar. 1964; *The Times*, 2 Mar. 1964.

123 *The Times*, 18 Nov. 1957.

124 *Daily Telegraph*, 1 and 5 Dec. 1957.

125 Tom Harrisson, *Living through the Blitz* (London, 1976), 316; Peter Clarke, *A Question of Leadership: Gladstone to Thatcher* (Penguin edn, London, 1992), 229.

126 Nigel Hamilton, *Monty: The Field Marshal, 1944–1976* (London, 1987); Young, *Bruce Lockhart Diaries, 1939–1965*, 539; Moran, *Churchill*, 632.

127 Young, *Bruce Lockhart Diaries, 1939–1965*, 670; Colville, *Fringes of Power*, 624.

128 Victor Feske, *From Belloc to Churchill: Private Scholars, Public Culture and the Crisis of British Liberalism, 1900–1939* (London, 1996), chapter 5; I owe the point about post-1945 European historians to Pieter Lagrou of the Institute d'Histoire du Temps Present, in Paris, speaking at a colloquium of

the Royal Historical Society in London, 16 Feb. 2002; Peter Wright, 'Mr Churchill and the War', in his *Portraits and Criticisms* (London, 1925), 136–7; Winston Churchill, 'To End War', *Collier's*, 29 June 1935; Caspar Weinberger, 'Winston Churchill, Visions and Leadership', address to the Churchill Society for the Advancement of Parliamentary Democracy, Toronto, 29 Nov. 1989.

129 Scott quoted in Roberts, *Eminent Churchillians*, 303.

CHAPTER 5: *'The Maker of Modern Ireland?': Churchill and the Celts*

1 Raleigh Trevelyan, *Address at the Memorial Service for Dr A. L. Rowse*, St Austell Parish Church, 4 Dec. 1997, printed by All Souls College, Oxford; A. L. Rowse, 'The Contribution of Cornwall and Cornishmen to British History', George Johnson Lecture, Steel-Hayne Agricultural College, Newton Abbot, 1969; A. L. Rowse, *Memories of Men and Women* (London, 1980), 1; *Belfast Telegraph*, 28 Jan. 1965.

2 Well into the twentieth century such official publications as Censuses continued to refer to 'Wales and Monmouthshire' and 'England, except Monmouthshire', though quite a large proportion of the 'Welsh' population had lived in Monmouthshire at least since the Industrial Revolution.

3 *The Times*, 13 Nov. 1951.

4 Randolph Churchill ed., *In the Balance: Winston S. Churchill Speeches, 1949 and 1950* (London, 1951), 181–9.

5 *The Times*, 16 Mar. and 29 June 1945, 17 July 1948, 11 Jan. 1949.

6 *The Times*, 28 and 29 Mar. 1945.

7 Churchill, *In the Balance*, 181.

8 *The Times*, 9 to 13 Feb. 1950.

9 Except, that is, for the places in South Yorkshire where the mine-owners themselves created Churchill Streets of colliery houses in the 1920s and 1930s as a form of thanks for his staunchness to their interests during the strikes of 1921 and 1926. This was unlikely to have endeared him to their occupants.

10 John Ramsden, *The Age of Churchill and Eden* (London, 1995), 228–9.

11 Randolph Churchill., *Winston S. Churchill*, vol. 2: *Young Statesman, 1900–1914* (London, 1967), 373–8.

12 Correspondence with Professor Alec Myers, Churchill's main historical adviser for the late-medieval period of the *History of the English-Speaking Peoples*; John Colville, *The Fringes of Power: Downing Street Diaries, 1939–1955* (London, 1985), 646.

13 Paul Ferris, *Richard Burton* (New York, 1981), 112–14, 140–1, 234, 245–9; Penny Junor, *Burton* (London, 1985), 77, 147–9; Melvyn Bragg, *Rich: The Life of Richard Burton* (London, 1987), 184, 579, 581–3.

14 Mary Soames ed., *Speaking for Themselves: The Personal Letters of Winston and Clementine Churchill* (London, 1998), 312.

15 *Scotsman*, 29 Apr. 1946, 16 May 1947, 29 May 1948.

16 *Scotsman*, 29 June 1945.

17 *The Times*, 29 Apr. 1946, 22 Feb. 1947, 28 Aug. 1948, 21 Feb. 1951, 28 Dec. 1954; *Scotsman*, 29 Apr. 1946.

18 Anthony J. Jordan, *Churchill: A Founder of Modern Ireland* (Westport, Ireland, 1995), 148.

19 *Scotsman*, 29 Apr. 1946, 15 Feb. 1950.

20 *The Times*, 6 June 1945.

21 *Scotsman*, 29 May 1948.

22 *The Times*, 21 May 1949, 15 Feb. 1950, 18 Oct. 1951; *Scotsman*, 21 May 1949.

23 *Scotsman*, 15 Feb. 1950.

24 *Scotsman*, 17 Oct. 1951.

25 *The Times*, 25 July 1952, 19 Nov. 1954.

26 *The Times*, 22 Feb. and 4 Mar. 1952, 17 June 1953.

27 Mary C. Bromage, *Churchill and Ireland* (Notre Dame, Indiana, 1964), 1–5; Jordan, *Churchill*, 9.

28 *Belfast Telegraph*, 25 Jan. 1965.

29 Bromage, *Churchill and Ireland*, chapters 2 and 3; Jordan, *Churchill* 28; Jeremiah MacVeagh ed., *Home Rule in a Nutshell* (London, 1912), v–vi.

30 Bromage, *Churchill and Ireland*, 72–94; Jordan, *Churchill*, 150.

31 Robert Fisk, *In Time of War: Ireland, Ulster and the Price of Neutrality, 1939–45* (Dublin, 1985), 62–5; Mary C. Bromage, *De Valera and the March of a Nation* (London, 1956), 172; Jordan, *Churchill*, 163–4; Allan Martin, *Robert Menzies*, vol. 1 (Melbourne, 1993), 323.

32 Tim Pat Coogan, *De Valera: Long Fellow, Long Shadow* (London, 1995), 519–20; Earl of Longford and T. P. O'Neill, *Eamon De Valera* (London, 1974), 315; Martin, *Menzies*, 338.

33 Fisk, *In Time of War*, 113–14, 116; Bromage, *Churchill and Ireland*, 124–5; Longford and O'Neill, *De Valera*, 355.

34 Dermot Keogh, *Twentieth Century Ireland: Nation and State* (Dublin, 1994), 114; Brian Girvin and Geoffrey Roberts eds, *Ireland and the Second World War* (Dublin, 2000); Longford and O'Neill, *De Valera*, 396–7; Peter Somerville-Large ed., *Irish Voices: Fifty Years of Irish Life* (London, 1999), 204.

35 Fisk, *In Time of War*, 116–17, 235, 250.

36 Coogan, *De Valera*, 549, 598; Bromage, *Churchill and Ireland*, 154–5, 167–71.

37 Longford and O'Neill, *De Valera*, 397; Coogan, *De Valera*, 600–5.

38 Fisk, *In Time of War*, 534–5.

39 Coogan, *De Valera*, 550–2.

40 Fisk, *In Time of War*, 201–11.

41 Coogan, *De Valera*, 592–3.

42 J. J. Lee, *Ireland, 1912–1985: Politics and Society* (Cambridge, 1989), 250.

43 Coogan, *De Valera*, 536, 544; Somerville-Large, *Irish Voices*, 204, 208, 245.

44 Fisk, *In Time of War*, 534–7.

45 Somerville-Large, *Irish Voices*, 245; Coogan, *De Valera*, 300.

46 *Irish Times*, 16 May 1945; *Belfast Telegraph*, 2 and 14 May 1945.

47 *Irish Times*, 18 May 1945, *Irish Press*, 18 May 1945, *Irish Independent*, 17 May 1945; Lee, *Ireland, 1912–1985*, 263–4; Fisk, *In Time of War*, 540; Martin Gilbert, *Winston S. Churchill*, vol. 8: *Never Despair, 1945–1965* (London, 1988), 12.

48 *Belfast Telegraph*, 12, 14, 16, 17 and 18 May 1945; J. J. Lee, *Ireland, 1945–70* (Dublin, 1979), 152.

49 *Irish Times*, 6 and 7 Mar. and 20 Sept. 1946.

50 Longford and O'Neill, *De Valera*, 393, 435–6; Coogan, *De Valera*, 646; *Irish Times*, 15 to 18 Aug. 1949.

51 Longford and O'Neill, *De Valera*, 441–3; Bromage, *De Valera*, 297; Anthony Montague Browne, *Long Sunset: Memoirs of Winston Churchill's Last Private Secretary* (London, 1995), 146; *Irish Press*, 17 Sept. 1953; *Cork Examiner*, 17 Sept. 1953; *Belfast Telegraph*, 17 Sept. 1953.

52 *Irish Times*, 30 Nov. 1954; *Irish Press*, 30 Nov. 1954.

53 *Belfast Telegraph*, 30 Nov. 1954; 13 to 16 Dec. 1955; Lord Moran, *Winston Churchill: The Struggle for Survival, 1940–1965* (Sphere Books edn, London, 1968), 497.

54 *Irish Independent*, 25 Jan. 1965.

55 *Irish Press*, 25 Jan. 1965; Longford and O'Neill, *De Valera*, 442; Coogan, *De Valera*, 574, 669.

56 *Irish Independent*, 28 Jan. 1965; US National Archives, State Department Papers, POL6, UK.

57 *Irish Times*, 25 Jan. to 1 Feb. 1965; Jordan, *Churchill*, 199.

58 'Corkcoin', *Specialised Catalogue of Irish Philately, 1865–1971* (Cork, 1972); Elizabeth Healy, *The Wolfhound Guide to Irish Monuments* (Dublin, 1998); Carol and Jonathan Bardon, *If Ever You Go to Dublin Town: A Historic Guide to the City's Street Names* (Belfast, 1988).

59 Bromage, *Churchill and Ireland*, xi–xiv; Longford and O'Neill, *De Valera*, 469–70.

60 Moran, *Churchill*, 330; Montague Browne, *Long Sunset*, 203.

CHAPTER 6: *'The Father of Europe'?: Churchill and the Europeans*

1 Martin Gilbert ed., *Winston Churchill and Emery Reves: Correspondence, 1937–1964* (Austin, Texas, 1997), 1–2, and *passim*.

2 *Ibid.*, viii, 8, 27, 44, 140–1, 182.

3 Paul Reynaud, 'Churchill and France', in Charles Eade ed., *Churchill by his Contemporaries* (London, 1953), 222; *Daily Mail*, 11 May 1946; *Daily Telegraph*, 13 May 1948, 10 and 12 Oct. 1950.

4 *Daily Telegraph*, 10 Oct. 1950; Robert Lewis Taylor, *Winston Churchill: The Life of a Great Man* (New York, 1954), iv.

5 *The Times*, 26 Apr. and 12 June 1945.

6 *The Times*, 26 and 28 Nov. 1949; Jean Monnet, *Memoirs* (London, 1978), 20, 22–4, 27; Lord Gladwyn, *Memoirs of Lord Gladwyn* (London, 1972), 139; Avi Shlaim, 'Prelude to Downfall: The British Offer of Union to France, June 1940', *Journal of Contemporary History* (July 1974), 27, 35, 53, 59.

7 François Kersaudy, *Churchill and de Gaulle* (London, 1981); David Stafford, *Churchill and Secret Intelligence* (London, 1997), 149–51; Monnet, *Memoirs*, 207–8; Ben Pimlott, *Harold Wilson* (London, 1992), 74.

8 John Young, *Britain, France and the Unity of Europe, 1945–1951* (Leicester, 1984), 2, 8.

9 Gladwyn, *Memoirs*, 157.

10 Duff Cooper to Churchill 2 Apr. 1946, and Churchill to Cooper, 7 Apr. 1946, CP 2/5; Douglas Johnson, 'Churchill and France', in William Roger Louis and Robert Blake eds, *Churchill* (Oxford, 1993) 5; John Young, *Winston Churchill's Last Campaign* (Oxford, 1996), 47–9; John Colville, *The Fringes of Power: Downing Street Diaries, 1939–1955* (London, 1985), 692; Anthony Montague Browne, *Long Sunset: Memoirs of Winston Churchill's Last Private Secretary* (London, 1995), 156.

11 Gilbert, *Churchill and Reves*, 293; Monnet, *Memoirs*, 25–6; Gladwyn, *Memoirs*, 330.

12 Jacques Arnavon, *Winston Churchill, ou l'ami de France* (Paris, 1944), 186; Duff Cooper, *Old Men Forget* (London, 1953), 341, 356–7; *The Times*, 4 and 10 Jan., 17 Feb., 12 to 19 June and 1 Aug. 1945; Pierre Gouhier, *Caen, Caennais, Qu'en reste-t-il?* (Paris, 1987), 271–2.

13 Cooper, *Old Men Forget*, 375; *The Times*, 7 Mar., 17 July and 16 Dec. 1946, 18 Jan. and 9 and 12 May 1947; Johnson, 'Churchill and France', 41.

14 Martin Gilbert, *Winston S. Churchill*, vol. 8 *Never Despair, 1945–1965* (London, 1988), 483; *The Times*, 19 Jan. and 16 Aug. 1948, 11 Aug. and 5 Oct. 1949, 1 Mar. and 29 June 1950, 15 Dec. 1951, 16 Nov. 1953, 8 Apr. 1954; author's correspondence with archivist, municipality of Angoulême.

15 *The Times*, 16 Sept. 1952, 2 Apr. 1954, 3 July 1965, 31 Oct. and 24 Nov. 1966, 16 May and 4 July 1967, 20 May 1969.

16 Author's correspondence with the municipal authorities in each of the named towns, and several others; council minutes, municipality of Rennes, 29 Jan. 1965.

17 *L'Ardennais*, 12 Aug. 1966; council minutes, municipality of Limoges, 19 Feb. 1965; *Le Populaire du Centre*, 1 Apr.

1965; minutes of the municipal council, Lille, 29 Jan. 1965; document FC 01236–4, archives of Le Havre; deliberations of the municipal council, Laon, 12 Feb. 1965; author's correspondence with municipality of Tours, Cabinet du Maire.

18 *The Times*, 12 May and 11 Nov. 1998; Reynaud, 'Churchill and France', 212; letter to the author from the Maire of Saint Vigor le Grand, 1 Sept. 2001.

19 Gilbert, *Churchill and Reves*, 51–7.

20 Gilbert, *Churchill*, vol. 8, 1057, 1141, 1239, 1256; *The Times*, 9 Jan. 1945.

21 *The Times*, 9 July and 9 to 19 Nov. 1945, 9 May 1946; author's correspondence with the city archivist, Antwerp; *Daily Telegraph*, 15 to 19 Nov. 1945.

22 *The Times*, 8 Apr., 24 to 30 Aug. and 11 Sept. 1946; John Ramsden, 'Mr Churchill Goes to Fulton', in James W. Muller ed., *Churchill's 'Iron Curtain' Speech Fifty Years Later* (Columbia, Missouri, 1999), 23–4; John Young, *Britain and European Unity, 1945–1999* (London, 2000), 17.

23 Paul-Henri Spaak, *The Continuing Battle* (London, 1971), 73.

24 *The Times*, 2 Jan. 1950, 20 Feb. and 8 Oct. 1953.

25 Gilbert, *Churchill and Reves*, 295, 308; Andrew Roberts, *Eminent Churchillians* (London, 1994), 42.

26 *The Times*, 17 July 1946, 5 Oct. 1967, 23 Oct. 1973; author's correspondence with city archivist, Antwerp; *Le Wolvendael*, Brussels, Nov. and Dec. 1967.

27 *The Times*, 15 Mar. and 3 Nov. 1945, 4 to 14 May and 12 June 1946, 7 to 11 May 1948, 4 Feb. 1949, 2 Nov. 1950, 1 Dec. 1954, 18 Aug. 1955, 10 and 11 Feb. 1956, 5 May 1960; *Daily Mail*, 11 to 14 May 1946; author's correspondence with the secretary of the advisory committee on street names, Rotterdam; *Winston Churchill in ons midden: zijn zegetocht door ons land, 8–13 Mei, 1946* (Amsterdam, 1946).

28 Gilbert, *Churchill and Reves*, 138.

29 *The Times*, 18 May 1945, 13 July 1946, 12 to 17 May 1948, 4 Nov. 1949; *New York Times*, 12 May 1948; *Churchill's Visit to Norway* (Oslo, 1949); A. Cammermeyer, *Mr Churchill in Norway* (Oslo, 1948).

30 *The Times*, 1 Jan. 1945, 22 Nov. 1946, 1 Dec. 1949, 5 May, 14 July, 2 Sept. and 10

to 12 and 30 Oct. 1950, 23 Jan. 1954; *Sydney Morning Herald*, 11 Oct. 1950; *Daily Telegraph*, 10 to 12 Oct. 1950; Tage Kaarsted, 'Churchill and the Small States of Europe: The Danish Case', in R. A. C. Parker ed., *Winston Churchill: Studies in Statesmanship* (London, 1995), 106–8.

31 *The Times*, 4 Nov. 1949, 7 Jan. and 14 May 1951, 7 Apr. and 5 May 1954, 10 May 1976; *New York Times*, 5 May 1950; *Finest Hour*, 109, 14–15.

32 Gilbert, *Churchill*, vol. 8, 901; *The Times*, 16 Oct. and 9 to 12 Dec. 1953; *Daily Telegraph*, 12 and 13 May 1948; Mary Soames ed., *Speaking for Themselves: The Personal Letters of Winston and Clementine Churchill* (London, 1998), 575; Montague Browne, *Long Sunset*, 133; US National Archives, State Department Papers, POL6, UK.

33 Gilbert, *Churchill*, vol. 8, 260–5; Leland Harrison to President Truman, 18 Sept. 1946, Harry S. Truman Presidential Papers, GF box 115, file 'Churchill, Winston, 1945–46', Truman Library; *The Times*, 24 Aug. to 21 Sept. 1946, 11 Feb., 8 May and 20 and 21 Sept. 1965; *Mr Churchill in Bern* (Bern, 1947).

34 K. W. Watkins, *Britain Divided: The Effect of the Spanish Civil War on British Political Opinion* (London, 1963), 84, 95, 203, 207, 210.

35 David Carlton, *Churchill and the Soviet Union* (Manchester, 2000), 122–8, 205; *The Times*, 31 Sept. 1945; E. S. Balanya, *Winston Churchill, vida de un hombre d'acción* (Madrid, 1944; war memoirs quoted in Christian Graf von Krockow, *Churchill, Man of the Century* (London, 2000), 147.

36 *The Times*, 8 Mar. and 3 Apr. 1946, 13 May 1949, 6 Feb. 1965; Martin Gilbert, *Churchill*, vol. 8, 78–9, 218, 600–2, 932; *Churchill, o estadista e o escritor* (No author given, Lisbon, 1957).

37 *The Times*, 19 to 24 Jan. and 4 to 8 May 1945; Gilbert, *Churchill*, vol. 8, 132–52.

38 Indro Montinelli, *Padri della Patria* (Milan, 1949); *The Times*, 15 and 16 Mar. 1951, 21 Apr. 1958.

39 *The Times*, 15 and 16 Feb. and 9 Mar. 1945, 14 to 28 Aug. 1954, 6 July 1963, 26 Jan. 1965.

40 *The Times*, 13 to 16 Feb. 1945, 23 Nov. 1954.

41 *The Times*, 23 Feb. and 20 to 27 Apr. 1945; Lord Cecil of Chelwood, 'Churchill the Man of Peace', in Sir James Marchant ed., *Winston Spencer Churchill: Servant of Crown and Commonwealth* (London, 1954), 26; Gordon Craig, 'Churchill and Germany', in Blake and Louis, *Churchill*, 21, 37.

42 *The Times*, 28 Feb. and 17 May 1945, 27 July 1949, 22 May 1950, 5 to 13 Dec. 1951, 30 April and 2 May 1953; Gladwyn, *Memoirs*, 260; Hugo Young, *This Blessed Plot: Britain and Europe* (London, 1998), 42; Robert Cole, *A. J. P. Taylor: The Traitor within the Gates* (London, 1993), 108; Lord Moran, *Churchill: The Struggle for Survival, 1940–1965* (Sphere Books edn, London, 1968), 631; Gilbert, *Churchill and Reves*, 319.

43 *New York Times*, 19 Mar. 1946; *The Times*, 13 July 1954; John Ramsden, *The Dam Busters* (London, 2002), 115.

44 *The Times*, 8 Dec. 1949, 5 and 8 Dec. 1951, 15 and 16 June 1953; Gilbert, *Churchill*, vol. 8, 574, 1070; Hans-Peter Schwartz, 'Churchill and Adenauer', in Parker, *Churchill: Studies in Statesmanship*, 173.

45 *The Times*, 2 June 1949, 8 Dec. 1951, 2 Dec. 1954, 22 Mar., 18 Apr., 11 May, 30 July and 8 Oct. 1956; Montague Browne, *Long Sunset*, 205–6; Gilbert, *Churchill*, vol. 8, 547, 1197, 1200.

46 Erhard's conversation with Wilson on 29 Jan. 1965 is minuted in the PREM file 13/317, Public Record Office, quoted in Stephen Barber, 'His Finest Hour: The Death and Funeral of Sir Winston Churchill', MA dissertation, Queen Mary and Westfield College, 1997, appendix B; Moran, *Churchill*, 731; *Sydney Morning Herald*, 6 Mar. 1949.

47 Gilbert, *Churchill and Reves*, 132–41, 177–9.

48 *The Times*, 28 Feb., 13 and 15 Mar. and 6 July 1945, 11 Mar., 22 Apr. and 11 Oct. 1948, 18 Nov. 1949, 27 July 1950, 19 Mar. 1951; Kenneth Young ed., *The Diaries of Sir Robert Bruce Lockhart, 1939–1965* (London, 1980), 514, 580.

49 *The Times*, 28 June 1947, 26 May 1948, 21 Aug. 1950, 24 and 26 Apr. 1951, 4 Jan. 1952.

50 *The Times*, 2 and 5 Dec. 1959, 4 Jan. 1962, 29 July and 1 Dec. 1964, 26 Jan. 1965, 11 Jan. 1967; *New York Times*, 25 Sept. 1966.

51 Author's correspondence with the Prague Historical Museum and with the British Embassy in Prague; Margaret Thatcher, *The Path to Power* (London, 1995), 27. The following sentence in Lady Thatcher's memoirs, 'British foreign policy is at its worst when it is engaged in giving away other people's territory,' would be seen as rather less supportive of Churchill in countries where his participation in the Yalta conference has given him a rather bleaker reputation; Ronald A. Smith, *Churchill: Images of Greatness* (London, n.d. but c.1995), 51.

52 Young, *This Blessed Plot*, 6.

53 Avi Shlaim, *Britain and the Origins of European Unity* (Reading, 1978), 68; Gladwyn, *Memoirs*, 141; Young, *This Blessed Plot*, 10–11.

54 *Collier's*, 4 Jan. 1947, 11–12; *Independent*, 25 July 1996.

55 *Herald*, Melbourne, 20 Sept. 1946; *Sydney Morning Herald*, 16 May 1947; Young, *Britain, France and Unity*, 108; Young, *This Blessed Plot*, 13, 17; John Young, 'Churchill's "No" to Europe: The "Rejection of European Union by Churchill's Post-war Government, 1951–2', *Historical Journal* (1985), 921.

56 Janet Morgan, *Backbench Diaries of Richard Crossman* (London, 1981), 49; Menzies diary, 11 Sept. 1948, Menzies Papers, series 13, box 397, National Library of Australia; Monnet, *Memoirs*, 273, 283, 315, 408; Spaak, *Continuing Struggle*, 200–2; Young, *This Blessed Plot*, 21; Gilbert, *Churchill*, vol. 8, 483–4.

57 Young, *Britain, France and Unity*, 116; Nicholas Crowson, 'The Conservatives and Europe since 1945', in Roger Broad and Virginia Preston eds, *Moored to the Continent: Britain and European Integration* (London, 2001), 176.

58 F. W. S. Craig, *British General Election Manifestos, 1918–1966* (Chichester, 1970), 123–4, 143–7, 159–61; Young, *Britain, France and Unity*, 185; Sean Greenwood ed., *Britain and European Integration since the Second World War* (Manchester, 1996), 46–7; Young, 'Churchill's "No" ', 923–37; Montague Browne, *Long Sunset*, 138.

59 John Ramsden, *The Age of Churchill and Eden, 1940–1957* (London, 1995), 195–6, 260–1.

60 *The Times*, 15 Sept. 1962; Montague Brown, *Long Sunset*, 272–6.

61 *Private Eye*, 25 Oct. 1962.

62 M. R. D. Foot, 'Winston Churchill', in Herbert van Thal ed., *The Prime Ministers* (New York, 1975), 686.

CHAPTER 7: *'An English-Speaking Union in my own Person': Churchill the American*

1 Martin Gilbert, *Churchill: A Life* (New York, 1991), 137; David Cannadine ed., *The Speeches of Winston Churchill* (Penguin edn, London, 1989), 226; John Colville, *The Churchillians* (London, 1981), 85.

2 Evidence of Clark Clifford, quoted in Kay Halle to Jim Rowe, for Senator Lyndon Johnson, 16 July 1959, Kay Halle Papers, folder 74(1), Kennedy Library. This story is broadly confirmed by the 1946 diary of Charles Ross, Truman's press secretary and another traveller on the same train, Charles Ross Papers, Truman Library.

3 *Washington Post*, 31 Jan. 1965; it was characteristic of the ambiguity that British newspapers tended to pay much less attention to the 'Anglo-US theme', and, when mentioning the United States in the context of the funeral, were more likely to dwell on Anglophile individuals like Eisenhower or to snipe at Lyndon Johnson for staying at home.

4 He was much less good at picking the coming men in American politics. Although he had met Franklin Roosevelt during the First World War, Roosevelt remembered this but Churchill did not, and he was one of many who neglected to make friends with Harry Truman before having to deal with him as President.

5 For Churchill in Canada see David Dilks, *Three Visitors to Canada: Baldwin, Chamberlain and Churchill*, Canada House Lecture series, no. 28 (London, 1985).

6 When hundreds of Canadians turned out to hear him speak at Winnipeg in 1900, Winston pointed out that the sum of £230 he had thereby earned in one evening was rather more than he had managed in such English cities as

Newcastle-upon-Tyne. Dilks, *Three Visitors*, 8.

7 *Sydney Morning Herald*, 7 Jan. 1952; *New York Times*, 14 Apr. 1961. Anthony Montague Browne, *Long Sunset: Memoirs of Winston Churchill's Last Private Secretary* (London, 1995), 144.

8 D. C. Watt, 'America and the British Foreign-Policy-making Elite', in his *Personalities and Policies* (London, 1965), 26–9. Christopher Hitchens, *Blood, Class and Nostalgia: Anglo-American Ironies* (London, 1990), 124.

9 Hitchens, *Blood, Class and Nostalgia*, 199; Donald Cameron Watt, *Personalities and Appeasement*, published lecture, University of Texas (Austin, Texas, 1991), 12.

10 Michael Wynne-Barker, *Bridge over Troubled Water* (Cambridge, 1996), 37, 42–4, 103–8; *Concord*, Newsbulletin of the E-SU of the Commonwealth, Dec. 1962.

11 Wynne-Barker, *Bridge over Troubled Water*, 104; *English-Speaking Union of the Commonwealth, Annual Reports* (1962), 26–9; (1964), 1; (1965), 14–15; (1966), 10–11; (1968), 4; *Concord*, July 1964; English-Speaking Union, *Ten Churchill Lectures* (London, 1998), 2.

12 Winston Churchill, 'To End War', *Collier's*, 29 June 1935, quoted in David Reynolds, *The Creation of the Anglo-American Alliance, 1937–1941* (London, 1981), 84; Roland Quinault, 'Churchill and Democracy', *Transactions of the Royal Historical Society*, 6th series, vol. 11, 213; Victor Feske, *From Belloc to Churchill: Private Scholars, Public Culture and the Crisis of British Liberalism, 1900–1939* (Chapel Hill, North Carolina, 1996), 224.

13 Nicholas John Cull, *Selling War: The British Propaganda Campaign against American Neutrality in World War II* (New York, 1995), 76; David Reynolds, 'Churchill the Appeaser? Between Hitler, Roosevelt and Stalin in World War Two', in M. Dockrill and B. McKercher eds, *Diplomacy and World Power: Studies in British Foreign Policy, 1890–1950* (Cambridge, 1996), 197–220.

14 Cull, *Selling War*, 72, 109; Susan A. Brewer, *To Win the Peace: British Propaganda in the United States during World War II* (London, 1997), 63–4;

Jonathan Sikorsky, 'From British Cassandra to American Hero', *Finest Hour*, 108, 2001; Richard Langworth, *A Connoisseur's Guide to Winston Churchill* (London, 1998), 202–11.

15 Murrow broadcasts, 10 May and 29 Dec. 1940, quoted in Sikorsky, 'From British Cassandra'; Cull, *Selling War*, 192.

16 Reynolds, *Anglo-American Alliance*, 86–7, 118–19, 139, 179–80; Colville, *Churchillians*, 92; Montague Browne, *Long Sunset*, 234; James MacGregor Burns, *Roosevelt: The Soldier of Freedom* (San Diego, California, 1970), 178–80; Sikorsky, 'From British Cassandra'.

17 David Culbert ed., *Mission to Moscow* (Madison, Wisconsin, 1980), 195, 201; Hitchens, *Blood, Class and Nostalgia*, 220; Yousef Karsh, *Faces of Destiny* (London, 1947), 52.

18 Sikorsky, 'From British Cassandra'; Hitchens, *Blood, Class and Nostalgia*, 145, 221, 315.

19 *Boston Globe*, 26 to 28 July 1945; *Chicago Tribune*, 27 and 28 July 1945; *Los Angeles Times*, 27 July 1945.

20 *New York Daily News*, 27 July 1945; *Washington Post*, 27 July 1945; *Philadelphia Inquirer*, 27 July 1945.

21 Eisenhower to Churchill, 26 Dec. 1945, Dwight D. Eisenhower Pre-Presidential Papers, Name file, box 22, file 'Churchill, 4', Eisenhower Library.

22 Gilbert, *Churchill*, 863–9; John Ramsden, 'Mr Churchill Goes to Fulton', in James W. Muller ed., *Churchill's 'Iron Curtain' Speech Fifty Years Later* (Columbia, Missouri, 1999), 15–47.

23 F. H. Harbutt, 'The Fulton Speech and the Iran Crisis of 1946: A Turning Point in American Foreign Policy', PhD thesis, University of California, Berkeley, 1979, 108–9; Stephen Ambrose, *Eisenhower: Soldier and President* (New York, 1990), 225.

24 Churchill to Truman, 8 Nov. 1948, Harry S. Truman Presidential Papers, GF box 115, file 'Churchill, Winston, 1947–50', Truman Library; John Young, *Winston Churchill's Last Campaign: Britain and the Cold War, 1951–1955* (Oxford, 1996), 110; John Colville, *The Fringes of Power: Downing Street Diaries, 1939–1955* (London, 1985), 654.

25 *New Republic*, 21 June 1948; *New York Times*, 20 June 1948; *San Francisco Chronicle*, 20 June 1948; *New York Herald Tribune*, 20 June 1948; *Yale Review*, Autumn 1946.

26 *American Historical Review*, vol. 54, 858; *New York Times*, 3 Apr. 1949; *Nation*, 2 Apr. 1949.

27 *San Francisco Chronicle*, 26 and 27 Oct. 1951; *Los Angeles Times*, 27 Oct. 1951; *Chicago Tribune*, 26 and 27 Oct. 1951; *Boston Evening Globe*, 26 Oct. 1951; *Boston Globe*, 27 Oct. 1951; papers prepared for general information, Harry S. Truman Presidential Papers, GF box 116, Churchill–Truman meetings, Truman Library; Winthrop Aldrich to Secretary of State, 6 Apr. 1954, Dwight D. Eisenhower Presidential Papers, International Series, box 19, file Eisenhower–Churchill, January to June 1954, Eisenhower Library; Robert H. Ferrtell, *The Eisenhower Diaries* (New York, 1981), 208, 222–4.

28 Princeton seminar file, 11–13 Dec. 1952, Dean Acheson Papers, box 89, Truman Library. On Churchill's overall relations with Truman, Eisenhower and Dulles, see Young, *Churchill's Last Campaign*; J. L. Harper, *American Visions of Europe* (Cambridge, 1994), 273.

29 *New York Times*, 19 Nov. 1957.

30 *Boston Globe*, 30 Nov. and 1 Dec. 1954; *New York Daily News*, 6 Apr. 1955; *New York Times*, 27 June, 19 Sept. and 14 Oct. 1955; *American Institute of Architects' Guide to New York City* (New York, 1995), 676.

31 *New York Times*, 8 July 1955, 10 Jan. 1956.

32 *New York Times*, 18 Oct. and 4 Dec. 1955.

33 See for example the *Argus*, Melbourne, 1 Sept. 1949; *Sydney Morning Herald*, 16 May 1947, 2 Apr. 1949.

34 *New York Times*, 25 Nov. 1955, 3 Jan., 28 Apr. and 11 May 1956, 1 Aug. 1957.

35 Charles Hays Sulzberger to Randolph Churchill, 4 Apr. 1963, Kay Halle Papers, folder C74(1), Kennedy Library.

36 Dulles to Eisenhower, 30 May 1955, Dwight D. Eisenhower Presidential Papers, International series, box 19, file 'Eisenhower–Churchill January–April 1955', Eisenhower Library.

37 The reason that Lafayette was not an

applicable precedent was that he had been made a citizen of the states of Maryland and Virginia during the Revolutionary War, and he therefore became an actual (not honorary) citizen of the USA when the Constitution made all citizens of a state citizens of the USA in 1787. There was therefore no prior case in which the honour had been conferred by Congress. Nevertheless, since Lafayette had never renounced French citizenship, his position remained anomalous under the definition later adopted in the Fourteenth Amendment, and in 1932 his great-great-grandson was actually denied admission to the New York Bar on the ground that he was not a US citizen. The State Department then exchanged diplomatic notes with the French Government to confirm Lafayette's exact status. Notes provided by White House for President Johnson, 25 Jan. 1965, Lyndon B. Johnson Presidential Papers, National Security files, Country file, UK, box 214, file 'Churchill funeral', Johnson Library; *New York Times*, 6 Apr. 1963.

38 *New York Times*, 8 May 1955.

39 *New York Times*, 29 July, 4 Sept. and 1 Dec. 1955. Rockefeller to Eisenhower, 26 Apr. 1955; Eisenhower's message to Congress, Eisenhower to Churchill, 26 Nov. 1955, Dwight D. Eisenhower Presidential Papers, International series, box 19, file 'Churchill, 1955–57, 4', Eisenhower Library.

40 *Washington Post*, 15 Apr. 1959.

41 John Ramsden, *The Age of Churchill and Eden, 1940–1957* (London, 1995), 326–7.

42 *New York Times*, 13 and 14 Oct. and 30 Nov. 1957; *Philadelphia Inquirer*, 13 Oct. 1957; *San Francisco Chronicle*, 13 Oct. 1957, 6 Apr. 1958.

43 Eisenhower to Churchill, 16 Apr. 1957, Secretary's note of meeting with Joyce Hall, 27 June 1957, Churchill to Eisenhower, 24 June 1957, Dwight D. Eisenhower Presidential Papers, International series, box 20, file 'Churchill, 1955–57, 3', Eisenhower Library; *New York Times*, 28 Oct. 1961, 23 Aug. 1964.

44 Eisenhower to Churchill, 14 Oct. 1957, Churchill to Eisenhower, 16 Dec. 1957, Dwight D. Eisenhower Presidential

Papers, box 20, files 'Churchill, 1955–57, 2 and 3', Eisenhower Library.

45 *Chicago Tribune*, 22, 24 and 29 Apr. 1958; *Argus*, Melbourne, 15 Feb. 1958.

46 Truman quoted in Christian Graf von Krockow, *Churchill, Man of the Century* (London, 2000), 93.

47 *Churchill the Painter*, exhibition catalogue, Nelson Art Gallery (Kansas City, Missouri, 1958), 3.

48 Eisenhower to Churchill, 3 Feb. and 30 Apr. 1958, Dwight D. Eisenhower Presidential Papers, International series, box 29, file 'Churchill, 1957–59, 4', Eisenhower Library.

49 Churchill to Eisenhower, 17 Oct. 1958, Dwight D. Eisenhower Presidential Papers, International series, box 20, file 'Churchill, 1958–59, 1', Eisenhower Library; *Sydney Morning Herald*, 13 Mar. 1960.

50 In preparation for the visit, such Anglophile newspapers as the *New York Times* warmed up their readers to the Churchill ancestry part of the story with such articles as 'Kin of Churchill numerous in US' (26 April) and 'Churchill claims Indians as kin' (3 May).

51 'Symbol of Britain', *New York Times*, 5 May 1959.

52 Montague Browne, *Long Sunset*, 161, 220–1; *New York Herald Tribune*, 11 May 1959; White House transcript of toasts at dinner on 8 May 1959, Dwight D. Eisenhower Presidential Papers, International series, box 20, file 'Churchill 1958–59, 3', Eisenhower Library. David Dimbleby and David Reynolds, *An Ocean Apart: The Relationship between Britain and America in the Twentieth Century* (London, 1988), 205.

53 Diary, May 1959, Dwight D. Eisenhower Presidential Papers, DDE Diary series, box 41, Eisenhower Library.

54 *Kansas City Times*, 31 Jan. 1958; Bess Truman quoted in Merle Miller ed., *Plain Speaking: An Oral Biography of Harry S. Truman* (New York, 1974), 237.

55 *New York Times*, 6 May 1959; Truman to Averell Harriman, 20 Apr. 1959, Truman to Churchill, 16 and 27 May 1959, Harry S. Truman Post-Presidential Papers, Name file, box 59, file 'Churchill, 1957–59', Truman Library;

Kansas City Times, 7 May 1959. Vaughan to President Davidson, March 1969, Harry Truman Post-Presidential Papers, Name file, box 60, file 'Churchill Memorial, Fulton', Truman Library.

56 The few personal remarks that Churchill made during the trip can only have helped his popularity with Americans in general and the President in particular; when he first arrived, he announced that he 'would not say everything I think' while in America, a comment generally taken as a rebuke to Montgomery. *New York Times*, 5 May 1959; Diary, week of 4 May 1959, Dwight D. Eisenhower Presidential Papers, DDE Diary series, box 41, Eisenhower Library.

57 *New York Herald Tribune*, 11 May 1959.

58 Eisenhower to Churchill, 26 May 1959, Dwight D. Eisenhower Presidential Papers, International series, box 20, file 'Churchill, 1958–59, 3'. A few weeks later, after Eisenhower had been in Europe, this mutual admiration society worked the other way round, with Churchill assuring him that his visit had been 'a tremendous success'. Churchill to Eisenhower, 16 Sept. 1959, Dwight D. Eisenhower Presidential Papers, International series, box 20, file 'Churchill, 1958–59, 2', Eisenhower Library.

59 Churchill to Kennedy, 13 Apr. 1961, John F. Kennedy Presidential Papers, President's Office Special Correspondence, box 28, file 'Winston S. Churchill, April 1961–March 1963', Kennedy Library; *New York Times*, 14 and 15 Apr. 1961; Martin Gilbert ed., *Winston Churchill and Emery Reves: Correspondence, 1937–1964* (Austin, Texas, 1997), 389.

60 Randolph Churchill to President Kennedy, 28 Oct. 1962, and Schlesinger to Kennedy, 26 Jan. 1963, John F. Kennedy Presidential Papers, White House Name file, General 487, 'Churchill'; Schlesinger to Kennedy, 9 Apr. 1963, President's Office Special Correspondence, box 28, folder 2, Kennedy Library.

61 Oral History interview, Kay Halle, Kennedy Library; CBS News transcript, 30 Nov. 1964; Beverly Nichols letter in *Daily Telegraph*, 10 Apr. 1963; Nigel Hamilton, *JFK: Reckless Youth* (New York, 1992), 335.

62 John Kennedy to Joseph Kennedy and two others, 4 Apr. 1963, John F. Kennedy Presidential Papers, White House Name File (Executive), box 487; Schlesinger to Pierre Salinger, 24 Jan. 1963, President's Office Special Correspondence, box 28, folder 1, Kennedy Library; *New York Times*, 25 Jan. 1963; Murray Kempton in the *Spectator*, 26 Apr. 1963, and, in a different version, in *New Republic*, 27 Apr. 1963.

63 Oral history interview, Kay Halle, Kennedy Library; *E-SU News*, vol. XII, no. 7, May 1965.

64 *Manchester Guardian*, 15 Apr. 1959; Halle to Kenneth O'Donnell, 6 Feb. 1963, O'Donnell to Halle, 23 Feb. 1963, Kennedy to Halle, 8 Mar. 1963, Kay Halle Papers, folder C74(1), Kennedy Library.

65 *Plain Dealer*, Cleveland, Ohio, 31 July 1962; James Reston to Halle, 21 July 1962, Goldwater to Halle, 31 July 1962, James Roosevelt to Halle, 1 Aug. 1962, Senator Young to Halle, 3 and 9 Aug. 1962, Horace Treharne to Ohio Reps and Senators, 23 July 1962, Kay Halle Papers, folder C74(1), Kennedy Library.

66 Halle to John Wyndham, Prime Minister's private secretary, 11 Aug. 1962, John Foster MP to Halle 20 Aug. 1962, Charles Wintour to Halle, 27 Aug. 1962; Kay Halle Papers, folder C74(1), Kennedy Library.

67 Schlesinger to Halle, 24 Aug. 1962, Young to Halle, 27 Sept. 1962, Kay Halle Papers, folder C74(1), Kennedy Library.

68 *Washington Post*, 3 Feb. 1963.

69 *Washington Post*, 9 Jan. and 13 Feb. 1963; *Chattanooga Times*, 16 Feb. 1962; *Baltimore Sun*, 21 Feb. 1962; *Boston Globe*, 28 Feb. 1962; Halle to Roy Larsen, *Time*, 25 Feb. 1962, Kay Halle Papers, folder C74(1), Kennedy Library.

70 Schlesinger to Halle, 22 Jan. 1963, Vice President Johnson to Mrs K. Thorne, 16 Oct. 1962, Halle to Larsen, 25 Feb. 1963, folder C74(1), Kennedy Library; *Washington Post*, 9 Jan. 1963; *Time*, 22 Feb. 1963; in this debate over precedents, both sides turned out to have a point, for an honour not used in the first two centuries of the Union was then used again within ten years, for Solzhenitsyn, and not long afterwards a

third time too, for Oskar Schindler, though this hardly amounted to a wholesale devaluation of the currency. For Solzhenitsyn at least, the case was undeniably exceptional, for he had been stripped of his Soviet citizenship when he went into exile and so was effectively a stateless person, while Schindler may already have been dead anyway.

71 Rep. Bolton's circular letter to constituents, 2 Feb. 1963, Halle to Roy Larsen, 25 Feb. 1963; transcript of Leonard broadcast, 8 Feb. 1963, Kay Halle Papers, folder C74(1), Kennedy Library.

72 *House of Representatives Report*, no. 57, 87th Congress, 1st session. *Congressional Record, House of Representatives*, 12 Mar. 1963; *Des Moines Register*, 14 Mar. 1963; *Congressional Record, Senate*, 12 Mar. 1963.

73 *Newsday*, 9 Apr. 1963; Berlin to Halle, 14 Mar. 1963, Kay Halle Papers, folder C74(2), Kennedy Library; *The Georgetowner*, 22 Apr. 1971; *Richmond Times Dispatch*, 3 May 1963; *Boston Record*, 4 Apr. 1963; *Philadelphia Inquirer*, 4 Apr. 1963; *Christian Science Monitor*, 9 Apr. 1963; *Plain Dealer*, 9 Apr. 1963; fundraising card, 9 Apr. 1973, in Kay Halle Papers, folder C75(1), Kennedy Library; Ben Tucker, *Winston Churchill: His Life in Pictures* (London, 1945), 231.

74 Papers relating to the ceremony, guest list etc. are all in the Kay Halle Papers, folder C75(1), Kennedy Library; Paul Fox, BBC, to President Kennedy, 13 Mar. 1963, Abba Schwartz, State Department, to President Kennedy, 9 Apr., Kennedy to Mayor of Clearwater, Nebraska, 18 Apr. 1963, John F. Kennedy Presidential Papers, White House Name file, box 487, Kennedy Library; *Daily Telegraph*, 10 Apr. 1963; Acheson quoted in the *National Observer*, 15 Apr. 1963; Schlesinger to Kennedy, 9 Apr. 1963, John F. Kennedy Presidential Papers, President's Office Special Correspondence, box 28, folder 1, Kennedy Library; *Daily Sketch*, 10 Apr. 1963; Montague Browne, *Long Sunset*, 319.

75 *New York Times*, 9 and 26 May 1963; *Washington Evening Star*, 9 May 1963.

76 *Gaelic American*, 5, 12, 19 and 26 May, 2 and 23 June 1945.

77 *Gaelic American*, 4 Aug. 1945, 2, 9, 16 and 23 Mar. 1946.

78 Speech in Belfast quoted in *Finest Hour*, 112, 54.

79 *Gaelic American*, 27 Oct. and 3 Nov. 1951, 19 and 26 Sept. 1953; *Boston Globe*, 10 Jan. 1952.

80 *Irish World*, 1 Dec. 1954, 9 Apr. 1955, 23 Apr. 1963, 23 and 30 Jan. and 6 Feb. 1965; *The Times*, 6 Sept. 1999.

81 *New York Times*, 11 June, 20 July and 3 Nov. 1963.

82 See for example the *New York Times*, *New York Daily News*, *Chicago Tribune*.

83 Will Yolen and K. S. Giniger, *Heroes of History* (Harrisburg, Pennsylvania, 1968), ix; Fae Korsmo and Michael P. Sfraga, 'Churchill Peaks and the Politics of Naming', *Polar Record* (2000), 131–8; *Washington Evening Star*, 16 Feb. 1971.

CHAPTER 8: *'The Lynchpin of the English-Speaking Peoples': Churchill and Canada*

1 George Drew to Georges Vanier, 3 Dec. 1964, George Drew Papers, vol. 404, Personal correspondence 1962–4, National Archives, Ottawa, ref. MG32C3.

2 With at least some Canadians this was indeed a problem, if not for many. A citizen urged Torontonians in 1980 to get Churchill's statue removed from their city and Churchill Boulevard renamed, for 'Churchill was no friend of Canada, or for that matter other former colonies.' The only evidence cited for this view was that the citizen's father had told him how Churchill carelessly sacrificed Canadian lives in Dieppe and Hong Kong in 1941–2: 'Winston Churchill was an Englishman first, a Britisher second, and if lives had to be sacrificed then colonials would be sacrificed.' *Toronto Globe and Mail*, 4 Nov. 1980. If there was an avalanche of letters supporting this view, they were not printed, and the statue was anyway not moved.

3 File note, Lester B. Pearson Papers, vol. 135, file 313.45, 'Visit to London, 1965', National Archives, ref. MG26N.

4 See Chapter One.

5 Winston S. Churchill, *My Early Life* (London, 1944 ed.), 377; Randolph S. Churchill, *Winston S. Churchill*, vol. 1: *Youth, 1874–1900*. (London, 1966), 543–4; Peter de Mendelssohn, *The Age of Churchill: Heritage and Adventure, 1874–1911* (London, 1961). 376; Martin Gilbert, 'Churchill and Canada', address delivered at the annual meetings of the Sir Winston S. Churchill Society, Edmonton, Calgary and Vancouver, May 1987.

6 Alan Rayburn, *Oxford Dictionary of Canadian Place Names* (Toronto, 1997), 76–7.

7 *Halifax Chronicle-Herald*, 25 Jan. 1965.

8 Mary Soames ed., *Speaking for Themselves: The Personal Letters of Winston and Clementine Churchill* (London, 1998), 337–8.

9 The Canadian Museum of Rail Travel, in Cranbrook, British Columbia, allows visitors to see the luxury in which Churchill travelled with CPR when in Canada, though the car on display was apparently used in 1943 rather than 1929.

10 Soames, *Speaking for Themselves*, 340–5.

11 John Plumpton, 'Churchill and Canada: Encounters with Canadians, 1900–57', in *Finest Hour*, 44, Summer 1984; Gilbert, 'Churchill and Canada'.

12 Soames, *Speaking for Themselves*, 341.

13 Speeches of 2 Nov. 1921, 3 Jan. 1927, 25 Nov. 1929, 20 Apr. 1939, included in Robert Rhodes James ed., *Winston S. Churchill: His Complete Speeches, 1897–1963* (London, 1974).

14 Martin Gilbert, *Winston S. Churchill*, vol. 7: *Road to Victory, 1941–1945* (London, 1986), 33–4; John W. Holmes, *The Shaping of Peace: Canada and the Search for World Order, 1943–57* (Toronto, 1979), vol. 2, 41.

15 *Ottawa Citizen*, Dec. 1941, Jan. 1942.

16 J. W. Pickersgill ed., *The Mackenzie King Record* (Toronto, 1960), vol. 1, 534.

17 Gilbert, *Churchill*, vol. 7, 467.

18 Gilbert, *Churchill*, vol. 7, 953, 969; Pickersgill, *Mackenzie King Record*, vol. 1, 534.

19 John G. Diefenbaker, *One Canada: Memoirs of the Rt Hon. John G. Diefenbaker* (Scarborough, Ontario, 1975), vol. 1, 187.

20 *Toronto Globe and Mail*, 27 July 1945.

21 *Vancouver Sun*, 26 July 1945.

22 *Toronto Telegram*, 27 July 1945; *Halifax Chronicle*, 27 July 1945; *Calgary Herald*, 26 and 27 July 1945.

23 See for example George Drew to Winston Churchill, urging him to come to Toronto to receive an honorary degree from the University of Toronto, 4 Feb. 1946, George Drew Papers, vol. 30, file 276.

24 See for example the *Calgary Herald*, 5 Mar. 1946, which chose to set its front-page report of Churchill's speech ('Churchill warns against Russia's "indefinite expansion"') immediately alongside reports of the Ottawa spy trial. The editorial on that day made the same link.

25 *Toronto Globe and Mail*, 28 June 1948.

26 St Laurent to Churchill, 17 Oct. 1951, St Laurent Papers, vol. 164, file U10 UK vol. 1, 'Personal and Confidential', National Archives, Ottawa.

27 Drew to Churchill, 19 and 27 Oct. 1951, Drew Papers, vol. 183, file 50, 'Churchill, Rt. Hon. W. S.'.

28 *Toronto Telegram*, 26 and 27 Oct. 1951; *Halifax Herald*, 27 Oct. 1951; *Toronto Globe and Mail*, 25 Feb. 1950, 27 Oct. 1951.

29 *Official Record, House of Commons Proceedings*, Canadian Federal Parliament, 13 Nov. and 13, 21 and 29 Dec. 1951.

30 *Toronto Globe and Mail*, 15 and 16 Jan. 1952; *Ottawa Citizen*, 15 and 16 Jan. 1952.

31 St Laurent Papers, vol. 164, file U10 UK, 'Visit of Rt. Hon. Sir Winston Churchill', National Archives, Ref. MG26L.

32 Lester B. Pearson, *Mike: The Memoirs of the Right Honourable Lester B. Pearson* (3 vols, Toronto, 1972–5), vol. 1, 234–6; *Official Record*, 4 Apr. 1952; *Monetary Times*, Mar. 1952.

33 *Official Record*, 29 Feb. 1952 (Edmund George).

34 See for example the *Official Record*, 18 Oct. 1945 (Thomas Church), 6 Dec. 1945 (Victor Quelch), 28 Mar. 1949 (Joseph Bradette), 6 Mar. 1950 (Donald Fleming), 30 Mar. 1950 (John Decore), 12 June 1950 (James Macdonnell).

35 *Official Record*, 20 May 1952 (George Drew).

36 *Official Record*, 1 Mar. 1950 (George Drew), 2 Feb. 1951 (Lester Pearson), 26 Feb. 1951 (Alistair Stewart), 16 Feb. 1953

(Lester Pearson), 1 Apr. 1954 (Lester Pearson), 26 Jan. 1955 (Donald Fleming).

37 See for example Drew Papers, vol. 30, file 276, 'Churchill, Sir Winston, 1947–63'.

38 *Official Record*, 17 Nov. 1949 and 29 June 1950 (Jean François Pouliot), 16 Feb. 1953 (Ernest Hansell), 20 Nov. 1953 (James Macdonnell).

39 High Commissioner, London, to St Laurent, 16 June 1954, St Laurent Papers, vol. 218, 'Visit of Rt. Hon. Sir Winston Churchill', 1954.

40 St Laurent Papers, vol. 218, 'Visit of Rt. Hon. Sir Winston Churchill', and vol. 285, 'Speech at Winston Churchill Dinner', 30 June 1954; *Winnipeg Tribune*, 29 July 1954.

41 *Edmonton Journal*, 29 and 30 Nov. 1954.

42 *Winnipeg Free Press*, 7 Mar. 1958.

43 *Official Record*, 5 Apr. 1955.

44 *Official Record*, 30 Nov. and 5 Dec. 1960, 30 Nov. 1962.

45 *Official Record*, 30 July 1964.

46 *Canadian Historical Review*, June 1957, June and Sept. 1958; *Saturday Night*, 9 Nov. 1956; *Canadian Forum*, June 1958; J. G. Maclelland to Churchill, 24 Apr. 1958, Churchill Papers, 4/28A.

47 Vincent Massey to Churchill, 13 Apr. 1959, John G. Diefenbaker Papers, file 311.21; Hugh Wallis to Diefenbaker, 12 June 1958, Diefenbaker Papers, files 313.25, 313.3 MI, and 843, microfilms in National Archives, ref. MG26M.

48 Churchill to St Laurent, 5 Nov. 1951, St Laurent Papers, vol. 164, file U10 UK vol. 1, 'Personal and Confidential'.

49 See for example *Toronto Globe and Mail*, *Halifax Chronicle-Herald*, *Edmonton Journal* and *Calgary Herald*, Jan.–Feb. 1965.

50 John English, *Shadow of Heaven: The Life of Lester Pearson* (Toronto, 1978), vol. 1, 200; Claude Bissell, *The Imperial Canadian: Vincent Massey in Office* (Toronto, 1986), 88–9.

51 Diefenbaker, *One Canada*, vol. 1, 195–6; Pearson, *Mike*, vol. 1, 155; Denis Smith, *Rogue Tory: The Life and Legend of John G. Diefenbaker* (Toronto, 1995), 120, 122; Plumpton, 'Churchill and Canada'.

52 Pickersgill, *King Record*, vol. 1, 328–30; J. W. Pickersgill and Donald Forster eds, *The Mackenzie King Record*, vol. 4 (Toronto, 1970), 36–41.

53 J. W. Pickersgill and Donald Forster eds, *The Mackenzie King Record*, vol. 3 (Toronto, 1966), 83–8, 180–6; English, *Shadow of Heaven*, 313; Pearson, *Mike*, vol. 1, 232–3; John Ramsden, 'Mr Churchill Goes to Fulton', in James W. Muller ed., *Churchill's 'Iron Curtain' Speech Fifty Years Later* (Columbia, Missouri, 1999), 15–47.

54 *Official Record*, 18 Mar. 1954 (St Laurent); St Laurent Papers, vol. 273, 'Speech at Banquet for Winston S. Churchill', 14 Jan. 1952, and vol. 285, 'Speech at Sir Winston Churchill Dinner', 30 June 1954; Dale C. Thomson, *Louis St Laurent, Canadian* (Toronto, 1967), 323, 348, 361, 388.

55 English, *Shadow of Heaven*, 79, 200, 216, 240, 248–9; John English, *The Worldly Years: The Life of Lester Pearson, 1949–72* (New York, 1992), 35; Pearson, *Mike*, vol. 1, 177, 234–6.

56 Peter C. Newman, *Renegade in Power: The Diefenbaker Years* (Toronto, 1973), 100; Peter Stursberg, *Diefenbaker: Leadership Gained* (Toronto, 1975), 72; Peter Stursberg, *Diefenbaker: Leadership Lost* (Toronto, 1975), 104; Smith, *Rogue Tory*, 525, 570, 578; Diefenbaker Papers, Series IV, file 313.02 'Churchill', file 818.21, P, 1958, 'Australia', file 312.214, 'Churchill', file 313.232, 'Churchill'.

57 *Official Record*, 20 Jan. 1955, 30 July 1964.

58 Drew Papers, vol. 30, file 276, 'Churchill, 1908, 1940–8', vol. 158, file 50, 'Churchill, Rt. Hon. W. S.', vol. 404, 'Personal correspondence, 1962–4'.

59 Drew to Major Bassett, 18 June 1965, Drew Papers, vol. 404, 'Personal correspondence, 1962–6'; *Toronto Telegram*, 18 Sept 1963, *Vancouver Sun*, 18 Sept. 1963.

60 Pearson to Drew, 30 Apr. 1964, Drew Papers, vol. 404, 'Winston Churchill Memorial Trust Correspondence, 1964–7', Drew to T. H. Symons, 5 Feb. 1965, Drew Papers, vol. 404, 'Personal correspondence, 1962–4'.

61 Drew Papers, vol. 408, various files on the Winston Churchill Memorial Trust; *Edmonton Journal*, 1 Feb. 1965; *Toronto Globe and Mail*, 2 Feb. 1965.

62 *Edmonton Journal*, 27 Jan. and 2 Feb. 1965.

63 Rayburn, *Oxford Dictionary of Canadian*

Place Names, 76–7; W. B. Hamilton, *The Macmillan Book of Canadian Place Names* (2nd edn, Toronto, 1983), 8–9, 173; Philip Smith, *Brinco: The Story of Churchill Falls* (Toronto, 1975), 4, 16, 36, 276.

64 *Toronto Globe and Mail*, 20 Sept., 27 Oct. and 2 Nov. 1977, 12 Feb. 1979; *Toronto Star*, 4 Oct 1977.

65 H. Cloud to George Drew, 21 Apr. 1965, Drew Papers, vol. 408, 'Winston Churchill Funeral'.

66 *Albertan*, 21 Apr. 1967, 29 Apr. and 4 May 1968, 20 Mar. and 25 Oct 1969, 10 Apr. and 8 May 1970, 26 Sept. 1974; *Calgary Herald*, 8 and 15 May 1969, 11 May 1970, 21 Jan. and 19 May 1973, 20 Sept. 1979, 16 Apr. 1980, 28 Feb. 1981, 20 Apr. 1984, 1 June 1986.

67 *Churchilliad*, magazine of the Churchill Society for the Advancement of Parliamentary Democracy, vol. 12, no. 1, Oct. 2000; Diefenbaker Papers, vol. 582, 'Memorials to Sir Winston Churchill, 1962–3'. For the International Churchill Society, see Chapter Twelve.

68 Drew Papers, vol. 30, file 276, 'Churchill, 1908, 1940–48'.

69 *New Westminster Columbian*, 25 Jan. 1965; *Vancouver Sun*, 23 and 29 Jan. 1965; *Edmonton Journal*, 25 Jan. 1965.

70 R. D. Cuff and J. L. Granatstein, *Ties That Bind: Canadian–American Relations in Wartime, from the Great War to the Cold War* (Toronto, 1977), 125ff; Holmes, *Shaping of Peace*, vol. 2, 99–100; English, *Worldly Years*, 12.

71 Cuff and Granatstein, *Ties That Bind*, 101; English, *Worldly Years*, 92.

72 St Laurent Papers, vol. 273, 'Speech at Banquet for Sir Winston Churchill', 14 Jan. 1952; *Official Record*, 29 Feb. 1952 (Edmund George), 20 Mar. 1954 (James Macdonnell, quoting Churchill).

73 *Edmonton Journal*, 27 Jan. 1965.

74 Joke as it undoubtedly is, the tendency of Churchill's Canadian admirers to refer to themselves as 'colonials' whenever Americans are present retains something of the flavour of that relationship even today.

75 Quoted from Morrison himself, in the programme of the International Churchill Society, 11th International Conference, Banff, 1994.

CHAPTER 9: *'The Brightest Gem in the British Crown': Churchill in New Zealand*

1 Research for this chapter was made possible by the award of a Churchill Fellowship by the Winston Churchill Memorial Trust in 1999.

2 John Ramsden, 'Mr Churchill Goes to Fulton', in James W. Muller ed., *Churchill's 'Iron Curtain' Speech Fifty Years Later* (Columbia, Missouri, 1999), 1–37.

3 Mark Garnett, *Alport: A Study in Loyalty* (Teddington, 1999), 84.

4 *NZ Parliamentary Debates*, 8 Sept. 1965, vol. 344, 2543.

5 Tom Brooking, *Milestones: Turning Points in New Zealand History* (Lower Hutt, New Zealand, 1988); Rex Monigatti ed., *New Zealand Headlines* (Wellington, 1963).

6 *Documents Relating to New Zealand's Participation in the Second World War, 1939–45* (Department of Internal Affairs, Wellington, 1951), vol. 2, 182–221.

7 This was suggested to me by Prof. Jock Phillips.

8 See for example the *Otago Daily Times*, 20 June, 5 Aug. and 13 Nov. 1942.

9 *NZ Parliamentary Debates*, 4 Aug. 1964, vol. 339, 1018.

10 The point was that the time difference made the official announcement of VE Day difficult to administer in New Zealand, where it therefore happened a day later (except in Christchurch, where graduating students jumped the gun). See Jock Phillips, 'The End of World War II', unpublished paper. I am grateful to Prof. Phillips for a sight of this paper.

11 Martin Gilbert, *Winston S. Churchill*, vol. 8: *Never Despair, 1945–1965* (London, 1988), 763. Since New Zealand had in fact urged the admission of Britain to Anzus Council meetings, he was correct in his view. See W. David McIntyre, 'From Dependency to Nuclear Free', in G. W. Rice ed., *The Oxford History of New Zealand* (2nd edn, Auckland, 1992), 219–30.

12 Quoted by Keith Holyoake in a speech in the House of Representatives, *NZ Parliamentary Debates*, 4 Aug. 1964, vol. 339, 1018.

13 *The Dominion*, 27 July 1945; *New*

Zealand Herald, 27 July 1945; *The Press*, 28 July 1945.

14 *NZ (House of Representatives) Parliamentary Debates*, 1, 24 and 31 Aug. 1945, 9 July 1947, vol. 268, 755, vol. 269, 320, 469, 501, vol. 276, 330.

15 Draft entry on Doidge for the *New Zealand Dictionary of National Biography*, vol. 5, forthcoming. I am grateful to Prof. Phillips for allowing me to see this; *Daily Express*, 27 May 1954.

16 See for example *The Press*, 7 and 8 Mar. 1946.

17 *The Press*, 29 Oct. 1951; *New Zealand Herald*, 29 Oct. 1951; *The Dominion*, 27 Oct. 1951.

18 *Otago Daily Times*, 11 Sept. 1952, 28 Feb. 1953, 9 Dec. 1954.

19 *The Press*, 30 Nov. and 1 Dec. 1954; *New Zealand Herald*, 1 Dec. 1954; *The Dominion*, 1 Dec. 1954.

20 *The Dominion*, 7 Apr. 1955; *NZ Parliamentary Debates*, 6 Apr. 1955, vol. 305, 170–3; for Nash see Keith Sinclair, *Walter Nash* (Auckland, 1976).

21 *NZ Parliamentary Debates*, 11 Sept. 1958, vol. 318, 1702, 29 June 1962, vol. 330, 561, 4 Aug. 1964, vol. 339, 1017–18; 27 Aug. 1964, vol. 339, 1632; Wellington *Evening Post*, 13 Dec. 1958.

22 See for example *The Dominion*, 21 Apr. 1956; *New Zealand Weekly News*, 24 Sept. 1958; *New Zealand Herald*, 12 Dec. 1956, 12 Sept. 1958, 1 Dec. 1964; *Otago Daily Times*, 12 Dec. 1959.

23 *Otago Daily Times, The Dominion, New Zealand Herald, The Press*, Wellington *Evening Post, New Zealand Weekly News*, 16 Jan. to 2 Feb. 1965.

24 *Otago Daily Times*, 28 Jan. and 4 Feb. 1965.

25 John Gunther, *Inside Australia and New Zealand* (London, 1972), 329.

26 *New Zealand Herald*, 27 Jan. 1965.

27 *NZ Parliamentary Debates*, 8 Sept. 1965, vol. 344, 2543.

28 *The Dominion*, 3 Feb. 1965; *New Zealand Herald*, 2 Feb. 1965; *Otago Daily Times*, 2 Feb. 1965.

29 *New Zealand Herald*, 3 Feb., 9, 11 and 16 Mar. and June, 1965; *The Dominion*, 4, 5, 11, 17, 18 and 19 Feb., 16 May, 21 June and 2 July 1965; *Evening Post*, 3 Feb. and 23 July 1965.

30 *NZ Parliamentary Debates*, 2 Sept. 1965,

vol. 344, 2470, 8 Sept. 1965, vol. 344, 2543.

31 *NZ Parliamentary Debates*, 19 July 1968, vol. 355, 647–50.

32 List of New Zealand Fellows Report, 1965–1996, and Guidelines for Prospective Applicants, 2000, Winston Churchill Memorial Trust, Wellington.

33 Wellington City map, 1999, Wise, Auckland.

34 G. W. A. Bush, *Decently and in Order: The Centennial History of Auckland City Council* (Auckland, 1971), 343–8.

35 Information from current telephone and business directories.

36 *Gazetteer of New Zealand Place Names*, Department of Lands and Survey, Wellington, 1968.

37 I owe much information on the Wellington suburb of Crofton Downs to the late David Hamer.

38 Information from the current parliamentary archivist, and from Felicity Connell, British Council, Wellington.

39 Mrs H. M. Elmslie to Sidney Holland, 2 Aug. 1945, and Holland to Elmslie, 8 Aug. 1945; Holland to Randolph Churchill, 24 Sept. 1947, Sidney Holland Papers, files 1/1 and 9/2, Alexander Turnbull Library.

40 Robert Muldoon, *Muldoon by Muldoon* (Wellington, 1977), 118.

41 Paul Freyberg, *Bernard Freyberg* (London, 1991), 98, 218, 562.

42 See correspondence and cuttings retained in the Fraser Papers, series 1 folder 3, series 4 folder 3, New Zealand National Archives.

43 *Inverness Courier*, 31 Dec. 1948; Fraser to Neil Beaton, 3 Apr. 1950, Fraser Papers, series 4 folder 6, series 2 folder 9, New Zealand National Archives.

44 Sinclair, *Nash*, 354.

45 Text of broadcast, 18 May 1945, Holland Papers, 70/5, Alexander Turnbull Library.

46 Holland to Ralph Etherton, 5 Sept. 1945, Holland Papers 1/1, Alexander Turnbull Library.

47 For example Peter Elliott to Holland, 26 Aug. 1945, Holland to Randolph Churchill, 24 Sept. 1947, Holland Papers 1/1 and 9/2, Alexander Turnbull Library.

48 Holland Papers, 16/3 and 26/5, Alexander Turnbull Library.

49 Holland to Churchill, 11 Nov. 1948;
Churchill to Holland, 12 Dec. 1948,
Holland Papers 16/3, Alexander Turnbull
Library; for similar co-operation in 1943,
see Barry Gustafson, *The First Fifty
Years: A History of the New Zealand
National Party* (Auckland, 1986), 197.

50 Churchill to Holland, 15 Feb. 1952,
Holland Papers 122/3, Alexander
Turnbull Library.

51 Though the nickname suited this policy
stance well enough, it was actually given
to him early in life to distinguish him
from an Australian cousin of the same
name. John Gunther thought that his
appeal to New Zealanders, explaining
his twelve years as Prime Minister, was
to be found in his understanding of
sheep-farming, his having had only a
self-education, and his having 'a first
name that his countrymen seem to
prefer above all others to give to their
male children'. In other words he was
stereotyped, however inaccurately, as a
genuine New Zealander. Gunther, *Inside
Australia and New Zealand*, 320–1. See
also Tom Brooking, 'Tobacco Road to
Pipitea Street', in Margaret Clark ed., *Sir
Keith Holyoake: Towards a Political
Biography* (Palmerston North, New
Zealand, 1997), 111.

52 Ross Doughty, *The Holyoake Years*
(Feilding, New Zealand, 1977), 22, 68,
102–3.

53 *New Zealand Parliamentary Debates*, 4
Aug. 1964, vol. 339, 1018, 8 Sept. 1965,
vol. 344, 2543.

54 *The Dominion*, 28 Jan. 1965.

55 Winston S. Churchill, *The Second World
War*, vol. 4: *The Hinge of Fate* (London,
1951), 3–17.

56 See for example *The Listener* (New
Zealand), 17 Aug. 1958, 22 Mar. 1957, 14
Mar. 1958.

57 Winston S. Churchill, *A History of the
English-Speaking Peoples*, vol. 4: *The
Great Democracies* (London, 1958).

58 Churchill Papers, 4/27, 4/435, 4/436,
4/439, 4/441, 4/67; *Sunday Times*, 16
Mar. 1958; *Daily Mail*, 17 Mar. 1958.

59 W. David McIntyre, 'Imperialism and
Nationalism', in Rice, *Oxford History of
New Zealand*, 342–3.

60 It was not reviewed in *The Listener*,
where all the previous volumes had
been reviewed at length, and did not get

a mention either in such obvious
journals as *Historical Studies*.

61 Quoted in Roland Quinault, 'Churchill
and Australia, the Military Relationship,
1899–1945', in *War and Society*, vol. 6,
no. 1 (May 1988), 43.

CHAPTER 10: *'Bad Stock':
Churchill and Australia*

1 Research for chapters 10 and 11 was
made possible by a period as a
Distinguished Academic Visitor at La
Trobe University's Institute of Advanced
Studies, and by a small grant from the
University of London's Central Research
Fund.

2 Michael Barson, *Cockburn: The Making
of a Community* (Cockburn, Western
Australia, 1978), 232.

3 Michael Davie, *Anglo-Australian
Attitudes* (London, 2000), 38.

4 Bill Gammage, *The Broken Years:
Australian Soldiers in the Great War*
(Harmondsworth, 1975), 276–9.

5 J. W. Fletcher, *Winston Churchill*
(Sydney, 1941), 37–41.

6 Ronald Blythe, *The Age of Illusion*
(London, 1963), 120–33; Churchill's
luncheon club speeches on 16 Dec. 1918
and 25 Apr. 1921 can be found in Robert
Rhodes James ed., *Winston S. Churchill:
His Complete Speeches, 1897–1963*
(London, 1974); 'Man in the Street', *The
Sporting English: From Front Line to
Body Line* (Sydney, 1933) Roland Perry,
The Don, 1908–2001 (rev. edn, London,
2001), 363.

7 The Melbourne *Herald*'s in-house index,
now in the Victoria State Library, began
indexing Churchill news stories on
separate cards in 1927, whereas most
British politicians except prime
ministers were subsumed in
miscellaneous alphabetical records.

8 Edgar Holt, *Politics is People: Men of the
Menzies Era* (Sydney, 1969), 71; Sir Earle
Page, *Truant Surgeon: The Inside Story of
Forty Years of Australian Political Life*
(Sydney, 1963), 66.

9 Quoted from Nixon's *Leaders*, in Sir
John Bunting, *R. G. Menzies: A Portrait*
(Sydney, 1988), 55.

10 W. J. Hudson, *Casey* (Melbourne, 1986),
38, 61.

11 Page, *Truant Surgeon*, 118.

12 W. S. Robinson, *If I Remember Rightly: Memoirs of W. S. Robinson, 1876–1963* (Melbourne, 1967), 146, 177. Robinson did not live to complete the book, one of the missing chapters being intended to describe his lifetime association with Churchill, but enough remains in the book to show their closeness, in part through the mutual friendship of Brendan Bracken. John McEwen quoted a tribute to Robinson by Churchill at his memorial service in 1963, Peter Golding, *Black Jack McEwen* (Melbourne, 1996), 33.

13 Melbourne *Herald*, 13 Dec. 1933.

14 Lady Mitchell, *Three-quarters of a Century* (London, 1940), 215.

15 Mary Soames ed., *Speaking for Themselves: The Personal Letters of Winston and Clementine Churchill* (London, 1998), 363.

16 Melbourne *Herald*, 6 Feb. 1935.

17 D. J. Wenden, 'Churchill, Radio and Cinema', in William Roger Louis and Robert Blake eds, *Churchill* (New York, 1993), 236–8.

18 *Sydney Morning Herald*, 30 Aug. 1945, 30 Oct. 1949; see also Fletcher, *Churchill*, 91.

19 See for example the photograph of Churchill, finger pointed like Kitchener in 1914, on an AIF recruiting poster used in a display at Myer's store, State Library of Victoria, photograph no. 1105781. 'Prime Minister visits Australian and New Zealand troops' is picture no. 1163378.

20 Fletcher, *Churchill*, 17.

21 Robinson, *If I Remember*, 195.

22 Page, *Truant Surgeon*, 312.

23 David Day, *Reluctant Nation: Australia and the Allied Defeat of Japan, 1942–45* (Melbourne, 1992), 98.

24 Kevin Perkins, *Menzies: Last of the Empire Men* (Melbourne, 1968), 111; Page, *Truant Surgeon*, 305.

25 Said to John Gunther and quoted in Nigel Hamilton, *JFK: Reckless Youth* (New York, 1992), 453.

26 David Day, *The Great Betrayal: Britain, Australia and the Onset of the Pacific War, 1939–42* (Melbourne, 1988).

27 Lord Moran, *Winston Churchill: The Struggle for Survival* (Sphere Books edn, London, 1968), 36–7. In the same tirade, Churchill remarked to his doctor that

'London had not made a fuss when it was bombed. Why should Australia?' Day, *Reluctant Nation*, 101.

28 Arthur Fadden, *They Called Me Artie* (Melbourne, 1969), 75–6, 77–8.

29 Richard Casey diary, 27 Dec. 1941 and 14 Jan. 1942, Casey MS, National Library of Australia, MS6150, series 4, box 24; Percy Spender, *Politics and a Man* (London, 1972), 31, 147.

30 Hudson, *Casey*, 130–2; P. G. Edwards ed., *Australia through American Eyes* (St Lucia, Queensland, 1979), 66–7.

31 Norton E. Lee, *Curtin, Saviour of Australia* (Melbourne, 1983), 35, 96, 98–100, 101, 131; Casey diary, 19–22 Mar. 1942, series 4, box 24.

32 Ken Buckley et al., *Doc Evatt* (Melbourne, 1994), 153.

33 Robinson, *If I Remember*, 189; Buckley, *Evatt*, 162, 185.

34 Hudson, *Casey*, 134; Paul Hasluck, *The Light That Time Has Made* (Canberra, 1995), 116–17 (a reprinted review of Norton Lee's *Curtin, Saviour of Australia*); *Canberra Times*, 27 July 1945; *Bulletin*, 27 Mar. 1965.

35 Casey diary, 27 July 1945, series 4, box 25. Casey had earlier heard one of Churchill's radio speeches for the election, and noted on 22 June that 'he repeated his hard-hitting attacks on the Labour Party and devoted himself but little to his own prospective policy'.

36 *Advertiser*, Adelaide, 27 to 29 July 1945; *West Australian*, 27 July 1945; *Argus*, Melbourne, 27 and 28 July 1945; *Sydney Morning Herald*, 27 July 1945.

37 *Canberra Times*, 28 July 1945.

38 *Mercury*, Hobart, 27 July 1945.

39 *Courier-Mail*, Brisbane, 27 July 1945; *Sydney Morning Herald*, 28 July 1945.

40 *Commonwealth Parliamentary Hansard*, vol. 184, 4910–11, HR, 2 Aug. 1945.

41 Moran, *Churchill*, 314; *Sydney Morning Herald*, 3 Aug. 1945, 10 Oct. 1946; *Courier-Mail*, 4 Aug. 1945; *West Australian*, 6 Aug. 1945; Ben Chifley, *Things Worth Fighting For* (Melbourne, 1953), 128–32; *Argus*, 8 Oct. 1946.

42 *Commonwealth Parliamentary Hansard*, vol. 184, 4960–1, HR, 29 Aug. 1945.

43 *Commonwealth Parliamentary Hansard*, vol. 187, 2727, HR, 18 July 1946; *Argus*, 19 July 1946.

44 *Commonwealth Parliamentary Hansard*,

vol. 198, 905, HR, 28 Sept. 1949; *Sydney Morning Herald*, 12 Aug. 1947.

45 *Western Australia Parliamentary Debates*, vol. 115, pp. 563–5, 11 Sept. 1945; *West Australian*, 17 Oct. 1945.

46 *Argus*, 16 Aug. 1946; Churchill to Menzies, 9 Aug. 1964, Menzies Papers, National Library of Australia, MS4936, series 1, folder 59.

47 Melbourne *Herald*, 21 May and 14 Dec. 1946, 11 Sept. 1947; *Sydney Morning Herald*, 30 May 1946, 1 May 1954.

48 Melbourne *Herald*, 26 Jan. and 19 Feb. 1949; *Sydney Morning Herald*, 22 Jan. and 25 Apr. 1950.

49 Melbourne *Herald*, 2 and 12 Jan. 1953; *Sydney Morning Herald*, 30 July 1949, 20 Apr. 1952, 16 Apr. 1955.

50 Melbourne *Herald*, 30 Apr. 1949.

51 Melbourne *Herald*, 14 Sept. 1946.

52 *Argus*, 17 July 1945.

53 *Sydney Morning Herald*, 19 Sept. 1945; *West Australian*, 6 and 19 Aug. 1945.

54 Melbourne *Herald*, 28 Feb. 1949, 10 May 1956; *Sydney Morning Herald*, 11 May, 17 July and 26 Aug. 1946, 16 Apr. 1947, 11 Oct. 1950, 12 Jan. 1953; *Argus*, 14 May 1948.

55 Melbourne *Herald*, 7 Sept. 1953; interview with Heather Henderson; Stuart Ward, *Australia and the British Embrace* (Melbourne, 2002), 84.

56 *Argus*, 21 and 22 Aug. 1948; *Sydney Morning Herald*, 18 Feb. 1954.

57 *Argus*, 8 July 1947; *Mufti* (Journal of the Victoria RSL), Aug. 1947.

58 *Commonwealth Parliamentary Hansard*, vol. 184, 5293, HR, 12 Sept. 1945, vol. 185, 5766, Senate, 21 Sept. 1945, and vol. 5999, Senate, 27 Sept. 1945.

59 *Commonwealth Parliamentary Debates*, vol. 187, 1793, HR, 26 June 1946, and 2442, HR, 12 July 1946; vol. 200, 3509, HR, 25 Nov. 1948; Melbourne *Herald*, 19 June and 4 July 1946; *Sydney Morning Herald*, 9 Jan. 1948; Chifley to Churchill, 21 July 1946, copy in the Menzies Papers, series 1, folder 57.

60 *Commonwealth Parliamentary Debates*, vol. 214, 1257–8, HR, 30 Oct. 1951.

61 *Western Australian Parliamentary Debates*, vol. 115, 341, Assembly, 23 Aug. 1945; *Victoria Parliamentary Debates*, vol. 219, 4247, Assembly, 25 Sept. 1945.

62 *Argus*, 14 and 19 Sept. and 6 and 9 Oct. 1945.

63 *Sydney Morning Herald*, 26 Aug. 1947; *Argus*, 1 and 4 Dec. 1947.

64 *Argus*, 17 Nov. 1946, Melbourne *Herald*, 14 Nov. 1947; *Mufti*, Feb. and July 1947.

65 *Advertiser*, 6 and 7 Mar. 1946; *West Australian*, 7 Mar. 1946; *Sydney Morning Herald*, 7 Mar. 1946; *Courier-Mail*, Brisbane, 7 Mar. 1946; *Argus*, 16 Mar. 1946; *Mercury*, Hobart, 9 Mar. 1946.

66 Allan Martin, *Robert Menzies: A Life* (Melbourne, 1999), vol. 2, 41; Percy Joske, *Menzies, 1894–1978* (London, 1978), 146; Chifley, *Things Worth Fighting For*, 137; *Commonwealth Parliamentary Debates*, vol. 186, 34, HR, 6 Mar. 1946, 439–40, HR, 20 Mar. 1946, 507, HR, 21 Mar. 1946, 558, HR, 22 Mar. 1946, 616, 26 Mar. 1946; James Killen, *Inside Australian Politics* (Melbourne, 1989), 284; *Argus*, 4 Feb. and 13 May 1946, 20 Mar. 1948; *Advertiser*, 5 Apr. 1955; *Sydney Morning Herald*, 7 Sept. 1949, 16 Feb. 1950.

67 *Advertiser*, 21 Sept. 1946; *Argus*, 20 and 21 Sept. 1949; Melbourne *Herald*, 20 Sept. 1946; *Mercury*, 20 Sept. 1946.

68 *Sydney Morning Herald*, 16 and 17 May 1947.

69 A. A. Calwell, *Be Just and Fear Not* (Adelaide, 1978), 106; *Sydney Morning Herald*, 18 Aug. 1947, 2 Apr. 1949.

70 Hudson, *Casey*, 248; David Lowe, *Menzies and the Great World Struggle: Australia's Cold War* (Sydney, 1999), 155–6, 167; Cain, *Menzies*, 63; Thomas Durrell-Young, *Australian, New Zealand and United States Security Relations, 1951–1986* (Oxford, 1992), 2; W. D. Macyntyre, *Background to the Anzus Pact* (London, 1995), 29, 353, 360–6; Spender, *Politics and a Man*, 266; G. Greenwood and N. Harper, *Australia in World Affairs* (London, 1957), 70–4; Martin, *Menzies*, vol. 2, 234.

71 Melbourne *Herald*, 16 May 1947, 19 May 1948, and *passim*; *Sydney Morning Herald*, 6 Oct. 1948.

72 Melbourne *Herald*, 21 Feb. and 30 Oct. 1948, 7 and 13 Oct. 1950; *Sydney Morning Herald*, 4 Oct. 1948, 3 Apr. 1949, 29 Apr. 1954; *Commonwealth Parliamentary Hansard*, vol. 201, 924, Senate, 3 Mar. 1949; Lee, *Curtin*, 96; Fadden, *They Called Me Artie*, 76.

73 Day, *Reluctant Nation*, 101; L. F. Crisp, *Ben Chifley* (London, 1970), 136;

Spender, *Politics and a Man*, 238; Ward, *Australia and the British Embrace*, 24; Casey diary, 25 June 1956, series 4, box 28; Winston Churchill, *History of the English-Speaking Peoples*, vol. 4: *The Great Democracies* (London, 1958); Rudyard Kipling, 'The Islanders' (1902); Melbourne *Herald*, 31 Oct. to 13 Nov. 1959; *Sydney Morning Herald*, 18 Mar. 1958.

74 RSL Papers, series 1, file 2211; Melbourne *Herald*, 14 Nov. 1947.

75 Melbourne *Herald*, 1 Apr. 1949.

76 *Advertiser*, 27 Feb. 1950; *Canberra Times*, 27 Feb. and 1 Mar. 1950; *Sydney Morning Herald*, 25 Feb. 1950; Menzies diary, 12 Aug. 1948, series 13, box 397.

77 *West Australian*, 27 Oct. 1951; *Canberra Times*, 27 Oct. 1951; *Courier-Mail*, 27 Oct. 1951; Melbourne *Herald*, 27 Oct. 1951; *Mercury*, 27 and 28 Oct. 1951.

78 Menzies to Churchill, 29 Oct. 1951, Menzies Papers, series 1, folder 57.

79 *Sydney Morning Herald*, 18 Nov. 1954.

80 *Sydney Morning Herald*, 25 Oct., 28 and 30 Nov. and 1 Dec. 1954, 4 Jan. 1955; Melbourne *Herald*, 5 Nov. 1954; *Commonwealth Parliamentary Hansard*, vol. 5, HR, 27 Oct. 1954; *South Australia Hansard*, 1954 vol. 2, 1580, 30 Nov. 1954; *Argus*, 1 Dec. 1954; *Advertiser*, 30 Nov. and 1 Dec. 1954; *Mercury*, 1 Dec. 1954; *West Australian*, 1 Dec. 1954; *Courier-Mail*, 1 Dec. 1954; Casey diary, 6 Apr. 1955, series 4, box 28.

81 *Victoria Parliamentary Debates*, vol. 245, p. 2932, Assembly, 21 Apr. 1955; *Canberra Times*, 6 Apr. 1955; *West Australian*, 7 Apr. 1955; *Courier-Mail*, 6 Apr. 1955; *Sydney Morning Herald*, 6 and 7 Apr. and 17 Aug. 1955; Melbourne *Herald*, 6 Apr. 1955.

82 See for example the *Age*, Melbourne, 23 Sept. 1958, 5 to 9 May 1959, 1 Apr. 1963.

83 *Sydney Morning Herald*, 30 Mar. 1947, 6 May 1951, 1 Mar. 1955; *Argus*, 1 Sept. 1945, 24 Aug. 1950; Melbourne *Herald*, 3 May 1947, 6 Dec. 1948.

84 Menzies to Churchill, 14 Nov. 1957, Churchill to Menzies, 6 Oct. and 31 Dec. 1958, Menzies Papers, series 1, folder 58; *Winston Churchill the Painter: Souvenir Catalogue of the First Exhibition of his Paintings* (Canberra, 1958).

85 *Advertiser*, 22 Mar. 1958; *Canberra Times*, 9 and 13 Aug. 1958; *Mercury*, 13 Aug. and

15 and 16 Oct. 1958; *Sydney Morning Herald*, 21 and 22 Aug. 1958.

86 I am grateful to Professor Graeme Davison for this information.

87 Menzies Papers, series 23, box 13, folder 14; *Argus*, 8 Oct. 1945; *Sydney Morning Herald*, 8 Oct. 1945, 12 Nov. 1946; RSL Papers, series 1, file 2205, National Library of Australia, MS6609; State Library of Victoria photograph collection, photograph no. 764591.

88 Information derived from personal observation and research in street maps and gazetteers; Alan Fasiley, *A Field Guide to the National Parks of Victoria* (Melbourne, 1982), 148; *Readers Digest Guide to Australian Places* (Sydney, 1993); *Bulletin*, 21 June 1965.

89 Richard and Barbara Appleton, *The Cambridge Dictionary of Australian Places* (Cambridge, 1992), 67; *Gazetteer No. 40, Australia* (Washington DC, 1957).

90 *Advertiser*, 4 Mar. 1965.

91 *Bulletin*, 12 June 1965; *Morwell Advertiser*, Feb. to May 1965; *Victoria Parliamentary Debates*, vol. 276, 2071, Assembly, 2 Dec. 1964, and vol. 277, 2071, Legislative Council, 23 Mar. 1965; Brian and Barbara Kennedy, *Australian Place Names* (Sydney, 1989), 218.

92 Page, *Truant Surgeon*; Robinson, *If I Remember Rightly*; Fadden, *They Called Me Artie*, 130; Day, *Reluctant Nation*, 11; Buckley et al., *Doc Evatt*, 185; *Sydney Morning Herald*, 27 Apr. 1953; Calwell, *Be Just and Fear Not*, 340–2.

93 Philip Ayres, *Malcolm Fraser* (Melbourne, 1987), 40; Ronald Conway, *Land of the Long Weekend* (Melbourne, 1978), 177; B. M. and Bernice Snedden, *Billy Snedden* (Melbourne, 1990), 112; James Walker, *The Leader: A Political Biography of Gough Whitlam* (St Lucia, Queensland), 223–4, 232; Gough Whitlam, *The Heart of the Matter* (London, 1974), 4; John Edwards, *Keating: The Inside Story* (Ringwood, Victoria, 1996), 50, 62, 135; Michael Gordon, *A Question of Leadership: Paul Keating, Political Fighter* (St Lucia, Queensland, 1993), 30–1.

94 Gerard Henderson, *A Howard Government?* (Pymble, New South Wales, 1995), 18, 32, 37; *Australian Financial Review*, 25 Nov. 2001.

95 *Advertiser*, 29 July 1964; *New South Wales Parliamentary Debates*, 3rd series, vol. 55, 2388, Assembly, 26 Nov. 1964; *South Australian Hansard*, 1964 vol. 1, 152, Legislative Council, 4 Aug. 1964; *Commonwealth Parliamentary Debates*, vol. S 28, 52, 18 Aug. 1964; Menzies to Churchill, 22 Sept. 1964, Menzies Papers, series 1, folder 59.

96 *West Australian*, 18 to 25 Jan. 1965; *Mercury*, 25 Jan. 1965.

97 *West Australian*, 26 Jan. to 1 Feb. 1965.

98 See for example the *Advertiser*, the *Age* and the *Sydney Morning Herald*.

99 Casey diary, 16 to 18 Jan. 1965; Melbourne *Herald*, 18 Jan. 1965.

100 *Australian*, 16 Jan. to 1 Feb. 1965.

101 *Advertiser*, 1 Feb. 1965; *Memorial Service for Sir Winston Churchill KG, St David's Cathedral, Hobart, 30 Jan. 1965*, State Library of Tasmania; *Mercury*, 1 Feb. 1965; *Sydney Morning Herald*, 1 Feb. 1965.

CHAPTER 11: *Robert Menzies, Worldwide Leader of the Churchill Appreciation Society*

1 Cameron Hazlehurst ed., *Menzies Observed* (Sydney, 1979), iii.

2 Sir John Bunting, *R. G. Menzies: A Portrait* (Sydney, 1988), 43.

3 Allan Martin, *Robert Menzies: A Life*, vol. 1 (Melbourne, 1993), 153, 155.

4 Kevin Perkins, *Menzies: Last of the Empire Men* (Melbourne, 1968), 51; David Day, *The Great Betrayal: Britain, Australia and the Onset of the Pacific War, 1939–42* (Melbourne, 1988), 44.

5 Hazlehurst, *Menzies Observed*, 182.

6 Hazlehurst, *Menzies Observed*, 191; A. A. Calwell, *Be Just and Fear Not* (Adelaide, 1978), 46.

7 Robert Menzies, 'Churchill and the Commonwealth', in Sir James Marchant ed., *Winston Churchill: Servant of Crown and Commonwealth* (London, 1954), 95.

8 Judith Brett, *Robert Menzies' Forgotten People* (Sydney, 1992), 215–24.

9 David Day, *Menzies and Churchill at War* (Melbourne, 1993); a contrary view is fairly briskly expressed in Gerard Henderson, *Menzies' Child: The Liberal Party of Australia, 1944–1994* (St Leonards, New South Wales, 1994),

166–9. Sheila Lawlor, writing at about the same time as Day, on the same period of war politics and using similar sources, did not think such a view of Menzies' motivation even worth mentioning, Sheila Lawlor, *Churchill and the Politics of War, 1940–41* (Cambridge, 1994). Allan Martin notes that no direct evidence to support Day's 'daring historiographical hypothesis . . . has yet been found'. Martin, *Menzies*, vol. 1, 354–5.

10 Martin, *Menzies*, vol. 1, 323, 327, 338.

11 Hazlehurst, *Menzies Observed*, 245; Sir Earle Page, *Truant Surgeon: The Inside Story of Forty Years of Australian Political Life* (Sydney, 1963), 308; David Day, *Reluctant Nation: Australia and the Allied Defeat of Japan, 1942–45* (Melbourne, 1992), 101.

12 Martin, *Menzies*, vol. 1, 327.

13 Allan Martin and Patsy Hardy eds, *Dark and Hurrying Days: Menzies' 1941 Diary* (Canberra, 1993), 162–4.

14 Perkins, *Menzies*, 113.

15 Hazlehurst, *Menzies Observed*, 216–17.

16 Martin, *Menzies*, vol. 1, 384; Anthony Montague Brown, *Long Sunset: Memoirs of Winston Churchill's Last Private Secretary* (London, 1995), 168.

17 Menzies to Churchill, 28 Feb. 1942, and Churchill to Menzies, 23 Feb. 1942, Menzies Papers, series 1, folder 57.

18 Interview with Heather Henderson, Menzies' daughter, Canberra, April 2001. Mrs Henderson thought that her father had rarely borne grudges and recalled him comparing himself to a sundial, since he only registered the sunny days of his life. This view would certainly be supported by such events as the generous parliamentary tribute that he paid after the death of Eddie Ward, his chief tormentor from the Labor side for years past. Menzies to Churchill, 1 Aug. 1945, and Churchill to Menzies, 10 Aug. 1945, Menzies Papers, series 1, folder 57.

19 Casey diary, 14 Jan. 1944, series 4, box 25; 14 Dec. 1949, series 4, box 26; Menzies diary, 12 Aug. 1948, series 13, box 397.

20 Menzies diary, 17 July to 11 Sept. 1948, series 13, box 397.

21 Melbourne *Herald*, 25 June 1949.

22 Menzies diary, 12 Aug. 1948, series 13, box 397.

23 W. J. Hudson, *Casey* (Melbourne, 1986),

218, 248; McEwen to Menzies, 24 Jan.
1965, Menzies to McEwen, 25 Jan. 1965,
Menzies Papers, series 23, box 445,
folder 15; Allan Martin, *Robert Menzies:
A Life* (Melbourne, 1999), vol. 2, 112.

24 Frederick Howard, *Kent-Hughes: A
Biography* (Melbourne, 1972), 163–84;
Perkins, *Menzies*, 207.

25 Papers relating to Cherwell's visit, Oct.
1953, and Menzies to Churchill, 5 July
1957, Menzies Papers, series 1, folder 55.

26 Menzies to Churchill, 30 Nov. 1959, and
Churchill to Menzies, 2 Dec. 1959,
Menzies Papers, series 1, folder 58;
Menzies to Churchill, 30 Nov. 1963, and
Menzies to Churchill, 30 Nov. 1964,
Menzies Papers, series 1, folder 59.

27 Churchill to Menzies, 2 Dec. 1956,
Menzies Papers, series 1, folder 59;
Hazlehurst, *Menzies*, 349.

28 J. D. B. Miller, *Sir Winston Churchill
and the Commonwealth of Nations*, John
Murtagh Macrossan Lecture, 1966
(St Lucia, Queensland, 1967), 23;
Menzies to Churchill, 20 Oct. 1961, and
Churchill to Menzies, 30 Oct. 1961,
Menzies Papers, series 1, folder 59;
Stuart Ward. *Australia and the British
Embrace* (Melbourne, 2002), 72, 147;
Sydney Morning Herald, 29 and 30 Oct.
and 12 Nov. 1948; Institute of
Commonwealth Studies Conference
Report, *Sir Robert Menzies*, 1978, 11.

29 Paul Hasluck, *Sir Robert Menzies*
(Melbourne, 1980), 17; Percy Joske,
Menzies, 1894–1978 (London, 1978), 265;
Michael Davie, *Anglo-Australian
Attitudes* (London, 2000), 129, 222;
Edgar Holt, *Politics is People: Men of the
Menzies Era* (Sydney, 1969), 110; Martin,
Menzies, vol. 2, 230.

30 Correspondence between Marchant and
Menzies, and Menzies' drafts for the
chapter, are in the Menzies Papers,
series 1, folder 57; Churchill to Menzies,
4 Nov. 1954, Menzies Papers, series 1,
folder 58.

31 Marchant, *Winston Churchill*, 91–9.

32 *Argus*, 23 Jan. 1950; Joske, *Menzies*, 314;
Ward, *Australia and the British Embrace*,
22; John Howard, *The Liberal Tradition*,
Robert Menzies Memorial Lecture
(Melbourne, 1996), 2; Sir Evelyn
Wrench, 'Churchill and the Empire', in
Charles Eade ed., *Churchill by his
Contemporaries* (London, 1953).

33 Russell Ward, *A Nation for a Continent*
(Rutland, Victoria, 1977), 360; 'Speeches
at Presentation', 15 Feb. 1974, Menzies
Papers, series 1, folder 62.

34 Institute of Commonwealth Studies,
Menzies, 5; Perkins, *Menzies*, 223;
Joske, *Menzies*, 337–40; Donald Horne,
The Lucky Country (Harmondsworth,
1967), 200; Martin, *Menzies*, vol. 2,
552.

35 Correspondence in Menzies Papers,
series 23, box 445, folders 2 to 5.

36 Correspondence in Menzies Papers,
series 23, box 445, folder 1.

37 Margaret Walters Auchmuty, *A
Perpetual Trust: The Story of the Winston
Churchill Memorial Trust Travelling
Fellowships* (Canberra, 1984), 4–11.

38 *Ibid.*, 16–19.

39 Auchmuty, *Perpetual Trust*, 18–20, 22;
Menzies Papers, series 23, box 445,
folders 6 and 7; Peter Sekuless and
Jacqueline Rees, *Lest We Forget: The
History of the Returned Servicemen's
League, 1916–1986* (Dee Why West, New
South Wales, 1986), 138–40; RSL Papers,
Jan. 1988 additions, box 84.

40 *Canberra Times*, 3 Feb. 1965; *Australian*,
6, 16, 20 and 26 Feb. 1965; Joske,
Menzies, 193; *Mercury*, 20 and 23
Feb. 1965; Ward, *Australia and the
British Embrace*, 96.

41 *Barrier Daily Truth*, 18, 22, 24 and 26
Feb. and 3 Mar. 1965; *Bulletin*, 13 Mar.
1965; *Newcastle Morning Herald*, 16, 18,
25 and 26 Feb. and 3 Mar. 1965.

42 *Bulletin*, 13 Mar. 1965; *Advocate*, 21 Jan.
to 18 Feb. 1965.

43 *Advocate*, 18 Feb. to 11 Mar. 1965.

44 Professor Carl Bridge, now Director of
the Menzies Centre for Australian
Studies in the University of London,
was then a boy scout collecting for the
appeal in Sydney, and had this
experience with Italian migrants.

45 *Morwell Advertiser*, 28 Jan. and 4 and 8
Feb. 1965; *Bulletin*, 13 Mar. 1965.

46 Brian Fletcher, 'Anglicanism and
Nationalism in Australia', *Journal of
Religious History*, vol. 23 (June 1999),
233, quoted in Ward, *Australia and the
British Embrace*, 25.

47 Clementine Churchill to Menzies, 29
Mar. 1965, Menzies Papers, series 1,
folder 59.

48 Auchmuty, *Perpetual Trust*; Winston

Churchill Memorial Trust, Annual
Reports (Canberra, 1966–74).

49 Menzies Papers, series 23, box 445,
folder 11; Horne, *Lucky Country*, 99; *Roll
Call, Official Organ of the Bicton-
Palmyra Sub Branch, RSL* (June 1980);
Menzies Papers, series 23, box 446,
folder 13.

50 Menzies Papers, series 23, box 446,
folders 15 and 16; *Mercury*, 22 and 23
Feb. 1965; Kirwan quoted in *Roll Call*,
June 1980.

51 I owe the persuasive suggestion of 'one
last rally' to Dr David Cuthbert; Calwell,
Be Just and Fear Not, 342.

CHAPTER 12: *The Man
of the Century – and of the Next?*

1 Malcolm MacDonald, *Titans and Others*
(London, 1972), 126.

2 Kingsley Amis quoted in Lawrence
Malkin's review of Randolph Churchill's
first volume of the official biography, in
Commentary, July 1967; Lord Moran,
*Winston Churchill: The Struggle for
Survival, 1940–1965* (Sphere Books edn
London, 1968), 761; *Times Literary
Supplement*, 21 May 1970; Peter
Hennessy, 'Churchill, still a force
without equal', *The Times*, 14 June 1983.

3 *Encounter*, Jan. 1966; A. L. Rowse,
Memoirs and Glimpses (London, 1986),
421, 427.

4 Robert Rhodes James, *Churchill: A Study
in Failure, 1900–1939* (Harmondsworth,
1973), ix–xi, 276, 354–5, 446; *Times
Literary Supplement*, 21 May 1970.

5 A. J. P. Taylor, Robert Rhodes James,
J. H. Plumb, Basil Liddell Hart and
Anthony Storr, *Churchill: Four Faces and
the Man* (London, 1969), 114, 243; *Daily
Telegraph*, 10 Apr. 1969.

6 Adam Sisman, *A. J. P. Taylor* (London,
1994), 354, 367; *Times Literary
Supplement*, 19 Aug. 1983.

7 *The Times*, 2 to 4, 10, 13, 16, 17, 21, 23
and 25 May and 3 June 1966; Moran,
Churchill; Winston Churchill, *His
Father's Son: The Life of Randolph
Churchill* (London, 1996), 469–77; *New
York Times*, 10 Jan. 1968; *Times Literary
Supplement*, 2 June 1966.

8 John Colville, *The Churchillians*
(London, 1981), 190–1.

9 John Wheeler-Bennett ed., *Action This
Day: Working with Churchill* (London,
1968), 7–12, 46, 193; John Colville,
Footprints in Time (London, 1976), 68;
John Colville, *The Fringes of Power:
Downing Street Diaries, 1939–1955*
(London, 1986); John Martin, *Downing
Street: The War Years* (London, 1991);
Anthony Montague Browne, *Long
Sunset: Memoirs of Winston Churchill's
Last Private Secretary* (London, 1995);
Times Literary Supplement, 28 Nov. 1968.

10 Richard Langworth, *A Connoisseur's
Guide to Winston Churchill* (London,
1998), 349–50, 362–70.

11 Churchill, *His Father's Son*, 85, 392.

12 *Times Literary Supplement*, 27 Oct. 1966,
26 Oct. and 21 Dec. 1967; Churchill, *His
Father's Son*, 395–7, 422–6, 465, 478–9;
Victor Feske, *From Belloc to Churchill:
Private Scholars, Public Culture and the
Crisis of British Liberalism, 1900–1939*
(Chapel Hill, North Carolina, 1996), 201.

13 Churchill, *His Father's Son*, 483–97;
Times Literary Supplement, 29 Oct. 1971,
9 Mar. 1973; *American Historical Review*,
1967, 1396, and 1973, 641–8; *History*, 1973,
133.

14 Martin Gilbert, *Churchill: A Life*
(London, 1991), 958–9.

15 *Times Literary Supplement*, 1 July 1983.

16 Henry Pelling, *Winston Churchill*
(London, 1974); William Manchester,
The Last Lion (London, 1983), and *The
Caged Lion* (1988); William Roger Louis
and Robert Blake eds, *Churchill*
(Oxford, 1993); R. A. C. Parker ed.,
*Winston Churchill: Studies in
Statesmanship* (London, 1995); January
2001 RHS conference papers in
*Transactions of the Royal Historical
Society*, 6th series, vol. 11; Frederick
Woods, *A Bibliography of the Works of
Sir Winston Churchill, KG, OM, CH*
(London, 1975); Eugene L. Rasor,
*Winston S. Churchill: A Comprehensive
and Annotated Bibliography* (London,
2000); Roy Jenkins, *Churchill* (London,
2001).

17 Vic Schuler, *Collecting British Toby Jugs*
(London, 1999), 104–5, 121–2, 135–6.

18 Ronald A. Smith, *Churchill: Images of
Greatness* (London, n.d. but c.1995),
118–35.

19 William A. Bredin, *Winston S. Churchill:
Catalogue of the Stamps of the World*
(Weston-super-Mare, 1998); James A.

Mackay, *Churchill on Stamps* (Amersham, 1966).

20 Kennedy to President Davidson, 7 Apr. 1963, John F. Kennedy Presidential Papers, White House Name file, box 487, Kennedy Library; *New York Times*, 16 and 20 Apr. and 1 Aug. 1964; records of the Winston Churchill Memorial, Westminster College, series 1, box 1; *Concord*, Newsbulletin of the E-SU of the Commonwealth, February 1968.

21 *New York Times*, 10 Sept. 1967, 8 May 1969; advance programme for New York Dinner, and various other papers relating to the Fulton appeal, in Harry S. Truman Post-Presidential Papers, Name file, box 60, folder 'Churchill Memorial, Fulton', Truman Library. See also Lord Hailsham *The Fulton Speech, Fifteen Years After*, Green Lecture (Westminster College, Fulton, Missouri, 1961). Other Green lecturers included Harry Truman, Mikhail Gorbachev, Margaret Thatcher, Lord Harlech and Winston Churchill MP (grandson of Sir Winston); James H. Williams, ' "An Imaginative Project": The Winston Churchill Memorial and Library Project, 1961–1969', unpublished dissertation, Westminster College, 1986.

22 English-Speaking Union, Washington DC branch, 'Churchill Statue' files; Halle to McVey, 12 Aug. 1963, Kay Halle Papers, folder C46(1), Kennedy Library; *Washington Star*, 7 Oct. 1965.

23 E-SU press release on unveiling, and commemorative programme, 9 Apr. 1966, Kay Halle Papers, folder C46(1), Kennedy Library; English-Speaking Union, Washington DC branch, 'Churchill Statue' files, and 'Dedication' file.

24 English-Speaking Union, Washington DC branch, 'Churchill Statue' files, and 'Time Capsule' file.

25 See Dwight D. Eisenhower Post-Presidential Papers, Eisenhower to Kennedy, 25 May 1963, Augusta-Walter Reed Series, box 2; Secretary's series, box 12; Charles Saltzman to Minnesota branch, E-SU, 1963 Principal File, box 44; 1964 Principal File, boxes 17, 34 and 50, Eisenhower Library.

26 Carl Gilbert to Charles Saltzman, 29 June 1965, Harry S. Truman Post-Presidential Papers, Name file, box 59,

file 'Churchill Foundation', and that file more generally, Truman Library.

27 *Concord*, July 1966.

28 *New York Times*, 19 May, 26 to 30 Nov. and 1 and 9 Dec. 1974; for Burton's attack on Churchill, see Chapter Five.

29 Eisenhower to Winston Churchill Society, Alberta, 24 May 1965, Dwight D. Eisenhower Post-Presidential Papers, 1965 Principal File, box 21, Eisenhower Library; Churchill Society of Alberta to Harry Truman, June 1967, Harry S. Truman Post-Presidential Papers, Name file, box 59, file 'Churchill, 1960–1964' (sic), Truman Library.

30 English-Speaking Union of the Commonwealth, *Annual Report* (1960), 3; *Concord*, Mar. 1965.

31 Montague Browne, *Long Sunset*, 334; E-SU *Annual Report* (1965), 1–2; Alan A. Bath, *A Survey of the Work of the Winston Churchill Memorial Trust, 1966–1983* (London, 1985), 1; Colville, *Churchillians*, 151–3; *News of the World*, 15 May 1938; Raymond Seitz, *Over Here* (London, 1998), 345–7.

32 Bath, *WCMT*, 2–4; *The Times*, 1 Mar. 1965; *Concord*, Mar. 1965.

33 *The Times*, 4 and 16 Feb., 4, 8, 10, 12 and 25 Mar. and 29 May 1965.

34 *The Times*, 2 July 1965; E-SU, *Annual Report* (1965), 12.

35 Bath, *WCMT*, 2–7, 23; Montague Browne, *Long Sunset*, 335.

36 Bath, *WCMT*, 7–23.

37 *Ibid.*, 25–105.

38 Denis Healey, *The Time of my Life* (London, 1989), 2; I am grateful to Professor Catherine Hall for explaining to me the naming patterns and use of 'Winston' in the West Indies.

39 Smith, *Churchill*, 69–72, 153–6.

40 The other parts of the United Kingdom have been discussed in Chapter Six.

41 For Liverpool, see *The Times*, 9 Mar. 1955; other information from current road gazetteers and street maps.

42 Montague Browne, *Long Sunset*, 307; 'Churchill, the native New Yorker', in British Airways *In Flight* magazine, October 2000; *www.churchill.com*; *The Times*, 11 June 1962, 21 May 1969, 16 Dec. 1974, 25 Jan. 2002.

43 Interview with Richard Langworth, 24 June 2001; Richard Langworth, '30 years, a History', *Finest Hour*, 100.

44 *Ibid*. ICS Conference programmes: Boston, November 1995, Jefferson City and Fulton, March 1996, Kent, October 1996; *Finest Hour*, 87.

45 Richard Ingrams and John Wells, *Mrs Wilson's Diaries* (London 1966), 104.

46 Ben Pimlott, *Harold Wilson* (London, 1992), 7, 265, 399, 451; Leslie Smith, *Harold Wilson* (London, 1965), 208; Harold Wilson, *Purpose in Power* (London, 1966), 25, 39–50; Anthony Shrimsley, *The First Hundred Days of Harold Wilson* (London, 1965), 25, 72; Ernest Kay, *Pragmatic Premier: An Intimate Portrait of Harold Wilson* (London, 1967), 41, 205; Paul Foot, *The Politics of Harold Wilson* (Harmondsworth, 1968), 155, 160.

47 Pimlott, *Wilson*, 388; Nelson D. Lankford, *The Last American Aristocrat* (London, 1996), 330; Andrew Roth, *Sir Harold Wilson: The Yorkshire Walter Mitty* (London, 1977), 11, 13, 44, 50.

48 Margaret Thatcher, *The Path to Power* (London, 1995), 73–4, 343; John Campbell, *Margaret Thatcher, the Grocer's Daughter* (London, 2000), 82, 84; Alan Clark, *Diaries: Into Politics* (London, 2001), 66; Ernle Money, *Margaret Thatcher, First Lady of the House* (London, 1975), 114; Robin Harris ed. *Margaret Thatcher: Collected Speeches* (London, 1997), 29–30, 231, 405, 624; Margaret Thatcher, *The Downing Street Years* (London, 1993), 829; Kay, *Pragmatic Premier*, 65.

49 D. W. Houck and A. Kiewe eds, *Actor, Ideologue, Politician: The Public Speeches of Ronald Reagan* (London, 1993), 35, 179, 195, 203, 328; Geoffrey Smith, *Reagan and Thatcher* (London, 1990), 29–34, 147, 166, 260–1; Hugo Young, *One of Us* (London, 1989), 396, 399; Harris, *Thatcher Speeches*, 236, 590, 626; Thatcher, *Downing Street Years*, 23, 193, 468; Christopher Hitchens, *Blood, Class and Nostalgia: Anglo-American Ironies* (London, 1990), 11; Caspar Weinberger, 'Winston Churchill, Visions and Leadership', address to the Churchill Society for the Advancement of Parliamentary Government, Toronto, 29 Nov. 1989.

50 S. E. Finer, 'Thatcherism and British Political History', in Kenneth Minogue and Michael Biddiss eds, *Thatcherism* (London, 1987), 127; Patrick Cosgrave, *Thatcher: The First Term* (London, 1985), 108; Peter Riddell, *The Thatcher Government* (Oxford, 1985), 207; Martin Holmes, *The First Thatcher Government* (Brighton, 1965), 58; Young, *One of Us*, 350; Julian Critchley, *Heseltine* (London, 1987), 136.

51 Norman Lamont, *In Office* (Warner paperback Books edn, London, 1999), 17, 41, 83; John Major, *The Autobiography* (Harper Collins paperback edn, London, 1999), 267, 498; Thatcher, *Downing Street Years*, 483.

52 *Finest Hour*, 93, 32.

53 *Time*, 31 Dec. 1999; *The Times*, 13 Aug. 2001; *Finest Hour*, 105, 16–20; *Daily Times*, Salisbury, Maryland, 13 Dec. 1999; Richard Langworth interviewed on *The Front Porch*, New Hampshire Public Radio/NPR, 16 June 2000; John Lukacs, *Five Days in May* (London, 1999).

54 Christian Graf von Krockow, *Churchill, Man of the Century* (London, 2000), 7–9.

55 *Ibid.*, 69, 72, 81, 103, 128, 170, 211–16.

56 Stephen Mansfield, *Never Give In: The Extraordinary Character of Winston Churchill* (Harding, Tennessee, 1996), 114–17, 194–7, 202–7; *Churchill Proceedings, 1994–95* (International Churchill Society, 1998), 111–13.

57 *Finest Hour*, 26, 110; *The Times*, 23 Aug. 2001.

58 *The Times*, 12–18 Sept. 2001, 29 Jan. 2002; *Finest Hour*, 18, 103, 112.

59 Eric Pooley, 'Mayor of the World', *Time*, 31 Dec. 2001. I am most grateful to Lisa Jardine for drawing this to my attention; *The Times*, 14 Feb. 2002.

60 *The Times*, 14 Feb. 2002; White House, Office of the Press Secretary, 'Exchange of toasts between the President and Margaret Thatcher, Prime Minister of Britain', 26 Feb. 1981.

INDEX

Cooke, Alistair, 128, 570
Coolidge, Diana, 84, 186
Cooper, Duff, 279, 281, 492
Coote, Sir Colin, 407
Cornwall, 225
Coronation (1953), 87–8, 397, 418, 501
Cosgrave, Patrick, 57–8, 578
Council of Europe, 268, 313, 317, 318
Courier-Mail, Brisbane, 446, 465, 467, 469
Coward, Noël, 19
Cowdrey, Colin, 507
Cowles, Virginia, 136, 138
Cowling, Maurice, 123
Cranborne, Lord, see Salisbury
Cranmer, Thomas, 146
Crete: Australian forces, 443; Australian losses, 436, 455; New Zealand losses, 415
Cripps, Sir Stafford: Churchill's attitude to, 134, 135, 192; Churchill's rival, 58, 444; lifestyle, 135; street names, 567; toby jug, 546; wartime role, 58, 77
Cromer, Lord, 560
Cromwell, Oliver, 130, 143, 150, 244, 367
Cronkite, Walter, 551, 552
Crookshank, Harry, 134
Crosby Kemper Lecture, 551
Crossman, Richard: apology for Milan allegation, 217; Churchill's eightieth birthday, 87; on Churchill's funeral, 20; on Churchill's parliamentary performance, 86; on European policy, 316; German policy, 303
Crowther, Bosley, 203
Cuba, 33
Cull, Nicholas, 333
Cunningham, Lord, 474, 567
Curtin, John: death, 447, 493; government, 72, 443; invitation to Churchill, 441, 453; relationship with Churchill, 444–5, 459–60; reputation, 481, 512–13, 515; US relations, 444
Curtiz, Michael, 336
Curzon, Lord, 41, 153
Czechoslovakia, 207, 309, 311–12, 365

D-Day, 65, 124, 247, 277
Dagens Nyheter, 295
Dahrendorf, Ralf, 330
Daily Express, 7, 9, 11, 12, 13, 14, 23, 135, 137, 241, 418, 433
Daily Herald, 44
Daily Mail, 18, 20, 23, 27, 59, 90, 157, 213, 277, 291, 434, 439
Daily News, Perth, 522
Daily Sketch, 365–6
Daily Telegraph, 16, 23, 54, 183, 185, 202, 212, 287, 294, 365, 366, 485, 530, 574, 589
Daily Worker, 203, 238, 450
Daley, Sir Denis, 97
Dalton, Hugh, 78, 166, 169, 191, 253, 303–4
Dardanelles (1915), 208, 218, 492, 529, 541
Dardanelles Commission, 44
Darlan, Jean Louis, 277
Darlington, freedom of, 104, 105–6
Darwin, 441, 442
Davidson, Lady, 54
Davies, Joseph, 336
Day, David, 436, 443, 466, 475, 490, 492
de Gasperi, Alcide, 83, 301
de Gaulle, Charles: career, 82–3, 275, 276–7; Churchill award, 112, 280; on Churchill's death, 3, 17; at Churchill's funeral, 14, 264, 280–1; European policy, 268, 361; memoirs, 279; relationship with Churchill, 274, 275, 276–7, 279–80, 282, 313, 338, 588; religion, 515; statue in London, 285; Tours meeting, 284; wartime broadcasts, 146
de Klerk, F.W., 27
De L'Isle, Lord, 511, 560
De Mille, Cecil B., 84
de Selincourt, Aubrey, 143
de Valera, Eamon: Churchill's victory broadcast against, 252–3, 367; civil war, 242; Hitler condolences, 251, 255, 264, 367; on invasion of Low Countries, 286; meeting with Churchill (1953), 258–9, 261, 368–9;

medallion, 349; Churchill's art
exhibition, 351–2, 470–1; at
Churchill's funeral, 16, 30–1; on
Churchill's memoirs, 195; Churchill's
US visit (1959), 353–6; D-Day
broadcast, 65; E-SU support, 555;
funeral tribute, 13, 31, 346, 506;
honours, 294; Indo-China policy, 210;
memoirs, 193, 199; paintings, 130, 349;
photographs of, 312; presidency, 341;
relationship with Churchill, 22, 31,
193–4, 196, 200–1, 325, 339–40, 341,
344, 494, 554; relationship with
Truman, 355–6; reputation, 83, 371;
secretary, 112; Stockholm summit
question, 296; Summersby
relationship, 197; on US attitudes to
Churchill, 128; wartime command, 551
El Salvador, 27
elections, British general: (1922), 226,
235; (1935), 235; (1945), 68, 69, 70,
71–2, 76, 78, 154, 187, 204, 234, 235,
367, 379, 430–1, 445–6, 492; (1950),
237, 318, 343, 464; (1951), 86–7, 235,
237, 318, 343, 381, 465; (1955), 235, 319
Eliot, T.S., 502
Elizabeth I, Queen, 5, 150
Elizabeth II, Queen: accession, 87, 150;
Australia visit (1954), 453, 460;
Churchill's death, 8, 14, 482;
Churchill's funeral, 5, 15, 29;
Churchill's tribute to, 87; Coronation,
88, 418; dinner with Churchill, 88–9;
Menzies appointment, 487, 505;
sculptor choice, 110; US visit (1958),
352; WCMT, 559; wedding, 140, 289
Elizabeth, Queen Mother, 562
Elliott, Walter, 148
Elton, Lord, 125
Emerson, Ralph Waldo, 190
Emmet, Robert, 369
Emporia Gazette, 163
Enchantress, Admiralty Yacht, 39, 40, 97
Encounter, 528
English Historical Review, 540
English-Speaking Union (E-SU):
banquets, 328, 488; chairmanship,

328–9, 507; Churchill Memorial
Trusts, 330; Churchill scholarships,
555–6; foundation, 328; honours
Halle, 364; Jenkins' address, 545;
relationship with Churchill, 329–30;
US fundraising, 31; Washington
statue, 24, 56, 366, 552–5; WCMT,
558, 559, 561
Epping constituency, 54
Epstein, Jacob, 109, 110, 547, 553
Erhard, Ludwig, 264, 307
Europe: Brussels speech (1945), 287–;
Churchill as European, 312–22;
United Europe campaign, 267; Zurich
speech (1946), 188, 267
European Coal and Steel Community,
316
European Defence Community, 318
European Economic Community (EEC):
Britain's entry, 563–4; Britain's entry
negotiations, 320–1, 402, 423, 452,
500; de Gaulle's veto, 361–2; origins,
319
European Union, 268, 312
Evatt, H.V.: Attlee congratulations
(1950), 464; British tour (1942), 441;
relationship with Churchill, 443,
444–5, 460, 479, 490
Evening Standard, London, 269, 270, 360
Evening Star, Washington, 203

Fadden, Arthur: Churchill motion, 446,
448, 449, 493; memoirs, 460; Menzies
cable to, 491; relationship with
Churchill, 443, 478–9
Fairbanks, Douglas Jr, 551
Falkirk, Churchill's visit (1945), 235
Ferguson, Sir John, 212
Ferrier, Neal, 80
Feske, Victor, 219, 220, 221, 539
Finer, Samuel, 578
Finest Hour (magazine), 569–70
Finest Hours, The (film), 203–4, 329, 553
Finland, 30, 34, 295
Fisher, Geoffrey, 145
Flanders and Swann, 225, 244
Fletcher, Brian, 517–18

Goldwater, Barry, 360
Gollin, Alfred, 80, 81
Gorbachev, Mikhail, 578
Gordon Walker, Patrick, 52
Gore, Al, 581
Gott, Richard, 209
Gough, Sir Hubert, 205
Graebner, Walter, 63, 130, 138, 142, 495
Graham, Katharine, 330
Grant, Lieutenant, 476
Graubard, Stephen, 143, 189
Gray, David, 250
Great War, 57, 61, 437–8
Greece, 25, 301–2
Green, Theodore, 345
Green Lecture, 551
Greene, Graham, 54–5
Greig, Morice, 562
Grenada, US invasion, 211
Grey, George, 434
Griffith, Arthur, 240
Grigg, John, 18, 21
Gromyko, Andrei, 247, 310
Guardian, 7, 8, 9, 10, 11, 18, 21, 485, 533
Gustav VI, King of Sweden, 296

Haakon VII, King of Norway, 292–3, 294
Hague: Congress, 92; speech, 155
Haig, Alexander, 330
Haig, Lord, 82, 438, 474
Hailsham, Lord, 54
Haldane, Lord, 98
Halifax, Lord: appeasement, 121, 122; Churchill's eightieth birthday, 502; Churchill's Fulton speech, 168, 169–71, 181; US Ambassador, 165, 168, 170; wartime government, 53, 581
Halifax Chronicle-Herald, 382, 393, 394
Hall, Joyce, 351, 353, 470
Halle, Kay, 88, 325, 337, 357–64, 552–3, 554
Hallmark Cards, 351, 470
Hamilton, Sir Ian, 238
Hamilton, L.W., 448
Hansell, Ernest, 387
Harbutt, Fraser, 163, 177

Hardy, Robert, 232, 233, 295, 569, 571
Harper, J.L., 345
Harriman, Averell: Churchill bust appeal, 553; Churchill's Fulton speech, 179–80; E-SU Churchill lecture, 330; Fulton Memorial, 551; Menzies' speech, 507; opinions on Russia, 155, 157; relationship with Churchill, 325, 335, 340, 356, 577; Washington statue of Churchill, 552; Winston Churchill Award, 577
Harrisson, Tom, 71, 218
Harrow School, 64, 149, 205
Harvey, Lucy, 423
Hasluck, Sir Paul, 445, 501
Haughey, Charles, 251
Havel, Václav, 311, 579
Headlam, Cuthbert, 62, 76
Healey, Denis Winston, 564
Hearst, William Randolph, 49, 326
Heath, Edward (Ted), 20, 82, 123, 321, 402, 589
Helms, Jesse, 581
Helsingin Sanomat, 295
Hemingway, Ernest, 129, 580
Hennessy, Peter, 527
Henry V, King, 150
Henry VIII, King, 133, 226, 546
Herald, Broken Hill, 513
Herald, Melbourne, 457, 459, 461, 464, 465, 468, 469, 485
Herbert, A.P., 131, 136
Herriot, Edouard, 274, 283
Heseltine, Michael, 578
Higgins, Trumbull, 218
Hill, Charles, 109
Hill, Christopher, 125
Hird, Dame Thora, 568
Hirst, Councillor, 107
History, 541
Hitler, Adolf: appeasement of, 144; Carter on, 210; Churchill on, 119, 157, 206, 207, 208; on Churchill, 45; Churchill near-meeting, 269; Churchill's policy, 52, 581; Czechoslovakia, 311; death, 82, 251, 255, 264, 367; European policy, 288;